REPERTORY IN REVIEW

REPERTORY IN REVIEW

40 Years of the New York City Ballet

BY
NANCY REYNOLDS

with an
introduction by
LINCOLN KIRSTEIN

THE DIAL PRESS
NEW YORK

Copyright © 1977 by Nancy Reynolds
Interviews by Charles France and essays by
Lincoln Kirstein, Walter Sorell and Nancy
Goldner, copyright © 1977 by The Dial
Press

Book design by Elaine Golt Gongora

Manufactured in the United States of America

First printing, 1977

**Library of Congress Cataloging in
Publication Data**
Reynolds, Nancy
  Repertory in review.
  Bibliography: p.
  Includes index.
  1. New York City Ballet.   I. Title.
GV1786.N4R48   792.8′4′097471   76-47686
ISBN 0-8037-7368-4

Grateful acknowledgment is made to the following for permission to quote from copy-
righted material.

Ballet: Used by permission of Richard Buckle.

Ballet Review: Used by permission of Marcel
Dekker, Inc.

The Boston Globe: Courtesy of *The Boston
Globe.*

The Christian Science Monitor: "Dance: Rob-
bins-Chopin; Balanchine-Gershwin" by Nancy
Goldner, Feb. 13, 1970; "Balanchine Ballet
Just for Melissa Hayden" by Nancy Goldner,
June 4, 1973; "Balanchine's 'Ivesiana' and
'Western Symphony' " by Margaret Lloyd,
Sept. 25, 1954; "Mooning Around" by P. W.
Manchester, Dec. 16, 1963; "Dances at a Gath-
ering? Robbins Returns in Triumph!" by Nancy
Goldner, May 23, 1969; excerpt from "Many
Premieres, Few Hits" by Nancy Goldner,
May 28, 1975. Reprinted by permission from
The Christian Science Monitor © 1954, 1963,
1969, 1970, 1973, 1975 The Christian Science
Publishing Society. All rights reserved.

Dance Magazine: Reprinted courtesy *Dance
Magazine.*

Dance News: Used by permission.

Faber and Faber Ltd: From *Stravinsky: The
Composer and His Works* by Eric Walter
White.

The Financial Times, London: Used by permission.

Robert Garis: Excerpt from article about Balanchine's "Jewels," *Partisan Review,* #4/68.
Excerpt from review of Ravel Festival,
Dance Life, October 1976. Used by permission.

The Guardian Weekly, Manchester: Used by
permission.

Harvard University Press: #923, "How the
Waters closed about Him" by Emily Dickin-
son. Reprinted by permission of the publishers
and the Trustees of Amherst College from *The
Poems of Emily Dickinson,* edited by Thomas
H. Johnson, Cambridge, Massachusetts: The
Belknap Press of Harvard University Press,
Copyright © 1951, 1955 by the President and
the Fellows of Harvard College.

High Fidelity: Used by permission of *High Fi-
delity/Musical America.*

Horizon Press: Excerpts from *Dancers, Buildings, and People in the Streets* by Edwin
Denby, copyright 1955, by permission of the
publisher, Horizon Press, New York. "Central
Park in the Dark" reprinted from *Ballet Chronicle* by B. H. Haggin, copyright 1970, by permission of the publisher, Horizon Press, New
York.

The Nation: excerpts from columns by Nancy
Goldner.

The New York Herald Tribune: Copyright ©
1935, 1936, 1939, 1943, 1944, 1945, 1947,
1948, 1949, 1950, 1951, 1952, 1953, 1954,
1955, 1956, 1957, 1958, 1959, 1960, 1961,
1962, 1963, 1964, 1965, 1966. Courtesy IHT
Corporation.

The New York Journal-American: Courtesy of
Hearst Newspapers.

New York Post: Reprinted by permission of
New York Post. © 1936, 1954, 1957, 1958,
1959, 1960, 1965, 1966, 1967, 1968, 1971,
1972, 1974, 1975, 1976.

The New York Times: © 1935, 1936, 1937,
1938, 1939, 1940, 1945, 1946, 1947, 1948,
1949, 1950, 1951, 1952, 1953, 1954, 1955,
1956, 1957, 1958, 1959, 1960, 1961, 1962,
1963, 1964, 1965, 1966, 1967, 1968, 1969,
1970, 1971, 1972, 1973, 1974, 1975, 1976 by
The New York Times Company. Reprinted by
permission.

The News: Used by permission.

Newsweek: "Return to Monte Carlo," June 30,
1969; "Eastern Omelet," February 14, 1972;
"Dreams of Glory," December 14, 1970; and
"The Sound of a Lifetime," February 9, 1970.
Copyright 1969, 1970, 1972 by Newsweek,
Inc. All rights reserved. Reprinted by permis-
sion.

The New Yorker: Excerpts by Andrew Porter
(December 9, 1972 and February 17, 1973),
by Arlene Croce (August 5, 1974, December
2, 1974, May 31, 1975, June 2, 9, 16 and 21,
1975, December 8, 1975, February 2 and 9,
1976, and May 31, 1976) and Calvin Tomkins
(June 1971). Used by permission.

Harold Ober Associates Incorporated: "Acro-
batics and the New Choreography" by Agnes
DeMille. Copyright 1930 by Theatre Guild.
Renewed. Reprinted by permission.

The Observer: Used by permission.

Partisan Review: excerpts from "The New York
City Ballet" by Robert Garis. (#4/68). Copyright © 1968 by Partisan Review. Used by permission.

Pitman Publishing Ltd.: excerpt from *Movement and Metaphor* by Lincoln Kirstein. Used
by permission.

Playbill: excerpts from "The Pleasure of Their
Company" by Arlene Croce, *Playbill,* New
York State Theater Edition, January–February
1970.

Praeger Publishers, Inc.: excerpt from *Movement and Metaphor* by Lincoln Kirstein (1971).

Time: excerpts from "Never Mind the Ginza."
Reprinted by permission from Time, The
Weekly Newsmagazine; copyright Time Inc.

Times Newspapers Limited: for reviews first
published in *The Times* and *Sunday Times,*
London.

University of California Press: From *Stra-
vinsky: The Composer and His Works* by Eric
Walter White. Copyright © 1966 by Eric
Walter White, reprinted by permission of the
University of California Press.

Village Voice: excerpts by Deborah Jowitt. Reprinted by permission of The Village Voice.
Copyright © The Village Voice, Inc. 1966,
1968, 1969, 1970, 1971, 1972, 1973, 1974,
1975.

*The World-Telegram, The World-Telegram &
Sun,* and *The World Journal Tribune:* Used by
permission.

ACKNOWLEDGMENTS

The inspiring and possibly paternal presence of Lincoln Kirstein has been a source of pleasure and support to me since we first worked together in 1967. Without his kindness and steadfast encouragement throughout, this book would probably never have been started, certainly never finished. In addition to contributing the opening essay, he frequently directed me to sources I might otherwise have overlooked and always had time to answer questions.

George Balanchine, more as essence than as being, is responsible for many of my ideas about dancing. In the flesh he granted me interviews and permitted me to watch him at work. Although I suspect he won't have much use for a book such as this, he often asked about my progress.

Other members of the New York City Ballet were most receptive; I was given access to files of all sorts and a key to the storage room, and I had the complete cooperation of the staff. Among the many who helped are Betty Cage, Edward Bigelow, Barbara Horgan, Carole Deschamps, and Mary Porter of the administrative department; and Virginia Donaldson, Marie Gutscher, and Larry Strichman of the press office. Their participation, however, as well as that of Mr. Balanchine and Mr. Kirstein, did not infringe upon my independence.

No one claiming to be a dance scholar or researcher could go far without consulting the immense resources of the Dance Collection, Library and Museum of the Performing Arts, Lincoln Center, of which Genevieve Oswald is Curator. In my many hours on the premises, I examined materials of every description: programs, clippings files, books, magazines, tapes, films, microfilm, photographs, original artwork.

A dance book of this nature would not be complete without abundant illustrations. For their endless patience and tact, and incidentally for the many hours of pleasure that looking through their photo files afforded me, I would like particularly to thank Fred Fehl and Martha Swope. Michael Avedon, Dwight Godwin, Donn Matus, William McCracken, and Michael Truppin also contributed to the tantalizing difficulty of narrowing down the final choice of pictures.

In locating foreign material, I had the generous assistance of many. Extensive translation and research were provided by Mary Clarke and Nesta Macdonald (England); Claude Baignères and Olivier Merlin (France); Horst Koegler and Inge Zürner (Germany); Susan Gould (Italy); and Beth Dean Carell (Australia).

For much of the time during the preparation of the book, my virtual collaborator was Charles France. He conducted interviews and made many substantive suggestions that have been incorporated in the text. It was extremely rewarding to work with someone whose admiration and perhaps even reverence for dance seemed to equal my own. Robert Cornfield also made useful recommendations along the way.

My interview with Tamara Geva was part of the Dance Collection's Oral History program.

Walter Sorell and Nancy Goldner kindly provided essays.

The Ford Foundation awarded me a most welcome grant.

David Vaughan graciously permitted me to listen to his tapes of Sir Frederick Ashton, from which I quote. His biography of Sir Fred, published in celebration of his fiftieth year as choreographer, was winner of the de la Torre Bueno prize for excellence in dance writing in 1976.

For the living history in the book, my deepest gratitude to the many performers and choreographers, past and present, who shared with me and Mr. France their thoughts and feelings about matters that deeply touch their lives. There is not space here to list them all—there are over fifty—but they know who they are, and their words will be found throughout the book.

Miss Horgan, personal assistant to Mr. Balanchine, and Ruth and Mark Schorer did me the enormous service of reading the final draft of the manuscript. Their comments and suggestions—and their encouragement—were both helpful and sustaining. The Schorers also shared with me some research for their forthcoming book on George Balanchine.

Katherine Rosenbloom and Alexandra Schierman coped cheerfully with the special difficulties involved in transcribing tapes replete with technical vocabulary. Stella Heiden brought to my attention some photographs I would not otherwise have known about.

In the transformation from manuscript to book, I was given expert assistance by Patricia Meehan, Nancy van Itallie, Jack Ribik, and Elaine Golt Gongora.

On the personal side, I owe more than I can say to my husband, who helped at all the right moments.

CONTENTS

Acknowledgments
Foreword

**RATIONALE OF
A REPERTORY** 1
by Lincoln Kirstein

**NOTES ON GEORGE
BALANCHINE** 13
by Walter Sorell

**THE SCHOOL OF
AMERICAN BALLET** 21
by Nancy Goldner

**1 STARTING
1935-1948** 33
**American Ballet
1935-1938** 36
Serenade 36
Alma Mater 39
Errante 40
Reminiscence 41
Dreams 42
Transcendence 42
Mozartiana 43
Concerto 44
The Bat 44
Orpheus and Eurydice 45
Apollon Musagète 46
The Card Party 50
Le Baiser de la Fée 51

**Ballet Caravan
1936-1940** 53
Encounter 53

Harlequin for President 54
Promenade 54
Pocahontas 55
The Soldier and the Gypsy 55
Yankee Clipper 56
Folk Dance 56
Show Piece 57
Filling Station 58
Air and Variations 59
Billy the Kid 60
Charade, or The Debutante 61
City Portrait 62

**American Ballet
Caravan 1941** 63
Time Table 63
Ballet Imperial 64
Concerto Barocco 66
Pastorela 69
Divertimento (Rossini) 70
Juke Box 70
Fantasia Brasileira 71

**Ballet Society
1946-1948** 71
The Spellbound Child 71
The Four Temperaments 72
Renard 76
Divertimento (Haieff) 77
The Minotaur 78
Zodiac 79
Highland Fling 79
The Seasons 80
Blackface 81
Punch and the Child 81

Symphonie Concertante 82
The Triumph of Bacchus
  and Ariadne 83
Capricorn Concerto 84
Symphony in C 84
Élégie 87
Orpheus 87

**2 THE COMPANY FINDS
A HOME: New York City
Center of Music and
Drama 1948-1954** 91
Mother Goose Suite 93
The Guests 93
Jinx 95
Firebird 96
Bourrée Fantasque 100
Ondine 102
Prodigal Son 102
The Duel 107
Age of Anxiety 108
Illuminations 110
Pas de Deux Romantique 114
Jones Beach 114
The Witch 115
Mazurka from "A Life
  for the Tsar" 116
Sylvia: Pas de Deux 116
Pas de Trois (Minkus) 117
La Valse 117
Lady of the Camelias 119
Capriccio Brillante 120
Cakewalk 120
The Cage 122
The Miraculous Mandarin 125

À la Françaix	126	Jeux d'Enfants	170	Electronics	213
Tyl Ulenspiegel	127	Allegro Brillante	170	Valses et Variations	214
Swan Lake	129	The Concert	172	A Midsummer Night's Dream	215
Lilac Garden	132	The Still Point	174	Bugaku	218
The Pied Piper	134	Divertimento No. 15	176	Arcade	220
Ballade	135	The Unicorn, the Gorgon, and the Manticore	177	Movements for Piano and Orchestra	220
Bayou	136	The Masquers	179	The Chase	222
Caracole	137	Pastorale	179	Fantasy	222
La Gloire	138	Square Dance	180	Meditation	223
Picnic at Tintagel	138	Agon	182	Tarantella	223
Scotch Symphony	140	Gounod Symphony	186	Quatuor	224
Metamorphoses	141	Stars and Stripes	187		
Harlequinade Pas de Deux	143	Waltz-Scherzo	190		
Kaleidoscope	143	Medea	190		
Interplay	144	Octet	192		
Concertino	144	The Seven Deadly Sins	192		
Valse Fantaisie	145	Native Dancers	195		
Will O' the Wisp	146	Episodes	195		
The Five Gifts	146	Night Shadow	199		
Afternoon of a Faun	147	Panamerica	201		
The Filly	149	Theme and Variations	202		
Fanfare	149	Pas de Deux (Tchaikovsky)	203		
Con Amore	150	The Figure in the Carpet	203		
Opus 34	151	Variations from "Don Sebastian"	205		
The Nutcracker	153	Monumentum pro Gesualdo	206		
		Liebeslieder Walzer	207		

3 CITY CENTER II 1954-1964

159

Quartet	161	JAZZ CONCERT	210	
Western Symphony	161	Creation of the World	210	
Ivesiana	164	Ragtime (I)	211	
Roma	166	Les Biches	211	
Pas de Trois (Glinka)	167	Ebony Concerto	211	
Pas de Dix	168			
Souvenirs	168	Modern Jazz: Variants	212	

4 "A HOUSE FOR DANCE": New York State Theater 1964-1976

225

Clarinade	227
Dim Lustre	227
Irish Fantasy	228
Piège de Lumière	228
Pas de Deux and Divertissement	230
Shadow'd Ground	230
Harlequinade	232
Don Quixote	234
Variations	240
Summerspace	241
Brahms-Schoenberg Quartet	242
Jeux	244
Narkissos	245
La Guirlande de Campra	245
Prologue	245
Ragtime (II)	246
Trois Valses Romantiques	247

Jewels	247	Symphony in E-Flat	291	Introduction and Allegro for Harp	321
Glinkiana	250	Concerto for Piano and Winds	292	Shéhérazade	321
Metastaseis & Pithoprakta	251	Danses Concertantes	292	Alborada del Gracioso	321
Haydn Concerto	253	Octuor	293	Ma Mère l'Oye	322
Slaughter on Tenth Avenue	253	Serenade in A	294	Daphnis and Chloe	323
Requiem Canticles (I)	255	Divertimento from "Le Baiser de la Fée"	294	Le Tombeau de Couperin	324
Stravinsky: Symphony in C	255	Scherzo à la Russe	296	Pavane	325
La Source	256	Circus Polka	296	Une Barque sur l'Océan	325
Tchaikovsky Suite	257	Scènes de Ballet	297	Tzigane	326
Fantasies	258	Duo Concertant	298	Gaspard de la Nuit	327
Prelude, Fugue and Riffs	259	The Song of the Nightingale	299	Sarabande and Danse (II)	327
Dances at a Gathering	259	Piano-Rag-Music	301	Chansons Madécasses	328
Reveries	265	Ode	301	Rapsodie Espagnole	329
In the Night	266	Dumbarton Oaks	301		
Who Cares?	268	Pulcinella	302	The Steadfast Tin Soldier	329
Sarabande and Danse (I)	270	Choral Variations on Bach's "Vom Himmel Hoch"	304	Chaconne	330
Suite No. 3	271	Requiem Canticles (II)	305	Union Jack	332
Kodály Dances	272				
Concerto for Two Solo Pianos	273			Postscript	337
Four Last Songs	273	Cortège Hongrois	306		
Concerto for Jazz Band and Orchestra	274	An Evening's Waltzes	307	Sources	339
Octandre	275	Four Bagatelles	308		
The Goldberg Variations	275	Variations pour une Porte et un Soupir	309	Notes	341
PAMTGG	280	Dybbuk	310		
Printemps	281	Bartok No. 3	313	Index	351
Chopiniana	281	Saltarelli	313		
Watermill	282	Coppélia	314		
		Sinfonietta	319		
STRAVINSKY FESTIVAL	286				
Lost Sonata	287	RAVEL FESTIVAL	319		
Scherzo Fantastique	287	Sonatine	319		
Symphony in Three Movements	287	Concerto in G	320		
Violin Concerto	289				

FOREWORD

When the idea of a documented history of the New York City Ballet was first proposed to me in 1971 by Robert Cornfield, I was skeptical. As a dancer, I had always found reading or writing about dance beside the point—one dances or perhaps one watches dance; anything else seemed irrelevant. And I was uncomfortably aware how poorly words serve dance. George Balanchine once said to Jerome Robbins, "We dare to go into the world where there are no names for anything. . . . We get our hands into that world just a little bit." Dancing ceases to exist the minute dancers stop, leaving no traces behind. Says Robbins, "Dance is like life . . . and [watching a dance] reminds people much too poignantly of their own mortality. So they say 'Books are better—or paintings or sculpture—because they can be touched. Because they will last.' " Because one does not have to catch them on the wing.

Formidable obstacles. However, in working with Lincoln Kirstein on his book *Movement and Metaphor,* I had begun to discover that words (and pictures) eloquently handled could be stimulating and informative about dance in quite another way than active participation. They made their own contribution, particularly where history was concerned.

Encouragingly, as enthusiasm for dance has become more and more widespread in this country during the past fifteen years, there is a greater amount of discriminating writing about dance than ever before (although writers remain hampered by lack of a working vocabulary to deal with the precepts of dance as an art form). Dance criticism is still a highly inexact and subjective affair, but the improvement has been enormous.

Upon reflection, it seemed that a chronicle of the New York City Ballet, unquestionably a major cultural phenomenon in mid-century America, was needed for the record. Perhaps now that dance has finally attained prominence in the world of the arts, such a work will have more than specialized interest.

Finally, and decisively in my case, there was the central fact of the existence of George Balanchine, whose period of activity has coincided with the flowering of theatrical dance in this country, although he is not a product of it. Such a creative artist appears far less frequently than once in a lifetime—like Mozart or Shakespeare (with whom he is frequently compared), he is preeminent not only for our time but for all time. I believe his vision would have manifested itself no matter when he lived, and that any contribution, however peripheral, I could make to preserving or disseminating some aspect of his work was worth attempting.

My aim has been to recall all the works performed by the New York City Ballet and its predecessor companies from the first *Serenade* in 1935. (I have excluded ballets that were parts of operas, movies, or created for television, and anything that was not primarily a dance work or that incidentally involved only one or two company performers, such as concert appearances by individuals in other than company context.) As sources I have used whatever came to hand—programs, critiques in newspapers and magazines, scenarios, letters, costume sketches, backdrop designs, Company records, posed and action photographs, snapshots, films, newspaper announcements, reviews, books, musical scores, publicity material, reminiscences of past and present participants, and of course my own firsthand observation over the years.

My interest has been not only to provide ascertainable facts, which include a listing of the creators involved in each ballet, an accurate record of the time, place, and cast of the initial performance, and significant subsequent casting (the cast lists make no claim to being comprehensive), but also to capture something of the atmosphere or effect of the works by giving the views of contemporary observers and key participants. I have occasionally used technical language in an effort to be specific as well as impressionistic and in the belief that some of the steps are particularly memorable or indicative of the flavor of the whole. Identifying them may be more meaningful to some spectators—and to the history- and research-minded—than subjective reactions.

Many imponderables come into play in attempting to

analyze—or even to describe—a dance piece, because any ballet that is maintained in active repertory is constantly changing. On the most obvious level, whenever a new dancer assumes a role, the look of the work is affected; a new interpreter may often, intentionally or not, change some of the steps to more congenial movements, or the choreographer may invent new ones more suitable to that individual. Or the choreographer may have second thoughts after a work is premiered and redo parts even when he is working with the same dancers. As years go by, changes in accent or execution creep in almost unnoticed. Most ballets are recorded only in someone's memory, an imperfect storehouse: not long ago, Balanchine was obliged to create a few new measures for the venerable *Concerto Barocco*, a piece now more than thirty-five years old, because in one section no one could recall the steps. In some of the more obvious cases, such as the continual reworking of *Swan Lake*, I have indicated the major changes. In others, alterations have been too slight or too frequent to be included.

In quoting from so many reviews, it is not my intention to leave the impression that critics have the last word in determining a work's value, but one must accept the fact that they often leave the only written record we have, and that their opinions, informed or otherwise, are part of the historical record. I have tried, however, to present only the most responsible and considered judgments by relying almost exclusively on the writings of experienced professionals of proven reputation. It should always be borne in mind that the repertory at any given time is made up primarily of old works, although novelties receive the most attention in the press.

Since we lack the ability to summon forth a work of dance for reference purposes, I felt that descriptive material was generally more suited to my intentions than philosophical or reflective pieces, even when those were of superior literary value. Accordingly, some of our most distinguished writers receive less space than they would warrant in a book devoted to dance criticism alone. There is an additional consideration, since the material available varied greatly in quality and amount: during the past fifteen years, as dance columns in newspapers and magazines have proliferated enormously, there has been a much wider range for selection and a generally higher level of writing to choose from than in the earlier years.

A similar situation exists with regard to photographs. Today's more sensitive cameras, superior lighting, and faster film mean that recent works are better and more frequently photographed than those of other years, though this, of course, is not a reflection of their quality as ballets.

Because even today comparatively little dance writing exists (in contrast, say, to literature on art and music), I have deliberately drawn as infrequently as possible from what is readily accessible—that is, available in book form—and concentrated instead on the more ephemeral pieces from newspapers and magazines, which often have more immediacy in any case. The books I have consulted are listed in the Sources and all are recommended for fuller information on various points. (I have also omitted plot summaries, musical analyses, and details of scenery and costumes if they could easily be found elsewhere.)

To present only the most relevant portions of the material consulted (which, quoted in toto, would have filled a volume several times larger than this one) and to avoid excessive repetition, I have had to fragment many excerpts. In the interests of readability I have not used the traditional ellipses, except when quoting in sequence two pieces published at different times or when there is a complete change of subject. Nonetheless, I have been as scrupulous as possible not to depart in spirit from the original or to quote out of context, though I could not always do justice to detailed arguments.

Originally I had planned to include an entire section on the Company's foreign and domestic tours, but as research progressed (and always bearing in mind the limitations of space), it became apparent that, overwhelmingly, with the exception of Ballet Caravan, the Company's development occurred in New York, and that to eliminate local material in order to include reviews from other parts of the world would be unnecessary elaboration. There was an additional deterrent: by and large, until very recent years, domestic reviewers were not trained dance writers, and their opinions lacked both conviction and interest.

A sampling of European notices is included, however. The tours to Europe were psychologically as well as financially important, for there the Company both measured and proved itself by international standards. Moreover, in the late 1950s, when the first transatlantic tours were undertaken, European critics were part of a tradition, unlike ours, in which ballet had been a fact of cultural life for many years—sometimes, as in France, for centuries—and this afforded them a markedly different perspective. From experience, their dance writing was more polished and assertive than our own. This is certainly no longer true, just as it is no longer the case that dance reputations can be made only abroad.

A significant fund of information has been the dancers and choreographers themselves, commenting on their intentions, their approaches, and their interpretations. Any quote not attributed to a printed source was generally taken from personal interviews conducted during the past four years; very occasionally, I have quoted reliable third parties; and infrequently, I have included remarks that appear in several places and are thus in the nature of common knowledge.

In the most fundamental sense, of course, the interpretive and creative artists are the source of all the material in the book.

N.R.
New York
May 1976

RATIONALE OF
A REPERTORY

by Lincoln Kirstein

Every ballet company possesses a repertory, a number of works that are repeated season after season, retaining the interest of a public even after many performances. Opera has its similar holding, and those drama companies supported by a state proclaim a national patrimony by continually restaging Shakespeare, Molière, Goethe, and Lermontov. In general, the international operatic repertory consists of Mozart and Gluck, with a few other eighteenth-century scores; the aggregate of Bellini, Donizetti, Rossini, Verdi, Wagner, and Bizet for the nineteenth century; Puccini and Richard Strauss for the twentieth. For ballet in the nineteenth century, apart from *Giselle*, whose music by Adam is the principal relic of the Romantic movement of the 1840s, there are the three masterpieces of Tchaikovsky and some lesser scores by Minkus and Pugni, Russian court-composers who so long and ably provisioned Marius Petipa. Of the three ballets by Delibes that represent the second half of the century, *Coppélia* alone is in active production. However, from searching in the library we find that dozens of separate and ambitious ballets were presented and their scores published, and that they enjoyed veritable success for a generation before they were retired, probably forever. The ratio of success to failure would perhaps have been one to four or five; out of the many that held the scene, we still have about half a dozen which might be revived in one form or another, usually by cannibalizing the music, altering the plot, and shifting the sequence of dances. (As far as true "authenticity" to any original choreography, of which there are few records and only the haziest memories, respectful echoes have long been legitimized.) However, all these lost ballets suited the taste of their times, gave pleasure to a large public in many cities,

and provided roles for important dancers.

The New York City Ballet, and its prior apprentice companies, was a direct heir of the principles of Diaghilev's Ballets Russes, inasmuch as the last ballet master, from 1924 through 1929, was George Balanchine. Diaghilev came to Paris with his magnificent aggregation of imperial Russian dancers in 1909 and altered the nature and format of the art. His separation from Russia, enforced by the October Revolution of 1917, also meant separation from the nineteenth-century system of government-supported companies based on a permanent subscription public, a state-imposed bureaucratic management of very conservative views, and a fixed association with a sister opera company which the ballet served when not occupied with its own repertory. Such a situation was stable, static, ingrown, but secure; it did not depend on private or foundation support or international tours.

With Diaghilev, touring became a necessity. He depended on international impresarios to place him favorably in the European opera houses when their own companies were not playing. A contemporary apparatus for travel, while elaborate, required drastic simplification from the former Russian format, a reduction in the number of dancers, the absence of trained children for the larger ballets, and elimination of elaborate scenery, panoramas, and mechanical effects. One recalls that in Petersburg when a scene demanded an open sea with a boat on it, a regiment of soldiers was on hand to creep under painted canvas, following a sergeant's orders to make waves. In Diaghilev's long fight for survival without the support of a Tsar's privy purse, the nineteenth-century repertory of full-length ballets, in great part, came to be replaced by shorter works, usually constituting a program of three one-act ballets with the addition of pas de deux. These might be mounted with fewer dancers and a smaller corps de ballet; in return, conditions prompted a constant stream of novelties of a nature which in Russia would have been taken as dangerous, frivolous, or inconsiderable. After 1917, the fact that Diaghilev was deprived of new additions of young recruits from the ballet academies was partially offset by his appropriation of advance-guard painters and composers stimulated by the atmosphere of Paris during the exciting if unsettled years following the First World War. The emphasis he allocated to new music and a novel lyric sensibility was almost as important as those elements remaining strictly within dancing itself. When, in 1921, he revived with magnificence Tchaikovsky's *Sleeping Beauty* (called *The Sleeping Princess*) with a great cast, its length and ponderous format determined its failure. It seemed as if the nineteenth century were truly dead. After that, he produced works of a confirmed, almost improvised triviality, involving the most fashionable figures in Parisian cultural politics. The efficiency of his professional dancers diminished; he was driven to accept even English girls and boys, although he Russified their names, and some were to become famous and successful. But the great period from 1909 to 1914 seemed to render harsh judgment on the later years of his decline, despite the presence of Stravinsky, Prokofiev, and the initial ballets of Balanchine.

After his early training at the Maryinsky Theater in Petersburg, it was in the last period of the Ballets Russes that Balanchine commenced his career. His education at school and then by Diaghilev determined the factors which, in combination, were to formulate the philosophy that directed his subsequent work. He had started by dancing in the whole of the nineteenth-century repertory, with the full panoply of the Imperial Theaters; these, while in a state of comparative confusion caused by war and revolution, were nevertheless conducted on a very grand scale. For Diaghilev, he was introduced for the first time to Western Europe and found quite a different court with new conditions. The state of Diaghilev's troupe at the time was vastly reduced; the need for constant novelty, often created in an atmosphere of haphazard improvisation and enforced ingenuity, stretched Balanchine's skills to their utmost. He was forced to use elements that would have been considered impossible or impractical in Russia. The audience he was expected to please was on a level of worldliness and sophistication quite alien to a boy brought up first in an imperial household that was strict and shut, and then released into the chaos of the revolutionary takeover of all culture by the first Bolshevik generation.

When it was proposed in 1933 that Balanchine transfer to America in order to establish his own school and company, he arrived with half a dozen productions just created for his Ballets 1933, a small troupe he managed that produced a single season in Paris and London, after he had terminated a brief association with the Ballets Russes de Monte Carlo (1932). This company had inherited not only many of the Diaghilev productions but also much of the personnel from the final five seasons up to 1929. Balanchine's 1933 ballets were also conceived in the spirit of Diaghilev's taste; the collaborators were taken from an advance-guard of painters and musicians, many of whom had been discovered, or at least first produced, by the Diaghilev Ballets Russes. Younger talents were those with whom Diaghilev would have probably chosen to work, had he survived. It was generally recognized that Les Ballets 1933, elegantly presented at the Théâtre des Champs-Elysées, the former scene of Diaghilev's and Stravinsky's early triumphs, represented a progressive spirit and effort, whatever its ephemeral fate, while the new Ballets Russes de Monte Carlo, competing at the same time in the old Théâtre du Châtelet, a big, popular city theater, under the direction of Léonide Massine, stood for the status and stability of the past. However, it presented ballets by Balanchine, notably *Cotillion* and *La Concurrence*, two considerable successes of the year before, when the new company had enjoyed the patronage of the Hereditary Prince of Monaco, who formerly had supported Diaghilev's novelties each spring in Monte Carlo. In 1933, Paris was still very much the queen of world taste; it was not only Madame Coco Chanel's dressmaking, but also her interest and cash that helped to give Balanchine the freedom he had come to desire. But always in his mind was the spectral, ancestral presence of Diaghilev; would he have approved of the new ballets?

It should be remembered that Balanchine came to the United States not only with some physical properties from his most recent work, but with a group of professional friends who had been his partners in the old Diaghilev company, and even before that, his teachers in the Imperial School. He recognized, before he left Paris, that the only possible long-term security of any future company with which he might be connected must depend on a school. At that time in America, there were many dance studios conducted by ex-Russian dancers who had remained after the disastrous U.S. tours of Diaghilev during the First World War. But there was no single academy with a diverse and proficient faculty, selective entrance requirements, and carefully graded students. With the model and criterion of his own schooling, Balanchine immediately set about founding an institution that, considering the difference in time, patronage, and a new country, at least pointed in the direction of the most professional training for young talents then available. Michel Fokine, Diaghilev's first ballet master and a historic figure in the Ballets Russes, with his wife, conducted a studio on Riverside Drive, but with no company as outlet. He had trained several excellent American dancers in the nearly two decades he had been in New York. Now, many of his best pupils came to enter the School of American Ballet, and to join Balanchine's venture.

When Balanchine began again to produce ballet, particularly new works for his fledgling company, the programs conformed to the Diaghilev principle of three one-act ballets for an evening. However, there were important differences. The works Balanchine presented were quite unknown to the American public; there could be no reliance on famous Diaghilev successes; and there was absolutely no possibility of reviving any renowned full-length ballets. Due as much to principle as economic necessity, there was no reliance on well-known personalities, although some were even then available. The best-known dancers of the younger generation at that moment were three "baby ballerinas," Tamara Toumanova, Tatiana Riabouchinska and Irina Baronova, whom Balanchine had originally selected in Paris for the initial season of the Ballets Russes de Monte Carlo (revived by him and René Blum, later to be taken over by Colonel de Basil.) But he was hardly in a position to invite any of these, although Toumanova had danced importantly in Les Ballets 1933; he kept to native Americans. The future of an American company must depend more on its repertory than on stars.

The star system, and its supportive publicity, guarantees a certain pre-sold focus that cannot be ignored. However, there is also another side to it. The star, except in special cases, is preeminently self-interested. A few state-supported companies have their own soloists and first dancers, but in general, a star is not attached to a single institution. There have been few periods in theatrical history when ballet has been able to support itself; like opera, it has depended on individual patrons, state subsidy, and the clever manipulation of devoted impresarios. The star is a pawn in the game, and frequently the morale and efficiency of a company can be diminished by an overemphasis on borrowed visitors who presume to save the situation. Early on, in New York, Balanchine determined his future philosophy: choreography was to take precedence over personal idiosyncratic performance; the company was to be dominant as a body; novelty, both in music and dance, was to be preferred over the established repertory. It would remain for other companies to perpetuate, within their potential, past precedent, and to present old works, both those inherited from the Russian Imperial Theaters and those created by Diaghilev.

The star system has many obvious advantages. It lodges the attention of a diffuse and inchoate public on single individuals—star names can be reiterated and merchandised like brands of soap or hair tonic until persistent repetition of a single face seems to insure a given magic value. In a company, this requires constant adjustment to individual needs and the expense in energy inherent in resolving competitive personalities. At the start of his first real independence (as today), Balanchine acted not only as artistic director, ballet master, and teacher, but also as manager. Like Diaghilev, he had the final word in every choice (while working for Diaghilev, he had been only charged with dancing). It was he who assigned schedules, programs, and roles. It was he who was the representative before the public as well as commander backstage. Balanchine could not help seeing the job of overall management from the unique position and viewpoint of the dancer, since he had been one all his life. This had its limitations, but now he was working with performers who, in truth, were more advanced students than full professionals. Their malleability, their lack of personal insistence, was a challenge and held a sympathetic appeal. There were no tenures to be respected, no hierarchies to be maintained, no old debts to be paid. The cost of physical production, particularly since the rehearsal of orchestras is always expensive where the hours needed to prepare new music are considered, required that scenery and costumes be subordinate elements. A new repertory, supported by unfamiliar music, old and new, for new and surprising dancers, has been the key to the continuity of Balanchine's work from 1934 to the present time.

However, audiences have their way, and naturally select or elect favorites for promotion to what is commonly agreed is "stardom." Over the years this has been true even for Balanchine's companies, whatever his own projection or preference. The public, denied the indulgence of individuals designated as "stars," invent these for themselves, all fitting the mold of "the Balanchine-dancer," a semimythological creature that exists in the half-world of journalism approaching its most gossipy. The Balanchine-dancer has become an identifiable entity based on a germ of truth. The European ballerina had previously been fulfilled in the public mind by the image of Anna Pavlova. She incarnated what was vulgarly conceived of as "soul," an approximation of the Romantic dancer Marie Taglioni, who filled the same function for the 1840s. Taglioni had implied an extraterrestrial atmosphere of ethereal melancholy or spirituality. It is quite unjust to allocate to Pavlova a single attribute, since she also danced the sprightly soubrette, the temptress, the femme fatale, and a variety of other roles. However, to the mass audience she arrogated to herself the canonization of ballerina, whose prime air was one of supramundane sad queenliness, a wistful regality, which, as the Dying Swan, imposed itself as symbol of the classic dance. Her "soul"—l'âme slave—was Russian in essence, deriving from aspirations to a supernatural or otherworldly realm, the province of sylph and faëry. Its truly Romantic origins sprang from the folk tales and legends of Germany and Central Europe, whose haunted lakes and dark streams were populated with ondines, pixies, and elves, theatricalized from the Frenchified versions of la Motte Fouqué, Heine, and Gautier.

To Balanchine, this notion of "soul" was anathema, and he identified it with the kind of commercial exploitation of Pavlova's world tours, which took her with a small supporting company to every quarter of the globe, in a repertory which hardly dignified her real talents, but which made her name a byword for ballet. He had liked to consider himself "American" even before leaving Russia; that is, he imaginatively identified himself with the world of ragtime, Jack London, Mark Twain, and the Wild West. America was the newest-found land, a vast continent of infinite resource and possibility with no built-in or hereditary prejudices, open to every chance. Its young girls were not sylphides; they were basketball champions and queens of the tennis court, whose proper domain was athletics. They were long-legged, long-necked, slim-hipped, and capable of endless acrobatic virtuosity. The drum majorette, the cheerleader of the high-school football team of the thirties filled his eye. These girls, embodied as dancers, had already appeared in musical comedies for three decades; corresponding to Anna Pavlova was their mistress, Ginger Rogers, whose partner was the incomparable Fred Astaire in Irving Berlin's top hat, white tie, and tails. Balanchine did not wish to impose an exhausted if correct "classicism" as an academy on top of their own strong stylization; he was to give their type a new turn which would transform their peculiar Americanism into a new classicism. One might recognize the abstract formula for a Balanchine-dancer, but in reality there would be never enough candidates to make up a whole company. Those that seemed to adhere most closely to this presumed ideal appeared to spread the atmosphere of their typicality over those less perfectly proportioned, but rather than a single physical model, it was in reality the quick and abrupt movements, the asymmetry and syncopation he suggested that lent to the aggregate corps the distinctive ideal of a particular American classic style and behavior. The pathos and suavity of the dying swan, the purity and regal hauteur of the elder ballerina, were to be replaced by a raciness, an alert celerity which claimed as its own the gaiety of sport and the skill of the champion athlete.

The true definition inherent in the Balanchine-dancer (and before him, to no ballet master had ever been attributed so definite a type) derived from Balanchine's personal conception of human movement, how it measured stage-space/stage-time based on the given meter of music. This was speed, and also steps; his dancers wore out more toe shoes in half the time of other companies, since his ballets, short as they were, contained more steps in twenty-five minutes than the old full-length four-act spectacles did formerly, with their heavy pageantry and parade, corps de ballets moving in unison deployment, and with the more brilliant variations, steps, and movement given only to the prima ballerina and a few soloists. Fokine had gone far in democratizing the corps de ballet; at least he had broken it down from its strictly hierarchical, quasi-military formality by giving individualized characters some special, particular movement of their own. He made a mosaic of motion that gave accent and variety to what earlier had been background or formally subordinate elements. Lacking stars, or refusing to project given dancers into an unwarranted prominence, Balanchine began by distributing virtuosity itself more evenly over his entire corps. But if one were to analyze this corps with attention, one would soon see that there was very little uniformity, except in a capacity to move fast. There would be tall girls and short ones and those between. His notion of a working company was a kind of visual organ with many stops; one needed blonde notes as well as brunette, with an occasional redhead. There would be approximate giantesses and token dwarfs; acrid and piquant notes were valuable and needed. The essential, without which no Balanchine-dancer could be imagined, was one whose motion was unrestricted, who did not resist his often extraordinary convolutions that deformed or denied the ordinary habit of how a dancer saw herself as beautiful, plus a capacity for ever-accelerating quickness. If one could imagine a slim arrow with the resilience of a snake

5

of toughened steel, headed by a thinking dart, this would symbolize the ideal Balanchine-dancer. For him, the European-trained, Russian-schooled ballerina moved far too deliberately, too much in a presupposed affectation of the noble or imperial manner. It was a high style, but a limited one. He preserved the style, but gave it a new accent, a playfulness, a dash and daring that rehabilitated old manners into new freshness. American gymnasia, high-school rallies, and track meets were based on a lean-muscled and economical virtuosity that heretofore, in theater, had been the common property of Broadway and Hollywood. Yet such is the definition of the academic classic tradition in all its rigor and anatomical analysis that without surrendering an iota of its authority, it could take on a new national shading and give it the novel vibrancy of another voice.

Balanchine's acute instinct for analytical consideration guided him. Presented with a new land and new material, he needed a new and appropriate repertory. The Diaghilev company had offered its precedents. Nijinsky, in 1913, had used the metaphor of tennis to canonize contemporary sentiment (in a game with *three* partners!). His sister, in the twenties, borrowed the manners of American vacationers on the Côte d'Azur. Jazz, the house party, vaudeville, and cinema all contributed to a new decorative ambiance, but their motivation was a rather naive pretext for novelty, not any innate stylistic expression. It was a violation of the fairy story, the nineteenth-century world, the repetition of historical revivals, the imitation of past epochs in rich dress that first seemed to fit the label "modernism."

But a more profound difference was formulated by Balanchine when, working on Stravinsky's eclectic yet progressive divisions, he started realizing a repertory that depended increasingly on movement itself, disdaining the usual appanage of theatricality, well-known dancers, or "shocking" themes. As for romanticism, the old habit of

returning to the Romantic decade of the 1840s was gone for good. Instead, there was born a new romanticism, as expressed by *Serenade*, his initial ballet designed for students in his school, which became the "signature ballet" for his companies for many years, just as the earlier and very romantic *Les Sylphides* of Michel Fokine had for two decades been a signature ballet for the Diaghilev company. Balanchine's lyric atmosphere, his own brand of romanticism, sprang also from the mysterious, the strange, and the obscure. But it was a mortal ambiance, with the confusion and frustration of human figures in their knottings and doublings, in their confusion of identities, in their ambivalence of emotion, and in their strange eloquence of unfamiliar yet heartbreaking gesture. Abrupt appearances and disappearances, the casual suspension of logic, the presence of double or triple meanings infused his dances with the super-reality of waking dreams. The dancers were invested less with special personalities than with the characteristics of an ardent mobility and the capacity to transform their bodies in motion into kaleidoscopic patterns that depended on the most intricate interplay of partnership, the weaving of limbs as if they were shuttling threads in a tapestry of plastic movement. In *Concerto Barocco*, for example, the double violins were Bach's, but Balanchine's correspondence to them could be a blonde and a brunette, a tall girl and a shorter one, while the relentless accompaniment of the grave duet was the constantly modulated steps of the small corps of eight and a single male supporting dancer; the totality seemed to sound and look in simple but absolute alliance with the body of strings. The dancers were abstracted from identifiable facial expression so that the essence of the music propelled its echo in motion, and the dance itself became as interesting and captivating as formerly might have been the personal quality of one single prima ballerina's dominant and isolated authority.

It was by no accident that Balanchine began to insist on

the use of the term "choreography" relative to the ballets he produced for Broadway. Before his time, dances in commercial shows were "arranged" by a professional dance arranger. When he worked for the final edition of the *Ziegfeld Follies* and in a later series of musical comedies for Richard Rodgers and Lorenz Hart and finally in Hollywood for the *Goldwyn Follies* (1938), his "numbers" were indeed miniature ballets. They were distinguished from other diversions by their musical originality, self-sufficiency, and style. His "choreography" drew attention to dance design, to the fact that it had its own integrity as part of the entertainment, and that the pattern was not an improvisation for star performers but a carefully formulated, predesigned map of movement. Naturally, it was the task of the choreographer to provide motion and gestures that enhanced a star's particular style, but the ex-vaudeville performers who had become musical-comedy luminaries in their own right were often restricted by the habit of years in which they had performed a single act with polished proficiency. Balanchine found new ways to make them surprisingly different while retaining their individual characters. In the musical *Cabin in the Sky* (1940), he was among the first to use black dancers, American, Cuban, and Puerto Rican, in a way that enhanced their own ethnic style without vulgarization or recourse to the prototypes of ordinary tap dancing, inherited from minstrel shows, ragtime, and early jazz. Balanchine was never expressly against the talents of stars, but only felt the limitation of an exhausted archetype which, for reasons of convenience or lack of energy, certain nominal stars persisted in fulfilling as their trademark.

There had been famous dancers at the court of Louis XIV; through the eighteenth century a number of extraordinarily gifted men and women, representing the peak of performance for their epoch, enlarged the capacity of movement by extending technique, introducing new steps, and later, with the aid of the stiffened toe shoe, de-veloping brilliant turns. What the star of one generation invented became the common property of the corps de ballet of the next. Thus the idiom was enlarged, although at certain periods it became frozen in rigid academic correctness and orthodoxy. This occurred in Russia in the later part of the nineteenth century; then through the revolution of Isadora Duncan from outside the academic tradition, and through the mastery of Michel Fokine within it, barriers were broken. Diaghilev tolerated, nay encouraged, every sort of heterodoxy in the classic language. However, when Nijinsky ceased to dance, his place as choreographer and first dancer was taken by Léonide Massine, who had not enjoyed strict classic schooling to any degree. He was an excellent character dancer, an assimilator of national forms, and a charming stylist, but his gifts did not extend to innovative choreography. His so-called symphonic ballets were rather elementary illustrations, decorating the more famous Berlioz, Beethoven, Tchaikovsky, and Brahms symphonies with tableaux vivants. There was no addition to the actual vocabulary of movement or gesture such as Balanchine had demonstrated in *Apollo* (1928), *Prodigal Son* (1929), and *Cotillon* (1932). Now, in America, Balanchine felt liberated to move as quickly as he chose toward an extension of those frames of movement that had always attracted him, but which the institutional nature of the Diaghilev repertory permitted only in fragments. Working with students who had no prejudice against novel arrangements, who as yet had gained no personal predilection as to how they might be best presented, gave Balanchine a liberty for trial and error that would have been impossible in a European company forced, in one way or another, to serve the religion of a star system.

Ballet was traditionally associated with opera; the diva was paired in reputation and drawing power with the ballerina. It became convenient, indeed necessary, for opera-house impresarios to exploit the acknowledged powers of extremely gifted men and women for their unique virtuosity. The ballet star feels that she (or, more rarely, he) is a reincarnation of past figures. Roles made famous in the nineteenth century—Swan Queen, Giselle, Princess Aurora—like Hamlet, Lady Macbeth, Carmen, or La Traviata, offer the challenge of historical comparison. These roles demand an authority, ambition, and experience that transcend ordinary novelty. A novel role or an unfamiliar ballet guarantees little but the interest and energy of conviction, an independence of discovery, taste, and spirit. There have been many, both students and a general public, who have been attracted by Balanchine's philosophy, and these have allied themselves with or as Balanchine-dancers. Nevertheless, some very able students from his school have chosen not to join his companies, feeling the limitations of his attitude a restriction. Some have left his authority for extended periods and have returned, possibly strengthened by the interim absence, to find what they had left to seek was finally to be discovered at home.

On a few occasions, gifted visitors have been drawn to appear and some have stayed. But it is not easy for them when the supreme authority derives from a ballet master, teacher, choreographer, and impresario in one person. However much visiting stars may hope to reconcile their attitudes to a new and an accountable situation, their innate resistance may leave them unsatisfied as far as any real integration into a company situation. Dominance is in their nature; it is the essence of stardom. After all, they have heard it legitimized by public acclaim. It is hard to tamper with this image; stardom enforces the mold; it becomes a negotiable security, worthy of exchange for its very particularities.

Balanchine's notion of material, his dancers, derives from his own morality. Dancers are angels, messengers of movement who are sent; the great magnetic impulse, activated by the Good Lord, is pleased to offer candidates with whom he can work, who have the impulse to work with or for him rather than primarily for themselves. It is their trust in his ingenuity and mastery that gives them confidence in him as someone from whom much may be learned, not alone through lessons, in school or on stage, but through the experience of dance in ordinary life. Those who are so magnetized have understood that Balanchine's attitude toward repertory roles is complex, synthetic, and based on interrelation, rather than an adhesion to what is commonly considered tradition. It by no means eliminates the past; he continually uses it, but in a manner transformed for the uses and conditions of a shifting present. Like no other living choreographer, he has danced the ballets of Petipa and Ivanov, from childhood. When he has, very occasionally, revived his version of some older work (the second act of *Swan Lake*, *Nutcracker*, *Coppélia*, *Harlequinade*), he has taken into consideration differences in time and technique between the original production and revivals, as well as the discrepancy in temperaments between the first casting and the dancers available to him at the present. He has been accused of reviving with lack of respect for the lost original, as if reproducing a ballet "authentically" were similar to restoring a damaged painting. Such comparison is false, for in the recovery of lost paint and design, there are no additions or amplifications. He has never hesitated to augment steps, alter the sequence of numbers, enlarge scenes or cut them, just as was the habit in the Imperial Theaters at the moment when the older ballets were first presented. Who is to decide what is more or less "authentic" when the observer was not present in the first place, to form a fixed and unalterable opinion? Also, a general accusation has been leveled against him for his disdain of stars, resulting in the canard that he has a lodged dislike of strong individualities. This has been proven obviously untrue over and over. It is merely that he is not attracted to personalities who wear roles like masks, rather than artists who, with transparent or translucent assurance, transform themselves into an incarnation of polymorphous personages, dictated by music however exigent, and the metric of steps under whatever variety of shaped motion.

The Balanchine-dancer, if indeed such a creature can be presumed to exist, is possessed of a temperament fascinated by the factors and the difficulties inherent in Balanchine's protean imaginative process, as displayed in the amazing variety of roles his repertory of over one hundred separate ballets offers. Those admitted to the New York City Ballet have already undergone some nine years of training in a school he supervises, but often find themselves, upon entering his company, virtually back at school again, grading themselves almost as beginners. The classroom exercises they have mastered are abruptly transformed into demands of a different and superior difficulty. There seems to be, at once, an acceleration of requirements needed for use in the particular steps of the repertory and a slowing down, or breakdown, in sustained analysis of separate movements. His daily company class, instead of being only academic exercises, turns into sessions of straining, forcing the extension of given capacity. Not only are new movements and seemingly even new muscles called into play, but the tension aimed at performance on stage requires a different sort of concentration and energy from that sufficient for achieving an academic correctness in tentative and permissive classical combinations.

Many have been surprised and even shocked by Balanchine's preference for very young dancers, fresh out of school, but these dancers have not yet managed to accrue habits, good or bad, and have no fixation on a developed identity or stylistic individualism. Relatively unfledged, they accept the demands of unfamiliar combinations, accelerated tempi, "impossible" steps, without prejudice. The requirements are a challenge and an excitement to many, but to others cause confusion, the reverse of release—the fear of failure. Entering a professional company is a crisis in any career, equal in its severity to the moment when a dancer feels that he or she must retire. Both are the ultimate facing and stretching of responsibility and personal possibility.

When one has watched Balanchine give company class and then compose on the same warmed-up bodies—composition being only a magnified extension of the class, even in its inversion or deformation—the dominant impression is a sense of economy, not only a lack of tentativeness, a spare use of time, but also the unfailingly appropriate use of particular persons who, for one reason or another, find themselves, after considerable time and experience, here in his rehearsal. He has often likened himself to both cook and gardener; the gamut of recipes or arrangements is infinite; tastes, scents, colors, their gradations, intensities, and values have no limit. The academic classic training is presupposed and makes the feast or the garden only that much more susceptible to efflorescence. While the aggregate of configurations can be forced into classifications of tall or short, thin or stocky, fast or slow, the subtle and unexpected differences and potentialities, in conformation, energy, and temperament, permit an endless source of materials to manipulate. The Balanchine-dancer is not characterized by physique, but rather by a metaphysical stance, the urge to satisfy a mastery of movement itself by surpassing the known or experienced limitations of habit and precedent. This does not mean that there are simply records to be broken, new tricks to be learned, but rather that movement and gesture in themselves are boundless language, past any lexicon to be verbalized or memorized. However, the greater number of those dancers who have been attracted to Balanchine come to see a vision that includes many recensions of the past but is actually aimed at a futurity of movement, which throws the ultimate weight or burden of roles on a handling of newness, the acceptance and forcing of an ever-amplified vocabulary.

To accept Balanchine's repertory, one must have accepted a person as well as a concept; he is stoic, impersonal, publicly nonverbal to the point of an almost pervasive silence; he can show movement, but neither writes nor describes it in speech. He deals in a kind of kinetic shorthand that takes some attention to accommodate. He has seldom sought dancers already famous. When the leading male dancer of his generation offered himself as a guest artist, Balanchine answered: "When you are tired of playing 'The Prince,' perhaps we can talk." Such talk could never take place. Association with Balanchine presumes a tacit submission, hope, conviction, or suspicion that he knows how to use dancers for their own best exploitation and development. It means they feel he has a clearer idea of their potential, however undefined or well formed, than they have. For many dancers this has not been easy. Yet over the years, as the multiple records in this book will show, he has attracted a great number of the most efficient dancers of his time trained in the United States, as well as a few from Europe.

Also, it is important to recognize that the repertory Balanchine has built over the last half century, first for Diaghilev, then for his own dancers, has been borrowed all over the world. There is scarcely a large ballet company in the United States, Canada, Australia, Japan, Israel, or Western Europe that has not at least one among his Bizet *Symphony in C;* Tchaikovsky *Serenade* or *Ballet Imperial;* Prokofiev *Prodigal Son;* or Stravinsky *Agon* or *Apollo.* He has been the Petipa of the twentieth century, and as Petipa benefited from his collaboration with Tchaikovsky, Balanchine enjoyed the lifelong and inestimable partnership with Stravinsky. Not only was he in the position of commissioning new works from the early thirties on, but later, he was able to appropriate many large orchestral scores never initially intended for theater, but

which received a new life and vivid existence from their use as ballet music. Their drive and kinetic impulse had almost cried out for a combination with dancing, and although the later Stravinsky works are by no means favored in the purely orchestral repertory, through Balanchine's devotion they are now continually heard as dance music. Balanchine without Stravinsky is almost unthinkable. The extraordinary joint compositions—*Duo Concertant, Violin Concerto, Symphony in Three Movements, Movements for Piano and Orchestra, Pulcinella* (with Eugene Berman's decorations)—represent a sequence of ballets unparalleled in the history of theater. It was Stravinsky's genius in discovering a new metric, the new division of time, that Balanchine translated, or transmuted, into novel meanings of space, new angularities, sonorities, shifts of accent and direction, the unused manipulation of an underlying systole and diastole of muscular energy that prompted increasingly the grandeur of the later Balanchine works. The composer could talk to the choreographer in his own tongue and on the same terms. Stravinsky knew the classic dance as Balanchine understood the language of the orchestra. From Stravinsky, Balanchine derived his creed: To make the audience "see the music and hear the dancing."

There are, of course, numerous choreographers who consider themselves musical, who can read a piano score and who are sensitive to the dynamics of orchestration. This gives them skeletal advantages when they come to compose, but often the analysis is superficial and the dancing follows or partially "illustrates" the music, without a very profound integration. Balanchine was trained as a musician at the Conservatory in Petersburg during his years as a ballet student; often, he has had no piano arrangements of orchestral compositions for his rehearsal pianist to use, so he has made his own reduction for piano from the full partition. Hence, when he comes to create steps, the blocking and structure are already a part both of an aural analysis and of a three-dimensional plastic design. An instance of this extraordinary musicality is Stravinsky's *Duo Concertant,* which is actually a double duet for two instruments and two dancers. There is here as much duration of sonority without steps or movement as that accompanying the dancing itself. Piano and violin spin their aural choreography in air the dancers seem to inhale; it overtakes them, or rather they take over the music in a complex weaving of mobile and sonorous complexity visibly activated, presenting a fusion of ear, eye, and mind. Although miniature in scale, the ballet fills a large stage with the concentration of this magical interchange.

In Balanchine's repertory there has also been a large variety of "experimental" ballets, which actually meant the employment of advance-guard or unfamiliar music, or music heretofore considered unlikely for dancing. This has recalled his extraordinary catholicity of taste, imagination, and daring. He used orchestral pieces of Charles Ives in 1954, twenty years before the popularity that this eccentric American composer finally gained among the nation's symphony orchestras. His use of Schoenberg's *Accompaniment-Music for a Motion Picture (Opus 34),* and his magnificent orchestration of the Brahms quartet, as well as the Brahms *Liebeslieder* song cycle; his recovery of the lost Bizet *Symphony in C* and of Gounod's forgotten symphony; his use of Anton Webern's music (in combination with Martha Graham, in *Episodes*), electronic music, the classical Japanese score of Toshiro Mayuzumi (*Bugaku*), and the extremely difficult "stochastic" score of Iannis Xenakis were balanced by an almost shameless assertion of his personal taste in the popular field. Who before him would have considered the marches of John Philip Sousa (*Stars and Stripes*), or George Gershwin's hit songs (*Who Cares?*) as possible for the classic dance?

In all of this it may be noted that with the possible exception of Rouault (*Prodigal Son,* inherited from the Diaghilev version of 1929), Chagall (*Firebird*), and Eugene Berman (Stravinsky's *Pulcinella*), few easel painters of distinction have been chosen to decorate his repertory. Diaghilev had introduced Bakst and Benois (before World War I), then Picasso, Matisse, Derain, Miró, and all the principal painters of the School of Paris from approximately 1917 through 1929. Painted curtains that served as prologues or visual overtures, or actual backcloths as scenery were, in essence, one-man shows that served to acquaint the Parisian public with a whole galaxy of first-rate painters. This was the period that, choreographically speaking and from the point of view of individual performers, was hardly Diaghilev's strongest. He was without the advantage of a ballet school to replenish his company. Apart from Stravinsky, who then seemed to have abandoned shock for pastiche, and whose scores of this decade came to be appreciated only in the following one, his composers belonged to the school of *musiquette,* in the wake of Erik Satie, synthetic jazz, perverse parody, and conscious deflation of the grand symphonic scale. Hence, the painters served an important role in providing an immediate visual impact, but it is their work, rather than the accompanying choreography, that is recalled, and it is their designs, more than any other single element (with the exception of Nijinska's *Les Noces,* with its exquisitely anonymous décor by Gontcharova), that have propelled their infrequent revival.

During the years when New York's Abstract Expressionist painters seized hegemony from the School of Paris as commanders of the world's visual advance-guard, it would have been only too easy to have utilized impressive backcloths blown up from the works of Jackson Pollock, Willem de Kooning, Clyfford Still, and many others. Any one of their pictures enlarged to the scale of the big State Theater proscenium would, at the rise of the curtain, have had its smashing effect. But, as with the star dancer, the currently fashionable easel painter proclaims and protects his own preeminence. A static design, however boldly brushed, remains stationary and is soon exhausted in the very boldness of its sweep. It is a reluctant and overwhelming partner to the kinetic core of the dance. A certain piquancy might have served publicity and the first few seconds of a performance, but the shock of the painting in its diminishing temporal effect would remain through the duration of the ballet, formidably unchanging. For some observers, this was a betrayal of one important aspect of the Diaghilev inheritance, a refusal to acknowledge the presence of big-time painting. The purely decorative aspect of Balanchine's repertory has sometimes been condemned as impoverished, when in actuality it has been intentionally stoic, bare, and uncompetitive.

For many years, there was the notion that ballet, and notably, Diaghilev's Ballets Russes, was a perfect consortium of dancing, music, painting, and poetry, if such can be attached to a lyric or atmospheric ambience. Nothing could have been further from the facts. In Diaghilev's first great period (1909–13), it was dancing (Nijinsky, Karsavina, Pavlova, Bolm), seconded by music (Debussy, Stravinsky), supported by scenery (Bakst, Benois). In his second period (1914–17), it was a picturesque exploitation of Russian folklore, and in his third (1917–29), it was painters of the School of Paris, Les Six (plus Stravinsky), with the greater body of choreography as incidental. There was never a perfect balance, and only in the first

years did the dancing as such predominate over every other element.

Balanchine has always claimed the priority of music as an incentive to propel his dancers, and while they have been often costumed by Madame Karinska in splendor, backgrounds were subordinate to stage lighting in order to project performers' tri-dimensional plasticity without the hindrance of bold, static outlines and competitive coloration. There are, of course, convenient generalizations to which many exceptions may be made, but as an over-all stylization, format, or frame, Balanchine has imposed a pervasive atmosphere derived from rehearsal hall and the classroom, the sites of a ballet's birth. The practice dress of black and white, a conventionalized uniform that is an approximation of nudity, reveals the human body in its essential polymorphic silhouette. It is motion measured by music that moves him, his dancers, and his audiences. That this movement, bare-boned or intricate, grandiose or ironic, playful or tragic, appears rich without ornament springs from a reasoning that is based on a multiplicity of highly selective choices that are, finally, unsentimental and stripped. These choices made after a lifetime immersed in music and motion differentiate his repertory in quality and in kind from any other. That it has found favor, in its paucity of alien or inessential elements, with so large a public on so rigorous a foundation, speaks strongly for the sense in its analysis and rationale.

NOTES ON GEORGE BALANCHINE

by Walter Sorell

Miracles happen in our time, if we consider them to be coincidental events surpassing all human expectation and having that extraordinary effect of wonder usually ascribed to a supernatural cause. The scientific mind of our age has felt compelled to reduce such miracles as the burning bush to the miraculous reality of a burning oil well, and the parting of the Red Sea to the tidal phenomenon it must have been. We are accustomed to operating with such down-to-earth notions as "timing" and "know-how," depriving ourselves of the belief in a destiny tied to the miracles of reality.

Such a miracle was the appearance of George Balanchine in the New World. Several coincidental phenomena conspired to bring about something that apparently had to happen right then and there. Serge Diaghilev was dead, and with him the Ballets Russes. Balanchine, the one great choreographic hope of its last phase, wandered aimlessly through the balletic desert in Europe searching for an artistic oasis. He tried to challenge fate with the creation of a new ballet company after his own taste when his short adventure with the Ballets Russes de Monte Carlo had come to an abrupt end. The company he founded was called Les Ballets 1933. Its title, indicative of the ephemera of ballet, was well chosen—the company did not outlive the year of 1933, and Balanchine clearly indicated his belief that the ballet company of his future should not try to live on the past glory of Diaghilev's Ballets Russes. In stressing the spirit of *tempora mutantur nos et mutamur in illis* he avowed the principles of his concepts: to use the heritage of his past for an experimentally creative and creatively experimental ballet company, international in its cultural outlook. To be a man of today one had to have been a man of yesterday's future.

Miracles of reality are caused by necessities and created by imminent needs, usually by the convergence of two needs. The second need came from across the ocean. Balanchine, at the age of twenty-nine and with about twenty ballet creations to his credit, was footloose. As he knew only too well, very few of his ballets could survive. As a result, his mind was restless. He dreamt of more than the opportunity to choreograph for one or another company, an opportunity that might have been offered more than occasionally. Nor would it have helped for him to accept a dancing part here and there. While working for Diaghilev he realized that he needed a company, more or less constant dancing material which he could fashion to his artistic heart's delight. This was Balanchine's dream when Lincoln Kirstein knocked at his door.

This Boston-born, Harvard-educated son of a wealthy family had seen the productions of Les Ballets 1933 and invited Balanchine to America. Kirstein was a young man of great culture and many artistic inclinations. Having been on intimate terms with all the arts—he could draw and play the piano, and had taken some dancing lessons—he could articulate whatever was close to his heart with the power of a passionate aesthete. He became a minor poet of great distinction, edited a well-thought-of literary magazine, *Hound and Horn*, and then founded one of the finest dance periodicals, *Dance Index* (1942–49). He had published a novel, *Flesh Is Heir* (1932), along with many essays on the arts. Later in his life, he wrote mainly on the dance. In the mid-thirties he brought out a scholarly work, *Dance: A Short History of Classic Theatrical Dancing*. It was the dance which had fascinated him from the earliest days of his awakening sensibilities. He had seen a great many ballets, including the Ballets Russes when he was

13

seventeen. By chance, he happened to attend Diaghilev's funeral in Venice in 1929, an experience that set his imagination afire. "Ballet became an obsession with me," he said, and felt with ardent conviction that it was his destiny to participate actively in it. His dream coincided with Balanchine's.

But there was more to it than the metaphor behind the word "dream" may insinuate. Both men's dreams were fortified by needs. In the late twenties and thirties there were many attempts to create American ballet companies in Chicago, Philadelphia, and San Francisco, while New York had developed into a stronghold of the first generation of modern-dance pioneers. A few Russians chose to stay in the States and run their schools, above all Michel Fokine and Mikhail Mordkin. One could not help using Russian teachers, but the spirit ought to have been American. An American classical ballet was the hope of Ruth Page, Catherine Littlefield, and Bentley Stone. The idea of ballets that were American in story and style caught fire in the thirties. *Filling Station* (Lew Christensen) and *Billy the Kid* (Eugene Loring) stood next to *Frankie and Johnny* (Ruth Page) and were followed by Agnes de Mille's Americana in the forties (*Rodeo, Fall River Legend*). Many of the works created by the modern-dance groups clung at the time to American folklore. The economic depression and its consequences played their part, though on a smaller scale, in a generally growing artistic awareness. This awakening to the consciousness of an American self was also reflected in literature (Fitzgerald, Hemingway, Dos Passos, Wilder). The old art of the ballet was about to be reborn in the New World. The accent had of necessity to be on America.

At the same time, Lincoln Kirstein was fully aware that only a Russian choreographer would be able to help him make his dream come true: to give America its own indigenous ballet, its own academy and company, to bring up generations of ballet dancers and educate an audience ap-

preciative of the balletic art made in the USA. He wanted to produce ballets mainly based on American history and folklore.

But where was the Russian genius to give this miracle the poetic touch of reality? It was not Fokine, Massine, or Lifar. Kirstein felt drawn to Balanchine, who was of his generation—only three years his senior—who danced music the way Kirstein thought ballets should be danced, and whose *Apollo* and *La Chatte* had inspired him. Balanchine, on the other hand, dreamt of long-legged girls à la Ginger Rogers and the freedom to begin anew. To be able to start across the ocean, far from the museum atmosphere of balletic tradition, seemed to be the very freedom he was searching for and the one holding the greatest possible promises. He was ready to pass the Statue of Liberty in the belief that the New World would be the beginning of a new life for him. Kirstein must have seen the great future of American ballet reflected in Balanchine's eyes when he agreed to accept the invitation. What Kirstein then envisioned was only his own wishful thought, but he felt convinced of Balanchine's being *the* man to help him make "the mirage" the "miraculous reality," as he called his ecstatic feelings at that weighty moment of balletic history.

We now know: the dream that both men dreamt became reality. Some of this reality was quite rugged and rough at times, as is the habit of all realities. But as long as destiny remained attached to the notion of the miraculous, all the nasty twists had to end with Fortune's smile. As a matter of fact, at least three times in those forty years after Balanchine's 1933 arrival in the States, Fortune put on her biggest smile for him. One was in 1948, when the New York City Ballet was instituted and—with the invaluable help of Morton Baum—given a home and the well-founded basis Balanchine needed to show the world what a Balanchine-shaped ballet company looks like. The second event of significance was when the Ford Foundation in cornucopian lavishness decided to bestow almost eight million dollars on the New York City Ballet and its affiliated companies, with nearly six million dollars going to the New York City Ballet and the School of American Ballet. The third event came about when the Lincoln Center Council began to build the New York State Theater.

Sometimes Balanchine appears to be in close contact with the gods via his intuitive vibrations, for he claims to have known all the time, while staging his ballets at the City Center on 55th Street, that one day he would have a theater at his disposal, a dream theater for the dance, with a deep stage, ample wing space, and room for plenty of scenery. He was so sure of it that he choreographed through all those years with a view toward one day executing the same ballets on a larger stage. Apparently there are now no more dreams left unfulfilled, except the obvious hopes of being able to go on creating ballets and more ballets while overcoming the daily hazards of mounting them, the human failures and inhuman strikes. No doubt it is an enviable position to be in.

The realization of these dreams was preceded by fourteen years of frustration, of starting companies which soon folded, of long years of separation from Lincoln Kirstein, of choreographic work wherever there was an opportunity for it. Only the School of American Ballet remained a bulwark that has held out with undiminished strength for all these forty years, and to this Balanchine has constantly remained attached.

The American Ballet was the first try, and a program including *Serenade* was shown on the Warburg family estate in White Plains, New York. But the company and Balanchine found scant response and, with the exception of Edwin Denby's great understanding and immediately positive reaction to Balanchine's genius, the critical appraisal was more than disappointing (some of it chauvinistic). The company had a short and unhappy marriage with the Metropolitan Opera House and was once briefly revived when Nelson Rockefeller asked Kirstein to send a ballet company to South America.

Meanwhile, Balanchine proved his versatility on Broadway and in Hollywood. However disappointing his work there may have been considered from a "higher" artistic viewpoint (whatever that may mean), it was a richer period for Balanchine than anyone was willing to admit, a period of Americanization. Lincoln Kirstein thought what he did was a waste of his abilities. John Martin, who vehemently expressed his dislike for Balanchine's ballets at that time, praised his light touch. Balanchine also choreographed four ballets for the Ballet Russe de Monte Carlo in those years and was happily reunited with Igor Stravinsky when he presented a gala evening at the Met, scoring his greatest success of that period with *Apollo, Le Baiser de la Fée,* and *Card Game.* After South America (1941), it was a long time before Kirstein and Balanchine got together again—not until 1946—to found Ballet Society, an organization for the connoisseur with some avantgarde tendencies. Two years later, the New York City Ballet was born.

Severely disappointed by the early folding of the American Ballet and its unnerving struggle with the Met, Lincoln Kirstein brought Ballet Caravan to life, a chamberballet group that stressed Americana thematically. In 1939, he told a reporter he would like to see productions of ballets based on "America's choicest folklore and history." Subsequently the American dance world experienced the extraordinary sensation of its own strength in ballet and modern dance, and in musicals on Broadway and in Hollywood. Many who heard the call of their soil tried to prove that this Gallic-Russian art could speak with an authentic American voice. Lincoln Kirstein was then no longer alone in his hope that an American classicism was about to unfold. Ruth Page, for instance, worked with a more Midwestern accent in the same direction, convinced that the land of the brave was ripe and ready for its own brand of classical ballet.

I recall a gathering of ballet luminaries at the Museum of Modern Art in the 1940s where Ruth Page—among some other speakers—gave a rapturous patriotic speech. After her, George Balanchine rose to speak, and all I remember were his first words, uttered in a heavy Russian accent: "I'm a Yankee!" (Prolonged laughter.)

I am not certain that he ever became a Yankee, but there can be no doubt about Balanchine having a great, if not the greatest, share in the development of an American classical ballet style. Thematically, *Western Symphony, Square Dance, Stars and Stripes,* and *Who Cares?* are ballets in the classical style with a thin veneer of the American idiom. They are probably as "American" as his sensuously poetic ballet *Bugaku* is Japanese. A new ballet, *The Birds of America,* was planned for the Bicentennial to extol James Audubon with a touch of Johnny Appleseed. The idea has apparently been dropped, but, as expressed in his *Complete Stories of the Great Ballets,* it would have evoked the image of "very good dancers" he had seen in his life, all of whom were "beautifully cold, like birds, with no warmth at all." But this is only one aspect of how Balanchine envisions his dancers.

What matters to him is never the step but the personality of the dancer. The vocabulary remains classical—although Balanchine has extended and streamlined it—but it is the American ballerina with her factual, natural, vigorous, and buoyantly dynamic look who embodies the Balanchine idiom. The dancer never seems to act for the benefit of the spectator; her body, carried by the music, is totally "with it" in such intensified concentration that the visual result already appears as one of relaxation and self-evidence.

Behind his accomplishments lies a philosophy of austerity. By reducing the danced image to its essence, Balanchine challenges the spectator's pleasure in absorbing the poetic symbolism of the moving body. Balanchine tends to exclude the allusive expressiveness in favor of a purely sensuous experience. Formal in structure and content, his ballets take on the look of a most intrinsic music-turned-into-movement visualization.

Music has always been to him the principal impetus for moving balletically. It would be an odd idea to imagine a Balanchine ballet without music, like, let us say, Jerome Robbins's *Moves.* As a boy, he took first to music before becoming a dancer and, undoubtedly, he became a choreographer only because destiny willed it that he should not compose. But compose he does, in his fashion, recomposing in another medium what the composer heard and notated. The composers on whom he relies are ever-present when he choreographs, present in such spiritual proximity that he will converse with them and convey to his dancers the impression that, for example, his intimate friend Mendelssohn, Mozart, Stravinsky, or Webern has just left the rehearsal room or was present at last night's performance.

Balanchine likes to deny that *he* creates. According to his version, "God creates; I only assemble." But then what an imaginative and masterly assemblage! Here the similarity with Stravinsky is striking, and Stravinsky's classic austerity has found the ultimate, most convincing balletic translation through Balanchine's works. He said that working on Stravinsky's *Apollon Musagète* in 1928 (still under Diaghilev's aegis) was the turning point of his life. Balanchine has responded to the vitality and intricate dynamics of Stravinsky's music with the astounding *Einfühlung* of someone who traveled similar creative routes. Stravinsky once described himself as an "inventor of music," enjoying the idea of arranging materials, of working with the precision of an architect. These are the levels on which the creative efforts of these two men met and found their stunning parallels: To be never the same, but always recognizable; to create a strong inner relatedness

16

of forceful formal structures lucidly organized with the excitement of immediacy and, here and there, with surprising wit; to manipulate materials meticulously, with calculated precision and bold sparseness—only to achieve, with a seemingly clinical impersonality, an emotional sweep and dramatic intensity. One understands Balanchine better when understanding Stravinsky, and vice versa.

Balanchine's tendency to austerity is also manifested in his preference for having his dancers perform in practice clothes. He regards with mistrust the theatricalization of costumes—if he is not telling a story ballet as *Don Quixote* or *Firebird*—because they take too much away from the beauty of the body line. Probably related is his predilection for giving the titles of his ballets the bare look of the composers' titles, a propensity which has become more marked with the years. I would rather accept the explanation that he wished to see his ballets closely identified with their music than that of the title being an invitation to music lovers who then "know what they're getting" and "don't have to look at the ballet if it bores them," as he claimed in a recent interview with Bernard Taper. Balanchine making such statements, however, cannot be taken too seriously. His basically gay disposition loves to shoot arrows of acid and whimsical wit, particularly when he thinks he faces a critical attitude; he fences off his imagined adversary with sarcastic asides. From time to time, this serious, mystically inclined man must need to break out into a facetious joke, as if needing to liberate himself from the hollow aspects of his environment. But he rarely loses patience or bearing, certainly not when at work.

Balanchine does not think of doing anything exceptionally great or unusual. He sees himself in the role of a high priest of the dance, serving his goddess Terpsichore. He is a romantic priest who, as Petipa's assumed heir, believes—in true pas de deux style—that the ballerina is and remains the focal point of ballet and that the male dancer's duty is to extol her beauty as dancer and woman in almost medieval fashion. But in contrast to Marius Petipa (who was more skilful in choreographing for the ballerina than for the male dancer, who often had to go to Christian Johannsen for help), Balanchine knows the danseur's implicit needs and potentialities. Nevertheless, the ballerina is the holy purpose for him, the major incentive to create a ballet. We all are differently mature and temperamentally more or less balanced on different levels. Where Balanchine's sensuous and sensual feelings are challenged, he may lose control of himself and, quite unwittingly, plunge himself into emotional adventures with a most chivalrous gesture with the risk of its quixotic aspects.

Bernard Taper mentions in his biography of Balanchine that even as a young boy, Georgei Balanchivadze "possessed a keen eye for feminine beauty." This keenness grew in him and measurably added to his fortune and misfortune as a male. But I dare maintain that this personal weakness—and I doubt we are justified in calling it so—has had an immeasurable share in the creative power of the artist. His feelings for the beauty of a number of ballerinas (to whom he was legitimately or less legitimately attached) have inspired him to a series of great works of lasting value. The private aspects of his attachments must be left to him and—since apparently little minds and cheap hearts thrive on it—to the business of the gossip columnists; the artistic consequences of his several attachments have so enriched the art that they even seem to mark various phases in Balanchine's choreographic development. After all, in serving "her," he could not help being inspired by her personality and the vision he had of her as a woman. This vision was decisive for the visualizations of his dance works.

It is amazing that in spite of the great emotional involvement that seems to motivate most of his works, it has often been pointed out that they are coldly clinical, athletic, and mechanical. He can be and has often been all of this. But equally he can be blamed for having been romantic, intricate, and emotional—and all this perhaps in a clinical, athletic, and mechanical way. He has undoubtedly been old-fashioned at times and then again very much avant-garde. He has counterbalanced what he smilingly calls "entertainment" with a highly poetic theater of the dance (a term I doubt he is fond of). He has choreographed nearly two hundred ballets since the twenties (he left Russia in 1924)—most of them in the last twenty-five years for the New York City Ballet.

He never compromised with his art, even while working on Broadway and in Hollywood or for the circus. Whatever he did he was genuine Balanchine. He is a choreographer with an open mind and has a way of surprising his most ardent followers with the unexpected. He certainly has one foot in the nineteenth century, upholding Petipa's legacy, but he was one of the first ballet choreographers to have his ballerinas roll on the floor (a conquest of the modern barefoot dancers), and he invited Martha Graham to choreograph *Episodes* with him to Webern's music. At one of his rare public appearances—it was at Cooper Union—he was asked what he thought of the modern dance. His reply: "I don't know any difference between ballet and modern dance. I only know good or bad dancing."

He could never have created a company to his heart's delight had he not had the School of American Ballet for the last forty years, where he and a staff of mainly Russian-trained teachers tutored his future ballerinas. He could observe them while they were still children and on their way to becoming *his* children, the willing instruments of his imagination.

He likes to compare himself to a sculptor and the dancers to clay whom he would approach with only a vague no-

tion of what he wants to mold. It is then that his Muse must kiss him—"on union time," as he is fond of saying. Like a sculptor, he breathes life into his material, giving his shapes form and expression. "The minute I see them," he once told me, "I become excited and stimulated to move them. I do not feel I have to prepare myself. All I know is the music, which I know intimately well. Of course, certain visualizations from listening to the score exist in my mind."

The most important thing for him is the movement itself. His imagination is challenged and guided by the human material, by the dancer's personality. He sees the basic aesthetic elements in the beauty of movement, in the unfolding of rhythmical patterns, and not in any possible meaning or interpretation. He feels that no single fragment of any choreographic score should ever be replaceable by any other fragment; each piece must be unique by itself, the inevitable movement.

To achieve what he sets out to accomplish, nothing is left to chance. He would not think of himself as a great dancer—a knee injury in 1927 has kept his dancing to a minimum—but while choreographing he moves with the dancers, shows, demonstrates, acts out, and dances all parts. He claims he only takes out of a dancer what is in her. Although he is basically a nonverbal person and thinks little of talking about the way he visualizes a phrase, he may stop from time to time to tell an anecdote to underline his point.

Balanchine has often pointed to a "kind of angelic unconcern towards emotion as a special charm of the American dancer." He has always dreamt of soulless angels with long legs and much vigor in them. These qualities correspond to his approach to pure ballet in which the moving body alone must create artistic excitement and evoke images of fantasy and human relationships. His ballerinas are angels, sylphlike creatures, because he chooses and wills them to be that way; they are dancers created in the image of his dream of what a dancer ought to be.

When Stéphane Mallarmé said that one does not write poetry with ideas but with words, he expressed in poetic terms what Balanchine thinks to be true in the dance. In many ways, Mallarmé anticipated Balanchine's essential beliefs by not seeing the dancer as a human being or the dance as a vehicle for emotional and intellectual statements. He envisioned the dancer as only half human, with the other and more important half being a symbol. Mallarmé asked for the elimination of her humanness because the human factors only distract from the visual miracle that unfolds. Mallarmé's postulate that in effacing herself, the dancer lets her motion create its own intrinsic meaning, is basically what Balanchine feels.

However, Balanchine does not follow Mallarmé to his speculative extreme that the function of the dancer's reality is to be nonreal, an ideal link between reality and dream. Balanchine's depersonalization is far more limited. The moving bodies cannot help being concrete manifestations onstage; their interrelations and the metaphors reflecting a tenuous likeness of human relationships are ever-present. The dancers may seem denuded of any personal emotional life, but they articulate, if nothing else, a mood, a very definite spiritual climate dictated by the music and adumbrated by the lines of their bodies. There is often something like a dramatic conflict in the movement per se, a bated inner tension usually dissolved through a surprising or an abrupt ending with the help of Balanchine's wry wit. We have to think only of such a sophisticated "abstract" construction as *Agon* or of a "mood" piece such as *Ivesiana*.

If prolificacy is the sign of genius, then no one can deny him this epithet. But he sees himself in a different light, as a craftsman before anything else, a professional maker of dances. With the attitude of an artisan, sure of himself and the mastering of his material, he does not mind being watched at work. There is a humility about him, genuine as far as his deep religious feeling is concerned, a bit feigned when it is acted out in public—for instance, by demoting himself and his co-workers from artistic directors to ballet masters for a company without stars. He seems to wear his simplicity with some pride, knowing only too well that his stature is much greater than perhaps his superstition may wish to acknowledge.

There are of course people who are dissatisfied with one or another aspect of the New York City Ballet and the way the Company is run. The one aspect which is the Company's forte is, in the eyes of many, its weakness: the fact that you can recognize Balanchine dancers from afar, that Balanchine and the School of American Ballet have produced the long-legged, young, and innocent-looking ballerina, full of energy, bounce, and brio. What a joy to watch them move to Balanchine's inventions! And yet they are typed in a uniform way of cool, unemotional, almost marionettelike precision. These lean, vigorous creatures are young. Some ballet lovers feel that Balanchine has sometimes been merciless to wonderful dancers who have put on weight or years by thinning out their roles.

Some people feel that having become an established institution, the Company is run with a certain disdain toward the public (which never can surmise the tremendous difficulties and intricacies of holding such an enterprise together) and that Balanchine, being a national figure ready for a figurative shrine or monument, seems to show an "either-you-believe-in-me-or-not" attitude.

However, the only real flaw that may be found about the Company is its being so very much a one-man show. Although this is the true miracle Balanchine has worked over all these years, some people have nevertheless been frightened by the lack of choreographies by other artists. When from time to time outsiders were invited, their works fell badly off as very minor tries. Taras, Moncion, d'Amboise, Clifford, Tanner, and Massine Jr., younger members of the Company, had their chances. But the question arises whether Balanchine should not have taken time off to help and labor with these young choreographers in a workshoplike fashion, giving their fledgling creations a more final *Gestalt*. Lately, Jerome Robbins's contributions have added a welcome note of variety to the Balanchine repertory, above all with *Dances at a Gathering* and his *Dybbuk* legend. Robbins, who also gives more attention to the male dancers, collaborated with Balanchine on the ballet *Pulcinella*. A great part of the audience (including some critics who may have written positively about it) felt unnerved by Robbins's experimental work, *Watermill*, but Kirstein and Balanchine kept it in the repertory, a great and artistically justifiable gesture.

But this brings up the most often asked question of who may be Balanchine's heir. It may be a moot question as long as he is around, but it is one with a built-in urgency. On the one hand, Balanchine admits that he will stop choreographing when he can no longer move and show the dancers what he means; but in the next breath he will claim that a Georgian lives to be a hundred and thirty-five, and he doesn't think of his final day. Since all the dancers are virtually his instruments and dependent on his virtuosity, neither he nor anyone else can imagine that this one-man company would not have to change drastically in other hands. The New York City Ballet is so very much Balanchine's company, associated with his highly personal style and concept, that it may be well and only fair to rename it when its master reaches his hundred-thirty-fifth year.

I have met George Balanchine personally only a few times. But whenever I have left him, I have had the ambiguous feeling of having known him intimately for a long time while being sure of never coming close to him. But this, I think, was precisely the impression he wanted to leave with me.

I remember the day when I was assigned to write an essay on Balanchine for the State Department magazine *America*, distributed in Russia and Poland. The editors sent me back to Balanchine with the idea of showing him the pictures accompanying my essay and having him give me his precise explanations for the necessary captions.

Balanchine sat with me in front of the pictures. He sniffed and then looked at the first set, saying very slowly, with deliberate pauses: "You see, I put Suzanne Farrell over there, not too far from Jacques d'Amboise—and then I said to Jacques, you step here with a—" Balanchine interrupted himself and turned to me: "You're the writer. This is your baby, you know better to say what you see—" and he shuffled the pictures together as if they were playing cards.

Balanchine rarely reads reviews and bothers little to know about what writers have to say about him. It too often makes little sense to him. Should he ever care to glance at what I have said here, the best comment I may expect is his favorite phrase: "Too fancy!" But it is a pleasant feeling to know that he will forgive me because he knows I love the dance, including most of his ballets, and am a writer who no more can help writing than he can help choreographing. Words are not his passion. He loves to listen to music. He also loves to cook. But cooking is not too far removed from choreographing. All he needs for it are the right ingredients, good measurements, precise mixing, taste, and a lot of imagination. And he is an incontestable master in all that.

THE SCHOOL OF AMERICAN BALLET

by Nancy Goldner

The School of American Ballet is an institution unique in America because its purpose is to train *professional* ballet dancers. Today, with ballet a widespread fact of cultural life, the desire to dance on the stage is relatively acceptable; in 1934, however, when the School of American Ballet opened, ballet was something Europeans did. The purpose of Lincoln Kirstein's invitation to George Balanchine to work in America was to extend ballet life as Balanchine knew it—the structure he was born into in Imperial Russia—across the ocean. Since Balanchine had already shown himself to be an outstanding and prolific choreographer by 1934, the key concept in America could afford to be permanency, the opportunity for a continual production of ballets. Choreographers need an ever-renewing supply of dancers; hence the rationale for a school-company relationship. Had Balanchine been primarily a teacher instead of a choreographer, the establishment of a school would have insured proper training—this we may assume, given his St. Petersburg schooling—but it would have been an incomplete, even sterile, undertaking. The School was not intended to offer the niceties of a liberal-arts education; it did not claim that ballet instruction had some intrinsic worth, and it certainly had no intention of shipping its graduates back to Europe. Its function was pragmatic: to prepare students for employment and to give Balanchine the material he needed. A significant, even symbolic, fact about the School of American Ballet is that in March 1934, just two months after the doors opened, Balanchine assembled his advanced students and began making *Serenade*. Just four months after that, the school had a performing wing, when *Serenade* was danced for an invited public at an estate in White Plains, New York.

Being a vocational school gives the School of American Ballet a simplicity of purpose but also means that it must operate on exact and exacting principles. Whereas people who enter medical school, for example, are old enough to know what they want and have the maturity to modify their lives according to the demands of their studies, the eight- and nine-year-olds who begin to study ballet cannot understand what they are getting themselves into. Usually their parents do not understand either, because it is not the custom in America to associate childhood with serious and hard labor. A child (the vast majority are girls) enters the School of American Ballet in a fairly blind state, buttressed perhaps only by a vision of *Serenade* as it is now performed by the New York City Ballet, or more likely by an experience with *The Nutcracker*, where she sees children not much older than herself dancing on stage. That is, if she is lucky, she enters the school with these visions. Very often it is her parents who have the visions. In the Soviet Union and Denmark, where ballet schools are subsidized by the state and where it is more generally and deeply understood that ballet is a consuming and long course of study, the little child is sent to a boarding school where all her needs are met; she is fed, clothed, instructed in academics, ballet and related fields of dance, stagecraft, and music; then she's bedded down at night. The School of American Ballet offers only ballet lessons, the point being that, in not being a boarding school, it does not have an apparatus that can become a kind of symbol of crossing a threshold. So it is more difficult for an American child than it is for a Russian child to discover what vocational training means.

Because the School of American Ballet has always been associated with Balanchine, and because from 1934 until the present Balanchine has always drawn most of his dancers from the School—whether for his various Broadway and Hollywood projects, the several predecessors of the New York City Ballet, or now the New York City Ballet—the school's professional orientation is so ingrained and ordained that the stakes inevitably become clear to students. This happens through a subtle psychological process—the School operates as though it were perfectly normal in American society for children to organize their lives around work. Naturally, the School accommodates itself to American life, but it is an accommodation. The School's expectation of professional interest and drive makes itself felt immediately.

First of all, every applicant is given an audition to see if she has sufficient promise and to determine what class her technique qualifies her for. (Auditions are held once weekly throughout the year.) Students already in their teens must qualify at least for the intermediate level. If they are not sufficiently strong for that level by the time they are fourteen, say, it is highly unlikely that they will ever become professional ballet dancers. Exceptions are made for boys, but only out of necessity. Beginning students from ages ten to thirteen are enrolled in an accelerated beginner course. Given its purpose, however, the School prefers beginners to be eight or nine years old (the Russian academies accept students at age nine) and to be *real* beginners, since it has found that most local training can be harmful and, at best, needs to be unlearned. For this group, "promise" means a well-proportioned body and, most importantly, flexible limbs and arched feet. The teacher who auditions does not ask the beginner to do actual ballet steps, but examines her feet and moves her back and legs to determine muscular temperament. At the end of the examination, the teacher asks the child to improvise to music, and notes if the child can move rhythmically and can adjust her movement to changes in tempi.

The eight- and nine-year-olds, in Children 1, attend classes only twice a week, but their hour-long baptisms are by fire, and the level of concentration demanded by the teacher is incredibly high. There is no "free movement," and since the students have so few steps at their command, there is little chance for variation. Moreover, since the students are so preoccupied with basics—standing up correctly, keeping stomachs pulled in, pointing feet, learning the muscular mysteries of turnout in the legs—the teacher can barely burden their minds with combinations of steps. At first they do four or eight battements tendus in each direction; not until later on in the year, or perhaps in the second year, are they asked to handle a more sophisticated but still very elementary combination, such as three battements tendus to the front and one to the side, three to the back and one to the side.

Of necessity, first-year studies are mostly drudgery and certainly no fun. A sense of progress or achievement is so hard-won that one can only marvel that any of the students have spirit left to feel it at all. Some react to the discipline and the humdrumness of the lessons by tuning out, so that they walk or dream themselves through class, or by becoming class cutups. As is always the case in life, boredom becomes a self-perpetuating cycle to failure. The more the student removes herself from the moment, the more difficult it is for her to jump into it later on, and so the more difficult it becomes to reap the rewards that encourage greater participation. However, a few children do learn the rare pleasure of doing something well, and all are spared the chaos of a half-baked education.

The School has a fixed schedule of attendance that gradually increases as the student progresses through the five Children divisions or the two older Beginner divisions (A1 and A2). Teachers do not take kindly to chronic absence, tardiness, or excuses of stomachaches while class is going on. They reprimand daydreamers and, while they realize that the child has just spent a whole day at academic school, they never openly acknowledge to the students that they know it is difficult to concentrate intensely right after a day's confinement in school.

Toward the end of the year, the teachers submit brief reports on their students. On these grounds, children are advanced, left behind, dismissed, or warned that they will have to make great progress the following year in order to continue at the School. In the beginning, teachers comment as much on attitude and brightness as they do on technical proficiency. In spring of 1974, six of the thirty-seven children in Children 1 class were asked to withdraw, mostly for reasons of discipline and laziness. The School's most thorough weeding occurs before the student enters the second Intermediate level, now called B2.

Obviously, however, the dropping-out process is two-way. Much of the enrollment drop is by attrition. Students cannot cope with competition, and lose sight, or never gain sight, of the connection between classroom exercises and dancing. For many entering their teens, sexual fantasies take precedence over everything else, leaving little energy to think about pliés. Like mathematics, ballet technique advances by geometric progression, and there comes a day when many find that they just cannot keep up.

Yet because ballet has become increasingly popular and seemingly more accessible, and because the School of American Ballet has that gigantic lollipop called *Nutcracker*, children—and their parents especially—are more likely to cling to dreams of ballerinadom than they were in the 1940s and early 1950s. Thus the faculty and administration must draw an increasingly "tough" line on enrollment. To parents, the School must seem harsh indeed. To children, who usually know better than their parents what is demanded of them as would-be professionals and how well they can live with that expectation, the School is probably more resolutely fair than harsh. For the School, whose business is to produce dancers, not

well-rounded, gracious young men and women or even first-rate amateurs, anything less than a tough line would negate its raison d'être.

The time slots given to classes are perhaps the School's most tangible expression of the all-consuming nature of a dance education.

Up to the first Intermediate level (B1), classes do not begin until 4:00 P.M. But B2 classes, the level at which the School does its most thorough elimination process, start at 2:30 P.M. Thus when a student enters B2, at about age fourteen, she must decide whether to enter a school with special hours, such as Professional Children's School, so that she can take the daily 2:30 class. Such private schools entail huge expense for the family and may even require a move into Manhattan. For the student, this means entering a much less "normal" world and making a formal declaration of intent regarding a career that neither she nor her teachers can yet guarantee. At this point, of course, parents and children want a firm word of encouragement from the School of American Ballet. But in most cases it cannot say, "Yes, you will be a dancer; the New York City Ballet wants *you*," because bodies and minds still go through drastic changes during adolescence. Also, beginning with the B2 level, technical demands grow disproportionately; this is the time when a young dancer's drive for excellence is severely tested and often broken. Thus the very structure of the School forces students to reckon with psychological stresses that most adults usually spend their lives avoiding, and they're reckoning at an age American society still calls childhood.

It is at the B2 level also that the required number of classes per week can discourage the less committed. Before this, boys and girls must attend four classes weekly, although many girls in B1 attend more. At B2 the number jumps to eight (six ballet classes and two toe classes). The boys, whose classes are separated from the girls', may still be taking four or five lessons a week, since they have probably started instruction at a later age. At the C and D levels, however, both sexes are spending most of their time at the School, squeezing in academics on the off-hours.

The boys have class every day with Richard Rapp, Stanley Williams, Antonina Tumkovsky, Peter Martins, or a guest teacher from 12:30 to 2:00 P.M.* From 2:30 to 4:00, they must take one or two supported adagio classes and a workshop class in preparation for the school's annual concert. There is an evening men's class from 5:30 to 7:00.

The advanced girls, split into C1, C2, and D levels, have ballet class from 10:30 A.M. to noon. From 2:30 to 4:00, the C1 girls have a toe class once a week, one variations class in which Alexandra Danilova teaches them dances from the standard Russian repertory, and one supported adagio class. At the same afternoon hour, the girls in C2 and D are attending each week one adagio class, two workshops with Danilova and Suki Schorer, and a variations class with Danilova. Advanced girls also attend three more evening ballet classes from 5:30 to 7:00. (They take nine classes weekly.)

As the spring workshop performance approaches, rehearsals are added to the schedule. Thus, advanced-level students, some as young as fifteen, may attend as many as thirteen classes a week. The School requires them to enroll for at least eight classes, but this is an arbitrary number. Ten classes per week (six morning classes and four specialized classes in the afternoon) would seem to be the minimum.

The School of American Ballet has always operated with exacting and rigorous standards. The faculty has always given classes designed to turn students into first-rate dancers, and the School has always demanded that advanced students attend at least eight classes a week. Yet, until a ten-year Ford Foundation grant was given the

School in 1964, and to a certain degree after that and into the present, the administration has had to negotiate an inherent contradiction: it wants only professional-caliber enrollment, but it must support itself through tuition. In the 1930s, 40s, and 50s, the student body had more dead weight as a result. During these decades, there were also fewer gradations of classes (for example, four Children's divisions instead of five, one B class instead of B1 and B2), which meant much larger class size, sometimes as many as thirty-five or forty in an evening C class, when professional dancers would join the students. Each of the School's residences (previous to the present Juilliard facilities), at Madison Avenue and Fifty-ninth Street (1934–1956) and Eighty-third Street and Broadway (1956–1969), had only two large studios and one smaller one. There simply was no space for more classes, nor could the administration afford to demand that teen-age students attend early-afternoon classes.

Larger classes with fewer highly qualified students mitigated to some extent the extreme professional air and the pressure to excel, which now flourish without restraint. Children in particular are helped immeasurably by today's smaller classes. The teacher's eye is felt more directly at a time when students' ability to motivate themselves is still developing, and individualized instruction can be truly enlightening. Today classes average around 20. Total enrollment is about 350, only 25 of them boys.

The School's success in expanding and refining curriculum and in drawing better students was in large measure due to the Ford Foundation program begun in 1964, but improvements would have occurred anyway, though not so quickly or thoroughly, because they had to happen. The entire dance field was expanding, and the "cultural boom" necessitated more and better dancers. The New York City Ballet itself was growing and its roots were deepening.

---

* In 1976 boys' classes were also taught by Andrei Kramarevsky, a former principal with the Bolshoi, and Jean-Pierre Bonnefous of the New York City Ballet.

Around 1960 Balanchine started to reform the School of American Ballet by hiring more faculty, instituting a special small class for the best students, and starting a complete male division. (Previously there had been only one or two men's classes a week.) In the early 1960s, when these programs had been in effect a while, the administration concluded that if the School continued to follow Balanchine's course it would plunge nicely into the red. It was also during this time that the Ford Foundation asked the school to draw up a proposal for a national program of ballet education. Like all historical processes, the growth of ballet, the City Ballet, and the School and the coming of the Ford Foundation grant converged in a mixture of coincidence and inevitability.

The Ford Foundation program was in two parts. The first centered around the School. Money was allotted for operating expenses and for renting space in the new Juilliard School at Lincoln Center. Although the School had always given some scholarships, the grant made it possible to offer more tuition scholarships, aid for private school, and living expenses of $200 a month (raised to $220 in 1975–1976) for students around the country who were thought promising enough to be transported to New York for study, either for the summer or for the entire year. The School had never found that New York alone could supply enough talent to justify its operation, and so the Ford grant enabled it to consider the United States its talent pool.

Yet even with this national scope, it does not have the resources of the Russian, Danish, or English academies to take full responsibility for nonlocal students' living arrangements. Seven younger students (ages fourteen and fifteen) live with Madame Guillerm, the mother of Violette Verdy, a principal with the City Ballet. The School tries to place other young ones with the families of local students, but sometimes a Ford Foundation scholarship necessitates the student's family moving to New York.

Older recipients, sixteen and seventeen years of age, live in residences approved by the School and often rent apartments together once they have been in New York for a while. Obviously, a move to New York is beset with complications, not the least of them the emotional one of leaving home and friends. Yet it enables those who want to become dancers *to* become dancers, not only through study but through the stimulation of competition and exposure to all of New York's professional dance companies. The New York City Ballet is a prime beneficiary, but a program that concentrates talent in one place is a boon to all.

The second part of the Ford Foundation program was designed to improve ballet education in the local community. Acting as administrator, the School was essentially an intermediary between the Foundation and the nation. School faculty and dancers from the City Ballet traveled to schools that applied for aid, watched classes, and recommended scholarships for local study, subject to yearly renewal. Matching grants were given to schools that wanted to set up beginner programs for children without the financial means for study. In many instances, the Ford representative taught at the local school for a day or so, while local teachers came to the school to observe. In the program's early years, Balanchine taught master classes at the School of American Ballet, which teachers from all over the country attended.

In the academic year 1971–1972, for example, 42 schools in 12 states were observed. The number of local scholarships awarded was 233 in 68 schools, and 8 beginner groups were operating. Scholarships to the School of American Ballet's 1972 summer course were given to 93 students from 52 schools, and out of that group, 12 won scholarships to the School for the following year. At the School itself, 79 students (34 of them boys) were on tuition scholarship, 41 of whom received additional aid for living expenses and academic tuition. Some scholarship students (as well as other students) participated in lecture-demonstrations led by Suki Schorer. For these 42 performances in metropolitan-area schools, the dancers received $30 a performance and $2 an hour for rehearsals. (No scholarship students are allowed to perform without the School's permission, and no dance engagements, such as the lecture-demonstrations, may interfere with regular classes at the School for any student.)

In 1973, this pilot program terminated. The Ford Foundation then approved a second grant of $1.5 million, covering the period 1974–1979, this time contingent on the School's raising equivalent funds. An additional $500,000 will be forthcoming if this money also is matched. The present grant is entirely for the operating expenses of the School; for the moment, the regional program has been suspended.

That the School of American Ballet is the official school of the New York City Ballet gives it distinct coloration beyond its professional orientation. Balanchine hires faculty, determines curriculum, and instigates new programs, such as those carried on just before and during the Ford Foundation period. Eugenie Ouroussow, the late executive director, and Natalie Molostwoff, who now holds the post, would not hire a teacher for a single class without Balanchine's permission, and all teachers have watched Balanchine teach. In the School's early years, Balanchine was a regular member of the faculty. Today he occasionally gives a class for the advanced students, but his place is in the theater, not the School. When openings develop in the New York City Ballet's corps de ballet, he asks advanced students to take his daily company class and to become apprentices for a season. In April 1974, during the period I was observing classes, he invited six girls into his company (which effectively wiped out level D class for the rest of the year). The faculty recommends students to his attention, but he does not necessarily follow their advice. Yet he draws all of his ensemble from the School (in 1974, sixty-two of the eighty-member company were graduates). Thus a student aiming for the New York City Ballet must study at its school.

Students are very much aware of the City Ballet's existence. Company members take class at the School, and ex-members Suki Schorer and Richard Rapp and present members Carol Sumner, David Richardson, Peter Martins, and Colleen Neary teach there. Company rehearsals are sometimes held if studios are available. Advanced students learn some of the Balanchine repertory (instead of the usual series of grands battements that end a class, Schorer gives her third-year children the grand battement combination from the end of Balanchine's *Stars and Stripes!*). And of course there are the ballets that use children from the School—*Nutcracker, Harlequinade, Pulcinella, A Midsummer Night's Dream, Don Quixote, Firebird, Coppélia,* and two ballets for the Stravinsky Festival, *Circus Polka* and *Choral Variations on Bach's "Vom Himmel Hoch."* With many students, there is much bugaboo about "getting into the company." As students mature—as they understand that they may not be material for Balanchine for reasons of physique and technique, or that Balanchine might not be the material for *them*— other companies might become "the" company. Since the School is considered to be among the best in the world, directors from dance groups all over the world use the advanced classes as their supply depots. The School's grapevine on auditions flourishes, and the administration actively tries to place those of its best students not likely to be candidates for the City Ballet, or who do not want it, with other professional companies. The School serves a global ballet community as well as Balanchine.

Students at the School of American Ballet learn standard ballet technique as it is taught in Russia and, with certain deviations, in England and Denmark. Essentially this is a technique taught by Russian-trained dancers and their students. Pierre Vladimiroff, the School's first teacher, from January 2, 1934, until 1968 (died 1970), was a graduate of the Imperial School of Ballet and was a leading dancer of the Maryinsky Theater, where Balanchine studied and performed in his youth. Anatole Oboukhoff, on the faculty from 1941 until his death in 1962, also had the same background, and so do present teachers Felia Doubrovska (Vladimiroff's wife) and Alexandra Danilova. Danilova was Balanchine's classmate, and Doubrovska was also an alumna of the Imperial School; both were with Diaghilev's Ballets Russes when Balanchine was its chief choreographer. Helene Dudin and Antonina Tumkovsky are graduates of the State Choreographic School in Kiev and were soloists with the Kiev State Theater of Opera and Ballet. Muriel Stuart was taught by Anna Pavlova from age eight and toured with her company. Stanley Williams comes from the Danish-Russian tradition, having graduated from the Royal Danish Ballet School and performed with the Royal Danish Ballet. Elise Reiman is the first of the School's staff to be a graduate of it and a member of Balanchine's early companies, American Ballet and Ballet Society, as well as New York City Ballet. Now Richard Rapp, Suki Schorer, and the present Company members provide more immediate links, but the major difference between their classes and those of the Russians is that they speak English better. Among the teachers, there are variations in emphasis, and all teachers have their own accents, apparent not only in what they choose to correct but in the amount of teaching they do. Some are more verbal and analytical; others let the exercises speak for themselves, so that students learn simply by doing. The ex-Company teachers are younger and so demonstrate more, but the older teachers set marvelous examples of regal carriage and of the use of épaulement, by showing how a slight shift in the shoulders or head can make the difference between an elegant and a dead-looking dancer.

The first two divisions are taught by Tumkovsky, Dudin, and Reiman. In Children 1, Tumkovsky goes from girl to girl at the barre, adjusting feet with a stick or her hands and making sure that elbows are rounded, pinkies are held out away from the other fingers, and that knees and backs are straight. She does not allow girls to turn their feet out to a full 180-degree angle if their knees must bend to support the legs in that extreme position. She does not allow them to lift their legs so high that their backs cave in. Certain steps at the barre are broken down into parts. In grand battement, the leg first points in tendu and then kicks. In rond de jambe the leg does not make a continuous circle but stops at the front, side, and back. However, even in the first year the students learn all the barre exercises that the advanced divisions do. Combinations in the center are very simple, and before each jump exercise, the children first practice it at the barre. To compensate, in a way, for the dryness of the class and to maintain a high energy level, Tumkovsky keeps the pace as quick as possible and talks in a loud voice. She ends the class on a dancy note by having the children chassé across the room. To tell the truth, this is the only part they seem really to enjoy. The rest is strange and even painful.

The students in Children 2 look markedly more alert and show more awareness of their bodies. They look more in one piece, and some already have bearing; they understand that heads must be held high in ballet. With these young children, Dudin is perhaps more concerned with their alertness than with technique. She scolds them gently when they do not pay attention, and when someone makes a mistake, she demands that the child figure out what is wrong. She will wait patiently, even if it means holding up the class for minutes, for the child to respond—and to respond with the *right* answer. Children learn from the start that details are everything. In one exercise that was done two by two, Dudin told them to look at each other before making a preparatory plié for emboîtés forward. The girls who did not first look at each other had to repeat the exercise until they did it correctly. In all levels all teachers stress the importance of épaulement—a croisé positioning of the shoulders must be croisé, en face must be en face, effacé must be effacé, écarté must be écarté. In the young divisions Reiman, Dudin, and Tumkovsky stop the class when students are hazy about these positions, and have everyone repeat the combination with greater clarity. In other words, students must learn that to do an assemblé en face when the teacher said to land in croisé is as big a mistake as doing a jeté instead of an assemblé. Details of this sort seem to be the hardest for children to learn, especially as the combinations become more complex and quicker. The advanced students work on the same problems, but the problems become more refined. They must find just the right amount of shoulder angle and must learn how to flow from one angle to another with just the right amount of motion.

In Children 3, the technical demands and complexity of combinations rise enormously, and one can see a noticeably greater strength in the legs and backs when compared to the two earlier divisions. At the barre the adagio exercises, with développés and dégagés, are much longer. Sumner and Schorer have the students do pirouettes at the barre in preparation for turns in the center. In the center the children do more things on one leg, which requires better balance and strong muscles for the supporting leg. Sumner reminds them that in preparations for pirouettes, the back leg should be straight (their first explicit exposure to one of Balanchine's few rules). Schorer stresses posture at the barre—straight backs, eyes straight ahead, buttocks taut, hips straight, no rolling over onto the front of the foot, and so forth. Like Tum-

kovsky, Dudin, and Reiman, Sumner and Schorer use the time at the barre for visiting each girl and making the necessary pushes and shoves. When the teacher grasps a girl's hips so that she finds she cannot swing her legs up so easily, a knowing smile passes between teacher and student. The student learns that there's quite a difference between throwing the leg up in any manner possible and throwing it up with the hip held in place. Yet in Children 4 and 5, when students must start striving for a high leg extension, Dudin will often raise a girl's leg much higher than the girl could achieve herself with her hips held in place. Thus the student must learn to work at a problem from both ends, to know when to let a high extension take precedence over hip placement and vice versa. Then when she starts taking Balanchine's class, she must juggle the two concerns again: she must get her leg *still* higher without bringing the hip out of alignment "too much"— but how much is too much?

Pointe work begins in Children 4, during the last fifteen minutes of each class. The girls wear especially light shoes, designed by Balanchine and a Capezio engineer. The most-stressed technical aspect, in this and the B toe classes, is the manner in which the girls rise on pointe. They must roll up, not jump. All movement must go through demi-pointe, and they must learn to use their pointe shoes as flexibly as their ballet shoes. This is one reason why Balanchine requires that girls from the intermediate levels on take ballet class in toe shoes. The students' constant striving for turnout and arched feet really comes into play with pointe work, and those who have not progressed in these areas find in toe work their Waterloo. Girls in Children 5 have a weekly one-hour class devoted specifically to pointe, and here they join girls in A2.

The convergence of the five Children divisions and two older Beginners' divisions in the elementary toe class is as good a measure as any of the older students' accelerated pace. The barre in A1 is about as quick, complicated, and strenuous as that in Children 3. Because their muscles are stronger, the older beginners are expected to use more gusto in forcing their legs up and out. In A2 they learn the same refinements taught in Children 4 and 5, and teachers tend to approach the steps more analytically and from an inner, or muscular, point of view. Richard Rapp can tell them to pull up on the standing leg, to press legs out in plié, to brush the leg in frappé with sharp attack— that is, he can use concepts a ten-year-old could not understand because she does not yet have enough muscular self-consciousness. Rapp and Reiman can expect them to work on the details of exercises; for example, sometimes in battement tendu with plié, they are asked to first bring the leg to fifth position and *then* plié. This method poses a much greater challenge to turnout and forces the student to turn her heel forward in tendu. These teachers stress the muscular spring and tautness that is at the very basis of ballet technique. They demand that rather than sit in plié, the student immediately rise with resilience. All leg movements must be sharply accented on the upbeat. In battement the leg must whoosh up and come softly down without collapsing. Frappés must be strongly accented out. Every movement must be rhythmically dynamic, fast at the outset and held for a split second at the finish. Reiman's students learn what "phlegmatic" means; Schorer speaks of limp macaroni. Stuart is perhaps the most theoretical of the teachers, and students do not take her class until they reach A2 and Children 5. Her central theme is that the buttocks must be pulled up and the back muscles down. Whereas other teachers ask students for more turn-out by asking them to turn their thighs out and push their heels forward (Tumkovsky and Dudin merely order, "more turn the leg out!!"), Stuart asks them to pull their buttocks up more. She also verbalizes more extensively the "secret" that students have been slowly discovering: muscular tension and control are hidden, and the head, neck, and arms—the parts of the body that are most likely

to display tension—must not be rigidly gripped, but held softly, with alertness.

In B1 girls are taught by Danilova for the first time. She does most of the barre right along with the students, but manages to keep her eye on them through the mirrors lining one wall of the studio. At the barre she gives ample time for balances at the conclusion of exercises done on demi-pointe and tends to give practical hints for balancing, such as keeping the front arm slightly above eye level in arabesque. After the barre, the girls do their own leg stretches, just about the only free movement ever allowed at the School of American Ballet. In the second half of the class, Danilova often teaches variations; at one class I watched, these were a simplified variation from *Sleeping Beauty*, a minuet to music from the same ballet, a tarantella, and a polonaise. She insists on careful épaulement, which she demonstrates in high style, and on moving exactly—but exactly—with the music. She reprimands girls who dance like wooden sticks and mimics them to make her point. Of all the teachers, Danilova seems to be most concerned with the ballerina style and with having students move slightly in anticipation of the beat.

B2 and the C and D classes are more of the same—just longer and harder. The fast exercises are faster; the slower ones slower. Combinations are trickier, requiring fast shifts in weight, and are longer, requiring more stamina. Whereas the less advanced grades do adagio movements on the flat foot in center work, now the students must rise onto demi-pointe as much as possible. Jumps are laced with batterie. Pirouettes must be triple or quadruple, although B2 girls are encouraged to give clean execution precedence over number, even if that means only a single turn. With B2 begins work on turns in arabesque, attitude, and à la seconde, and by C they are par for the lesson.

At this level students meet two more teachers, Williams and Doubrovska. Williams's time is spent mostly with men's classes and the C and D classes, but he does teach one B2 class a week. Doubrovska normally instructs only the C and D classes, but when D was temporarily suspended in mid-April 1974, she was assigned to one B2 class and now teaches B2 regularly. Doubrovska stresses virtuoso aspects—balances, big jumps, and, especially, turns. She spends much time on the use of the arms for turns and has a hawk's eye for chests and backs that are anything less than regally held. At the barre she gives some exercises, such as grands battements and ronds de jambe, at a very quick pace, almost as fast as Balanchine. She wants square hips, a taut and highly pulled-up torso, and proper placement at the conclusion of a big jump so that the student can move from jump to jump easily and quickly. Herself a model of elegant carriage, she constantly reminds her students not to collapse after a combination, but to be en garde and gracious all the time. Épaulement is a means of presenting oneself to the audience. Presentation of self is the real significance of turnout, Doubrovska implies. With Doubrovska and Danilova, the student begins to perceive herself as performer.

Williams is perhaps the most idiosyncratic teacher. Whereas all the teachers at all levels jump back and forth between basic and refined corrections, Williams directs all comments to the refinements that interest him most. He seems to be envisaging the students as *his* ideal dancers. (I write *seems* because understanding exactly what Williams is after is almost an intuitive process, with sporadic flashes of recognition.) He seems to be primarily interested in a sustained legato quality of movement. Whereas Rapp, Reiman, and Schorer often want exercises to be separated (and hold!, and hold!, and hold!), and whereas the other teachers are not so explicit about this but imply it by exhorting students to be more energetic and forceful, Williams wants exercises to be done in one sustained and steady breath, and he wants this sustained

rhythm without a loss of tension. To communicate this, he says that he wants the leg to "go through" fifth position, rather like electrically charged taffy. In one B2 class I observed, which, as Williams acknowledged to the class at the end, was one of the most intense he taught, he told them that in an exercise in which the leg développés front, goes into passé, and then into arabesque, he wanted the leg to go through passé on one count, like "pulling thread through a needle." A stop in passé, or for that matter in fifth position in battement and fondu exercises, is a rest and "you've lost it," "it" being that string of tension. In adagio combinations and in adagio class, Williams always wants a sense of movement even if the body is still. In adagio class he repeatedly tells the girls not to think about balancing in promenades but about their "position." If the girls are not in position, the movement "dies." What Williams is getting at here is the problem of occupying space vibrantly and authoritatively when the body is static. For supported turns in adagio class and in unsupported turns in regular ballet class, he always tells the students not to think of the turn but of the passé or attitude. He wants an illusion that the turner is always facing front, trying to pull a single clear, crystallized image out of a blur. Williams speaks of what to think and what not to think. In the men's classes, he says not to think of a jump as a jump but as a plié, so as to get that continuity of movement between the floor and the air. He is more interested in ballon, less in elevation, more interested in a clear position in turns, less in the number of turns. More than any other teacher, Williams makes dancing a mental exercise, a matter of concentration. Most of the boys are not advanced enough to grasp or make use of his subtleties. Because he forces dancers to rethink what they are doing, while the other teachers force them merely to think of a thousand familiar things at once, the students tend to look more amateurish in his classes than in others'. But because the girls ordinarily are stronger and more experienced than the boys, their weakness proceeds from strength; they can afford to experiment on this very high level.

Do the teachers prepare students for Balanchine? It is not difficult to pick out those technical emphases Balanchine will be happy to see in his Company class, yet most of them would please most teachers. When teachers ask for energy, a high carriage of the chest, high leg extensions, extreme turnout when the leg is in effacé or à la seconde, a taut plié, springy glissades with the accent in fifth, assemblés with the legs together in the air, a straight back leg in preparation for pirouettes, precise definition of all the shoulder and head positions; when teachers work for speed; when they design combinations that develop quickness in weight shifts; and when they ask that combinations be done in reverse so as to develop mental flexibility and to discourage a habit-forming approach to movement—they are preparing students for Balanchine. The one important exception to Balanchine-teacher accord is Williams's demand that battement, fondu, and frappé series be one steady flow. Balanchine wants them separated, with a slight accent out and a larger accent in fifth position. There is also a difference in ports de bras. The teachers want arms to move in a long line and at standard distance from the body. Balanchine likes the arms closer to the body in transitional movements, so that the elbows are more prominent, and wants a bigger-than-life silhouette once the pose is hit. Generally Balanchine wants a more voluptuous look in arm movement; Schorer calls the look "juicy." Also, Balanchine wants the thumb more prominently displayed than some teachers call for. In rond de jambe some teachers want the accent out, whereas Balanchine usually wants it without accent; here Williams is in accord with Balanchine. Perhaps Rapp in his men's classes and Schorer in her advanced classes are the most doctrinaire Balanchinians, but all the other teachers share their methods qualitatively if not quantita-

tively. As I have written, in most cases it is a matter of emphasis.

On the other hand, no class at the School of American Ballet really prepares a student for Balanchine. First of all, there are physical matters less superficial than one might suspect. As many as eighty may attend Company class in the State Theater's big rehearsal studio. Dancers hang off the rafters, and it takes a while to find one's comfortable rafter. Then, the dancers wear individually concocted warm-up costumes. They seem to take special delight in the contradictory effect of raggedy leotards and assorted bulky woolens wrapped around their beautiful, sleek bodies. The overall effect is as dizzying as a vista of Neapolitan clotheslines such as even Eugene Berman could not duplicate in his sets for *Pulcinella*. Classes at the School are conducted at a quick clip, but Balanchine's classes are in another time zone. There is absolutely no break between the left-foot and right-foot exercises at the barre. There is barely a break when Balanchine explains what exercise he wants next. He mumbles a word or so, or makes a gesture with his hands, and the dancers go to it with what an outsider perceives to be magical anticipatory speed. At the School the barre is from thirty to forty minutes long; the class, ninety minutes. In Balanchine's one-hour class the barre is only twenty minutes, yet every exercise is covered. Balanchine condenses barre work by cutting out the frills and by setting a fast tempo.

Condensing involves heightening. Balanchine's classes are designed to present normal academic exercises and combinations in their most heightened, or difficult, form. This is the crux of the matter; and this is what no student is prepared for. The tempo for each exercise is as fast or as slow as is necessary for it to be just beyond the reach of possibility. Balanchine seems to be especially fond of a series of battements tendus and jetés that becomes faster and faster until teasingly close to the impossible. Because this series has no rest break or pliés to stretch the muscles in the opposite direction, it is extremely hard on the thighs.

The series will often be continued in the center of the room, where the dancer has no barre for support. To make matters more difficult, the arms are held down so that the dancer cannot use them to balance herself. Since the tendus go in rapidly changing directions, they call for extremely strong backs and great agility in weight shifts. Whereas an adagio combination at the School grows progressively longer, in Balanchine's class it can be longer than long. At one class I observed, he had the dancers do twelve consecutive développés on each foot; as a fillip, each was done in a different position or with different ports de bras. In the School, arabesque penché is common; in Balanchine's class the dancers must do ports de bras while in that position. Hardly anyone can do it without falling over, but falling and stumbling are common features in the professional class. Balanchine's class is truly a place to experiment, to sport with ideals, to look ungainly. Because it is the exact opposite of the performance situation, where everything must go smoothly and effortlessly, it is a haven. Yet it takes time for newcomers to discover that a situation where the premiums are on struggle and failure *is* a haven. Newcomers must develop trust, bravery, and a sense of humor before they can experience the exhilaration of a Balanchine class. In addition, a pre-warmup at the barre is a virtual necessity.

The classes assume an extra difficulty because Balanchine wants each step to be a musical and visual statement. A single développé is an aria unto itself. The movement may perhaps be done on one count but have two climaxes—when the foot leaves the ground for the ankle, and when the moving leg leaves the supporting leg as it unfolds into an extension. Again, this is not in contradiction to what is taught at the School, but an intensification. Sometimes a combination or a series of them will be built around the use of dynamics. In one class the theme was combinations with soutenu, itself an easy step. The idea was to whoosh around in the soutenu, freeze for a fraction of a second, and then whoosh into the next step, a pas de bourrée. A further complication was that the pas de bourrée was supposed to be as fast as the soutenu, which is impossible to really achieve.

In other words, Balanchine wants the dancer to have as much flexibility with his body as the musician has with his piano or violin. When done with Balanchinian dynamics, movements are easy to see and exciting to watch. But I think the crucial factor is their imitation of musical stress. It has been said many times now that watching Balanchine ballet is like seeing the music. His "eye music" is usually attributed to choreography, but the fact is that the musicality of his ballets is built right into the technique, just as the drama of Graham's ballets is built right into her technique. One may deduce from this that technique is not an *a priori* system of rights and wrongs. At the School of American Ballet, technique *is* a historically proven system of rights and wrongs enabling a dancer to dance for anyone and endowing him with a base for forms other than ballet. For Balanchine, technique is a pragmatic and on-going search for a style of moving that will please him once it is seen on the stage. His classes are workshops for the dancers, but they are also preliminary exercises for Balanchine's work as a choreographer.

1
STARTING

1935–1948

On New Year's Day, 1934, following an announcement in the newspaper, the School of American Ballet, 637 Madison Avenue, New York City, held its first auditions. George Balanchine, clearly interested in forming a professional company as soon as possible, selected intermediate and advanced students, some of whom had already been professionally employed. There were few beginners, and no children. Balanchine already had a reputation among those who had been to Europe, and even in America he was beginning to be recognized because the Ballet Russe de Monte Carlo had toured with two of his ballets in the repertory, *Cotillon* and *La Concurrence*. Lincoln Kirstein was known for his editorship of the literary magazine *Hound and Horn*. A nucleus of the first student body and, later, the first company was formed by the well-trained pupils of Catherine Littlefield of Philadelphia. Believing in Balanchine, she sent him her advanced girls as well as her sister Dorothie, who became Balanchine's first assistant.

Within a few months, Balanchine had begun creating ballets, and on 9 June 1934, the first viewing of *Serenade*, *Mozartiana*, and *Dreams*, for an invited audience, was held on a platform erected on the lawn of the Warburg family home in White Plains, New York. (Edward Warburg, a Harvard classmate of Kirstein's, was providing some money for School and Company.) Seven months later another stage was made available, also through Kirstein, at the Wadsworth Atheneum, Hartford, Connecticut, the Avery Memorial Theater. The group, now called the Producing Company of the School of American Ballet, gave four performances, 6–8 December. Not too long afterward, after a "preview" night in Bryn Mawr, Pennsylvania, the American Ballet gave its first season in New York in a professional setting, the Adelphi Theater, opening 1 March 1935 for a week's run. Despite the absence of known dancers other than guest artists Tamara Geva and Paul Haakon, the engagement was successful enough to

be extended another week. Following this, however, the dancers found themselves in a situation they would face again and again: no work. In fact, the entire fourteen years leading up to the formation of the New York City Ballet were a series of stops and starts—two weeks here, six months there, constant disbanding, reformation, in theaters, movie houses, and high-school auditoriums, with long months of unemployment and nothing definite for the future. (Even Ballet Society, the direct forerunner of the New York City Ballet, performed only about four times yearly.) Balanchine kept busy with Broadway musicals, a Hollywood film, engagements in Europe, a stint as ballet master of the Ballet Russe, and Kirstein always had irons in the fire (including one not of his own design, in the service of the U.S. Army), but many dancers dissipated their prime performing years in one abortive enterprise after another. (Most kept returning whenever a new Balanchine venture was announced, however. Then, as now, many felt that, after exposure to him, dancing elsewhere was not worthwhile.) America was simply not ready for more (and, in the forties, much of the talent around was siphoned off to either Ballet Theatre or Ballet Russe); even the initial seasons of the New York City Ballet lasted only three weeks, with extensive layoffs in between.

Two reasons for the slow start were the ignorance of the American public and the tyranny of the Russians in the dance field. The only classical dancers ever seen by most Americans were Pavlova, years before, and, starting in 1932, those in the Ballet Russe. Therefore, in the public and often in the critical mind, only the Russians could dance ballet. (The Ballet Russe was full of non-Russian Europeans, and even Americans who had Russified their names, but this, of course, was not publicized.) Members of the American Ballet noted with some cynicism that the very Balanchine works they had first performed to an indifferent reception were praised when they reappeared in the 1940s in the repertory of the Ballet Russe. If there was any dance in those days of which Americans were capable, it was modern dance. And the moderns had as their ally the most influential critic in print, John Martin of *The New York Times.*

During the thirties and forties, there were only two professional dance critics operating—Martin and Edwin Denby. (Usually music critics, or persons even further removed from dance, reviewed performances, if they were reviewed at all.) Denby was "sold" on Balanchine; Martin, emphatically, was not. Moreover, Denby was in Germany when the American Ballet began, and after returning to America wrote for a bimonthly music magazine; he only briefly had a daily forum, when he was on the staff of the *Herald Tribune* in wartime. Martin had the spotlight at the *Times.* So he and Kirstein went to war—in print, behind the scenes, in letters, on the telephone. (As Anatole Chujoy has observed, it turned out they were both fighting for the same things—against the dreary schmaltz of endless *Scheherazades* and for the primacy of dance unencumbered by phony theatrics.) Not until the very late forties and early fifties did Martin begin to embrace Balanchine's concept of movement (although he had in isolated cases admired some of his ballets for many years) and to decide that an "American" ballet could be and had been created through the efforts of a person he had long considered a talented but insubstantial foreigner. (Just before the war, and permanently afterward, Walter Terry, the first person to train expressly as a dance critic—Martin and Denby were ex-performers—became the regular, and progressive, critic on the *Herald Tribune.*)

In the fall of 1935, the American Ballet embarked on a transcontinental tour, which ended abruptly two weeks later, no farther west than Pennsylvania. But soon after, the American Ballet Ensemble reported for rehearsals as the resident dance group of the Metropolitan Opera. This association, despite its promise of stability and almost year-round work for the dancers, was not a happy one, although it lasted until the spring of 1938. The essential problem was that of opera houses everywhere, even the most glamorous in Europe—they are *opera* houses, in which ballet is ever a stepchild. Dancers performed in all the chestnuts—*Aïda, Carmen, Samson*—and were allowed a few nights or partial evenings of their own. Balanchine mounted the short-lived *Orpheus and Eurydice,* and the next year staged his first Stravinsky festival of three works, with the composer conducting. After leaving the Met, he went to Hollywood to choreograph the movie *Goldwyn Follies,* taking some of his dancers.

Meanwhile, to provide summer employment, a group of twelve organized a touring ensemble called Ballet Caravan. Principals were the Christensen brothers, Eugene Loring, and, the following season, Marie-Jeanne. Kirstein immediately became interested and began providing scenarios, composers, and scene designers; with his encouragement, the subject matter was mainly American.

He engaged Frances Hawkins as business manager (this would have invaluable repercussions later), and, through her association with Martha Graham, who was teaching a summer course at Bennington, the Caravan opened there 17 July 1936. The enterprise caught on, and the Caravan remained in existence until 1940, touring twice to the West Coast and spending a week in Havana, often performing—usually to the accompaniment of one or two pianos—in gyms and movie houses to audiences that had never seen ballet before. However, they rarely appeared in New York. "It was marvelous training, but definitely of the summer entertainment type," says Hawkins. "It was not considered desirable to book the company into New York."

In 1940, there was again a void for the dancers, although they managed to hang on for another six months by performing twelve times daily in *A Thousand Times Neigh* at the Ford Pavilion of the New York World's Fair, in a little skit about horses and motor cars choreographed by William Dollar. In 1941, headed by Balanchine and Kirstein, the American Ballet Caravan was formed and undertook a six-month tour of South America for the U.S. State Department (engineered by Nelson Rockefeller), traveling by slow boat, car, bus, and train, under the shadow of incipient war. Leading dancers were Dollar, Lew Christensen, Gisella Caccialanza, and Marie-Jeanne.

During the war years, there was no employment, although sporadic attempts were made to give concerts. The New Opera company presented a month of *Ballet Imperial* in November 1942. The American Concert Ballet, made up of Balanchine alumni, gave one performance in 1943. In 1945, Balanchine took a group to Mexico to appear in operas, and he staged *Apollo* at the Belles Artes. But there were hiatuses everywhere.

Then, late in 1945, Kirstein got out of the Army. On 5 November 1945, he and Balanchine presented some students at Carnegie Hall in conjunction with Leon Barzin's National Orchestral Association (Barzin would become Balanchine's music director). In September 1946, Kirstein arranged *An American in Paris* for television, choreographed by Todd Bolender. And in November 1946, Ballet Society, a Kirstein enterprise, again with Frances Hawkins, gave its first performance. Ballet Society was dedicated to presenting "lyric theater" on a Diaghilevian scale, featuring specially commissioned music, décor, and choreography, but for subscription audience only, with no critics (they came, but weren't supposed to write reviews, which they did anyway). Operas (including *The Telephone* and *The Medium*) were also given, as were purely musical works and dancing other than ballet.

Ballet was the featured product, however, and Balanchine at last had a platform of his own from which to operate. This accounted for the presence of such established professionals as Maria Tallchief, Nicholas Magallanes, Mary Ellen Moylan, Herbert Bliss, Francisco Moncion, Gisella Caccialanza, and Lew Christensen, but most of the dancers were students. (*The* student discovery of these performances was Tanaquil LeClercq.) However, the venture was self-consuming. It did not seek a large public and thus could not realize much money from ticket sales. The policy of presenting new works at each appearance meant that most were retired after one or a very few showings. The dancers could not make a living. And, in its catch-as-catch-can existence, the company had to perform wherever space was available, with constant changes of location, so its reputation was that of an arty, impermanent, expensive plaything. Hawkins real-

ized that this situation, not to mention the central fact that Kirstein was completely running out of money, could end only as all the previous Kirstein-Balanchine efforts had ended, and it is she who is given great credit for engineering the move to City Center, for encouraging Kirstein to approach the essential Morton Baum. The Company, now called the New York City Ballet, first appeared there as an affiliate of the New York City Opera, on 11 October 1948. Three months later, it performed as an independent component of City Center. Was New York at long last ready for a resident ballet troupe? It seemed the time had come.

AMERICAN BALLET 1935–1938

SERENADE

CHOREOGRAPHY: George Balanchine

MUSIC: Peter Ilyitch Tchaikovsky (Serenade in C for String Orchestra, op. 48, 1880), arranged and orchestrated by George Antheil

COSTUMES: Jean Lurçat (1935) (William B. Oakie, Jr., 1934); Candido Portinari (1941); uncredited tunics (1948); Karinska (1952)

DÉCOR: Gaston Longchamp (1935 and 1936 only; since then danced without décor)

LIGHTING: Jean Rosenthal (1948); Ronald Bates (1964)

PREMIERE: 1 March 1935, Adelphi Theater, New York (first presented 6 December 1934 by the Producing Company of the School of American Ballet, Avery Memorial Theater, Hartford, Conn.)

CAST: *Sonatina:* Leda Anchutina, Holly Howard, Elise Reiman, Elena de Rivas; 13 women; *Waltz:* Anchutina, Sylvia Giselle (Gisella Caccialanza), Howard, Helen Leitch, Annabelle Lyon; 10 women; *Elegy:* Howard, Kathryn Mullowny, Heidi Vosseler, Charles Laskey; 8 women, 4 men

OTHER CASTS: (1941, with *Russian Dance*) Marie-Jeanne, William Dollar, Lorna London; since 1948, solo parts have been taken by virtually every principal dancer in the Company

To think of *Serenade* as old might be misleading. The point the ballet itself set out to prove was the very timeless news of the academic ballet technique." [1]

One day after class in 1934, when the School had been in operation a few months, Balanchine dismissed the boys and clapped his hands for attention. "Mmmm," he said, "I think we'll start something." There had been seventeen girls in the class—and what he "started" was the first ballet especially for his American dancers (all of the other works during the first season would be imports, with the exception of *Alma Mater*, which came a bit later and was not classical ballet); what he started was *Serenade*. From all accounts, some of Balanchine's early dancers were excellent technicians; few, however, had had much stage experience, either because they were very young, or because few jobs were available. What he proceeded to create was a ballet of patterns, a ballet of constant movement, a ballet to train an ensemble. Every dancer did something a little different; there was no posing around watching soloists perform; everyone was a full participant; the stage was a moving floor. Says Anchutina, "We ran and ran and ran."

Although clean technique was called for, few were given the opportunity to display flashy difficulties. There were a number of direct quotes from the classroom—a stageful of girls standing in first position, multiple pirouettes with arms above the head, rather routine adagio sequences with the men, piqué turns in a circle en masse; because of this, and the modesty needed to perform it, *Serenade* reminded Denby of a graduation exercise. Virtuoso ability was not required, except in some demanding solo passages; more necessary were a lift in the torso, limitless breath, a soaring line, and the ability to sustain a phrase and to move and move and move. *Serenade* had little to do with "steps" and everything to do with dancing.

Terry wrote (in what Balanchine considers one of the best descriptions of the ballet):

"The movement inventions of *Serenade* are numberless but among the images retained in the mind are those of a diagonal line of girls, peeling off from their formation one by one and rushing into the wings like a wave from the sea; a grand jeté by a girl into the arms of a man with a sudden reversal in midair from a forward to a backward propulsion; the quiet patterns of a kneeling ensemble of girls as they open their arms in accented pauses along the path of an arc; the traveling turns of the girls culminating in a huge spinning circle; a figure in arabesque, her leg grasped by strong male hands, pivoted slowly in two complete turns while she herself remains motionless." [2]

There are other moments: a delicate waltz for a couple, in which the woman is just lifted off the ground, like a breath; plunging arabesques by the full corps that give the effect of cascading water; the climax of the first movement, when a large group suddenly dissolves into the opening formation, each girl with arm raised as though shielding herself from a brilliant sun; the exquisite pose, from Canova, in which the reclining ballerina gazes up at her standing partner, framed by the rounded arms of the "angel" figure behind him.

Then there was the "story"—or was there a story? Much was hinted—love, rejection, mourning—nothing specified. There were no characters; these were dancers, not people, who anguished, following the swelling and ebbing of the score. "It's all in the music," says Balanchine, and indeed, we do not know why—or whether—Tchaikovsky grieved. So, too, with Balanchine's dancers: they seem to yearn, but without object.

The course of composition is well documented—seventeen girls were there the first day, nine the second, someone arrived late, someone fell, and Balanchine incorporated it all into his design. Since the 1950s, the solo parts have been divided among three to five women, two men; earlier, the female solos were danced by a single ballerina (with a second female soloist for the Elegy); but in the original production, there were no leading parts—the solo steps were shared by all the girls, with nine given slight prominence over the others. In the beginning the ballet comprised three sections only, the Sonatina, Waltz, and Elegy; the so-called Russian Dance, the fourth movement in the score but inserted by Balanchine before the closing Elegy, was not added until 1941, for the Company's tour of South America (Balanchine had choreographed it a year earlier for the Ballet Russe de Monte Carlo). This movement was for a brilliant "jumper" supported by four strong girls, in contrast to the lyrical flavor of the Waltz and Elegy sections and somewhat related to

Serenade. Left: **Students of the School of American Ballet. June 10, 1934. Woodland, White Plains, New York. First performance.** (*Courtesy Marie-Jeanne.*) *Right:* **The American Ballet. 1935. Kathryn Mullowny, Hortense Kahrklyn, Charles Laskey, Elena de Rivas.** (*Photo Vandamm.*)

the vigor of the opening. Today's familiar look of flying tulle drenched in blue was not always the case; for many years the dancers wore tunics of various designs.

Serenade has for some time been considered the "signature piece" of the New York City Ballet—the epitome of a work in which no one merely decorates the stage and where, despite solo moments, no "star" dominates. (Japanese critic Eguchi described it as "A masterpiece of sheer musical movements. The end result: no dancers remained in our memory; only the structural beauty of extreme refinement." [3])

But the ballet has had its detractors. Martin dismissed it as "serviceable rather than inspired" after his first viewing in 1935; and there are reports that the opening-night audience *laughed*. But the *Dancing Times* critic, even in the earliest days, was taken, and he provided what is perhaps *Serenade*'s first good notice: "Contains some of Balanchine's most unusual groupings, breathtaking in the sheer beauty of their arrangement. The Elegy is a little masterpiece of choreographic design." [4] The Met management must also have approved; it was performed there.

Some time later Martin softened a bit, although he continued throughout the 1940s to mistrust what he considered Balanchine's striving for superficial effects: "As a composition it is fresh, impeccably neat and chic, with an admirable musicianship always evident under its line and phrase. It is almost a pure abstraction, with only a hint of classroom 'center practice' in its opening movement and a vague suggestion of a program in its final sec-

tion. For those who have the inclination to go with the choreographer along his rather rarified way, the experience is eminently worth the effort for the first two movements. For the final one, there may be reservations. It is referred to in the program notes as somber and tragic, but it proves instead to be both lush and disingenuous." [5]

In 1949 Hering discussed what many considered the specious emotional content in *Serenade*:

"The ballet seems dated. The reason has nothing to do with years, but rather with the underlying concept. It is a piece of theatrical deception. On the surface it is the very essence of lyricism. There is a little theme of youth, awakening, and unrequited love woven with the utmost delicacy through one of Balanchine's typical music visualizations. But if you probe beneath the movement to weigh the theme and its relative importance to the ballet, you have the feeling that Balanchine takes very serious emotions and uses them as a convenient excuse for his pretty patterns. The result is cold and strangely naive." [6]

In contrast, a bit later, Smith wrote: "It has aged not a whit. The *jeune-fille* quality of the corps de ballet is a profoundly imaginative conception; and the composition of the work is masterly. Balanchine here achieves classic simplicity without becoming brittle or sophisticated. A challenge to younger choreographers to preserve the fine taste and nobility of ballet tradition." [7]

By 1953, Hering would be calling it "the sum-total of dance experience, Balanchine's votive offering to the art he

serves. The dew of discovery lies glistening upon it." [8] Ten years later, Terry expressed what has become the general feeling about this enduring ballet: "Presents that beauty which is the province of dance alone, the beauty of highly trained bodies moving rhythmically through space, experiencing adventures in design, exploring the air in leaps, exploiting the endless possibilities of movement sequence. There is beauty also in the almost intangible theme of *Serenade*, in the communication of romantic searching, of waiting, of longing, of finding. Led by the wonderfully lyric Adams, the space-slashing brilliance of Wilde, the movement delicacy of Jillana, and the gestural sensitivity of Magallanes, the Company once again gave new life to one of the most perfect of romantic ballets." [9]

At the same time, Martin was writing: "This aged but perennially lovely piece is always full of surprises. Divided up in ever new combinations, tall girls where small ones formerly appeared, lyric ones replacing bravura ones, it takes on something of the quality of a kaleidoscope. Fortunately, it is basically that kind of piece, and the variations played upon it by its choreographer make it continually inviting." [10]

Forty years after its creation, *Serenade* flourishes still, found in repertories throughout the world. Perhaps all that remains to be said is that it has always been a favorite among dancers. In contrast, perhaps, to some of Balanchine's more technically difficult ballets, in which the performer may feel inadequate, *Serenade* makes dancers feel beautiful.

Serenade. **Left: New York City Ballet. Mid-1950s. Tanaquil LeClercq, Nicholas Magallanes, Jillana.** (*Photo Kiehl.*) ***Above right:* New York City Ballet. Early 1960s.** (*Photo Fred Fehl.*) ***Lower right:* New York City Ballet. Mid-1960s.** (*Photo Martha Swope.*)

Critics in Europe, and even in Russia, were (mostly) enthusiastic from the beginning:

England:

"The music is readily danceable, with an obvious emotional quality and a kind of lyric wistfulness. Then again, Balanchine made this ballet before he had fallen in love with academic austerity. He was nothing if not a classicist, but in *Serenade* it was a classicism which still left room for some touch of romantic warmth within its strict conventions. The opening and more especially the concluding passages are examples of that 'classicism plus' which is the most individual and most enduring of ballet's contributions to art." [11]

"In concerted dances the patterns are striking, and striking too is the way the groups change from one formation to an-other: but it is in passages where only two or three dancers are employed that suggestions of human tragedy emerge. There is a touching duet in which a ballerina circles in pas de bourrée and the man waltzes in counterpoint around her; and in the sweet despairing slow movement [Elegy], there is a moment where the choreographer turns sculptor, and the lovers form a beautiful group with a mysterious other woman. In the moment of stillness and parting she moves her arms, and it is as if the Angel of Fate had flapped her wings; and life continues." [12]

Italy:

"The devil—so goes an old proverb—is not as evil as he is depicted: abstraction is not as abstract as they say. Balanchine repeatedly affirms that his choreography is not narrative; but he admits to being inspired by 'romantic abstraction' in *Sere-nade*, evoking images of Destiny, Love, Longing, and Death. The dancing contains a love story or at least the sentiment of love." [13]

Germany:

"A masterwork of geometrical poetry. It sparkles. And yet, the style and theme of the ballet are tiring. Aestheticism and sentiment take away the inner tension, the ballet becomes soft and full of blurred pathos; the final transfiguration is of bombastic beauty." [14]

Russia:

"A beautiful spectacle distinguished by a fresh balletic style and an original choreographic vocabulary." [15]

"In this work, Balanchine declares himself heir to the traditions established by L. Ivanov and M. Fokine in *Swan Lake* and *Chopiniana*. From the first measures he introduces the innovative 'dance of the arms' to interpret Tchaikovsky's music—a world of contradictory emotional urges, lyric meditations, doubts, limpid sadness, and the trouble-fraught quest for happiness. Balanchine enriches the classic dance of his predecessors with the new body movements, . . . 'single-voiced' and 'multi-voiced' modulations of the corps de ballet, retardations and accelerations of the dance melody, changes in rhythm (not only inward but outward), plastic caesuras, and so on. It is no wonder that Balanchine's staging of this work has remained alive for nearly forty years in many of the world's theaters." [16]

ALMA MATER

CHOREOGRAPHY: George Balanchine

MUSIC: Kay Swift (including "Boola Boola," "Bright College Years," "Stein Song"), orchestrated by Morton Gould

BOOK: Edward M. M. Warburg

COSTUMES: John Held, Jr.

DÉCOR: Eugene Dunkel

PREMIERE: 1 March 1935, Adelphi Theater, New York (first presented 6 December 1934 by the Producing Company of the School of American Ballet, Avery Memorial Theater, Hartford, Conn.)

CAST: *1. Introduction: The Heroine*, Sylvia Giselle (Gisella Caccialanza); *The Villain*, William Dollar; 6 *Girls*; *2. Entrance of the Hero—Snake Dance: The Hero*, Charles Laskey; *The Photographer*, Eugene Loring; 6 *Girls*, 4 *Boys*; *3. Waltz*: Caccialanza, Laskey, Dollar; *4. The Knock-Out-Dream-Wedding and Nightmare: The Bride*, Heidi Vosseler; *The Groom*, Laskey; 14 *Girls*, 5 *Boys*; *5. Morning Papers, and The Duel: The Janitor*, Dollar; plus entire cast; *6. Salvation Rhumba: Nell*, Kathryn Mullowny; *7. Finale*: entire cast
Villain also danced by Paul Haakon

An early review, referring to *Alma Mater* as "the first of the burlesque ballets," supplied this account of the action: "College life as the wishful freshman sees it. The fantasy gallops instantly into a farcical phantasmagoria. Yale has apparently just won a game and the dumb but handsome halfback hero is lifted high on the shoulders of his cock-eyed college mates. A photographer snaps our hero draped against the Yale fence. The snake dance zig-zags to the goal posts [human], which are plucked from their sockets. The villain, keen, corrupt, and coonskin-coated, dashes upon the stage with the beautiful but dimwit heroine, both on a bicycle built for two. One blink of those mascara'd orbs and the halfback is knocked for a loop. The villain, curse him, again knocks our hero for a whole row of loops, while he is picking daisies for his sweetie. Dreamland. Our hero hesitates between becoming Queen of the May or getting married, but fortunately chooses the altar. A wedding march is strangely like the football victory song. Then, behold our pantied bride! Children, dozens of them, each with a college letter on his sweater, immediately spring from the union and destroy their dream papa. Comes the dawn. A janitor with a Phi Beta Kappa key sweeps up the pieces. Our hero has it out with ye villain in a rotogravure forest. Whoops! A rain squall. There goes that photographer fellow off to heaven on his storm umbrella. You get the pattern?" [1]

The final "Salvation Rhumba" was danced by a Salvation Army lady who stripped in the process. Few pairs of toe shoes were involved in this number; Loring remembers some "Chaplinesque" movement on the part of the photographer. Definitely something new in ballet scenarios.

Martin called it "thoroughly amusing. . . . [but] relatively unimportant, not because it fails in any degree to do what it sets out to do, but only because it is really a revue sketch rather than a ballet." [2]

Said Warburg of his first (and last) ballet, "It's serious satire" (as probably any comment on life at Yale by a Harvard man would have to be).

Alma Mater was a great success with audiences. The real puzzle was how Balanchine, recently arrived from life in Paris, Monte Carlo, Copenhagen, and Leningrad, had the vaguest idea what he was doing. According to Ruthanna Boris, a member of the ensemble, "He got it from us. The ballet was divine! It opened with kids in the corps dressed in shorts, bush hats, little jackets, lying on the floor reading the funny papers. That was because on Sundays when we rehearsed we did the same—read funnies and chewed gum. He thought these things were very American." Says Balanchine, "I didn't know anything. I was swimming. Once they took me to see football, and, of course, I had been to soccer in England. It's practically the same thing—well, that is, there's a ball and they're running."

Alma Mater. **Entrance of the Hero. Charles Laskey aloft.** (*Photo Gray-O'Reilly.*)

ERRANTE

Choreographic fantasy by Pavel Tchelit-chew and George Balanchine

CHOREOGRAPHY: George Balanchine

MUSIC: Franz Schubert ("Wanderer" Fantasy), arranged by Charles Koechlin

COSTUMES, LIGHTING, DRAMATIC EFFECTS: Pavel Tchelitchew

PREMIERE: 1 March 1935, Adelphi Theater, New York (first presented 10 June 1933 by Les Ballets 1933, Théâtre des Champs-Élysées, Paris)

CAST: *Woman in Green*, Tamara Geva (guest artist); *Two Men*, William Dollar, Charles Laskey; *3 Youths; Shadows, Angels, Revolutionaries, etc.*, 13 women

OTHER CASTS: *Woman*, Daphne Vane, Marjorie Moore; *Men*, Nicholas Magallanes, David Nillo

There is a mystique to *Errante*. Though very little performed, and dismissed by Martin (and some others) as "cosmic nonsense, [approaching] the record for choreographic silliness," it left a marked impression on those who appeared in it and other dancers who saw it. Says Balanchine, "It's impossible to describe [in terms of movement]; it's all visual," and it is clear that a great deal of the ballet's impact derived from Tchelitchew's effects. Says Dollar, "Tchelitchew had a great flair for theater, a great flair for dressing dancers beautifully (clothing them in a state of undress, really), and a wonderful sense about color, line, and staging. The décor was just white, but there were different colored lights on it for every mood. The central character—a woman—was barefoot and had a green train about twenty feet long."

The décor was made of white lamp-shade-type material, which was saturated with color from the lights from time to time. Says Magallanes, "It was as though huge white window shades came down and formed a sort of a circle. Sometimes it looked pearllike, sometimes colored." At times it looked like cellophane. Todd Bolender remembers the ending: "a cloud—a huge piece of chiffon—floated down and covered the woman. A lovely finish."

If hard to describe, it was equally difficult to say what the ballet was "about."

Interpretations ranged from Balanchine's ideas about the Russian Revolution ("we had red flags going through there," says Lew Christensen) to "the private life of Tchelitchew—revolution, tempestuous love affairs." The ballet was presented in New York without program note, but for the South American tour, a brief introduction was offered to audiences: "Inside a translucent column pass strange and giant images of the world, sometimes in shadow, sometimes in diffused light. A woman appears to flee from herself, from the angels, the flag bearers, and from a moon in eclipse. In an agitated yet hieratic manner the figures move on. It is the disequilibrium of a dream."

The important characters in the woman's adventures/hallucinations/reminiscences are two men and a child who lays a flower on the stage. Much of the choreography revolved around the woman's train. She also had some giant backbends. Says Dollar, "The two

Errante. **William Dollar (center).**

men in her life were dressed alike: you never knew one from another. We spent a lot of time wrapping and unwrapping her train. Balanchine did very unusual groupings and strange adagio movements. It was impressionistic, disconnected, like someone remembering. Or she might have been dying."

Geva recalls, "I think it was based on a poem: 'Your home is *there*, where you are

not.' Everything the woman touched fell apart; it was kind of negative, really. And at the end, I was left alone, and suddenly a rope ladder appeared, really only a shadow in back of that scenery, which was transparent. One of the men was climbing up, and I was chasing—almost like Petrouchka was chasing something. Then he disappeared and I started violently dancing by myself, and at the end of that total despair, a big piece of white silk was released from above, and it covered me. They had fans which made it float like a silken white cloud, and as it descended you could see my body standing, and then I went on my knees, and more and more until I flattened myself and was covered. The stage was white and the walls were white, and there was nothing but this sense of emptiness and space, absolutely spherical. The decor was incredibly gorgeous in its simplicity; it looked like a sugar cathedral, all elongated, flying somewhere up into the wings, and illuminated from the inside. It was kind of like a dream—for instance, the train: in dreams, sometimes, you want to run forward, but you feel pulled back by some force, and this train gave a feeling that I was always running against odds, physically and emotionally. The ensemble was faceless at the beginning, but at one point they came out like angels with wings growing out of their breasts instead of their backs. It was a unique thing—surprises every minute."

When the ballet was first presented in England (summer of 1933), the *Dancing Times* reviewer wrote:

"The German atmosphere was much in evidence in [this] fantastic and highly introspective study of the morbid workings of the mind of a woman searching for her lost love. There are moments perilously close to the ridiculous, notably when the woman falls through the legs of an apparently dead body, some very beautiful effects are obtained by the use of flowing draperies and the clever lighting of the almost bare stage, and the grouping of the dancers reaches from time to time a high level of artistic excellence. The ballet is made up of 'posturing' rather than dancing in the commonly accepted meaning of that word." [1]

In a later production (Ballet Theatre, 1943), Kolodin would refer to the "posturings" as "calisthenics" and consider the work "a revelation of the kind of freakishness that was the vogue in ballet in the mid-30s."

After the debut of the American Ballet,

the *Herald Tribune* ran the following unsigned notice:

"The sustained atmosphere of phantasmagoria. Geva, pulled back in her every movement by a [long] train, to symbolize the helpless feeling of one who flees in a nightmare, evoked applause. There were some rather stagy effects, as when Geva utilized the body of her dead lover as the stretcher on which she was almost carried off by a funeral cortege; a finale in which the hero, in silhouette behind the panel, climbed a rope ladder; and a remarkable moment when ribbons wove serpentine patterns across the stage. So startling were some of the effects that there were bursts of poorly suppressed laughter, quickly shushed by the more rapt members of the audience." [2]

Errante was performed by the Company at the Met; it was greeted with fervor on the South American tour of 1941: "We are still submerged by the spirit of the marvelous conception. There are colors which it is not possible to translate into letters. There are emotional effects which we can only barely reflect. The Company has produced in this plastic fantasy a work not derived from anything else or capable of imitation. It is a manifestation of a single emotion conceived and constructed out of a group of emotions one day meeting and merging to crystallize into a work that for all its divinity yet has human connotations. And all of this out of the simplest materials one could desire." [3]

Other critics were equally effusive. Moore was—literally—a sensation.

REMINISCENCE

CHOREOGRAPHY: George Balanchine

MUSIC: Benjamin Godard, orchestrated by Henry Brant

COSTUMES, DÉCOR: Sergei Soudeikine

PREMIERE: 1 March 1935, Adelphi Theater, New York

CAST: *Brighella:* Eugene Loring; *Entrée:* 12 women; *Pas d'Action:* Kathryn Mullowny, Charles Laskey; 4 men, 12 women; *Valse Chromatique:* Leda Anchutina; *Barcarole:* Elena de Rivas; *Canzonetta:* Gisella Caccialanza; *Fragment Poétique:* Annabelle Lyon; *Tarantella:* Ruthanna Boris, Joseph Levinoff; *Saturn:* Paul Haakon (guest artist); *Pas de Trois:* William Dollar, Holly Howard, Elise Reiman; *Finale:* ensemble

---

I knew of Godard because when I was in Russia and studied piano we all played Godard. When I came here nobody had heard of him and in France nobody had heard of him. So I went around saying, 'Godard, Godard,' and I found lots of things he wrote besides the piano music. It's cute, nice, melodic."—Balanchine

After deciding on the music, Balanchine set out to choreograph a classical, plotless work ("You know, the way I usually do—variation, coda, pas de deux, and finale"). It was called simply "Variation" in rehearsals, but when the time came to choose a title, *Reminiscence* was selected—"because it was in the style of the old times—on pointe," said Balanchine; thus, after the fact, the ballet took on the character of graduation exercises at the Maryinsky. A fulsome program note provided a lengthy description, calling it "An evocation of the mood of pure classical theatrical dancing, with a traditional atmosphere as of the old theatres of Russia and France at the end of the last century. It is set in a huge palace ballroom, lit with candelabras and hung with tapestries. It opens with a figure from the old Italian commedia, dancing his welcome to the audience. Then in a long single file the corps de ballet enter in the first entry, clad in gold tutus and crowned with gilt leaves. Cavaliers in violet enter gravely for the Pas d'Action, a brilliant arrangement of men supporting the girls on the floor and in the air, culminating in a tableau. Then in rapid succession follow a series of solo numbers; examples of all the various moods and forms of the art of ballet. There is a grand ballerina, a dashing Italian mistress of Hussars, a Venetian Barcarole danced eccentrically by a girl in the costume of a Carpaccio page, a pair of peasants in a Tarantella, a boy dressed as Saturn who whirls in a silver ring, and a pas de trois of two girls and a man clothed in pure white. This number is the climax, a superb composition of fire and technical virtuosity. Then with mounting rapidity all the dancers, in character, reenter and weave the stage with their interlacing figures until the curtain falls on a pyrotechnical display of thrilling movement."

For Martin, *Reminiscence* was "the real hit of the evening [opening night of the American Ballet]. . . . It is not calculated to cause any sort of sensation, but it is exactly the sort of thing that one would expect to find in the repertoire of what is at present actually an apprentice group with guest stars." [1]

He was just about alone in this opinion. Wrote the *Dancing Times* correspondent: "The whole is rather suggestive of *Aurora's Wedding*. . . . Has thus far proved the most popular ballet in the repertoire—a rather astonishing fact when one considers America's oft-professed fondness for the ultra-modern in art." [2]

Engel: "Forthright in its appeal, but each dance so purposely called to mind something that we have seen more expertly done by the Russian ballets, that the result was unsatisfying." [3] Kirstein was the most gloomy: "To me, it represented everything banal, compromising, and retardative in the philosophy of what we should not be doing; a pastiche, a concession to the Ballets Russes public at one remove, a betrayal of Diaghilev's *avant-gardisme;* ten steps backward." If this assessment seems particularly harsh, it should be remembered that, at this, the first unveiling of his company, Kirstein was trying to prove a point about American ballet.

Encouragingly, the technical equipment of the dancers was given high praise ("Fouettés and batterie followed bewilderingly, young women attained attitudes not reached before and seemed to pause in midair."—*Herald Tribune*). "Dainty" Anchutina "fairly flew" through the Valse Chromatique; Caccialanza remembers her demanding Canzonetta in an Italian style ("no picnic"); the Tarantella was "spirited" (says Boris, "The whole thing was based on a chase. I ran and he ran; he chased me all over the studio. He was a very fast kid and so was I; between us it was a very fast Tarantella"); Haakon "brought to life the Manship 'Prometheus' in Rockefeller Center with his Saturn dance" (spectators remember his triple air turns); Dollar "executed some remarkable *tours de force.*"

Very early on, the part of the major domo was eliminated. Several months later, for performance at the Metropolitan, when Haakon was no longer available, the Saturn dance was dropped; a Mazurka was added to display the talents of Anatole Vilzak, who had been premier danseur with Diaghilev and became Balanchine's assistant at the Met and a teacher at the School. (The Mazurka was danced with Rabana Hasburgh and ensemble.) A Valse and Grand Adagio were also added, and the Pas d'Action removed. Balanchine never revived this ballet.

DREAMS

CHOREOGRAPHY: George Balanchine

MUSIC: George Antheil

SCENARIO, COSTUMES, DÉCOR: André Derain

PREMIERE: 5 March 1935, Adelphi Theater, New York (first presented as *Songes* 7 June 1933 by Les Ballets 1933, Théâtre des Champs-Élysées, Paris)

CAST: *The Ballerina*, Leda Anchutina; *The Polka*, Gisella Caccialanza, Paul Haakon (guest artist); *The Acrobat*, William Dollar; *The March: The Knave*, Edward Caton; *2 Buffoons*; *6 (female) Pages*; *The Can-Can*, Holly Howard, 8 women; *The Lady and The Prince*, Kathryn Mullowny, Charles Laskey; *The Finale*, entire cast; *The Epilogue: The Fairy Queen*, Mary Sale *Ballerina* also danced by Annabelle Lyon

As first presented in Paris, *Songes* was a vehicle for Tamara Toumanova, to music of Milhaud, and with striking costumes and décor by Derain. In America it was given a different score ("We couldn't find Milhaud," said Balanchine), and among the young dancers of the American Ballet there was as yet no star.

The theme was evoked in a rather overwrought program note. An excerpt: "Dancer! Artist!! After all, then, what is the artist? She is a human being who accepts no limits, and who, even better, cannot imagine them possible. Her dreams magnify, amplify, multiply. Her spirit, avid for perfection, fills her heart with an overflowing love. She subdues her fragile body from which emanates— the charm, the beauty, the fervor, which soon, in their turn, all other hearts, bodies, and souls will love. . . ."

It is the story of a famous dancer, lonely in her personal life, who falls asleep and encounters in her dreams and nightmares a series of strange creatures who are not what they seem (a rat turns into an acrobat in one episode). At the end "a rose fairy appears. She mothers the little ballerina, protects her from the dreams, which fade with her. The dancer awakes."

New York, unlike Paris, received the ballet coolly. "Scarcely worth the labor that has been spent on it," wrote Martin; "trivial in subject matter." [1] "Without Toumanova, it seems meaningless and banal." [2] The ballet was performed very little; in fact, it was dropped after the first season. The costumes, however, proved durable and useful, reappearing in *Divertimento* (1941) and *Mother Goose Suite* (1948). Despite their elaborateness and weight, they did not prevent "real dancing."

Neither Balanchine nor his dancers considered *Dreams* "much of a ballet."

TRANSCENDENCE

CHOREOGRAPHY: George Balanchine

MUSIC: Franz Liszt ("Mephisto" waltz; Ballade; 10th, 13th, 19th Hungarian rhapsodies), arranged and orchestrated by George Antheil

SCENARIO: Lincoln Kirstein

COSTUMES: Franklin Watkins

DÉCOR: Gaston Longchamp

PREMIERE: 5 March 1935, Adelphi Theater, New York (first presented 6 December 1934 by the Producing Company of the School of American Ballet, Avery Memorial Theater, Hartford, Conn.)

CAST: *Mephisto Waltz: The Young Girl*, Elise Reiman; *The Young Man*, Charles Laskey; *The Man in Black*, William Dollar; 10 women, 4 men; *Ballade: The Mesmerism*, Reiman, Dollar; *The End of the Man in Black*, Dollar, 4 men; *The Resurrection:* 16 women, 6 men

Transcendence was more a quality, an atmosphere than a story. It had a very strange, mystical kind of feeling for me," says Eugene Loring (who appeared in the corps). In Martin's opinion, it was "totally obscure. It has the quality of phantasmagoria and some of its incidents are of distinct power, but it remains largely incomprehensible." [1]

Another reviewer considered it to be "dramatic and macabre. The title refers to the period of Liszt and Paganini, when technique and virtuosity were transcendent, when living and dying themselves were the culmination of technique and

Transcendence. Elise Reiman, William Dollar.

virtuosity." [2] *Dancing Times*, admitting that the "literal meaning" of the action was unclear, called *Transcendence* "a beautiful thing. Balanchine weaves patterns of startling originality with the bodies of his dancers. He is merciless in the demands he makes upon them; each work bristles with difficult feats." [3]

Indeed, almost no one can recall the story, which concerned a hooded man (an abbé? Liszt? the devil?) who steals a girl from her lover, transfixes her, and is finally foiled by the fiancé. (There was mention of a "frenzied finale.") The underlying premises—a virtuoso male dancer as equivalent of these technically prodigious music-makers (who, many were convinced, were possessed by the devil), which was, in Kirstein's words, "a suitable pretext for the unlimited possibility in musical dance-drama"; the trickery of disguise echoing Paganini's and Liszt's mesmeric appeal, which they achieved in part through extramusical means, hence deceptively—were more provocative than the story line, if hardly danceable. Balanchine, who is known for bringing out specific gifts of particular dancers, was said to have played beautifully to Dollar's fine-schooled classicism and acrobatic abilities.

MOZARTIANA

CHOREOGRAPHY: George Balanchine

MUSIC: Peter Ilyitch Tchaikovsky (Suite No. 4, "Mozartiana," op. 61, 1887)

COSTUMES, DÉCOR: Christian Bérard

PREMIERE: 28 September 1935, Westchester County Center, White Plains, N.Y. (first presented 7 June 1933 by Les Ballets 1933, Théâtre des Champs-Élysées, Paris; first in America 6 December 1934 by the Producing Company of the School of American Ballet, Avery Memorial Theater, Hartford, Conn.)

CAST: 1. *Gigue*, Hortense Kahrklin, Joseph Levinoff, Jack Potteiger; 2. *Menuet*, 8 women; 3. *Preghiera*, Annabelle Lyon; 4. *Theme and Variations:* a. *Pas de Six*, 6 women; b. *Promenade*, 2 men, 5 women; c. *Scherzando*, Annia Breyman, Elise Reiman; d. *Pas de Quatre*, 4 women; e. *Clochettes*, Gisella Caccialanza, Elena de Rivas, Potteiger; f. *Pas de Deux*, Holly Howard, Charles Laskey; 5. *Finale*, entire cast

Mozartiana. **Preghiera. Annabelle Lyon.** *(Photo Paul Hansen.)*

Mozartiana had been Balanchine's first new work to Tchaikovsky—"always, for dancing, Tchaikovksy," says he.* Many would follow. The program speaks of a "visualization of Mozart's melodies," Petipa-like choreography, and gypsies and peasants in a gay square, "perhaps in Italy." Passing comments and the score itself bespeak emotional undertones (Kirstein wrote that it "incorporated some of Balanchine's most mysterious and touching psychological ambiguities, capitalizing on the fragile quality of post-adolescent dancers"); and Tchaikovsky's swelling melancholy is instantly discernible through the Mozartean sun.

It would also seem that there was some "distortion" in the choreography; wrote one correspondent of the Paris production: "To music of Mozart and with such dancers one expected something in which beauty of line was predominant, but Balanchine seems to have gone out of his way to caricature some of the poses of the classical dance." [1]

Denby confesses himself confused by his first viewing of *Mozartiana* (Paris, 1933), but "it wouldn't stay out of my mind. I couldn't understand a thing that was going on. Parts didn't make any sense at all. But I went to the other programs, and nothing else was as good for me." Later he would consider it "brilliantly complex, full of surprising realizations, and poignant interchanges, and a subtle, very personal fragrance." [2]

In 1933 Balanchine had had Toumanova; in America, lacking a star of her magnitude, he divided some of her sections among the girls. In the original White Plains performances (9–10 June 1934), there were other problems: girls were forced to assume the parts of boys. Making her debut there, in the Preghiera, was a tiny girl who would become the first of a small number of American ballerinas to inspire Balanchine's most special and personal attention, for whom he later created two of his most memorable and lasting works, *Ballet Imperial* and *Concerto Barocco*—Marie-Jeanne.

Mozartiana was performed during the Company's abortive tour across country that was abandoned after two weeks; it was also given at least one showing at the Metropolitan (1936). In 1945 the Ballet Russe de Monte Carlo revived it. At that time, Denby called it "sunny, another of Balanchine's pocket masterpieces which restore to ballet its classic clarity and joyousness." [3]

Martin was somewhat less enthusiastic: "Follows essentially the oh, so familiar

---

* He has written that, after several years with Diaghilev in which he was assigned mostly contemporary music, he was only too happy to turn to the "classics—Bach, Mozart, Tchaikovsky—with the permanent exception of Stravinsky, who is always a classic." (*Center*, Sept. 1954)

formula. It is cool, clean, difficult, and de-vised. It has its ensemble movement in which everybody plays 'London Bridge' like mad, its slow movement devoted to chicly lugubrious sentimentality, its adagio section in which a ballerina is assisted in the performance of odd inventions, the virtues of which lie not in expressiveness or beauty or formalism but only in differentness. If these variations are measured in those fractions of millimeters which chiefly delight the esthete, they are nevertheless present, valid, and sensitive, beyond peradventure. There are authority, superb technical competence, imagination, and musicianship always to be found in Balanchine's work; it is only range and, above all, matter that they lack." [4]

Dancers remember it as very beautiful. To Caccialanza, it was "very classical, not so different from his classical steps today" (1974). According to Ruthanna Boris "It was all very technically difficult and nice—a lovely score. I think it was way ahead of its time, and the costumes were a bit old-fashioned. Parts of 'Emeralds' [from *Jewels*] remind me of what we did—lots of marvelous arms and beautiful pictures forming, a very delicate thing. It didn't last long; maybe it wasn't sensational enough."

Above: Concerto. (Photo Mark Cassidy.) Below: The Bat. **The Poet with Identical Ladies. Gisella Caccialanza, Lew Christensen, Olga Suarez.** (*The Dance Collection, New York Public Library. Courtesy Lew and Gisella Christensen. Photo George Platt Lynes.*)

CONCERTO
in 1937 called
CLASSIC BALLET

CHOREOGRAPHY: William Dollar and George Balanchine

MUSIC: Frédéric Chopin (Piano Concerto No. 2 in F minor, op. 21, 1829)

PREMIERE: 8 March 1936, Metropolitan Opera, New York

PIANO SOLO: Nicholas Kopeikine

CAST: William Dollar, Holly Howard, Charles Laskey; ensemble of 45

Originally approaching it as a training piece at Balanchine's urging, Dollar, the Company's premier classic dancer, was surprised and delighted when *Concerto* turned out well enough to receive public performance. Says he, "Years later, I was grateful for Balanchine's pushing me into choreography (and teaching), but at the time, all I wanted to do was dance. He was the one concerned about my future." Dollar was responsible for the two outer movements; the center was a Balanchine adagio for Howard, considered the first of his "American beauties," partnered by Laskey, in which Dollar made a brief dramatic entrance.

The ballet was presented on one of the "popular" (low-priced) Sunday concerts that the Met offered from time to time, to which the performance of ballets was generally (but not always) restricted. Dollar dealt mainly with group formations.

Wrote Denby: "Swift, pleasant, interesting, [Dollar's] choreography shows an honest and well-grounded talent. [Balanchine sometimes] minimizes detail for the soloist or the ensemble, and avoids technical feats, [building] instead on unmistakable clarity of groupings and

directions; on rapid oppositions of mass, between single figures and the group; and above all on an amazing swiftness of locomotion. Dollar now uses [this style] very well. He has been able to add to it interesting feats, where they are worth doing. In addition Balanchine has contributed a middle section which is more elaborate both in detail and in feeling, which fits in astonishingly with the more abstract speed of the rest, heightening it with its greater warmth." [1]

THE BAT

Character Ballet

CHOREOGRAPHY: George Balanchine

MUSIC: Johann Strauss (mostly from *Die Fledermaus*, 1874)

SCENARIO: Lincoln Kirstein

COSTUMES, LIGHTING: Keith Martin

PREMIERE: 20 May 1936, Metropolitan Opera House, New York

CAST: *The Bat*, Holly Howard, Lew Christensen; *The Poet*, Charles Laskey; *The Masked (Identical) Ladies*, Leda Anchutina, Annabelle Lyon; *The Gypsies* (later called *Hungarian Dancers*), Helen Leitch, William Dollar; *The Can-Can Dancer*, Rabana Hasburgh; *The Ladies of Fashion*, 4 women; *2 Coachmen*; *Can-Can Dancers, Officers, Ladies and Gentlemen*, ensemble

OTHER CASTS: *Bat*, Todd Bolender, André Eglevsky, Helen Kramer; *Poet*, Lew Christensen; *Masked Ladies*, Gisella Caccialanza, Olga Suarez; *Can-Can Dancer*, Beatrice Tompkins; *Hungarian Dancer*, Marie-Jeanne

Participants in *The Bat* remember it as a light, waltzy diversion, with colorful ballroom costumes, mysterious characters, disguises, and the barest hint of a story: "It is an evocation of the atmosphere of Old Vienna, when the Waltz King reigned. In a park, which could well be the Prater, a series of confusing and mysterious encounters takes place. A young poet enters in search of inspiration; however, he is confounded by two beautiful but identical ladies. Hungarian gypsies invade the scene, which climaxes in a gay can-can. Soon the park is empty, save for the shadow of the bat." (Program note for South America.)

The role of the bat was performed by two dancers, who separated and "covered everybody" with one giant wing each, then got back together again at the end. Anchutina had a "perpetual motion" solo that was memorable ("mostly jumping en pointe"); the Hungarians/Gypsies stomped around in boots.

The Bat was the first independent ballet choreographed by Balanchine at the Metropolitan while the American Ballet Ensemble (as the Company was billed) was in residence. It became a part of the repertory and was performed about a dozen times over the next two seasons (including the Met spring tour of 1938). Always presented with an opera (or once with highlights from several operas), on its opening night it followed *Lucia*, and

thereafter it accompanied *Cav* and *Pag*, *Hansel and Gretel*, *Bartered Bride*, and *Butterfly*. Thus it was always written up—always in generalities and with brevity—by music critics.

"The American Ballet Ensemble was heartily applauded for its attractive dancing and groupings in the second part of the program," came at the end of a long column on *Lucia*.[1] "Likable and well-contrasted epilogue in the evening's entertainment."[2]

"Dancers, in bright raiment, against a luminous blue-green background, romped fast and merrily through the time allotted while the orchestra played Strauss music none too well. The bat was a dual personality—each half in spangled black. If he—or they—filled the cast with terror, the audience had nothing but pleasure of the whole show."[3]

Plot and music being what they were, dance critics might not have found anything more illuminating to say.

ORPHEUS AND EURYDICE

Opera in two acts (four scenes)

Stage production conceived by George Balanchine and Pavel Tchelitchew

MUSIC: Christoph Willibald von Gluck (first produced 1762; in Balanchine's staging, the final scene was omitted)

COSTUMES, DÉCOR, LIGHTING: Pavel Tchelitchew

PREMIERE: 22 May 1936, Metropolitan Opera, New York

SINGERS: *Orpheus*, Anna Kaskas; *Eurydice*, Jeanne Pengelly; *Amor*, Maxine Stellman; *Chorus*

CAST: *Orpheus*, Lew Christensen; *Eurydice*, Daphne Vane; *Amor*, William Dollar; *Shepherds and Nymphs, Furies and Ghosts from Hades, Heroes from Elysium, Followers of Orpheus*, ensemble

ACT I, scene 1. At the tomb of Eurydice
ACT I, scene 2. Entrance to Hades
ACT II, scene 1. The Elysian Fields
ACT II, scene 2. The Gardens of the Temple of Love

Orpheus was the only opera staged by Balanchine while the American Ballet was

in residence at the Metropolitan. The total visual concept was his responsibility, and in this case, that was saying quite a lot: he was doing far more than moving bodies around. His dancers carried the action (the singers were invisible in the pit), and he engaged Tchelitchew not merely to provide some clothes and backdrops but to create an entire hermetic world, a place where no horizon defined sky or land, suffused with an unnatural light that articulated form and modeled surface, where dancers and scenic objects, undifferentiatedly draped in identical translucent cloths, became structures. All this Tchelitchew made, according to Kirstein, using chicken wire, dead branches, cheesecloth, light, and flying wires for the dancers. Kirstein explained. "The four scenes of the drama were revealed, first, as our everyday world of domestic loss and personal tragedy wherein the rest of the uncaring world busies itself apart, undeterred by individual death or the survivor's loneliness. Then we pass to a public hell of suffering, deprivation, and loss of personal freedom. From here, we ascend to a limbo of suspended animation where an echoing dream-life maintains its negative image of lost free-will and abnegation. Finally, there are the celestial, eternal regions, a lunar landscape of metaphysical imaginings, a world of sense and order above our small world of loving or hating."

Warburg financed the visual spectacle, the Metropolitan the musical.

The reception of *Orpheus* is well documented: passive lack of enthusiasm on the part of the audience, vilification on the part of the critics (*music* critics, of course). "Ranks as the most inept and unhappy spectacle this writer has ever seen in the celebrated lyric theater; absurd as an interpretation of the opera. Ugly, futile, impudent, meddlesome, wholly ineffective in performance. There is farfetched and ridiculous maneuvering on stage, arbitrary and vaguely symbolic choreography."[1]

"The [scenery] might be described as a mixture of a convict ship and Sing Sing prison. The dancers who postured and fidgeted through it helped matters very little."[2]

Chotzinoff found the choreography "Hardly startling. The poses and gestures were very much like what one sees in the usual solemn ballets of our numerous dance groups. [All] behaved in the routine manner with which we have been made familiar."[3]

What was going on? It is hard to believe that the work actually did come close to being as dreadful as described. For Chujoy, the answer was simple: "So far as the opera audience was concerned, *Orpheus* was not an opera." What sounds like a flippant remark may be near the truth, for ballet-lovers are rarely the same people as opera fans. Each art has its own conceits, and initiation into one specialized world in no way prepares the spectator for the other. If anything, it may fill him with preconceived notions and thus have a negative effect.

A quite different view of the work was expressed by the novelist Glenway Wescott, who wrote a long letter published in edited form by *Time* magazine (which had roasted *Orpheus*), in which he insisted that despite the critics, there were many in the audience, without a public forum, who were "not disappointed":

"The present *Orpheus*, the only original undertaking of the opera association this season, gave as much pleasure to a certain public as offense to the critics. By virtue of the strange new scenes and 20th-century dances, I was more deeply moved by the ancient myth and 18th-century music than ever before.

"I am one who has believed that the Russian school of dancing has had its day, which has made me dubious of the effort of the company directed by Balanchine. [But] this *Orpheus* is the only ballet I can think of that Isadora Duncan would have approved whole-heartedly, [and] if I were to make a list of the dozen most exciting and inspiring things I have seen in the theater, three of [Balanchine's] choreographic works would be on it: *Apollo*, *Prodigal Son*, and *Errante*. But by this general admiration I am not at all disposed to admire all that he does; quite the contrary. *The Bat*, for example, bores me. Now may I repeat that [*Orpheus*] gave me greater satisfaction and interested me more than any other art-event of the past season? *Time*'s reporter says that the dance of the three principals together at the end of the opera suggests 'a Japanese tumbling act.' No doubt this comparison was scornfully intended. Yet it might be read as a compliment. For to those of us who find classic operatic pantomime ludicrous and of waning significance, the acts of acrobats often seem very fine." [4]

Orpheus had two performances. Although the brouhaha it engendered has been amply recorded, it is less easy to discover what actually occurred on stage (see Kirstein, *The New York City Ballet*).

Orpheus and Eurydice. Daphne Vane.

The opera has three set dance sequences (Hades, Elysian Fields, and Shepherds and Shepherdesses, here omitted). Says Loring of the Dance of Hades, "There was a marvelous scene in which we were to whip the damned soul. We made flying entrances from four directions. Very exciting—leaps, running, jumping on the stage—but behind a scrim, unfortunately, as we discovered only at the last minute."

For the rest, it was loosely said that the action of the libretto was mimed by the dancers. Says Christensen, "My movements were mostly slow (no jumping). I played the harp everywhere and carried Daphne Vane all over the place. It kept moving—we were going into hell, coming out of hell, going through hell, dragging Eurydice along. The Dance of Hades was quite large, and there was another sequence with trees on cloth or gauze. Amor descended from the sky."

What did the dancers do during the arias, in which there is no action and the words are repeated several times? According to Ruthanna Boris:

"We looked beautiful and moved 'appropriately'—slow walking, bending. But it's too superficial to say that it was 'walking' and 'gesturing'; in many ways, it was a kind of organic movement growing out of what was happening—as though people were talking to each other. This has nothing to do with 'pantomime'—but it's relating—body language. Actually, it was full of those marvelous encounters that happen all through Balanchine's works, which nobody pays any attention to—*Liebeslieder*, *Serenade*—there's no 'story,'

but people are always transacting something together."

Says Balanchine (1975), "I think you could call it classical movement—classical without toe shoes. Pavlik's things were very beautiful. The dancing was mostly a series of pas de deux (except for the dance numbers). But, can you imagine, it was *two hours* of singing! I choreographed the whole thing. For that, you have to be young, with energy. I wouldn't *start* anything so impossible today!"

"Beauty" is the single word most often encountered (except in the columns of music critics) in descriptions of *Orpheus*.

APOLLON MUSAGÈTE
in 1951 called
APOLLO, LEADER OF THE MUSES
since 1957 called
APOLLO

CHOREOGRAPHY: George Balanchine

MUSIC: Igor Stravinsky (1927–28; commissioned by Elizabeth Sprague Coolidge)

COSTUMES, DÉCOR: Stewart Chaney (1937); Tomás Santa Rosa (1941); Karinska (1951; costumes only); since 1957, danced in practice clothes without décor

LIGHTING: Jean Rosenthal (1951); David Hays (1964)

PREMIERE: 27 April 1937, Metropolitan Opera, New York (first presented 12 June 1928 by Diaghilev's Ballets Russes, Théâtre Sarah-Bernhardt, Paris)

CAST: *Apollo*, Lew Christensen; *Terpsichore*, Elise Reiman; *Calliope*, Daphne Vane; *Polyhymnia*, Holly Howard; *Leto, Mother of Apollo*, Jane Burkhalter; 2 *Nymphs*

OTHER CASTS: *Terpsichore*, Marie-Jeanne; *Calliope*, Olga Suarez; *Polyhymnia*, Marjorie Moore

REVIVAL: 15 November 1951, City Center of Music and Drama, New York, as *Apollo, Leader of the Muses*

CAST: *Apollo*, André Eglevsky; *Terpsichore*, Maria Tallchief; *Calliope*, Diana

Adams; *Polyhymnia*, Tanaquil LeClercq; *Leto*, Barbara Milberg

OTHER CASTS: *Apollo*, Jacques d'Amboise, Conrad Ludlow, Peter Martins, Edward Villella; *Terpsichore*, Diana Adams, Suzanne Farrell, Allegra Kent, Patricia McBride, Kay Mazzo; *Calliope* and *Polyhymnia*, Karin von Aroldingen, Gloria Govrin, Melissa Hayden, Jillana, Sara Leland, Marnee Morris, Patricia Neary, Mimi Paul, Francia Russell, Suki Schorer, Carol Sumner, Patricia Wilde

SCENE I, the Birth of Apollo: Leto, Nymphs, Apollo
SCENE II, Olympus: Variation of Apollo; Pas d'Action (Apollo and Muses); Variation of Calliope; Variation of Polyhymnia; Variation of Terpsichore; Pas de Deux (Apollo and Terpsichore); Coda—Apotheosis (Apollo and Muses)

Apollo. 1960s. Jacques d'Amboise. (*Photo Fred Fehl.*)

Ballet began when Terpsichore touched Apollo's finger, as on the Sistine ceiling God touches Adam's, and inspired a pas de deux in which movement became form and bodies learned to speak and sing—a pas de deux that whenever it is re-enacted holds implicit in its plastic images all dance, past, present, and future. This symbolic moment, when Terpsichore joined her sisters Polyhymnia and Calliope on equal terms, was first shaped in mortal beauty on June 12, 1928, on the stage of the Théâtre Sarah-Bernhardt in Paris." [1]

Apollo is the oldest Balanchine ballet in the New York City repertory, yet its appeal is not historical; and its stature is that of a seminal work that is wholly contemporary. It is the first ballet on which Balanchine collaborated with Stravinsky (although not the first he had choreographed to Stravinsky's music), and Balanchine considers it pivotal in his own development. Over twenty years after its creation, in a rare moment of analysis, he wrote: "*Apollo* I look back on as the turning point of my life. In its discipline and restraint, its sustained oneness of feeling, the score was a revelation. It seemed to tell me that I could dare not to use everything, that I too could eliminate. I began to see how I could clarify, by limiting, by reducing what seemed to be multiple possibilities to the one which is inevitable." [2] What was a turning point for Balanchine was, of course, a turning point for twentieth-century choreography.

Of equal importance to this reductive

principle was Balanchine's "rediscovery" or "reaffirmation" in *Apollo* of classical technique—previously, according to Chujoy, "he had leaned toward the modern, which in 1928 meant the grotesque." [3]* This also proved paramount for Balanchine ("Technique is the floor"). He wrote: "*Apollo* is sometimes criticized for not being 'of the theater' [because] it has no plot. But the technique is that of classical ballet, which is in every way theatrical, and it is here used to project sound directly into visible movement." [4]

But Balanchine's classicism was classicism with a difference (indeed, his style has come to be referred to as "neoclassicism"). The five positions were there, the jumps, beats, turns, the arabesques of old, the perfect feet—but so were heels, turned-in legs, protruding hips, outstretched palms, contractions in the torso, arms in new configurations not found in any ballet dictionary. Some movements even had a maneristic awkwardness—Polyhymnia's torso-twists with her finger on her lips, two Muses hanging from Apollo's arms, jumping with obvious effort, Apollo's swivel-pirouette in which both knees touch the ground in descent. Says Alexandra Danilova, who was in the original Diaghilev cast, simply: "Instead of going on the toes, you went on the full feet . . . everything was so new."

Critical acceptance of *Apollo* was not immediate. Not until some thirty years after its premiere did it begin to acquire

---

* Grotesque dancing is what we today would call character dancing.

its present reputation for just the simplicity and inevitability of which Balanchine spoke. (In 1937 it was given only two performances and proved to be a much greater success on the Company's 1941 tour of South America.) For a long time the ballet was considered quirky, eccentric, very much of the moment, and contrived (perhaps in earlier years such formations as the "troika," the "swimming," and the "wheelbarrow" seemed forced). After its initial American presentation as part of the Stravinsky evening at the Metropolitan, Martin found it to be "Remote and mannered; created in [a] period when novelty and eccentricity were valued as pure esthetic gold." [5]

As late as 1951, when he had become in general favorably impressed with Balanchine (a conversion which began in 1947), Martin wrote: "*Apollo* will never, in all probability, be popular. For him it has enormous personal importance. Perhaps it should be revived from time to time, since historical milestones in the ballet are evanescent; but to ask us to admire it for its intrinsic virtues is another matter. It still seems a very young and dated effort." [6]

Sabin, by contrast, felt that although "the work seems rather pallid today, it is almost wholly free from gaucheries of experimentation or sophistication gone stale. The movement has many fine, characteristic Balanchine touches, such as the intertwining arms and fingers, and is often freshly inventive from Apollo's second variation on, through his pas de deux with Terpsichore to the apotheosis with all

Apollon Musagète. Left: **American Ballet Ensemble (Metropolitan Opera). 1937. Lew Christensen, Holly Howard, Daphne Vane, Elise Reiman.** (*Photo Dwight Godwin.*) *Right:* **American Ballet Ensemble (Metropolitan Opera). 1937. Lew Christensen.** (*Photo Richard Tucker.*)

three Muses. Frequent tableaux of poses keep the ballet somewhat static—legitimately so, considering its nature and its style—but the transitional movement is occasionally awkward or seemingly illogical, and there are some grotesqueries that are no longer as witty as they may have seemed in the beginning." [7]

Hering also had reservations: "Kirstein once said that *Apollo* was 'conscious, constructed and deliberate art.' And in these words lie both the ballet's strength and its weakness. For despite the fascination of its movement experimentation, the grandeur of its final sections, and its enkindling theme, its very deliberateness has divested the ballet of passion. As with all genuine works of art, *Apollo* may be understood on two levels. There is its literal self—the sunny image of a poet growing up. And there is its symbolic self—the picture of an artist maturing. In style, *Apollo* has the same duality. On one hand, it is a model of classic order and discipline. On the other, it is a clever combination of athleticism and willful distortion. It is as though the choreographer were trying to see how far he could deviate from the classic structure and still be able to snap back to it." [8]

From the beginning, the ballet also had a few champions. In 1938 Denby called it a "masterpiece." In 1945 he wrote that "*Apollo* is about poetry, poetry in the sense of a brilliant, sensuous, daring, and powerful activity of our nature. It depicts the birth of Apollo in a prologue; then how Apollo was given a lyre, and tried to

make it sing; how three Muses appeared and showed each her special ability to delight; how he then tried out his surging strength; how he danced with Terpsichore, and how her loveliness and his strength responded in touching harmony; and last, how all four together were inspired and felt the full power of the imagination; and then in calm and with assurance left for Parnassus. . . . *Apollo* is an homage to the academic ballet tradition—and the first work in the contemporary classic style, but it is an homage to classicism's sensuous loveliness as well as to its brilliant exactitude and its science of dance effect. . . . So *Apollo* can tell you how beautiful classic dancing is when it is correct and sincere; or how the power of poetry grows in our nature; or even that as man's genius becomes more civilized, it grows more expressive, more ardent, more responsive, more beautiful. Balanchine has conveyed these large ideas really as modestly as possible, by means of three girls and a boy dancing together for a while." [9]

It was not until a 1957 production that the ballet began to win wholehearted praise. This was probably due to d'Amboise's assumption of the title role; he was the first since Christensen to realize, physically and instinctually, the unmannered, untutored boy-man of Balanchine's conception. In addition, the work was given in practice clothes. This, wrote Martin in reaction to the innovation, was "a wonder-working change. Now the place is a well-defined stage area, the

characters are dancers so clad, and the action is a purely choreographic construction. If there are many hangovers from the original pantomimic implications behind many of the phrases, they are now primarily and convincingly motivations for technical creation. If, also, some of the invention remains self-consciously over-inventive, at least it has ceased to seem chichi." [10]

D'Amboise was the ranking Apollo for the next fifteen years.

With the passage of time, the look of *Apollo* has changed a great deal. The original production was marginally Greek (despite the pastoral "primitive" settings of Bauchant): Apollo wore a tunic, was birthed by Leto, and ascended Mt. Olympus; the Muses, however, belted with Chanel cravats, departed somewhat from the traditional image. Balanchine spent many years dispensing with the Greek look (which he felt had nothing intrinsically to do with his ballet): first the chariot disappeared (it couldn't get across the Andes); Apollo and his Muses began dancing in practice clothes; the laurel crown was removed; Mt. Olympus became a flight of stairs. Balanchine's Apollo had never been the Sun God. Says he, "Apollon Musagète is the *small* Apollo, a boy with long hair." To Christensen, his first American Apollo, he said, "You are a woodcutter, a swimmer, a football player, a god." Says Marie-Jeanne, "He wanted an unformed, unmajestic Apollo. He said that he had in mind a soccer player when he did it for Lifar. Lew had a kind of jerky

Left: Apollo, Leader of the Muses. **New York City Ballet. 1951. Maria Tallchief, Tanaquil LeClercq, Diana Adams, André Eglevsky.** *Right: Apollo.* **New York City Ballet. Late 1950s. Allegra Kent, Patricia Wilde, Jillana, Conrad Ludlow.** (*Photos Fred Fehl.*)

movement, a roughness. He was tall enough to wear a little skirt. The hairs on his head, chest, and legs were gilded, so when the lights turned on him, he shone."

After Leto gives birth to Apollo, he appears completely wrapped in winding cloth (this Russian custom is supposed to keep the child's body straight), then begins to live and breathe and soon pirouettes himself out of his bandages, appearing almost naked. "At that moment, out of the darkness," says Eglevsky, "you're as if blinded by the sun, and you twitch like an animal, cornered." Later it appears that Apollo learns to walk, to feel his manly strength, to manipulate an instrument, his lute, and finally to harness three goddesses. (At the same time, he is tamed by them. Says Balanchine, "He is a wild, half-human youth who acquires nobility through art.") Glenway Wescott, bearing in mind the playful nature of the relationships, suggested calling the ballet "Apollo's Games with the Muses."

Balanchine has said that the primitive (or naive) aspect of the original décor and the primitive nature of the young and rough Apollo influenced his choice of movement. And the music—melodic, lyrical, nonpercussive (it is for strings only), and highly complex rhythmically— provided hiatus, stasis, unexpected moments of suspension, and "awkward" juxtapositions, all of which were used in the characterizations. What Martin calls "pas de bourrée on the heels," when dancers appear to be shuffling, was inspired by

the naive school of painting, by the likes of Douanier Rousseau (or Bauchant himself), whose canvases were peopled with little woodenlike figures who might move in such a stiff and graceless manner.

A few observers thought this did not do justice to a lofty subject. Balanchine tells a story that after the first performance in Paris, a famous Russian critic accosted him: "Young man," he demanded, "tell me, where did you see Apollo walking on his knees?" To which Balanchine replied, "Mr. So-and-so, you know what I want to ask you: Where did you ever see Apollo?" And Balanchine continues, "He isn't 'walking on his knees'—he's dancing."

As for style, Balanchine has told some of his young interpreters to look at Greek vases and friezes—his figures often make planar pictures, with a twist in the torso, as if arrested for an instant between two sheets of glass. Schorer mentions a "Mercury" position, "all turned in"; Tallchief speaks of a kind of German feeling for *plastique*—in which one is aware of the configuration of the body as a body, rather than as the instrument for executing steps. The final tableau can be read only frontally; two formations in particular—the chariot (Apollo driving the Muses as horses), and the moment where the Muses raise their legs to different heights as if from a single nucleus, like the spokes of a wheel—are obvious references to frieze motifs.

Of her variation (Calliope), Schorer says, "You have speech that comes from deep inside you. Balanchine said that be-

fore an utterance you contract through the body, then clutch your heart as if wounded by an arrow, then emote. When you run forward, you speak a little, addressing yourself to one side, then to the other, as if in a Greek amphitheatre. Speech grows weaker and weaker; finally there's nothing. Then you get an idea. As you start running, you regain your strength. The idea is that you're going to write. There's one step in particular that you do falling off pointe—not in a refined manner rolling through the foot—you archaically fall."

Eglevsky speaks of many such "unfinished" moments.

Says McBride, "The Terpsichore role is very jazzy, the variation especially. The rhythm is interesting—it's delay, then you change the rhythm in it. In the adagio, the designs are actually very simple."

Eglevsky: "In the Coda, you come out with a big jump, then twist in the air; then there's a slide and stop; slide and stop. You don't know where you are. Mr. B. said, 'You have no bones in your back. Slide like rubber.'"

Apollo clearly called for a different way of moving and responding. It is a way that still looks modern today, and yet a way that Balanchine, for all his subsequent forays into modernism, has not specifically developed (except, perhaps, in *Four Temperaments*)—a modern path that has no direct offspring, yet opened up a whole new world.

Apollo was performed during the sec-

Apollo. **New York City Ballet.** *Left:* **Late 1960s. Suzanne Farrell, Peter Martins.** *Right:* **1960s. Edward Villella, Patricia McBride.** (*Photos Fred Fehl.*)

ond Stravinsky Festival, 24 June 1972, reportedly for the last time in a Balanchine company.

England:
"The first of the masterpieces, and the groups still seem the inventions of a master sculptor. This is an elemental vision of the birth of art." [11]

Germany:
"Besides his intensification of dance, Balanchine tells the whole plot only by means of physical movement. As is the case with any great work, one keeps discovering new aspects—this time, the wonderful pas de deux, at the beginning of which Terpsichore sits so humanly on Apollo's knees, or the short pas de deux of Polyhymnia and Calliope, with the enchanting mirroring diagonal, or the 'troika' pas de quatre on the way to the apotheosis." [12]

THE CARD PARTY
in 1951 called
THE CARD GAME

Ballet in Three Deals

CHOREOGRAPHY: George Balanchine

MUSIC: Igor Stravinsky (*Jeu de Cartes,* 1936; commissioned by Lincoln Kirstein and Edward M. M. Warburg)

SCENARIO: Igor Stravinsky and M. Malaieff

COSTUMES, DÉCOR: Irene Sharaff

PREMIERE: 27 April 1937, Metropolitan Opera, New York

CAST: *Joker,* William Dollar; *Queens: Hearts,* Annabelle Lyon; *Spades,* Leda Anchutina; *Diamonds,* Ariel Lang; *Clubs,* Hortense Kahrklin; *4 Aces* (women); *4 Kings; 4 Jacks; 10, 9, 8, 7, 6, 5 of Hearts; 10, 9, 8, 7 of Spades*

REVIVAL: 15 February 1951, City Center of Music and Drama, New York, as *The Card Game*

CAST: *Joker,* Todd Bolender; *Queens: Hearts,* Janet Reed; *Spades,* Jillana; *Diamonds,* Patricia Wilde; *Clubs,* Doris Breckenridge; (*4 Aces* now men)

The argument for *The Card Party* was appended to Stravinsky's original score: "The characters in this ballet are the chief cards in a game of Poker, disputed between several players on the green cloth of a card-room. At each deal the situation is complicated by the endless guiles of the perfidious Joker, who believes himself invincible because of his ability to become any desired card.

"During the first deal, one of the players is beaten, but the other two remain with even 'straights,' although one of them holds the Joker.

"In the second deal, the hand that holds the Joker is victorious, thanks to four Aces who easily beat four Queens.

"The third deal is a struggle between three 'flushes.' Although at first victorious over one adversary, the Joker, strutting at the head of a sequence of Spades, is beaten by a 'royal flush' in Hearts. This puts an end to his malice and knavery."

Kirstein pointed out that the game was played literally according to Hoyle. Stravinsky was in constant attendance from about halfway through the rehearsal period. According to an article by Kirstein, "The creation of *Jeu de Cartes* was a complete collaboration. When Stravinsky saw the first two deals he expressed an enthusiasm, an interest, and a criticism which was as courtly as it was terrifying. He would appear punctually at rehearsals and stay on for six hours. During successive run-throughs of the ballet he would slap his knee like a metronome for the dancers, then suddenly interrupt everything, rise, and, gesticulating rapidly to emphasize his points, suggest a change. This was never offered tentatively but with the considered authority of complete information. Thus, at the end of the first deal, where Balanchine had worked out a display of the dancers in a fanlike pattern to simulate cards held in the hand, Stravinsky decided there was too great a prodigality of choreographic invention. Instead of so much variety in the pictures, he preferred a repetition of the most effective groupings. On another occasion he composed some additional music to allow for a further development in the choreography." [1]

Said Balanchine, "Stravinsky and I attempted to show that the highest cards—the kings, queens, and jacks—in reality have nothing on the other side. They are big people, but they can easily be beaten by small cards. Seemingly powerful figures, they are actually mere silhouettes."

As the Joker, Dollar, who had acrobatic training, had a variation in which he did a roll-over onto his belly, slowly came up, then did pirouettes, bent back, and again rolled over.

Despite these promising ingredients, Martin was not impressed. He wrote, "The theme of a series of poker hands upset by the wandering of the joker offers obvious possibilities of formalism to a mind which likes to build on such a basis. However, though it has its moments of humor, it is difficult to follow on the stage and loses most of its point accordingly. With his knack for revue, Balanchine could undoubtedly have handled it more effectively if he had had more experienced dancers to work with, and if, above all, he had been freed from the incubus of Stravinsky's score. Just why the musical setting for a poker game should quote from every musician from Rossini to Ravel is not readily apparent, nor why it

should be involved, calculated, and arbitrary in phrase. It is difficult to be light, witty, and clear of design against such a counterweight." [2]

When revived, the ballet was scarcely more enthusiastically received. Chujoy wrote, "The current version has been changed to advantage. A few simple pantomimic moments have made the action clearer and the humor more specific. It is a frothy musico-balletic joke, sure to amuse at first seeing. There is doubt whether it can have a wide appeal." [3]

Hering: "A series of long-winded poker deals with a kind of dressed-up literalness. With the exception of charming solos for the four queens, it is a music-hall piece and does not belong in the repertoire of this distinguished company." [4]

And Martin, as before: "One of the arider collaborations of Balanchine and Stravinsky. A thin and tedious work." [5]

It seemed that not only the cards, but the ballet, suffered from two-dimensionality. (For the record, however, Denby gave it a rave when it was produced by the Ballet Russe de Monte Carlo in 1940; and Haggin, who had remarked on its "thinness and brittleness" in 1941, found it a "masterpiece" ten years later.)

The Card Party. **American Ballet Ensemble (Metropolitan Opera). 1937. Queen of Hearts and Joker. Annabelle Lyon, William Dollar.** (*Photo Maharadze.*)

LE BAISER DE LA FÉE
in 1950 called
THE FAIRY'S KISS

Ballet-Allegory in four scenes

CHOREOGRAPHY: George Balanchine

MUSIC: Igor Stravinsky (1928), inspired by the music of Tchaikovsky

---

SCENARIO: Igor Stravinsky, based on a tale of Hans Christian Andersen ("The Ice Maiden")

COSTUMES, DÉCOR: Alice Halicka

PREMIERE: 27 April 1937, Metropolitan Opera, New York

CAST: *The Fairy,* Kathryn Mullowny; *The Bride,* Gisella Caccialanza; *Her Friend,* Leda Anchutina; *The Bridegroom,* William Dollar; *His Mother,* Annabelle Lyon; FIRST TABLEAU, *Prologue: Mother; Two Winds; Snowflakes,* Anchutina, 21 women; *Fairy; Her Shadow,* Rabana Hasburgh; *8 Mountaineers;* SECOND TABLEAU, *The Village Festival: Peasant Boys and Girls; Bridegroom; Bride; Bridesmaids,* Anchutina, 7 women; *A Gypsy (Disguised Fairy);* THIRD TABLEAU, *Inside the Mill: Dance of the Peasant Girls,* Anchutina, 16 women; *Pas de Deux, Bride's Variation, Coda (Bride, Bridegroom, Friend, ensemble); Scene: Fairy* and *Bridegroom;* FOURTH TABLEAU, *Epilogue (Berceuse de demeures éternelles): Fairy* and *Bridegroom*

REVIVAL: 28 November 1950, City Center of Music and Drama, New York, as *The Fairy's Kiss*

LIGHTING: Jean Rosenthal

CAST: *Fairy,* Maria Tallchief; *Bride,* Tanaquil LeClercq; *Friend,* Patricia Wilde; *Bridegroom,* Nicholas Magallanes; *Mother,* Beatrice Tompkins; *Shadow,* Helen Kramer

I dedicate this ballet to the memory of Peter Tchaikovsky by relating the Fairy to his Muse, and in this way the ballet becomes an allegory, the Muse having similarly branded Tchaikovsky with her fatal kiss, whose mysterious imprint made itself felt in all this great artist's work." (Stravinsky, note appended to the score.)

Le Baiser de la Fée. **Left:** **American Ballet Ensemble (Metropolitan Opera). 1937. Gisella Caccialanza, Stravinsky, William Dollar taking curtain call.** (*Courtesy Lew and Gisella Christensen. Photo Richard Tucker.*) **Right:** **New York City Ballet. 1950. Nicholas Magallanes, Maria Tallchief.** (*The Dance Collection, New York Public Library. Photo George Platt Lynes.*)

Baiser is a rarity—a modern fairytale ballet. It has mystery, magic, "the hand of fate"; a make-believe story in a far-away setting; a hero, a villain(ess), a lovely bride; elaborate scenery; even quotations from Tchaikovsky—all the elements that recall the traditional ballet classics. Balanchine and Stravinsky placed it firmly in the twentieth century, however. Denby was impressed with its theatrical potential: "It has a range of expression that includes the brutality of the peasant dances, the frightening large mime gestures of the fortune-telling scene, the ominous speed-up of the wedding party, the hobbled tenderness of the bridal duet, the clap-of-thunder entrance of the veiled Fairy, the repulsive dissolution of the last scene; all of it fascinating and beautiful." [1]

The story is recounted by Hering, who saw the work as "in the romantic tradition, colored with a spare, modern irony": "In a magically lighted snowstorm, a fairy implants a kiss upon a babe lost by its mother. The boy grows to young manhood, and we find him dancing at a village festival. Left alone, [he] is enticed by a gypsy (fairy disguised). Later, when he is dancing with his bride, the fairy again appears. And in a fanciful final scene, the young man can be seen climbing a huge net to reach the fairy and dwell with her forever. *Baiser* depicts the eternal renunciation of the artist. It may also be understood to portray the inability of a young man to wean himself away from an image of ideal womanhood and attach himself to a real woman." [2]

Here is another telling of the story: "First there is the Fairy's glittering ap-

pearance with her black Shadow. She swoops over the baby in devouring benevolence and the figure beside her moves ominously through the same arc of space—a device that fills the theater with instant mystery and dread. Later she is herself her Shadow, prowling through the village. She descends on the Boy in a series of constricting rectangles to wrestle for his soul. Rough and brutal, she thrusts him from left to right until she seizes his head in triumph and forces it to the ground. Finally there is the searing encounter in the mill. She confronts him suddenly, a towering apparition and, helpless, he embraces and carries her rigid form away with him. Raising her veil [only then realizing she is the Fairy], he rushes off in panic but returns in painful submission. Dragging one knee after another, he pulls the Fairy from behind, down over his body in an extreme arabesque penché. Her head seems to touch the ground. She draws back and we see them both tense and anguished. So, their hands locked, they move in an open-and-shut diagonal across the stage with an effect of mounting, cruel sensuality. The Fairy then glides with her prey into the sea. 'The Ice Maiden,' says Andersen, 'kissed him and he grew stiff with cold and sank. She stood with one foot pressing him down and so they floated out of sight.' " [3] Some fairytale!

Despite its promise, there have always been reservations about *Baiser* as a ballet, and Balanchine is said to have remained dissatisfied with his several versions: the ballet is by nature episodic; the relationships between the characters are im-

possible to make clear through dance alone; and the ending presents enormous problems technically. Although he has mounted the ballet for several companies, its life in his own troupes has been brief.

Balanchine first choreographed it for his Stravinsky evening at the Met. It is relevant to look at Martin's general impression of Balanchine's work at the time, before going on to his review. He wrote: "It is necessary always to accept the fact that for Balanchine the dance, as he has expressly stated, is purely spectacular and should strive only for the attainment of sensuous pleasure. That he believes such pleasure is best attained by tenuous rather than robust means is apparently characteristic of his personal approach. It should not be surprising, then, to discover that the three ballets he has presented should be without substance and trivial." [4]

Of *Baiser* in particular he continued, "It is couched in a style that is deliberately reminiscent of the romantic ballet of the post-Taglioni period of the last century. It does not attempt an exact reproduction of the style, but it pays it a somewhat more objective tribute. It is more consistent, contains more choreographic body and fuller phrases than any of Balanchine's other ballets, and puts him far more on his mettle as a choreographer instead of a deviser of tricks. To be sure, there are passages which come crashing through the style like a herd of wild anachronisms. It is a distinct shock, for example, to see the unearthly fairy wrap one leg about her young protégé's torso, or the bridegroom dragging his leaning bride across the room with the point of her toe scraping the floor all the way. But in the main the feeling of the composition is true and sensitive." [5] Some years later, he would consider it "one of Balanchine's most admirable creations. It has great charm and style, and musically, dramatically, and choreographically it is all of a piece." [6]

The revival was welcomed in principle, but in the end *Baiser* was once again judged a beautiful, worthy, but imperfect work. New choreography was added to the interludes between scenes; the Bride and Bridegroom had a new (lovely, lilting, intimate) pas de deux. Martin wrote with evident pleasure of the snowstorm scene: "Beautifully danced and superbly lit. Balanchine's fantasy is rich and delicate, and the following scene, with the peasants dancing outside the inn, is another joy and delight, wonderfully vivacious and inventive."

He concluded (as did other critics) that it was "a beautiful work waiting for the right production." [7]

For Sabin, it was "wonderfully subtle in its blending of tenderness and fierce inexorability." [8] Haggin, who had admired the ballet for years, mentioned in particular the two pas de deux (Fairy-Bridegroom, Bride-Bridegroom).

Tallchief was praised for the "startling frozen passion" she brought to her role. (She considers this one of her finest parts.) Magallanes, who has a special fondness for the ballet, describes some of the highlights of the 1950 production: "Even the scenery was choreographed. In the big snow scene, first there was the Mother, like Liza, alone with her baby. She abandons it, and the Fairy arrives, dancing with her Shadow in the snow—a marvelous effect. Later, there is a big celebration, with the Bride and Bridegroom. That all fades away, and the Fairy comes in again, disguised. Maria looked like Dolores del Rio, with big earrings, loose hair. She circles the boy, then grabs him and reads his palm to wonderful music. Then there's quite a wild dance, where she dominates him. She turns, her leg goes over his head, he'd be under. Then she'd be wrapped around him. The music got slow, she went behind him and pushed him forward, around the shoulder blades (he was standing), then went in the same forward direction past him, pointing toward the wings. Then she'd push him again, and go past him again, pointing. It was a marvelous exit."

BALLET CARAVAN 1936–1940

ENCOUNTER

Classic Ballet in one act

CHOREOGRAPHY: Lew Christensen

MUSIC: Wolfgang Amadeus Mozart (Serenade in D major, K. 250, "Haffner," 1776)

MEN'S COSTUMES: after the drawings of J. G. von Schadow

WOMEN'S COSTUMES: after traditional sources

PREMIERE: 17 July 1936, College Theatre, Bennington, Vt.

DANCERS: ensemble of 12

Encounter, the first work in the Ballet Caravan repertory, was also Christensen's first ballet. Believing that Mozart's complete composition was too long to sustain a plotless classical work, he used only four movements initially, one of which was a pas de deux for himself and Gisella Caccialanza (subsequently danced by Helen Stewart and Marie-Jeanne). Later programs indicate that he eventually used all six movements (Allegro, Minuetto, Andante, Minuetto, Adagio, Allegro). According to the program, the ballet "in the purest classic style, recreates, in the mood of dancing, dramatic pantomime, and costuming, the spirit of the 18th century. The musical forms of one of Mozart's loveliest compositions are translated into visual patterns which suggest the atmosphere of a formal garden with various romantic exchanges and encounters."

The ballet was, in Christensen's words, "completely inspired by Balanchine. The trick was that Annabelle Lyon and Ruby Asquith looked alike, so they kept switching places behind a curtain, giving the impression that one person had danced for an hour. We chose Mozart because it *sounded* easy—and we had to start somewhere."

Reviewers, unaccustomed to writing about pure dance works, usually took refuge in describing the costumes, which, according to the program (often quoted directly in the reviews), were essentially "based on designs created for the Viganos, a celebrated Italian dancing partnership, man and wife, who revolutionized the whole field of the ballet a century ago. These clothes were a reform over the traditional male dress which heretofore had insisted upon a wide flaring stiff skirt, which made free movement nearly impossible."

Wrote Norton, however, with more perspicacity, "There is nothing pretentious about *Encounter*; it is purely decorative, lyrical dancing, delightful in conception and distinctly beautiful in execution." [1]

The performers remember it as a derivative work, but a serviceable one, which remained in the repertory for several seasons. A report in *American Dancer* gives some idea of the disarming modesty and perhaps naïveté not only of this ballet but also of the troupe itself in its first season: "Most cleverly contrived. Almost entirely technical, it nevertheless weaves a little story and refreshing lightness of atmosphere into the dance and the entrances and exits of the dancers. The manner, style, and virtuosity of everyone was a joy. They gave elegance and meaning to every phrase of the music, to every point of a toe. It was presented without flaw on the tiny stage; the name Mozart printed against the black velvet curtain completed the picture." [2]

Wrote Lloyd, "The point lies not so much in analysis of [this and the other] productions as if they were major works of art—which they are not—but in the question of what they have accomplished and whither they are tending." [3]

HARLEQUIN FOR PRESIDENT

Ballet-Pantomime after the Italian popular comedy

CHOREOGRAPHY: Eugene Loring

MUSIC: Domenico Scarlatti (sonatas), originally played on one piano, later orchestrated by Adriana Mikeshina

SCENARIO: Lincoln Kirstein

COSTUMES: Keith Martin

PREMIERE: 17 July 1936, College Theatre, Bennington, Vt.

PIANIST: David Stimer

CAST: *Harlequin,* Eugene Loring; *Columbine,* Annabelle Lyon; *Captain Zerbino,* Lew Christensen, married to *Leonora,* Gisella Caccialanza; *Captain Bimbombo,* Harold Christensen, married to *Isabella,* Ruthanna Boris; *Captain Grillo,* Charles Laskey, married to *Fracasquina,* Rabana Hasburgh; *The People,* Ruby Asquith, Albia Kavan, Hanna Moore; *The Doctor,* Erick Hawkins

Columbine later danced by Asquith, Marie-Jeanne

In *Harlequin,* Loring used the stock characters of the commedia dell'arte in a series of tableaus to comment on a situation of timely relevance. His object was "to satirize the way we Americans elect a President." Audiences, however, might not have suspected this from the somewhat cryptic program note, which read: "Harlequin loves Columbine who is not impressed. The People are upset over Harlequin's melancholy and decide he must be sick. The Doctor can find no cure. So the People suggest that if all the Captains are married, Columbine will not want to be left single, hence must take Harlequin. The marriage they arrange confuses everyone. News comes that the President is dead. In the election campaign, the Captains, as candidates, urged on by their jealous Wives, kill each other. The People, by a process of blind-man's buff, elect Harlequin, the sole survivor. Columbine consents to be first lady."

In the light of Loring's intentions, the most telling episode was the blind-folded selection of Harlequin to office. Also im-

portant were the relationships between husbands and wives. They married each other with (literally) eyes closed, and each wound up with "what seemed to be just the wrong person." But perhaps not— Loring paired weak with strong, and there was much exaggerated pulling and pushing around among them, recalling a major occupation of commedia characters over the past few hundred years. The Doctor is called to Harlequin's aid when rigor mortis has set in (another stock situation). Says Boris: "It began with an empty throne, and three stooges—the People in their white faces—came in with black handkerchiefs, weeping and sobbing. Various couples appeared and campaigned. Harlequin was chasing Columbine, who was busy doing other things. There was a final big campaign, with the stooges running around undecidedly from one candidate to the other. In the end it is Harlequin who is on the throne." As a final irony, after Harlequin *is* President, Columbine "decides she likes him a little better."

Loring, who was not himself an accomplished classical technician (although an excellent performer in other types of

Harlequin for President. **Eugene Loring.**

roles), used what he calls "free-form movement," which included some ballet steps, some non-ballet steps, and some broad pantomime, which was, he says, more realistic than the traditional gestures of the commedia. Asquith remembers it as "raw and very energetic." Says Fred Danieli, "Loring was marvelous at comedy, which is the most difficult thing. In dance, where you don't speak, after you fall flat on your face to get a laugh, what then? He could find something."

The ballet was a success with both audiences and critics, although there is one recorded instance—a performance at a "swanky garden party" on an Easthampton estate—where the vividness of the satire "caused some of the starchy guests to exit." [1]

In general, spectators agreed with the reviewer who wrote: "A spirit of fine caprice prevailed. It is full of clownish antics. With studied awkwardness, Loring did a highly entertaining enactment of the unwitting Harlequin."

The youthful Terry wrote, "Harlequin, Columbine, the Doctor, and the Captain have been making successful appearances since the long-past debut of the commedia dell'arte, and their freshness, their romantic actions, and their humorous complications have not diminished during the passage of centuries. *Harlequin* brings these lovable characters and their ridiculous actions back to us again. This ballet-pantomime was a vital and hilarious bit of theater." [2]

The costumes, it is reported, used highly un-Italian combinations of "mauve, burnt orange, and nile green, with pink, lilac, and black."

PROMENADE

CHOREOGRAPHY: William Dollar

MUSIC: Maurice Ravel (*Valses Nobles et Sentimentales,* 1911)

COSTUMES: after Horace Vernet

PREMIERE: 18 July 1936, College Theatre, Bennington, Vt.

CAST: *1. Promenade,* ensemble; *2. Venus and Adonis,* Annabelle Lyon, Charles Laskey; *3. The Three Graces with Satyr,* Eugene Loring, 3 women; *4. Apollo and Daphne,* Rabana Hasburgh, Lew Christensen; *5. Hercules and Omphale,* Ruthanna Boris, Erick Hawkins; *6. Echo and Narcissus,* Gisella Caccialanza, Harold Christensen; *7. Promenade,* ensemble

---

In the Empire period, decorated with motifs from the antique, things Greek were all the rage, and one can imagine the smart set getting together at a party and playing at the roles of famous Greek lovers. The opening and closing promenades commented on the latest vogue in ballroom dancing to sweep Europe at the time—the waltz. The ballet was described by one performer as "a style on a style." Many of the dancers were impressed with the musicality of Dollar's choreography. Critics, however, were not favorably inclined, although all liked the rich red and white costumes. Most felt, finally, that the classical choreography fit neither the Empire style of the costumes nor the romanticism of the music.

An exception was Biancolli, who wrote: "A feast for the eyes. Sets out to satirize a society—the French middle class of post-revolutionary days, with its search in classic culture for models in manners and art. In 'Venus and Adonis,' done over in approved bourgeois 'simplicity,' an elegantly brittle pair mimicked the antique episode. In another, one watched three garishly garbed Graces dallying about with a Satyr. The 'Apollo and Daphne' myth was graphic enough, for all its frills and fluting, but the 'Hercules and Omphale,' with a highly decorative Lydian Queen, took first honors. A prevailing note of youthful freshness and a good amount of technical accomplishment gave unfailing interest to the ballet." [1]

POCAHONTAS

Ballet-Pantomime in one act

CHOREOGRAPHY: Lew Christensen

MUSIC: Elliott Carter (1936; commissioned by Ballet Caravan)

SCENARIO: Lincoln Kirstein

COSTUMES: Karl Free, after the engravings of Theodore de Bry

PREMIERE: 18 July 1936, College Theatre, Bennington, Vt.

CAST: *Princess Pocahontas,* Ruthanna

Boris; *King Powhatan, her father,* Harold Christensen; *Captain John Smith,* Charles Laskey; *John Rolfe,* Lew Christensen; *Priest,* Erick Hawkins; *Indians,* 6 women

---

OTHER CASTS: *Pocahontas,* Leda Anchutina, Gisella Caccialanza, Marie-Jeanne; *Rolfe,* Fred Danieli

---

Pocahontas seems to have been completely formed in Kirstein's head before Christensen, the choreographer, heard anything about it. It was Kirstein who came up with the concept (influenced by a boyhood acquaintance who had been doing work on the subject in Virginia), researched the period, and commissioned the music. He required of Carter, presumably among other things, a finale that "should sound like an 'American-Indian' version of *Apollo.*" (Critics and dancers alike found the score Stravinskian.)

The costumes were based on contemporary impressions of Indians: "In 1585, Thomas Hariot wrote his famous *Voyage to Virginia,* with a 'marvelous and honestly true description of the savages.' John Smith was sent out to take portraits of the Indians on the spot, and his drawings, brought back to Europe, were the models for a series of magnificent plates engraved by the great Flemish technician de Bry. The drawings frequently resembled imperial Romans more than the tribesmen of the Chickahominy, but they served as the pictorial ideal of the New Continent for many generations." (program note)

Other influences on Kirstein were Hart Crane (*The Bridge*) and Degas (*Young Spartans Exercising*). The story of the ballet was a simple one: Smith and Rolfe are captured by the Indians, then saved through the intercession of Pocahontas, who marries Rolfe and leaves with him for England. (The action was broadened in a reworked version to include a Medicine Man and some Warriors.) Pocahontas wears a short Indian tunic until the final scene, when she appears in an Elizabethan wedding gown. The program note commented soberly that "no attempt has been made to reconstruct either music or dance from archeological sources, since little remains."

Christensen confessed himself perplexed by the task. "I never could make the story and music come out together. Then there was the challenge of reconciling some sort of Indian feeling with classical technique. I didn't have the ex-

perience; it was too much of a job for me at that point. I worked on it and worked on it; after the fourth revision, it had to be abandoned."

Says Boris, "It was stylized, in the manner that one might turn sideways, for instance, to convey Egyptian movements. But I wore toe shoes and did some arabesques. At the end, in a costume of wire and tulle, I had a huge translucent globe of the world, and I bourréed forward feeling like Martha Graham doing imperial gestures."

One reviewer mentioned "the treatment of the virgin forest," with the dancers dressed as trees. (Rolfe and Smith became lost in the woods.) Beaumont wrote that the girls were in costumes of fruits and flowers, the men in serpents, animal heads, and birds' wings. He referred to the choreography as "baroque and pseudoheroic." [1]

Martin took a dim view of the proceedings: "Modernistic and stuffy. The costumes are in the manner of the old-fashioned cigar-box Indian and after the first amusing glimpse, their pseudo-naïveté begins to grow irksome. The music is so thick it is hard to see the stage through it." [2]

Chapman called it "What Smith, Rolfe, Powhatan, and Pocahontas would have done if they'd known about dissonant brasses and the post-Wigman school of movement." [3]

Others were cheerier, particularly enjoying "the mystery of the forest primeval."

Says Boris, "It was my first leading role, so naturally I thought it was the greatest ballet ever done."

THE SOLDIER AND THE GYPSY

Character Ballet in seven scenes

CHOREOGRAPHY: Douglas Coudy

MUSIC: Manuel de Falla (*The Seven Popular Songs,* 1914)

COSTUMES: Charles Rain

PREMIERE: 17 August 1936, Colonial Theatre, Keene, N.H.

CAST: *The Gypsy,* Rabana Hasburgh; *The Soldier,* Douglas Coudy; *The Bullfighter,* Lew Christensen; *The Cigarette Girl,* Gisella Caccialanza; *The Great Lady,* Annabelle Lyon; *The Brigand Chief*, Charles Laskey

OTHER CASTS: *Gypsy*, Ruthanna Boris; *Soldier*, Erick Hawkins

Boris, an excellent Spanish dancer, was the Carmen figure. Lloyd wrote, briefly: "Tells the story of Carmen in pantomime and stylized Spanish rhythms. It is an animated, refreshing version of the familiar tale, enhanced by the essential Hispanicism of the de Falla excerpts." [1]

To the *New York Sun* reviewer, it was "The most ambitious work of the evening and the most colorful, although Coudy's treatment of his Iberian material may be described as clever rather than distinctive." [2]

Biancolli called it "bold and vivid." [3]

Coudy had been trained as a character dancer, which was evident in two works he choreographed for Ballet Caravan. He was also the Company manager and alternated with Lew Christensen in giving class to the dancers on tour.

YANKEE CLIPPER

Ballet-Voyage in one act

CHOREOGRAPHY: Eugene Loring

MUSIC: Paul Bowles (1937; commissioned by Ballet Caravan)

SCENARIO: Lincoln Kirstein

COSTUMES: Charles Rain

PREMIERE: 12 July 1937, Town Hall, Saybrook, Conn.

CAST: *The Farm Boy*, Eugene Loring; *The Quaker Girl*, Albia Kavan; *Sailors*, 5 men; *Gana (Argentina)*, Ruthanna Boris; *Himone (South Seas)*, Marie-Jeanne; *Tahitian Girls*, 4 women; *Kagura (Japan)*, Helen Stewart; *Adat (Indochina)*, 2 women; *Maou Fa (West Africa)*, Ruby Asquith; *Shems (Morocco)*, Rabana Hasburgh

Yankee Clipper started with an appealing theatrical concept: a restless young man, with whom the audience could sympathize, sails around the world, stopping in exotic ports (which provide opportunities for unusual dances). In his dreams he continually visualizes the girl he left behind, and he finally returns home only to find that wanderlust possesses him still.

Loring was after something of more dimension than a simple series of episodes: "The Boy goes to many different places, and in each country they give him a stick. At the end he weaves all these sticks together; in other words, he has found a new and more mature philosophy. When he gets back to his sweetheart in New England, he wants to give her this. She takes it and pulls on one of the sticks; the whole interwoven design falls apart.

"In the music, there were some traditional tunes, but you wouldn't recognize them; Bowles was extremely avant-garde. The way we worked was that I would figure out where I wanted the Boy to travel (where logically a clipper ship would go), then give this to Paul, and he would invent the music. In the Balinese section, he wanted a quart milk bottle, half filled with water, hit by a silver dollar. In the African section he had written, 'Here, no conducting is necessary.' The conductor—when we finally got one (we worked mostly with one or two pianos)—was not too happy!"

The ballet was enthusiastically received. Loring had taken a universal subject, given it an American slant, and handled it deftly. Terry was especially pleased: "First-rate ballet entertainment. Proved that Americans can dance American themes and still employ the great traditions of the classic ballet. The voyage takes the boy to exotic ports, subjects him

Yankee Clipper. **Eugene Loring, Albia Kavan.**

to the bullying of experienced sailors, and finally it makes a man of him. The foreign dances made no pretense of being authentic, and they were shown to us as the humorous eyes of fun-loving American sailors would see them. Particularly successful were the three Japanese *—two of them were as shy as we would expect Japanese girls to be, and the other was a veritable Gilbert-and-Sullivan Katisha with gnashing teeth and machinating gestures. The strange movements of the Indochina dancers were broadly burlesqued, with head wobblings, fingers and arms describing definitely weird designs, and utterly blank expressions. The dance of friendship [with Lew Christensen] was splendidly choreographed and excellently executed by the brusquely self-conscious sailor who tried to make the young lad's life a happier one through friendship, understanding, and protection. Loring's mime as the frightened and bullied boy was finely delineated in form and subtly yet profoundly shaded in emotion." [1]

Martin: "At present the company has both the faults and the compensatory virtues of youthfulness, but its approach is fresh and unpretentious. Loring gave a delightful performance of the central role. He has managed to keep a dramatic unity in his theme in spite of its many episodes, and its tinge of nonsense remains constant without becoming monotonous. Occasionally [it] suffers a momentary lapse of style, but on the whole this is an original and substantially made work. Bowles, without sacrificing anything of cleverness, has provided a sustained musical groundwork." [2]

An interesting point: here was a rare instance of a ballet for men. Exotic ladies appeared from time to time, but the Boy, of course, was the leading character, and he and his sailor pals/acquaintances were part of almost every scene.

FOLK DANCE

Character Ballet in one act

CHOREOGRAPHY: Douglas Coudy

MUSIC: Emmanuel Chabrier (selections)

COSTUMES: Charles Rain

PREMIERE: 15 July 1937, Town Hall, Saybrook, Conn.

* Originally a solo, this dance soon became a trio.

Folk Dance. **Eugene Loring, Marie-Jeanne.** *(Photo Dwight Godwin.)*

Show Piece. **Marie-Jeanne, Fred Danieli, Eugene Loring.** *(Photo Dwight Godwin.)*

CAST: *Sardana,* 3 couples; *Siciliano,* Helen Stewart, Harold Christensen; *Moresco,* Ruthanna Boris; *Karrika Dantza,* Marjorie Munson, 2 women (later Fred Danieli, 3 women); *Volta,* Rabana Hasburgh (later a trio); *Saltarello,* Ruby Asquith, Eugene Loring; *Asturiana,* Marie-Jeanne, Erick Hawkins; *Aurresku,* ensemble

F*olk Dance* was a group of theatricalized national dances from the Latin countries, in the tradition of third-act divertissements in nineteenth-century ballets and popular for the same reasons. It had bright costumes and an atmosphere of gaiety; all the dancers were on stage, smiling sunnily.

The program described the individual numbers: "The *Sardana* is an ancient Catalan chain-dance resembling the seventeenth-century *contropaso.* The *Siciliano* is a semi-classic version of a Sicilian pastoral. The *Moresco* shows the traces of Moorish influence as it was absorbed by the Spaniards. *Karrika Dantza* is a Basque street-dance, having an Iberian origin, but which is more common to the French side of the Pyrenees. The *Volta* is a Portuguese dance of flirtation using characteristic finger-cymbals. The *Saltarello* or 'little leap' is one of the few Italian peasant dances which gives as much prominence to the boy as to the girl. In the *Asturiana* of northern Spain there is more steady dignity than is found in the southern dances. The *Aurresku* is a dance of courtship used in the Basque country."

Although a number of critics found it entertaining, Terry had reservations: "Sought to catch the spirit of the native dances of Spain and Italy. In this it failed, for the dancers appeared as a group of Americans having a gay time in costumes that were alien to them. They performed with their customary vigor, enthusiasm, and infectious good humor, so the proceedings were by no means dull; but we would rather see this company dancing American themes with their robustness and agreeable satire, or strictly classical ballets." [1]

Clearly Terry, following Martin's attitude toward American ballet, was beginning to look to the future.

SHOW PIECE

Ballet Workout in one act

CHOREOGRAPHY: Erick Hawkins

MUSIC: Robert McBride (1937; commissioned by Ballet Caravan)

COSTUMES: Keith Martin

PREMIERE: 15 July 1937, Town Hall, Saybrook, Conn.

CAST: *1. Introduction,* Eugene Loring; *Parade and Dance; 2. Scherzino,* Jane Doering; *Waltz,* Lorna London; *Romance,* Ruby Asquith; *Trio; 3. Jig,* Douglas Coudy; *Pizzicato,* Albia Kavan; *Air,* Lew

Christensen; *Waltz; 4. Bolero,* Ruthanna Boris; *5. Pantomime and Imitation,* Loring, ensemble; *6. Round,* Marie-Jeanne, Fred Danieli; *7. Zarabanda* (later *Nightmare*), Rabana Hasburgh; *8. Threesome, Foursome; 9. Adagio,* Marie-Jeanne, Danieli; *10. Workout and Finale*

S*how Piece* was expressly designed to show off the company's technical virtuosity in a classical work with a modern character. In this it was not completely successful, according to Martin, who wrote: "While its choreography is intricate, it is seldom genuinely brilliant. Its style is dry and arbitrary and its main design choppy and unclimactic. The music is similarly inclined to dryness and is too involved to make ideal stuff for dancing." [1]

Carter, though more positive, came to essentially the same conclusion as Martin: "The work has a great deal in its favor. There is little fuss and pretension about it. Straightforward, with no attempt to build up elaborate atmosphere, it shows young people doing ballet dances in bright costumes before a black curtain. The choreography was ingenious and, within the limitations of the classic steps, had imagination. Probably because of a certain formlessness and lack of emphasis in the music, the ballet did not achieve a natural and theatrical articulation. This somewhat clouded the brilliance of the dancing." [2]

To a non-dance critic like Norton, however, it was "brightly entertaining." [3]

This was Hawkins's first ballet and he

left the dancers a lot of leeway to develop their own parts. Some appreciated this; others resented it. Says Boris, "I felt exploited. All I can remember is stomping around on my sore toes, banging castanets, with a little hat that kept slipping. I didn't realize I was getting a chance to do my own thing."

Danieli: "The idea was good, although not well realized. We rehearsed endlessly, but Erick didn't have the experience to decide what he wanted. We had a series of benches, each painted a different color, as props. They fit over one another, like tubular furniture, but the bottoms were rounded, so they were never stable. Loring came out and placed them around—or misplaced them. The variations were classical in a sense, although the line wasn't classical; it was angular."

The ballet was highly serviceable and appeared on many programs.

FILLING STATION

Ballet-Document in one act

CHOREOGRAPHY: Lew Christensen

MUSIC: Virgil Thomson (1937; commissioned by Ballet Caravan)

SCENARIO: Lincoln Kirstein

COSTUMES, DÉCOR: Paul Cadmus

PREMIERE: 6 January 1938, Avery Memorial Theater, Hartford, Conn.

CAST: *Mac, the Attendant,* Lew Christensen; *Roy & Ray, Truck Drivers,* Douglas Coudy, Eugene Loring; *The Motorist,* Harold Christensen; *His Wife,* Marjorie Moore; *His Child,* Jane Doering; *The Rich Girl,* Marie-Jeanne; *The Rich Boy,* Fred Danieli; *The Gangster,* Erick Hawkins; *The State Trooper,* Todd Bolender

OTHER CASTS: *Mac,* Danieli, William Dollar; *Rich Girl,* Gisella Caccialanza; *Rich Boy,* Bolender

REVIVAL: 12 May 1953, City Center of Music and Drama, New York

CAST: *Mac,* Jacques d'Amboise; *Roy & Ray,* Robert Barnett, Edward Bigelow; *Motorist,* Stanley Zompakos; *Wife,* Shaun O'Brien; *Child,* Edith Brozak; *Rich Girl,* Janet Reed; *Rich Boy,* Michael Maule;

Gangster, Walter Georgov; *Trooper,* John Mandia

Rich Boy also danced by Jonathan Watts

F*illing Station* was the first popular hit in the Ballet Caravan repertory. It was American, all right, decidedly so; its connection with classical ballet was more tenuous. Vaudeville, comic strips, slapstick, and acrobatics were closer relatives. There was only one "straight" (balletic) role in the piece—the lead, Mac, and here, Christensen choreographed to his own strengths: he was a former vaudeville performer, so his measures were full of exciting tricks, spins, cartwheels, and popular dances. (The roles of the Rich Girl and her escort were fairly serious in the beginning, but became more and more comic with the passage of years, culminating in a genuinely hilarious portrayal by Reed and Maule in 1953.)

The story of this "roadside fable" concerns an ordinary day in the life of Mac, in a gas station somewhere in America. He

Filling Station. **Ballet Caravan. *c.* 1938. Jane Doering, Harold Christensen, Marjorie Moore.**

is visited first by truckers, old friends, then by an obnoxious family (very broadly played): the befuddled father needing a map; the bossy mother, overstuffed in overalls; the bratty little girl. As evening falls, an obviously rich and equally obviously inebriated young couple (whom Kirstein called "vaguely F. Scott Fitzgerald") stagger in. A gangster then visits the scene, and when a state trooper arrives, a shoot-out takes place, with the girl in the path of the bullets. As her

corpse is carried off, Mac looks around and sighs, opens his tabloid, and sits back, awaiting the next round of customers.

Audiences loved it. It was not so much that it was a "good" ballet (with so many gimmicks, that might have been difficult), but the novelty of the subject matter, the humor with which some of the admittedly corny bits were put together, and the exuberance of the performers won the day.

Filling Station was included in the Caravan's first coast-to-coast tour, so reports came in from all over the country.

Dallas: "A vivid directness of experience. Full of observation of details and people all of us see every time we take an automobile trip. One could hardly witness this piece without perceiving clearly exactly the goals Kirstein is driving at in his blast at the Russian school and his departure upon an American way. It is not adverse criticism to point out the company has yet only scratched the surface of what it has set out to do." [1]

"Thomson has woven frontier cadences, honky-tonk syncopation, good old movie-house agitators, and the Suzy Q into a serviceable and not too conspicuous score. Choreography ranged from intricate and exciting ballet tricks to tumbles, cartwheels, and the old 'adagio act.' The gags of the departed two-a-day were employed unblushingly, including one about the restless child at the portals of the restroom." [2]

San Francisco (Frankenstein): "A tale of encounters under neon and chromium, with a filling station attendant wrapped in cellophane, that concludes with a choreographic chase somewhat after the fashion of movie comedy. It immortalizes perfect American types, and there is never a hint anywhere either of Gershwin or of that equally common and equally false Americanism that has its source in the French music hall." [3]

Boston: "A somewhat timid step taken in a new direction. It is more impressive for what it promises for the future than in what it achieves. It doesn't give enough opportunity for the kind of technical brilliance which makes good ballet a great show. It is pictorial rather than dramatic: it lacks climax. [But] probably never before has such a setting been utilized in the ballet, which has always been a rather pompous art. If the Caravan group proved nothing else, they made it plain that gasoline is potentially as fragrant as the most delicate perfume in the realm of the dance." [4]

At least one critic in South America, while reporting that the audience had a wonderful time, did not care for these overdrawn (North) American types: "The music shows vivid rhythm and realism, but the choreography uses and abuses sarcastic elements. It is a variety show, well executed, but in his burlesque movements, Christensen did not show any individual or creative orientation." [5]

Filling Station was a collaboration in the full sense of the term. Kirstein had the idea originally, then he and the Christensen brothers thrashed out the excesses and cut it down to size. Thomson was invited to compose. Says Lew Christensen: "Virgil and I worked on it inch by inch—though sometimes he would fall asleep during rehearsals." (Others remember him doubled over with laughter.)

Says Thomson: "We shaped the story into a ballet scenario, with timings for the different numbers. The longest was the pas de deux. Lew said, 'I can last five minutes on that. Beyond five minutes, I don't know too many new things to do.' It opens with a tango. The music is absolutely normal, middle-class America for the time—tunes that everyone would have known, such as tangos, two-steps, waltzes, and a Big Apple (once as popular

as the Charleston). There was no rock then, and jazz was still pretty special.

"I think I made a contribution to the costumes. Paul had never done costumes and he was worried. I said, 'Couldn't we make little comic-strip costumes, as in *Popeye the Sailor?*' The family—especially the Little Girl—had to have comical clothes. The comic-strip idea gave Paul a start."

In 1953 *Filling Station* was revived by the New York City Ballet—perhaps partially, as Kirstein explained in a pre-curtain speech, to show the roots of the current repertory and how far native ballet had come since 1938, but largely, one suspects, to showcase the emerging abilities of d'Amboise, destined to become the first American premier danseur trained entirely by Balanchine, and who at the age of eighteen had just the fresh-faced good looks and unstrained kinetic response to be perfect in the role. Terry commented on this fortunate casting: "The part seems tailor-made for his youthful exuberance and for his remarkable physical prowess. Muscular elasticity—a quality which usually disappears with maturity—was evident in the high and resilient leaps; jumps which found the body resting easily in air; leaping

turns, apparently motivated by coiled springs, which described slow-motion arcs in space; rollovers, cartwheels, tumblings, rough-house. There were also slow and sustained pirouettes, impeccable entrechats, and the disclosure of a young but beautifully schooled dance technique." [6]

D'Amboise went on to become for many years the Company's principal male stalwart in the classical divertissements (for a while sharing this role with Eglevsky), dancing all manner of princes and cavaliers (as well as tragic heroes and demi-caractères). He was tall enough to partner Balanchine's leggiest ballerinas, and his dancing always had a touch of daring as well as virtuosity. He lacked the ultimate as a stylist, however, and in the course of his long career, he found few roles as congenial as was Mac, the all-American boy.

For Martin, the ballet was far more "engaging" than it had been in 1938. Much credit for this probably goes to Reed's excruciatingly funny Rich Girl. Balanchine, unhappy with the downbeat ending, changed it so that the besotted heroine does not really die, but revives to give the audience a good-bye wave as she exits on the shoulders of her "pall-bearers."

The revival was well received, but with more than a slight smile at the ballet's gaucheries. And by this time, of course, it had lost its pioneering connotations.

Filling Station. **New York City Ballet.** *c.* **1953. Michael Maule, Jacques d'Amboise, Janet Reed.** (*Photo Frederick Melton.*)

AIR AND VARIATIONS

CHOREOGRAPHY: William Dollar

MUSIC: Johann Sebastian Bach (*The Goldberg Variations,* 1742), arranged for two pianos by Trude Rittmann; later orchestrated by Nicolas Nabokov

COSTUMES: Walter Gifford (1938); Eudokia Mironowa (1939)

PREMIERE: 25 April 1938, Winthrop College, Rock Hill, S.C.

CAST: Marie-Jeanne, Lew Christensen; Marjorie Moore, ensemble

OTHER CASTS: Gisella Caccialanza, Leda Anchutina; William Dollar, Fred Danieli; Lorna London

Thanks to his tutoring by Rittmann, Dollar was able to give *Air and Variations* musical integrity as well as choreographic interest. Using Marie-Jeanne as the theme—the constant that appears in and out of every number—he constructed a series of variations in which the dancers more or less paralleled the progression of the individual voice-parts, not merely the melodic indications. Each variation used a different number of dancers, and there was no corps, in the sense of a group of dancers moving in one bloc. Says Dollar, "I was turned over to Trude to become well grounded in the construction of the music. Then she played all the rehearsals and would tell me when I was using someone incorrectly, musically speaking. A fascinating experience. We worked like dogs."

The entire piece could not be used. As Dollar explains, "Ballet was still so unpopular and unknown that half the music was plenty." At the first performance, seventeen sections were listed; at times this was cut to thirteen.

As an excellent classical dancer, Dollar had a particular feeling for men's steps and partnering, with which the ballet was replete. According to women he worked with, he also understood pointe work and created a most challenging role for Marie-Jeanne.

Most reviews were quite favorable: "Dollar's ingenuity has served him admirably in inventing appropriate and telling movements and patterns to reflect Bach's musical metamorphoses. With a group of ten, he has cannily utilized the full ensemble only for climactic purposes and has divided his group into varying units, sometimes permitting a single male or female to convey his intentions, at others combining dancers of both sexes, or using combinations of female dancers exclusively [Marie-Jeanne remembers an adagio in which she was partnered by three couples]. The results are always arresting." [1]

"Dollar has seen to it that the clarity, design, and fluidity of the music are complemented by the dance." [2] "Straightforward choreography devoid both of sentimentality and of reliance on the 'living sculpture' that too often relates such ballets to the tableaux they exhibit in the circus with albino horses and ladies in white. It was all movement, all pattern, it was all a play of lightly dynamic forces, and it had the good sense to avoid making its patterns too closely after those of the music." [3]

Martin's was one of the few negative reactions. He found the music unsuitable for dancing.

BILLY THE KID

Character Ballet in one act

CHOREOGRAPHY: Eugene Loring

MUSIC: Aaron Copland (1938; commissioned by Ballet Caravan)

SCENARIO: Lincoln Kirstein

COSTUMES, DÉCOR: Jared French

PREMIERE: 6 October 1938, Chicago Civic Theater

CAST: *Billy*, Eugene Loring; *Mother and Sweetheart*, Marie-Jeanne; *Pat Garrett, his friend*, Lew Christensen; *Alias*, Todd Bolender; *Dance Hall Girls; Mexican Women; Ranchers' Wives; Cowboys*

OTHER CASTS: *Billy*, Fred Danieli, Michael Kidd; *Mother and Sweetheart*, Alicia Alonso, Margit de Kova; *Pat Garrett*, Harold Christensen

1. The open prairie: The Pioneers, ensemble
2. A street in New Mexico (ca. 1877): Billy, his Mother, Pat Garrett, Alias (as Mexican), ensemble
3. Billy kills his Mother's murderer, Alias (as Cowhand)
4. Billy grows up (ca. 1885), kills Alias (as Land Agent)
5. Billy cheats Garrett at cards, kills Alias (as Sheriff)
6. Billy captured by Garrett, now sheriff. Battle
7. Dance after battle: Cowboys, Gun-Girls
8. Billy in prison, kills Alias (as Jailer), escapes
9. Billy lost, betrayed by Alias (as Indian Guide)
10. Billy finds his Mexican sweetheart
11. Garrett, led by Alias (as Guide), kills Billy
12. Billy's funeral (ca. 1886)
13. The open prairie: The Pioneers

Billy was Ballet Caravan's biggest hit—with audiences and critics—and the only work produced during the Caravan's existence to have a life in repertory to the present day (it has been performed by Ballet Theatre since 1940). By 1942 Martin was already referring to it as "something of a classic." The subject, of course, was a perfect one for capturing the public imagination, and Loring's treatment—stylized gesture, pantomime, and a lot of running and jumping and "horseback riding," with little in the way of orthodox ballet vocabulary—made it very accessible. Martin described Loring's methods: "He came to dance by way of acting and has an instinct for characterization and dramatic procedure that dominates his approach to composition. His ballets have nothing of the quality of 'pure' dance, but employ a medium that is essentially a heightening and an abstraction of acting, orchestrated according to the principles of dance form." [1]

He also had a feeling for suspense,

Air and Variations. **William Dollar, Marie-Jeanne (right).**

drama, and humor. His idea was to evoke the flavor of the West and use it as a background for Billy's special story; thus scenes lending color alternated with those that advanced the plot. Martin continued, "His characterization in general is achieved by discarding everything except some one essential aspect of the individual as a variation on a type and allowing the specific action to play around this as a core. His Old West is peopled by galumphing cowhands, dazzling vulgarians of the dance halls, busy ranch women, peasant girls from over the Mexican border, and a liberal sprinkling of two-gun men. They are no less vivid because they have been lightly sketched and with a deliberate quirk of stylization. They play cards incessantly, fight with and without guns, have a bit of time for lovemaking, and generally convince you they are alive and active. Loring employs various contrapuntal devices—[sometimes a broad kaleidoscopic method], sometimes two or three rather tightly knit independent motifs, and [also] smaller and more concentrated scenes where the situation demands." [2]

Bohm commented on the intentional air of unreality surrounding the murders and other violent episodes. And Vitak wrote: "The story was at all times clear and stimulating in its dramatic style. The motif of cowboys riding was a highly amusing bit of rhythmic originality, an inspiration which, without being obvious, acts as a sort of theme of the work, just as the rhythm of horseback riding pervades the descriptive score." [3]

Terry was almost convinced: "With some judicious cutting, should become what it just misses being—a virile, exciting, and honest re-creation of a rip-roaring epoch in America's past." [4]

Martin also felt that cutting, or, as he put it, "thinning" was in order; there was simply too much in it for audiences to easily absorb. He also mentioned several effects that he felt did not quite come off: "In every case Billy's victim is 'Alias' in various characterizations. This is inherently an amusing device giving a certain unity to an essentially episodic plot and lending a touch of fatalistic suspense to the individual scenes. The scheme of the work, however, is already too full to bear it. [Kirstein pointed out, however, that the recurring single Nemesis solved the problem of corpses littering up the stage.] The love scenes employ a rather coldly conventionalized type of ballet

Billy the Kid. Marie-Jeanne, Eugene Loring. *(Photo Dwight Godwin.)*

adagio, and the use of pointes at least raises a question. When just before his fatal shooting, Billy actually speaks a phrase in Spanish, the stylistic integrity of the piece suffers a momentary lapse. All these things, however, have certain justifications in principle." [5]

Almost forty years later, Loring comments on his most lasting and successful theater work: "I had never been west of the Mississippi, but Kirstein, in his abrupt manner, gave me *The Life and Times of William Bonney.* 'Read this,' he said. 'See if you can get a ballet out of it.' I made an outline and Copland and I worked together filling in the duration of the action. We decided, for instance, that the most violent sound was silence, and that's why it's only at the end, when Billy gets killed, there is the musical equivalent of a shot. Other than that—every time Billy kills someone—the shooting is in silence. There was some discussion as to whether we should use real guns; but I thought it should all be done in what's called sense-memory—no props. The steps are not very balletic, but each time just before he fires, he does a double pirouette, double air turn—then shoots. To me, this isn't a technical thing, but an emotional one. It seemed to me that before doing such an act, one would be in a state of white heat—an explosion of temper would go through the body—and that's how he expresses it. It's a vivid movement, just before he does something memorable.

"No one ever knew of a real girlfriend, so that's why the part of the Sweetheart is on pointe. It's like a mist, a dream. I was criticized for that—mixing boots and toe shoes. But I assumed, because Billy associated a great deal with Mexican girls

and prostitutes, that it would be a dark, Latin, sensuous person. Marie-Jeanne, the original, and then Alicia Alonso both had those qualities. To this day, they're the best ones in the part I've seen.

"I tried not merely to tell Billy's story, but to show that he had to die. The march at the beginning and the end symbolizes the establishment of law and order, which destroyed his world."

Kirstein wrote of the ending that it "Concludes not with Billy's personal finish, but with a new start across the continent, this time the march taken up a little more solidly by benefit of one more step achieved in the necessary ordering of the whole generation's procession. It's a flag-raising more than a funeral. Billy's lonely wild-fire energy is replaced by the group force of the many marchers." [6]

Some years after its premiere, Denby compared *Billy* to the newer *Rodeo*, "our other serious American ballet. *Rodeo* is about the West as it is lived in: *Billy* is about the West as it is dreamed of." [7]

Says Loring, "There were some places we couldn't play it because it was not a fit subject for a ballet. But elsewhere . . . In San Francisco an old fellow—a surviving pioneer—came backstage and told us that the ballet was 'just as it happened—except that Billy really shot left-handed.'"

On the Company's tour of South America, where the work had a great success, Danieli in the title role was acclaimed as "better than John Wayne."

CHARADE
or,
The Debutante

Ballet Romance in one act

CHOREOGRAPHY: Lew Christensen

MUSIC: American songs and social dances, including melodies by Stephen Foster and Louis Gottschalk, and variations on "Good Night, Ladies," arranged by Trude Rittmann (1938)

SCENARIO: Lincoln Kirstein

COSTUMES, DÉCOR: Alvin Colt

PREMIERE: 17 October 1939, Lancaster, Pa.

CAST: *Blanche Johnson, the debutante,*

Marie-Jeanne; *Trixie, her younger sister,* Gisella Caccialanza; *Mr. Johnson, their father,* Harold Christensen; *Minnie, the maid,* Ruby Asquith; *Wilmer J. Smith, a young man,* Lew Christensen; *7 female guests* (Sissie Rover, Clarice & Birdie Stout, Melba Jones, Emmy Vale, Lily Pond, Mollie Fair); *6 male guests* (Dick & Rod Rover, Jeff West, Charlie Baker, Clarence Todd, Phineas Hall)

Charade was designed to take advantage of the comic flair of Caccialanza and the virtuoso techniques of Lew Christensen and Marie-Jeanne (her vocabulary included double sauts de basque, for a start), in a gay little tale set to a medley of polkas, schottisches, waltzes, a varsovienne, and a galop—ballroom dances that were taught in America around the turn of the century. The steps, mostly balletic, were combined with theatricalized bits of these social dances. The costumes recalled "tutti-frutti ice cream, pink cake, and lace party favors." The time was 1900.

Says Christensen about the plot line, "It was a very complicated story, but it worked. A young debutante was having a coming-out party, and her younger sister was sent to bed, so the sister came down in her nightgown all gussied up, put a lampshade on her head (this was Lincoln's touch), and made an entrance in disguise. All the boys liked her and avoided the debutante, and that's when the trouble started. The father had to come in and break it up; and so he distracted them by putting on a game of charades. Everyone got a letter—C-H-A- -A-D-E—but the R was missing. The little sister had it, and the father had to chase her around the room to get her to cooperate." The names of the characters were chosen with some deliberation.

Critics mostly found it delightful (with the exception of Martin, for whom it was "a low comedy rumpus in which energy and activity largely substitute for choreography," [1] although from that comment it sounds as though he enjoyed himself).

Terry wrote that this concoction was "Not only an exceptionally good ballet; it's first-rate entertainment by the best theater standards. The choreography was ingenious, the costumes perfect. From the waist up the lassies were clad in period costumes, but even here the turn of the century was not neglected, for white lace panties were much in evidence. A superb madcap performance by Caccialanza, who in lampshade and veil

Charade, or The Debutante. **Marie-Jeanne.** (*Courtesy Lew and Gisella Christensen.*)

threw the party into a fit as a mysterious lady." Equally important for the company, Terry continued, "The dancing was spirited, with ensemble work that ought to shame the Russian ballets." [2]

Chujoy, who was ordinarily not too taken with frivolous subject matter, found it "a whimsical bit of stagecraft produced in the best theatrical manner." [3]

Kolodin saw some interesting forerunners: "A fetching bit of Americana. Christensen has not hesitated to borrow liberally from the method of Massine in such ballets as *Beau Danube* and *Gaîté Parisienne*. Indeed the work begins somewhat as a Mauve-decade version of Balanchine's *Cotillon*. But what happens from that point onward is wholly original and thoroughly entertaining." [4]

Says Fred Danieli, "We used to depend a lot on humor in dance. Much of that's lost today—now everybody's so serious."

CITY PORTRAIT

Ballet-Document in one act

CHOREOGRAPHY: Eugene Loring

MUSIC: Henry Brant (1939; commissioned by Ballet Caravan)

SCENARIO: Lincoln Kirstein

COSTUMES: Forrest Thayr, Jr.

PREMIERE: 23 October 1939, Four Arts Club, Mobile, Ala.

CAST: *1. Rain in the Street: 3 Bums* (male); *The Little Girl,* Lorna London; *Passers-by,* 7 women; *2. Tenement Quarrel: A Mother,* Beatrice Tompkins; *A Father,* Todd Bolender; *Their Elder Daughter,* Gisella Caccialanza; *Their Younger Daughter,* London; *Their Son,* Michael Kidd; *3. Love in the Street: Elder Daughter; Her Boy Friend,* Newcomb Rice; *4. The Office Workers,* ensemble; *5. The Manhole,* 3 men; *6. The Drugstore Cowboys,* Kidd, ensemble; *7. The Public Square: Tough Girl, Nice Girl, Street Orator, Hungry Drunks, The Crowd* (added later: *Little Girl, Blind Man*)

City Portrait (a "dour tenement-street pantomime" [1]) was probably ahead of its time. Unrelievedly pessimistic, it dealt with unexalted subject matter and unglamorous characters. As such, it did not appeal to audiences and even depressed some of the performers. Loring didn't attempt to sweeten things up: "The idea of *City Portrait* was disillusion. The effects of living under those conditions, especially when you are poor, destroys the family. The city was New York."

Says Fred Danieli: "It reminded me a

little of Sokolow's work—the quietness, the dim lighting, and the dancing."

Bolender: "Genie had a beautiful eye for situations—the picture, the look of the contemporary scene."

The music was described in the program: "full of contemporary rhythm of the city indoors and out; the noise of street bands and mechanical pianos." Diamond complained that it contained traces of Mozart, "the atmosphere of Bach" [in the pas de deux], a Vienna waltz, "swing," and "a few measures of the Beethoven *Moonlight* with wrong notes added. Paper is inserted into the sounding board of the piano, the strings of the piano are struck with the hand—all excellent sonorities in themselves, but not all the mechanical pianos and hand organs in the world play as many wrong notes as Brant has inserted into his score." [2]

Sabin, however, mentioned "biting irony beneath the platitudes." [3]

About the work as a whole, critics were divided between the negative and the somewhat favorable, with reservations. "[One recognizes] Loring's gift for characteristic movement. His street youths move like urchins, the gestures and pantomime of the 'Tenement Quarrel' have been authentically observed, and the manhole workers are similarly in character. Some of the episodes are overlong, and the mental slant is not too original." [4]

Martin: "Where Loring has chiefly missed fire is in the attainment of sufficient dramatic unity to pull his composition together. The work has no center and provides nothing with which the spectator can identify himself. A family of five runs predominantly through the action but without enough accent to hold the episodes together in one piece. [The characters] emerge not only as an oppressed but an oppressive crew. Some of the movement is beautifully revealing, retaining the quality of realism and capturing at the same time the colors of abstract design." [5]

"Loring clutches wildly for novelty with the result that many of the movements are startlingly unrelated to the idea at hand." [6] "Intellectually he has done his task well, but no communicative value is transmitted to the audience. The variety of colloquial gestures does not clarify the quandary which exists in the scenario." [7]

AMERICAN BALLET CARAVAN 1941

TIME TABLE

CHOREOGRAPHY: Antony Tudor

MUSIC: Aaron Copland (*Music for the Theatre*, 1925)

COSTUMES, DÉCOR: James Stewart Morcom

PREMIERE: 27 June 1941, Teatro Municipal, Rio de Janeiro, Brazil (open dress rehearsal 29 May 1941, Little Theatre of Hunter College, New York)

CAST: *The Girl*, Gisella Caccialanza; *Her Boyfriend*, Antony Tudor; *High School Girl*, Lorna London; *High School Boy*, Charles Dickson; *Three Young Girls*, June Graham, Mary Jane Shea, Beatrice Tompkins; *Two Marines*, John Kriza, Newcomb Rice; *Lady with Newspaper*, Georgia Hiden; *Soldier*, Jack Dunphy
Boyfriend also danced by Lew Christensen

REVIVAL: 13 January 1949, City Center of Music and Drama, New York

CAST: *Girl*, Marie-Jeanne; *Boyfriend*, Francisco Moncion; *High School Girl*, Tanaquil LeClercq; *High School Boy*, Roy Tobias; *Three Girls*, Ruth Gilbert, Ruth Sobotka, Beatrice Tompkins; *Two Marines*, Walter Georgov, Jack Kauflin; *Lady*, Hiden; *Soldier*, Edward Bigelow

Time Table. **New York City Ballet. 1949. Tanaquil LeClercq as High School Girl, Roy Tobias as High School Boy.** (*Photo Konstantin Kostich—Graphic House.*)

Time Table, created for the Company's South American tour, was the first ballet Tudor choreographed on American soil (although, to be truthful, he was still tinkering with it on the gangplank of the ship that took the dancers to Rio). It concerned wartime partings and reunions at a railroad station.

"I prefer to find music first and then look for an idea, since the other way around is terribly difficult," Tudor says. "This ballet was considered to be so 'American,' but you know we have armies in England, and it could just as well have happened there. I saw such things in World War I. And my costumes were

roughly that period. The three girls were sort of flappers. It wasn't terribly sad, because at the end a husband comes home just as the boyfriend leaves, on the same train."

Already in Tudor's vocabulary were those steps that dancers find so excruciating to do. Says Caccialanza, "They're wonderful, when you think about it—just what you don't expect. But almost impossible. He used to give walk, walk, walk, then rise to toe with no plié, no support. In his ballets you had to keep looking for opportunities to sneak up onto pointe."

By the time the ballet was officially seen in New York (1949), Robbins's *Fancy Free* and Tudor's own *Pillar of Fire* were already established as contemporary masterpieces, and *Time Table* was felt to be no more than their pallid forerunner. There were also the expected reservations about Balanchine dancers' ability to project so different a style. The highlight of the piece was the sensitive pas de deux of the girl and the boy, and the whole, to Sabin's mind, was suffused with nostalgia, wrote "Tudor's favorite mood in ballet. [*Time Table*'s] main fault is lack of choreographic development. The horseplay of the two young marines offered Tudor an excellent opportunity, but he gives them almost nothing to do. The minor figures are only faintly sketched in, with the result that the action drags when the principals do not dominate the stage. Nevertheless, Tudor has captured the poignance of youth and parting." [1]

Wrote Hering in a similar vein, "In the love duets one caught occasional glimpses of the Tudor who was to burst forth with *Pillar*. There were the ecstatic slow adagio passages, the plasticity and attention to dramatic detail. It was choreography and dance-acting of tenderness and poetry. But in his lighter group material Tudor was trapped by the kind of banality that often characterizes Massine's ballabiles. He adhered to the rhythmic structure of the music with little attention to its essential character." [2]

Terry: "Slight material, treated in a manner that suggests a musical-comedy interlude. Pleasant enough, but hardly worthy of the choreographer's known skills." [3]

Martin: "Definitely minor, but charming and atmospheric and wonderfully made." [4]

BALLET IMPERIAL
since 1973 called
CONCERTO NO. 2

CHOREOGRAPHY: George Balanchine

MUSIC: Peter Ilyitch Tchaikovsky (Piano Concerto in G major, op. 44, 1879)

COSTUMES, DÉCOR: Mstislav Doboujinsky

PREMIERE: 25 June 1941, Teatro Municipal, Rio de Janeiro, Brazil (open dress rehearsal 29 May 1941, Little Theatre of Hunter College, New York)

PIANO: Simon Sadoff

CAST: Marie-Jeanne, William Dollar (principals); Gisella Caccialanza; Fred Danieli, Nicholas Magallanes; 2 female demisoloists; 16 women, 6 men

REVIVAL: 15 October 1964, New York State Theater (staged by Frederic Franklin)

COSTUMES, DÉCOR: Rouben Ter-Arutunian

PIANO: Gordon Boelzner

CAST: Suzanne Farrell, Jacques d'Amboise; Patricia Neary; Frank Ohman, Earle Sieveling

NEW PRODUCTION (*Concerto No. 2*): 12 January 1973, New York State Theater

COSTUMES: Karinska

PIANO: Gordon Boelzner

CAST: Patricia McBride, Peter Martins; Colleen Neary; Tracy Bennett, Victor Castelli

OTHER CASTS: Merrill Ashley, Melissa Hayden, Violette Verdy; Conrad Ludlow; Marnee Morris, Suki Schorer

I. Allegro Brillante—Antante
II. Andante non troppo
III. Allegro con fuoco

Ballet Imperial was created to show South America that the classical tradition was alive and well in the North—South America, with its ornate opera houses in Rio, Buenos Aires, Lima; the United States, where Ballet Caravan had danced in high school auditoriums, and where a Balanchine company had not performed for four years (and would have to wait an-

other five for a single concert, again in a high school): no wonder proof was needed. Balanchine decided against another *Sleeping Beauty* or *Giselle*; he was not interested in reviving the classical tradition, but in revitalizing it (and how could he bring from America a ballet with kings and queens?). Hence, his homage to the old by means of the new.

As Martin would write (some years later), "It would be a grave mistake to imply anything old-fashioned in any respect except the psychological setting [of *Ballet Imperial*]. The virtuosity of the old academic style, the grandiloquence of manner, even the conventional mime [Balanchine] has looked back on with a certain tenderness but with an artistic objectivity as well, which allows him to treat it purely as choreographic material and to compose it freely and imaginatively." [1]

Kirstein noted, "*Ballet Imperial* is not an American ballet. It is a Russian ballet danced by an American company."

Fortunately for his purposes, Balanchine had as first ballerina Marie-Jeanne, who is still remembered thirty years later for the brilliance and speed of her jumps and beats and the clarity of her movements ("She took off like greased lightning," said a colleague). The ballet was created as a vehicle for her.

To achieve the imperial idea, Balan-

Ballet Imperial. Above: New York City Ballet. 1964. *Opposite, above left:* American Ballet Caravan. 1941. South America. Marie-Jeanne. (*Courtesy Marie-Jeanne. Photo Schulmann.*) *Above right:* New York City Ballet. 1960s. Violette Verdy. (*Photo Fred Fehl.*) *Bottom: Concerto No. 2.* 1970s. Patricia McBride, Peter Martins. (*Photo Martha Swope.*)

chine used sumptuous music, an expansive back drop showing a Neva embankment, regal costumes, massed effects, a ballerina part still considered perhaps the most difficult in his repertory, and a liberal helping of what he called "old Russian corn"—touches of schmaltz here and there to match the super-soulful moments in the music. (Terry has referred to the ballet's "heightened elegance, slightly forced brilliance, and over-all quality of delicate caricature." [2])

But the framing is the least of it; the real glory of *Imperial* is its dancing, a non-stop outpouring of kinetic exuberance.

As Lederman observed, "The theme of this ballet is grandeur, and it is projected for 35 minutes in a power drive of unflagging intensity. When this almost ceaseless flow of movement is over, we are, astonishingly enough, not worn but

happy and elated. Balanchine is always urging people to *look* at dancing. This is an invitation few choreographers can really afford to give. In *Imperial*, where the stage is always so full of people, no one ever gets lost, everyone, everything is perfectly spaced." [3]

Wrote Denby: "It begins with a solemn, pompous, vaguely uneasy mood, groups and solos that turn into brilliant bravura; then comes a pantomime scene, with softer dances; then a third section, even more vertiginously brilliant than the first, in which everybody shines, individually, in clusters, the boys, the girls, and stars, and all in unison. The musicality of the choreography is as astonishing as its extraordinary ease in affording surprises and virtuoso passages." [4]

Paralleling the music, the ballerina has her most dashing solo work (piano en-

trance and cadenza) in the first movement, while the ensemble is often stationary, as a backdrop; the second movement, mournfully melodic, is the least complex in its groupings, as it is the least complex musically; in the third, the ballerina and her cavaliers are leaders, not set-off soloists, of the constantly moving group actions. McBride describes her first appearance:

"You don't have time to have a nice, an easy entrance. You're on and brilliant right away. It's the shock of it more than anything. There's a step you can't count on—I could practice it all day and still not be sure if it would come out—a swivel after which you have to stop on a dime, exactly. There's another part that's incredibly difficult because of the speed. You have to be so clear, you have to be so on top of the music. Your legs have to be

like your arms—very expressive. And the music starts slow and becomes faster and faster and faster. You need a lot of stamina. And, of course, you're dancing to the cadenza—there's no conductor's beat. And with the pauses, it's essential to stop exactly when the pianist does. Very tricky. After the first movement, it's a breeze, very enjoyable. It may be my most difficult part. Always a challenge. It's wonderful as a dancer to have something like this, though, because it makes you work." "Brutally demanding" is another name for the ballerina role.

Wrote Lederman, "Absolutely dazzling is [her] supported, stuttering retreat on toe from which the arms and legs open out to the widest horizontal as she is dragged, with only one foot touching, around the stage. Or the circle of limping steps from which her partner appears to take flight in a series of brisés with its climax of entrechats." [5]

The male role—perhaps in the Petersburg tradition, perhaps due to Balanchinian predilection—is more subdued. The noble cavalier is most frequently relegated to a support for the ballerina, and at one or two points carries her elegantly on his shoulder all over the stage ("about forty million miles," says one veteran of the part). Elsewhere, he acts as central pillar in a formation involving about thirty girls. The secondary soloists—one woman, two men—have more academic measures than is usually the case in Balanchine works. They do straightforward steps from the classroom, frequently in unison. This is unusual for a woman, since the featured big leaps, beats, and pirouettes are male specialties. The original female soloist, Caccialanza, was noted for her jumps.

Ballet Imperial was performed by a group called the American Ballet, presented by the New Opera, at the Broadway Theater, November 1942, with Mary Ellen Moylan, William Dollar, and Gisella Caccialanza, a last gasp in the Balanchine-Kirstein collaboration before the war suspended their joint activities.

When the ballet was revived in 1964, it was praised for its choreography but not for its performance, costumes, or setting. The dancers were not considered grand enough and the investiture too grand, or in some cases too gaudy.

In 1973, when it was unveiled as *Concerto No. 2*, Balanchine had made a number of changes. Gone were the Alexander Column, the two-headed eagles, the view of St. Petersburg, the tutus, little Russian hats, the epaulettes and the pantomime. In their places were a plain cyclorama as background, mid-calf-length chiffon dresses, and a new pas de deux. Kisselgoff wrote:

"There was not a tutu in sight [in] Balanchine's best known homage to the Russian ballet tradition. Contrary to advance rumors, the previously elaborately designed ballet was not performed in practice clothes. There is no doubt, however, that *Ballet Imperial* has become less imperial. The velvets and capes have given way to stylized Romantic attire. At first view, it provokes some very mixed feelings. In its tribute to the classicism of Petipa and its reverence for the score, it became a Balanchine signature piece. Now presented only as pure dance, it does not seem quite as interesting on its own. Or perhaps time is needed to adjust to this latest instance of giving a romantic veneer to what had been classic glitter." [6]

Most dancers, however, preferred the new costumes, with their softness and flow. Says McBride, "It's much nicer now without the mime. It's all dancing. Balanchine put in some new music for the new pas de deux. And the costumes affect your style. I feel much freer in chiffon, more open. The little crown on your head keeps you feeling elegant."

CONCERTO BAROCCO

CHOREOGRAPHY: George Balanchine

MUSIC: Johann Sebastian Bach (Double Violin Concerto in D minor)

COSTUMES, DÉCOR: Eugene Berman (as of 13 September 1951, performed in practice clothes and without décor)

PREMIERE: 27 June 1941, Teatro Municipal, Rio de Janeiro, Brazil (open dress rehearsal 29 May 1941, Little Theatre of Hunter College, New York)

CAST: Marie-Jeanne, William Dollar (principals); Mary Jane Shea (soloist); 8 women

OTHER CASTS: Diana Adams, Suzanne Farrell, Melissa Hayden, Allegra Kent, Gelsey Kirkland, Tanaquil LeClercq, Sara Leland, Patricia McBride, Mimi Paul, Janet Reed, Maria Tallchief; Frank Hobi, Conrad Ludlow, Nicholas Magallanes, Peter Martins, Francisco Moncion, Nolan T'Sani; Adams, Karin von Aroldingen, Doris Breckenridge, Ruth Gilbert, Leland, Marnee Morris, Colleen Neary, Patricia Neary, Suki Schorer, Carol Sumner, Patricia Wilde

Vivace
Largo ma non tanto
Allegro

Concerto Barocco is a supreme challenge to dancers—and to audiences. It is a ballet especially for the legs and feet, chastely precise, and demanding the utmost in refinement of movement and musicality. There are no histrionics, no abandon, only totally tempered, contained technique. The movement is as exacting, yet also as expansive, as Bach's regulated score: rigorous control is at the center of the singing line. The ballerina must be mistress of impeccable, quick footwork, have deliberateness yet freedom in the arms, flexibility in the torso, and, in the adagio section, the ability to sustain a phrase almost forever with the smoothness of soft butter. There is nothing static in the ballet; in drawing out the lines, there is a constant sense of movement.

The corps girls, customarily chosen only from among the most promising for their line and style, shimmer in their modest deportment like eight cultured (perfect) pearls on a necklace, interspersed at measured intervals. They maintain their bearing throughout, for they never leave the stage. Even the ballerina is absent for only a few seconds. (The second ballerina and the partner do not appear in all the movements, however.) It is the sustained tension that has made many dancers—soloists and corps members alike—consider *Concerto Barocco* their most demanding role.

Under the heading "Balanchine Makes Polyphony Visible" Willis described it: "Captures the soul of polyphony in patterned space. It assigns one girl to each solo line and goes on from there to explore the relationships between small group and large, fast measure and slow, soft terrace and loud. In the adagio, the principal soloist acquires a male partner and takes to the air with the singing melody for one of the most poetic displays of strength and agility this choreographer has produced. In the third movement,

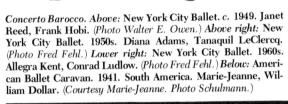

Concerto Barocco. Above: New York City Ballet. *c.* 1949. Janet Reed, Frank Hobi. *(Photo Walter E. Owen.) Above right:* New York City Ballet. 1950s. Diana Adams, Tanaquil LeClercq. *(Photo Fred Fehl.) Lower right:* New York City Ballet. 1960s. Allegra Kent, Conrad Ludlow. *(Photo Fred Fehl.) Below:* American Ballet Caravan. 1941. South America. Marie-Jeanne, William Dollar. *(Courtesy Marie-Jeanne. Photo Schulmann.)*

the dancers' arms outline and emphasize the offbeat attack which this music needs for life." [1]

The ballet was created for the Company's tour of South America in 1941; it was first seen in New York in the fall of 1943, danced by the American Concert Ballet, a group of Balanchine dancers headed by Todd Bolender, William Dollar, and Mary Jane Shea, whose attempts to form a troupe in the vacuum left after the dissolution of the American Ballet Caravan unfortunately came to very little. (It produced two ballets, however—Bolender's *Mother Goose Suite* and Dollar's *Five Boons of Life*—later called *The Five Gifts*—which appeared in the New York City Ballet repertory.) Denby wrote of *Concerto Barocco*: "It is straight dancing, animated, complex, and completely clear. There is no deformation of gesture, but the variety of invention in the choreography is unparalleled. In the adagio the lifts are breathtaking as well as unheard of. And the syncopations of the first and third movements are wonderfully apt and American." [2] (Denby was the first critic to call the ballet a masterpiece, a view now common.)

Barnes sounded the same note many years later when he wrote: "The three hallmarks of the American classic style are poetry, athleticism, and musicality, and these three graces are exquisitely exploited by [*Concerto Barocco*]. It is a cool ballet, poised disarmingly on the verge of understatement, effortlessly paralleling the sustained yet weaving lines of Bach's music. The choreography is austere, and controlled, and as beautiful as Euclidean geometry." [3]

In 1945, *Concerto Barocco* was presented by the Ballet Russe de Monte Carlo, without costumes. Wrote Denby, "Balanchine has set his ballet so happily to Bach's *Concerto for Two Violins* that the score may be called his subject matter.[*] The correspondence of eye and ear is at its most surprising in the poignant adagio movement. At the climax, the ballerina, with limbs powerfully outspread, is lifted by her partner, lifted repeatedly in narrowing arcs higher and higher. Then at the culminating phrase, from her greatest height, he very slowly lowers her. You watch her body slowly descend, her foot and leg pointing stiffly down-

* Balanchine's use of Bach for concert dance deserves attention. Doris Humphrey is perhaps the only other major choreographer of the time to find Bach suitable for dancing.

Concerto Barocco. **New York City Ballet. 1970s. Gelsey Kirkland, Conrad Ludlow.** (*Photo Michael Truppin.*)

ward, till her toe reaches the floor and she rests her full weight at last on this single sharp point and pauses. And in the final adagio figure, the ballerina, being slid upstage in two or three swoops that dip down and rise a moment into an extension in second [later, arabesque]—like a receding cry—creates another image that corresponds vividly to the weight of the musical passage. But these 'emotional' figures are strictly formal as dance inventions. The introductory vivace is rather like a dance of triumph, strong, quick and square; while the concluding allegro is livelier and friendlier, with touches of syncopated fun and sportive jigging. Both these sections have sharply cut rhythms, a powerful onward drive and a diamond-like sparkle in their evolutions. There are many lightning shifts in the arm positions and yet the pulse of the dance is so sure its complexity never looks elaborate." [4]

For all its lofty purity and beauty, the first and third movements, as Denby suggests, have a certain quirkiness. Says Schorer (who performed the soloist role), "More difficult than precision in technique is exactitude in timing—the syncopation. He works for hours to get that right. It's as though an ounce makes all the difference. And for all its refinement, he likes it 'jazzy.' There's one place where the corps almost does the Charleston on pointe. In some of my most brisk and classical movements, he kept saying, 'Make it jazzy. Lead with the hip.'" Shades of Apollo's Muses!

The ballet was on the opening-night program of the Company's first appear-

ance as the New York City Ballet (as an affiliate of the opera), 11 October 1948, which may give some notion of Balanchine's feelings about it. It was presented with costumes. Martin, who had previously (1945) commented on its "narrow range," now found it a "good" ballet.

Hering wrote, during the same season, "Takes the prize for sheer quality of movement. It is a compositional tour de force. The minute polyphonic detail is all there in the quick movements of arms and heads, and in the long interweaving melodic lines for soloists. It provides Balanchine with the kind of richness and complexity to whet his choreographic appetite." [5]

Most critical comment of the evening centered on *Orpheus*, which shared the program and was considered a more important work. (Time seems not to have borne out this estimation; both have been major—and lasting.)

In September 1951, *Concerto Barocco* was performed with the girls in black tunics; a number of years later, black was changed to white. The dance has been in the repertory continually since the debut of the New York City Ballet.

Europe reacted with restrained enthusiasm to the rigors of Bach cum Balanchine; but since the Company did not appear in England until 1950, or on the continent until 1952, Balanchine's special classicism and pure-dance aesthetic were still novelties when the first reviews were written.

England:
"A rarefied style of dance imagery. It is one of Balanchine's strongest statements of the fact that a ballet is a spectacle of dancing, and any illumination of character or suggestion of personality comes only incidentally from the dancer's manner of demonstrating that he is primarily, in this context of Time and Space, a creator of a fascinating pattern of movement." [6]

Germany:
"A masterpiece of absolute dance, a beautiful and terrible radicalism that forms a style. Even though this most modern form of classical dance may be a byway, it nevertheless teaches us the beauty of abstract gesture and a scenic play of forms, fulfilling thus a function similar to abstract painting. Aesthetic dangers lie only in the possibility of abusing the music. The first and third movements, with their baroque

lightness and gaiety, stand the addition of movement well; but there are some doubts in the case of the Adagio, since the music is so complete that even the addition of artistry and immaculate taste seems forced." [7]

PASTORELA

Ballet-Opera in one act

CHOREOGRAPHY: Lew Christensen and José Fernandez

MUSIC: Paul Bowles (1941), from traditional songs, orchestrated by Blas Galindo; words by Rafael Alvarez

SCENARIO: José Martinez

COSTUMES: Alvin Colt, from traditional sources

PREMIERE: 27 June 1941, Teatro Municipal, Rio de Janeiro, Brazil (open dress rehearsal 27 May 1941, Little Theatre of Hunter College, New York)

SINGERS: James Doyle, Preston Corsa

CAST: *Eremitano (Hermit),* John Kriza; *El Angel Miguel (St. Michael),* Charles Dickson; *El Angel Luzbel (Lucifer),* Lew Christensen; *El Indio (Indian),* Fred Danieli; *6 Pastores (Shepherds); 3 Diablos (Devils); Gila, the cook,* Gisella Caccialanza; *4 women*

REVIVAL: 15 January 1947, Hunter College Playhouse, New York (Ballet Society)

CAST: *Hermit,* Paul d'Amboise; *St. Michael,* Jacques d'Amboise; *Lucifer,* Lew Christensen; *Cook,* Beatrice Tompkins; *Boy,* Luis Lopez

Pastorela, commissioned by Nelson Rockefeller, was composed as a gesture for the Company's goodwill tour of South America. Based on an Indian Nativity play, as enacted in a remote Mexican village, it was probably just as quaint and folkloristic for the cosmopolitan audiences of Buenos Aires and Rio as it would be for New Yorkers. *Pastorela* was given some sixty times in Latin America (though never in Mexico), to favorable response: "In the dance ensembles, the primitive music, the Mestizo dance and music, a work of great beauty has been produced." [1]

It was later presented by Ballet Society, with twelve-year-old Jacques d'Amboise, a student at the School, making his debut as St. Michael.

The words and music were adapted from songs remembered by Martinez, whose father had participated in the pageants. Fernandez provided the authentic Mexican accents in the choreography (there is a cockfight between St. Michael and Lucifer, a hat dance at the end). In the story, shepherds are on their way to Bethlehem to see the Child. As they sleep one night, they dream that they are tempted by Lucifer and his devils, but St. Michael subdues the evil ones. The shepherds arrive at the manger and offer their gifts. St. Michael is seen dragging Lucifer and his henchman away in chains.

Says Christensen, "As a ballet, it was much too unpretentious to be more than pleasant. Basically, the shepherds move from one side of the stage to another, and there are little interludes along the way."

Back in New York, Chujoy wrote: "Simple, naïve, captivating folk pageant.

More in the nature of pantomime than anything else. Enjoyable, relaxing, it owes its charm to the utter simplicity of its elements." [2]

Terry dissented: "Not very exciting. Captures something of the simplicity but little of the earthiness and fervor present (or latent) in the Mexican material." [3]

Two excerpts from the songs (in translation):

The Hermit:
"From these wooded mountains
I see some shepherds coming
Going to see the newborn Babe
Who will redeem mankind."

The Shepherds:
"Let's go, Grandad, let's go
Let's go to Bethlehem
To see the Virgin Mary
And the Child as well
What is that light there
That shines so bright?
Is the manger on fire,
Or is the sun coming up?"

Pastorela. **Ballet Society.** 1947. (*Courtesy Lew and Gisella Christensen. Photo Richard Tucker.*)

DIVERTIMENTO

CHOREOGRAPHY: George Balanchine

MUSIC: Gioacchino Rossini (*Matinées Musicales*, *Soirées Musicales*, overture to *La Cenerentola*), selected and orchestrated by Benjamin Britten

COSTUMES, DÉCOR: André Derain (from *Dreams*)

PREMIERE: 27 June 1941, Teatro Municipal, Rio de Janeiro, Brazil

CAST: *March: King*, Todd Bolender, *6 Attendants*; *Canzonetta: Flower Lady*, Marjorie Moore; *Tyrolean Dance*, Marie-Jeanne; *Polka: Couple in Black and White*, Gisella Caccialanza, John Kriza; *Bolero: Lady in White*, Olga Suarez; *Tarantella: Ladies in Red*, 9 women; *Nocturne*, Marie-Jeanne, Fred Danieli; *Finale*, ensemble

Divertimento was done specifically as a closing ballet for South America and has never been performed anywhere else. It was a series of short dances (which Danieli remembers as the most popular items on that tour) and included a show-stopping number for Marie-Jeanne. Says she, "Balanchine used to have to whip up ballets at the drop of a hat—I mean literally in one day. The Tyrolean Dance was one of the most brilliant things I have ever done—all on toe, very sharp, very exciting. I used to have to do encores; that was something new—and sometimes almost impossible. But it was very thrilling—a marvelous variation." Says Magallanes, "The ballet was like a big costume party, and at the very end a rat arrives—an uninvited guest. They chase him into one wing and out another, trying to find out who he is. Finally they get the costume off, and underneath, he is an acrobat. Balanchine, who was full of tricks in those days, said, 'Let's fool them, because they don't know who is under the rat costume.' So the kids poked him and kicked him, and then he took his mask off."

Critics found *Divertimento* pleasant: "The dances are effective for their polychromy as well as for their folkloristic expression. The choreographer has become light and euphoric." [1]

"A collection of gay and gracious dances, some imitating folk dance, some sentimental." [2]

Divertimento. **Nocturne. Marie-Jeanne, Fred Danieli.** (*Courtesy Marie-Jeanne. Photo Schulmann.*)

JUKE BOX

CHOREOGRAPHY: William Dollar

MUSIC: Alec Wilder (1941; using songs as below)

SCENARIO: Lincoln Kirstein

COSTUMES, DÉCOR: Tom Lee

PREMIERE: 4 July 1941, Teatro Municipal, Rio de Janeiro, Brazil (open dress rehearsal 27 May 1941, Little Theatre of Hunter College, New York)

CAST: *Man with Nickels*, William Dollar; *Bartender*, John Taras; *College Widow*, Yvonne Patterson; *Nice Girl*, Marjorie Moore; *Football Hero*, Lew Christensen; *2 Teammates*; *Drum Majorette*, Lorna London; *Boys and Girls*

TIME: Present. After a football game. About 6:00 P.M.

PLACE: A midwestern college town. Late fall. The Log Cabin Bar & Grill

Juke Box was, of course, created to bring a little of our vernacular culture to the Southern Hemisphere. "However," says Dollar, "we didn't choose just any popular music—Wilder was a long-hair, the kind of Bach of the 'hot swing' style. The ballet was full of corny touches—the college widow, the football hero, a rockette sequence. There weren't any ballet steps in it; the kids could more or less do what they wanted. Nobody wore pointe shoes."

Wilder based the score on some of his own songs. A music and action synopsis follows:

1. Opening. Bar & Grill
   "Kindergarten"; "Flower Pageant"
2. College Widow and 6 Men
   "Her Old Man Was Suspicious"
3. Entrance of Boys and Girls from Washrooms
   "Sea Fugue Mama"
4. Cheerleader. Athlete and 6 Girls. College Widow fails to make the Athlete.
   "His First Long Pants"
5. Man and College Widow
   "Debutante's Diary"
6. General Dance. Initiation: Jitterbug Speciality.
   "The Children Meet the Train"
7. Pas de Deux Blues: Grand Adagio
   "Please Do Not Disturb"

8. Miracle of the Juke Box: Coda
    "Neurotic Gold Fish"

Juke Box was a good-humored addition to the repertory. The reviewer of *La Critica* wrote: "Wilder is a master of instrumentation and counterpoint, apart from his feeling for the modern North American dance. Jazz music, treated in contrapuntal manner and developed with irresistible power, gives the dancers an opportunity to prove their splendid control and good taste. They show how even the frivolous can be raised to an unexpected level." [1]

The ballet was premiered on an "all-American" program on the Fourth of July, which also included *Charade* and *Billy the Kid.* It was never performed in the United States.

FANTASIA BRASILEIRA

CHOREOGRAPHY: George Balanchine

MUSIC: Francisco Mignone (piano concerto)

COSTUMES, DÉCOR: Erico Bianco

PREMIERE: 27 August 1941, Teatro Municipal, Santiago de Chile

PIANO: Simon Sadoff

CAST: Olga Suarez, Fred Danieli, Nicholas Magallanes, ensemble

This work was choreographed by Balanchine during the South American tour and was seen only there. His collaborators were Brazilian. Balanchine says that he did it "as a gesture." Danieli remembers it as an ensemble ballet with a hint of a story: a girl finds herself in a jungle, with natives. The music utilized Brazilian dance forms, including the samba—one reviewer mentioned the "carioca ambience" and the "undulating grace" of the rhythms from the tropics.

The ballet was well received: "Based on folkloric motifs of Brazil, excellently conceived to the inspired and fertile music of Mignone. Interprets in felicitous fashion moments of great beauty based on the customs of the country. It received a careful interpretation, full of beauty and emotion." [1]

BALLET SOCIETY 1946–1948

THE SPELLBOUND CHILD
in 1975 called
L'ENFANT ET LES SORTILÈGES

Lyric Fantasy in two parts

CHOREOGRAPHY: George Balanchine

MUSIC: Maurice Ravel (*L'Enfant et les Sortilèges,* 1925)

POEM: Colette (translated by Lincoln Kirstein and Jane Barzin)

COSTUMES, DÉCOR: Aline Bernstein

PREMIERE: 20 November 1946, Central High School of Needle Trades, New York

CAST: (Each role performed by dancer on-stage and singer offstage. Casting given below only for important dance roles.) *Child* (sung and danced), Joseph Connolly; *His Mother; Armchair; Bergère; Clock; Tea Pot; Chinese Cup; Fire,* Elise Reiman; *2 Shepherdesses; 2 Shepherds; Princess,* Tanaquil LeClercq; *Teacher Arithmetic; 10 Numbers; Black Cat,* William Dollar; *White Cat,* Georgia Hiden; *Big Frog; 4 Little Frogs; Tree* (sung only); *7 Dragonflies; Nightingale; Bat; Squirrel; Little Squirrel; Owl.*

REVIVAL: 15 May 1975 (Ravel Festival), New York State Theater, as *L'Enfant et les Sortilèges*

COSTUMES, DÉCOR: Kermit Love (supervising designer: David Mitchell)

LIGHTING: Ronald Bates

CAST: *Child* (sung and danced), Paul Offenkranz; *Fire,* Marnee Morris; *Princess,* Christine Redpath; *Black Cat,* Jean-Pierre Frohlich; *Gray Cat,* Tracy Bennett; *Dragonfly,* Colleen Neary; other characters as above.

This work must have a particular appeal for Balanchine. He choreographed its first stage presentation for the Monte Carlo Opera in 1925, where he met Ravel: "Yes, he was there. At that time it was nothing amazing. He played. I did not understand French, but I understood the music. I staged the performance in French with the Diaghilev dancers. Then I came here, and I said, 'Lincoln, why don't we stage *L'Enfant et les Sortilèges?*' He translated it—and we did."

This was for the first Ballet Society program. To initiate the Ravel Festival, marking the hundredth anniversary of the composer's birth in 1975, he staged it for a third time.

In Colette's libretto, the naughty little boy, rebelling against his environment, is made to seem even smaller and more menaced by his surroundings because of the huge size of the furniture. He embarks on a course of destructiveness, but is eventually redeemed through his sympathy for a wounded squirrel.

Musically, this "magic opera" is a delicate, multicolored, exquisitely polished, but rather arty work. (Ravel's contention that it was composed "in the spirit of American musical comedy" is far off the mark.) There are definite problems in staging it. The leading singer is a little boy, which means that vocally, and in movement, the role will never be outstandingly performed. (In recordings a mezzo sometimes sings it.) In French or English, the words are difficult to understand. And it is basically a story that few find touching. Perhaps, as Ned Rorem has suggested, it is unstageable. Ravel's brother thought it could be realized visually only as an animated cartoon. In any case, the opportunities for dancing are extremely limited. It is in individual effects—musical and, potentially, visual—that it can be enchanting. Highlights of the 1975 production were the giraffelike Mother (whose face is never seen), the Fire variation, paper peeling

The Spellbound Child. **Ballet Society. 1946.**
Tanaquil LeClercq as the Princess.

off the walls, the moving armchair, and
the mysterious garden scene, filled with
the wings and tendrils of moths and
dragonflies. Says LeClercq of the earlier
version, "The stage was much smaller, of
course, and the costumes weren't so
fancy. This made it more childlike, I
think."

Critics then and now mostly found it to
be not worth the effort.

1947. Martin: "Dull and dated in
itself and inept in its staging." [1]

Berger: "The score has an element of
mischievousness in the notes of the blues
and in the ragtime of American operetta
of the 20s. The slide-whistle, cheese-
grater, and whip add fun and titillating
sounds to the orchestration. The singers
chant intriguing imitations of cats meow-
ing and frogs croaking. The present plan
is admirable and, with more lavish stage
machinery, the work might fruitfully be
mounted for more general public con-
sumption." [2]

"A waste of everyone's time and talent." [3]

"Certainly not in keeping with the organizations's basic purpose." [4]

1975. Herridge: "Remains stubbornly
a showpiece for the costumes, sets, and
singers. There is a grumpy over-stuffed
armchair that lumbers around his room, a
methodical grandfather clock, a dainty
Chinese cup, a shimmering fire, a stern
math man, flirtatious cats, and imperti-
nent frogs. They are given amusingly appropriate movement by Balanchine. For a
while, the novelty has a whimsical charm,

but it finally palls as the opera continues
for 40 minutes." [5]

Barnes: "Rather less than spellbinding.
The child looks awkward and graceless
surrounded by dancers, yet musically
the performance was sufficiently distinguished, and the costumes, scenery, and
lighting have the right mixture of grotesque fantastication and toyshop prettiness. The choreography had spurts of
brilliant invention (watch, for example,
for the frogs or a pas de deux for cats that
out-felines Petipa), but these are dragged
back by the limitations of the stage
form." [6]

THE FOUR TEMPERAMENTS

CHOREOGRAPHY: George Balanchine

MUSIC: Paul Hindemith (*Theme with Four
Variations* [*According to the Four Temperaments*], for string orchestra and
piano, 1940; commissioned by George
Balanchine)

COSTUMES, DÉCOR: Kurt Seligmann (as of
November 1951, performed in practice
clothes and without décor)

PREMIERE: 20 November 1946, Central
High School of Needle Trades, New York

PIANO: Nicholas Kopeikine

CAST: A. THEME, 1. Beatrice Tompkins and
José Martinez; 2. Elise Reiman and Lew
Christensen; 3. Gisella Caccialanza and
Francisco Moncion; B. FIRST VARIATION:
Melancholic, William Dollar; Georgia
Hiden, Rita Karlin, 4 women; C. SECOND
VARIATION: *Sanguinic*, Mary Ellen Moylan,
Fred Danieli, 4 women; D. THIRD VARIA-
TION: *Phlegmatic*, Todd Bolender, 4
WOMEN; E. FOURTH VARIATION: *Choleric*,
Tanaquil LeClercq, 3 "Theme" couples,
Moylan, Danieli; Dollar, Bolender, ensem-
ble

OTHER CASTS: *Melancholic*, Herbert Bliss,
John Clifford, Moncion, Richard Rapp;
Sanguinic, Merrill Ashley, Suzanne Farrell,
Gloria Govrin, Marie-Jeanne, Melissa Hay-
den, Marnee Morris, Colleen Neary, Maria
Tallchief, Patricia Wilde; Jacques d'Am-
boise, Anthony Blum, Nicholas Magal-
lanes, Frank Ohman, Jonathan Watts;
Phlegmatic, Arthur Mitchell, Moncion,
Rapp; *Choleric*, Diana Adams, Joan
Djorup, Renee Estópinal, Govrin, Allegra
Kent, Patricia Neary

Balanchine says that around 1940,
when he had a little extra money from his
Broadway shows, he asked Hindemith to
write a piece for one of his musicales.
"Every month or two weeks I had musicians—I remember Milstein—I did unknown music. They would come and play.
I had lots of food and I invited friends. I
did this by myself, alone. I had a nice
apartment, two pianos, and friends.

"I asked Hindemith if he could do
something with piano and a few strings,
something I could play at home. He did
the piece, but instead of writing in Italian
or German—allegro, presto, schnell—he
wrote a temperament for each variation.
It's just a direction. Everybody thinks
that 'Sanguinic' means you cut yourself,
or somewhere else you cry. No."

Thus, "pensive," "confident," "impas-
sive," and "angry" are the moods reflected in the *Four Temperaments* score.

Musically speaking, what Hindemith
wrote was a three-part theme with four
variations. In the variations, he frequently respected the melodic sequence
of the theme, but transformed it completely through new rhythmic values,
so that it was unrecognizable. (He also
used free melodic derivations and traditional variation devices.) The complex
rhythms were to give the dancers a great
deal of difficulty. Says Mitchell, "There
was one little section of seven or eight
counts. Balanchine told me he'd spent
years trying to get people to do it correctly. Believe me, I worked on that spot.
I'd go back after performance, discreetly,
and he'd say, 'Nope.' Or occasionally he'd
say, 'Not Bad.' It was the rhythm, not the
steps. Several things were going on at
once. The actual steps were just kind of
like a tricky tap dance. Throughout Phlegmatic, you had to keep the rhythmic thing
going with your feet, while the body is
supposed to be loose, boneless. Sometimes when you start accenting, the body
becomes jerky. To get the accents with
the feet and retain fluidity in the body—
that was the challenge."

It was planned to mount a work called
The Cave of Sleep to this music for the
Company's South American tour in 1941.
Tchelitchew designed fantastic costumes,
with which he intended to completely
overshadow music and dancing. Not un-
surprisingly, his drawings were rejected,
and the work was shelved. Little did anyone know that the designer eventually
chosen, a man interested in black magic

and probably having a special affinity for the *real* four temperaments or "cardinal fluids" of ancient and medieval physiology—Blood, Phlegm, Black Bile ("melancholy") and Yellow Bile ("choler")—would do yeoman's duty in camouflaging dance.

In 1946 Balanchine choreographed a work to the score for the opening program of Ballet Society.

In terms of pure movement, *Four Temperaments* is unique. It would be easy to think of successors—*Agon, Episodes, Violin Concerto, Symphony in Three Movements*—but almost impossible to name any forerunners. *Apollo,* perhaps, distantly. But for the most part, *Four Temperaments* as a movement vocabulary sprang full-grown, from nowhere one could name. The "inverted" (or "distorted") look of it is distinctly modern; yet its movement is more firmly and obviously grounded in the classical technique than Balanchine's other "avant-garde" works. It is full of long phrases of classical steps, where later works use them in isolation.

As Denby put it (1947), "Novel aspects of classic ballet technique—aspects apparently contrary to those one is accustomed to—are emphasized without ever breaking the classic look of the dance continuity." [1]

A number of years later, Miller wrote: "Balanchine speaks perfect ballet. But he is like the foreigner who, though at home in a host tongue, knows the color value of mispronouncing and misaccenting, of running two languages together. He is also a great one for locomotion. Steps that in ordinary ballet are but preparation for a spectacular leap or turn are, for him, of great intrinsic interest, dividing, varying, speeding, and building a sentence. They are like notes to the composer. . . . The technical problems are many. Balanchine grafts certain traditional movements onto one another. He is also one to borrow from other dance movements, even non-dance sources. He makes a kind of dance bestiary and like the great draughtsman he is, he doesn't show the sutures. Every flow of movement is continual, audacious, right, inevitable." [2]

Says Caccialanza, "After two or three days of rehearsals, Balanchine said to us, 'What do you think you are?' None of us knew. We said, 'Worms? Insects?' 'No,' he said, 'you're not insects'; then grandly, 'you're temperaments.' We asked what he meant, and he said, 'I'll explain it to you.' But he didn't, really. We just moved."

Four Temperaments, it was generally agreed, got Ballet Society off to a most auspicious beginning. Denby's awed reaction: "Unpredictable and fantastic the sequences are in the way they crowd close the most extreme contrasts of motion possible—low lunges, sharp stabbing steps, arms flung wide, startling lifts at half height, turns in plié, dragged steps, révérences, and strange renversés; then an abrupt dazzle of stabbing leaps or a sudden light and easy syncopated stepping. Neither sequences nor figures look familiar. But it is the pressure and shift of the musical as well as of the dance images that is the heart of the piece: no choreography was ever more serious, more vigorous, more wide in scope or penetrating in imagination. And none could be more consistently elegant in its bearing." [3]

Chujoy: "As in all Balanchine ballets, it is the dancing that matters, and [this] contains some of the most complicated and yet most satisfying dancing ever invented by this brilliant choreographer." [4]

Hering: "The three theme statements and their subsequent variations contain sequences of pure movement that leave one gasping at their inventiveness. They have an almost ruthless quality as though the bodies used in their fabrication should be discarded for new ones after each performance." [5]

Yet the work was criticized on the grounds that the steps had nothing to do with any "four temperaments" and that the costumes—"theatrical to the hilt"—made for confusion. As the years went by and the ballet continued to be performed, critics stopped complaining about the first problem as irrelevant; and by 1951, the costumes, long since simplified, were discarded altogether, an action that won almost unqualified praise.

The notorious costumes and décor, of astounding virtuosity in themselves, obscured the dance design, and were, in addition, not constructed with the dancing body in mind. There are doleful tales of various obstructions—mittens (which made partnering difficult), breastplates that knocked together, long skirts covering legs, cumbersome headdresses, including some bonnets that looked like sunbursts, and a horn—all this and more, plus décor, were crowded onto the small high-school stage. The Sanguinic ballerina seemed to be wrapped in bandages, the Phlegmatic costume was considered to represent a mushroom, or possibly Don Quixote. Says Danieli, "The

costumes arrived, as usual, about 30 minutes before the curtain went up. Balanchine took a pair of scissors and went around snipping everywhere." The easel painter as full collaborator had become the painter as tyrant.

Since its reappearance in 1951, without costumes, the ballet has rarely been out of the repertory for long, although it is sometimes rested for several seasons at a stretch. The choreography has remained essentially the same since the beginning (Balanchine made a few changes in the Choleric section in 1975).

The curtain rises in silence. Three pas de deux follow, each a part of the Theme. "In these seemingly modest dances—all too often overlooked because of the four major variations—one may discover a remarkable syllabus of dance movement. This syllabus invites attention to the simple flexion and the pointing of the foot (a ballet basic) and goes on from there to establish the essential kneebends, leg extensions, turns, jumps, ports-de-bras, darts, lifts, allegros, adagios, and finally, distortions and extensions—including hints of angular archaisms—into new areas of action." [6]

That is just the beginning. The ballet contains two most unusual parts for men—the Melancholic, with its movement definite yet soft (originally with touches of the acrobatic), supported by several lanky, high-kicking women; and the quizzical Phlegmatic, in which the man suddenly finds himself bending over and wrapping his hand around one ankle or staring at the hands attached to his outstretched arms as if he had never before noticed they were there. Between them is a virtuoso pas de deux—Sanguinic—in which the ballerina performs all manner of small, light jumps and beats, and is partnered in movements of some brutality. For the final variation (Choleric), an Amazonian woman flies through the air, crashes to the ground, violently exits, is later literally thrown around by male partners, while surrounding her, four couples perform pas de deux that seem to defy gravity: the women are held upside down by their partners or in splits that almost touch the floor, but remain just off it with an obvious sense of strain. They are also manipulated in arabesques or other off-balance poses with such ferocity that one fears their supporting legs will simply be ripped from their sockets. All of the partnering work, beginning with that of the three Theme couples, can be seen as highly erotic encounters. In the final moments, the entire company is on stage, and the tension is much lessened as they perform in unison (or in groups) large consonant movements, and the music, rather sweetly and unadventurously, gathers itself together in a kind of final golden glow. (Balanchine, apparently least satisfied with this part, made several versions of the ending before the premiere.)

Terry analyzed the work's dynamics: "The total effect is quite modern-dance in quality, for fluid torsos, archaic arm patterns and breath rhythms (as opposed to purely musical rhythms) are apparent, yet a closer search will show that the fundamental structure is balletic. . . . Rhythmically, he uses his dancers on the beat, against the beat, on the phrase, in syncopation or poised on a flow of sound. It follows also that accents vary, not only as to placement but as to degree of sharpness. Dynamic contrasts are made through movements which range from the most gentle and lyrical to the harsh and vibrant. Gravity is dealt with excitingly as one dancer defies its commands through aerial action while another plays with it in precarious balance and still another succumbs to its pull and sinks floorwards. Directional possibilities are explored through stage paths which are straight, curved, spiraled, oblique, weaving; and these directional designs may be augmented by movements up and down as well as by those which are horizontal. The volume of space is defined, invaded, redistributed by patterns which call for single figures, duos, ensembles, or combinations thereof. It is the very stuff, undiluted and unobscured, of dance. . . . Technical and stylistic perfection is not the goal, but frighteningly enough, the starting point. The ballet is, I think, the most imaginatively wrought of all contemporary, nondramatic ballets. Balanchine's relating of music and action is almost twinlike in its maintaining of separate yet mystically bound artistic identities, and his extensions of movements belonging to the ballet d'école into free gesture and exploratory action are as exciting as anything to be found in the theater." [7]

Some years later, Barnes also mentioned modern dance. He too caught the ballet's irregular rhythmic surface: "The ballet is of historic as well as historical importance, for it marked Balanchine's new style of 'character classicism' [defined elsewhere by Barnes as the use of gesture for its emotive and aesthetic effect

rather than its narrative meaning], which was to play a vital part in the development of American ballet. Now [1965] it is obvious that Balanchine has been influenced, and beneficially influenced, by American modern dance. But looking at the convoluted beauty, the gently askance classicism of *Four Temperaments*, with all its wit, gravity, and secretive passion, one must wonder whether this influence—or rather mutual reaction—has not been felt longer than most people imagine. For, oddly enough, it is a work that could only have been choreographed by an American. Its force and beauty depend to a great extent upon the juxtaposition of symmetry with quirkiness. A serene, unhurried panoply of movement is suddenly penetrated by a sharp, jagged gesture; or one line of movement will be slowly unfolding with endearing eccentricity, while at the back of the stage the dancers will be going about their classic business with the conventional predictability of bank clerks." [8]

Referring to the brilliantly polished 1975 presentation, Croce * described the ballet with penetrating vision: "When in the opening statement we see a girl, supported on her pointes, turning from side to side and transferring her weight from one foot to the other as she turns, we see her do it with finicky grace: she lifts and lowers the free foot, curls it around the standing leg, and carefully flexes it before arching to full pointe. We see, in short, a foot becoming a pointe—nature being touched to artificial life. The Theme is full of elementary particles, jostling, caroming, crisscrossing space in strokes that define the boundaries of the territory Balanchine will invade. In the [second pas de deux] the side-to-side turns have become full revolutions, rapid finger-turns marked off by the girl's pointe as it taps the floor. In the third, the finger-turns are taken in deep plié with one foot held off the ground in passé position. The weight on that one supporting pointe looks crushing, but there is something about a woman's pointe that makes it not a foot—that makes it a sign. The image created by the third girl as she is spun is blithe, even comical; could Balanchine have been thinking of the bass fiddle the forties jazz player spins after a chorus of hot licks?

_____
* Considered by many the most perceptive dance critic now writing, a worthy heir to Denby.

"In Melancholic, we have an expansive field of vision, but the solo dancer does not seem to know how much room he has. His space is penetrated by menacing diagonals for the entries of the corps. The corps is a small menace, but they are enough to block and frustrate his every attempt to leap free. He leaps and crumples to earth. We recognize this man: his personal weather is always ceiling zero. In Sanguinic, for a virtuoso ballerina and her partner, the vista is wide, the ozone pure and stinging. The ballerina is an allegro technician; she is also a character. She enters and pauses. Her partner is expectant. But she pauses and turns her gaze back toward the wings. For a moment she seems to wear a demure black velvet neck ribbon, and then she is bounding like a hare in the chase, an extrovert after all. Sanguinic takes us to the top of the world, and twice we ride around its crest, its polar summit (a circuit of lifts at half height). In these two thrilling flights, the camera eye pivots on the pinpoint of a spiral, once to end the trajectory, once to start it. We see, as in some optical effect of old cinema, a scene spread from the center of its compass, then re-spread in reverse.

"The topography of the ballet shrinks in Phlegmatic to the smallest it has been since the Theme. Phlegmatic is indolent, tropical, given to detached contemplation, to pretentious vices. The male soloist languishes, and loves it. Slowly he picks up invisible burdens, lifts them, and clothes himself in their splendor. Slowly, self-crowned, he picks up his right foot and studies it. His little dance with the corps includes cabalistic gestures toward 'his' floor, and he hovers close to the ground, repeating his mumbo-jumbo (a syncopated time-step) as if he expected the ground to answer him. The confined, floor-conscious world of Phlegmatic and Melancholic returns redeemed in the next section, when Choleric, that angry goddess, executes her climactic ronds de jambe par terre. Here we have the traditional dénouement of an eighteenth-century ballet, in which Mt. Olympus hands down a judgment on the mess mortals have made. Choleric enters in a burst of fanfares and flourishes, kicking the air. Her fury must be appeased, assimilated by the ballet's bloodstream. The entire cast collaborates in the process. Key motifs are recapitulated in tempi that charge them with new vitality. We are racing toward the finality of a decision,

The Four Temperaments. Above left: **Ballet Society. 1946. Phlegmatic. Todd Bolender.** *(Photo Carl van Vechten.) Below left:* **Ballet Society. 1946. San-guinic. Fred Danieli, Mary Ellen Moylan.** *Above right:* **New York City Ballet. Mid-1960s. Choleric. Patricia Neary (center), with (clockwise from left) Marnee Morris, Mimi Paul, Carol Sumner (2nd, 3rd, 1st themes), Melissa Hayden (Sanguinic).** *(Photo Fred Fehl.) Center right:* **New York City Ballet. Late 1960s. Melancholic. Susan Hendl, Richard Rapp.** *(Photo Fred Fehl.) Below right:* **New York City Ballet. Early 1960s. Phlegmatic. Arthur Mitchell (center).** *(Photo Fred Fehl.)*

and then it comes. Those ronds de jambe are a space- and air-clearing gesture. Three circles traced on the ground: it is the most wonderful of the ballet's magic signs; the vastness of it incorporates all bodies into one body, all worlds into one planet. After a silence in which nobody moves, the great finale begins its inexorable massed attack. All the parts the ballet is made of are now seen at once in a spectacle of grand-scale assimilation. Apotheosis. We see a succession of sky-sweeping lifts; we see a runway lined by a chorus of grands battements turned to the four points of the compass. The lifts travel down the runway and out as the curtain falls." [9]

One critic who never warmed up to *Four Temperaments* was Martin. Initially, commenting that the costumes nearly "stifled" it, he found "nothing very advanced." [10] Once the costumes were removed, life improved a little, but he felt the music did not entirely fit the work. "It is rich and flavorful music and handsome choreography, but the two work more than a little at cross purposes. The ballet misses fire, in spite of its many brilliances of composition, chiefly because Balanchine's choreography echoes only the form of the music and misses its texture and perhaps even its content to a degree. The music is neo-Gothic, and though Balanchine has put the danse d'école through all sorts of imaginative deviations, they all fall quite within the classic frame." [11] He asserted that "strictly from the standpoint of movement, it is certainly one of Balanchine's most inventive works." [12]

Where did this movement come from? Says Tallchief, "He'd play the pieces copiously on the piano, one note after another. Then we'd go to the studio, and out of his lumbering piano would come this incredible new movement. One would think that the body had been placed in every possible position in relation to the time and the space, yet you get to the studio and he would have this music completely in his mind, and there would come another way of putting that body into use."

But although the movement was so different, his dancers did not find it difficult to assimilate. Says Danieli, "After ten years of working with Balanchine, I had gotten used to his requirements—quickness, precision, abrupt shifts in direction, cleanness in execution, brilliance, instant response, not being able to 'fake.' It's all

there, only differently combined. In what he wants from the trained body, he has been eminently consistent. Of course, the steps were difficult. But for ten years I'd been associated with that kind of thinking and feeling."

Critics in Europe were intrigued.

London:
"Yet another indication of Balanchine's masterly feeling for style. He has the formal certainty to draw previously divergent threads together, in the Choleric section. Idiomatically he extends the neo-classical procedures to suit Hindemith's music, which is at once classical in thought and romantic in ideals. One of the two or three most interesting ballets this company has shown us." [13]

Germany:
"Enthusiasts of dressage would probably be the most appreciative audience for these études. Never has music been more musically interpreted by dance movement, never have the classical formulas of movement been concentrated in a more precise and inspired way. The dancers, much to the surprise of the audience, performed quite unpretentiously, without series of pirouettes or acrobatic jumps; rather, they executed all with a cool verve that was most satisfactory. In these variations it became evident that men like Dalcroze had not worked in vain." [14]

France:
"Resembles no other ballet. He uses the purest classical language, which yet becomes an entirely new idiom, with enigmatic alliterations worthy of James Joyce and spatial volumes as fascinating as the prisms of Max Ernst. As he himself says, he 'sees music and hears dance.' " [15]

RENARD

Ballet-Burlesque for Singers and Dancers

CHOREOGRAPHY: George Balanchine

MUSIC, TEXT: Igor Stravinsky (1916–17)

ENGLISH VERSION: Harvey Officer

COSTUMES, DÉCOR: Esteban Francés

PREMIERE: 13 January 1947, Hunter College Playhouse, New York

SINGERS: William Hess, William Upshaw (tenors); William Gephart, Leon Lishner (baritones)

CAST: *The Fox,* Todd Bolender; *The Rooster,* Lew Christensen; *The Cat,* Fred Danieli; *The Ram,* John Taras

OTHER CASTS: *Rooster,* Francisco Moncion; *Cat,* Herbert Bliss

Renard, here in a new version, staged for the first time in America, was a work that lent prestige to its sponsors, but was a succès d'estime rather than a robust theatrical offering. Martin for one, wrote, "An important event. Here is a work extremely difficult to produce, destined always to be unpopular, and yet of greatest interest. Marks Stravinsky's transition from a merely progressive force in the lyric theater to a radical one. Its action is merely illustrative of the literary fable which is sung as its musical background,

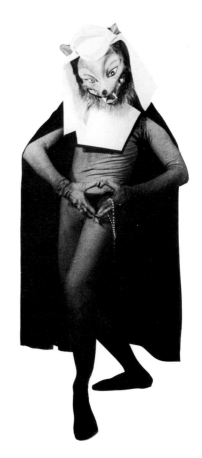

Renard. **Todd Bolender as the Fox (disguised as a nun).** (*Photo Carl van Vechten.*)

and offers even Balanchine little opportunity. It is easy to see why its first productions were [not] successful. But it is a kind of historical milestone in the modern ballet, and has been treated handsomely." [1]

For Kirstein, "on its small scale it was as perfect a production as could be imagined." Being more a mimed show than a dance vehicle, however, its life in a ballet company was necessarily short. (It was given five times.)

Others found it less Olympian. Wrote Chujoy, "gay and imaginative, it would make an excellent matinee piece for children." [2] (He was later to consider it "overwhimsical, overdressed, and overproduced, a long and rather pointless joke, and dated, to boot." [3])

Terry was simply uninterested in the concept: "The brilliant and often imaginative costumes in no way compensate for choreographic lack. Balanchine has given his roosters and foxes a few capers but very little dancing and that on a plane suitable to a minor Sunday school pageant." [4]

The story, from Russian legends, concerns the attempts of the Fox, at one point disguised as a nun, to lure the Cock from his perch. Although he succeeds twice, in the end he is tricked by the Ram and the Cat, who strangle him. Stravinsky introduced sounds to imitate an old Russian instrument, the *guzla* ("a kind of fine, metal-stringed balalaika").

Though technically negligible in dance terms, *Renard* was not without problems for the performers. Says Taras, "It was one of the most difficult things to learn, one of the first ballets where we did nothing but count. Having come from Ballet Theatre, where everything was melodic and fitted, it was quite a challenge. But there was great satisfaction in knowing you'd gotten to the end without having lost your way. The costumes were rather marvelous."

DIVERTIMENTO

CHOREOGRAPHY: George Balanchine

MUSIC: Alexei Haieff (1945)

LIGHTING: Jean Rosenthal

PREMIERE: 13 January 1947, Hunter College Playhouse, New York

Divertimento. **Maria Tallchief, Francisco Moncion.** (*The Dance Collection, New York Public Library. Photo George Platt Lynes.*)

CAST: Mary Ellen Moylan and Francisco Moncion (principals); Gisella Caccialanza, Tanaquil LeClercq, Elise Reiman, Beatrice Tompkins; Todd Bolender, Lew Christensen, Fred Danieli, John Taras

Ballerina role also danced by Maria Tallchief

Prelude
Aria
Scherzo
Lullaby
Finale

Haieff's *Divertimento* is a ballet much talked about but little seen, a perfect chamber work for a leading couple and four supporting couples, with all the parts taken by soloists. It is reputed to have been extremely beautiful, and there have been many suggestions that Balanchine revive it. He always refuses, claiming that he has forgotten every step, and that, anyway, even if he could remember them, he wouldn't remount it, because he has used all the movements one way or another in his subsequent ballets and people would

see that he has merely been cribbing from himself over the course of the past thirty years.

Divertimento was quite successful with the critics. For Terry, it was "an out-and-out joy. It is a delicious piece of classical dance with undercurrents of contemporary rhythmics, and it permits a lively group of Americans to pep up the danse d'école with their innate love of hoofing. . . . There are the familiar steps and attitudes of the traditional ballet, even something of its etiquette, but Balanchine has flavored them with the zest of today's popular dance and intensified them by adding torso movements usually associated with the technique of modern concert dance." [1]

Wrote Chujoy, "Staged with a fine sense of line and form. Its most notable achievement was the choreography for a group of men, who for once had something to dance. The pas de deux, although technically very difficult, succeeded in conveying the lyric quality of the dance. The ballerina's variation was not so successful. Choreographically set in a very slow tempo, it appeared intellectual rather than artistic, and lacked the inspiration which distinguishes a theatrical performance from a difficult classroom exercise." [2]

Martin found it "engaging, gay, vivacious, inventive," though derivative of some of Balanchine's other works,[3] and Hering wrote, "Reminds one of *Interplay*, but instead of being brash and extrovert, *Divertimento* is by turns lyrical and sweetly dignified even in its most exuberant moments. It is an idealized youth. Another of those perfect weddings of movement and music." [4]

The ballet was clearly very special for its dancers. "One of Balanchine's little gems," says Danieli, who is echoed by almost everyone who ever performed it. "A jewel," says Tallchief, "with one of the most beautiful adagios ever, to a lovely piece of music." LeClercq calls the adagio "dreamy—a blues pas de deux that is fabulous, absolutely divine, just heavenly. The ballerina had sort of a pussy-cat step which was very pretty. Sometimes turned in, kind of floozy, like two tango dancers. Just a dream. The variation [Lullaby] was not popular, but very difficult. Lots of balancing, piqué on a bent knee, fouetté on a bent knee, and everything right on top of the music. The rest of us had little solo moments, stepping out of the group. The tone of the ending was cute and perky." One step was described by Melissa Hayden as "sort of a swing kick, doing a rond de jambe in front of yourself . . . after a battement into fourth position, you slid the back leg over and you did a flip, a slide. The ballet was very short. It was like a breath."

London was much less enthusiastic: "The chief interest is the adagio, an extremely interesting composition in which the ballerina moves sur les pointes almost sur place, the dance being conveyed by subtle inflections of the movement made by one raised leg, by the execution of sweeping curves, and by constantly varying the torso line in relation to the pose of the head and limbs." [5]

"Balanchine construes Haieff's happily bad piece in terms of giggling if athletic teen-agers, who prance and cavort around the stage with energetic mien and little aim. Tallchief's superb physique and eloquent movements triumphed over dress; particularly expressive were the rapid curvilinear sweeps of her flexed legs as she hovers supported by her partner. For the rest, the choreography was a forceful reflection of vapidity." [6]

THE MINOTAUR

Dramatic Ballet in two parts

CHOREOGRAPHY: John Taras

MUSIC: Elliott Carter (1946–47; commissioned by Ballet Society)

SCENARIO: Lincoln Kirstein

COSTUMES, DÉCOR: Joan Junyer

PREMIERE: 26 March 1947, Central High School of Needle Trades, New York

CAST: *Pasiphaë, Queen of Crete*, Elise Reiman; *Handmaidens; Bulls; Minos, King of Crete*, Edward Bigelow; *Cretan Workers; Greek Boys and Girls; Theseus*, John Taras; *Ariadne*, Tanaquil LeClercq

Theseus also danced by Francisco Moncion

I. THE PALACE OF MINOS: *Pasiphaë, Handmaidens;* PASHIPHAË AND THE BULLS
II. COMPLETION OF THE LABYRINTH: *Minos; Cretan Workers;* THE SACRIFICE OF THE GREEKS: *Boys and Girls;* THESEUS AND ARIADNE; THE LABYRINTH (THE FIGHT WITH THE MINOTAUR): *Ariadne;* THE SURVIVAL OF THE GREEKS: *ensemble*

The Minotaur gave an opportunity to Taras, who had expected to be Balanchine's assistant on the piece but wound up taking it over. Needless to say, the score, scenario, and visual aspects had been shaped without him. It was generally considered that he was saddled with "turgid" music and rather overwhelming scenic effects, but, he says, "The costumes were very interesting—kind of Cretan, with the body cut in half, one side in shadow, one side in light, and I could use this choreographically. There was also a great white screen, suggesting the labyrinth, which helped me, as well as an episode where Tanny was being pulled by a real string around her waist (indicating the struggle between Theseus and the Minotaur in the labyrinth)—all these influenced my movement. I coped with the music as best I could at the time. The only real dancing was the pas de deux between Ariadne and Theseus."

The Minotaur was looked on by most critics as a training piece, an interesting experiment that could be retired quite quickly. (It was given only twice.) Martin: "Just the kind of thing Ballet Society should be sponsoring. The choreography works well with the scenery and especially the costumes to achieve an archaic remoteness. It is inclined to be thin, however, and remarkably static. Its best moments consist of some ingenious group formations, and, characteristically, its dramatic high point has nothing to do with dancing, but consists of some tugging at the offstage end of a rope." [1]

Terry: "One of the most beautiful productions I have seen, but the choreography was far less interesting than the set and costumes. Except for the bulls,

The Minotaur. Tanaquil LeClercq (center).

much of the design seemed to be 'planned pictures' rather than the result of dramatic compulsion or search for symbol." [2]

Chujoy: "The pas de deux was staged on a very shallow and narrow plane and consisted of a few repetitious steps and poses." [3]

It was at this performance that critics discovered LeClercq, who was labeled "the find of the evening."

The elaborate production was reviewed by art and music critics as well.

ZODIAC

Contemporary Ballet in one act

CHOREOGRAPHY: Todd Bolender

MUSIC: Rudi Revil (1946; commissioned by Ballet Society)

COSTUMES, DÉCOR: Esteban Francés

PREMIERE: 26 March 1947, Central High School of Needle Trades, New York

CAST: *Libra*, Virginia Barnes; *Gemini (Sun)*, *Twin*, William Dollar; *Gemini (Moon)*, *Twin*, Todd Bolender; *Capricorn*, Job Sanders; *Aquarius*, Pat McBride; *Aries*, Janice Roman; *Cancer*, Ruth Sobotka; *Leo*, Jean Reeves; *Pisces*, Irma Sandré; *Sagittarius*, Joan Djorup; *Scorpio*, Marc Beaudet; *Taurus*, John Scancarella; *Virgo*, Betty Nichols; *The Earth*, Gisella Caccialanza; *The Sun*, Edward Bigelow; *The Moon*, Gerard Leavitt

One believes there is a fundamental order in the universe, but, to presume: Libra, the Scales, is the balance of pure reason. What if violence were done to Libra?" (program).

Bolender personalized the hypothesis, relating it to postwar conditions, where the normal order has been lost, people have developed false values from their displacement, and the potential for losing balance is great. So despite the costumes, the set (showing spheres, lunar landscapes, and the head of Zeus), and an astrological diagram, with the circle of the Zodiac divided into twelve houses and twelve signs, designed by a noted astrologist for the ballet program, it did not deal with astral bodies.

The action was described by Hastings: "The Scales are kidnapped by Gemini

Zodiac. **Betty Nichols as Virgo.**

(danced acrobatically); all was 'thrown out of whack,' and anything became legitimate. This led the girls to become whores and the men bandits. The Twins were split, and no order was possible until they were reunited. The Gemini masqueraded as the Sun and the Moon, and assumed the prerogatives of dictators. Personality, rather than guns, was the instrument of force, and the Earth was at the mercy of Gemini. Decay and chaos set in as Earth and the false Moon dance together, but then the Earth took hold and with great effort returned all to normalcy." [1]

Everyone commented that the lighting was exceedingly dim. Wrote Chujoy, "To the naked eye none of the premise was visible. Moreover, few of the characters were recognizable. With the exception of some interesting choreographic moments for the Earth and Gemini, the dancers just posed and moved in and out, much too often in single file. A little more dancing and much less desire to 'épater le bourgeois' would have helped a great deal." [2]

Martin: "Total form vague and inconclusive." [3]

Terry: "Some fragments of exciting dance but lacks the linear discipline and tight pattern inherent in the zodiac diagram designed for the work." [4]

Says Bolender (1974), "I've mostly forgotten it now. It was like a step along the way—it takes so long to learn how to become a choreographer, just forever to know what you're about." *Zodiac* was given once.

HIGHLAND FLING

Romantic Ballet in three scenes

CHOREOGRAPHY: William Dollar

MUSIC: Stanley Bate (1947; commissioned by Ballet Society)

COSTUMES, DÉCOR: David Ffolkes

PREMIERE: 26 March 1947, Central High School of Needle Trades, New York

CAST: *Bride*, Gisella Caccialanza; *Groom*, Todd Bolender; *Sylphide*, Elise Reiman; *Bridesmaids*, Tanaquil LeClercq, Beatrice Tompkins; *Minister*, José Martinez; *Friends*, 8 couples; *Sylphides*, 10 women

VILLAGE GREEN: *Minister, Friends*
ENTRANCE OF BRIDE AND GROOM. CEREMONY OF THE MAGIC CIRCLE.
DANCE OF THE SYLPHIDES AND GROOM
PAS DE DEUX: *Sylphide and Groom*
WEDDING DANCES:
　Bride, Groom, ensemble
　Bride, ensemble
　LeClercq, ensemble
　Tompkins, ensemble
　Bride and Groom
　Ensemble

Highland Fling was premiered the same night as *Zodiac* and *Minotaur*—three new ballets by three young choreographers, all with specially commissioned scores and décors. Balanchine was not represented, and there was some grumbling about that. (He was in Paris staging *Le Palais de Cristal* [*Symphony in C*] for the Opéra.) The evening was generally praised for its spirit of experimentation, although none of the ballets was considered outstanding, and a meal of so many new elements was felt to be a bit rarefied. One reviewer suggested that an older work of Balanchine be revived from time to time on the programs. He also asked whether *everything* about each work had to be new. Weren't there some suitable scores for ballets already in existence?

Highland Fling was the most admired work of the three. Described as "a contemporary ballet based on Romantic themes," and a "combination of the Romantic style with theatricalized folk material" (in this case, Scottish), it did not have the same story as *La Sylphide*, but the

Highland Fling. Todd Bolender, Lew Christensen, Gisella Caccialanza (**center**), Elise Reiman (**right**).

same ingredients. In this case, the bridegroom does not follow the Sylph who attracts him, but under her spell he is lost in reverie for a while, then snaps back to reality, and the wedding goes on as planned.

The ballet was a moderate success and was given three showings on Ballet Society programs. The choreography won more praise than the music or sets. Terry: "Dollar handles his dual material easily and with no transitional jerks, moving his character of the Scottish bridegroom from a wedding ceremony to an enchanted realm of sylphs and back to the earthbound patterns of the folk dance. Happily, [he] omits the stereotyped pantomime of former days and replaces it with appropriate dramatic action; further, his folk patterns are theatrically more compelling than folk interludes probably were in the ballets of a century ago. The flavor and style of romantic ballet, however, are maintained.

"The choreography boasts many distinguished dance moments, among them the formal bridal processional; the floating quality of the Sylphide, achieved by keeping her in some form of the arabesque for much of her dancing; a beautiful wedding dance by the bride, performed with joyous feet, released body energy, and an air of delight. The final section of the ballet, composed of six wedding dances, is too long, for not only is it top-heavy in respect to the earlier portions of the ballet but its very length carries the beholder too far away from the memory of the initial ceremony and of the interlude with the Sylphide." [1]

Severin: "The Sylphide interlude was

fantastic for its treatment rather than its theme. Picture a glade of silver birches, sylphides dressed in white romantic tutus, and recall the airy, floating quality Fokine gave them. Then imagine them dancing in the bold, incisive style of Balanchine. Completely fascinating! The group dances and some of the six wedding dances, especially the third, on pointes, by LeClercq, were also amusing; Dollar succeeded completely in synthesizing Scottish folk dances with the *danse d'école.*" [2]

The consistently above-average notices given to Dollar's ballets through the years, and the remarks of dancers he worked with, indicate a talent for choreography, particularly classical choreography, that he did not fully develop.

THE SEASONS

CHOREOGRAPHY: Merce Cunningham

MUSIC: John Cage (1947; commissioned by Ballet Society)

COSTUMES, DÉCOR: Isamu Noguchi

PREMIERE: 18 May 1947, Ziegfeld Theatre, New York

CAST: *1. Prelude I:* Orchestra; *2. Winter:* Merce Cunningham; *3. Prelude II:* ensemble of 8; *4. Spring:* ensemble; *5. Prelude III:* Tanaquil LeClercq, Gisella Caccialanza, Beatrice Tompkins; Cunningham; *6. Summer:* ensemble; *7. Prelude IV: as III; 8. Fall:* ensemble; *9. Fi-*

nale (Prelude I): Caccialanza, Cunningham, ensemble of 8

Cunningham wrote for the program, "I have tried to use the materials of myth, the wending of a span of nature's time, in my own terms. And if time and the seasons are inseparable, it seems to me that time and dancing are hardly less so. The preludes that announce each season attempt to catch moments that might exist in a life, or in any fraction of human time."

The Seasons was a close collaboration among choreographer, composer, and designer. Cunningham had recently left Martha Graham and had been teaching modern dance at the School of American Ballet. In *The Seasons* he used neither Graham-type contractions and floor work nor the more avant-garde and personal movement he was to develop later. The dancers remember the movements as rather simple. Cage's score was his first for large orchestra. Both worked very hard to make something that would be congenial to ballet dancers. Says LeClercq, "They were extremely nice—and serious. So many choreographers are swamped by their music; not Cunningham. He really knew his business. He gave you the counts and they worked. It was a pleasure. We wore a kind of leotard. The stage was very spare in an Oriental manner. There was a back projection of snow in the winter section. For spring, the girls tied on little tails. This always got a terrific laugh, which made Merce angry."

The work was quite successful and was performed again during the New York City Ballet's initial season.

Martin found it "an extremely interesting work that improves markedly on acquaintance. It is simply the story of a cycle of the seasons, visualized in a naïve, elemental manner that suggests almost the furtive, playful, and unreasoning subjectiveness of some curious kind of small animals. The designs, with their succession of beautifully formalized symbols carried or worn by the dancers, and the final masks of autumnal sleep and wintry death, make of nature a huge and formidable force, and the reactions of the living creatures are keyed to it beautifully in the choreography. Cunningham appears to be not only the leader of the group but also a sort of demon of the year." [1]

Sabin called it "Experimental and challenging. Evokes a primitive world.

The movement is a blending of modern dance and ballet." [2] Terry mentioned the "resiliency of jumps, space-slicing cut of the long leaps, almost mercurial shifts in direction, wonderfully controlled dynamics, poise in pose. It is a loosely knit work which I do not yet find entirely satisfying as a theatrical entity." [3]

For Chujoy, however, the work was "more amusing than important or even interesting," and Haggin wrote that "nothing in it makes sense to me." [4]

BLACKFACE

CHOREOGRAPHY: Lew Christensen

MUSIC: Carter Harmon (1947; using themes of Stephen Foster: "There's a Good Time Coming," "Oh, Boys, Carry Me Home," "Nelly Bly," "Swanee River," "Camptown Races")

COSTUMES, DÉCOR: Robert Drew

PREMIERE: 18 May 1947, Ziegfeld Theater, New York

CAST: *Interlocutor,* Fred Danieli; *Mr. Tambo,* Paul Godkin; *Mr. Bones,* Marc Beaudet; *White Girl,* Beatrice Tompkins; *Colored Couple,* Betty Nichols, Talley Beatty; *3 White Couples; 3 Creole Couples*

1. Gentlemen, Be Seated
2. Introduction of Interlocutor and End Men
3. Soft Shoe
4. Cake Walk
5. Oleo
6. Finale

The American minstrel show was perhaps our first entirely national theatrical form. Initially it consisted of white men in blackface, imitating or parodying songs and dances of Negro slaves. The form of the original minstrel troupe entertainment, which achieved international popularity as early as the 1830s, was a kind of staged ritual, composed of apparently improvised numbers directed by an Interlocutor as Master of Ceremonies, who was fed jokes and pretexts for sketches by the two End Men, Mr. Bones and Mr. Tambo. The Colonial Slave Laws of 1740 had forbidden Negroes to use drums, since it was feared that their tribal instrument would incite to insurrection.

Hence, bones as clappers, castanets, blacksmith's rasps, handclapping, and heel beats were a substitute for percussive accompaniment. The soft-shoe number was a basis of twentieth-century tap-dancing" (program).

Blackface, despite a promising pretext, was not successful, and was given once. Says Christensen, "I had just gotten out of the Army, and I had all kinds of emotional things about the black man and helping him out. I tried to put this into a minstrel show. It would probably work better in the seventies, but at the time it fell flat."

Terry wrote that the ballet was "consistently dull. The minstrel-show theme should lend itself to balletic translation but Christensen garbled it along the line, omitting the bravado, the wit, and the gaudy glitter of the original form. He has kept something of the exuberance but this is not enough." [1]

PUNCH AND THE CHILD

Character Ballet in three scenes

CHOREOGRAPHY: Fred Danieli

MUSIC: Richard Arnell

SCENARIO: Fred Danieli and Richard Arnell

COSTUMES, DÉCOR: Horace Armistead

PREMIERE: 12 November 1947, City Center of Music and Drama

CAST: *Father* and *Punch,* Herbert Bliss; *Mother* and *Judy,* Beatrice Tompkins; *Child,* Judy Kursch; *Fishwife* and *Polly,* Gisella Caccialanza; *Peg Leg* and *Constable,* Charles Laskey; *Streetcleaner* and *Hangman,* Victor Duntiere; *Professor,* Luis Lopez; *Puppeteer* and *Devil,* Lew Christensen; *Musician* and *Doctor,* Edward Bigelow

Punch was another of the Ballet Society offerings that was, in Danieli's words, "an experiment in theater, not really in dance. We had new music, costumes; I did some research; we had an elaborate libretto." The work was compared to *The Nutcracker,* in that a child, in her imagination, is transported into another world—here, the world of Punch and

Punch and the Child. Herbert Bliss as Punch. *(The Dance Collection, New York Public Library. Photo George Platt Lynes.)*

Judy, with her mother, father, and others around assuming the puppet roles.

Arnell wrote that the ballet's scenario "Considerably expands the old legend. Using the 'stage within a stage' of Pirandello, the ballet is divided into three parts. The first, a scene of daily life at a seaside town, includes many familiar figures, begging musicians, holiday makers, lovers, policemen, and a great many children. In the background is the proscenium of a Punch and Judy theater, but when a storm arises, all the people are driven off the beach, and the show is canceled. On a darkened stage, a little girl returns and enters the curtains of the theater. With the sudden appearance of a life-size Punch, the second part of the ballet begins. The traditional episodes are enacted at a furious pace, culminating with Punch's defeat of the Devil himself. Then, in the epilogue, Punch runs into the puppet theater, closes the curtains in the girl's face, and disappears, leaving her outside. She tries in vain to find him. The sun shines, people return to the scene and the puppet man begins his Punch and Judy show. The child wanders disconsolately away."

The ballet was well received and was performed for a brief period by the New York City Ballet. (It was dropped when Danieli left the company, however.)

Wrote Hering: "The sets! the costumes! The people of the street and the child's parents are encased in exaggerated or inflated grotesqueries calculated probably to give them the appearance they would have in the eyes of a small but imaginative child. The interior of Punch's home is luxurious and forbidding, which is as it should be to surround the fascinating but ugly characters that people this puppet classic. The puppets wear make-up and costumes in the style of Cruikshank, and the effect is perfect." [1]

Herridge: "An unpretentious work about a child who discovers fantastic caricatures of the people in her everyday life. It is not merely a grown-up's fairy land for children. It is the real world seen through the eyes of a child, with a child's peculiar cruelty, his lack of moral judgment, his irrationality." [2]

Martin: "Choreographically it has all sorts of invention and imagination. Clearly a work of distinction that needs only time and repetition to acquire its proper theatrical dimensions." [3]

Terry: "Sustains a story-book atmosphere and boasts several engaging episodes." [4]

Says Danieli, "I'll never forget—Bea Tompkins got an ovation the first night. Her part was full of very fast footwork, in high laced boots. I think the work did sort of capture the essence of Punch. There were two sets of costumes—the father was about six feet wide, the mother very thin—shredded. The idea was to establish these characters with certain movements in the first part, movements which the Punch people also used. There was a marvelous set within a set with demons. The tie between the child's imagination and the real world is a doll she keeps, which Punch had given her."

VIOLA: Jack Braunstein

CAST: *Allegro Maestoso:* Tanaquil LeClerq, Maria Tallchief, 22 women; *Andante:* LeClerq, Tallchief, Todd Bolender, 6 women; *Presto:* LeClercq, Tallchief, Bolender, 22 women

OTHER CASTS: Diana Adams, Lois Ellyn, Melissa Hayden, Jocelyn Vollmar

Symphonie Concertante was a plotless ballet with a very close relationship to its music. In description, Denby wrote that it was "kept fresh by successive brief entrées." [1] Says LeClercq: "There were no individual variations. The adagio was really a supported pas de trois—one ballerina did a step with the man, then stood aside while he partnered the other. It was pretty music, nice steps, nothing bravura." The ensemble work was frequently described as "complex."

The effect of the ballet was debated. For Martin it was "Perhaps Balanchine's most boring work, at least up to the Presto. Contains many difficult and subtle adagios, but it is not very rewarding to watch. . . . Nearly smothers Mozart with a large and busy ensemble and many inventive but tedious passages for his two leading figures." [2]

Sabin was even less enthusiastic: "How an artist of such generally good taste could use one of Mozart's most eloquent scores as background music for an exhibitionistic exercise in the most brittle and empty academicism is inexplicable. Each entrance or ornament in the music is dutifully and quite literally echoed by a stylistically inappropriate movement on the stage, with complete disregard for the fact that the function of those elements in the score could not possibly be duplicated in such a fashion in the choreography." [3]

Terry, however, found it "marvelous, elegant in manner, as refreshing in its movement patterns as the music which is its base" [4]

Haggin: "In Balanchine's ballets, as in Mozart's concertos, the mind, the language, and the style, the formulas are always the same, but the completed forms are constantly new. Over and over again Balanchine has used the formula of the adagio supported by male dancer, and here, in the slow movement, was another adagio, different and again wonderful." [5] And Denby wrote of the "delicate, girlish, flower-freshness of the piece" [6]

Says Tallchief, "It was beautiful—just pure classical dancing and quite difficult. It was no great audience-pleaser, and I always wondered whether Balanchine had done it as a learning exercise because there were no furbelows or frills. It was like taking your medicine every day."

Balanchine has written, "The music is long and difficult; to the inexperienced

SYMPHONIE CONCERTANTE

Classic Ballet in one act

CHOREOGRAPHY: George Balanchine

MUSIC: Wolfgang Amadeus Mozart (Symphonie Concertante in E-flat, K. 364, 1779)

COSTUMES, DÉCOR: James Stewart Morcom

LIGHTING: Jean Rosenthal

PREMIERE: 12 November 1947, City Center of Music and Drama (first presented 5 November 1945 by students of the School of American Ballet, Carnegie Hall, New York)

VIOLIN: Hugo Fiorato

Symphonie Concertante. **New York City Ballet. Early 1950s. Tanaquil LeClercq, Diana Adams.**

listener it might be boring. The ballet, on the other hand, fills the time measured by the music with movement and seems to shorten its length. What seemed dull at first *hearing* is not so dull when the ballet is first *seen*." [7]

Opinions varied in London as well: "As an experiment in demonstrating how close the relationship between music and dancing can be, it is a triumph of choreography but the result is completely untheatrical." [8]

"Though over-energetic and lacking repose, it follows Mozart so intelligently that had other choreographers showed equal consideration for the music on which they based their talents we should have had none of the controversy about symphonic ballet." [9]

THE TRIUMPH OF BACCHUS AND ARIADNE

Ballet-Cantata (*in Italian*)

CHOREOGRAPHY: George Balanchine

MUSIC: Vittorio Rieti (1947; commissioned by Ballet Society)

COSTUMES, DÉCOR: Corrado Cagli

PREMIERE: 9 February 1948, City Center of Music and Drama

SINGERS: Eileen Faull, soprano; Leon Lishner, bass; chorus of 40

CAST: INTRODUCTION (*Prelude and chorus*): *Major Domo*, Lew Christensen; *Spectators*, 6 couples; BACCHUS AND ARIADNE (*Chorus*): *Bacchus*, Nicholas Magallanes; *Ariadne*, Tanaquil LeClercq; SATYRS AND NYMPHS (*Tarantella with chorus*): *Satyr*, Herbert Bliss; *Nymph*, Marie-Jeanne; *6 Satyrs, 6 Nymphs*; SILENUS (*Aria for solo bass*): *Silenus*, Charles Laskey; MIDAS (*Chorus*): *Midas*, Francisco Moncion; *2 Discoboles; Little Girl*, Claudia Hall; *Young Girl*, Pat McBride; INVITATION TO THE DANCE (*Aria for solo soprano*); BACCHANALE (*Chorus*): *ensemble*

This choral ballet employs words from a Florentine carnival-song written by Lorenzo de' Medici, called the Magnificent. It celebrates Youth and Age, sacred and profane love, in verses derived from classical Latin verse, which are divided into ballet entries" (program note).

Bacchus was a kind of moving pageant, a series of episodes elaborately dressed and produced. The singers were visible through the windows of the building that formed the backdrop. It was successful as a novelty and was presented again during the first season of the New York City Ballet, but probably the expense of production precluded a long life, and, in any case, the work was definitely of an "occasional" nature. (In the Renaissance, such spectacles were designed for a specific event and retired after a single presentation.)

Highlights were the pas de deux of Bacchus and Ariadne, described by Magallanes as a "very pretty, leaves-in-the-hair, nude-looking, drapery kind of thing"; a wild and vivid solo for Marie-Jeanne, which she remembers as one of the most effective of her entire career, very staccato, very fast, show-stopping; and the sequence where Midas and his favorite wife and child turn to gold (painted gold on one side, they performed in profile; when they turned, they were gold). At the end there was a great processional— the "triumph"—in which Bacchus and Ariadne were borne on the shoulders of the other dancers.

Says Magallanes, "It wasn't completely ballet, but rather the kind of collaborative theater presentation that Ballet Society attempted. Everybody had a hand in the rehearsals. The composer was there. The painter was there. Mr. Balanchine was there."

Wrote Krokover, "A brilliant conception, and certainly the novel form of the work and music entitles it to serious con-

The Triumph of Bacchus and Ariadne. Left: Nicholas Magallanes, Tanaquil LeClercq. (*Photo R. F. Ganley.*) *Above:* Francisco Moncion, Herbert Bliss, Marie-Jeanne (center).

THE TRIUMPH OF BACCHUS AND ARIADNE

sideration. In many ways the ballet is constructed like a seventeenth-century masque, with some dancing stage effects, dumb-shows, and an anti-masque complete in itself. Sheer dance seems to be secondary, and in such a number as 'Midas,' it dwindles to practically nothing. The anti-masque ('Silenus') is a bass solo during which a heavily made-up Silenus waddles grotesquely around the stage. The opening duet between Bacchus and Ariadne has a few moments of rather derivative footwork, and only in one instance did Balanchine appear to extend himself choreographically—'Satyrs and Nymphs.' The concluding Bacchanale was completely out of character with the rest of the work: the sudden flurry of before-the-footlights activity destroyed the previous mood." [1]

Terry: "Not an exciting work, either in the technical or the dramatic sense, but an absorbing one, for it is a choreographic parade and a colorful one." [2]

Martin: "It is very slow getting started, the soprano solo near the end stops the action in its tracks, and there are some fairly dull passages elsewhere. But the dance of the nymphs and satyrs is brilliant, and the Silenus episode is amusing." [3]

Chujoy: "The complexity of the ballet and the fact that each number was stylized rather than presented in an obvious manner made for difficult watching. To get full enjoyment, one must see it again and again." [4]

CAPRICORN CONCERTO

CHOREOGRAPHY: Todd Bolender

MUSIC: Samuel Barber (Capricorn concerto for flute, oboe, trumpet, and strings, 1944)

COSTUMES, DÉCOR: Esteban Francés

PREMIERE: 22 March 1948, City Center of Music and Drama

CAST: *Earth,* Maria Tallchief; *Sun,* Herbert Bliss; *Moon,* Francisco Moncion; *Stars,* 8 women, 4 men

For Bolender, this was a "second brush with outer space" (after *Zodiac*). The ballet was not successful, despite pleasing music and a virtuoso role for Tallchief. Wrote Martin: "In Bolender's choreographic zodiac, the earth is unashamedly egocentric, with the sun and the moon as her satellites and all the other stars staying pretty well put around the outside. This makes for monotony." [1]

Chujoy: "Some excellent dancing, but choreographically derivative. Although workmanlike and even streamlined, it suffers from being purely mental. The choreography is more mathematical than artistic; it has body but no soul." [2]

SYMPHONY IN C

CHOREOGRAPHY: George Balanchine

MUSIC: Georges Bizet (Symphony No. 1 in C major, 1855)

COSTUMES: Karinska (Fall 1950)

PREMIERE: 22 March 1948, City Center of Music and Drama (first presented as *Le Palais de Crystal* 28 July 1947 by the ballet of the Paris Opéra)

CAST: *1st Movement:* Maria Tallchief, Nicholas Magallanes; *2nd Movement:* Tanaquil LeClercq, Francisco Moncion; *3rd Movement:* Beatrice Tompkins, Herbert Bliss; *4th Movement:* Elise Reiman, Lew Christensen; in each movement, 2 demi-solo couples, 6–8 women (depending on size of the company); finale: entire cast

OTHER CASTS: *1st:* Diana Adams, Karin von Aroldingen, Melissa Hayden, Patricia McBride, Marnee Morris, Colleen Neary, Patricia Neary, Suki Schorer, Violette Verdy, Patricia Wilde; Jacques d'Amboise, Anthony Blum, Jean-Pierre Bonnefous, Richard Hoskinson, Robert Maiorano, Peter Martins, Ivan Nagy, André Prokovsky, Earle Sieveling, Jonathan Watts; *2nd:* Adams, Lois Ellyn, Suzanne Farrell, Hayden, Allegra Kent, Gelsey Kirkland, Kay Mazzo, Mimi Paul, Verdy, Heather Watts; Dick Beard, Adam Lüders, Conrad Ludlow, Martins, Nolan T'Sani; *3rd:* von Aroldingen, Merrill Ashley, Gloria Govrin, Hayden, Kent, Sara Leland,

Symphony in C. 1st movement. Diana Adams, Jacques d'Amboise (center). *(Photo Kiehl.)*

McBride, Marie-Jeanne, Christine Redpath, Janet Reed, Giselle Roberge, Schorer, Verdy, Lynda Yourth; Robert Barnett, Bonnefous, John Clifford, Deni Lamont, Paul Mejia, Jerome Robbins, Peter Schaufuss, Kent Stowell, Heigi Tomasson, Edward Villella, Robert Weiss. (4th, less consequential than the others, performed over the years by an even greater number of principals, soloists, and other dancers than the first three.)

Symphony in C was originally created for the Paris Opéra, and one can imagine that Balanchine, whose own dancers were performing four times yearly in high schools, truly enjoyed exploiting the resources of one of the grandest state-supported opera houses in Europe. In Paris ornate gold framed row upon row upon row of dancers, clothed to resemble "neon-lit particles" and backed by scenery described as a mixture of Louis XIV and World's Fair 1900. It contained a staircase, balconies, galleries, "lion-poodles, chubby-faced demons, and clusters of crystal."

It was fifteen years before Balanchine had sufficient amplitude—in stage space or in personnel—to achieve similar effects with his own company, although he presented a cut-down version of the ballet in New York immediately afterward. (He never was interested in finding equivalent costumes or sets.) Many feel that some of Balanchine's most important ballets, such

as Orpheus and Agon, lost impact when transferred to the New York State Theater, which had a much larger performing space, and, especially, a much larger proscenium than the Company had ever had before. Symphony in C, however, created so long ago, appeared in the new theater to the manner born.

New York audiences, now accustomed to the white tutus and black men's tights and leotards that have always dressed the ballet, might be surprised to learn that in the Paris original, each movement was a different color; in the finale, with fifty-two dancers, the stage was divided into color areas. In New York, Balanchine couldn't have duplicated this for many years because his dancers were so busy doubling from movement to movement. (Although fifty dancers, many of them students, were rounded up for the Ballet Society presentation, during the early years of the New York City Ballet it was often performed with forty or fewer.)

Despite the known bureaucracy of the Paris Opéra, the length of the work (about thirty minutes), and its extremely full quotient of dancing, the choreography was completed in two weeks. (Critics seeking to identify evolutions in Balanchine's work shouldn't bother in one area—his facility for putting steps together remains unchanged, at least since 1947.)

There is no way to describe Symphony in C and scarcely any way to evoke it; a fresh zestiness invests the music of the

first, third, and fourth movements; the second is a lightly mellow adagio, led by the oboe. Balanchine directly echoed the musical form in places, setting a little fugue in the adagio movement and a jaunty Scottish folk dance in the third. The first two movements are for ballerinas, the first authoritative, the second delicate and weightless. In the third movement, for jumpers, the man and woman have parts of equal importance, and the dancing radiates a youthful exuberance. The fourth-movement soloists appear briefly, and soon make way for a kind of recapitulation, in which, separately, the soloists from the first three movements, with their respective corps and demi-soloist entourages, have another showing. The corps forms a three-sided box as the stage is filled with dancers. For the last few minutes, up to the final pose, the entire cast performs the same complicated beaten jumping steps, moving in a bloc. The impact of so many, in unison, really *dancing* has a tremendous excitement that builds and builds. (Porter called the finale "surely the grandest thing danced since Petipa dreamed up the Kingdom of Shades scene of *La Bayadère*." [1])

Despite a certain pro-Lifar (and thus automatically anti-Balanchine) faction in the press, the Paris production was quite well received, heralded as "a well-constructed work at last!" Wrote Maurice Purchet: "Written entirely in the most orthodox classic vocabulary, it will introduce sev-

Symphony in C. Left: 2nd movement. Tanaquil LeClercq, Francisco Moncion (center). *Right:* 3rd movement. Suki Schorer, Paul Mejia (right). (*Photos Fred Fehl.*)

eral innovations to the language of the dance. Balanchine knows how to make a work both coherent and well structured—in a word, solid—under its appearance of lightness and ease. There is a variety in its figures—solos, duos, pas de quatres, the couples and ensembles alternate as easily as the straight lines, the curves, the circles. The continuity of the ballet is not broken from the first measure to the final galop by any pause, by any interlude." [2]

Most New York critics were highly enthusiastic. Chujoy: "If there ever was any doubt that Balanchine was the greatest choreographer of our time, this doubt was dispelled when the curtain came down on his *Symphony in C*. Here is a classic ballet that will go down in history as the finest example of this thrilling art form. Symphonic ballet at its greatest, it builds with ever-mounting force to a thrilling climax. The fifty dancers on the stage at the same time not only give exhilaration to the final movement of the ballet, but make all other ballets seem puny and pale. And all the strength of the ballet is achieved by dancing alone. The finale topped everything seen in ballet hereabouts for a long time." [3]

Terry: "A show-off piece, frankly and unashamedly, and since showing off is and always has been one of the basic reasons for dance action, the work is on perfectly solid ground. It presents the body singly and in proximity with other bodies in beautiful fashion, in designs which are decorative, in motions which are exciting,

in attitudes of linear loveliness. Sometimes it is mercurial, with racing steps and flashing leg-beats, and sometimes it is lyricism itself, with slow-motion beats and gently sustained adagio. Again it explores the air in leaps, in jumps, in spiralings, or tests the pull of gravity in posed arabesques, in partial falls arrested just before completion. The beauties, the glitters, and the show-off wonders of the work are easily discernible." [4]

Martin's was the only sour note, and very sour it was: "Balanchine has once again given us that ballet of his, this time for some inscrutable reason to the Bizet symphony. Up to the middle of the third movement [when the critics had to leave], he had used virtually all of his familiar tricks, some of them charming, some of them forced, and some of them slightly foolish. One thing he can almost be guaranteed to deliver, however, is showy and gratifying material for his ballerinas, and here he has certainly not failed." [5]

According to Robbins, a performance of this work in 1949, particularly LeClercq in the adagio, so moved him that he asked Balanchine if he could become affiliated with the Company in some capacity—dancer, choreographer, whatever was needed. It was in this part that Farrell, a very special star of the late sixties, returned to the Company after an absence of five years, on 16 January 1975. Others who have had particular success with the adagio are Kent and Paul. The second and

third movements have always been the audience favorites. *Symphony in C* is as popular—and admired—today as ever.

Critics in Europe were equally won over. In London, Barnes somewhat overstated his case; rare indeed would be the class he cites in his review of the work: "I have heard the opinion expressed that this ballet shows no more than would be shown in a classroom enchaînement by a teacher of genius, and it is true that Balanchine uses few movements that would not be performed in a typical class. However, a poet is not judged as great on the strength of a recherché vocabulary; he is judged not on the words he uses but by the way he uses them." [6]

"Here the patterns of the corps are half the battle. Of geometry Balanchine makes a paean. How breathtaking when the white-clad girls forming three sides of a square do simple battements tendus with port de bras!" [7]

Italy:
"A crystalline, transparent construction, it bursts out, by the movements of the corps, in such a way as to seem an uninterrupted succession of electrifying lines of invention and fantasy, warmed up by a pure lyricism that well adapts itself to the 'classical' and Mozartean music of Bizet with a fabulous richness of ideas and an inexhaustible variety of inventiveness." [8]

Symphony in C. **Finale.** (*Photo Fred Fehl.*)

Germany:

"Ballet in its purest, most fascinating form. There is no fussing about with meaning—there is quite simply dance. In this pure exercise, each step, the transition to the next one, each jump, and each gesture have the glitter of indescribable proficiency and become pure magic. *This is perfection.*" [9]

Russia:

"Sparkling. A veritable cascade of dancing in its brilliance, virtuosity, and total absence of trickery." [10]

ÉLÉGIE

CHOREOGRAPHY: George Balanchine

MUSIC: Igor Stravinsky (Elegy for solo viola, 1944)

PREMIERE: 28 April 1948, City Center of Music and Drama (first presented 5 November 1945, by students of the School of American Ballet, Carnegie Hall, New York)

VIOLA: Emanuel Vardi

CAST: Tanaquil LeClercq, Pat McBride

Balanchine has said that he "tried to reflect the flow and concentrated variety of the music through the interlaced bodies of two dancers rooted to a central spot of the stage." LeClercq found *Élégie* "very pretty. Two rather wild girls, just twining—bare feet, with hair flowing."

Chujoy wrote: "A minor work, more daring than artistic." [1]

Denby: "Two young girls with hands entwined, turning, rising, interlacing, spreading, crouching, and folding in a long, uninterrupted, beautiful adagio sequence." [2]

Dance Observer: "There is more to this duet than meets the eye, but even its surface convolutions are fascinating to watch." [3] Given three times.

ORPHEUS

Ballet in three scenes

CHOREOGRAPHY: George Balanchine

MUSIC: Igor Stravinsky (1947; commissioned by Ballet Society)

COSTUMES, DÉCOR: Isamu Noguchi

LIGHTING: Jean Rosenthal

PREMIERE: 28 April 1948, City Center of Music and Drama

CAST: *Orpheus*, Nicholas Magallanes; *Dark Angel*, Francisco Moncion; *Eurydice*, Maria Tallchief; *Leader of the Furies*, Beatrice Tompkins; *Leader of the Bacchantes*, Tanaquil LeClercq; *Apollo*, Herbert Bliss; *Pluto; Satyr; Nature Spirits; Friends to Orpheus; Furies*, 9 women; *Lost Souls*, 7 men; *Bacchantes*, 8 women

REVIVAL: 24 June 1972 (Stravinsky Festival), New York State Theater

CAST: *Orpheus*, Jean-Pierre Bonnefous; *Dark Angel*, Moncion; *Eurydice*, Melissa Hayden; *Leader of the Furies*, Deni Lamont; *Leader of the Bacchantes*, Gloria Govrin; *Apollo*, Michael Steele

OTHER CASTS: *Orpheus*, Edward Villella; *Dark Angel*, Herbert Bliss, Arthur Mitchell; *Eurydice*, Diana Adams, Pat McBride, Kay Mazzo, Violette Verdy; *Leader of Bacchantes*, Allegra Kent

Orpheus was the most important three-way collaboration to come out of Ballet Society and the only such ballet produced during its existence that has endured virtually unchanged to this day. The collaboration between composer and choreographer was described as closer than any other in the history of ballet (possibly matched later by another effort from the same team, *Agon*). Each scene was discussed and plotted as to its exact number of seconds before the music was composed. Stravinsky then came to most of the rehearsals and conducted the premiere. (Stravinsky writes that Orpheus, as a subject, was Balanchine's idea; Noguchi was Kirstein's, and effectively precluded any "Greek" look. Originally, it had been planned that Tchelitchew design the work.)

Stravinsky was, if anything, more precise than Balanchine. Says Tallchief, "I remember one rehearsal. I had a marvelous death scene. Any performer wants to drag out a death scene as long as possible. Stravinsky turned to George and said, 'How long is it going to take Maria to die? She must do it in five counts.' Well, I did. I had to! After that command was given,

the conductor never looked at my death scene. I got my five counts and he went right into Nicky's music."

The ballet was designed for a stage long and narrow, like a shelf; hence what some have called its frieze-like effect. (Except for the Furies, the Bacchantes, and the pas de deux between Orpheus and Eurydice, Manchester wrote, "the rest develops two-dimensionally, to be observed as one might slowly cast one's eyes along an ancient frieze that tells a story, revealing itself one portion at a time." [1])

The ballet's intimacy may have derived from the stage specifications. In addition, the two leading men, both of stunning theatrical presence, were not strong classical dancers—thus another reason for intimacy: theirs was not a large-scale virtuosity. However, the presence of the pyrotechnical Tallchief did not inspire technically supercharged measures for Eurydice either. The most intense movement was that for the head Bacchante, and here timing—split-second nervous response to the music—was more responsible for her impact than technical difficulties.

Another shaping factor in the work's small scale was, of course, the preeminent one: Stravinsky's luminous score. Wrote Martin: "The music is remote, hieratic, tender with the memory of distant emotion, purified and distilled by time and perspective. It is also, in spite of the refinement of its texture, eminently of the theater—the truly lyric theater where action is translated into aesthetic significance." [2]

Stravinsky had been studying the music of Monteverdi, "so it is not surprising that his score had something of the same translucent emotion and noble proportions as Monteverdi's own *Orfeo*. Restraint is its distinguishing characteristic. With the exception of the Dance of the Bacchantes, all the music is pitched *mezza* or *sotto voce*. Orpheus's lyre is translated into sound in terms of the harp." [3]

A synopsis of the action, from Stravinsky's score (where the episodes are not numbered): [4]

SCENE ONE:
1. Orpheus weeps for Eurydice. He stands motionless, with his back to the audience. Some friends pass, bringing presents and offering him sympathy.
2. "Air de Danse."
3. "Dance of the Angel of Death." The Angel leads Orpheus to Hades.

Orpheus. Left: **Orpheus and Friends (Scene One). Jean-Pierre Bonnefous as Orpheus.** *Right:* **Pas de Deux. (Orpheus and Eurydice before the veiled curtain). Nicholas Magallanes, Maria Tallchief.** (Photos Fred Fehl).

4. *Interlude.* The Angel and Orpheus reappear in the gloom of Tartarus.
SCENE TWO:
5. "Pas des Furies" (their agitation and their threats).
6(a). "Air de Danse" (Orpheus).
7. *Interlude.* The tormented souls in Tartarus stretch out their fettered arms toward Orpheus, and implore him to continue his song of consolation.
6(b). "Air de Danse" (concluded). Orpheus continues his Air.
8. "Pas d'Action." Hades, moved by the song of Orpheus, grows calm. The Furies surround him, bind his eyes, and return Eurydice to him. (Veiled curtain.)
9. "Pas de Deux" (Orpheus and Eurydice before the veiled curtain). Orpheus tears the bandage from his eyes. Eurydice falls dead.
10. *Interlude* (Veiled curtain, behind which the décor of the first scene is placed).
11. "Pas d'Action." The Bacchantes attack Orpheus, seize him, and tear him to pieces.
SCENE THREE:
12. "Orpheus's Apotheosis." Apollo appears. He wrests the lyre from Orpheus and raises his song heavenwards.

The ballet's emotional center is the pas de deux, when Eurydice, her body entwining Orpheus's, tempts him to look at her. As he finally rips away his blindfold, she is drawn away under the curtain, "like a dead leaf." The dramatic die is cast with the entrance of the Dark

Angel, in the first scene. Moncion speaks of his "menacing presence and static mobility." The action climax comes when the Bacchantes destroy Orpheus. This was one of LeClercq's finest roles. Says Magallanes, "She was very fragile, very slim. This made her more ferocious, like a whiplash."

The designs were described as a "kind of stone-age Greek," dissociating the action from any period. The most exciting effect was the lightninglike descent of a white silk curtain, which fell and swirled in a dramatic zig-zag, as the audience gasped. Also, Noguchi designed a rope element as part of the Dark Angel costume, which Balanchine incorporated into the choreography.

Most critics were very favorably impressed.

Martin: "Balanchine has treated it with the utmost simplicity. He has told the story with complete directness and a minimum of ornamentation. He has used gesture sparingly but with intuitive invention, and only in the scene between Orpheus and Eurydice does he allow the familiar flavor of the ballet adagio to creep in. The relationship between Orpheus and the Dark Angel is eloquently established in the first scene and admirably maintained to the end, with an especially fine passage in the Underworld, where Orpheus plays for Pluto. The destruction of Orpheus by the Bacchantes carries great dramatic conviction, and the closing scene of Apollo at the tomb

and the symbolic apotheosis is a superb achievement of ritual fulfillment. . . .

"Against the serenely meditative score, Balanchine has conceived a profoundly touching action that is part gesture, part choreography, part theater movement, and Noguchi has drawn the whole thing together texturally and visually, giving it accent and phrase by a motile decor of supreme eloquence." [5]

Chujoy: "An intricate poetic design so pure and so right in its details that it appears simple and crystal clear even at first seeing. There are no pantomime or histrionics to explain the action. The movements are sparse and economical, yet they not only project the plot but produce in the spectator an almost religious feeling, as if he were present at some mysteries." [6]

Many critics mentioned ritual. For some of them, spareness meant bleakness, ugliness, or thinness. One critic called *Orpheus* "a murky bore." Sabin wrote, "*Orpheus* depends on the inspiration of the dancers and the integration of the performance for its emotional effect. It is a profoundly subjective conception, uneven in texture and confused in idiom, but full of strokes of bold invention. The score has a directness and unity of style that Balanchine did not achieve in his choreography." [7]

There is no doubt that the work is delicate and depends a great deal on the precise delineation of many small details. Terry appreciated this when he wrote:

"It is not an easy work to perform, being neither virtuosic nor merely decorative. If it is to communicate anything, its gestural patterns must be clearly defined and they must also, through the slightest of dynamic shadings, project a sense of emotional compulsion." [8]

There is some feeling that *Orpheus* is dwarfed by the large stage of the New York State Theater. Nevertheless, it was extremely well received when it was remounted for the Stravinsky Festival in June 1972, and Bonnefous was praised for the poetry of his conception.

The ballet won an excellent critical reception in London: "Uncompromisingly modern. There hardly ever can have been so Spartan an apotheosis as this ascent of the lyre to heaven. But the highly abstract movements develop a grave beauty so that the central episode of Eurydice's journey back from the Underworld has a greater vividness than any literary or operatic presentation of Orpheus. His Eurydice conveyed by sinuous physical envelopment of him the insinuation into his mind of the intolerable longing which made him cast off the symbolical bandage of his eyes. The ele-ment of strangeness in décor, dance, and music was successful in conveying that occult power which in Orphism connected Bacchus with Apollo through Orpheus. The ballet tapped some of the deeper, unexplicit implications of the myth." [9]

"Some beautifully composed movement indicates that, while the 'blinded' Orpheus cannot see his Eurydice, he is conscious of her nearness. There are other poetic moments when Orpheus is leading Eurydice from Hades to Earth, trying bravely to ignore her, while she, fearing to have lost his love, wraps her body about his, until, unable to bear the torment of her despair, he [looks]. The setting is almost Brancusi-like in its emphasis upon pure form; but the passage through the Shades is imaginatively conveyed by the lowering of a glaseous curtain shot with light." [10]

"The episode of the red- and yellow-haired Thracian women who tear Orpheus to pieces seems curiously right amidst the sinister and strange costumes and scenic objects." [11]

"Gauntly modern but effective. Not a pretty ballet." [12]

Orpheus. Above: **Pas d'Action (Bacchantes attack Orpheus). Nicholas Magallanes, Tanaquil LeClercq.** (The Dance Collection. New York Public Library. Photo George Platt Lynes.) *Below:* **Underworld (Scene Two). Melissa Hayden (Eurydice), Jean-Pierre Bonnefous (Orpheus), Francisco Moncion (Dark Angel.** (Photo Martha Swope.)

2

THE COMPANY FINDS A HOME
New York City Center of Music and Drama

1948–1954

On 11 October 1948, the New York City Ballet appeared for the first time at City Center as an affiliate of the resident opera company, with a program of *Concerto Barocco*, *Orpheus*, and *Symphony in C*; its premiere season as an independent constituent followed in January. Among the first principals were Maria Tallchief, Marie-Jeanne, Tanaquil LeClercq, Beatrice Tompkins, Jocelyn Vollmar, Nicholas Magallanes, Francisco Moncion, Herbert Bliss, and Todd Bolender. Within the next year or two they would be joined by Melissa Hayden, Janet Reed, Patricia Wilde, Jerome Robbins, and only slightly later by Diana Adams; already in the corps de ballet were Jacques d'Amboise and Jillana.

Thus the Company's distinctive profile for the first ten years or so of its existence was discernible almost from its inception. For dancers tended to come and to remain. Balanchine inspired loyalty and a sense of mission; dancers themselves went around town distributing printed announcements of coming seasons. Says Tallchief, "We were young, we were enthusiastic, we were doing beautiful things." Other stellar dancers associated with the Company during these early years, but who did not remain permanently, were Nora Kaye, Hugh Laing, and, for a nine-year stay, André Eglevsky.

The Company's image was one of dedicated integrity, deriving first and foremost from Balanchine's and Kirstein's direct approach to pure dance unadorned (gone were the overdressed spectacles of Ballet Society—the easel painter was dismissed from a primary conceptual role in the creation of ballets, a banishment that seems to be permanent), and also possibly due to the fact that Balanchine was, frankly, working to a large extent with inexperienced dancers who were not always a match in showmanship for those in longer-established companies; then, of course, there was the matter of money, or the lack of it: the Company could afford neither to dress its ballets nor to mount expensive publicity campaigns.

Despite this background, however, there was one star in the glamorous mold of international ballerinas, who needed no apology on the grounds of youth, inexperience, lack of support by expensive productions, or a non-European upbringing, and this was Tallchief. Her clean strength, speed, and absence of mannerism came to be considered the "new" American technique; Tallchief herself came to personify the New York City ballerina.

The Company began to catch on. The loyal audience—never enormous but constantly enlarging—remained. For it, as well as for the dancers, there was the excitement of being in on the beginning of something destined for greatness. Balanchine created ballet after ballet after ballet. His resources seemed limitless.

In 1950 the Company made its first trip to London. Both Kirstein and Chujoy have described the significance of the visit: Europe was still not only the cradle but the capital of ballet; without its imprimatur, the Company, despite its successes in New York, might still be considered provincial. And Kirstein, an Anglophile, had an intense need to succeed in England. Balanchine, aware of international standards, sequestered his solo dancers for special two-hour classes for months before the visit. (Balanchine as teacher deserves a chapter—perhaps a book—to himself.)

And the Company was a success, despite frequent reference in the English press to American gymnastics and emotional coolness. Indeed, critical acclaim from London did bring it up a notch in the dance world's esteem (much as New York's stamp of approval was to usher in a new era of recognition for the Sadler's Wells). Further tours followed—in 1952 to England and the Continent and in 1953 to the Continent, with a long stay in Italy.

From the start, the Company had found a champion in Martin. The man who in 1935 had advised Kirstein "to shake hands cordially with Mr. Balanchine and get to work starting an American ballet," who had received *Serenade* with something less than hot-blooded enthusiasm, and who had once believed that Balanchine's true métier lay in choreographing Broadway musicals, now considered the New York City Ballet as "probably the most forward-looking company in the world and one of the finest." This is not to ignore the contributions of other critics (Terry, for instance, expressed his approval of the Company on many occasions), nor to imply that any critic's opinion is necessarily the last word on the subject—either for Balanchine and Kirstein or for the ballet audience; it is only that their voices are more audible than others, and a favorable notice gives a psychological boost to the participants whether or not it does anything to influence artistic policy or the public taste. And Martin's change of heart seemed particularly significant, since he had been a devoted observer of the dance scene for more years than had any other critic, and he wrote on a continuous basis for the most prestigious journalistic organ.

Behind the scenes, finances continued to be an almost desperate problem, but to public observers the Company seemed to be leading from strength as it gathered its forces in the fall of 1953 to mount its first full-length production, with accompanying scenic and publicity regalia—*The Nutcracker*.

MOTHER GOOSE SUITE

Classic Ballet in five scenes

CHOREOGRAPHY: Todd Bolender

MUSIC: Maurice Ravel (*Ma Mère l'Oye* [suite], 1908, orchestrated 1912)

COSTUMES, DÉCOR: André Derain (from *Dreams*)

PREMIERE: 1 November 1948 * (first presented 1943 by American Concert Ballet)

CAST: *Young Girl*, Marie-Jeanne; *Spectator*, Beatrice Tompkins; *Hop O' My Thumb*, Todd Bolender; *Bird*, Una Kai; *Prince*, Dick Beard; *Beast*, Francisco Moncion; *Clouds*, 7 women; *4 Couples*; *Little Girls*, 4 women

PAVANE: *Girl, Clouds*
ENCHANTED GARDEN: *Girl, Couples, Little Girl*
HOP O' MY THUMB: *Girl, Hop, Bird*
ENCHANTED PRINCESS: *Girl, Prince, Little Girls*
BEAUTY AND THE BEAST: *Girl, Beast*

OTHER CASTS: *Young Girl*, Nora Kaye, Janet Reed; *Hop O' My Thumb*, Herbert Bliss, Jerome Robbins; *Prince*, Roy Tobias; *Beast*, Todd Bolender, Michael Maule

The ballet was described in the program as "a fantasy in which the spectator dreams of her adventures as a young girl."

Says Bolender, "It's a story of remembrance. As it begins, I had clouds floating across, so that you get the sense that this is a situation of reaching back into time. A woman—the Spectator—walks diagonally across the stage (wearing a beautiful dress that Balanchine found in an old trunk), and as she crosses, from the opposite direction comes the Young Girl, and they meet in the center, not recognizing each other, but with just a momentary kind of awareness. The Spectator sits on the side of the stage, where she remains for the entire ballet. As each of the sequences occurs, it is as though she were reliving it—the painful and the pleasurable, climaxing with 'Beauty and the Beast.' First comes the development of the Young

* This and all subsequent premieres until 24 April 1964 took place, except where noted, at the City Center of Music and Drama, New York City.

Girl. Different couples walk into the 'Enchanted Garden,' and she realizes she is unrelated to any of them—it's kind of an identification thing. Out of this crowd she meets 'Hop O' My Thumb,' with whom she has a very peculiar kind of relationship: he is extremely evasive, always escaping from her. After this there is a kind of Chinese fantasy. It is as though, not having made an identification with herself, the Young Girl retreats somewhat. At one point she covers her face with a peculiar veil, almost like a scar. The 'Enchanted Princess' is an uglyduckling story. The Girl becomes beautiful, the Prince dances with her, and the background figures give a sense of people liking her, a joyous situation, but she leaves, runs, and jumps into the arms of the Beast. This is where the whole idea comes together. The Beast is finally unmasked by figures—the Clouds from the opening scene—and becomes a handsome Prince. He carries her away, and at the same time the Spectator stands up, turns and looks at the mask that has been left on the stage. She picks up her skirt and turns away, walking toward the back, perhaps not wishing to remember too much."

Bolender says the ballet is not for children and that his ideas derived from the Ravel score rather than traditional Mother Goose stories. The distant music, with its exotic instrumentation and shifting modalities, was a major element in the unspecified dream world where the ballet occurs.

The work was praised for its atmosphere and the suitability of the score to the theatrical concept. Terry wrote that Bolender "succeeded in capturing much of the eerie loveliness of the music." [1] Chujoy complained of a "lack of choreographic substance" [2]; others agreed, but considered that the evocation of fantasy more than made up for scant ingenuity in the choreography itself. "Lovely," "tender," "wistful," and "poetic" were the words most often used to describe the ballet. Martin called it "A completely enchanting little work, characterized by delicacy of imagination and beautiful taste. It has caught quite magically Ravel's mood and flavor as well as his formal invention." [3]

Terry: "Finds its greatest distinction in its evocation and sustaining of a mood. It is really a dream, and like a dream it hovers between reality and fantasy. The link between the two is the dreamer who

sometimes sees herself as a participant and again as a ghostly, remote observer. The choreographer has succeeded quite remarkably in suggesting the unhurriedness, the frustrations, the fantastically complex but somehow logical (to the dreamer) dramatic involvements of a dream." [4]

More specific descriptions of details of the ballet were offered by Denby in his review of the original production: "Has the feeling both solitary and intimate, like that of a child's daydream. I liked the way the movement seems to wait a long time and then flare up all at once; or how sometimes the space is very empty and then peculiarly crowded. I liked the tree that once picked up a little girl and carried her to a garden seat; and the slow clouds. But I wished the chief character had danced more, and that the many slow arm movements had held my interest better. The piece seems almost to make a virtue of indecision; but it has a quality of time that is not derivative, and serious workmanship is evident throughout." [5]

London enjoyed the ballet, both for itself and as a contrast to the predominantly Balanchine repertory.

"To parts of the body which dance as well as the legs, Kai as the Bird added the wonderful tresses of her hair. There was more of suggestion and fantasy in this slender and pleasing ballet than this company has hitherto shown to be within its emotional range." [6]

"Described, accurately, as 'a classical ballet.' Its classicism, however, is far removed from the austerities of Balanchine's postwar interpretation of the term. It is a wistful, tenuous piece, suggesting rather than telling a number of fairy-tales and depending for its success much more on its affinity to the elegiac lyricism of Ravel's score than on any choreographic inventiveness. It is far from being an important work, but it is a pleasant, because comparatively unusual, item among the severely academic ballets most favored by the company's artistic directors." [7]

THE GUESTS

CHOREOGRAPHY: Jerome Robbins

MUSIC: Marc Blitzstein (1949)

PREMIERE: 20 January 1949

CAST: Maria Tallchief, Nicholas Magallanes, Francisco Moncion; *First Group*, 5 couples; *Second Group*, 3 couples

OTHER CASTS: Melissa Hayden, Nora Kaye, Tanaquil LeClercq; Frank Hobi, Jerome Robbins

The program note explained that the ballet "concerned the patterns of adjustment and conflict between two groups, one larger than the other." It was Robbins's first work for the Company, the product of a close collaboration with the composer. Said Blitzstein at the time, "[After deciding on a theme], I would make a musical sketch or core of each section, which both of us considered, kicked around, and flayed alive till it was right. [Robbins then went off to make dances to it.] It is a wild and perilous experience working with someone of [his] drive, imagination, and genius." [1]

Robbins described the process of refining the idea:

"Marc and I had the idea of wanting to do something about minorities and majorities, and we tried many, many ways. Originally it was a very literal, specific ballet which had to do with the competition among people who worked in a department store. It turned out that the winners happened to be a black and a white. But the more we worked on it, the more we decided to try to get away from those specifics. (As a matter of fact that's the same approach I wanted to take for *Dybbuk*—to get away from the concrete details.) We wanted to see whether we could do a classic ballet telling a story with that content. I was already trying to move things away from those specific theater qualities—maybe because I was able to do them in theater. I wanted to do it in dance where it couldn't be any other way. The host [was defined] by his quality of movement. He was commanding; the movement was very cut. There was a very good pas de deux.

"Balanchine once described the subject as 'the cluded—the included and the excluded.' He was very touching: he came in to watch a couple of rehearsals—which made me nervous—then he went out and returned half an hour later with masks, because he knew I needed masks, and he'd gone out and shopped for them, and wanted me to try them. He was—and

The Guests. **Maria Tallchief, Jerome Robbins, Nicholas Magallanes.** (*The Dance Collection, New York Public Library. Photo George Platt Lynes.*)

always has been—enormously aiding, helpful, trying to make it work for you, interested, and devoted."

The ballet received lengthy and thoughtful reviews. Hering made the point that *Guests* promised much for the future: "It has all the potentiality of a new-born child—small and perfectly formed, but as yet not quite coordinated." She suggested that the development—of the ballet and of Robbins as choreographer—would be fascinating to watch: "It is a semi-abstract study of the bitter problem of social stratification and snobbery and its effect upon two young people, stated not with the dispassionateness of satire, but with the closer concern of social commentary. The situation is set by the entrances of ten accepted ones (the clique, as it were) and six unaccepted ones. They dance in two separate circles and bow frequently to the arbiter—all very formal, very social. This is followed by a masking episode in which two of the uninvited ones obtain masks and melt into the clique. There is a lyric solo by one of the masked boys followed by an exquisitely danced solo by one of the masked girls, and a lovely duet for the

two. Then comes unmasking and discovery. An elect boy has fallen in love with a non-elect girl. The two are separated by the ubiquitous arbiter. They try to achieve acceptance by either group—are rejected by both, and finally go forth together. Robbins has spent most of his time on the idea-content and structure of his ballet, and he has received understanding support from Blitzstein, whose musical score is ideally suited to Robbins's style. In the lyric middle section [the music] has a haunting, very young quality that is Blitzstein at his best. But Robbins has evidently not yet made up his mind what the prevailing tone of the introduction should be." [2]

Smith found the ballet, originally titled *The Incident*, "a compassionate social comment, handled with a delicacy and restraint that make its message more affecting than the tractarian documents of many of our socially-conscious modern dancers." [3] He, like almost everyone else, believed the pas de deux to be the high point.

Martin, on the other hand, was surprisingly negative and almost ill-humored about the ballet, considering it "disappointing, quite obvious, somewhat overstated. Scarcely lived up to what might be expected from such collaborators." [4] Within a year, however, he had changed his mind (Robbins had done some overhauling in the interim):

"The work originally was not impressive except for a brilliant pas de deux. [Now] the theme is the same, the choreographic scheme and production are the same, but what emerges is a taut and brilliant theater work with a style all its own.

"There is nothing personal or emotional about any of it. Yet because the premise is clearly stated as one with relevance to human experience, the unfolding composition teems with meaning and pertinence and bitter comment. It is also sharply emotional in effect, for all its coolness of approach." [5]

Terry wrote of the choreography, "Robbins has, for the most part, used the vocabulary of the classic ballet, but his application of gesture and of dynamic accent has given freshness and emotional luminosity to a traditional way of dance. Further, he has used balance and unbalance in the placings of his groups to good dramatic effect and has explored the spatial areas of his theater with masterful use of direction." [6]

Tallchief remembers her "lyrical" variation, with lovely arm movements, and the beautiful pas de deux in which "I was up in the air *most* of the time, in almost every conceivable position."

The score was described as "continually melodious; and though its harmonic scheme is predominantly quite dissonant, the sound and texture of the music are full of pathos. Intrinsically American [although not] in the conventional jazz-and-local-color fashion." [7]

The London press was enthusiastic: "He has done something which looks simple but is not. He has, with small modifications, married an entirely classical technique to a tiny sketch of a story—a story which is all mood and atmosphere and which never tries to say anything which could be better said in any other medium. Because of his delicate sense of the dramatic, his sense of music, and, above all, his respect for the limitations of the classical dance, he has turned his forbidding little scenario into a work rich in imaginative suggestions. He also produced an excellent pas de deux—classical again but with nuances of angularity." [8]

"The solos and pas de deux are as beautiful and expressive as anything the Americans have given us, full of tender youthful gestures of diffidence and awakening love. Blitzstein's music, which tends to the use of brass and low strings, has some attractive dissonances which help to produce an atmosphere of tension and mystery." [9]

JINX

CHOREOGRAPHY: Lew Christensen

MUSIC: Benjamin Britten (*Variations on a Theme by Frank Bridge for string orchestra,* 1937)

SCENARIO: Lew Christensen

COSTUMES: Russell Hartley

DÉCOR: Jean Rosenthal

PREMIERE: 24 November 1949 (first presented 24 April 1942 by Dance Players)

CAST: *Jinx, a clown,* Francisco Moncion; *Wirewalkers,* Janet Reed, Ruth Sobotka, Frank Hobi; *Equestrians,* Herbert Bliss, Barbara Milberg, Barbara Walczak; *Bearded Lady,* Beatrice Tompkins; *Strong Lady,* Georgia Hiden; *Tattooed Lady,* Dorothy Dushok; *Ringmaster,* Val Buttignol

OTHER CASTS: *Jinx,* Todd Bolender; *Wirewalker,* Barbara Bocher; *Equestrian,* Harold Lang; *Bearded Lady,* Melissa Hayden

Based on the atmosphere of theatrical superstition, the element of chance in all spectacular performance. It is set in a small circus troupe which is continually dogged by a set of mishaps. The clown, Jinx, is blamed for the bad luck, as he always seems to be present when an accident occurs. The performers finally kill him, but find that they have not rid themselves of the 'jinx,' whose spirit returns to harass them" (program note).

Jinx was a useful ballet within the context of a Balanchine-dominated repertory, providing dramatic roles, atmosphere, and plot. It was, according to Hering, "a challenge to the [Company], which is notably weak in dramatic movement. (True, this is a calculated weakness, for both Balanchine and Kirstein favor dance as a pure art designed to transmit emotion and mood without the aid of dramatic gesture and literary plot.)" [1]

Its theme was that of a person lusting after an ideal and being rejected, then returning for revenge, said Moncion; however, it was felt that *Jinx* did not quite make its point. Chujoy wrote that it "succeeded in creating an atmosphere of mystery and suspense, but failed in telling the story in terms that would be understandable to the spectator. The fate of the clown is worked out in a rather ambiguous fashion. Based on an excellent idea; there is enough material for a good ballet." [2]

"A dramatic and convincing ballet, small in scope, concentrated in action. The dances are simple and episodic in form, the costumes are colorful without being too literal. And the Britten score, with its dry, whirring strings, is properly melodramatic. Now it remains for *Jinx* to

Jinx. Final scene. (*Photo Melton-Pippin.*)

be given the stylistic treatment it richly deserves." [3]

Both Martin and Terry shared these sentiments and felt, in addition, that the performance of the title role was not all it might be.

Terry: "A hint of malevolence, a tinier hint of pathos, were apparent, but these attributes of [Jinx's] character were not sustained, and since they were not, the key to the ballet's integration of scenes and sequences was occasionally lost. [However], Reed was wonderfully appealing, and Bliss performed a delicately macabre duet with her quite beautifully. Tompkins did a magnificent job in transforming the Bearded Lady from a laugh-getting figure into a completely sympathetic, tragic woman. Its sequences of actual circus performing—equestrians, wirewalkers, clowns, freaks—are witty and kinetically skillful. The interweaving of theatrical superstition with performing aplomb makes for a dramatically arresting theater experience, and at its best *Jinx* is just that." [4]

All reviewers expressed the hope that Christensen would do further work on the ballet ("a work of inherent stature, unusual and impressive," said Martin), which he did, to excellent effect: "A stunning, atmospheric, taut new version which holds the attention unflaggingly. Perhaps it is a bit more of a melodrama than it was before." [5]

As often during that first London season, critics, starved for plots and characters, and feeling overwhelmed by what they considered "gymnastic" American technique and a plethora of "heartless" Balanchine abstractions, welcomed a ballet with a story line that dealt in a clear fashion with the emotions. *Jinx* was considered commendable—"a modest curtain-raiser." [6]

"Has a scenario that is a cross between *Pagliacci* and *Petrouchka*, danced to the music of Britten without damage or inconvenience to either art. There are stylized dances for tight-rope dancers and equestrians; there is a bearded lady who loves the clown Jinx, who is also a Jonah. Bolender played him with a fine suggestiveness and he was supported by the other ten, who had well-defined character dances to execute. Christensen has certainly compassed a ballet of admirable concentration and dramatic impact." [7]

"If not a masterpiece, it will appeal to many ballet-lovers and whets the appe-

tite for more of its composer's creations. The power of Jinx is revealed not so much in his own movements, though both Bolender and Moncion make him an impressive figure, as in the fear and loathing which the others show to him. Most remarkable is the skill with which Christensen has arranged his story so that each incident exactly matches the moods of the contrasting sections of Britten's music." [8]

FIREBIRD

CHOREOGRAPHY: George Balanchine

MUSIC: Igor Stravinsky (*Firebird*, 1909–10 [Third Suite, for reduced orchestra, 1945])

COSTUMES, DÉCOR: Marc Chagall

LIGHTING: Jean Rosenthal

PREMIERE: 27 November 1949

CAST: *Firebird*, Maria Tallchief; *Prince Ivan*, Francisco Moncion; *Prince's Bride*, Pat McBride; *Kastchei*, Edward Bigelow; *Chief Monster*, Beatrice Tompkins; *8 Maidens, 19 Monsters*

OTHER CASTS: *Firebird*, Melissa Hayden, Kay Mazzo, Patricia Neary, Mimi Paul, Violette Verdy, Patricia Wilde; *Prince Ivan*, Herbert Bliss, Robert Lindgren, Conrad Ludlow, Michael Maule

NEW PRODUCTION, 28 May 1970, New York State Theater

CHOREOGRAPHY: Balanchine and Jerome Robbins

CAST: *Firebird*, Gelsey Kirkland; *Prince Ivan*, Jacques d'Amboise; *Prince's Bride*, Gloria Govrin; *12 Maidens; 12 Youths; Kastchei*, Paul Sackett; *28 Monsters*

OTHER CASTS: *Firebird* (after 18 June 1972, in new costume), Karin von Aroldingen, Colleen Neary; *Prince Ivan*, Jean-Pierre Bonnefous, Peter Martins, Lorca Massine

Balanchine, no matter how avant-garde he becomes, has never turned his back on tradition or forgotten his Russian roots and the sumptuous ballet productions of his youth. His *Firebird*, though innova-

tive and spare, and danced to "modern" music, evokes the pomp and enchanted atmosphere of yesterday's fairy tales. Stravinsky's famous score is too well known to benefit from discussion here, except to mention one technical point: "The composition posed an interesting problem—how to differentiate in musical terms between the natural and the supernatural elements in the action. Stravinsky took [a] hint [from Rimsky Korsakov's *Golden Cockerel*]: The music for Ivan, the Maidens, and the hymn of thanksgiving in the finale is all strongly diatonic in character, whereas all the magical element, including the music for the Firebird and Kastchei, is conjured out of one chromatic interval, the augmented fourth." [1]

The ballet provided the new Company with its first box-office hit. It was warmly praised by all of the dance critics, and even drew a rave from the flippant *Time* magazine, whose coverage of serious dance events in those days was rare: "When the curtain went up on Chagall's brilliant red-and-blue sets, the audience gasped with pleasure. . . . Balanchine had scrapped Fokine's original Russian-folk-dancey choreography completely, put his more Oriental Bird and Prince on more acrobatic tiptoe. The flashing first-scene duet brought a touchdown roar from the audience." [2] The New York City Ballet was on the map.

Other views:

Terry: "What could be pleasanter than to have an old classic, which had been showing the unkind ravages of time, reborn into a new (or almost new) classic sparked with contemporary vitality? The story of the ballet remains, inevitably, slight if not altogether pointless. It still concerns a prince who captures the Firebird and is given one of her magical feathers in return for her release. Later, when he is interrupted in his wooing of a princess by a band of demons, the feather is waved, the Firebird comes to the rescue and the hero weds his heroine. So much for that. Now let us get on to the dancing, for herein lies the excitement of the new *Firebird*.

"Balanchine has devised some magnificent movements for the title figure. They are fluttering, flashing, soaring and, at the proper moments, they fairly flame with dynamic tension and speed. In his own miraculous way, Balanchine has again taken the academic ballet for his basic stuff of dance and through freshness of sequence and of accent, through the incorporation of freely created but related actions, has made this traditional language of dance seem contemporary without in any way marring its classic nature. Tallchief gave a performance of historical proportions. Moncion, turned out in a really superb Tartar makeup, made a splendid prince.

"The folklike episodes of the princess and her ladies have been pleasantly devised and seem not only less interminable than those of the original version but quite entrancing. The magicians and demons are not, it must be confessed, very frightening, but they are lively, and Balanchine has accorded them some unusually effective group patterns to accomplish. A slight irony seemed to touch this section, for Balanchine gave his demons just a hint, the merest hint, of jive and an adapted Charleston movement or two. Very engaging and right, I would say, since no one seemed to take the demons seriously." [3]

Martin: "It is a beautiful, sensitive, balanced ballet, and a joy and delight to watch. *Firebird* is the first ballet Stravinsky wrote for the Diaghilev company back in 1910, and in Fokine's choreography, with the original Golovine scenery and costumes, it was a magical work in its day, unlike anything we had ever seen. Most of the ballet audience today is too young to have seen it then, and remembers it, if at all, only in the wretched form in which it was presented by the De Basil company a few seasons ago, with different décor, with half the choreography forgotten, and with a kind of apologetic awareness of being dowdy and déclassé.

"In 1945 we saw another and considerably happier version. Stravinsky had cut the score drastically, though without sacrificing anything of its essential spirit or color; Chagall had designed a superbly imaginative and evocative production, and Markova danced the title role. There was, however, a lack of unity in the work as a whole, for Bolm's choreography had been keyed to another style, and that mysterious enkindlement which takes place when a piece of art is right somehow did not occur. In the present production we have the same score; the same magnificent Chagall scenery and costumes; plus a choreography that has captured the spirit of both music and décor and created in its own right a joyous and formally vivacious piece of pure theater.

"Balanchine obviously remembers what

Firebird. 1949. Maria Tallchief. *(Photo Weisenfeld.)*

fun a fairy tale can be; and because he remembers it as an adult with a sense of humor, he manages to be nostalgic with a delightfully objective quirk. He has never been more freshly inventive nor used his perhaps not-so-fresh devices from other ballets with more aptness. Undoubtedly Tallchief has been his inspiration. Hers is the key role, and he has built for her astonishing virtuosity almost as if he were challenging it. Yet there is nothing of the circus about it; there are fabulous acrobatic tricks in it, but they are invariably justified by the fact that the role is that of a magic bird who has been captured and is struggling for her freedom. Tallchief keeps this always before us, and as she gives us each of the choreographer's inventions, he is ready with another for her, as if he were actually feeding creatively on her performance. Certainly we have never seen a Firebird performed and choreographed with such uncanny unity.

"But in the long scenes in which Tallchief is not on stage, there is no falling away whatever of artistry. The dance of the Bride and the eight maidens goes its sweet and gentle way without excitement but with complete winsomeness in its unpretentious inventions. The scene of the monsters is wonderfully grotesque and full of comment, but all the while you are smiling at its humors, a dramatic tension is building as dramatic tensions can build

only in fairy tales when the prince is in danger. It is a moment of high climax indeed when, after he has dashed about the stage frantically waving the magic feather of the Firebird, she actually comes to his rescue bearing a gleaming sword for him to slay the evil magician with. Rarely has a work of art, pushing the dangerous middle age of forty, when any work of art is so likely to look its blousiest and most bedraggled, been so happily restored to its own true youth and vigor." [4]

Chujoy, as a Russian, would seem well equipped to discuss certain folkloristic details. Like others, he found the ballet "as exciting a choreographic poem as has been seen in quite a while," and went on to mention that "incidentally, Moncion's type of Mongoloid Prince [was] historically correct." He continued his critique, "The weakest part of the ballet was the pantomime, or lack of it, between the Firebird and the Prince at the beginning. The scene does not make clear the very important moment of the release of the Firebird by the Prince and the meaning of the magic feather. The wedding wants more pomp and more people on the stage. The cake with its lighted candles looks much more like a birthday cake and clashes with the décor. The traditional Russian Bread-and-Salt on a tray covered with an embroidered towel would be much more in place." [5]

Hering, however, found the final scene "most satisfying, entirely free of corny celebration dances. There wasn't a trace of tarnished device in the entire ballet." She also mentioned the décor and the music, which she felt must have been an inspiration to Balanchine:

"Sets are dotted with flying brides and animals, but it is the vibrant color and sense of movement that predominate. Shades of red riotously intermingled, whole gamuts of pastels, and the costumes range from the jewellike appliquéd velvet of the Prince to a veritable bouquet of color-splashed muslin for the maidens. [The score, too] is full of bits of incidental color—the muttering forest music, the orientalism of the maidens' dance." [6]

A lone dissenter was Haggin, who seems to have been reacting as much to the press adulation as to the ballet itself. While he felt that *Firebird* was a "fine work," he found *Le Baiser de la Fée* of "greater stature and power" and the *Firebird* pas de deux not more inventive than the two pas de deux in *Baiser*. He also implied that, for all Tallchief's excellence, her emergence was not exactly news: "I would say that the clarity, elegance and brilliance of Tallchief that are exciting in *Firebird* have been evident and exciting for some time." [7]

The fact remains that it was the role of the Firebird that established the reputation of Tallchief, not only as "the first among equals" in the New York City Ballet, but as the leading "home-grown" (American-trained) ballerina, the first of international importance. The eminent dance scholar Moore wrote prophetically of the Firebird's embodiment in the person of Tallchief:

"[She] has found a role that fits her like a glove and may become her personal symbol. She dances like a flame, but is no mere acrobat. She dances equally with the tips of her darting, glittering fingers and with her expressive eyes, which mirror perfectly the fear and then the growing confidence of the captive bird. One of the loveliest passages is the haunting Berceuse, which she dances alone." [8]

Terry found her feats "breathtaking. In off-center spins, in sudden lifts, [her movements] seem to defy gravity, and in their alert, graceful, and sharp explorations of space, they define the characteristics of a magical, air-born creature." [9]

For Hering, "Her intense portrayal set the key for the entire production. It seemed as though Balanchine had conjured up terrible technical traps for her, forgetting her as a young woman and thinking of her a magical bird. And Tallchief was caught in the spell. The strange off-axis turns, the sharp développés, the driving jetés, were brilliantly encompassed as she progressed, transfixed, through the action. It was maddeningly beautiful and somehow not quite human." [10]

Says Tallchief herself, "[That role] was better suited to me than anything else I ever danced, but I didn't think I was a Firebird until Balanchine *made* me a Firebird. It was very difficult, because after the opening variation, you immediately go into the pas de deux. Breathwise and musclewise it was very demanding. He did the variation first and then the pas de deux; we didn't really do it all in one stretch. It was only when it was all together and I finally went through it without stopping that I realized it was practically impossible. The variation contained many low, fast jumps, near the floor, lots of quick footwork, sudden changes of direction, off-balance turns,

turns from pointe to pointe, turned-in, turned-out positions, one after another. It was another way of moving. . . . There was no time."

And Moncion: "The ballet was made for Maria, and she went after it like a demon, as if possessed, with ferocity. That is certainly one of Balanchine's greatest strengths, apart from his creative abilities—being able to compose a frame for a person that suits him or her exactly. Balanchine didn't comment much on the Prince's character; it was Lincoln who suggested something exotic, but I actually arrived at the Eastern Tatar look myself. Then, some years later, Mr. B. decided that Prince Ivan was not a Tatar but a Romanov."

Although *Firebird* was "Tallchief's ballet," others successfully danced it—and were touched by it—during the twenty-year period it remained in the repertory.

Says Hayden: "Maria was cold, statuesque, like a ballerina—a 'hot-ice' kind of feeling that was tremendous, tremendous power. I couldn't do it that way; I was very involved emotionally. I think Balanchine would have preferred less involvement. The role is that of a creature, not a woman, except in the Berceuse. Frank Moncion was exotic and sexy, because that is his personality; but my relationship with the Prince was always birdlike."

Verdy: "What I love about Firebird is the quality of entamed independence of that bird who has a mission, who cannot be caught by anybody in particular, who cannot afford to belong to any one person because of its mission. She's afraid to be captured—not an ordinary animal fear of bird being caught by man, but the fear that what she carries will stop there. So she tests the Prince to find out what his intentions are, and once she's satisfied with the motive, you can see that she was never really that afraid—the distance she kept was to test and check. What I adored was the Berceuse, because for a moment there was regret at seeing him leave with his bride—regret at not being part of the ordinary—at being left alone once more. She is not completely a bird, no. Balanchine explained that 'fire' and 'bird' don't really go together—how could you represent it? So in a sense it's a moment of magic or a creature that doesn't exist, something that you cannot really pinpoint. It's half a monster. He was always unsatisfied that, in a sense, it could never be properly solved."

Surprisingly, perhaps, Balanchine is

quite negative on the subject of *Firebird* as a ballet: "Right from the beginning it didn't work. You can never make it convincing that the ballerina really is fire—she's just a dancer in a red tutu. The story is too complicated. First, the Russian legend is not about a firebird—it's a bird that is made of gold. Like the sun, you can't look at it because it's so glittery. The story is about eggs, pike, ducks, apples, and Kastchei lives thousands of years. You can't make a ballet out of it. There is nothing but beautiful music—much better to listen to than to see. The costumes we got [from 1945 version] were rags—just awful—so the monster scene was completely in the darkness. The ballet became just the pas de deux for Tallchief and Moncion."

Firebird was among the ballets shown in the Company's first trip abroad, when the troup visited London in 1950. The English greeted it with varying degrees of disapproval. With a single exception, critics found Balanchine's treatment inferior to the Fokine version.

"A poor emancipated creature. Where are the golden apples of yesteryear? Tallchief caught some of the glitter of the bird but none of her aloof supernatural magic. The whole was danced without the slightest trace of the atmosphere of Stravinsky's music against a décor containing motifs of smartness quite alien to Russian fairyland. Perhaps this company is too immature for imaginative and romantic ballets." [11]

"Inexcusable." [12]

Buckle was the exception: "Fokine's has atmosphere, agreed, but so has Victoria Station. Balanchine's *Firebird* is an exciting ballet with dancing in it; and as the elemental creature Tallchief has the most spectacular part of her career. Pecking, darting, swooping and posing in the dark, enchanted garden, she was glorious. The dances for the girls were simple and delightful; and the crowd of supers at the wedding was not much missed. (We got a cake instead.) Masked monsters and witches, I admit, never live up to the designer's sketches. Chagall's settings are as Russian and magic as Gontcharova's and perfectly in keeping with the rich mysteries of Stravinsky's score." [13]

Two years later, he had other thoughts: "In 1950 I defended *Firebird* against all the other English critics because I thought the magnificent dancing role Balanchine created for Tallchief justified his concomitant depredations; now I have

Firebird. *Top:* **1960s. Berceuse. Violette Verdy.** *(Photo Michael Avedon.)* *Left:* **1970. Gelsey Kirkland, Jacques d'Amboise.** *(Photo Martha Swope.)* *Above:* **1949. Final scene, Pat McBride, Francisco Moncion.** *(Photo Fred Fehl.)*

99

Firebird. 1972. Karin von Aroldingen, Peter Martins. *(Photo Martha Swope.)*

changed my mind. *Firebird* is essentially a ballet of atmosphere, and this is unfortunately lost in the New York City version, together with the golden apples, the magic egg containing Kastchei's soul, the sixty supers necessary to lend glory to the processional, and a third of Stravinsky's score." [14]

Germany:

"The impression made by the production, thanks especially to the elemental yet refined décor and costumes of Chagall, is ravishing. The Russian fairytale suits Stravinsky's score perfectly." [15]

Italy:

"Although visually the ballet was pleasing, we had hoped for more. Much of our disappointment stems from the rigid choreography. It is said that Balanchine had the approval of the composer for his reworking of the original Diaghilev model. This was not enough. It should be possible to have brilliant new choreography that yet does not introduce foreign elements into the fairy tale." [16]

By 1969, Balanchine had decided that the production should be renewed for the facilities of the State Theater. He ac-

quired all of Chagall's drawings, and Karinska went to work. Here Balanchine dressed the Firebird in gold. To portray her, he chose the seventeen-year-old Gelsey Kirkland, of whom he said, "She's still a baby, just coming out of the awkward age. But I didn't want a woman. I didn't want a personality or a passionate performance. I wanted a bird, one of God's natural creatures. I wanted a storm that even when it's raging is unemotional. I didn't want people. I wanted Chagall." [17]

Kirkland was compared to "a hummingbird rather than a majestic creature of fire and spirit." [18] As for the new pas de deux, which was highly demanding and completely different from the Tallchief version, Sealy wrote, "Very beautiful. In the watery arcs and shimmering, arrested bourrées, there is truly the vision of a man dancing with a bird." [19] But most critics found the new steps, which included a new variation for the Firebird, more difficult (and awkward) than dazzling. Robbins was responsible for the new monsters' dance. He asked Balanchine for guidance. "Well," said Mr. B., "there are sweet costumes, and funny. So, instead of some bogey man it would be nice to have something more gay and

lively, like a fairy tale. It's to show off those costumes." The Robbins choreography was generally considered the best in the ballet—"*echt* Chagall," Sealy called it. But basically, the new *Firebird* (with the exception of the pas de deux) was not so very different from the old. And, lacking the excitement in the leading character, it disappointed almost everyone. "Not the definitive *Firebird* we had hoped for," wrote Belt. [20] The costumes were glowingly praised.

Two years later, Balanchine changed his idea again. Said he, "In *Firebird*, everyone is a monster. It's a strange world. All of a sudden you can't have a ballerina in a tutu come in and start turning. I took the Firebird and made her a Chagall woman, like the figure on the front curtain, so now she looks like part of the mysterious world. Most important is the music accompanying Chagall—Chagall and Stravinsky. There is no Balanchine in there. You're not supposed to do anything. Just let the costumes flow. It's like a moving exhibit."

This version was unveiled on the opening night of the Stravinsky Festival, 18 June 1972. The Firebird is now so encumbered with long skirt, train, and wings, holding a bunch of roses in one hand, that she has difficulty doing any dancing or even working with a partner. It's hard to find any spectator who likes this *Firebird*. Barnes wrote, with some understatement, "The role has declined somewhat in stature over the years." [21]

BOURRÉE FANTASQUE

CHOREOGRAPHY: George Balanchine

MUSIC: Emmanuel Chabrier (*Marche Joyeuse*, 1888; *Bourrée Fantasque*, 1891; "Prélude" from *Gwendoline*, 1885; "Fête Polonaise" from *Le Roi Malgré Lui*, 1887)

COSTUMES: Karinska

PREMIERE: 1 December 1949

CAST: *Bourrée Fantasque:* Tanaquil LeClercq, Jerome Robbins; 8 women, 4 men; *Prélude:* Maria Tallchief, Nicholas Magallanes; 2 female demi-soloists; 8 women; *Fête Polonaise:* Janet Reed, Herbert Bliss; 2 demi-solo couples; 6 women, 4 men; followed by full cast

OTHER CASTS: *Bourrée Fantasque:* Diana Adams, Mimi Paul, Patricia Wilde; Todd Bolender, Harold Lang, Arthur Mitchell; *Prélude:* Adams, Melissa Hayden, Nora Kaye, Allegra Kent, LeClercq; Frank Hobi; *Fête Polonaise:* Carolyn George, Kent, Patricia McBride, Suki Schorer, Barbara Walczak, Wilde; Jacques d'Amboise, Hobi, Conrad Ludlow, Eugene Tanner, Jonathan Watts

Melodious, colorful, full of comic touches, dash, high spirits, elegance, lots of difficult dancing, and massed effects created by a horde of dancers on stage, *Bourrée Fantasque* must be considered—along with *Stars and Stripes*—as the ultimate in "closing" ballets. Some of the antics included, in the first movement, the amusing use of fans, dancing on flat feet, the ballerina misjudging her "reach" and kicking her partner, falling off pointe, the tangle of elbows that resulted when partnering didn't go smoothly—all tossed off with insouciance and immensely elegant style; in the third movement, the pyrotechnical tours jetés of the ballerina, supported high above the head of her partner—a full arm's length above; and the rather kitschy finale that featured much jumping up and down by the ensemble, multiple pirouettes by the ballerinas, and, at the end, the entire company whipping their arms round and round as if winding up to pitch softballs.

Most of the critics found it grand entertainment, although Martin's attitude was that it was not exactly a masterpiece—only "gay, energetic, young, spirited, and generally charming," and Chujoy was quite a bit more negative: "funny it may be; good ballet, no." [1] Both Terry and Hering had a wonderful time, as did the majority of spectators for more than a decade. (Curiously, the revival in 1967 did not last very long.)

Terry: "Sheer delight. Last evening's audience guffawed, sighed, and cheered as the ballet progressed along an unexpected route from horseplay through tender romance to a flamboyant, circuslike finish. The fun is spontaneous and not at all contrived, the romantic section is fresh yet easy in its movement patterns, and the closing polonaise incorporates practically every known trick for bringing down the house. The new work is listed as a classical ballet and it is just that. It spoofs ballet and it takes a fleeting jab at the choreographer's own tendency to wind dancers into daisy chains and it tosses in activities which border on the acrobatic, yet its vocabulary, both balletic and gestural, is primarily academic and its choreographic form is as flawless as that to be found in any one of Balanchine's pure-dance masterpieces.

"Much of the opening movement finds its humor in pure kinetics. The dancers commence a familiar balletic enchainement and instead of arriving at a normal resolution culminate their activities in pleasantly zany actions which have a muscular and ironic logic if not an academic one. If the ballerina extends a hand, why grasp it? why not lay your head upon it? If male partners have wondered what the ladies are doing with their feet in an adagio, why not let them function on their own for a moment while the gentlemen lie on the floor where proper analysis may be achieved?

"LeClercq and Robbins were nothing short of triumphant. LeClercq's wide and innocent eyes and her long legs projected the wit of her sequences to perfection, and Robbins, agile as a leprechaun and twice as mischievous, created a character which must be classed with his immortal Hermes in *Helen of Troy.* Just to prove it could be done, Balanchine jumped from this frolic to the sweetly sentimental Prélude, which starred Tallchief and Magallanes, and made us not only accept but be captivated by a totally new mood. It is wistful and searching in quality, a

Bourrée Fantasque. **Tanaquil LeClercq, Harold Lang.** (*Photo Walter E. Owen.*)

reverie of romance. The Fête Polonaise appeared to bring every dancer in New York upon the stage. What with runs, leaps, beats, and swiftly moving mass patterns, the stage seemed about to burst, but by some miracle, form remained discernible and the curtain came down upon a choreographer's dream (or maybe nightmare) of a sure-fire finale. Reed and Bliss launched this section in sprightly fashion, but were soon lost, along with the other principals, in the whirl of group action." [2]

Martin: "Balanchine has translated the general exuberance and vivacity [of the music] into most ingratiating choreographic terms. In this he has been admirably served by the costumes of Karinska. They are prevailingly black, touched with saffron or turquoise, silver or cerise, with gloves or fans, flowered headdresses or black butterflies, all set against swathes of white gauze draperies and a blue cyclorama to make a chic and lovely stage.

"The work, unfortunately, starts better than it finishes. Its first movement is a real gem, entirely off the beaten track, turning the typically flavorsome stuff of Balanchine in the direction of a well-mannered romp. There is comedy not only in the unexpected distortions of classic movement and in the wonderfully amusing use of groups of three figures together in quietly outlandish design, but also in the relations of the individual dancers to each other. The other sections revert pretty thoroughly to the commonplace, or rather, to the Balanchinian commonplace. The second movement has some excellent adagio, but as a whole is inclined to be pointless. The final section is in the same general vein as the final movement of the *Symphony in C,* piling entry upon entry and group upon group until a climax is built almost by sheer mass. There are moments here which, with due apologies all around, might almost have been composed by Massine. But, of course, it is effective, even if it is not genuinely distinguished." [3]

Hering: "Like a French Christmas tree, dazzling and sleek and sophisticated—with plenty of impishness to spare. [At first] one had the sinking feeling that here was going to be another one of those pumping can-can ballets à la Offenbach. We should have known better! Barzin gave the rousing Chabrier score a lift and a twang that evoked foolish things like champagne and "mais oui" even before the curtain went up. And when it did, the fun really started. A row of black-clad youngsters were soon followed by LeClercq and Robbins in a madly mischievous pas de deux. The second mood was as nostalgic as the first was abandoned. Tallchief and Magallanes performed with the languid tenderness of a romantic sigh. Unfortunately, the sustained quality was occasionally interrupted by a static pose for the corps de ballet or the complicated arms for which Balanchine has a predilection. But there was nothing static about the third section. Reed was swung in wide, airy arcs by her partner. And the accumulated corps de ballet and soloists massed for a leaping finale that left the audience laughing and shouting bravo in a single breath.

"Despite all the wonderful antics, it is more than a showpiece. It is a master stylist's amalgam of French flavor and Russian classic technique geared to the very special exuberance and speed of young American dancers." [4]

European critics, on the whole, enjoyed *Bourrée*. Few, however, wrote about it at any length; most merely referred to it, almost in passing, as a bright and happy finale. An exception was England's Monahan, who, surprisingly, felt that the ballet, which contains so many unorthodox steps and formations, was too classically hidebound:

"Here, once more, we were shown an application of the severe classicist Balanchine's theories. Balanchine nowadays seems to reject everything except the classroom steps; he aims at variety only by varying the number of his dancers. It may be a corrective to those kinds of choreography which bury dance under a load of symbolic mime; and it certainly expresses the belief of one of the most authoritative choreographers that it is only the dance—and preeminently the classical dance—which can preserve a ballet against rapid obsolescence. But even the most salutary theories can become a bit too fanatical. The evidence of *Bourée Fantasque*—coming after those several other Balanchine ballets which have been seen here recently—is that if the choreographer would set his dance to music which was not devised for ballet, then the unadorned, unmodified classroom movements are not enough. Certainly they should be the basis of the choreography, but they need to be applied with fairly free and sensitive inven-

tiveness. Failing that, such a ballet as *Bourrée Fantasque* can only seem sadly unmusical and, frankly, dull. We know that Balanchine is very far from being unmusical or dull: his *Cotillon* of twenty years ago (also set to Chabrier's music) is a reminder of what he can do when he does not bedevil himself with theorization." [5]

"The most memorable and delightful ballet this company has presented." [6]

Italy:

"With *Bourrée Fantasque*, in which Balanchine let his fancy loose, the evening closed with a veritably triumphant burst of wild dancing, with a sense of dynamism, and an almost frenetic bursting forth, not without a trace of acrobatics." [7]

"Balanchine seems to have known how to combine a tone of brittle irony with the delicate lyricism of a poetical mood in a ballet of festive variety and color." [8]

ONDINE

Romantic Ballet in three scenes

CHOREOGRAPHY: William Dollar

MUSIC: Antonio Vivaldi (*The Seasons*, published 1725)

COSTUMES, DÉCOR: Horace Armistead

PREMIERE: 9 December 1949

VIOLIN: Hugo Fiorato

CAST: *Ondine*, Tanaquil LeClercq; *Matteo*, Francisco Moncion; *Giannina*, Melissa Hayden; *Hydrola*, Yvonne Mounsey; *5 Fishermen; 10 Peasant Girls; 10 Naiads; 3 Tritons*

Matteo, a young fisherman, after joining other peasants and fishermen in preparation for the Festival of the Madonna, attempts to catch a fish for supper. Instead, his net brings in the naiad Ondine, who tries to lure him to her underwater realm. Matteo, already in love with a peasant, Giannina, resists the naiad. But Ondine, infatuated, transports him in a dream to the marine world where she lives under the rule of Hydrola, Queen of Waters. At the Festival, Ondine lures Giannina into the water, substituting her-

self for the peasant girl. However, Matteo is not long deceived; Ondine, in despair, is carried under water by Hydrola, who restores Giannina to her lover" (program note).

The ballet was given for one season only; despite all the right ingredients—tragic romance, fantasy, sea spirits, and peasants—it was felt to be disastrously served by the inappropriate music (which Dollar had not wanted to use in the first place). Martin even called for Pugni, composer of the original score (1843): "With some good corny music to go with a fascinatingly corny plot, Dollar might well find inspiration for some choreographic invention with style and excitement instead of the labored measures he has here turned out." [1]

Terry dealt at greater length with the choreographic substance: "A waterlogged *Giselle*, bogged down in the choreography, *Ondine* seems endless for several reasons. The fisherman's separations and returns to his betrothed seem to be repeated again and again with little variation in the manner of their accomplishment, and the naiad is required to go through her luring act a comparable number of times. The actual dances are not very inventive in their movement and pattern details, and most of them are cast in either of two dynamic areas: lustily folksy or swoony. There are, however, moments of dance beauty. The emergence of the water sprites from the waves are nicely conceived, and portions of a pas de deux for the fisherman and his girl are quite beautiful. The waits between such high points are unbearably long and the ballet, I fear, finds its characteristics in these attenuations." [2]

PRODIGAL SON

Ballet in three scenes

CHOREOGRAPHY: George Balanchine

MUSIC: Sergei Prokofiev (op. 46, 1929)

COSTUMES, DÉCOR (added July 1950): Georges Rouault

LIGHTING: Jean Rosenthal

PREMIERE: 23 February 1950 (first presented 21 May 1929 by Diaghilev's Ballets Russes, Théâtre Sarah-Bernhardt, Paris)

Prodigal Son was the first revival from another era to be presented by the young company. It had been the last work choreographed by Balanchine for the Ballets Russes and premiered only three months before Diaghilev's death. The notion was suggested to Balanchine by Boris Kochno, who was thinking not so much of the Bible but of a Pushkin tale, "The Station Master" (also known as "The Postmaster"), which describes a series of pictures of the parable that hang on the wall of a little posting station somewhere in Russia:

"In the first picture a venerable old man in nightcap and dressing gown was bidding farewell to a restless youth who was hastily receiving his blessing and a bag of money. Another displayed in vivid detail the dissolute conduct of the young man, who was depicted seated at a table surrounded by false friends and shameless women. The last of the series showed his return to his father; the good old man, still in his night cap and dressing gown, ran out to meet him; the prodigal son knelt at his feet." [1] The ballet portrays these three episodes.

As was often the case with Diaghilev productions, this one was a collaboration among composer, choreographer, and designer. Says Balanchine of the trio: "I could talk to Prokofiev, but he wouldn't talk to me. [Rouault] never spoke. But in the middle of a rehearsal, he began balancing a chair on his nose. Still, I finally got it through my stupid head what art and music were, especially new art and new music." [2]

And Kirstein has written of the creation: "Rouault was one of the few artists of the School of Paris who had any religious inpiration. Diaghilev had always collected icons; his early exhibitions organized for

Prodigal Son. **Scene I. Edward Villella.** (*Photo Fred Fehl.*)

the West indicated what became a real preoccupation. Prokofiev's score echoed a gravity showed by Diaghilev's physical decline. Rouault had followed his master, Gustave Moreau, in a revival of Byzantinism, which was an important factor in fin de siècle art. When Prokofiev arrived from Moscow to supervise orchestral rehearsals, he was scandalized by what he saw of Balanchine's choreography. Deep in post-Stanislavsky 'realism,' he wanted real glass goblets, real wine, real cushions, and three-dimensional scenery. As for the dancing, what he found was a shocking mixture of nightclub acts infused with formal classicism." [3]

Reviews of the first performance in New York were mixed, with much discussion of whether or not the ballet (or some of the steps in it) seemed "dated." ("Remains essentially a museum piece," said Chujoy [4]; "has unmistakably the marks of an era about it. It is not dated in the sense of being passé, but has rather the air of being a classic of its time," wrote Martin [5]; says Robbins, "Possibly in 1929 it was shocking—but you remember they were used to *Sylphides* then.") The work was widely hailed for its historical interest; it also proved a milestone in the dancing career of Robbins. And, in contrast to the many plotless ballets in which pure

dance is the subject matter, *Prodigal Son* also had dramatic situation, characterization, and expressionistic décor.

Terry: "Our old friend the gamut was accorded another run. Whether the revival resembles the original, I cannot say, but I am inclined to believe that it may, for some of its less happy moments of choreography may thusly be blamed upon the passage of time and associated changes in style. There are portions which are deeply touching, superb in their inventions; there are others which are both appropriately and believably erotic, and there are others which must be classified as unadulterated foolishness, dramatically and kinetically. Unfortunately, the foolish or the dull passages predominate.

"The initial sequence, showing the bumptious son at home, concerns itself mainly with a demonstration of the boy's physical agility. The agility is admirable but it is hardly sufficient to establish a situation which involves father, sisters, servants, and something of the magnetic quality inherent in a home. Since the son is to return later, the reason for his determination to return should have been clearly delineated in the initial scene. The second scene takes us to the site of revel. Here there is an absorbing duet, and

Prodigal Son. Left: **Scene I. Francisco Moncion.** *Right:* **Scene II. Diana Adams, Edward Villella.** *(Photos Fred Fehl.)*

there are also some impressive moments when the drunken youth slides the length of a tilted table or is robbed of his money or suffers his first moments of shame. But it is also in this scene that most of the foolishness occurs. The [mentally deranged] Drinking Companions engage in activities which appear to have little bearing on the development of the plot or even upon the creation of mood. There are grotesqueries, but they are not pertinent. The brief closing scene, on the other hand, is simple and profoundly moving. There are empty moments and attenuated measures in which the broken boy drags himself about, but the closing bit, when the lad struggles into his father's arms, is beautifully conceived." [6]

Martin: "Here is unquestionably the finest work of the late Diaghilev period. It is a sturdy, substantial, and meaty piece of choreography, with enough fresh and creative material in it to supply ten ballets. It is not merely inventive, however; it is also imaginative, which is not always the same thing. The Balanchine of the classic idiom and the musical visualization is nowhere in evidence. He has here told the familiar Bible story in a style of complete originality, which reflects the lusty music and adds rich flavors of its own. It is gauche and cruel, funny and naive, las-

civious and tender, and its physical and mental energy, though not its skill and artistry, could scarcely belong to anyone but a young choreographer of twenty-five. It moves with direct and sweeping dramatic force, through fantastically perceptive and daring episodes, to a conclusion of irresistible emotional conviction.

"That such results could have been achieved without Robbins in the central role is dubious in the extreme, for here is a performance to wring your heart. It is dramatically true and it touches deep; there is not a movement that is not informed by feeling and colored by the dynamism of emotion. Yet it is done with complete simplicity and lack of straining for effect." [7]

Moore: "The often-described acrobatics of the orgy scene are certainly present. The appalling wrigglings and squirmings of the Drinking Companions and the alluring contortions of the Siren combine to produce an effect of degradation which is revolting but highly convincing. Occasional moments, such as the imitation of the ship, seem today a little forced and consciously clever." [8]

Sabin: "Looks much more old-fashioned to us, in some ways, than *Swan Lake* or *Giselle*. Very wisely, Balanchine

has left the mark of the 1920s strongly stamped upon it. It has many characteristics of the ballet, music, and literature of that dynamic decade. The mixture of styles, alternating between slangy informality of idiom and serious and elevated emotionalism, the incessant attempt to be clever and different, the desire to shock, the combination of sophisticated wit with the most unabashed use of vaudeville devices—all these earmarks of the 1920s are to be found. The temptation scene was as full of tricks as an acrobatic act, and as naive as the old motion pictures of Theda Bara. The Siren climbed over tables, drinking companions, and everything else within reach, and ended up in an embrace with the Prodigal Son so complicated that they had to be helped apart. In the final episode, Balanchine resorted to mime, and since it was too long in the first place, it dragged, in spite of the efforts of the performers." [9]

Now more than forty years old, the ballet continues to be performed. Compelling reasons for its long success are the two leading roles, which provide stunning opportunities for their interpreters—the Son, in particular, is one of the rare great dramatic male figures in ballet.

Robbins's performance clearly shaped the ballet. Many years later he recalled:

"It was a thrilling experience in every way. George showed it to me very fast, as he always does—he's very quick and very accurate—and I remember Doubrovska [Felia Doubrovska, the original Siren] came to rehearsals also. It was a wonderful role to work on. When he shows you what he wants, he does a performance, he's deep into a role. There is a particularly difficult part in it, which is after the boy is robbed and worked over by the bacchanale group and they leave, and there is a long, long stretch of very, very slow movement, mostly crawling around—the trap of it was to keep away from self-pity there; a lot of the movements are asking for sympathy. The most difficult part is to sustain that.

"[As for 'acting'], I think [that comes when] a dancer devotes himself totally to the steps—I don't just mean technically but fulfilling the impulse of the movement to the music and understanding what the choreographer is about and what are the relationships on stage. Even in 'non-dramatic' ballets there are relationships going on; it's a question of relating yourself to your circumstances.

"Opening night; I remember, Maria went absolutely blank, and I was sitting on the floor and looked up at her and said through my teeth, 'Sit on my head'—which was the movement she had to do next."

Tallchief felt herself unsuited to her role, not dramatically but physically: "Emotionally speaking it was very good, but the configurations had so much to do with length of limb: there were times when I was supposed to wrap myself around Jerry, and the length of my arms and legs was simply not sufficient."

Balanchine has said that the Siren should not only overpower the Son, but loom over him physically as well. The part was taken to great effect by Mounsey and later by Adams. Says Moncion, another highly successful Prodigal Son: "Yvonne [Mounsey] had the size and a kind of smoldering sensual quality, almost like a movie star. Maria and Jerry had been kind of cool. Diana [Adams] was very beautiful, and again, cold and aloof—ice cold, cold as a snake . . . people are drawn to snakes. The role of the Prodigal is one you can really develop. I thought first of the figures as being very decorative in style and looks, taking sculptural poses, but later I came to feel that, for instance, when the Siren enters, I must glue my attention to her rather than sit

like a peacock—that's where the fascination should begin—and I also involved myself with the men."

Martin wrote of Adams's performance: "Here is no elegant and elite seductress, but a cheap wanton, who goes through her tricks as if for the thousandth time, animated only by greed. She is well aware of the fact that she has an easy victim, and scarcely troubles to hide her contempt. One has never seen the role played this way by any other dancer, and what it adds to the power of the work is inestimable." [10]

In 1959, Villella assumed the title role and made it his own for more than a decade (a number of observers, including Barnes, have suggested that his presence was the main virtue of the ballet). His impetuousness was ideal. Manchester: "Even the young thickness of his black hair seems to participate in the passion which drives him to the innermost heart of the character. The impatience to be gone, the barely tolerated moment of quiet as he kneels to receive his father's blessing, the wide-eyed eagerness at his first view of the sophisticated world, the helpless involvement with the evil which he gradually comes to sense even as his innocence crumbles before it, the bitterness of despair after disillusionment, and the final return in shame; all this is done most beautifully and, at the end, heart-rendingly." [11]

Denby, of course, has seen all the Sons, and he discussed some of their differences in an interview with Arlene Croce and George Dorris:

"How was [Robbins] as the Prodigal?"

DENBY: "Wonderful. Very simple. The whole physical force of it wasn't so great as [Villella's], and I don't remember that leap in the first scene that's always striking in [Villella's] version, nor even any spins as terrific as [Villella's]. But the line, the continuity of emotion, was very strong, and the development of emotion from scene to scene. And the detail in the pantomime business of the scene after he is robbed. The ship used to be much better than it is now. They used to row it and they've forgotten about that. They've forgotten it's a ship, I guess. But you used to see tiers of oars . . . And the two servants have a different dance now. The old dance was an anti-dance dance, as if these people couldn't dance. It worked very well. It was very advanced. It was very wild and open."

"[There is] that marvelous thing in the

photographs that I looked for when I first saw the ballet but didn't find—the trough of hands, the Siren pouring the wine down a trough the boys form with their hands, into the Prodigal's mouth."

DENBY: "[In 1950 there was] a famous avant-garde business in which the courtesan is screwed by each one of the boys in turn, very fast. It consisted of nothing at all, and it was so shocking. There was that bench and she lay down on it at one end and the boys ran—like insects—all across the bench and over her and out again, and it gave you very distinctly an image. But they left that out some years ago. It made her more of a character, somehow. It made an enormous contrast between her hieratic appearance when she first comes on and does her solo."

"That's when you're seeing her as if through the Son's eyes. Then presumably she gets progressively less remote, less grand, less mysterious."

DENBY: "One can understand that tradition of a courtesan who is very grand."

"It seems to me that many of the movements the Siren does indicate that she comes from perhaps a certain caste—that wonderful movement where she kneels on the floor and strikes her breast and then strikes her back—"

DENBY: "I'm not sure that's not one of those things that's actually in the Ghedra [a dance performed in Southern Morocco, entirely on the knees]. They might have seen it sometime or other, Balanchine and Diaghilev."

"Although we never did see him, I imagine that Moncion must have been extremely monumental and moving in Prodigal."

DENBY: "Yes, he was. And he did the plastique, the shifting from one dance or pose to another, much better than anybody else. That's what he always has been very good at."

"Did he do the last section of the ballet, the final third, as a series of abstract gestures or did he make explicit pantomimic references? It seems to me that there are indications in that choreography and in the music, too, for explicit things the Son should do to show the audience what is happening to him at that period and that Villella doesn't do. At one point you should see, for example, that the Son has to beg and that it's humiliating to him. Or when he finally gets home you should see that he falls down and kisses the ground. Now, I guess that Lifar [the original Prodigal] did those things but Villella gives a

Prodigal Son. **Scene II. Jerome Robbins.**

more abstract feeling, a more generalized emotional tone to that whole section, as if maybe you really shouldn't see anything explicit. . . . Balanchine used to dance, or mime the Father. Did you see him?"

DENBY: *"I think so. I saw some very beautiful hand gestures."* 12

Balanchine's images—the Siren pouring wine down a trough of hands, or turning into the prow of a ship, her cloak the sail, with the Drinking Companions as oarsmen—are vivid. Some of the finest writing about *Prodigal,* about just this feature of the choreography, came from a young American dancer who saw the Diaghilev version—Agnes de Mille:

"One of the roughest of these dances and by far the most effective is the love duet in *The Prodigal Son.* Doubrovska as an ancient Biblical courtesan full of splendor and wickedness hangs against the Prodigal's body, her arms locked over his bent elbows, her wrists dangling, her long slender legs bent so that her toes trail in the air, her knees moving slowly in rhythm with his steps. He crosses the stage languorously under this sensual burden. She sits before him and with frenzied strength jumps to her toes. He wraps her about his waist like a belt and with feet spread apart watches her slide down his body to the ground where she lies in a coil, hand clutching ankle, spine tense as

a sprung trap. He sits beside her, swings toward her, away from her, tries to lift himself from the floor, sinks back, and twists into her arms in an inextricable tangle. This scene constitutes one of the most important seductions to be found on any modern stage.

"Aside from the subject matter of the returned wanderer, which has been important for approximately two thousand years, the method of treatment is worth noticing as a useful development of the adagio. Imaginative concepts hitherto seldom expressed except with words, the moods and imagery that words connote, can be wrought into visual form by the same hackneyed acrobatic stunts. It is with vigorous wiles that the courtesan lures the Prodigal into her power, as we have seen, and vigorously she makes known her triumph. Her attendants immediately smother him in her crimson train. She mounts to the shoulders of one of them and stands looking down a good ten feet at her subdued lover. In this device, a tumbling trick, Doubrovska opens up an entirely new field for theatrical expression. Literally she towers over her prey. No actress by voice or presence could dominate the situation more completely.

"The effect produced by exaggerated human gestures and imitation of animal

movements by a chorus of twenty-four young men in *The Prodigal Son* far outreaches the attacks on modern civilization in any of our expressionistic dramas. . . . Bald as eggs, dressed identically, moving identically, crowded together as closely as possible, the dancers hop over one another's back, circle around alternately squatting and rising, rear themselves into architectural formations, crawl down each other to the earth again, scramble about sideways in ridiculous positions like crabs. Their movements are those of children at play, their attitude that of sinister, super-sophisticated adults. They are abortions, gargoyles, abnormal, undeveloped creatures found in the drawings of Beardsley and Alastaire. They range themselves in serried ranks and open and shut their mouths, goggle their eyes, stick out their tongues, wiggle their hands in their ears, thumb their noses. They are the epitome of all the gossiping, scandalmongering neurotics the world has bred. They seize the Prodigal, strip and rob him, bind him to a pillar, and hiding behind it so that only their hands can be seen pat him up and down. The humiliation of their touch on his body is almost more than he can suffer. Long after they have gone he remains rigid with arms stiff at his sides and fingers quivering in anguish.* Then in an excess of shame and grief he turns to the wall and pulls himself up until his body hangs pilloried, shrunken with loathing, knees drawn taut. In this manner he comes to the earth. In this manner he crawls away. He thrashes in the dust, draws himself into a knot, kicks free, turns feverishly over and around and back again. Broken, prostrate at the feet of his father until he receives some sign of welcome, he embraces the patriarch's ankles, takes hold of his waist, his shoulders, lifts himself up into the man's arms and clings there safe and comforted, folded like a child in his father's mantle. Those who watch hide their face from the gentle wonder of the scene. Lifar's crippled progress away from the city of sin is as realistic an expression of remorse as the most intense acting. In the one case the outward trappings of

---

*Balanchine says that the bald heads were his invention: "Then I had them put on crowns of flowers—Christ wore a crown—because they were bare-headed and they were celebrating, with wine, because they had stolen. I shaved the heads and put on flowers to make them sinister. There's no sex to them, you know—they're insects, awful and terrible. Disgusting looking."

grief are exactly reproduced, in the other the symbol of the grief itself." [13]

In London, where *Prodigal* was not particularly well received in 1950, Browse mentioned a consideration that had once been a vivid theoretical issue, but which had been more or less "settled"—or buried, at least by Balanchine, et al.—some years previously:

"Raises the interesting question whether 'easel' painters are suited to theatrical designing. And this ballet is one which confirms my opinion that the greater the artist, the less wise it is to invite him to collaborate in a production on the stage. Rouault's costumes and décor for *Prodigal Son* could not fail to be impressive, but it seems that his personality has been too strong for the choreographer, and that the ballet, instead of being the free invention of Balanchine working hand in hand with designer and composer, has suffered, through being dominated by the middle partner. Apart from this, and for all its merits and invention, *Prodigal Son* is not as telling as it should be. Balanchine is apt to work up to a splendid climax and then immediately to negate it through lack of timing. In the scene of the Prodigal's debauchery, after a most effective hurling of the Siren across the feasting table into the arms of the Drinking Companions, the revelry—without a pause—continues at the same fast and furious pace, and the choreographer throws away the point up to which he has been building. The pas de deux between the Siren and the Prodigal is tedious in its length and in its overstriving for novelty; the best parts of the ballet are the opening and closing scenes where the dignity of Christensen as the Father evokes the tender atmosphere of parental understanding." [14]

1965: "Relics have a value; in the world of ballet, any work which tells us something about the history of the Diaghilev company, particularly if it also tells us about the early stages of Balanchine's choreography, cannot be entirely insignificant. That is nearly, but not quite, the limit of the present value of *Prodigal Son*." [15]

"A bad work of genius; a Balanchine ballet, as we discovered in 1950, for people who do not like Balanchine ballets." [16]

France:

"It suffices to see *Prodigal Son*, created forty years ago, to be convinced that Bal-anchine is certainly the greatest choreographer of our century, whom all balletic generations must acknowledge. Everything is already there—the power, the emotion, and the revolutionary technical conceptions, which were to be tirelessly exploited in the future by Kurt Joos, Lifar, Roland Petit, Béjart, and Robbins: the monstrous little men recalling *The Green Table,* the trembling hands *Notre Dame de Paris,* the scene of seduction evoking the adagio of *Prometheus,* and so on." [17]

Germany:

"Balanchine's realization of the Bible story of the *Prodigal Son*, set to Prokofiev's dry, metallic music, vacillates between story and pure movement, and the narrative and the acrobatic elements don't always mix. There are magnificent effects, such as those of the drinking companions and their drunken back-to-back dance, with legs bent and wide apart, running quickly across the stage, and the amazing 'play of limbs' between the Son and the seductive Siren. But the plot drags, and the opening and closing scenes, at the Father's house, are rather sentimental." [18]

THE DUEL

CHOREOGRAPHY: William Dollar

MUSIC: Raffaello de Banfield

COSTUMES: Robert Stevenson

PREMIERE: 24 February 1950 (first presented 24 February 1949 as *Le Combat* by Ballets de Paris de Roland Petit, Princes Theatre, London)

CAST: Melissa Hayden, William Dollar, 3 men

OTHER CASTS: Barbara Walczak, Patricia Wilde, Francisco Moncion

In contrast to the bulk of the repertory, *The Duel* provided a drama of high theatricality, with suggestions of the richness and exoticism of the heroic past. As described in the program note for the work, "The ballet, laid in the days of the Crusades, tells of the first encounter of Clorinda, the pagan girl, and Tancred, the Christian warrior, and of their final meeting—a mortal duel. Only after he has wounded her fatally does Tancred dis-cover that his masked assailant is the girl he loves. Suggested by Cantos III and XII of Tasso's poem *Jerusalem Delivered*."

The Duel provided two juicy leading roles, particularly the female one. Terry wrote of Hayden as Clorinda, "A bravura performance that I seriously doubt could be equaled by any other soloist of the ballet." He also approved of the ballet itself: "It is introduced by warriors, establishing scene, mood, and movement theme. They are Crusaders, it is a battlefield, the atmosphere is tense with imminent conflict, and the pawing feet and resilient bodies suggest not only horses and their riders but alert combatants. The duel itself is beautifully conceived. It is just right in its evocation of the medieval beauties of a matched fight, for its participants are proudful, handsome, swift and graceful of action, fearless and quick, but not crafty. The death scene is touchingly realized; the placement of the mortal wound, the unmasking of the girl, the comprehension and despair of the Crusader who has caused the death of his beloved, are all realized in unpretentious but highly expressive dance terms." [1]

Martin agreed as to the work's quality and mentioned in particular the variety Dollar was able to introduce in the horseback movements.[2] Moore was struck by these as well, and found the closing moments, when Tancred carries the body of Clorinda across his saddle, especially skillful.[3] Chujoy admired the dancing but considered the dramatic development weak.[4]

Not only the audience but also the dancers felt the enormous change from Balanchine. For instance, Walczak says, "It was in dancing *Duel* that I realized that Balanchine could be restricting emotionally, in the sense that technically his things were very difficult, timing was very difficult, the requirements were so special. The outcome was that at the end of a performance you felt that, all right, I did it better, I did it worse, but you always felt that you fell below what he wanted—and what he had made you want. And so you were rarely satisfied. Whereas when you danced the classics, or Fokine (*Les Sylphides*), or *Duel*, it was just a little bit easier, or just a little freer emotionally, or a little more dramatic, and there was a tremendous emotional fulfillment, because you had time to *enjoy* dancing. To feel good about it. To feel that you really could dance after all, that you really could look beautiful."

The Duel. Melissa Hayden, Francisco Moncion. (*Photo Walter E. Owen.*)

In London too, *Duel* was well received: "It is not uneloquently told. Dollar's invention is striking, whether in the virile footwork of the sparring knights, the suggestion of armed combat without recourse to weapons, or the portrayal of Clorinda's last pitiful moments. Banfield's music, flamboyantly dramatic, partners the choreography successfully." [5]

"Calculated to please those among us who ask nothing better than to die in a madness of kissing and a welter of blood. The music is dramatic, full of 'wars and rumours of wars'; Dollar's choreography is effective . . . and Hayden throws herself with splendid masochistic fury into the part of the lucky girl." [6]

AGE OF ANXIETY

CHOREOGRAPHY: Jerome Robbins

MUSIC: Leonard Bernstein (Symphony No. 2 for Piano and Orchestra, "Age of Anxiety," 1949)

Based on the poem of the same name by W. H. Auden

COSTUMES: Irene Sharaff

DÉCOR: Oliver Smith

LIGHTING: Jean Rosenthal

PREMIERE: 26 February 1950

PIANO: Nicholas Kopeikine

CAST: Tanaquil LeClercq, Todd Bolender, Francisco Moncion, Jerome Robbins (protagonists, appearing in each scene)
THE PROLOGUE
THE SEVEN AGES
Yvonne Mounsey, Pat McBride, Beatrice Tompkins; 5 women, 5 men
THE SEVEN STAGES
Melissa Hayden, Herbert Bliss, Dick Beard, Shaun O'Brien; 16 women
THE DIRGE
Edward Bigelow; 5 women, 5 men
THE MASQUE
Full cast
THE EPILOGUE

OTHER CASTS: Hayden, Nora Kaye, Hugh Laing, Roy Tobias

This ballet was inspired by Bernstein's symphony and the Auden poem on which it is based. It follows the sectional development of the poem and music and concerns the attempts of people to rid themselves of anxiety.

1. The Prologue: Four strangers meet and become acquainted.
2. The Seven Ages: They discuss the life of man from birth to death in a set of seven variations.
3. The Seven Stages: They embark on a dream journey to find happiness.
4. The Dirge: They mourn for the figure of the All-Powerful Father who would have protected them from the vagaries of man and nature.
5. The Masque: They attempt to become or to appear carefree.
6. The Epilogue (Program note.)

Without question the ballet marked a major step in the development of Robbins as choreographer. He was already exhibiting his now-familiar trait of posing an almost insurmountable challenge for himself—and overcoming it. Here he found his initial motivation in a talky philosophical poem in which the characters engage in seemingly undanceable activities ("discussing the life of man from birth to death"). However, he quickly left the literary program behind (Martin advised viewers not to read the poem beforehand, because it had little direct bearing on the dance).

He wrote: "[The ballet] is quite as obscure as Auden's poem and just as unavoidably unresolved. But if you are interested in seeing one of the most sensitive and deeply creative talents in the choreographic field tackling his most profound and provocative assignment with uncompromising vision, you will find the piece completely fascinating. His intuition is uncannily penetrating, his emotional integrity is unassailable, and his choreographic idiom is lean and strong and dramatically functional. He has a fine theater sense, can evoke an atmosphere by means that are somehow never definable, and knows how to get from his dancers qualities that perhaps even they themselves are not aware that they possess." [1]

As for the action, Terry wrote "I cannot offer a synopsis, for it is not a story; it is an experience," [2] which he described thus: "Robbins has made it very clear that the individual is very much alone in his battle with anguish and doubt. True, the four find solace in simply being together and warmth in the sharing of their fears, but each is continually adventuring along his own paths in search of peace. They recall, in dance, the ages of man from birth to death, and nowhere do they find security. They dream and their dreams mock them by aping their empty actions. They cry out for a super-being—a dictator, a household god, a benevolent despot, a shaman—to assume their anxieties, but the super-one inevitably tumbles from his contrived and false elevation. By acting carefree, they hope to become so, but again they fail. Finally, each alone nears the answer he seeks by finding faith, the promise of faith, in his own being." [3]

The ending was open to interpretation. As Martin saw it:
"In the poem there is a short peroration in which the poet seems to imply a return to mystical religion as the answer; in Bernstein's music comes the dawn in a kind of glorious technicolor, and Robbins's four figures simply bow to each other with a new peace, which has come from nowhere discernible and separate. . . .
It is [Robbins's] intention in the finale to show that his four principals, after an emotional discussion of life's darknesses and possible paths of refuge from them, have found, if not an actual solution, at least an awareness of each other as people and a certain fellowship to strengthen their meeting of daily problems as they arise." [4]

Says Robbins, "There were four protagonists, not specific characters. There was no pantomime; it was all expressed in pure dance." The dance content of the work won praise on its own. Wrote Terry, "The choreographer has created dance

designs of sufficient physical beauty, power, and imaginativeness to rouse those who would ignore the theme. . . . The choreography, of course, cannot be completely divorced from its dramatic line, but if it could, one would find that Robbins has also created a masterpiece of dance architecture, wonderfully detailed and ofttimes monumental in its dramatic use of spatial areas, large and small, high and low, constricted and horizonless. . . . Among the many aspects of choreographic genius are Robbins's use of recurring movements to establish characterization and mood as well as formal structure, his employment of emotional gesture as a potent replacement for pantomime, his way of building a pattern from a simple walk or a commonplace action into a complex dance, his skill in using processional patterns for his group by way of creating a sense of passing time or an endless parade of humanity, and his faultless use of shifting dynamics and varied rhythmic accents to give color and shading to the unfolding story." [5]

Said Hering, the characters "are removed to a world of mood haunted by the inspired melancholy and looming protectiveness of the big city. He makes no attempt to lean upon the literary framework. It speaks instead with the infinite eloquence of the kinetic language. In other words, Robbins has penetrated into that fluid realm where only movement speaks." [6]

The strongest sections, visually and emotionally, were felt to be the Seven

Stages, the Dirge, and the Masque. Sabin described the Seven Stages as follows: "Aided by Smith's evocative backdrops, which have a de Chirico flavor in their spatial sensitivity, Robbins has used the solo figures in a contrapuntal relationship with the corps de ballet that is psychologically powerful. In one striking episode, the characters are mimicked by Doppelgänger, at the rear of the stage, to uncanny effect." [7]

Hering considered the ballet to be "a harrowing, tormented, labyrinthine experience with a company of crimson-clad, faceless figures, in which [the four] come together literally and through the means of four dream counterparts." [8] (Robbins says the idea for the mirror images came to him while he was watching a rehearsal in which understudies were copying the movements at the back of the stage.) The "Colossal Dad" was represented as "a gigantic figure from childhood imagination, a sort of wizard on stilts." [9] The Masque, with jazz elements in music and dancing, was "a brilliant statement of a forced gaiety to blind one's self to one's own basic cynicism and fear." [10]

Krokover mentioned something that was to prove most important later on: "It is a work close to our time: a product that could be of this decade and no other. In some respects it is too close, and this observer has the strong feeling that the next generation will find it remarkably dated." [11]

Age of Anxiety did not wear well, and within four years Martin would write,

Age of Anxiety. **Left: The Prologue. Francisco Moncion, Todd Bolender, Tanaquil LeClercq, Roy Tobias. Right: The Dirge. Edward Bigelow (center).**

"It begins to seem quite old-fashioned. Perhaps this is because when one has really grasped its boldly complex design, there is not so much substance there as one had believed. Or perhaps this is an age of different anxieties, less selfish and more universal." [12]

Working on the ballet remains vividly in the memory of many of the participants.

Says Moncion, "We spent a great deal of rehearsal time working out the relationships between the four. This is the substructure. Each comes in separately in a kind of ritualistic walk, they meet, they touch, and they become acquainted. That bond stays. Then he takes each one through various phases. It ended with what he called the Masque—a kind of jittery cocktail party where everybody goes to pieces. Then it closes as it began, only in the reverse. They get together again, they touch, they do their obeisance, then they go away separately, into a glorious technicolor sunset, with chimes and bells and chords—it was very effective.

"The corps de ballet were more symbols than people, dressed in sleeveless red leotards and wearing fencing masks—therefore faceless. They become obstructions, they become hurdles, they become alleys. There was a section where they were like turnstiles and we had to break through them; they lined up in various directions and we had to find our way out of the maze; they shifted directions, which caught us against the wall."

Bolender: "We already knew the story, and we would often speak of ourselves as those characters. Jerry would occasionally say a word or two, because he's very good at giving sharp, clear characterizations of both movements and psychological states. Often by criticizing the movement you could get through to the character. There was an urgency about the movements always. It was sustained as though in a tension, then would burst out and move into something else. We always appeared to be on the move, about to break and go into another area. He incorporated ballet kinds of steps rather beautifully and managed to use symbolism that didn't have a heavy connotation. It was so light and beautifully done. He seemed to focus the very word *anxiety* in his movement—jagged, almost unrelated things, like tics sometimes, throughout the body. Everyone would move in exactly the same way, to the same degree. Since the ballet was dealing with the times we lived in, he

used movement that one could associate with from the street, for instance, but then heightened so that it came out quite a different color. It is always an extraordinary experience working with him; he'll talk and talk and talk, and at the end you may not be able to repeat what he has said, but you'll have a vivid impression of what he wants."

England:

"Will give us enough to talk about for the remainder of the season. Usually these psychological or metaphysical ballets suffer from pretentiousness. This one does not, though heaven knows it is unintelligible enough. The ballet fits its music and its theme (which is nightmarish enough to satisfy the gloomiest Central European) and has an undeniable conformity with modern life. The choreography employs stylized gestures, jazzified rhythms, plain walking and running, and plenty more. The four strangers, who seek escape from this un-American pessimism, were danced with powerful deliberation." [13]

"For those who have had somewhat of a surfeit of abstract ballets in which the detailed pattern of the music is embodied in complicated movements, sometimes hardly removed from ugliness and repeated from one ballet to another like clichés, the two works by Robbins (*Age of Anxiety* and *The Guests*), in which every movement is surcharged with emotion and meaning, have come as a welcome relief." [14]

Italy:

"The post-World War I German choreographers were already struggling with such themes; here we find them in a ballet, served up as a 'perfect' cocktail, in which, however, the venom is neutralized. We miss the tragic vibrations in the theme." [15]

ILLUMINATIONS

Ballet in one act

CHOREOGRAPHY: Frederick Ashton

MUSIC: Benjamin Britten (*Les Illuminations,* for tenor and strings, 1939)

Words from Arthur Rimbaud (*Les Illuminations: Painted Plates,* 1871–72)

COSTUMES, DÉCOR: Cecil Beaton

LIGHTING: Jean Rosenthal

PREMIERE: 2 March 1950

TENOR: William Hess

CAST: *Poet,* Nicholas Magallanes; *Dandy,* Robert Barnett; *Sacred Love,* Tanaquil LeClercq; *Profane Love,* Melissa Hayden; *Drummer,* Barnett; *King and Queen,* Shaun O'Brien, LeClercq; *Being Beauteous,* LeClercq, with 4 men; *Birdcage Woman, Postman, Waiter, Chef, Painter and Poster Sticker Assistants, Chimney Sweep, Kiosk Lovers, Soldiers, Train Bearers, Acolytes, Herald, Bishop, Coachmen*

OTHER CASTS: *Poet,* Hugh Laing; *Sacred Love, Queen,* and *Being Beauteous,* Diana Adams, Jillana, Carol Sumner, Dido Sayers, Maria Tallchief; *Profane Love,* Jillana, Nora Kaye, Marie-Jeanne, Barbara Milberg, Charlotte Ray, Sallie Wilson; *Dandy* and *Drummer,* William Weslow

REVIVAL: 7 April 1967, New York State Theater

CAST: *Poet,* John Prinz; *Sacred Love,* Mimi Paul; *Profane Love,* Sara Leland; *Dandy* and *Drummer,* Robert Weiss

OTHER CASTS: *Poet,* Jean-Pierre Frohlich, Robert Maiorano; *Sacred Love,* Nina Fedorova, Sumner; *Profane Love,* Karin von Aroldingen, Gloriann Hicks, Linda Merrill

I. Fanfare: "Alone, I hold the key to this savage sideshow."
II. Dreamtown: "Suburban Bacchantes weep . . . barbarians dance nocturnal rites. . . ."
III. Phrase: ". . . I have hung golden chains from star to star . . . and I dance."
IV. Antiquity: ". . . Supple son of Pan. . . ."
V. Royalty & VI. Anarchy: "A man and a woman proclaim they would be king and queen."
VII. Being Beauteous
VIII. Sideshow
IX. Farewell: "Departure amid novel sounds, and love."

Illuminations was described in the program as "A sequence of danced pictures (*tableaux dansants*), or charades, in which images suggested by Rimbaud's poems and symbolic incidents from his violent life are interwoven on the musical pattern." Terry called it "A theatrical adventure in which our guide is a daring, unconventional, half-mad figure." [1]

This was Ashton's first ballet for the Company, and quite unlike anything it—or he—had done before (when the ballet was greeted with some disapproval in London, it became clear why he had never been able to stage anything in such a style for an English company). The work combined poetry, song, and stunning visual sequences, with a strongly literary underpinning. Its effect was intellectual as well as visceral. Of this, Chujoy wrote, "Like *Age of Anxiety, Illuminations* dealt with a lofty theme, not the simple tale of individuals. It identified and gave substance, as it were, to the ideas and aspirations Kirstein had always held about the lyric theater—a mirror of humanity as a whole. . . . Many people felt at the time that *Age of Anxiety* and *Illuminations* justified the existence of the New York City Ballet." [2]

Kirstein is said to have remained very fond of it. It was he who brought the various elements together. (In fact, some years later, Barnes suggested that the influence of Kirstein was implied throughout in a work so different from anything else Ashton ever did.[3]) The idea for the ballet, however, had been in Ashton's mind for several years, as he recalls, "Around the end of the War, I became tremendously fascinated by Rimbaud as a character, and when I heard Britten's music in a concert, I immediately wanted to do a ballet to it. In fact, I mentioned it to Bérard, but these discussions were very tentative. I suppose it was intended for Covent Garden, although possibly for the Ballets des Champs-Élysées; I don't remember. Years later, after Bérard had died, Lincoln came along and put it all into motion. I've always found Rimbaud a very obsessive personality, and I read a great deal about him. I found him one of the most tragic of human beings; I used to weep reading his books.

"For the ballet I wanted to have a kind of realism—poetic realism, you might say; that is, I wanted realistic elements in it, but not too stressed. It was a problem how to dress it, and finally I think Lincoln arrived with a lot of books, including a whole book about Pierrot, and I decided that this would be the look of the ballet, except that Rimbaud would be dressed

Illuminations. Left: **Nicholas Magallanes, Melissa Hayden.** (*Photo Walter E. Owen.*) *Below:* **Dreamtown.** (*Photo Melton-Pippin.*)

more or less realistically. The music dictated, of course. It was set to some of the ideas of the poems, and I illustrated that. I think I was perhaps the first person to put a colored boy on the ballet stage [Being Beauteous section]. This was an allusion to Rimbaud's devoted Ethiopian servant, and it was also to suggest Rimbaud's African life. In fact, the ballet had all sorts of allusions running through it, due to my having read so much about him."

Ashton talked at length with Martin about the ballet and later said he liked what Martin wrote about it. Martin gave a kind of synopsis and then went into some of the underlying ideas of the scenario:

"A passionate and rebellious poet views his life as a grim and vulgar sideshow, a world of dirty and bedraggled Pierrots who have no idea what he is up to; he hangs his beautiful visions defiantly on the stars. Pulling him in opposite directions are two women—the white-clad figure of what is called in the program Sacred Love, and the voluptuous and overwhelming figure of Profane Love. The latter he yields to totally but rejects ultimately with violence. The former he visualizes as a queen, and tearing the crown from the head of her king, dons it himself and overturns the pattern of his society. In a vision he sees her as 'a Being Beauteous' borne aloft, but 'amid whistlings of death and circles of muffled music'; and from the ranks of the barbaric sideshow of Pierrots, the figure of Profane Love emerges to direct his murder. Following still the dream of his pure vision, he walks entranced into immortality.

"So far, so good; but under this lovely romantic exterior Ashton has packed stuff of harsher and more violent character. He has told us much of the essential story of Rimbaud's actual life, including his virulent personal relationship with the older poet, Paul Verlaine, a relationship that all but destroyed them both, before the world and in their inmost natures. By lifting the whole theme into terms of high abstraction, Ashton has managed to tell an untellable story and to do it without the slightest color of offense, with passion but dignity.

"[He] utilizes with wonderful adroitness the facts of Rimbaud's turbulent life as a thread to bind [the scenes] together, translating sordid and brutal elements of a singularly violent existence into symbols and themes that are in themselves creations of pure poetry. Nowhere has he done this more successfully than in his distillation of the negative forces that played upon Rimbaud—Verlaine is the first of them to come to mind, of course—into a single female figure of Profane Love. There are episodes which touch into memory the war of 1870 and the Commune, and there are doubtless scores of other passing references that the Rimbaud scholar will light upon. What is important, however, is that on this basis of factual truth, hinted at lightly, transformed into dramatic abstractions, or merely brushed across the composition,

he has built a substantial, perfectly communicative work of art. Certainly you do not have to know Rimbaud to follow it and be moved by it." [4]

As for the production, Martin found the costumes "too pretty" for the subject matter (agreeing with other reviewers) and Britten's music "cold," if "charmingly used." Magallanes seemed to him more the "conventional" poet—"dreamy, sweetly unhappy, pictorially tormented"—than the brutal and sordid Rimbaud, although later he found the portrayal had darkened. Chujoy agreed that Magallanes seemed "just" a poet.

Terry wrote, "We are shown a youthful rebel who seeks to experience life quickly, violently, avidly. The scenes suggest, sometimes specifically and again elusively, a few of those experiences of sacred and profane love, dreamy solitude, pagan adventure, beauty, ugliness, falsity. As in the poems, fragments of adventure, glimpses, hints are given rather than episodes, and so *Illuminations* emerges as a series of fragments, some eloquent, others teasingly misty, and a few disappointing. [As a series of] 'danced pictures,' it follows then that the ballet has little opportunity for dramatic development, for cumulative choreographic effect. It must find its theatrical unity in the figure of the poet who participates in or beholds the successive charades and in the mood of fantasy which pervades the work as a whole. In the main, Ashton has been successful." [5]

He complained of some "awkward choreographic contrivings and unnecessary acrobatics," however.

Some years later, Barnes would find it "not so much about a poet as about being a poet. It takes Rimbaud's lightning-flash visions and intuitions, placing them onstage with a thunderous kind of vividness. It takes the dirt and squalor of his life, the garbage can from which he picked—self-indulgently—his diamonds and seems to summarize them in a brisk series of images, so that it is an essay in metaphor rather than biography."

He went on to describe the movement: "The choreography is simple. It has much of the ritual that Ashton admires and produces so well, it has a strong classic feeling, even to a grand adagio for a ballerina and four cavaliers [Being Beauteous] and it also has something of the clutching eroticism that Roland Petit had [around 1950] just popularized and almost sanctified in his ballet *Carmen*. The staging also con-

tains some very direct imagery. The poet runs across the stage literally trying to hang stars into the sky. He stands at a pissoir and urinates, while at the end a nameless figure (not Verlaine but his shadow) shoots the poet in the wrist, with a real dummy pistol shot producing real dummy blood. The total effect of the ballet, with its unpretentious yet wonderfully effective choreography, its apt if clashing symbols, and its crazy feel for words and music, all this, is extraordinary. It adds up to something much more than the sum of its parts—which might, I suppose, also be true of Rimbaud's poetry." [6]

Watt: "Everything that happens seems terribly important and terribly inconsequential at the same time—youthful torments to be remembered warmly." [7]

Chujoy mentioned the device of having the Profane Love wear one toe shoe and one bare foot. In the mind of the choreographer and perhaps of the audience, this gave her more license for suggestive, "modern-dance style" movement, and formed an additional point of contrast with the decorous and balletic Sacred Love. LeClercq recalled the Being Beauteous adagio in which the ballerina is partnered in a number of precarious balances, lifts, and turns by four men, including a series of arabesque turns on pointe with a partner catching her by one arm. It was Balanchine who helped her most, technically, with this section. She found Ashton very detailed and helpful throughout.

So did Magallanes, who says of him: "Ashton was marvelous. Highly musical. He showed everything he wanted absolutely. He'd had this idea for a long time, and he explained everything to me, got me to read books. He was very literary in what he was doing—an entirely different approach from Mr. Balanchine. The actions were more or less right there in the songs. For me, it's a beautiful ballet—a good theater piece. There are little things today that weren't in the ballet as it was created. Some interpreters insist on putting in extra steps for technical display. Ashton's steps weren't that difficult but were so totally appropriate. Today there are some different values, although I restaged it exactly as it had been in the original. I remembered every step. But ballets do change over the years—in both subtle and unsubtle ways."

When Ashton was in New York creating *Illuminations*, he was questioned about the differences between British and

American dancers. He had answers ready: "Yours are less disciplined, but more electric, more rhythmic, less inhibited. You have to *pull* [suggestive] actions and gestures out of our dancers; yours understand immediately and express them easily. And your dancers are all so healthy. I couldn't work mine so intensely. Strange things happen to muscles unfed by steaks. . . . One thing I've learned during this visit is what 'Keep Out' means to an American. It says 'Come In.' When I put this sign on the rehearsal door, we drew a full house—mostly mothers. A very good audience."

Critics in London, home of Ashton, Britten, Beaton, and even, briefly, of Rimbaud, were interested in but not really taken with *Illuminations*. They showed much concern with "fitness": the fitness of representing Rimbaud's poems by danced images, the fitness of using music with voice to accompany ballet, the fitness of the realistic portrayal of sexual intercourse on stage.

"Smart masquerade is indeed the very last style one would have imagined as suitable to Rimbaud. Britten has given the choreographer a formal lead, choosing for his leitmotif a single phrase at the end of the long prose-poem 'Parade': *J'ai seul la clef de cette parade sauvage*; and he uses it with wonderful effect. By placing the lyric fragment 'Départ' at the end of his musical composition he has also provided the choreographer with a telling finale. Scene II, in which the poet wakes, one by one, by varied devices, the scattered groups of masqueraders, contains some delightful inventions, and the dancer reveals something of the creative joy of the poet and of his startled reaction to the hollow beings he has recklessly called into existence. One feels that the choreographer is hampered by the slightness of the musical material in the beautiful slow movement which Rimbaud calls 'Phrases.' The solo dance of the poet is extremely brief and uninventive. In fact, the scene designer has taken over and suspends some pretty tinsel shapes to hold the chain which the program tells us is being hung from star to star. It is this scene which first brings home to one the fundamental mistake of choosing an existing musical score, complete in itself, and incapable of adaptation to the needs of the choreographer. The exquisite scene (in Rimbaud and Britten), entitled 'Antique,' suggests a sylvan satyr solo, but is ren-

Illuminations. **Being Beauteous. Tanaquil LeClercq.** (*Photo Melton-Pippin.*)

dered by a realistic erotic rough and tumble, chiefly on the ground, in which Sacred and Profane Love compete for the attentions of the poet. This unstylized display was not justified by the text or the music. I enjoyed the scarlet pomp and wild movement of Scene V, as a spectacle, though it is surely quite alien to the spirit of Rimbaud's 'Royauté'—that fragile lyric in which a man and woman on the public square, superbly dreaming, achieve royalty for a day.

" 'Anarchy' is Ashton's version of the elemental turmoil of 'Marine'; the poet leaps upon and scatters these too real monarchs and their fatuous retinue, snatches the crown, and lies prostrate with his head hanging over the footlights, while the slow, lovely 'Being Beauteous' is danced. For that remote and solitary Being among the snows, surrounded by sighs of death and ringed by muted music, we are given Sacred Love, or Columbine, handed about by a ring of posturing youths, with naked torsos and tight satin trousers *de fantaisie*. In 'Parade' we have a scene of savage violence, where the poet, quite distraught, is acrobatically savaged by high-hatted coachmen with whips and S.A. men disguised as pierrots, one of whom shoots him at the instigation

of his abandoned mistress. The choreography here was very effective, though the realism of the pistol shot and the bloody arm belongs surely to another stage than ballet. The final scene of apotheosis, 'Départ,' seems to have been inspired by that extraordinary autobiographical passage near the end of 'Mauvais Sang,' in *Une Saison en Enfer*. It is finely imagined by both Ashton and Beaton. This ballet raises again the question continually lurking in the background, of what music is suitable to dancing." [8]

"What you get is not beauty, nor significance, nor revelation, but just plain grossness." [9]

"[The poems] defy translation into dancing; their meaning is too esoteric, too personal. 'Antique' is the most realistic presentation of physical love yet seen in ballet. Much may be excused on the ground of dramatic effect; but this time the limit has been exceeded. True art is to suggest, not to imitate." [10]

"Ashton has certainly succeeded in a circuitous way in conveying some of the poet's bright vision, which combines naivete with a terrible sophistication. Beaton's ink-spattered townscapes and skyscapes form an appropriate décor, though his Pierrot costumes are almost too bizarre and pretty—one notices them too much. It is also harder to take in the choreography when everyone is dressed differently.

"I was not at all shocked by the exhibition of love-making, and its natural conclusion: but what does surprise me is that the idea of fitting a ballet, with dancing, décor, and dresses, to music which is already busy accompanying a poem should have been seriously considered. There is nothing wrong with dance accompanied by song, but these songs are unsuitable. The ballet occupies our attention to the exclusion of Rimbaud's words. To encumber the poems with a ballet was wasteful and an error of taste." [11]

PAS DE DEUX ROMANTIQUE

CHOREOGRAPHY: George Balanchine

MUSIC: Carl Maria von Weber (Concertino for Clarinet and Orchestra, 1811)

COSTUMES: Robert Stevenson

PREMIERE: 3 March 1950

CAST: Janet Reed, Herbert Bliss

This ballet proved something of an enigma to both audience and critics. Martin titled one of his columns "To Laugh or Not to Laugh"—and was unable to answer his own question. Critics in London were equally at a loss. Did Balanchine intend to be funny?

The choreographer told Chujoy that he had not intended a parody, but a stylization of the romantic pas de deux. If so, audience laughter was out of place.

Wrote Martin, "What to do? Balanchine is skating on very thin ice, indeed. This is too bad, for the choreography in itself is both brilliant and charming. . . . He has selected the music, followed it loyally in period, form, and flavor, and has dressed his two dancers in rhinestones galore. Nature, obviously, takes its course. It cannot avoid being funny." [1]

Terry: "I have been told that Balanchine casually compared it to the display tactics of the coloratura soprano. It is by no means a cartoon, for its fundamental style is true to tradition and its designs are quite as lovely as any you would find in a pas de deux by Petipa or by Balanchine himself in a serious vein. His humorous comments are to be found in wry sequences of movement; in repetitions of such pleasantly foolish conventions as the parading about of the ballerina by her cavalier or in their bowings and scrapings to each other; in resolutions of poses by means of overly complex hand signals and graspings and in the sweet vacuousness of expression with which the protagonists contemplate their assignments." [2]

England:

"The solo instrument in Weber's little Clarinet Concertino seems to be imitating the flowers of bel canto, to be taking all the principal parts in turn of a miniature opera, so it was an ingenious idea of Balanchine's to invent a *Pas de Deux Romantique* to go with it. The antics of passionate operatic lovers may seem tragic and sublime from one point of view, ridiculous from another: having chosen an impartial central position, Balanchine has backed far into the distance so that the lovers' frenzy seems less an expression of personal rapture and despair than the fulfillment of a preordained ritual common to the whole species. This is all a fanciful and roundabout way of saying that the pas de deux has a special quality that is easily missed: it is neither a display of spectacular dancing in the grand manner, nor is it a skit. It is a classical duet with suggestions of demi-caractère." [3]

JONES BEACH

CHOREOGRAPHY: George Balanchine and Jerome Robbins

MUSIC: Juriaan Andriessen (Berkshire Symphonies [Symphony No. 1 for orchestra], 1949, dedicated to Serge Koussevitsky)

COSTUMES: Jantzen

PREMIERE: 9 March 1950

CAST: *Sunday:* Melissa Hayden, Yvonne Mounsey, Beatrice Tompkins, Herbert Bliss, Frank Hobi, 22 women, 9 men; *Rescue from Drowning:* Tanaquil LeClercq, Nicholas Magallanes, 2 couples; *War with Mosquitoes:* William Dollar, Hobi, Tobias, 7 women; *Hot Dogs:* Maria Tallchief, Jerome Robbins, and full company

hate mosquitoes. I think if I give them free advertising, they may be kind to me later."—Balanchine

Possibly *that* was the motivation; the fact that Jantzen contributed the bathing suits also helped. Perhaps Robbins needed a new piece to work on; undoubtedly the company could use what Kirstein persistently refers to as "a novelty." In any case, there was an air of expediency to the proceedings, with results about what one would expect from such a mixture. Chujoy referred to this frolic as "a whimsical bit of what Diaghilev used to call 'ballet sportif.' The ballet is much too long for its scope, and the last two movements could be dropped. The second movement is the high spot. The company needed a closing ballet and this is it." [1]

Hering supplied somewhat more detail: " 'Sunday' pictured a huge group of attractive young people lolling and chatting, with the usual silly frolicking that one sees on a beach and several hilarious entrances and exits by Tompkins as an aggressive little female resolutely chasing a big handsome man. Then an almost classic solo for Hayden. 'Rescue' combined artificial respiration and love. Although the choreography often verged on the acrobatic, LeClercq has such an unfailing dramatic sense that her wilting rag-doll dance (with Magallanes tucking her hands between her shoulder blades and breathing into her mouth) seemed sweetly sad. In the third movement, seven pretty little female mosquitoes pricked their way daintily on toe shoes around three robust reclining males. A mighty battle ensued and ended with the men standing in triumph like big-game hunters over the inert form of—one mosquito. In the finale the choreographers resorted to the usual ballabile technique and only hinted at a boy and girl roasting and sharing a single hot dog, and a subsequent rivalry between said boy and his friend over the girl." [2]

Robbins describes the collaboration: "George asked if I would help him. I said fine, but how do we do it? We worked it out this way, and it's one of the most exciting experiences I've had. I was in one room working on one ballet, and he was in another room working on *Jones Beach*. He started it, did about one and a half or two minutes of the first movement, and gave the dancers a break. Then he came into my room and said, 'Okay, you pick up where I left off.' And so when they came back again, they ran through what they had done, and I just started right there, without any preparation, and went on for another minute and a half or two. I took a break and showed him what I had done, and *he* went on. It was his theory—absolutely valid at the time—that I should do more ballets; I was doing about one a year (I was also doing about a show a year). He'd say, 'Keep doing and keep doing, and every so often you'll do a great one.' He was trying to free me. We did the first movement that way, then we did the finale that way also. He did 'Mosquitoes' for three girls, then asked me to take it, and I changed it to three boys, which worked out better. And so we played in and out of each other's work, very elatingly. And the kids—the dancers—didn't know *what* was going on!"

In London, where a program note identified the locale as "a magnificent municipal beach resort within an hour's drive of New York City, created by the great Commissioner of Parks, Robert Moses," the ballet was received with about the same benign indulgence as in New York:

"Balanchine's idea comes from a symphony by Andriessen which suggested to him the 'vivacious nonsense that takes place among the young people at such a resort.' It is a light-hearted affair, particularly well suited to this company's penchant for the athletic and acrobatic, but though the movement is riotous and spontaneous in effect, there is an underlying sense of form which derives in the first place from Balanchine's scrupulous regard for the music's own tripartite planning throughout. This in the slow movement necessitates a dramatically illogical return to lifelessness with the recapitulation after a resuscitated middle section, but LeClercq, who is splendidly rescued by Magallanes, simulates unconsciousness with such pliant and willowy beauty of movement as to make truth a secondary concern." [3]

Jones Beach.

THE WITCH

CHOREOGRAPHY: John Cranko

MUSIC: Maurice Ravel (Piano Concerto No. 2 in G Major, 1931)

COSTUMES, DÉCOR: Dorothea Tanning

PREMIERE: 18 August 1950, Royal Opera House, Covent Garden, London

PIANO: Nicholas Kopeikine

CAST: *The Fair Girl*, Melissa Hayden; *Her Lover*, Francisco Moncion; *Owl Heads*, Robert Barnett, Michael Maule; *Bald Heads*, Edward Bigelow, Jacques d'Amboise; *Witches*, 8 women

The Witch was premiered in London, but, due to copyright problems, it was never seen in the United States. Hayden: "Cranko saw something in me that I myself didn't recognize . . . I think he perhaps intended a deeper meaning than what he explained to me. At any rate, for me, the Girl was innocent of the evil powers that she had—I might even have been a personification of Woman. There is an opening pas de deux—highly erotic, full of the complicated lifts and almost acrobatic movements Cranko later became known for, as well as suggestive ones, such as rolling on the floor. All of a sudden, out of the woodwork, strange witch-like creatures appear, and the Girl is surrounded by them and is transformed from a peasant into a witch herself. Then there is an interlude with ghoulish figures—like monkeys—in which I am torn apart and thrown through the air, and I become frantic. There is also a mirror image—a sequence where the Girl and the Lover dance together, and behind a scrim two dancers copy the movements. At the end of the ballet I am again in my peasant dress. The Lover dies, but the Girl can't free herself from him."

Critics were not notably enthusiastic. Most felt the treatment rather histrionic and the choice of music poor. Wrote Buckle, with his customary panache: "This ballet, which sits with some incongruity on Ravel's Second Piano Concerto, is another variation on the Gothick nightmare theme. Two lovers have a rendezvous at the ruined castle of Otranto—which turns out surprisingly to be built of red brick. The evil spirits who haunt the place infect the girl with their black magic so that she becomes a vampire and kills her beloved with a kiss. Formal beauties tend to go by the board when choreographers try to be gruesome and frightening, and it hardly matters how badly one dances if one is wearing an owl mask and a dead flamingo on one's skirt. There is no denying Cranko's talent but he must invent four classical ballets to Mozart before indulging in any more romantic expressionism." [1]

MAZURKA FROM "A LIFE FOR THE TSAR"

CHOREOGRAPHY: George Balanchine

MUSIC: Mikhail Glinka (1836)

COSTUMES: Karinska

LIGHTING: Jean Rosenthal

PREMIERE: 30 November 1950

DANCERS: Janet Reed and Yurek Lazowski (guest artist); Vida Brown and George Balanchine; Barbara Walczak and Harold Lang; Dorothy Dushok and Frank Hobi

This brief interlude was a pure character work, the kind of thing that would serve as court divertissement in a full-length classical evening. Possibly Balanchine was prompted by the presence of Lazowski, an outstanding character dancer, and Lang. He himself performed on opening night—to an ovation.

Reviews mentioned the ebullience of the performers, the attractive costumes, and the general gaiety of the proceedings. According to Chujoy, Balanchine had last appeared on stage in Mexico City, 1945.

SYLVIA: PAS DE DEUX

CHOREOGRAPHY: George Balanchine

MUSIC: Léo Delibes (1876)

COSTUMES: Karinska

Sylvia: Pas de Deux. **Maria Tallchief, André Eglevsky.** (*Photo Fred Fehl.*)

PREMIERE: 1 December 1950

CAST: Maria Tallchief, Nicholas Magallanes

OTHER CASTS: Melissa Hayden, Allegra Kent, Patricia Wilde, Jacques d'Amboise, Herbert Bliss, André Eglevsky

Sylvia was clearly designed around Tallchief's technical virtuosity. Not long after its premiere, Eglevsky made his debut with the Company in this ballet (17 February 1951), and Tallchief found a partner whose bravura dancing matched her own. The two performed the ballet together all over the world (Eglevsky also made his final appearance with the Company nine years later in *Sylvia*), and both remember it as one of their most beautiful and exciting vehicles. Says Tallchief, in admiration: "George always found Delibes music very danceable (as do I). André was incredible; I don't know anyone else who could have done it. The steps, the partnering, the timing—turns, balances, promenades—it was a tour de force. [Balanchine] incorporated for me some very lovely ports de bras that were reminiscent of a French style (rather than the grand Russian manner one might expect in a virtuoso pas de deux). It was charming, with different-looking steps that were still purely classical. It was a wonderful and very artistic showpiece."

Eglevsky: "It was such an elegant thing. The girl's variation was exquisite. In the coda, Maria did a series of relevé turns en attitude en avant with arms closed at unbelievable speed—unbelievable—and clean, clean, clean!"

Wrote Hering, "Only a master stylist like Balanchine could take the hackneyed *Sylvia* ballet music and choreograph it so exquisitely that it sounded as pearly fresh as the day it was written!" [1]

Terry wrote of *Sylvia*'s undeniable excitement ("greeted with shouts of delight") and of its value in a repertory: "A new grand pas de deux—complete with entree, adagio, two solos and coda—has been sorely needed in the profession. The old favorites, such as those known as Black Swan and Bluebird or the extracts from 'Nutcracker' and *Don Quixote*, have delighted audiences for a half-century but even they need respite from repertories from time to time. Yet a grand pas de deux, a really grand one, is almost an essential item in any company's roster of ballets, for it is the dance equivalent of the opera's coloratura aria, the drama's soliloquy, the circus's top aerial act. In *Sylvia* the ballerina balances endlessly (and breathtakingly) on pointe, accomplishes multiple turns, turns in a batch of entrechats-huit (even the men dancers rarely do more than six), bounces on toe, and does everything short of back-flips. Yet all the tricks are strictly balletic, threaded together into lovely patterns and resolved into aristocratic dance. Balanchine has not only augmented traditionally spectacular actions with fresh steps, but he has also added further spice to the occasion by making the whole work rich in rhythmic variety. Furthermore, it ranges, dynamically, from the delicate to the forceful and it treats with accents which are at times gentle and at other times dramatic in their percussiveness. Tallchief responded to every item of choreographic demand in a performance which surely represented a supreme example of virtuosity and a superior manifestation of classic beauty. In her solo, Pizzicato Polka, or in the lovely adagio with her partner or in the final flashing coda, she made one conscious of dance strength and dance beauty, of effortlessness, of complete command of a magnificently disciplined body. So superb was she that technical definitions fled the mind and the beholder was simply content to describe her performance in one word, 'Wow!' " [2]

Italy:
"The pas de deux from the highly celebrated *Sylvia* of Delibes, a sample of the most elegant and fantastic virtuosity, whose place in a ballet is like a brilliant cadenza in a sonata, recalled for a moment that flowery period of dance which excited the muses of the poets and turned the heads of rulers and financiers." [3]

PAS DE TROIS

CHOREOGRAPHY: George Balanchine

MUSIC: Leon Minkus (from *Paquita*, 1881)

COSTUMES: Karinska

PREMIERE: 18 February 1951 (first presented 1948 by Grand Ballet du Marquis de Cuevas in somewhat different form)

CAST: Nora Kaye, Maria Tallchief, André Eglevsky

OTHER CASTS: Melissa Hayden, Allegra Kent, Patricia Wilde

Another display piece happily fulfilling its function—to delight and excite.

"Nobody could carp about Balanchine's

Pas de Trois. **Maria Tallchief, Melissa Hayden (kneeling), André Eglevsky.** (*Photo Fred Fehl.*)

wonderful *Pas de Trois*, for it pretends to nothing but sheer 'danciness,' and dancing it to the hilt were Tallchief, Eglevsky, and Kaye, stomping happily to the corny music." [1]

"Not so exciting as *Sylvia*, it is nevertheless a spectacular tour de force which makes great demands on the dancers and gives the public its money's worth. Eglevsky evoked a storm of applause with his very first soubresaut battu (or was it a cabriole?) high in the air, hanging there for seconds." [2]

"Such a performance could make even the most jaded believe wholeheartedly in the genius of all concerned—Balanchine, the dancers, and even Minkus, whose middle-class but thoroughly danceable score took on the brilliance of the whole." [3]

Hayden describes the choreography: "It had Cecchetti-type choreography with lots of recognizable classroom steps. The feeling was bouncy and light, with many small jumps and runs. The first female variation was very quick, finishing with very fast piqué, piqué, chainé, chainé, chainé, entrechat-six, arabesque. The second variation had many more balances, beginning with big beats. One particularly difficult step for the ballerina was a kind of sissonne in penché, very deep, coming up to pointe in attitude. No one's ever really done it outside the studio. At the end we all did Cecchetti ballonnés

across stage. It was great fun to dance and most effective. The Glinka Pas de Trois, for instance, was more difficult but not as showy."

LA VALSE

CHOREOGRAPHY: George Balanchine

MUSIC: Maurice Ravel (*Valses Nobles et Sentimentales,* 1911, orchestrated 1912; *La Valse,* 1920)

COSTUMES: Karinska

LIGHTING: Jean Rosenthal

PREMIERE: 20 February 1951

CAST: VALSES NOBLES ET SENTIMENTALES: *First Waltz:* overture; *Second Waltz:* Vida Brown, Edwina Fontaine, Jillana; *Third Waltz:* Patricia Wilde, Frank Hobi; *Fourth Waltz:* Yvonne Mounsey, Michael Maule; *Fifth Waltz:* Diana Adams, Herbert Bliss; *Sixth Waltz:* Adams; *Seventh Waltz:* Bliss, Brown, Fontaine, Jillana; *Eighth Waltz:* Tanaquil LeClercq, Nicholas Magallanes; LA VALSE: LeClercq, Magallanes, Francisco Moncion; 16 women, 9 men

REVIVAL: 1 May 1962

CAST: *Eighth Waltz* and *La Valse,* Patricia McBride, Nicholas Magallanes, Francisco Moncion; other variations, Victoria Simon and Michael Lland; Carol Sumner and Richard Rapp; Jillana and Bill Carter

OTHER CASTS: *Eighth Waltz* and *La Valse:* Suzanne Farrell, Sara Leland, Kay Mazzo, Maria Tallchief; Jean-Pierre Bonnefous, Richard Hoskinson

I had intended this as a kind of apotheosis of the Viennese waltz, linked, in my mind, with the impression of 'un tournoiement fantastique et fatale.' "—Ravel

As a ballet, *La Valse*, with its dramatic overtones and rich atmospheric effects, marked a departure for Balanchine—or perhaps, as Chujoy suggests, a return to a vein of feeling he had abandoned many years before:

"If any choreographer can be credited with creating a new style in classic ballet, it is, of course, Balanchine. And if one must have a label for Balanchine's style, it could be called neo-classic with excellent justification. In *La Valse*, however, Balanchine has chosen a different style. If we still want labels, neo-romantic would suit nicely. Balanchine's *Cotillon*, to Chabrier's music, was more or less in that style. *La Valse* is permeated with the spirit of the romantic period of the 1830s and still more with the sense of futility which pervaded Europe some thirty years ago, when Ravel wrote the music, and which, justifiably or not, makes itself felt at the present time. 'We are dancing on the edge of a volcano,' Ravel quoted Comte de Salvandy in his notes to *La Valse*, and this short statement is the underlying motif of both the music and the choreography.

"Structurally, Balanchine has used seven of the eight *Valses Nobles et Sentimentales* as an approach to his main theme, expressed in *La Valse* proper, and to establish the various figures who later take part in the denouement of his theme. Choreographically, each of the seven waltzes is different in mood and style, all of them are integral parts of a mounting feeling of restlessness, at some times hidden, at others apparent, but never obviously justified until they culminate in a grand ball with all the couples 'dancing on the edge of a volcano.' Death finally enters in the form of a man dressed all in black (Moncion), who presents black jewels to a dancer all in white (LeClercq), dresses her in black, and dances her to death. If at some moments in the middle of *La Valse* the ballet seems on the verge of falling to pieces, it is not an accident or a choreographic mistake of Balanchine. It was Ravel himself who wrote about the disintegration of the waltz. All Balanchine did was to follow the music and give it a choreographic justification." [1]

Martin wrote of the ballet's fascination: "The movement themes, the wisps of character, the hints of piquant decadence that are established in the sequence of waltzes are developed steadily to the macabre climax, when the scene itself has become an overpoweringly sickly hedonism, a dainty madness. If it is all extraordinarily beautiful to look at, rich in invention and eloquent in gesture, sumptuous in costume and voluptuous to the ear, there is nevertheless a deceptive power beneath its surface that carries a real emotional wallop." [2]

Hering described more of the action: "The whole dance is done with a shrug of the shoulder and a toss of the head that camouflage the most intricate of choreographic detail. There is a blasé trio with

La Valse. Left: **Tanaquil LeClercq, Francisco Moncion.** (*Photo Walter E. Owen.*) ***Right:*** **Eighth Waltz. Suzanne Farrell, Nicholas Magallanes.** (*Photo Martha Swope.*)

much hand-posturing; a sparkling pas de deux for Wilde and Hobi; an airy one for Mounsey and Maule. Adams and Bliss strike a note of delicacy and refinement in their duet, and they seem to make contact with each other on a human level. But this is torn asunder by the re-entrance of the three first figures, who surround Bliss and finally leave him in isolation. All the couples who have thus far danced skitter across the stage like dry leaves and leave in their wake the final couple, LeClercq and Magallanes, who carry the mood progression to a state of decadent sophistication.

"Diaphanous curtains part to reveal a huge space backed by tall black archways made of floating fabric and lighted with clusters of tiny lights. In this area of Cocteau-like splendor, dancers dart and whirl in great masses of intoxicating color. Crimsons, pinks, oranges, violets, and white emanate from their underskirts and are punctuated by the gleaming black waistcoats and tights of the men. Suddenly, in the midst of the fevered activity, a dark figure enters. It is death, and he chooses the decadent girl in white as his partner. She dies and is carried off the stage by her lover, only to be brought on again and held aloft while the crowd continues its heedless whirling." [3]

One moment, the beginning of *La Valse* proper, was closely observed by Croce: "The waltz itself begins like a movie out of focus. It is very dark and everything is in disarray. We still don't know where to look. Dancers—one, then in twos and threes—cross and recross the stage like

swallows. A boy arrives looking for his partner. On a sudden premonition he turns and a spotlight picks out the deadly trio standing completely still at the back of the stage. (Have they been there all along?) Again they are blind, one arm covering their eyes, the other flung to the heavens. They look like crosses in a graveyard.[*] He approaches and they seize him. Now a line of boys runs on, and with them, we scan some mysteriously far-off horizon, which begins to pitch and dip as if in a landing on the moon. Then, as the mists clear, a line of girls. They find the boys just in time, for with a mighty crescendo the stage suddenly rights itself, we touch down, and everything coalesces in a smash of *luxe, calme et volupté*. But only for a moment." [4]

La Valse may have been the quintessential role of LeClercq, not only for its angular sophistication and doomed half-innocence, which she was superbly equipped to project, but for the eerie parallel between her waltz with Death and her real-life paralysis from polio in 1956. She recalls her feelings about the ballet:

"I just adored it. First of all, I liked to watch in the wings before I came on, watch the other people, watch the costumes. I found that it got me in the mood to look at the other people waltzing around, with the gloves—they looked so pretty. So I would come out and do the first variation [Eighth Waltz]—the atmosphere was lovely, it was like going to a

---

* Terry saw them as "the three Fates in the guise of courtesans."

party. There wasn't anything terribly hard in the variation, and yet you could work within what you had and make it different. Balanchine said to think of German-style contractions for it—a feeling for 'plastique.' For the La Valse section, the dramatic mood grew completely out of the steps—he didn't say anything about acting or reacting at all. He doesn't usually. You just do the steps somehow, with the expression that he demonstrates. Today [1974], the steps have changed; I think perhaps there is more dancing and less posing in the variation. The second part is the same, and the impact of both is the same.

"I felt that my character put on the [black] jewelry, looked at herself in the mirror and really liked it, was rather eager to plunge into the gloves, then got the coat and thought how fabulous, and began to waltz away—almost mindlessly."

Denby writes of her magical articulation while being dressed by Death; indelible also is her motion of drawing back in fascinated horror as she first views herself in Death's mirror, clothed in black. "The way I remember Tanny's marvelous gesture of putting on the [long black] gloves was that when she put her hand into the glove she threw up her head at the same time, so that it was a kind of immolation, you felt, like diving to destruction. That's what the atmosphere is about. The difficulty was, how do I get my hand into that glove without seeing where I'm putting it? It was a very interesting theatrical problem. My memory tells me that she never even looked at the glove, but that's really impossible. So she must have been able to look at the glove without any emphasis and then put her whole emphasis on diving into it, including the movement with her head." [5]

Haggin, considerably less taken than most, felt that LeClercq's theatrical presence was the chief justification for the ballet, which he called "sheer nothingness. What Balanchine did was to bring into operation his extraordinary powers as a theater artist, and to create with the color of costumes in a play of darkness and light the excitement there would not be in the movement alone." Her duet with Magallanes he termed "strangely perverse." [6]

Moncion, although not so named in the program, was specifically called "Death" by Balanchine. The dancer recalls that "Balanchine definitely asked me if I wanted to be Death. The quality Tanny gave to the character was a kind of discon-

tent and then an avidity—not really greed—for reaching out to something new, a discontent not assuaged by the man she has met [Eighth Waltz]. Somehow, with the Death figure, it is the allure of the unknown that tantalizes her. She clutches the necklace, tries it on, and suddenly something fulfilling begins to happen. She looks into the broken mirror, which distorts her, and recoils. Always Death is leading her, leading her—at that point she's completely mesmerized. . . . Sometimes Balanchine watches things for years without saying anything, then makes a change. Just a short time ago [1974], he said to me, 'You know, I've always wanted to have the figure of Death somewhere in the first section as a premonition'—many people have felt there should be an inkling of his presence—so now, twenty years later, there is a special place for him in the Eighth Waltz. The figure appears from nowhere in the spotlight, suddenly and only for a moment, just as she is going off, and it's very frightening. Balanchine was pleased."

In 1962, the ballet, which had been abruptly dropped when LeClercq became ill, was revived. As if to continue the spell, there was a death in McBride's family while she was learning the role. McBride brought to it an otherworldly, almost vampire-like characterization, with a quality of sophistication that Leland also found; Mazzo and Farrell played the role more as an innocent young girl. *La Valse* was performed during the Company's Ravel Festival in the spring of 1975.

London critics barely nodded at *La Valse;* those in Italy enjoyed it; and the German reviewers seemed to identify with tragic and sinister undertones.

London:
"The evocative music was a strange choice for so meticulous, neo-classically minded a choreographer as Balanchine and, in the event, not a very successful choice. Some of the groups are poetic and striking; but the mystery of *La Valse* and the wistfulness of certain of the *valses* are not suggested." [7]

Italy:
"There is a current of foreboding and regret, until the finale, ablaze, signals the overflowing of repressed emotion. The choreographic effect derives from contin-

uous, ingenious, ever-new variations on the waltz, building to a climax with a rush of suggestive movements, of a drama not quite expressed." [8]

Germany:
"A poetic interpretation of Ravel's own homage to Vienna, what Erich Kleiber called 'waltzes poisoned with absinthe.' " [9]

LADY OF THE CAMELIAS

CHOREOGRAPHY: Antony Tudor

MUSIC: Giuseppe Verdi (selections from five early operas)

After the novel of Alexandre Dumas fils

COSTUMES, DÉCOR: Cecil Beaton

LIGHTING: Jean Rosenthal

PREMIERE: 28 February 1951

CAST: *Marguerite Gautier,* Diana Adams; *Armand Duval,* Hugh Laing; *Armand's Father,* John Earle (Antony Tudor); *Prudence,* Vida Brown; *M. le Comte de N.,* Brooks Jackson; *Guests,* 4 women, 5 men

Scene 1. Paris, 1848. Party *chez* Prudence.
Scene 2. In the country two months later.
Scene 3. Paris. Several months later.
Scene 4. Marguerite's bedroom.

The Company wanted a vehicle for its newly arrived stars, Adams and Laing, and it had in its possession some elaborate Beaton costumes and scenery. These and the Camille story they handed over to Tudor; he selected the musical excerpts.

Tudor found the package uncongenial: "When you take a narrative like that you're bound to have something rather formless as a dancing structure. And then you're saddled with telling a whole story."

Reviewers mentioned that much of the action unfolded in gesture; says Tudor, "Once you get into those big crinolines, it's difficult to move. I wanted the partygoers just to float around very quietly; the dancers had trouble *dancing* my movements. There were really only two dance sections: the death scene and a pas de deux when they'd gone to the country.

Lady of the Camelias. Diana Adams, Hugh Laing. (*Photo Walter E. Owen.*)

I liked that very much."

In this the critics all concurred; the pas de deux was the highlight. Martin: "[Here] echoes of the old romantic ballet style combine with free gesture to create an enchanting moment of rapturous young love."[1]

Terry: "Tudor's familiar use of movement to penetrate the feelings of the heart was much in evidence [in the pas de deux]. Gestures of tenderness, some gently sweet and others playful, were mated with larger actions indicative of soaring happiness, of surging love. The death scene, too, with its faltering solo and its brief and sad duet, communicated emotional values clearly and, to a degree, affectingly." He found the rest "curiously uneven. As a dramatic entity it is weak in its present form, for one leaves the theater with the feeling that he has seen a few absorbing fragments from the romantic adventure of two ill-starred individuals surrounded by characterless figures who impede and clutter up the presentation of a duet."[2]

Chujoy also mentioned the fragmentary nature of the treatment, but attributed this to the short time available to Tudor (who is known to prefer a long preparation period). For Martin, what he called the "dialogue of movement" was in the beginning quite arresting: "In effect, a choreographed novel of the late nineteenth century. It contains a minimum of pure dance; its action unfolds in terms of what might be called abstract dialogue, varying from a hint of the formal

miming of the nineteenth-century ballet, through fairly natural gesture, to a heightened expressiveness of inward feeling when the situation touches deeper emotional levels. There could scarcely be a more inspired method of approaching the story of *Camille*. Tudor has caught the period and the conventions of the novel superbly, and has translated them bodily into a new medium."[3]

Later, he found it "unconvincing."

Says Tudor, "I wasn't doing the ballet for myself; I was doing it for the costumes and scenery, I was doing it for Diana and Hugh. I was a short-order cook."

CAPRICCIO BRILLANTE

CHOREOGRAPHY: George Balanchine

MUSIC: Felix Mendelssohn (*Capriccio Brillante* for piano and orchestra, op. 22, 1825–26)

COSTUMES: Karinska

LIGHTING: Jean Rosenthal

PREMIERE: 7 June 1951

PIANO: Nicholas Kopeikine

CAST: Maria Tallchief and André Eglevsky; Barbara Bocher, Constance Garfield, Jillana, Irene Larsson

Ballerina role later danced by Tanaquil LeClercq

In *Capriccio Brillante*, says LeClercq, the piano was on stage and the dancers were grouped around it, wearing tutus of black and white—like piano keys. "Because it was for Maria, her variation and every exit were *full* of turns." The ballet seemed clearly to have been whipped up to fill a repertory gap somewhere.

Wrote Martin, "Another of those service pieces that circumstances require from Balanchine every so often. It is not especially capricious, nor, truth to tell, especially brilliant, but it has taste and integrity and is admirably performed."[1]

For Terry it was "Sweet and neat —even ingenious at times. It is small, and Balanchine has not been pretentious. He has created an incident rather than a ballet."[2]

Chujoy: "A great deal of choreographic invention, which at times is too subtle and intricate to reach the general spectator. It is a dancers' ballet if there ever was one."[3]

CAKEWALK

CHOREOGRAPHY: Ruthanna Boris

MUSIC: Louis Moreau Gottschalk (7 short pieces) and 3 minstrel tunes (as below), adapted and orchestrated by Hershy Kay (1951)

COSTUMES, DÉCOR: Robert Drew (from *Blackface*) and Keith Martin (from *The Bat*)

LIGHTING: Jean Rosenthal

PREMIERE: 12 June 1951

CAST: *Interlocutor* and *Louis, the Illusionist,* Frank Hobi; *Endmen* and *Moreau* and *Lesseau,* Tanaquil LeClercq, Beatrice Tompkins; *Wallflower* and *Hortense, Queen of the Swamp Lilies,* Janet Reed; *Freebee Leader* and *Wild Pony,* Patricia Wilde; *Venus* (attended by *Three Graces*), Yvonne Mounsey; *Harolde, the Young Poet,* Herbert Bliss; *Auxiliary Ladies and Gentlemen,* 8 women, 2 men

OTHER CASTS: *Interlocutor,* Roy Tobias; *Wallflower,* Boris, Barbara Fallis, Tompkins; *Freebee,* Carolyn George; *Venus,* Irene Larsson; *Harolde,* Stanley Zompakos

IN THE FIRST PART
"Grand Introductory Walkaround"
"Wallflower Waltz"
"Sleight of Feet" (Interlocutor)
"Perpendicular Points" (Endmen)
"Freebee"
"Skipaway" (all)
PART SECOND
by Louis the Illusionist, assisted by Moreau and Lesseau, and featuring Venus and her Three Graces, a Wild Pony, and Hortense and her lover, Harolde
PART THIRD
Gala Cakewalk (in which all are invited to participate)

Cakewalk was quite a departure for the Company in both style and substance. According to Hershy Kay, the entire score was based on the cakewalk rhythm. The following melodies (all by Gottschalk except for the minstrel tunes) were used:

Grand Walkaround, "Bamboula"; Wallflower Waltz, "Won't You Buy My Pretty Flowers?" (minstrel); Sleight of Feet, "Josiphus Orange Blossom," and "Adolphus Morning Glory" (both minstrel); Perpendicular Points, "La Gallina"; Part Second (Venus, Wild Pony, Hortense and Harolde pas de deux), "Marche des Giberos," "The Maiden's Blush," "Orpha," "The Water Sprite"; Gala Cakewalk, "Pasquinade." Gottschalk, a New Orleans-born American of mixed European parentage, achieved spectacular popularity during the last century on his concert tours throughout America, playing his own piano compositions and conducting his orchestral works, while shunning Beethoven and other concert masters. His unusual and original compositions made lavish use of Creole and other American folk themes and rhythms. He and his music were just as spectacularly forgotten after his death.

Boris describes her detailed research: "Lincoln asked me to do a ballet: 'I don't care *what* it is,' he said, 'but please try to do it in costume. If we do *one* more ballet in leotards, they'll kill us.' In the warehouse I came across the costumes from *Blackface*, which had been a very serious ballet about black and white in the South in the antebellum period, and when I saw them, the idea of *Cakewalk*—a classical ballet in the form of a minstrel show—was

born. Since I needed more people, we used *Bat* dresses also, with decorations sewn on by me. (On opening night Lincoln was sitting in the back winding flowers around the swing.)

"I knew I needed music with an early American feeling, but *not* Stephen Foster. Lincoln suggested Gottschalk, whom nobody had heard of then—except for Balanchine, because Gottschalk had been famous in Russia. I did a lot of research on minstrels and discovered that around the period of *Giselle* [1842], minstrel shows were putting on caricatures of this kind of ballet. Hortense, Queen of the Swamp Lilies, is a kind of *Giselle*. And of course everybody was very busy with necrophilia in those days. Finally, I found a lady in her eighties who had been a cakewalk dancer and I took some lessons from her."

Critics seemed to have a good time. Audiences have been enjoying the ballet for years (in this and other repertories). The reviews show why.

Terry: "Breezy and witty—a really fine bit of Americana, a lusty folk ballet which translates something of the form, the characteristics, and the genial boisterousness of the old minstrel show into the dance language of the contemporary theater. The cast, whether they are cake-walking or not, [all] employ the vocabulary of ballet. What Boris has done, however, is to color these move-

ments with the inflections and the accents of folk dance, with the rhythms and mannerisms of the minstrel show. The result is a theater piece which is polished but sturdy, rich in humor and (for some) nostalgia, imaginative and irresistibly good-natured.

"There is no story to *Cakewalk*, but incidents and specialties tumble one upon the other with fine generosity. The Interlocutor, of course, supervises all and the Ends keep discipline on the distant flanks, but these three also have opportunities to dance as well as to introduce such wonderful numbers as The Wallflower Waltz, Sleight of Feet, Freebee, the dances of the Wild Pony or Hortense, Queen of the Swamp Lilies, and inevitably the mass cakewalk. Minstrel music of Gottschalk provided the dancers not only with superb support but also seemed to drive them to dance, such were the infectious rhythms of the score." [1]

Hering: "Boris made generous use of the open-hearted and frankly sentimental flavor of the minstrel period, and she received inspired cooperation from Kay's orchestration of music by Gottschalk. To froggy horns, foolish tambourines, and tearful calliope effects, the dancers cavorted through a series of charming genre pieces. The prize was The Wallflower Waltz, a wilting solo for Reed. While all of the other dancers performed their solos eagerly, none of them equalled Reed in achieving the perfect balance between satire and good old corn. Wilde was a bit too much the ballerina in her leading of the Freebee, but she later redeemed herself as a headstrong pony in a solo that contrasted delightfully with Mounsey's handsome and commanding Venus tableau and Reed's moon-bathed pas de deux with Bliss. Again Reed managed just the right tongue-in-cheek quality—this time a blending of Taglioni and Mary Pickford. As a company, New York City Ballet needs works like *Cakewalk*. For it requires them to drop their elegance and restraint and romp like vaudevillians." [2] Other highlights were a solo featuring Hobi's deft and tricky footwork, which he tossed off with insouciance, and a duet for the Endmen (one tall, one short, both sleek in long black tights) that was resolutely "tongue-twisting" in its perverse shifts from tip toe to flat foot.

Almost all the reviewers urged some cutting, however; and during the next year, Boris shortened and revised.

Cakewalk. Patricia Wilde, Frank Hobi. (*Photo Fred Fehl.*)

The English took to the ballet even more, reacting to the American subject: "A tremendously enjoyable new piece. Not a neo-classical abstraction, nor an orgy of symbolism; it is a period piece called *Cakewalk*, and it sets out to amuse; it amuses—hugely. An old-time concert party is the subject. Ladies and gentlemen cavort with an exuberance almost indecent on a stuffy evening. Sparkle is really the mark of *Cakewalk*. It is of the genre of *Rodeo* and *Billy the Kid*, vivid, unspoiled, and ebullient. And since these are some of America's, and the company's, most endearing characteristics, *Cakewalk* may be claimed as a happy contribution to the national dance. . . . Lively choreography, gay décor, and a splendidly vulgar score, brilliantly orchestrated." [3]

"Evokes a minstrel entertainment in Mississippi showboat tradition. Really belonging in a music hall, it includes burlesques of old-style 'turns,' which, if trite in humor, are entertaining for their period atmosphere." [4]

THE CAGE

CHOREOGRAPHY: Jerome Robbins

MUSIC: Igor Stravinsky (Concerto in D for string orchestra, "Basler," 1946)

COSTUMES: Ruth Sobotka

LIGHTING: Jean Rosenthal

PREMIERE: 14 June 1951

CAST: *The Novice*, Nora Kaye; *The Queen*, Yvonne Mounsey; *The Intruders*, Nicholas Magallanes, Michael Maule; *The Group*, 12 women

OTHER CASTS: *Novice*, Melissa Hayden, Allegra Kent, Gelsey Kirkland, Tanaquil LeClercq, Patricia McBride; *Queen*, Gloria Govrin, Janice Groman, Una Kai, Irene Larsson, Patricia Neary, Sallie Wilson; *Intruders*, Bart Cook, Robert Maiorano, John Mandia, Francisco Moncion, Richard Rapp, Roy Tobias

There occurs in certain forms of insect and animal life, and even in our own mythology, the phenomenon of the female of the species considering the male as prey. The ballet concerns such a race or cult" (program note).

"I don't see why some people are so shocked by *The Cage*. If you observe closely you must realize that it is actually not more than the second act of *Giselle* in a contemporary visualization."—Robbins

Despite Robbins's 1951 disclaimer, *The Cage* provoked a lot of controversy, particularly in Europe, where there was an official attempt to ban it in The Hague (unsuccessful). As late as 1966, Barnes called it "a repulsive bit of misemployed genius," suggesting that, for some, the shock has not diminished with the passage of years. The ballet was part of the Stravinsky Festival in 1972 and continues to be performed—giving it a lifespan of most respectable proportions. The role of the Novice was a personal triumph for Kaye (and Hayden would later enjoy a great success in the part).

The ballet had the impact of an onrushing train; both Chujoy and Martin felt it to be Robbins's best work.

Chujoy called it "Tremendously exciting, beautiful in the savagery of its contents, thrilling in its choreographic development." [1]

Martin: "More compact in design, more inventive in movement, more devastating in dramatic power than anything that has preceded it. It is stimulating to have an artist speak out with such unbridled venom; the courage to be honest, even though unpleasant, is all too rare. Robbins now seems likely to become the first major choreographer in the native field." [2]

Terry commented more specifically: "Either of two distinct vocabularies (both English) would serve to describe it. The first might be used in an Army barracks; the second might be heard at a seminar concerned with the science and the philosophy of antagonism existing between the sexes. The second would be more suitable to a discussion of a work of art, savage as it may be in its comment upon an aspect of sexual behaviour. There is no discernible protest against matriarchy, the current topic of 'momism,' or the powerful place of woman in modern society. Subtlety of such nature is absent, for *The Cage* deals not so much with woman as with the female and, specifically, with those species of female, real or imagined, which destroy the male. The ballet does not specify the insect, the animal, or the human, although attributes of each are indicated in the movements. Rather is the work a primitive ceremonial which cele-

brates with a certain aloof frenzy this terrifying digression from the accepted social pattern of modern man. It is as forthrightly primitive—perhaps primal would be a better word—as, say, Martha Graham's *Dark Meadow*, but it has no sweetness in its treating with sex because, unlike the Graham work, it lacks love and hope. It is, instead, a rite of blood and destruction and eternal hate.

"The stage for *The Cage* is designed to suggest a great web, a snare. The female dancers too wear costumes which hint at the glittering lights of the insect shell, which accentuate the length of weapon-like arms and legs. In this setting, lighted in somber mysteriousness, and with these brief and tight costumes, the female dancers move. A ceremony is underway. The Queen, a compelling amazon, regal in stature, strong in action, conducts the rite and removes the mask, or is it a cocoon? or a shell? from the face of the Novice. The ceremony continues. Wild, strange and perfectly ordered. An Intruder enters. The Novice strangles him by pressing her knees against his neck until he is dead. A second Intruder enters, handsome and virile. The Novice hesitates. Does she tease him or is she tempted to succumb? The Queen, however, drives her to the kill and the alien is destroyed, the community of females secure.

"Robbins has created a startling, unpleasant but wholly absorbing theater piece. The movements, with a few exceptions, are not only pertinent to the theme but they drive its meaning to the fore with passion and clarity. Not since Doris Humphrey's *The Life of the Bee* has a choreographer been so successful in depicting and evoking the communal existence, fascinating and somewhat fearsome, of nonhuman life. His group designs, deep and acute of line, are in themselves exciting, and the drama which springs from them cuts like a knife, burns like a sting. *The Cage* was designed for the unique dramatic gifts of Kaye, and she dances the Novice with ferocious brilliance. Except for her moment of temptation, she is frighteningly inhuman, provocative, and glitteringly feral." [3]

Many years later, indicating that the force of the ballet was undiminished, Mishkin was able to write this judgment: "With a stage setting consisting of nothing but a variety of varicolored strings hanging down from the flies, suggesting a cobweb, and with Hayden giving an almost incredibly electrifying performance as the

The Cage. **The Group.** (*Photo Martha Swope.*)

Novice (supposedly an insect emerging from its chrysalis and then coming to maturity with the seizure of a male Intruder), *The Cage* stood as a superb, if grim and at times even revolting work. But as somebody once noted in another connection, life in the raw is seldom mild." [4]

In 1955, Robbins discussed in some detail a few of the sources of his theme, interpretation, and specific movement. It took over a year after hearing the music for the subject matter to come to him, and the treatment took longer still. Says he, "Its conception was not deliberate or conscious—a series of things came together at the right time." "It all began (or at least the spark that touched off the creative explosions was applied) when Robbins bought a recording of Stravinsky's *Apollon Musagète*, which happened to have the *Concerto in D for Strings* on the other side. When Robbins played this, his reaction was: 'What a dramatic work this is!' He felt that Stravinsky must have had a dramatic plan in the music, although he knew that this was probably not true in a literal sense. But there was something 'terribly driven, coerced, compelled' in the music. He was overwhelmed by the economy of the score—not a wasted bar. He conceived of the first movement as

militaristic, defiant, full of challenge. The second was the expression of love and tenderness, of individual human emotion. In the third there was a melodramatic chase, action, pursuit, and final solution. There were the general concepts on which the structure was built.

"At least part of the inspiration for the subject material came from a dancer. But interestingly enough, not from the artist who first took the role of the Novice and made it her own. At the time when *The Cage* was first being conceived, Kaye was not a member of the New York City Ballet, and some of the things that went into the work were originally suggested by the personality and development of LeClercq, who did not dance the part of the Novice until long after Kaye had made it famous. As Robbins explains, 'I am very touched by the people I work with, and I am very sensitive to LeClercq's dancing. In those days, her movement had a quality that made me think of a young animal coming into its own, like a gauche young colt, soon to become a graceful thoroughbred. There was a kind of aura about her, the spirit of the adolescent emerging into the sensitive woman.' It was from these impressions that he struck upon the idea of a novice initiated into a primitive cult, an idea which was to play such an impor-

tant part in the ballet. Later, when the role was created by Kaye, who had joined the company meanwhile, her 'terrific drive and forcefulness and difference of personality gave it a different coloring.'

" 'It arrived as a whole concept in my head,' [said Robbins]. 'It's about a tribe of women. A young girl, a novice, is to be initiated. She doesn't yet know her duties and capacities as a member of the tribe nor is she aware of her innate instincts. She falls in love with a man and mates with him. But the rules of the tribe demand his death. She refuses to kill him but she is again ordered to fulfill her duty, and when his blood actually flows, her animal instincts are aroused and she rushes forward to complete the sacrifice. Her affection yields to her tribal instinct.' It was only when the ballet was almost completed that Robbins realized that it 'touched a hidden unconscious sense of animalistic destruction usually withheld according to rules of human society.'

"In the ballet the figures appear as insects, but that was not part of the original concept. Robbins first thought in terms of a tribe of Amazons [*The Amazons* was the ballet's working title]. He read through the Greek myths about them, including the killing of Hippolyte by Hercules. But, in his ballet, the situation was to be reversed, the woman was to be the killer, not the man. He completed the whole opening section to the point where the mask is removed from the Novice's face. But he did not like it. 'It was what I call "square."' He said to himself in discouragement, 'Oh, God! I can see them in tunics and shields!' While searching for other aspects of this subject, he found a book on spiders and suddenly there was a clue. These were not merely to be girls or Amazons, but they were to be partly animal or insect.

"In every ballet Robbins has found that at some point he hits the key or color that fixes the style. And so the animal-insect primitive-ritual quality persisted throughout the new work. In his notes he has called the ballet 'a phenomenon of nature.' As he trained the dancers, Robbins was exhilarated by the new possibilities for his choreography. 'I did not have to confine myself to human beings moving in a way that we know is human. In the way their fingers worked, in the crouch of a body, or the thrust of an arm, I could let myself see what I wanted to imagine. Sometimes the arms, hands, and fingers became pincers, antennae, feelers.' The flip of the Novice's hand, in which the movement seems to continue after the hand has stopped, was suggested by a chipmunk. The first appearance of the Novice was altogether conceived in this animal-insect atmosphere. 'The whole first variation is her examination of the world around her. She is like an animal that has just been born, acutely conscious of her skin and eyes and nose. Everything is too hot, too bright, too overpowering in odor. All these things are reflected in the choreography. And yet *The Cage* has no pantomime, it is all pure dance.'

"Robbins went to see a motion picture about bees and their life in the hives. He did more research on the phenomena of cults and killing in human society. One day, at the zoo, he noticed the effortless movement of a tiger's tail as it whipped from side to side. That suggested another movement idea for the ballet. 'All the time I was working on *The Cage*,' says Robbins, 'I had a very special eye out looking for material. The "eye" becomes a sort of Geiger counter which starts to tick in the brain and emotions as you approach a subject of value to you. It is not by freak chance that one stumbles on these subjects. They are there in existence all the time, but the artist, tuned to his special subject, tracks them down, discards or se-

The Cage. Nora Kaye, Nicholas Magallanes. *(Photo Walter E. Owen.)*

lects them, and finally reinterprets them.' One day Kaye came out of the shower after a rehearsal and he happened by her dressing room before she combed her hair. He was fascinated by the effect he saw, hair plastered like a helmet over her head, and thus the hair-dress of the Novice came about. Another time, a lighting rehearsal had just ended. The network of ropes and strings, one of the most evocative elements of the setting, was taut, as it had been from the beginning. Rosenthal, having finished with her lighting sheet, shouted, 'Strike it!' Just as the bars were relaxed and the ropes slackened, Robbins turned and noticed the effect. Thus was born the striking touch at the beginning of *The Cage*, when the network is pulled up taut as if to symbolize the tightening of the action. At the close, it is again relaxed.

"'I had to be economical. The music said "Break it clean." I had to make my points very strong and very clear.' The opening movement of the ballet is a striking instance. The first thing that the dancers do is to thrust out their hands and throw back their heads. 'It is like a scream of triumph,' explained Robbins.

"While he was working on the choreography for Broadway's *The King and I*, Robbins had studied Oriental dancing and had been fascinated by the stretching of the hands and the hyperextension of the arm and elbow. All of these observations now served him in *The Cage*. Many of the positions he used were archaic in style. They had a stone-like quality and

were reminiscent of primitive drawings and sculptures. 'I had to work hard with the corps initially, but once they understood and felt physically a quality I was after, they went ahead like wildfire. Stravinsky's score is stinging; it really pulls your guts out of you.'" [5]

Robbins maintained a deliberate ambiguity as to the precise nature of the protagonists. Some of the movements definitely had human connotations (the group's prancing on pointe with heads thrown back, mouths open, arms extended tautly forward, as if in a victory celebration of some primeval beings); others recalled lower forms of life: the girls sliding their palms up and down their arms and legs, as if removing slime. Other movements, such as the group's sitting on the floor with their thumbs in their mouths, are more provocative than explicit. Still others—as when the Novice wrings the first Intruder's neck between her legs—are nothing if not literal. In all, *The Cage* is quite a mixture of movements that Terry called "balletic, expressional, gestural, and primitive."

Hayden discussed working with Robbins and her own concept of the role: "If you give one performance that looks the way he wants it to, he wants that performance reproduced. I always enjoyed *The Cage*. The role is very satisfying. It's a well-constructed ballet, with a beautiful pas de deux, and a variation that's perfect. It's a tremendous challenge because you cannot do it as yourself; you have to do it in a very objective way, as though you're watching someone else dancing it. Often when you're dancing a movement, you feel it a certain way, but with Robbins I would practice the movement looking at it, and if it looked a certain way, I would try to recapture the look, rather than feeling it: that is, I worked on the role intellectually. Robbins didn't want anything personalized—'Don't be maudlin,' he'd say. In the look—the action—the drama was realized."

Great Britain:
"Robbins is one of the very few Americans who can play successfully with cosmic or abstract ideas and can express them in an idiom at once up to date and classical. His idiom is always personal, sharp, and intelligent. His theme, this time, is certainly forbidding; he has expressed it both forcibly and tastefully." [6]

"Too much fuss has been made over *The Cage*, Robbins's fantastic ballet of life, in which the female novice kills her mate, egged on thereto by the Queen of the species and her satellites. Horrible it certainly is. The dancers' angular movements and emphasis on pointes convey uncannily the atmosphere of the insect world, a few weblike ropes hanging from above by way of décor. Kaye even more uncannily portrays the gradual unfolding and awakening of the novice, shaking each limb as if discovering its power. Magallanes, a fine dancer who deserves a better fate, is kicked around unmercifully before and after being done to death. One is reminded of what Samuel Johnson once said about a woman's preaching: 'It is not done well; but you are surprised to find it done at all.' The quotation is not entirely apt. It is done superlatively well. The wonder remains that it is done at all." [7]

France:

"*The Cage* has lost none of its force—quite the contrary. In a completely new manner and with an inhuman ferocity, Robbins has constructed the masterpiece of his young career. We shall never forget this rite of insects, which evokes, in its Picasso-like groups and its shadowy depths reminiscent of Redon, the loves of another world, or another planet inhabited by some form of life we can barely imagine." [8]

Italy:

"The modern touch, the inventiveness of certain figurations, which, however, remain always within the sphere of a traditional, classical background, define the character, the style, the temperament, and above all, the age of Robbins. Although a spiritual and technical son of Balanchine, Robbins belongs to the succeeding generation; his choreography is stern but tormented, personal, and expressive. Within this 'cage' is a metaphysical tale of a fantastical and primordial world of natural phenomena. Insects—their struggle for existence, their severe laws for the survival of the species, and the sexual drama for the preservation of the species—are schematically evoked with highly suggestive movements and emotion-filled group patterns. Robbins, deriving from the heart of Balanchine, represents the promise of American choreography." [9]

Japan:

"The most celebrated item in the repertoire. The 'philosophy' behind this strik-

ing creation has never been classified as a secret: 'The male amounts only to food for the female.' The number is a gripping study in sensualism. And as a famous Japanese litterateur once put it, 'it represents the cream of the art of organization.' " [10]

THE MIRACULOUS MANDARIN

CHOREOGRAPHY: Todd Bolender

MUSIC: Béla Bartók (*The Miraculous Mandarin*, op. 19, 1919)

Libretto after Melchior Lengyel

COSTUMES, DÉCOR: Alvin Colt

LIGHTING: Jean Rosenthal

PREMIERE: 6 September 1951

CAST: *The Woman*, Melissa Hayden; *An Old Man*, Frank Hobi; *A Young Man*, Roy Tobias; *A Blind Girl*, Beatrice Tompkins; *The Mandarin*, Hugh Laing; *6 men*

Mandarin also danced by Bolender

PLACE: Any city street, anywhere in the world

Written as a ballet, *Mandarin* has tempted many choreographers, probably because it has a strong and "realistic" story line—in fact, the first two productions were banned on grounds of immorality. There is also, of course, the Bartók score. Bolender used the same characters and general setting as the original, but changed the relationships; all the same he found himself with a Central European expressionist melodrama on his hands, what Martin called a cross between *The Cabinet of Dr. Caligari* and *M*, and a work firmly rooted in the twenties. Thus the ballet was clearly a period piece. Because of this and the libretto's violence, and because Bolender chose to use "choreographic pantomime" rather than dance to tell the "heavy" story, reception was mixed. Martin alone gave a completely favorable review, and in this he was as much concerned with the Company's successful performance of such an alien style as he was with the ballet itself. ("It seems a good thing for the company

The Miraculous Mandarin. **The Men, the Woman, the Mandarin.** (*Photo Melton-Pippin.*)

to have done, for it destroys once and for all the theory that it is an exclusively Balanchinian company that can dance only daintily tutued musical abstractions in strictly virtuosic vein." [1]

Bolender described his approach: "I was overwhelmed by the sound of the music, but the original story didn't make any sense—all that killing for no reason. Who was the Mandarin, finally? A figment of her imagination? A real situation? So I changed the emphasis. I made the Woman the central character, not the Mandarin, as he was in the libretto. I used the idea of a war and what war does to people, especially what happens to people in cities—planes, guns, bombs. The Woman was then a lost person, as were the Men, so that explains the violence—they're like animals trying to survive. The Mandarin could be in her imagination. I had him dressed in a way that gave him a kind of extraordinary beauty. It could be another side of herself—the side she would esteem. This, of course, only went through my mind. What comes out on stage *is* a Mandarin. I tried to make it a very realistic situation. The set was beautiful—like matchsticks put together to create a number of levels, with staircases leading up to them so there could be movement in all directions. I also added another character—the Blind Girl. This person was to be the counterpart of the Woman, the part of her she didn't know or understand. The Blind Girl shows up for the first time just a moment before the Mandarin appears at the very top platform. It's almost as though it's a premonition of a horrible experience the Woman will have to face. At one point the Blind Girl keeps reaching for her, and finally the Woman shakes her off, but only to find the Mandarin at the top of the stairs, watching. There follows a marvelous romantic pas de deux, and then the gang takes over, trying to kill him, and she lets it happen until the hanging (which was *very* realistic), when she realizes that she loves him and that he is, perhaps, a part of her, whatever she wants to hold onto. And this is something else I added: I had her pull him down from the noose. There is just one last moment when he seems to come to life, then there's another pas de deux in which he's a lifeless body. At the same time the Blind Girl is walking through and stands at the place where the Mandarin first appeared. When he finally collapses definitively, and the Woman just sits there with

the dead body in her lap, the Blind Girl sits down, feeling her way, and the lights go down on the two of them. The implication is that through hideous violence, the Woman is trying to find herself. I used movement related to gesture; or rather, I took gesture and turned it into dance movement. There were so many realistic situations, but I didn't want it to be primarily acting."

Martin called it "a distinguished effort all around. It is a grim and sordid underworld tale of a prostitute, her gang of cutthroats, and her mandarin lover, who has to be killed half a dozen times before he can be compelled to stay dead. It is almost unrelievedly violent. There are undoubtedly heavy philosophical arguments in Melchior Lengyel's scenario, but they are basically unadaptable to the choreographic idiom and emerge, if at all, surrounded by a dense fog. The music, the idea and the incidents add up to a fairly representative picture of that neurosis which was Central Europe at the time of the first World War. Indeed, its present production may very well be thirty years too late and several thousand miles too far west. Nevertheless, for those with strong stomachs, it has an intense sadistic excitement about it.

"Bolender has done a superb job. There is little opportunity for any sustained line of movement, for the piece is a pantomime rather than a ballet, but he has created remarkably intuitive phrases and gestures, and for all the excess of action over dancing, there is not a moment that is less than vibrantly tense and alive. Hayden's performance is sheer black magic. She is part maenad, part Gorgon; her alternations of rigid extensions and complete relaxations, the sharp clarity of her pointes, her kind of physical voracity, all stem from an inner compulsion that is overwhelming in its power. Laing meets her vehemence with that curiously potent stillness of his which has real dominion in it. As for Bartók's difficult score, it is aimed directly at the nervous system, and though it seems a little self-conscious about it, it manages to produce every reaction it strives for." [2]

A more common opinon was Terry's: "That the choreographic quality does not consistently parallel the brilliant beauties and powers of the music must be admitted, but Bolender has fashioned dance passages and even scenes stunning in design and emotionally eloquent. If some movements seem derivative of Tudor or

Robbins, others are fresh and free, and if certain actions are but thin kinesthetic echoes of the music's dramatic intent, others join the score as co-equals in a theatrical experience. Not only was Laing's performance a remarkable one—dynamic, superbly paced, remorseless in its sensuality—but also the choreography here reached its peaks of dramatic power. The whole scene built, as the gentle Mandarin, attracted to the streetwalker, let his desire generate to the point that brutal buffetings, a stabbing, and a hanging at the hands of the girl's accomplices could not still a passion until it had found satisfaction." [3]

For Hering, "Sometimes it was disturbingly mature; other times it was gauche and inexpressive. The opening scene in which the six young ruffians stand in watchful waiting and discharge their nervous energy on scuffling among themselves sets a fine mood of subdued evil. And the whole first half of the ballet—Hayden as the girl tossing in boredom on top of a high, stair-decorated platform, her bitter encounter with the old man, the young man, and the blind girl—presents a sharp picture of a soul in furious and purposeless torment. And the first appearance of the Mandarin is something to remember. He stands bathed in soft light atop the platform and the girl stands below, a distance away, her back to the audience, trembling violently, and with the orchestra screaming like a soul in purgatory. But somehow the ballet does not grow beyond this point." [4]

Wrote Chujoy, in sum: "Despite its defects, an exciting, disturbing work." [5]

À LA FRANÇAIX

CHOREOGRAPHY: George Balanchine

MUSIC: Jean Françaix (Serenade for Small Orchestra, 1934)

SCENERY: Raoul Dufy

LIGHTING: Jean Rosenthal

PREMIERE: 11 September 1951

CAST: Janet Reed, Maria Tallchief, André Eglevsky; Roy Tobias, Frank Hobi

OTHER CASTS: Melissa Hayden, Jillana, Todd Bolender

Before the early-fall season of 1951, LeClercq sprained her ankle, causing postponement of the planned revival of *Apollo*. Balanchine concocted this "balletic anecdote"—also known as a "balletic hors d'oeuvre"—in a hurry to fill the gap.

Terry wrote all that could be written: "Tasty indeed. It is neither big nor opulent and it pretends to no choreographic complexities. Rather is it a little joking game, as gay as the music to which it is set.

"The plot—if one could call it that—is merely an excuse for making fun in dance terms. A little girl (Reed) and two boys (Hobi and Tobias) are playing happily when in bounces a handsome athlete (Eglevsky). He tosses aside his tennis racket and, frightening off the two youths with some well aimed leg-beats, woos the maiden. But soon a winged ballerina (behaving for all the world like a fugitive from *Giselle*) in the person of Tallchief floats in and lures the fickle youth away from his new love to her own misty world. The story continues with the departure, accomplished by floating bourrées and rippling arms, of the ballerina, the return of the original trio, the second interference by the athlete, the re-emergence of the ballerina and her sudden stripping into a brilliant bathing-suit affair, a few more steps, and finish. One can see that

this is hardly a profound study of human behavior. But why should it be? It is great good fun to be permitted to chuckle at ballet." [1] To this, Martin could only add, "Quite delicious." And along the same gastronomic lines, for Krevitsky it was "a choreographic bon-bon. Even the pun of the title is undisturbing, because it fits so well to the music of Jean Françaix." [2] To Hering, however, it was "merely a sketch." The chief novelty was that Eglevsky, for once, was not a premier danseur noble, but a mortal tennis player.

TYL ULENSPIEGEL

CHOREOGRAPHY: George Balanchine

MUSIC: Richard Strauss (*Till Eulenspiegel's Merry Pranks*, op. 28, 1895)

COSTUMES, DÉCOR: Esteban Francés

LIGHTING: Jean Rosenthal

PREMIERE: 14 November 1951

CAST: *Tyl Ulenspiegel*, Jerome Robbins; *Nell, His Wife*, Ruth Sobotka; *Philip II, King of Spain*, Brooks Jackson; *Duke and Duchess*, Frank Hobi, Beatrice Tompkins; *Woman*, Tomi Wortham; *Tyl as a Child*, Alberta Grant; *Philip II as a Child*, Susan Kovnat; *Spanish Nobility*, 2 women, 2 men; *Soldiers*, 6 men; *Peasants*, 8 women; *Inquisitors*, 4 men; *Crowd*, 8 women
Tyl also danced by Todd Bolender, Hugh Laing

Tyl was the most lavish production yet in the life of the three-year-old company. The title role was another great success for Robbins. (Echoing the sentiments of everyone who has ever worked with Balanchine, he observed, "As a dancer, I got some of the best notices of my life for Tyl, but I never came anywhere near the gusto and the earthiness that he achieved when he was demonstrating it for me in rehearsal.") For various reasons, among them Robbins's departure and a warehouse fire that destroyed all of the costumes and props, *Tyl* did not remain in the repertory more than a few seasons.

The program note indicated that Balan-

chine's Tyl derived from Flemish sources and that the character was something more than a cheerful practical joker: "Lower Saxony, Flanders, and Poland dispute the origin of Tyl Ulenspiegel, presumably an historic personage who lived in the first half of the fourteenth century. Written versions of his adventures appeared some time at the end of the fifteenth century, and translations into English, French, Danish, and Dutch quickly followed. A Flemish edition of 1520 served as the basis for an epic novel by Charles de Coster written in the last century, which has become a Belgian classic. This story, showing Tyl as liberator of Flanders from the Spanish invaders under the cruel Duke of Alba, inspired Balanchine's ballet. Conceiving the ballet in the spirit of the late Gothic, Francés has recreated for our time a vision of an epoch framed between the harsh nobility of Zurbarán and the savage fantasy of Hieronymus Bosch."

Chujoy succinctly summarized the general impression made by *Tyl Ulenspiegel*: "No other ballet contained so much theatrical (not necessarily choreographic) invention, and no other was so much handicapped by the shortness of the musical composition. In this detailed, complicated pantomime, rather than a ballet in the accepted sense, Tyl just did not have a chance. No sooner had he begun a scene, or a prank if you will, than the music drove him right out of it. There was not even enough time to achieve what stage directors call 'establishing' the scenes, let alone for developing them. One doubts whether the spectators [on] opening night saw more than half of what Balanchine staged for Tyl. Only repeated seeings made it possible to have more than just a cursory impression of what was happening on the stage." [1]

His spectator's view is fully corroborated by Robbins's backstage view: "There were just a few moments where there was what you might call 'dance-pattern choreography.' The rest of it was not. The whole thing was a race. I timed it out once—the ballet was fifteen or sixteen minutes long, and I had to handle twenty-three props or costume changes in that time. It worked mostly, but it was a very unfortunate ballet for the corps, who were mostly behind masks or dressed as cripples and in rags, so they would be apt to goof off, and at the moment you needed something, they might not be right there. It was a hard ballet to do, al-

À la Françaix. André Eglevsky. (*Courtesy André Eglevsky.*)

Tyl Ulenspiegel. Above: **Beatrice Tompkins (center), Jerome Robbins (right).** (*Photo Walter E. Owen.*) *Right:* **Jerome Robbins.** (*Photo Melton-Pippin.*)

though I enjoyed it, but it was really like getting through an obstacle course. I think out of all the performances I did, I remember feeling happy about three or four of them—times when it all came together. George was terrific in showing that—the way he would blow his nose, or wipe his face, or look at a girl, he showed me a Tyl that I wish I could do. It was such a terrific character. And he had it fully. It had a rough and peasant and basic volume to it, which I didn't feel I ever could get to. He would show what the attitude toward the other people was."

Other critics were struck by various details; all felt the work had a certain breathless quality.

Martin: "Tyl's pranks in the present version are no less merry and no less pranksome, but when they are given thus a moral issue and a passionate cause to animate them, they do far greater justice than is generally done choreographically to the substance and the sardonicism of the Strauss music.

"We are given the key to the piece in a prologue, set to a loud, sustained roll of drums, in which the child Tyl and the child Philip II of Spain play chess at a

huge table, the one moving a loaf of bread, the other an armada across the board. Their continuing struggle forms the body of the work. Tyl is insolent, obscene, grotesquely ingenious in his endless devices for humiliating the Spanish Duke and Duchess, and at length the invaders depart with their galleons as the great flag of the Flemish eagle flies triumphantly over the walls of the city. It is all richly medieval in feeling—coarse, sumptuous and violent.

"So much for intent; as for accomplishment, it is still a work in progress. Its developments follow so quickly on each other's heels that the line is not always clear. Technically there is still work to be done on lighting and mechanics. There is very little dancing in it; it is all mime and choreographic action. For this reason, especially, time and performance are needed to develop it into the driving and pungent work that it is inherently." [2]

Terry: "Robbins, the dancer, triumphed—if Balanchine, the choreographer, did not. This production is an elaborate one—possibly overelaborate with respect to properties—and visually handsome, but as striking as the decor is and as

pictorially arresting as the Balanchine ensemble designs are, it is Robbins's performance which captures and revitalizes the spirit and the purpose, the wit and the warmth of a great legend. Robbins permitted us to see the contradictory elements of Tyl's nature. He made us love him and laugh at him, disapprove of him and weep for him as he capered disrespectfully and irresistibly throughout his fantastic adventures. He made a myth into a human being, an unlikely one perhaps, but human none the less. Other characters—the King of Spain, a Duke and his Duchess, soldiers, peasants—rarely came to life, scarcely had dimension. Because Tyl's antagonists tend to be cardboard, the magnitude of his conflicts is somewhat lost." [3]

Smith: "The ballet is really not a ballet but a serio-comic pantomime. In a series of disguises that pass by so swiftly that it is difficult to recall them in detail—as a beggar, a monk, a painter, an old woman—Tyl plays a series of practical jokes—sometimes childish, sometimes lewd, sometimes cruel—on Philip and his retinue. At the climax of the music, which in Strauss's program accompanies the hanging of Tyl, the proceedings take on a wry twist. For a moment Tyl stands as limp as Petrouchka; then, picking up a convenient skeleton from the floor, he tosses it to a couple of hungry animals nearby, who proceed to dismember it and gnaw at the bones while Tyl comes brightly back to life and Philip replaces him as a corpse, to be carried off in state by his retainers. In this somewhat surrealist fashion the character of Tyl as the deathless liberator of his people is equated with the figure of the legendary prankster. Despite the uncommon profusion of properties, costumes and supernumerary characters, it is essentially a one-man show." [4]

As Kirstein said, "The ballet received unanimous approval from those who felt we usually skimped on decoration," and, indeed, the elaborate costumes and sets were reviewed in art columns as well: "At the climax, when Tyl is fighting off the Spanish soldiers, the backdrop suddenly evanesces into a sheet of fire, in which the owl, like the heart in a human body, stands silhouetted as a steadfast symbol of Tyl, courage, liberty, etc. Perhaps this is one of those cases where the set is so exciting and, far from being just a setting, actually participates in the action, that one almost forgets the ballet itself." [5]

Genauer, who felt the flavor of Bosch had been captured "remarkably well," mentioned one picturesque detail: "When Robbins dumps a Spanish nobleman into a barrel so a rear view of him is seen from the waist down, with legs kicking wildly, the audience is literally getting one of Bosch's pet images." [6]

Tyl was performed just a few times abroad; it was given first in Edinburgh: "The part of Tyl offers a rare opportunity for character dancing and mime, of which Laing missed nothing. His pranks, now in the mock dance of death and again as the mock monk, kept the audience about as breathless as the Spaniards." [7]

SWAN LAKE

CHOREOGRAPHY: George Balanchine (after Ivanov)

MUSIC: Peter Ilyitch Tchaikovsky (op. 20, 1875–76)

COSTUMES, DÉCOR: Cecil Beaton (1951); Rouben Ter-Arutunian (1964)

LIGHTING: Jean Rosenthal (1951); Ter-Arutunian (1964)

PREMIERE: 20 November 1951

CAST: *Odette, Queen of the Swans*, Maria Tallchief; *Prince Siegfried*, André Eglevsky; *Benno, the Prince's Friend*, Frank Hobi; *Pas de Trois*, Patricia Wilde, 2 women; *Pas de Neuf*, Yvonne Mounsey, 8 women; *Von Rothbart, a Sorcerer*, Edward Bigelow; *Swans*, 24 women; *Hunters*, 8 men

Over the years, nearly all the male and female principals have danced the leads in *Swan Lake*.

There was a good deal of speculation as to *why* Balanchine mounted yet another *Swan Lake*. The program note was almost apologetic about the enterprise ("the first older work to be revived in sixteen years of collaboration between Balanchine and Kirstein in some fifty works"). The whole notion of reviving the classics seemed the very antithesis of the ideals of both Balanchine and Kirstein, particularly in the case of this ballet, which was already in the repertory of practically every ballet company worthy of the name. Balanchine has since demonstrated, both obliquely and explicitly, that he is not opposed to traditional stories, to lavish costumes, or even to frankly "old-fashioned" choreography. *Nutcracker*, *Harlequinade*, and *Coppélia*, to name but three examples, are rooted in tradition. *Raymonda Variations* and *Cortège Hongrois* recall at one remove the spectacles of his Russian youth. *Figure in the Carpet*, *Midsummer Night's Dream*, and *Don Quixote* show him to be quite at home with a well-dressed stage.

Early headlines caught the gist of *Swan Lake*'s critical reception: "Young at Fifty-Six"; "Balanchine Puts Zing into *Swan Lake*." His major contribution (in addition to speeding up the tempo), was to completely rechoreograph the group sections. As Manchester wrote, "The corps de ballet becomes the protagonist. [This] *Swan Lake* [is] a ballet for the ensemble and not a showpiece for a ballerina." [1] Balanchine took music from the second and fourth acts; the music for the Prince's solo, although in the original score, had not been used previously. As for choreography,

only the adagio, the Swan Queen's variation and coda, and the pas de quatre were from the Ivanov version, and the first entrance of the swans was based on the traditional steps. Reaction was highly favorable: Just about everyone admired the group choreography and the stunning pas de trois—in which Wilde performed jumps and beats worthy of a man—and there was also wide agreement that the Swan Queen was a forbiddingly distant and unemotional creature.

Terry: "Lest this report cause the traditionalist to shudder with apprehension, let it be said at once that this is still *Swan Lake*. The meeting of the Queen of the Swans and the huntsman Prince is very close to that with which we have become familiar through other stagings. Furthermore, Balanchine has, I think, kept his innovations within the style of Petipa, and within the general framework of the choreography which Petipa's assistant, Ivanov, devised. What, one may ask, is the result of such tinkering with a presumably inviolate classic? The result, choreographically speaking, is fine, really fine, for Balanchine actually did not tinker or patch. He renewed a work of art. And so beautifully has he accomplished this task that he is certain to disappoint many, for *Swan Lake* is now a creation for a dance company and not merely a vehicle for a star.

"This *Swan Lake* belongs to the corps de ballet. For the twenty-four girls who compose the ensemble of swans, Balanchine has created passages and patterns of miraculous beauty. They floated, they poised, they soared, and they moved, not simply back and forth and up and down (as they tend to do in the traditional version), but also in circles, arcs, and spirals as if the stage had become their lake in which they could find the mirror of their own endless beauties of motion. For subensembles, Mr. Balanchine restored not only the pas de quatre (unchanged), but also added a pas de trois and created a group dance for nine little swans. The pas de trois, headed by the resilient, sharp, fleet and generally remarkable Wilde, turned out to be a show-stopper, a splendid dance in its own right and excellent as a contrasting element in a generally lyrical piece. The impeccable corps met the challenge of its new starring role with grace and aplomb, and it must be reported that its engaging qualities of performing were enhanced by the handsome backswept tailfeathers. With every motion these snowy plumages wavered delicately, and in the bouncy pas de quatre, they bobbled delightfully, perkily.

"Tallchief was a beautiful Queen of the Swans. Royal bearing was maintained throughout, yet there were tremulousness and delicacy also and, of course, a grandeur of balletic line which few of her ballerina colleagues could hope to match. Missing was warmth. There was gleam but little glow in a characterization which requires the projection of romantic urgency as well as of dance architecture. Eglevsky was gallant and danced his brand new (and brief) solo handsomely, but he, too, slighted the dramatic potential. For the production itself, there is nothing but praise. Beaton's black and white and grey scenery provides a superb background—thematically and visually." [2]

Martin: "Once one has registered astonished disapproval of the wasteful expenditure of energy and taste [involved in reviving *Swan Lake*], there remains nothing but praise for the way the dubious assignment has been executed. Though it is fundamentally the same old one-act excerpt that everybody knows backward and forward, Balanchine has put his hand to it with characteristic magic. Most of the major foolishnesses and minor irritations that clutter the familiar version have been deleted, and many fine and ingenious alterations and additions have been made. The Prince has a completely new variation (and about time, too) set to unfamiliar music; each of the two assistant swan queens has a variation, one designed around Wilde's sensational technical powers, set to music that is generally omitted, and the other, less successfully achieved for (and by) Mounsey and a group of eight, set to a lovely Russian dance. The ending has been altered more or less after the manner of the final scene in the fourth act, employing the music for that scene, to admirable dramatic and poetic effect.

"But the greatest change has to do not with even such major details as these, but rather with the whole concept of the choreography and its emphasis. It is no longer an exhibition piece for a ballerina filled in with perfunctory ballabili; it is instead basically a large-scale ensemble work with solos. The Swan Queen is still the center of interest, but she does not carry the burden of the interest upon her slim shoulders. The corps de ballet dominates the composition, and what it has to

do is alive with design and vitality, and verve that is altogether without precedent. There are no sagging tempos, no lapses from birdlike animation into the familiar bored and sentimental slouching. Things really move.

"It is probably, also, quite the handsomest *Swan Lake* visually that anybody can recall. Beaton has designed a great black-and-white wilderness after the style of the late fifteenth-century German engravers, and has costumed his huntsmen in rich reds. (The Prince's costume alone seems commonplace.) . . . Whether his treatment is flattering to the music is open to question. The swan theme is here given to us virtually in its entirety without the leavening of the many contrasting tunes and rhythms which surround it in the complete score. Since it is sentimental in the extreme, it is inclined to become cloying and banal. In general, the score is strongly supported in the full work, by the re-creation of the old-fashioned mime, the old-fashioned romantic style; Balanchine by taking away these supports is inclined to demand of Tchaikovsky something more classic, more absolute, perhaps, than he meant to compose.

"But it is a stunning production, with grandeur and magic about it, and one can only hope that its successful realization will satisfy all Balanchine's revivalist compulsions and set no precedents." [3]

Over the years there have been many changes—the pas de trois and pas de quatre have been dropped, a valse bluette for three swans has been added. The Prince's variation is often omitted. The Swan Queen's traditional solo no longer exists; to her music, a number of new variations have been designed in which the Queen is supported by four swans. (Each ballerina has her own version, tailor-made, like a cadenza.) There is a new ending to the famous adagio, which involves the corps de ballet; and parts of the adagio itself have been changed. (Eglevsky recalls, "Our pas de deux ended in the traditional manner: little battu, single pirouette, battu, double pirouette, and fall. After about a year Mr. Balanchine called us in and said, 'I spoke to Tchaikovsky last night, and he wants us to make a new ending.' ") Long ago the Prince's friend Benno disappeared. The Queen's flying entrance in the coda has replaced the traditional series of piqué arabesques with sharp turns of the body. For the move to the New York State Theater in 1964, the bal-

let was outfitted with new scenery, costumes, and lighting.

A quarter of a century later, Balanchine's *Swan Lake* is still performed frequently—although possibly in the words of one of Odette's interpreters, "that's the one ballet he would appreciate none of us asking him to rehearse."

How does Balanchine see ballet's most famous heroine? He has spoken of birds in general as cold and unemotional; he once told Violette Verdy, a performer with a highly inflected style, who projects a great sense of involvement, "For my taste, the real Odette is more cold, more unobtainable, not dramatic." As usual with Balanchine, characterization derives principally from movement. Says Tallchief, "The movement never really stops, it just goes on and on and on, and that's the way he demonstrated. In *Swan Lake*, it's so much more than the steps. There's always room for a little finger that's just the right way, or a head movement. It was one of the most difficult things I ever did. I remember when George choreographed it; I could see what he wanted, but then I couldn't do it. I think that he perhaps had in mind Spessivtzeva,[*] whom he always admired. Technically it wasn't difficult at all as compared to my other roles, but it was the interpretation . . . George could do it. He left my role more or less in the traditional version. I thought what he did at the very end was beautiful; the whole stage was alive with movement." (In the final moments of the ballet, the entire corps, on a motif of small running steps and continuously undulating arms, moves from pattern to interwoven pattern, never pausing.)

Barbara Walczak recalls "Balanchine coaching particularly Tanny [LeClercq] and Diana [Adams], demonstrating in a manner that was incredibly beautiful— and none of them quite caught it. His major comment was always 'larger, wilder, more creaturelike,' especially in the case of the very long-legged ballerinas. He seemed to be asking for more than anyone was able to give. In addition, all of the ballerinas were very tense about this role."

Later views:

"The recently added jaunty coda to the pas de deux would kill any romantic mood that might have been engendered by the

---

[*] Balanchine staged a *Swan Lake* for Spessivtzeva in 1929 (Diaghilev's Ballets Russes).

Swan Lake. Above left: Early 1960s. Nicholas Magallanes, Allegra Kent. *(Photo Martha Swope.) Center left:* Early 1960s. Violette Verdy. *(Photo Fred Fehl.) Bottom:* Mid-1960s (new production). Edward Villella, Patricia McBride. *(Photo Martha Swope.) Below:* Mid-1950s. Maria Tallchief, André Eglevsky. *(Courtesy André Eglevsky.)*

adagio itself. This still seems to me a most unhappy afterthought of Balanchine's." [4]

"Balanchine's *Swan Lake* is not *Swan Lake*, of course, but it is Balanchine—in one of his purest crystal-clear classical moods." [5]

"Balanchine's production is based vaguely on the Ivanov original and shows him in a rare, uncertain mood. He seems unable to decide whether he wants to do an out-and-out Balanchine ballet to the Tchaikovsky music, or whether he wants to revive, or perhaps he would say resuscitate, the original Ivanov choreography. The result lacks the courage of what are presumably his convictions. This is a fairly feeble *Swan Lake*, and personally, I have seen so many feeble *Swan Lakes* that the very words make me think not of ballet but blood transfusions. . . . An eccentric Odette . . . an intrusive and vulgar solo for the Prince." [6]

"Since the Company described [Balanchine's unusual version of *Swan Lake*] as 'a contemporary commentary on a classic masterpiece,' its brisk, breezy pace was not a surprise. Balanchine has indeed given the work a fresh look. No four little swans and no languor." [7]

One might have expected extensive analysis from Europe of *Swan Lake*. In the fifties, there was little in the European experience against which to compare *Pied Piper*, *Age of Anxiety*, *Concerto Barocco*, *Divertimento*, *Orpheus*, and *Four Temperaments*, but *Swan Lake* touched on a ballet tradition with which *everyone* was familiar. The "new" *Swan Lake*, however, did not appear to generate a particularly vivid response. But in Australia, it was the unquestioned hit of the four-month 1958 engagement. (This was because it was *Swan Lake*, not because it was a new *Swan Lake*.)

England:
"Balanchine has taken Ivanov's finest work, replacing certain portions with his own arrangements, often inventive and theatrically effective, only they do not always match Ivanov's choreography either in style or feeling. The music includes borrowings from the last Act, and Tchaikovsky's tempos are sometimes ignored, the final ensemble being quickened to a galop. The growing craze for taking a classic and 'injecting new life in it,' as the formula runs, will, unless checked, gradually dissipate what should be rigorously treasured. Beaton's swan-

maiden costumes with their absurd wings assist neither dancers nor illusion. Von Rothbart, once an owl, has become a man-at-arms." [8]

"Considerably refurbished. He has left none of the choreography intact save the lovely adagio and the tedious pas de quatre for the cygnets. It is the sort of treatment which provides balletomanes with happy, inconclusive argument. On the one hand, it is true that *Swan Lake* was, from the start, the least exactly preserved of Tchaikovsky's ballets. There is also the high authority of Diaghilev—he had no compunction about adapting Tchaikovsky and Petipa (or Ivanov) to suit his taste. On the other hand, there is no doubt that by now *Swan Lake*, Act II, has settled down to an accepted convention, and it is perilous to break such conventions. In fact, some of Balanchine's alterations are effective and pretty; others are ill-judged, and the finale, taken at a sprinter's pace, does real damage to the spirit (to say nothing of the letter) of the original." [9]

Reports from Italy and Germany were rather inconclusive and seemed to skirt the issue of Balanchine's innovations.

Italy:
"Despite its exquisite realization, it has not, on the surface, discovered new expressive values." [10]

"Petipa's choreography, restudied and renewed by Balanchine, does not gain much. And we must confess that certain measures of the old version and some of the expressive moments as performed by our own dance troupe are not inferior." [11]

Germany:
"*Swan Lake* was awaited with great excitement. Beaton designed a shadowy backdrop with the feeling of a subtle graphic. The literal, Lohengrin-style swans drawn along the back at the beginning of the ballet did not suit it exactly. Tallchief danced with great bravura, creating the atmosphere of a fairy tale and making the Swan Queen an otherworldly creature. We have never seen such a perky pas de quatre. The deportment of the corps de ballet was in appropriate high classic style." [12]

Australia:
"An artistic revelation. The ballet purists may be horrified, but, to this critic, the ballet has been remolded closer to the heart's desire." [13]

LILAC GARDEN

CHOREOGRAPHY: Antony Tudor

MUSIC: Ernest Chausson (*Poème* for violin and orchestra, op. 25, 1896, dedicated to Eugène Ysaÿe)

COSTUMES: Karinska

DÉCOR: Horace Armistead

LIGHTING: Jean Rosenthal

PREMIERE: 30 November 1951 (first presented 26 January 1936 as *Jardin aux Lilas* by Ballet Rambert, Mercury Theatre, London)

VIOLIN: Hugo Fiorato

CAST: *Caroline, the Bride-to-Be*, Nora Kaye; *Her Lover*, Hugh Laing; *The Man She Must Marry*, Antony Tudor; *The Woman in His Past*, Tanaquil LeClercq; *Guests*, 4 couples

OTHER CASTS: *Caroline*, Diana Adams; *The Man She Must Marry*, Brooks Jackson; *The Woman in His Past*, Yvonne Mounsey

SCENE: The lilac garden of Caroline's house

Lilac Garden, with its story of desperate partings and even more desperate meetings, has been breaking hearts for fifteen years. It would seem to be one of the very few ballets destined for immortality." [1]

Originally created for the English company of Marie Rambert, it was imported for the repertory of Ballet Theatre in 1940,* where it is still being danced. The program of the first American production gave the following summary:

"Caroline is about to enter upon a marriage of convenience, but gives a farewell party before the ceremony. Among her

---

* When Tudor was still new to America, Martin gave this assessment of his (and others') place in the choreographic hierarchy: "Tudor belongs to the extremely small fellowship of ballet choreographers who can take hold of the academic tradition and bend it to their uses instead of being taken hold of by it and bent to its uses. It is a fellowship which boasts the name of Fokine at the head of the list, of course; Nijinska after him; Balanchine in his own particular department of meringue and whipped cream; and young Eugene Loring as a light just rising above the horizon." (*NYT*, 21 July 40)

guests are the man she really loves, and the woman who, unknown to her, has been her fiancé's mistress. The ballet is a series of meetings and partings and interrupted confidences, until at the end Caroline, without the opportunity to take a final, tender farewell of her lover, has to leave on the arm of her fiancé."

At the time of its first U.S. performances, Martin wrote of the ballet: "In Tudor's hands the tearful little tale is neither tenuous nor sentimental, but warmly alive and aglow with intuition and revelation of inner feeling. The poignancy that he succeeds so admirably in achieving derives less from the immediate circumstances in which his characters find themselves than in the basic problem that lies beneath the circumstances, the conflict between the human passions and the conventions of ordinary living. The formality of the garden party, its movements highly stylized and unreal, constitutes the dominating background for the torrent of feeling that breaks through only in flashes of reality, inhibited almost before they come into being. It is this fundamental conflict that makes the essential drama of the piece, and Tudor has managed superbly to capture its essence in the comparatively minor romantic episode he has selected for his plot. With sure and simple strokes his choreography projects haste in leisure, turbulence in ordered calm, mute desperation and constraint. This is a remarkably free dramatic use of the academic dance, in every way modern and in a sense even anti-classic." [2]

A few years later, Lawrence added: "No central character exists. This ballet advances not only the wreckage of two pairs of lives, but the emptiness of a whole social system that demands the marriage of convenience. The dominant note is that of frustration. A Tudor [characteristic]—that of hurried entrance and exit—is [integrally used]: both couples make frequent appearances at dramatic intervals, as individuals and in pairs. Other guests appear, pass them by, exit quickly." [3]

In 1951, prompted by the presence of Kaye and Laing in the New York City Ballet, Tudor revived his work, and it was given new costumes and scenery. The critics were enraptured.

Wrote Martin: "Tudor has restaged it as if he had only just conceived the idea and was still under the spell of its fresh inspiration. The entire cast has been touched by the contagion and the work

Lilac Garden. **Nora Kaye, Antony Tudor.** *(Photo Melton-Pippin.)*

emerges as a heart-breaking romance. Kaye is altogether incomparable; a rich, warm womanliness pervades her characterization, and subtleties of movement managed to convey her controlled desperation with the utmost poignance. Visually, the production is so far superior to the old one that it seems to provide a third dimension to the action." [4]

Terry, in describing Kaye's performance, gave a clue to the Tudor style: "It is a modern classic; it belongs to the world of dance. The undeniable star was Kaye. Every dance movement, each gesture revealed the tormented heart of the girl or mirrored the fleeting ecstacies experienced in the quick and furtive embraces with her beloved or disclosed the wrenching conflict between duty and desire. A rise onto the pointe of the toe slipper or a pirouette no longer represent mere physical skill but, rather, define

emotion in terms of eloquent movement." [5]

Manchester wrote, simply: "With the choreographer himself, Kaye, and Laing in their well-loved roles, this revival could hardly fail, but even so one was hardly prepared for the beauty and wonder of this production." [6]

Hering: "Since 1936 it has stood as an exquisite monument to the Fokine-inspired idea that gesture may be firmly motivated psychologically and dramatically and yet have wings of its own. *Lilac Garden* has an atmosphere so concentrated emotionally and yet so gossamer in texture that the dancers seem to be moving in a dream world—a world of the real beyond the real where all time is snared in one timeless moment." [7]

All reviewers praised the scenery; most also praised the costumes. In disagreeing, Tudor revealed some of his opinions about other aspects of the ballet. He says, "They were divinely beautiful costumes, but the people wearing the costumes could not have had the thoughts my people had. The ambience of the family was in the wrong place. It became a rich family. My ladies aren't rich. Caroline's family is falling on worse days, trying to keep up a respectable picture—otherwise, why is she going to marry that other man? And the scenery was a kind of eighteenth-century French Watteau, very different from my slightly decayed garden; this was anything but decayed. I think really it's the difference between my middle-class, petit-bourgeois background, and Lincoln's."

Much has been written of Tudor's unique handling of psychological themes, his gripping projection of internalized emotions, and his ability to create a sustained dramatic mood. Less space has been given to Tudor's style of movement, his use of and/or rejection of a classical dance vocabulary—in short, how his dances look, as opposed to the feeling tone they project. Terry mentioned, for instance, the "sharp yet fluid transition from gesture to large-scale movement." [8] Sabin spoke of "exciting lifts [and] the art of tension and release." [9]

Tudor achieves his effects by understatement and connotation. He rarely uses literal gestures; he uses nuance. As for the steps underpinning the work, audiences are often unaware of the specific movements, for particularly important to a realization of the Tudor style is the idea that muscular effort or academic preparation for a step should be invisible. Tudor does use a large range of classical movements—extensions, leaps, supported adagio—but in a context that makes them hard to recognize. And although they don't always look it, Tudor's steps are technically difficult, the more so in that they are supposed to appear completely effortless. According to LeClercq, "The steps are uncomfortable; exactly where you don't want to go—*that's* where you go. In a certain way, it seems anti-ballet. In *Lilac Garden* the steps are very hard, and you have to act at the same time; the lifts were difficult, but Tudor managed them with me very well. He does a great deal of coaching, much more than either Robbins or Balanchine; it takes the form of a running commentary that has nothing to do with the steps and everything to do with motivation. The ballet was wonderful to dance, and the dress was fabulous—a dream dress that you could really move in—long and in Italian silk. It was lovely."

Barbara Walczak, one of the Guests, describes some of the difficulties, particularly formidable for Balanchine dancers: "*Every* movement had a meaning, no detail was too small. At one point, we shivered in the first chill of evening; at another, we were wishing on a star. It was quite a change from working with Balanchine, where everything was on counts. Here, there was super-romantic music and no counts, so to perform on the music—often some rather awkward lifts—in character, in a long costume, and with style, was an enormous challenge. Tudor knew exactly what he wanted, although he couldn't always explain it vividly. One had to sense it; and you had the feeling that you were either suited to his requirements and could do it, or you were simply unsuited and unable—that it was something you couldn't learn to do."

Says Tudor, "I hate counts, I really hate them. I make the dancers listen to the music until they really know it; actually, with patience, you can do it with almost anyone."

England:
"Intense, sentimental, by no means unmoving." [10]

Italy:
"A highly mediocre musical text, the product of nineteenth-century salon sentimentality, provides, however, a splendid background for this story. No longer

do we have music and dance—one complements the other in such a way that sounds seem to be mingled with gestures, fused in a single fabric of language and expression. Tudor's fluent choreography thus serves this rather banal, pathetic little tale of unhappy love, which continually hovers on the verge of cliché, but, amazingly, within the strictest limitations, achieves a valid psychological and emotional realization of its theme." [11]

THE PIED PIPER

CHOREOGRAPHY: Jerome Robbins

MUSIC: Aaron Copland (Concerto for Clarinet and String Orchestra, with Harp and Piano, 1948, written for Benny Goodman)

LIGHTING: Jean Rosenthal

PREMIERE: December 4, 1951

PIPER (solo clarinet): Edmund Wall

DANCERS: Diana Adams and Nicholas Magallanes; Jillana and Roy Tobias; Janet Reed and Todd Bolender; Melissa Hayden and Herbert Bliss; Tanaquil LeClercq and Jerome Robbins; 16 women, 7 men

This was Robbins's fourth work for the New York City Ballet (not counting parts of *Jones Beach*), and quite different from any of the preceding ones. He was beginning to establish a pattern—a pattern of not repeating himself and a pattern of creating successful ballets.

Piper was fun for performers as well as audience. Says LeClercq, "What did I do? Well, I chewed gum and did a jazzy little dance. It was easy—and no toe shoes! We even got paid for providing our own 'costumes.'"

Terry enjoyed the fun: "To use an appropriately slangy term, a real beaut. Has its slang movements, such as the thumbing of noses, but it is also balletic, jazzy, lyrical, frenzied and ever-responsive to the compulsion of rhythm. As a matter of fact, the ballet's only connection with the folk tale of Hamelin is to be found in responsiveness to music. Robbins's Piper works his magic upon a group of dancers.

"The curtain rises upon an empty stage. A ladder or so, a section of a theatrical flat, and doors leading to backstage

quarters are all we see. Through the dimness, the Piper approaches. He is a man dressed in ordinary street clothes and he carries a clarinet. His amblings lead him eventually to a music stand, stage left and front. He glances at a musical score, adjusts a light so that he can see, tootles tentatively, and then bursts into Copland's Concerto for Clarinet and String Orchestra. A little light filters through the dimness as the dancers enter. The music is slow, a trifle sad, and two of the young pursuers of sound, Adams and Magallanes, commence to dance a fairly gentle, almost formal pas de deux. Jillana and Tobias enter. Doors open, letting in more light, obliterating a few of the shadows, but not so many of them but what a pair can dance, backs to audiences, with their silhouettes reflected in giant size against the walls. The tempo changes, the lights come up, Reed and Bolender enter, and soon the stage is flooded with people ensnared by the now wild, insistent, cajoling, dictating notes of the music. Hayden, Bliss, LeClercq and Robbins himself join the throng in an intricate, unpredictable and throbbing kinetic response to the Piper and his abettors in the pit. They do the Charleston, they lie on the floor in a vast vibrating mass, they freeze into contorted immobilities, they pretend to resist or they yield crazily to a screaming command of the clarinet, to an irresistible rhythmic pattern, to a musical jolt, to the lash of a cadenza, to the tickle of a single pointed note.

"And yet *The Pied Piper* is by no means a disorderly, illogical ballet. It has form in stage design, in movement contrasts and parallels, in spatial patterns; and it has kinetic logic. This kinetic element (which is, of course, present in all dance) is the key to this ballet's purpose and power. The majority of the movements in the work may be classified as kinetic pantomime. In other words, the movements have meanings but they are neither literal nor symbolic meanings. They are kinetic, they make muscle-sense. In this specific instance, the music is the stimulus, the body reacts or comments upon it immediately and impulsively and instinctively. It is danced pantomime in its purest, most primal, most potent form." [1]

Martin: "Basic elements of both the academic ballet and jazz, with a slightly rambunctious sense of play as the fusing agent. If classicism does not imply too lofty a tone, this is actually a classic idiom in its own terms, and a very responsive

The Pied Piper. (*Photo William McCracken.*)

one. . . . More fun than a box of monkeys, and a pronounced hit, but it is not really top-drawer Robbins. At its premiere it exhibited two main difficulties. One was that it was done on a bare stage without even a cyclorama, which was both distracting and utterly without esthetic pleasure. The other was that Robbins had apparently conceived an amusing idea for Copland's clarinet concerto and tried to twist the form of the music to fit. The result was that the slow opening section, which did not conform to that idea, was started off in half a dozen directions, as if the choreographer were merely improvising until he came to the part that suited his purpose. When that part arrived, he really went to town, it is true, and the hilarity and the ingenuity of the invention, together with an especially brilliant and engaging performance by Reed, proved completely irresistible. A work of great talent and individuality it unquestionably is, but it is a mite on the shallow side and is still in need of structural carpentry." [2]

Europeans, of course, seized on the Ballet's American quality, and most of them were delighted by it.

England:

"Other choreographers besides Robbins show intelligence and musical sense, but few of them have so personal a style or such deftness. And of all the leading choreographers he is the most emphatically and unmistakably American. Per-

haps just because his choreographic style is so American and because that is precisely what a European audience would want of an American choreographer, there is a tendency in this country to overvalue Robbins's work to the detriment of, say, the later works of Balanchine: the American way in ballet is relatively unfamiliar over here, the traditional classical way is not. *The Pied Piper* is a joke which goes on too long, and its latter part does not quite fulfill that high promise of the elegiac pas de quatre with which it begins: those are its obvious limitations. Yet it is an extremely apt and competent work, marked with a thoroughly American rhythm; marked, too, with Robbins's characteristic audacity. The dancers come on stage in their practice-tights and dance, as it were, involuntarily to the piper's tune. Indeed, there is little to it when it is set down on paper, but as a choreographic spectacle it is thoroughly satisfactory." [3]

Germany:

"A real surprise. As a kind of danced 'show,' it falls into no known school of movement either in technique or in spirit. . . . The clarinetist begins to play, and from all sides dancers appear, bewitched, first only a few, then large numbers, in bright shirts and tights. In steps and boogie-woogie accents and belly-dancing movements they scurry across the stage. They knock off splits in the air as though they were throwing around pieces of spaghetti. They shake their

shoulders, lie down on the floor, and begin all over again, reacting to the enticement of the clarinet. It's a capital work, received with great enthusiasm." [4]

Italy:

"Completely American. The background is the undressed stage, with some clutter of cases in the back and lights that seem to play without direction. The Piper emerges from the darkness, attracting dancers. His sounds animate them like marionettes who live solely on music and rhythm. First there are languid movements for couples. Eventually, the compelling music drives everybody into a frenzy. At the end they rebel against the Piper, who disappears in a puff of smoke. Full of modern rhythms and the dance styles of today, the ballet creates the effect of most agile humor, but it never tries to overdo the joke." [5]

BALLADE

CHOREOGRAPHY: Jerome Robbins

MUSIC: Claude Debussy (*Six Épigraphes Antiques,* piano pieces for four hands, 1914, orchestrated by Ernst Ansermet, 1939; *Syrinx* for unaccompanied flute, 1912)

COSTUMES, DÉCOR: Boris Aronson

LIGHTING: Jean Rosenthal

BALLADE

FLUTE: Frances Blaisdell

CAST: Nora Kaye, Tanaquil LeClercq, Janet Reed, Robert Barnett, Brooks Jackson, Louis Johnson (guest), John Mandia

Ballade was not well received; a major criticism was that, despite a fairly insistent but unspecified underlying premise, the intent of the ballet was elusive. This was frustrating for the spectator. Robbins, however, was eminently sure of what he was doing. As he explained it (in 1974): "In a way it's about what happens to roles when people aren't dancing them. There's that Petrouchka costume lying on a rack somewhere, or there's the role in limbo—I'm not necessarily talking about Petrouchka; it's only when someone gets into that role that the role comes to life—exists again—and then when that person stops, the role collapses. The roles are endowed by whatever artist happens to dance them. And to me that's sort of what was underneath it all. The costumes were all based on the Picasso circus and clown people, so they are *performers* more than anything else. Along comes the man who gives them life, and they get up and perform their roles, then he takes the balloons away and they collapse again. And they wait in limbo until someone else comes along. . . . The snow [made it] cold to begin with; as the man comes on, the snow stops. It's the state of hibernation until something happens. Then there's a little twist—Tanny's rebellion at her existence and letting go of her balloon. At the end, they all collapse again, except Tanny. She can't collapse because she's let go of the force that gives her life—or sleep. She's in a state of nowhere, really, while everybody else is in hibernation. Of course, it doesn't matter whether people see what I was after, as long as it has a logic; people may not know exactly what it is, as long as they feel some sense behind it." He is thinking of reviving it.

Chujoy expressed his puzzlement. "This is a ballet that absolutely demands a program note [which it did not have]. The curtain rises on a dim stage peopled by half a dozen figures huddled on chairs against a backcloth. Snow is falling heavily, adding to the melancholy of the scene. A balloon-vendor enters, places a balloon in each inert hand, and walks away. The balloons endow the puppets

with life, and each rises to his or her feet with the pull of the balloon.

"This is a striking opening, but after that Robbins seems completely at a loss. The characters are all broken-down fugitives from the commedia dell'arte or Toulouse-Lautrec, but their functions are never made clear. Three boys dance together, but for no particular reason. Kaye, in an unbecoming Harlequin leotard and tights, caricatures many of the movements of *The Cage*, but the audience is plainly not intended to laugh. LeClercq, also *en travesti*, is a Pierrot who makes cabalistic signs on the floor and then lets her balloon float away. If only we knew of what the balloons are symbols, what the dance of the three boys means, or what the Kaye-Harlequin and the LeClercq-Pierrot represent, all the rest might fall into place.

"As it was, only one episode came to life. This was the dance in which a terrifyingly silly Columbine is wooed by one of the three boys. He, poor fool, cannot understand that she is not a living creature until she shows him her heart filled only with sawdust. It sounds ridiculously sentimental, but as performed by Reed and Tobias it has a pitiful quality, and the shaking out of the sawdust becomes a horrible moment of realization." [1]

Martin said: "cute, cloying, and self-conscious" and complained that the costumes were ugly. [2] For Hering, it was "a feeble bit of misanthropy whose cute theatrical tricks titillate rather than move." [3]

Terry, also somewhat baffled, called it "enormously poignant, enchanting. Sweet and tender and nostalgic, but what does it recall? Nothing very specific, admittedly. Robbins has created fresh, unforced, wonderfully simple movements which never actually led to a neat, tidy, and thoroughly dead resolution. But this might be, might it not, the true dance symbol of youth, eager to explore many exciting avenues but not interested in arriving at a final destination, an unalterable decision, too soon?" [4]

BAYOU

CHOREOGRAPHY: George Balanchine

MUSIC: Virgil Thomson (*Acadian Songs and Dances*, 1947)

COSTUMES, DÉCOR: Dorothea Tanning

LIGHTING: Jean Rosenthal

PREMIERE: 21 February 1952

CAST: *Boy of the Bayou*, Francisco Moncion; *Girl of the Bayou*, Doris Breckenridge; *Leaves and Flowers*, Melissa Hayden, Hugh Laing, 2 couples; *Starched White People*, Diana Adams, Herbert Bliss, 2 couples

The ballet describes the gentle mysteries and murmurings of a place where life, plants, and waters fulfill unseen destinies and the people living there who play, with poetic awareness, their part in its history. The spirit of the Bayou calls, and from the moss-hung forests come those who hear this call, to dance" (program note).

The ballet was, not surprisingly, drenched in atmosphere. Setting and music ("bewitching") were highly praised; the dance treatment was not.

Wrote Martin, "[The music] has wonderful possibilities for the right choreographer. Its underlying matter concerns the magic and the power of the land and water of the Bayou country; and over this constant base, as it were, there flit fragile and transient folk tunes, as if people were important, perhaps, but no match for the nameless mystery of enduring nature. Choreographically there is nothing of either the folk or the flora of the region, nor any formal values to compensate. An entirely new approach is clearly called for." [1]

Terry was more favorably impressed: "It has much to recommend it. It has atmosphere, soft and inviting, which may be sensed at the opening and closing of the ballet as the Boy of the Bayou poles his tiny boat along labyrinthine paths beneath dim and mysterious trees. There are moments of headiness also when the Boy, resembling a Cajun Puck, wafts a heavily scented flower under the noses of a fairly proper couple from the town and a pair representing figures from the fertile bayou forest, thus creating a union between those of the village and those of the land, or between man and nature. Not all is gentle poetry. There are lively dances that remind [us] that the Acadians like to dance until sleep comes upon them. As an entity, however, *Bayou* tends to leave the viewer discontented." [2]

Says Moncion, "It was a series of rather

disconnected elements. Balanchine resolved the conflict by mixing up the groups: the Starched White People were drawn to the Nature group, and they ended up paired differently. And that was helped along by the Boy, who was something like the figure of Oberon, because he broke up the pairs and brought about other relationships. At one point there was a Girl of the Bayou . . . but the ballet did limp along."

Both Thomson and Stravinsky had advised Balanchine to use different music, feeling that this suite—"little songs and dances from Acadian folklore"—was too choppy. But, says Thomson, "George was stubborn."

CARACOLE

CHOREOGRAPHY: George Balanchine

MUSIC: Wolfgang Amadeus Mozart (Divertimento No. 15 in B-flat major, K. 287, 1777)

COSTUMES: Christian Bérard (from *Mozartiana*)

PREMIERE: 19 February 1952

CAST: Diana Adams, Melissa Hayden, Tanaquil LeClercq, Maria Tallchief, Patricia Wilde, André Eglevsky, Nicholas Magallanes, Jerome Robbins; 8 women

OTHER CASTS: Yvonne Mounsey, Herbert Bliss

Allegro
Theme and Variations
Minuet
Andante
Finale

Caracole was one of Balanchine's pure dance compositions, set to what he reputedly considers the finest divertimento ever written. And it had another Balanchine hallmark: lavish use of principal dancers—here, in a work of thirty minutes, five ballerinas and three premiers danseurs. The steps of *Caracole* were lost many years ago (Balanchine has since created a completely new ballet to this music—*Divertimento No. 15*), but it is remembered with great fondness by its dancers as being particularly challenging—and flattering—to perform (another Balanchine hallmark). The rather

fanciful title in French means "half-turn"; according to Kirstein, it is "apparently a form of the Latin 'conchylium,' snail and conch, from its twisting and turning in a compact form. In horsemanship: a half turn to right or left; loosely, any turn or twist in zig-zag course, as in capering about."

Caracole was a ballet for ballet-lovers. Rather surprisingly, a write-up appeared in *Time* magazine (according to which "the title fit the dances like a leotard"). Even more surprisingly, *Time* quoted the *Daily News:* " 'Enchanting, stimulating, beautiful, active, lively, lovely, colorful, unusual, and just plain sound ballet,' said the *News*. Balanchine wowed them again. The Finale, with the full company on stage, sent the critics racing hot-eyed for their typewriters." [1]

In quite another vein, Denby wrote, "Despite its hard clothes [he disliked the costumes], *Caracole* is a heavenly piece to see, and everybody knows it immediately. If you watch the steps, in the variations, for instance, a single step or brief combination will flash out oversharply visible, so astonishing is the contrast to the step before it. There is not one novel 'expressive' gesture to tax your nervous sympathy; not one step twisted or odd, each limpidly departs from and returns to a neutral equilibrium; everything is academic convention; nothing but the body

in plastic motion in beauty—the dancer appearing effortlessly fantastic." [2]

Martin, "Certainly the most flashing and brilliant composition Balanchine has given us, at least since *Theme and Variations*. Quite obviously the choreographer was in love with the music. The strongest sections are the Theme and Variations and the Andante. The variations for Tallchief and Wilde are breathtakingly rapid, rhythmic, and ingenious; that for Eglevsky may well be the most intricate passage ever created by Balanchine for a man. The Andante is an amazingly complex series of pas de deux put together into a total form with ensemble passages, and it is a joy and delight." [3]

Hering discerned not a classical but a baroque and rococo flavor. For Terry, "The formula—classical steps, straight lines and curved lines, interweavings and parallelisms, mass motions and solo designs—may be familiar but it has [here] produced a new and delightful work of art." [4] Making something fresh from traditional sources is also a Balanchine hallmark.

London critics were considerably less enchanted; in general, they were not wholly receptive to the Balanchine "abstractions":

"One of Balanchine's tactful essays in choreographic setting of eighteenth-cen-

Caracole. **Andante. Tanaquil LeClercq, Nicholas Magallanes.** (*Photo Fred Fehl.*)

tury music. Some of it, notably the variations, is imaginatively treated, but not the Andante, which is misconceived from a musical point of view." [5]

"The rhythm is exactly translated into steps. Sometimes the choreography has almost the precision and unemotional quality of 'drilling to music.' " [6]

LA GLOIRE

Ballet in three scenes

CHOREOGRAPHY: Antony Tudor

MUSIC: Ludwig van Beethoven (Overtures: *Leonora III*, 1806, *Coriolanus*, 1807, *Egmont*, 1810)

BOOK: Lincoln Kirstein

COSTUMES: Robert Fletcher

DÉCOR: Gaston Longchamp

LIGHTING: Jean Rosenthal

PREMIERE: 26 February 1952

CAST: *La Gloire*, Nora Kaye; *2 Handmaidens to Lucretia*; *Sextus Tarquinius* and *Hamlet's Stepfather*, Francisco Moncion; *The Pleiades*, 6 women; *Orion*, Jacques d'Amboise; *Artemis*, Una Kai; *Hippolytus* (*Stepson to Phaedra*) and *Laertes*, Hugh Laing; *Ophelia*, Doris Breckenridge; *3 Players*; *Hamlet's Mother, the Queen*, Beatrice Tompkins; *The Dancer in Gray*, Diana Adams

SCENE: The stage of a state repertory theater

La Gloire is the last work created by Tudor for the New York City Ballet, although his *Dim Lustre* was revived there some years later, in 1964. Tudor's "psychological" ballets, heavily dependent on atmosphere, theatrical effects, and acting ability, are not particularly well suited to the talents of most New York City Ballet performers. Two of the three dancers most closely associated with him (Kaye and Laing) did not remain with the Company long (Adams stayed), and when they left, his ballets lost their most effective interpreters. The life of *La Gloire* was short.

The basic criticism was one with which Tudor concurred: the inappropriateness of the music. Says he, "The score absolutely overwhelmed it. You can't get the whole thing going with those Beethovian blasts."

Martin wrote, "Three Beethoven overtures played end to end would make any group of dancers look puny. His story shows us a declining tragedienne. As she plays, we are supposed to see through to her personal tragedy. But even with a few offstage interludes to show her a bit more directly, this is an almost impossible assignment for a dancer, against the voice of the Titan roaring in the pit." [1]

In addition to being too imposing, the music was also too short for all the material Tudor wanted to cover, including the relationships between Lucretia and Tarquin, Phaedra and Hippolytus, Hamlet and Ophelia. In particular, the backstage drama—the aging star threatened by aspiring younger artists—was neglected.

Wrote Terry, "Tudor has achieved few striking, penetrating differences in the sequences of characters which La Gloire herself plays. Perhaps intentionally, she is at her most magnificent at the close when young heroines are denied her and Hamlet is her role. But this triumph, this late glory does not seem to relate to the intimations of anguish suggested, oh so sketchily, in a brief scene in the dressing room. He has given Kaye some superb gestures, which speak of pride, arrogance, fear, and dedication, and he has from time to time augmented these with dance actions indicative of La Gloire's

La Gloire. **Nora Kaye as Hamlet.**

personal ways and theatrical prowess, but too much unfinished business, too many gaps, make this ballet seem like an outline, rather than the synopsis, of the life of a star. The corps members often merely wander, intrude, and provide remote support to the plays within the ballet." [2]

On the other hand, for Hering "The actress's whole existence was there—the tense dressing-room moments, the great scenes on stage, and the flirtations with the leading men in the wings. And the whole was punctuated with Tudor's matchless ability to fuse dramatic gesture and dance impetus. [However], the relationship between movement and music was often questionable." [3]

Marie Rambert is said to have felt it conveyed the backstage atmosphere better than any work she had ever seen.

Tudor himself remains very fond of the idea and has been looking for suitable music for the past twenty-odd years, so far without success. He especially liked the Hamlet sequence with the Players "and the understudy hovering in the background" (several critics also thought this the high point). If he ever does find the right music, "I'd probably use different stories, and, of course, with different rhythms, the steps would be new."

Even in England, where the critics seemed at times to be crying out for a ballet with a story line as relief from a repertory they felt to be top-heavy with abstract works, *La Gloire* was not a success. Most criticism, as in America, centered on the choice of music and the sheer amount of drama that was struggling to unfold. The *Times* had this tidbit: " 'Cecil B. de Mille,' runs a famous quatrain, 'Was persuaded, much against his will,/To leave Moses/Out of the Wars of the Roses.' Not so Tudor, who contrived to bring into one ballet Lucretia, Phaedra, and Hamlet, fitting the action of these three plots, together with some backstage business, to the overtures which Beethoven composed for quite different dramas." [4]

PICNIC AT TINTAGEL

Ballet in three scenes

CHOREOGRAPHY: Frederick Ashton

MUSIC. Sir Arnold Bax (*Garden of Fand,* 1916)

COSTUMES, DÉCOR: Cecil Beaton

LIGHTING: Jean Rosenthal

PREMIERE: 28 February 1952

CAST: *The Husband (King Mark)*, Francisco Moncion; *The Wife (Iseult)*, Diana Adams; *Her Maid (Brangaene)*, Yvonne Mounsey; *Her Lover (Tristram)*, Jacques d'Amboise; *His Rivals (The False Knights)*, Stanley Zompakos, Brooks Jackson; *Her Chauffeur and Footman (Heralds)*, Alan Baker, John Mandia; *The Caretaker (Merlin)*, Robert Barnett

OTHER CASTS: *Husband,* Roland Vasquez, Zompakos; *Wife,* Melissa Hayden; *Lover,* Herbert Bliss; *Maid,* Una Kai, Irene Larsson

Picnic at Tintagel. Diana Adams, Jacques d'Amboise, Yvonne Mounsey. *(Photo Fred Fehl.)*

Today a mist-swept ruin, the Cornish Castle of Tintagel has been considered for centuries as the scene of the love story of Tristram and Iseult, which has inspired writers from the time of Geoffrey of Monmouth to Tennyson, Swinburne, Richard Wagner, Thomas Hardy and Jean Cocteau. It is imagined that a party of tourists in 1916 (the date of the composition of the score), visits the castle. Overcome by the atmosphere that lurks among the ancient stones, they find themselves involved in an echo of the famous tragedy. When they recover their sense of time and are recaptured by the present, the power of the legend persists" (program note).

Chujoy summed up the ballet's virtues: "Exactly the kind of work the company needed, telling a story succinctly without depending on program notes to eke out choreographic vagueness, and giving the dancers one of their rare opportunities to characterize.

"It had a handsome set with a fine transformation scene, wonderfully colored medieval costumes and some 'amusing' ones for the picnickers. And it had an Ashton pas de deux out of his top drawer. The warm audience response indicated that the story ballet still had a strong appeal when the story is told with as skillful a mixture of mime and dance as it is here. Ashton's craftsmanship was everywhere in evidence, and in the passage for Iseult and Tristram he also showed us Ashton the fine and sensitive artist." [1]

The ballet additionally provided the seventeen-year-old d'Amboise with his first leading role; and the passion, femininity, and beauty of Iseult suited Adams perfectly. Ashton himself is fond of *Picnic:* "The story was my idea. I like the notion of two people falling almost desperately in love, against their own volition, with an outside force plunging them into it. I'd also read the book by those two ladies [*An Adventure,* by M. Moberly and Eleanor Jourdain, 1931, in which the authors recount how they stumbled on the court of Louis XIV in full panoply on a visit to Versailles], and the ballet has that same idea of going back in time. It had a very nice pas de deux for Tristram and Iseult, and a marvelous kind of *coup de théâtre,* because the change to the past was so terrifically quick—they were able to do it in seconds—and when the light went on again they were immediately at court. It always got a round of applause."

Martin wrote, "A typically British ballet, if not a typical Ashton ballet, with its accent on story told in large part in mime. It constitutes the only ballet of this type in the local company's repertoire. It is extremely simple and unpretentious, it is expertly planned, beautifully realized in stage terms, smart and stylish. A party visits the ruins of the Castle of Tintagel, where Merlin, or at least his spirit of magic, inhabits the body of the caretaker. Among them are a young wife, her husband, and a young man who might be her lover at the slightest opportunity. This fact becomes very clear to all of them in their romantic surroundings, and when the two young people raise their wine glasses, the wine becomes the potion of Tristram and Iseult for a flashing moment in their minds. Before they have finished drinking, they have relived the tragic love story, and when the husband breaks the spell by taking away the glasses, they return to their motoring a bit disturbed by the general awareness of the potential relationships. Ashton has made the middle section wonderfully romantic, with all the magic of Round Table days, and he has designed a lovely pas de deux as well as some crisp and lively formal dramatic action. But he has managed to frame it all in a delicately sophisticated sense of humor, which keeps it from being lush or whimsical. His characters are likewise cleanly drawn, with the simplest and most direct of strokes, whether in the period of the legend or in the early automobile-and-duster era." [2]

Terry: "At the close of the piece, the first scene and costumes are restored as the frightened group leaves and the caretaker picks up two gleaming swords, relics of a dream. Or was it a dream? . . .

"Ashton's drama is concerned with an ominous moment preliminary to crisis. At the picnic, desire of the lovers for each other and the swelling anger of the husband draw close to catastrophe. The same situation, lived to its completion in fulfilled passion, betrayal, and death through the fantasy of Tintagel revisited in antiquity, is but a second of thought in the minds of the distraught trio. The drama is of the instant; only implications of drama are permitted to span long reaches of time. The love duet itself is a work of great beauty. Even its prelude is remarkable, for he has given the waiting Iseult movements which proclaim her yearning for Tristram, her impatience in awaiting his arrival. The steps are classical—little running bourrées on pointe—but the hips move ever so slightly with each step and the result is unbelievably sensual. The duet is an extension of this into wider, freer movement, into patterns which celebrate the sought-for wonders of proximity." [3]

SCOTCH SYMPHONY

CHOREOGRAPHY: George Balanchine

MUSIC: Felix Mendelssohn (Symphony No. 3 in A minor, op. 56, "Scotch," 2nd, 3rd, and 4th movements, 1842)

WOMEN'S COSTUMES: Karinska

MEN'S COSTUMES: David Ffolkes

DÉCOR: Horace Armistead

LIGHTING: Jean Rosenthal

PREMIERE: 11 November 1952

CAST: Maria Tallchief, André Eglevsky, Patricia Wilde; 8 couples

OTHER CASTS: Diana Adams, Suzanne Farrell, Melissa Hayden, Allegra Kent, Kay Mazzo, Patricia McBride, Violette Verdy; Jacques d'Amboise, Herbert Bliss, Jean-Pierre Bonnefous, André Prokovsky, Peter Schaufuss, Edward Villella; Karin von Aroldingen, Sara Leland, Patricia Neary, Susan Pilarre, Barbara Walczak, Sheryl Ware

Vivace non troppo
Adagio

Allegro vivacissimo—Allegro maestoso assai

According to the program, "Balanchine [like Mendelssohn] wished to evoke the sweep and freshness, the brilliance and strength inherent in the Highland landscape. He has invented a classic ballet based on atmosphere and music, with an affectionate nod to the romantic tradition that made the hero of La Sylphide a Highlander." The ballet proved more durable than might originally have been expected; it is still in the active repertory. It irritates many because it cannot be too closely questioned: it is a ballet that hints at much but explains nothing ("Agreeably indefinite," wrote Terry [1]).

Manchester: "The first movement is an excuse for some lively dancing 'in the Scottish style'—a brilliant balletic pastiche for eight boys in Highland costume and a Scots lassie who spurs the ground with her steely pointes or flies above it. With the end of this movement the leading male figure (Eglevsky) enters and from then to the end there is an abrupt change of mood and style. We are tantalized with expressions and gestures which look as though they mean something but actually do not. If one is prepared to accept this discrepancy, then there is beauty to spare in the extended pas de deux which occupies almost the whole of the second movement. It is a most lovely and poetic conception, danced with the tenderest sensibility by Tallchief, who performs steps of the utmost difficulty without for a moment abandoning her new-found gentle radiance.

"The final movement brings back the whole corps de ballet, with the girls in Balanchine's favorite arrangement of eight performing movements in canon form, two by two. These ballabiles are no more interesting than they commonly were in the real Romantic ballet and Balanchine does not seem to have known how to introduce Wilde into the proceedings. The ballet therefore breaks in two, but as both halves are full of felicitous invention it is perhaps churlish to do more than mention the fact." [2]

As Kent said, "There were theories—I was too sylphlike, not sylphlike enough; I was really a sylph, I was a girl pretending to be a sylph. Finally Balanchine said, 'Just dance it!'"

Wrote Hering, "To look for any special artistic conviction would be to make un-

duly heavy demands upon it. It is little more than a pleasant patchwork of styles and historical fragments." [3]

On the other hand, the ambiguities can be enticing for some. Wrote Barnes, "It is the quality of mystery that appeals, or, for that matter, tantalizes. Who is this young laird roaming through an impossibly romantic gloaming, or who is this sylph, protected it seems by an entire regiment of Her Majesty's Highlanders, who so mysteriously seduces him? The answers are quite unimportant—only the questions matter, only the atmosphere of Sir Walter Scott, the strange spirits flitting through even stranger glens." [4]

In any event, the ballet contains many attractive elements, including gay scenery and costumes and hints of Scotland in the dancing, and, in particular, a challenging ballerina role that requires a high level of technique tempered by lightness, grace, and the quality of an otherworldly vision. It was a new kind of part for Tallchief, whose reputation had been built on brilliance. (She has said, however, that she attempted something of the same style in the second movement of Bourrée Fantasque.) Choreographically, the ballet contains many steps, gestures, and poses allusive of the romantic era. For instance, to simulate flight by wires, which had propelled sylphs, fairies, gods, goddesses, and sometimes an entire corps de ballet heavenward in the preceding century, Balanchine had the ballerina thrown across the stage by a group of men into the arms of her cavalier.

Of the ballerina figure, Terry wrote: "Tallchief, flying through space with gossamer lightness, sweetly rejecting gravity as she balanced effortlessly on pointe, was lovely in her elusiveness. [The Scotsman] is obviously fascinated with her but she is unattainable, and [their] episode is built upon their brief meetings, partings, touchings and withdrawals. It is an appealing poetic sequence, for the movements are light and swift and exquisitely designed. When two boys toss Tallchief high in the air, she sails forward as if the air were her natural home, and Eglevsky catches her high on his chest as if she were without weight." [5]

Martin: "If perhaps one has wondered in advance how Balanchine could possibly build one of his customary musical abstractions upon this score, the answer is simply that he has not attempted anything of the sort. What he has done is considerably more interesting, for he has built rather a dramatic abstraction upon it. What emerges is very like some forgotten ballet by Coralli or Mazilier or Perrot, of which the actual plot has faded into oblivion but all the dramatic scenes, the moods and formalities remain. For this kind of treatment the music is admirable.

"Choreographically Balanchine has touched lightly on Scottish themes, but always entirely within the frame of the nineteenth-century ballet. [The] long adagio, wonderfully danced with its scenes of sadness, of nameless dramatic interference, of romance, even of the supernatural. This is by all odds the finest of the three movements, in both invention and atmosphere.

"This is perhaps not to be classed among the foremost masterpieces of Balanchine, but it is a sweet and winning work, beautifully made, beautifully produced, and beautifully danced." [6]

The ballet was not particularly well received in Europe. One French critic, for instance, felt that the hints of tragedy were pretentious rather than evocative: "Adds nothing to Balanchine's reputation.

The dresses are dreadful, the backdrop deplorable, and with the characters hinted at here, I would have preferred a more full-bodied love affair, such as that of *La Sylphide*. In a singularly unsuitable Scottish beret, Eglevsky performed beats and jumps and other measures of courtship whose significance escaped me. The lovely Tallchief, more beautiful than ever, made a graceful sylph, but one whose essence was completely vague. *Scotch Symphony* is, at bottom, rather insipid." [7]

Italy:
"This traditional choreography seems to be a new attempt to freely refresh aspects of nineteenth-century style. But we can't help saying that despite the picturesque costumes and scenery, the ballet does not engage the attentions or interest." [8]

METAMORPHOSES

CHOREOGRAPHY: George Balanchine

MUSIC: Paul Hindemith (*Metamorphoses on Themes of Carl Maria von Weber,* 1943)

COSTUMES: Karinska

LIGHTING: Jean Rosenthal

PREMIERE: 25 November 1952

CAST: Tanaquil LeClercq, Todd Bolender, Nicholas Magallanes; 16 women, 8 men

Metamorphoses was *rather* mad, with its costume effects of old bustles, scenery of bedsprings, pas de deux with the male on his knees, and a finale in which the stage was aflutter with giant wings. The music is a boisterous and rousing affair, with sweeping rhythms and jazzy, colorful, and exotic percussive effects. (The principal theme of the second movement is derived from a Chinese melody Weber found in the musical dictionary of Rousseau, published 1786.) As Martin implied, the ballet owed at least as much to Hindemith and Karinska as to Balanchine:

Scotch Symphony. **Left:** **Allegra Kent, Edward Villella.** (*Photo Fred Fehl.*) **Right:** **Michael Maule, Patricia Wilde, Frank Hobi.** (*Photo Walter E. Owen.*)

Metamorphoses. Left: **Tanaquil LeClercq, Todd Bolender.** *Above:* **Ensemble with Tanaquil Le-Clercq (facing front).** *(Photos Fred Fehl.)*

"On the very free adaptations and variations [from Weber], Balanchine and Karinska have really gone to work and turned out an idiotic, visually gorgeous, richly humorous extravaganza. Metamorphoses is right! It is a large ensemble work with the full company on stage almost all the time. The basic costume, though perfectly decorous, has the intent of nudity; upon this [Karinska] has added in each movement some little bits of identifying regalia—minimal trunks, wee tutus, masks, antennae, and the like. They are all perfectly beautiful, as gay as a lark in spirit, backed in one movement by some charming Chinese panels let down from the flies, and lighted with genuine magic.

"Balanchine hits his real stride in the second movement, and he has let his fantasy run free. It is a stunning job and ends with a wonderfully grotesque adagio for LeClercq and Bolender. The first movement, about acrobats, is built in effective mass designs, and the last is considerably hampered choreographically by the huge wings attached to the dancers' arms. But it is all never less than theatrically brilliant and true to the form and the spirit of the music." [1]

Hering saw the ballet with less humor: "*Metamorphoses* is merely chic. It is a cold dance to warm music—a costume designer's feast and a choreographer's fam-

ine. It is almost inevitable to outline it in terms of its ingenious but garish costumes. In the opening section the dancers resemble grub worms (or lambchops or French poodles, depending upon one's imagination). Clad in flesh-colored tights and leotards with the thighs outlined in shirred satin, they kick and plunge energetically in unison. Dainty bell-like forms are lowered against the black backdrop, and a plaintive oriental theme accompanies a sort of hotcha version of *The Cage.* The dancers wear sequined bras and fanciful wired headdresses with trembling feelers that transform them into stylish insects. The ballet ended in cheerful banality when Magallanes flapped on with enormous wings to chase the beetle. The entire corps joined in the flapping and used their wings to create the kind of geometric patterns one sees in presentation house finales." [2]

Manchester, too, had criticisms, but found the overall effect "exhilarating." Somewhat in the same vein, Terry wrote: "A colorful, sometimes impudent and pictorially stunning ballet whose thematic pattern suggests the transitions of creatures from earthbound figures to gossamer-winged insects to great birds. These metamorphoses are not accorded profound exploitation in the choreography. There is no sense of churning creative processes nor intimations of conflict

among species. The Balanchine touch is to be found in the fine and mobile patterns of the ensemble, in gestures which are sensitive but not always sensible, in complex adagio designs, and in a theater craftsmanship which few choreographers can hope to match. . . . handsome but slight, adept but not very deep, diverting but not stimulating, and visually splendid." [3]

One of the decided assets of *Metamorphoses* was that it offered LeClercq, with her unique theatrical personality, one of her most distinctive roles. (Speaking of her sinuous elegance, a fellow dancer remarked that "Tanny was like Garbo when she danced.") She describes the ballet: "George said that in the first movement we were like acrobats. We were dressed in leotards. I was in turquoise and a little bit of gold—a new material that had just come out and had a little bit of elastic in it, and it really *fit*. Nicky was in fuchsia. We didn't do that much acrobatics; he lifted me a bit; it was very cute. Then I went off and put on a headpiece and a mask and—this was so clever—a sort of a little bra, you know, the kind a Balinese or Indian dancer would wear. It fastened in the front—just two little fasteners—and came with very light wings. And then I stepped into a little bikini that had tubular horsehair around that made a kind of a fluffy tutu. That's the part I did with

Todd, who was like a bug. It was a beautiful, beautiful adagio. He was on the floor and on his knees the whole time and partnered. George had said, 'I'd like to pose myself a puzzle: how can I make an adagio with the man only getting up as high as his knees?' This man, looking like a bug, shiny, crawling around, and . . . dancing. It was really amazing. Todd had to have knee pads because he got very sore. It was a little bit maybe like *Bugaku*, but not as acrobatic and intense. He partnered, for instance, by giving me support around my knee (the *Serenade* supported-promenade-in-arabesque idea), and I would do arabesque, à la seconde, and then bend the knee and bring it front, then switch legs and he would hang onto the other knee. I think George had seen the Balinese dancers, so the adagio had a Balinese flavor (the way *Bugaku* is slightly Japanese). Then we went rushing out, took off the masks, and got two enormous wings. The last movement was lots of wings and lots of running around with poses—not much dancing."

Says Bolender, "My first reaction when I got into that outfit—knee pads and a great hump of shell on my back—was that the movement should have the look of a heavy, soft creature, perhaps like a turtle—a kind of life that has existed forever, eternal, like breathing. Not a fast-moving beetle, but something very slow. This kind of movement would play down any kind of relationship between male and female. The girl was a sort of butterfly, a gorgeous, elegant, long creature, against this earthy, black, ageless kind of thing. The feel of my hands as I would lift

them was always as though I were pushing them against air, or even through something."

HARLEQUINADE PAS DE DEUX

CHOREOGRAPHY: George Balanchine

MUSIC: Riccardo Drigo (from *Les Millions d'Arlequin*, 1900)

COSTUMES: Karinska

LIGHTING: Jean Rosenthal

PREMIERE: 16 December 1952

CAST: Maria Tallchief, André Eglevsky
Also danced by Janet Reed

This is one Balanchine display pas de deux that did not get top reviews, despite the presence of Tallchief and Eglevsky. For one thing, there was a certain amount of coy characterization associated with Harlequin and Columbine, not much suited to either principal. For another, critics found the passages of virtuosity, while definitely present, to be isolated. And, as Martin remarked, "With the music of Drigo, we come pretty close to the bottom of the barrel."[1]

Of this early pas de deux, Terry wrote: "A balletic trifle if ever I saw one, [it] produces two figures distantly related to the coquettish Columbine and the impetuous

Harlequin. A few random gestures hint at these characters, but for the rest, the duet is a display piece. Tallchief's multiple turns are longer and faster then ever; balances, requiring split-second timing with the partner, are perfectly done, and prancings sur les pointes are as frisky as one could wish. Eglevsky has some remarkably exciting passages in the coda, but his solo is twittery, as if too much action were crammed into a tight rhythmic phrase."[2]

Martin was harsher: "Notably lacking in urgency. Balanchine looked point-blank at period corn and gave it to us straight."[3]

KALEIDOSCOPE

CHOREOGRAPHY: Ruthanna Boris

MUSIC: Dmitri Kabalevsky (*The Comedians*, 1940)

COSTUMES: Alvin Colt

LIGHTING, DÉCOR: Jean Rosenthal

PREMIERE: 18 December 1952

CAST: Melissa Hayden, Patricia Wilde, Herbert Bliss, Todd Bolender, Francisco Moncion

OTHER CASTS: Jillana, Frank Hobi

Kaleidoscope was frankly a serviceable

Harlequinade Pas de Deux. **Maria Tallchief, André Eglevsky.** (*Photo Fred Fehl.*)

Kaleidoscope. **Patricia Wilde, Herbert Bliss, Todd Bolender, Frank Hobi, Melissa Hayden.** (*Photo Fred Fehl.*)

and perky diversion, whipped up in a hurry. Boris describes her general intent: "It was kind of a relay race of ideas, the way when you look through a kaleidoscope the colors pass and become something else. Each costume was a different color. It was also something of a show-within-a-show—they dance for each other as well as with each other."

The ballet, the critics found, served its unexalted purpose well. Terry called it "a jovial work in which everyone dashes, dances, and prances with fine spirit. The music supplies [Boris] not only with motivations for fleetness and joy of action, but also for making frolic. Her ballet has a good many agreeable jokes in it, some of them dealing with situation but several of them true muscular jokes, kinetic surprises. There are thin spots, and a few of these danced anecdotes are stretched beyond their worth, but *Kaleidoscope* is engaging if not particularly substantial. The title is mirrored in the attractive décor, in the stunning costumes, in the decorative locomotions of the dancers, and in the subject matter. Thematically, Boris treats with a relay race, with Spanish-flavored activities, with classical dance at its most regally foolish, and with other matters open to satire." [1]

Hering added a bit more description: "A leisurely dance-play in which leaping and turning and wearing funny hats followed each other with good-natured ease. The scene designer did an equally imaginative job with a proscenium decoration of colored Mondrian-like squares and four little booths where the dancers perched to rest and hang their headgear." [2]

INTERPLAY

Ballet in four movements

CHOREOGRAPHY: Jerome Robbins

MUSIC: Morton Gould (*American Concertette*, 1943)

COSTUMES, DÉCOR: Irene Sharaff

LIGHTING: Jean Rosenthal

PREMIERE: 23 December 1952 (first presented 1 June 1945 as part of Billy Rose's *Concert Varieties*, Ziegfeld Theater, New York)

PIANO: Simon Sadoff

CAST: Janet Reed, Michael Maule (pas de deux); Todd Bolender (2nd movement); 3 women, 2 men

OTHER CASTS: Carolyn George, Allegra Kent, Sara Leland, Patricia McBride, Kay Mazzo, Dorothy Scott; Jacques d'Amboise, Herbert Bliss, Conrad Ludlow, Kent Stowell, Roy Tobias (pas de deux); Robert Barnett, Arthur Mitchell, Jerome Robbins (2nd movement)

FIRST MOVEMENT: Free-Play—full cast
SECOND MOVEMENT: Horse-Play—Bolender
THIRD MOVEMENT (pas de deux)—Reed, Maule
FOURTH MOVEMENT: Team-Play—full cast

Interplay was Robbins's second ballet—coming a year after his astounding and fresh *Fancy Free*—as well as his second ballet hit. He deliberately attempted a non-story ballet as a contrast to his first work. And he cast himself in it, giving eight performances a week in the *Concert Varieties* for a solid month. Then the show closed. The ballet soon became a staple of the Ballet Theatre repertory. At that time, Martin wrote of it, "Pure abstraction. The idiom is altogether Robbins. He has employed the basic approach of the classic ballet and its vocabulary to make a slightly jazzy, quite contemporary, American kind of dance. And he has done it quite easily and authoritatively. This might be considered as the foundation of an American mid-forties classic style." [1]

And Denby wrote, "Of serious interest for being, of all the ballets by American-trained choreographers, the most expertly streamlined in dance design. The intellectual vigor, the clear focus of its craftsmanship suggest that Robbins means to be and can be more than a sure-fire Broadway entertainer, that he can be a serious American ballet choreographer." [2]

What Robbins created was some boisterous hijinks for a group of all-American kids (vintage 40s)—kids who could dance like demons. Leaps, cartwheels, spins, multiple air turns, a duel of fouettés, comic bits, silly stuff, jive, and jitterbug—energy exploded all over the stage. Then the lights lowered, the music became pensive. The dancers sat on the sidelines or lay on the floor staring into the audience, while two appealing youngsters (perhaps only close pals, not yet lovers) performed a soft blues duet in the same jazz idiom as the more extroverted measures. At the end, as they sat together, the lights went up, and the competition was on again.

Without exception, the critics found the New York City Ballet's "sophisticated ambience entirely unsuited" (Chujoy) to a fully satisfactory rendition of the piece: "The company is far too classical and has far too little sense of play to make the most of Robbins's jazzy little escapade. There was not much swing and twinkle to it. Surprisingly enough, not even its technical demands were as well met as they should have been when it began to get over into the showy category." [3]

"[It] is a series of playful or wistful improvisations—with shreds of imitations of other dance styles—bits of flirtation—and a contest with the dancers choosing teams. Its charm lies principally in the ability of the dancers to throw themselves into its wild turns and jazziness with a total lack of inhibition. At its first performance, the dancers did not have the whip-cracking zest that one associates with *Interplay*." [4]

"The New York City Ballet has never been fully at ease in this brisk and jazzy work. The sporting instincts were missing. Smiling effort [was substituted] for genuine liveliness." [5]

Despite its reception, the work was performed by the New York City Ballet for many years, providing quite a contrast to the rest of the repertory, and offering both technical and stylistic challenges to a number of the younger soloists, many of whom were on their way to becoming principal dancers.

CONCERTINO

CHOREOGRAPHY: George Balanchine

MUSIC: Jean Françaix (1932)

COSTUMES: Karinska

LIGHTING: Jean Rosenthal

PREMIERE: 30 December 1952

PIANO: Nicholas Kopeikine

CAST: Diana Adams, Tanaquil LeClercq, André Eglevsky

It was technically difficult, especially hard on the breathing. There were cute

Top: Interplay. **Horse-Play. Arthur Mitchell, Ruth Sobotka, Sonja Tyven.** *(Photo Fred Fehl.)*
Center: Concertino. **Tanaquil LeClercq, André Eglevsky, Diana Adams.** *(Photo Fred Fehl.) Bottom: Valse Fantaisie.* **Diana Adams, Patricia Wilde, Nicholas Magallanes, Tanaquil LeClercq.**
(Photo Fred Fehl.)

things—my variation, the pas de trois with the girls, very involved with arms and feet. One of the girls would kick and I would stumble on the foot up in the air, look around, and wonder what it was doing up there." (Eglevsky.)

Thus the humor in what Martin called "the merest wisp of a pas de trois." For Terry, it was "Gallic fluff."

Martin continued, "[Eglevsky] is all dressed up for the evening with two engaging ladies. He is never left alone with either of them (they are not that careless), and they let him out of their sight only long enough for an oh-so-impeccably nice little variation." [1]

Terry: "Because it is unpretentious, does not offend. LeClercq and Adams appear as very elegant cancan dancers, busy with pony trots, light actions of several kinds, and even some smooth and very aristocratic attitude turns. Assisting them is Eglevsky, agile and foolishly gallant." [2]

VALSE FANTAISIE

CHOREOGRAPHY: George Balanchine

MUSIC: Mikhail Glinka (1839)

COSTUMES: Karinska

PREMIERE: 6 January 1953

CAST: Diana Adams, Melissa Hayden, Tanaquil LeClercq, Nicholas Magallanes

OTHER CASTS: Barbara Fallis, Allegra Kent, Dorothy Scott, Barbara Walczak, Patricia Wilde

A short-order novelty that turned out to be a charming work. Balanchine displayed his talent for minute variation of detail and nuances of rhythm and accent." [1]

This "trifle" remained in the repertory eight or ten years. (In 1967, Balanchine choreographed another Glinka ballet, *Glinkiana*, one section of which used the same music and the same title.)

Martin: "Balanchine has set three of his most enchanting ballerinas to moving in a kind of perpetuum mobile, dainty, lilting, fleet, and studded with brilliance. A partner attends them all, less to dance in his own right than to serve as an adjunct to their dancing. They are clad in filmy, subtly shaded elegance, with jeweled headdresses and long streamers to take them back to Glinka's own Russia. The music, winning and melodious, with no break, no change of tempo, passes from persuasiveness to virtual hypnosis, and it is easy to realize why once the genteel waltz was considered an instrument of the devil." [2]

WILL O' THE WISP

CHOREOGRAPHY: Ruthanna Boris

MUSIC: Virgil Thomson (selections from *Acadian Songs and Dances*, 1947; Passacaglia from *Louisiana Story*, 1948)

COSTUMES, DÉCOR: Dorothea Tanning (from *Bayou*)

PREMIERE: 13 January 1953

CAST: *Those of Today*, Frank Hobi, 3 men; *Those of Yesterday*, Ruthanna Boris, 2 women, 2 men; *That of the Place*, 9 women

Spreads the pond her base of lilies
Bold above the boy
Whose unclaimed hat and jacket
Sum the history.
—Emily Dickinson
(program note)

According to Boris, "The story was a *Giselle* idea. A girl who had been betrayed on her wedding day committed suicide and was buried in unconsecrated ground in the swamp. She waited there to find a lover. One boy got involved with her, then realized what he had gotten into and tried to get away, but the swamp closed in on him. I decided the Spanish moss would be girls. They were lying on stage from the beginning, as part of the set, and when the boy fell asleep, the swamp began to come to life. There was suspense because the audience saw the swamp moving, but the boy didn't."

The ballet suffered the same fate as *Bayou*—poor reception and a brief life. It was felt, as in the case of *Bayou*, that music, décor, and costumes again overwhelmed the choreography, and that Boris had not provided choreography of

note. Hering found the most to praise: "The dramatic structure was nicely balanced. Four boys cavorted playfully after a turn in the old swimmin' hole. One of them curled up and went to sleep. The others left him. The sleeper was awakened by some amorphous-looking spirit people called Those of the Place. And after a bit of *Sturm und Drang*, he was enticed to a watery grave by an imperious-looking naiad who was one of Those of Yesterday. The boys returned; found their playmate's abandoned sweater; and wandered off. The grove was left empty. And the naiad glided across in silent triumph. The ballet started off promisingly—with the boys indulging in a nice combination of pantomime, athleticism, and a flavor of popular dance. But as the corps went into action, the lines and shapes of the choreography became confused, the gesture insignificant. Yet, despite its movement emptiness, the ballet has caught a wistful, poetic atmosphere. And so it may well be worth additional work." [1]

Others were considerably more negative.

THE FIVE GIFTS

CHOREOGRAPHY: William Dollar

MUSIC: Ernö Dohnányi (*Variations on a Nursery Rhyme*, for orchestra and piano concertante, op. 25, 1913)

Based on a story by Mark Twain ("The Five Boons of Life")

COSTUMES: Esteban Francés

PREMIERE: 20 January 1953 (first presented 1943 by American Concert Ballet)

CAST: *The Youth*, Todd Bolender; *The Fairy*, Melissa Hayden; *Pleasure*, Carolyn George; *Death*, Yvonne Mounsey; *Fame*, Jillana; *Riches*, Patricia Wilde; *Love*, Irene Larsson; *Another Youth*, Jacques d'Amboise; 4 women, 4 men
Fairy also danced by Marie-Jeanne, Barbara Walczak

The *Five Gifts* had an indifferent reception. Dollar's choice of music was criticized. Manchester wrote: "The essentially light-hearted character of the music

is completely ignored. The pompous, heavily orchestrated opening is the composer's playful way of pointing up the silliness of the one-finger picking out of the childish tune which follows. Had Dohnányi wanted to be serious he would hardly have chosen that particular song as his musical foundation." [1]

The story was faulted for not making much sense: A Fairy offers a Youth five gifts. He chooses all others over Death (which seems logical enough), but for this he is punished—condemned to old age—while the Fairy shows him another Youth who chose Death in preference to the other gifts. For reasons not made clear, this was the proper choice. Was the Fairy a good or an evil spirit?

As for the choreography, Martin felt "There was much to admire as well as sections inviting restlessness." [2] For Terry, the ballet overall was "pedestrian," but he also found interesting parts. Said he, "Strong and striking in its group actions and in those measures allotted to some of the men, and tending toward thinness and unimaginativeness in the patterns fashioned for the feminine principals. The initial episode, in which the Youth becomes enmeshed in yards of cord manipulated by the good-sized ensemble, is pictorially arresting, [and] the scene boasts much in the way of dramatic force. There is a harsh implacability in the weaving of the design itself and here one senses the inauguration of a conflict which is supposed to become more specific shortly. Whenever the ensemble returns throughout the course of the ballet, the dynamic pitch increases and the movements themselves take on character, emotional colorings. But everything tends to sink and to waver when actual incident is involved, for those passages in which the Youth must choose among five gifts, much of the movement reverts to the academic, to the dynamically frail. [The gifts] are given steps and patterns which do not seem far from the classroom, and the special nature of each is indicated fleetingly, if at all. It follows that one is hard put to recognize which gift is which and why the Youth selects one in preference to another. With this occurring, the dramatic line fades away." [3]

Hering mentioned "freshness" in the solos, and "an atmospheric starry sky for backdrop." [4]

AFTERNOON OF A FAUN

CHOREOGRAPHY: Jerome Robbins

MUSIC: Claude Debussy (*Prélude à l'Après-midi d'un Faune*, 1892–94)

COSTUMES: Irene Sharaff

DÉCOR, LIGHTING: Jean Rosenthal

PREMIERE: 14 May 1953

CAST: Tanaquil LeClercq, Francisco Moncion

OTHER CASTS: Melissa Hayden, Jillana, Allegra Kent, Irene Larsson, Patricia McBride, Kay Mazzo, Mimi Paul; Jacques d'Amboise, Peter Martins, Arthur Mitchell, Helgi Tomasson, Edward Villella

PLACE: A room with a mirror

Afternoon of a Faun. **Francisco Moncion, Allegra Kent.** (*Photo Martha Swope.*)

Debussy's music was inspired by a poem of Mallarmé's which was begun in 1865, supposedly for the stage, the final version of which appeared in 1876. The poem describes the reveries of a faun around a real or imagined encounter with nymphs. In 1912 Nijinsky presented his famous ballet, drawing his ideas from both the music and the poem, among other sources. This pas de deux is a variation on these themes" (program note).

Robbins describes the genesis of his then-daring use of the famous music—daring because of its previous, seemingly definitive associations:

"*Faun* came out of a couple of sources. First of all, my fascination with the original: I grew up on all those legends of Nijinsky in *Petrouchka*, *Schéhérazade*, *Faun*. And then watching it. That dropped somewhere into my head. Then one day in class, little Eddie Villella, who was standing next to me as a kid, suddenly began to stretch his body in a very odd way, almost like he was trying to get something out of it. And I thought how animalistic it was . . . he didn't know what he was doing, and that sort of stuck in my head. At another time I walked into a rehearsal studio where Louis Johnson was practicing the *Swan Lake* adagio with a student girl, and they were watching themselves in the mirror, and I was struck by the way they were watching

that couple over there doing a love dance and totally unaware of the proximity and possible sexuality of their physical encounters. And that was curious to me. The combination of all those things—even Edwin Denby talking once about how long the phrases were in the original choreography—sort of stuck in my head. And then I started. I wasn't ever quite sure whether the mirror should be straight front or offstage, right angles [to the audience]. I rehearsed it both ways, and each way is interesting. When the dancers' attention is to the side, it's easier for the audience to watch—they are sort of looking in—but when it's straight front, I think something much more arresting happens. . . . It was choreographed on Tanny, and that's the closest to what I had in mind, although Eddie and Patty [McBride] are very, very into that also. Tanny also had a terrific sexuality, underneath—the possibility of that—which was much more interesting than the obviousness of it. I always thought the girl had just washed her hair and just had on new toe shoes and a new clean practice dress and came into the studio to preen and practice."

Since its opening, the ballet has never been out of the repertory, and it has been performed by other companies as well. "Hypnotic" and "atmospheric" were the words most often used in describing its effect, with "erotic," "narcissistic," and "sensuous" not far behind. It has also been called "a perfect work." LeClercq and Moncion were widely praised.

Hering gave a lengthy description: "The atmosphere begins to accumulate even before there is any dancing. When

the curtain first rises, there is a fragile nylon drop downstage. The music stirs, and a light slowly rises behind the drop. The outlines of a dance studio are revealed. The nylon melts away, and one sees a tawny male creature asleep on the floor. He stretches. He arches his back and curves slowly from side to side. In mood he is very much like the faun of the old Nijinsky ballet. In appearance he is a boy alone in a dancing studio. The music draws him languidly to his feet. After a few tentative stretches, before a mirror (imagined on the audience side of the stage), he drifts to a corner of the room and curls on the floor, asleep again.

"Along a corridor behind the translucent back wall a female of unbelievable elegance picks her way on pointe. She glides into the studio, becomes aware of the sleeping male, but is more attracted by her own image in the mirror. The sleeper sits up like a startled faun. And slowly, hypnotically, with the music sifting through the space around them, they intertwine in a dance for two—or rather, for three. For the mirror is always there. After each moment of near-contact, they stare wide-eyed into its surface.

"Suddenly they drop to the floor, sitting in that ever-alert manner of dancers and wild creatures. The boy brushes a kiss on the girl's cheek. She stares into the mirror, brings her hand slowly to her cheek, and leaves. The boy dances alone, trying to capture the atmosphere of her presence. As the music dies, he sinks slowly to the floor and sleeps." [1]

Krevitsky: "One of the most sustained studies in focus and one of the most objective boy-girl relationships in all ballet.

The room, with china silk walls and bars, with the proscenium opening acting as the mirror wall, does much to establish the diaphanous quality of the impressionistic work, clearly inspired by Debussy. Rosenthal has done a masterful job with it. For simplicity of means, for directness in the handling of the theme, for brilliance of characterization, and for doing a contemporary work within the framework of the music, Robbins and the collaborators are to be highly praised." [2]

Terry: "Here, indeed, is an absorbing study, a sometimes shocking but exquisitely cool biography of the dancer who cherishes his own body-being, the only instrument his art possesses, just as the singer cherishes his voice or the violinist his Stradivarius. Although *Afternoon of a Faun* is not explosive physically, it is intense dynamically, and when the few large movements come, they appear as sharp and shining peaks of ecstasy in a pattern of sensual action which has not only omened their emergence but made them inevitable. It is true that there are not many flashy steps, but there is a great deal of movement, of gestural revelation, even of dynamic pause, and since human ardor is just as exciting as a batch of brisés volés (and perhaps more pertinent to the lives of most of us), the Robbins work strikes me as a major creation of its genre." [3]

Manchester: "Alas it is the girl in the mirror who receives the kiss. Before *Faun* is halfway through we have the feeling that the dancers we are watching have become the reflection, not the reality." [4]

Martin was the least drawn to the ballet. After praising the performances and the physical look of the work, he wrote, "Certainly the choreography does no violence to Debussy's music." [5]

LeClercq describes work on the ballet: "Jerry did it more quickly than any other I have known. He didn't say much, only that it was a summer day, and this was helped along by the wind machine billowing the silk. I don't recall his saying anything about the kiss. But he said it was sort of an interlude after class—and you come in and look at yourself and try out things to sort of assess how you look, and then you see him. I think the dancers know each other very well. The hair, fixing the toe shoes—Jerry uses what's around."

One quality that differentiates the performances of the girls is that some—like Mazzo—do it very literally, very rea-

Afternoon of a Faun. Francisco Moncion, Tanaquil LeClercq.

listically, while others, particularly McBride, are totally, eerily removed. "I think I was removed," says LeClercq.

Moncion: "Jerry had been looking around for a mood piece; he had already done *Ballade* to Debussy but didn't feel he had finished with the idea. The languor of the people was his; he read Mallarmé, and the gestures he used were evocative of Mallarmé's faun—such as pushing through the reeds on a hot, humid afternoon. Rosenthal invented the design—with a wonderful sumptuous, sensuous feel, a wonderful idea, the sheen of white silk. And the rippling comes—cool—just when the action on stage gets hot. Tanny never was innocent (unlike some later interpreters who have been winsome nymphets); with her, the awareness was already all there, an element of knowing what it was about and being, in a way, provocative—not obviously, but just leading very carefully from one thing to another in a very subtle way. I remember a Martin review of Jacques [d'Amboise] and Jillana in which he said he preferred their girl-meets-boy approach, as opposed to the neurotic tensions that existed between me and Tanny. But ours was the original conception. Jacques told me that he couldn't do it my way—it wasn't him—and that he approached it like a young swaggering truck driver, an *American*."

Moncion hit on the fact that in such an atmospheric work, with so little dancing, and where mood is of the utmost importance, the whole nature of the piece changes with each new interpreter.

The ballet was very well received in Europe.

France:
"Robbins places his 'faun' in a dance studio. As the curtain rises, he is sleeping on the floor. Slowly he wakes up, begins indolently to exercise, facing the public, his mirror. He is a beautiful dancer, but for the moment his thoughts are not on work. Slowly he abandons it; sliding to the floor, he seems to sleep again. Then the 'nymph' appears—a dancer in a work outfit, severe and pure. She begins to practice seriously right away. She tries to involve the man, but still he is elsewhere. He is more than a fellow dancer; it is 'nymph' that he sees in this chaste young girl. Gently he caresses her hair; all his sensuality is in this gesture. She responds with an academic dance gesture that excludes his desire: it is one of the great moments of dance. But nature speaks: the insistence of the faun seems to gain over the resistance of the nymph. Gently at first, then more voluptuously, she gives herself over. The inevitable seems to be happening. But then the faun, impatient, places a seemingly modest kiss on the cheek of the nymph. She is suddenly sobered: as if drawn from a bad dream, she comes back to herself: severe and pure, she disappears on her pointes, while the faun, 'impure,' unsatisfied, sinks again into his heavy reverie. This echoes the music, step by step, marvelously, and responds to the profound requirements of the poem. Robbins's inspiration seems to have attained truth itself." [6]

"Guardians of traditionalism have complained with indignation that Debussy's masterpiece has been profanely treated. But the score is perfectly respected, and as for the choreography, if respect for tradition means piously to preserve the most shaky antiques of the past century, then one must go all the way and revive such works as *Le Papillon*. Nijinsky's *Faun*, let's be frank, is no longer possible. The horned head, wriggling derriere, the little beating foot motions, the costume of hair—all this seems to me an affectation of the early century, just as old-fashioned, if not more so, than *Le Spectre de la Rose*—androgyny in petals. Robbins's *Faun*, with its own kind of frankness, its corporal mystery, and its own reincarnated nymph casts a spell ten times more potent." [7]

Italy:
"An absolute masterpiece, worthy of a

place beside the most important choreographic creations of the past and present. To the courage of attacking a theme already handled by others, Robbins adds the courage of his conception. Something is present that transmits to the steps and positions an extremely tangible vibration. The undercurrent of violent sensuality at the base of the choreography expresses itself in terms of a chastity, one could say a sense of religiosity: it is again the dance as expression of the divine in the forces of nature, as Robbins has also created in *The Cage*. The choreography is simple, unadorned, expressed in absolutely common dance vocabulary; but the talent of Robbins established around this vocabulary an aura of awe and wonder, and makes of it the expression of one of the most intense dramas of nature, the drama of the woman who all at once feels the awakening of her femininity." [8]

THE FILLY
or,
A Stableboy's Dream

CHOREOGRAPHY: Todd Bolender

MUSIC: John Colman (1953, commissioned by Ballet Society)

COSTUMES, DÉCOR: Peter Larkin

PREMIERE: 19 May 1953

PIANO: John Colman

CAST: *Stableboy*, Roy Tobias; *The Mare*, Diana Adams; *The Stallion*, Nicholas Magallanes; *The Foal*, Ellen Gottesman; *The Filly*, Maria Tallchief; *Jockeys*, 7 men; *Horses*, 7 women

The Filly was not a success, and Bolender felt this as keenly as anyone: "I loved the idea at first; in particular, there was something quite theatrically wonderful in a tiny child (the Foal) suddenly turning into Maria Tallchief! It could have been enormously effective. But the composition of the music was delayed for several years, and during that time too many hands became involved. There was an additional problem: the ballet embraced to some extent one of the tenets of Ballet Society—the idea that the serious easel-painter was a collaborator equal to the dance- and music-maker; and

it was an idea whose time had passed. Finally it was finished, but far from my original concept. I only saw one performance."

The Filly was a story ballet; in fact, it was felt that Bolender spent too much time on the story and not enough on characterization or choreography.

Martin wrote, "Deals with the life of a filly from before she is born until, in the mind of her adoring trainer and attendant, she wins all the honors of the track and, rejecting all the eager jockeys, chooses him to be her rider. Perhaps there is a ballet here and perhaps not. In any case, it should definitely have been more choreographic. Colman's score is tremendously busy; so much so, indeed, that one would require four ears to discover its relationship to what is going on on stage." [1]

Terry put his finger on the choreographic lulls: "The principal dancers are all horses and the equine conceit of his theme has so fettered the choreographer that no one really gets an opportunity for any extended, cumulative dancing of the sort which celebrates the dance skills of the human." [2]

Wrote Sabin, "Ingenious in capturing the aroma of the stable, but the ballet is a bundle of tricks and amusing bits of pantomime rather than a choreographically unified and interesting composition. Larkin's set, which shows a decorative stable and yard, was excellent, and the Coney Island-style additions in the dream sequence were ingeniously handled." [3]

FANFARE

CHOREOGRAPHY: Jerome Robbins

MUSIC: Benjamin Britten (*The Young Person's Guide to the Orchestra*, op. 34, 1945)

COSTUMES, DÉCOR: Irene Sharaff

LIGHTING: Jean Rosenthal

PREMIERE: 2 June 1953

CAST: *Harp*, Yvonne Mounsey; *Percussion*, Todd Bolender, 2 men; *Oboe*, Jillana; *Clarinets*, Carolyn George, Roy Tobias; *Violas*, Irene Larsson, Jacques d'Amboise; *Double Bass*, Brooks Jackson; *Trumpets*, Frank Hobi, Michael Maule; *Tuba*, Edward Bigelow; *Piccolo, 2*

Flutes, 3 First Violins, 3 Second Violins, 3 Celli, 4 Horns (all women); *Major Domo* (spoken), Robert Fletcher

OTHER CASTS: *Harp*, Jillana, Larsson, Patricia Neary, Charlotte Ray, Francia Russell, Dido Sayers; *Percussion*, Deni Lamont, Richard Rapp

REVIVAL: 15 January 1975, New York State Theater

CAST: *Harp*, Colleen Neary; *Percussion*, Bart Cook

I. Theme by Purcell: Entire Orchestra
Variations by Sections:
1. Woodwinds
2. Brass
3. Strings
4. Percussion

II. Variations by Instruments
Woodwinds
  Piccolo and Flutes
  Oboe
  Clarinets
  Bassoons
Strings
  Violins, First, Second
  Violas
  Celli
  Double Bass
  Harp
Brass
  Horns
  Trumpets
  Tuba and Trombones
Percussion
  Drums, Cymbals, Gongs, etc.

III. Fugue: Entire Orchestra

Fanfare was created in celebration of the coronation of Queen Elizabeth II, 2 June 1953. Says Robbins of the occasion, "Lincoln, as he always does, sent me a ton of books. He's marvelous that way. . . . A great big collection of books on heraldry and coronations was deposited at my door. So that had some influence on the 'royalty' of it all."

The program noted that the theme upon which the music was based was from Henry Purcell's incidental music for *Adelazar, or the Moor's Revenge*, by Mrs. Aphra Behn. Britten wrote the music to display the orchestra, and the ballet follows his plan exactly. Slightly on the contrived side (one dancer referred to it as the prepackaged, frozen-food ballet), *Fanfare* was nevertheless a splendid presentation piece and undeniably clever. It

Fanfare. **Opening ensemble.**

dressed the stage.

As Manchester wrote, "There is so much happy invention in the choreography, and it is so good to see the bravely colored pennants hanging from the flies and the crisp, gay costumes of a stage full of dancers that *Fanfare* should be a most welcome occasion for a long time to come." [1]

Terry found the proceedings equally festive: "A gay and frolicsome work employing the distinctive talents of thirty-four dancers divided into groups—and subdivided into individual instruments. The plan has provided Robbins with magnificent opportunities for the creating of mass action and of delicate detail, and he has functioned in both areas with wit and brilliance. *Fanfare* is courtly but its courtliness is suffused with good humor and peppered with mischief. Not only has Robbins selected and invented movements and, particularly, rhythmic phrasings which appear to be visualized characteristics of the instruments portrayed and the themes allotted to them, but he has also found the special brands of fun associated with, say, the tuba, the double bass or the bassoons. One sees speed and lightness in the dancing of flutes, gliding in the celli, soaring in the clarinets, ripples and sweeps in the harp, and fine pomposity in the percussion." [2]

The slightly less enchanted side was represented by Martin, who said the ballet suggested "a combination of *Card Party* and *Peter and the Wolf*," [3] and Hering, who wrote: "Robbins's phenomenal kinesthetic memory is [both] delight and detriment; it often prevents him from digging deeply into himself for movement ideas." [4]

As for the instruments themselves, each had its own different and distinctive bit of business (offering the dancers a number of prized mini-parts): "His bassoons more than live up to their reputation as the low comedians of the orchestra. There is a charming pas de deux for the violas; a truly delightful entry for the first and second violins; and a solo for the harp in which the glissando becomes a forward handspring, and her final pose, with body arched away from the floor, has all the elegance of that most gracious of instruments. Last and best comes the percussion, where Robbins cuts loose with his acute sense of the ludicrous and gives a thorough going-over to the whole of the 'kitchen department.' " [5]

"His bassoons are a pair of soft-shoe hoofers, the trumpets bounce through a mock duel. The tuba and trombones are a big-mouthed drill sergeant and his strutting underlings. And the percussions are everything from fanny-wiggling strippers to Chinese dancers à la *Nutcracker* to flamenco dancers. The feminine members do not for the most part share in the humor. The oboe has high, sustained extensions and splits. And the harp has an acrobatic solo that ends with her balanced on her chest, as though she were doing a swan dive on the floor." [6]

Fanfare was performed for years, traveling to Europe and Japan. It received less than enthusiastic notices in London in 1965, where considerable annoyance was expressed that this was the sole Robbins ballet presented (as compared to more than twenty by Balanchine and one by d'Amboise):

"A pleasant triviality (danced better by the Danes). It appears as if America cares less for its greatest native-born choreographer than it should." [7]

"A coarse, musically insensitive piece with one or two good inventions that are not good enough to save it." [8]

Italy:
"Not what one might have expected after *The Cage, Age of Anxiety,* and *Fancy Free.* There are some elements that certainly derive from Massine, others that resemble, but perhaps too cautiously, *Fancy Free,* and much that is academically inspired. If it all lacks a certain choreographic urgency, it is infused with lively spirit and well-constructed measures. Robbins does not seem quite to have achieved what he intended: a visual realization of what Britten extracted from Purcell's theme." [9]

In 1975, after some years out of the repertory, the ballet was revived with a large number of minor changes in the steps (and a few in the costumes) but with the ceremonial feeling and the humor intact. The most notable difference was a completely new variation for the bassoon, which made him an acrobat rather than a clown who could barely stand without help; in addition, the horns were now danced by men.

CON AMORE

Choreography: Lew Christensen

MUSIC: Gioacchino Rossini (Overtures to *La Scala di Seta*, 1812, *Il Signor Bruschino*, 1812, and *La Gazza Ladra*, 1817)

SCENARIO: James Graham-Lujan

COSTUMES, DÉCOR: James Bodrero; Esteban Francés (March 1954)

PREMIERE: 9 June 1953 (first presented 10 March 1953 by San Francisco Ballet, San Francisco Opera House)

CAST: *Captain of the Amazons*, Sally Bailey (San Francisco Ballet); *10 (female) Lieutenants and Soldiers; The Bandit*, Jacques d'Amboise; *The Lady*, Nancy Johnson (San Francisco Ballet); *Her 3 Suitors; The Husband*, Herbert Bliss; *Amore*, Edith Brozak

OTHER CASTS: *Captain*, Gloria Govrin, Yvonne Mounsey, Sonja Tyven, Violette Verdy, Patricia Wilde; *Bandit*, Conrad Ludlow, Kent Stowell, Edward Villella; *Lady*, Karin von Aroldingen, Melissa Hayden, Marian Horosko, Jillana, Jane Mason, Janet Reed

SCENE 1: The Amazons and the Bandit
SCENE 2: The Husband's Return
SCENE 3: A Triumph of Love

*C*on Amore, an out-and-out farce, enjoyed a long life in the repertory. In addition to giving the audience a lot to laugh about, it provided three juicy comic roles in the Captain of the Amazons, the Ban-

dit, and the Lady. Of these, the first two also offered a chance for virtuoso technical display.

Martin: "Certainly Christensen never has produced more resourceful choreography. . . . A ballet with, of all things, a genuinely fine and funny scenario, ingenious, theatrical, and eminently Rossinian." [1]

The ballet reflected Rossini in period as well as in humor, as Terry pointed out: "Thematic, dramatic, and pictorial materials of the nineteenth century are present throughout. Each episode is filled with action. Christensen, fusing actual dance with some magnificently satirized ex-

Con Amore. Above: **Scene 2. Jillana, Deni Lamont.** (*Photo Martha Swope.*) **Below:** **Scene 1. Edward Villella, Violette Verdy.** (*Photo Fred Fehl.*)

amples of traditional mime and stock gesture, keeps things spinning at a giddy pace, and his danced comments upon the theater styles of an earlier age are rich in affectionate but hearty humor." [2]

Manchester gave some details of the plot: "It would be difficult to imagine a more unpromising sounding scenario than this one, which starts off with two entirely unrelated stories, one a gentle ribbing of a typical ballet of the Romantic period, with Amazons in tutus and soldierly tunics first capturing a Bandit and then falling in heaps for his masculine charms, and the other a typical—one might almost say the only—French farce, with a Lady, her Lovers, and her Husband in the usual time-worn situation involving a great deal of hiding behind doors. But these two apparently irreconcilable plots are most surprisingly brought together by the ingenious device of having the Bandit from Plot No. 1 flee from the lovesick Amazons right into the drawing-room of Plot No. 2 at the point where the imbroglio has reached an unmanageable climax. From then on all parties become so entangled that it is necessary to introduce a deus ex machina to sort them out. The deus in this case is a cupid who comes on practically smothered in garlands and shoots arrows in all directions until everyone is tied up with someone, and who cares with whom? I would have sworn beforehand that this was precisely the kind of ballet which could not amuse me in any circumstances, but Christensen's simple-hearted gaiety and very genuine ability to tell a story in dancing is disarming, and *Con Amore* romps merrily along its unimportant but entertaining way." [3]

OPUS 34

CHOREOGRAPHY: George Balanchine

MUSIC: Arnold Schoenberg (*Accompaniment-Music for a Motion Picture*, op. 34, 1930)

COSTUMES: Esteban Francés

DÉCOR, LIGHTING: Jean Rosenthal

PREMIERE: 19 January 1954

CAST: *First Time:* Diana Adams, Patricia Wilde, Nicholas Magallanes, Francisco Moncion; *9 women; Second Time:* Tan-

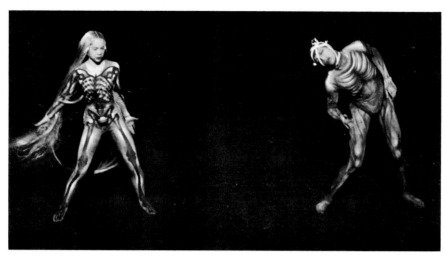

Opus 34. Second Time. Jillana, Herbert Bliss. *(Photo Fred Fehl.)*

aquil LeClercq, Herbert Bliss; 6 women, 10 men

Second Time also danced by Jillana

A Balanchine "weirdie" and no two ways about it. The program note—typical Kirstein—was no help at all: "Opus, the Latin word for work, is the root of a large number of English words, including opera, operatic, operation, operative, and operational." The music was played through twice without pause.

Sylvester headed his review "Lots of Guts in This Ballet," and he continued, "The new ballet might better be called *Operation Ghastly*, since it is probably the first dance work ever inspired by compound fractures, blood transfusions, and scar tissue. *Opus 34* has the following ballet novelties: Yards of bloodstained bandage. Scalpels. Bloody hands. Death shrouds. Aches and pain. All these and more.

"During the course of *Opus 34*, which among other things is staged with a sort of lopsided choreography, people are anaesthetized and wrapped in the mantle of new blood. They are enfolded in the black shrouds of death. And for a smash finish, Balanchine turns on a set of hospital amphitheater lights which are pointed at the audience and momentarily blind the first ten rows. *Opus 34* was halfway through its second part before the first nervous laugh came from the audience. There was considerable shocked laughter thenceforth." [1]

For Haggin, the ballet (First Time) was "a demonstration of how much more ef-

fectively Balanchine uses [elements of modern dance] than the modern dancers themselves." [2] *

Martin decided that Balanchine was indulging in a "tantrum" after a string of docilely produced classical variations: "It is a fairly perverse little piece that the balletomanes are going to hate violently, for it is markedly anti-classic, has not so much as a single pirouette, and is out-and-out German Expressionism of the period around 1930, when Schoenberg wrote this score. Actually the work as a whole has very much the quality of one of those experimental movies, morbid, solemn, and a bit skimpy, yet not without an undeniable fascination.

"The first time, the stage action is in abstract terms, and if it was not done exactly this way by Laban twenty years ago, it is only because the idea did not occur to him. The movement is altogether in his idiom, torso, grotesqueries, and all. The second half is in terms of dramatic gesture, with literal story suggestions and a total absence of dance movement. It is equally old-fashioned, however, and equally Central-European. The whole stage action, indeed, fits the design, the content and the period of the score with remarkable fidelity; yesterday it would all have been a great scandal. It is extremely well done, and it is, in its own way, highly

---

* This was not the first or the last time modern dance was mentioned as an influence on Balanchine (see *Four Temperaments,* for example). By about 1959, with *Episodes,* when it became evident that Balanchine was fully as "modern" as any modern dancer, the subject dropped. It is not recorded how much, if any, modern dance Balanchine had seen when he choreographed the contractions in *Apollo* (1928).

effective, and a remarkable demonstration of how much can be done with nothing but pure skill to work with." [3]

Sabin observed that the score contained the indications Threat, Danger, Fear, and Catastrophe, and that *perhaps* these had inspired Balanchine. But who knew? LeClercq says he never explained: "In the first part they did odd things. One I remember: the whole stage of dancers, each with one leg forward, shook their calf muscles. In the second part we wore stockings over our faces, so that the features were mashed in. A Frankenstein effect. After the operation, a huge black china silk seemed to cover the stage, swallowing me up from time to time, with dancers underneath whom you never saw. Then a cylinder came down, black mesh that you could see through, and lit from inside. There was something red left on the stage, which I picked up at the end and put over my shoulders—blood?—just before the lights were turned on the audience. Balanchine didn't explain what he was after—horror show, bride of Frankenstein—but I think he was amused by it, and I don't think he considered it a major work."

Moncion: "The first part was one of his white abstractions, quite similar, amazingly enough, to Xenakis [*Metastaseis and Pithoprakta*, 1968], but at the time completely unique. We clambered over one another. In the second part he had some marvelous effects. There were hosts of nurses and attendants pulling blood-soaked bandages into a kind of web over two big tables which concealed two forms. Tanny LeClercq wore a long gray wig. Boys dressed in black were under a huge black cloth, and she was lifted by them, so that you saw this creature rising and then being engulfed in all this black and disappearing, and then coming up again. It was absolutely eerie, obscenely eerie, having the connotation of foulness and death—this long, lanky, skeletal body dissolving in a morass of black. Then Herbie [Bliss] disappeared into a disjointed column—a phallic ring or tube that he strapped himself into. In the last section, Tanny started walking in a seductive and beguiling manner downstage. A curtain rose in the back, exposing a huge klieg light that went on behind her, blinding the audience. This drew *such* a reaction— people screamed and yelled. It was like an insult, like flinging something foul in their faces, like a pail of cold filth. Some were enraged."

THE NUTCRACKER

Classic Ballet in two acts, four scenes, and prologue

CHOREOGRAPHY: George Balanchine

MUSIC: Peter Ilyitch Tchaikovsky (1892)

Based on E.T.A. Hoffmann's tale, "The Nutcracker and the Mouse King" (1816)

COSTUMES: Karinska

MASKS: Vlady

DÉCOR: Horace Armistead

LIGHTING, PRODUCTION: Jean Rosenthal

PREMIERE: 2 February 1954

CAST: ACT I, SCENE 1: Christmas Party at the Home of Dr. Stahlbaum, Nuremberg, c. 1816
Dr. and Frau Stahlbaum, Frank Hobi, Irene Larsson; *Their Children, Clara and Fritz*, Alberta Grant, Susan Kaufman; *Maid; Guests: 4 Parents, 11 Children, 2 Grandparents; Herr Drosselmeyer*, Michael Arshansky; *His Nephew (The Nutcracker)*, Paul Nickel; *Toys: Harlequin and Columbine*, Gloria Vauges, Kaye Sargent; *Toy Soldier*, Roy Tobias
(*Drosselmeyer* also played by William Dollar, Shaun O'Brien, Richard Thomas)
SCENE 2: The Battle Between the Nutcracker and the Mouse King (choreography by Jerome Robbins)
Mouse King, Edward Bigelow; *Nutcracker; Clara; 8 Mice; 19 Child Soldiers*
SCENE 3: The White Forest and the Snowflake Waltz
Nutcracker; Clara, Snowflakes, 16 women
Boys choir (40 voices) from St. Thomas Episcopal Church

ACT II: Confituerenburg (The Kingdom of the Sugar Plum Fairy)
Sugar Plum Fairy, Maria Tallchief; *Her Cavalier*, Nicholas Magallanes; *Little Princess*, Grant; *Little Prince*, Nickel; *Angels*, 8 girls; *Divertissements: Hot Chocolate (Spanish Dance)*, Yvonne Mounsey, Herbert Bliss, 4 couples; *Coffee (Arabian Dance)*, Francisco Moncion, 4 children; *Tea (Chinese Dance)*, George Li, 2 women; *Candy Canes (Buffoons)*, Robert Barnett, 6 teen-age girls; *Marzipan Shepherdesses (Mirlitons)*, Janet Reed, 4 women; *Bonbonnière (Mother Ginger and Her Polichinelles)*, Edward Bigelow, 8 children; *Waltz of the Candy Flowers, Dewdrop*, Tanaquil LeClercq, *Flowers*, 2 demi-soloists; 12 women

APOTHEOSIS: The Walnut Boat

NEW PRODUCTION: 11 December 1964, New York State Theater

COSTUMES: Karinska

DÉCOR, LIGHTING: Rouben Ter-Arutunian

VIOLIN: Earl Carlyss

CAST: ACT I: *Dr. and Frau Stahlbaum*, Roland Vazquez, Penelope Gates; *Mary and Fritz*, Sylvia Blaustein, Jean-Pierre Frohlich; *Herr Drosselmeyer*, Shaun O'Brien; *His Nephew*, José Luis Greco; *Toys*, Karen Morell, Margaret Wood, Robert Rodham; *Mouse King*, Michael Steele Boys' Choir from Church of the Transfiguration (The Little Church Around the Corner)

ACT II: *Sugar Plum Fairy*, Allegra Kent; *Her Cavalier*, Jacques d'Amboise; *Hot Chocolate*, Victoria Simon, Earle Sieveling; *Coffee*, Gloria Govrin; *Tea*, Deni Lamont; *Candy Cane*, Richard Rapp; *Marzipan Shepherdess*, Suki Schorer; *Mother Ginger*, David Richardson; *Dewdrop*, Patricia McBride

At the time of writing (1974–75), *The Nutcracker* is well on its way to its 700th performance by the New York City Ballet; so an attempt to give alternate casts would require a lengthy list of all the principal dancers—and many others—who have performed with the Company since 1954.

It is a well-known bit of theater lore that *The Nutcracker*, one of the most popular ballets ever created, was not successful in its first production in St. Petersburg, 1892, although the Tsar had complimented Tchaikovsky after seeing the dress rehearsal, and the composer himself seemed pleased with it. Just a few days after the opening, however, he wrote to his brother, "This is the fourth day on which the periodicals have been carving up my latest creations." His music was criticized as being "too symphonic" (which implied that it was a poor background for dancing), and ballet lovers complained that the ballerina did not make an appearance until late in the evening. Some years afterward (1899), Konstantin Skalkovsky, a critic, gave a blunt opinion: "Generally speaking, *The Nutcracker* was staged mainly for children; for the dancers it contains very little; for art—exactly nothing. Even its music was rather weak."

And yet, are tales of the ballet's failure perhaps inflated to make a good story? For, according to Chujoy, *The Nutcracker* remained in the Russian repertory continually for thirty-seven years.[1] And it is worth noting that when the suite from the ballet was first given in concert by the Russian Music Society (19 March 1892), five of the six numbers had to be encored. One of Tchaikovsky's special prides in connection with the score was his use of the celesta, a silvery-toned keyboard instrument that had only recently been invented, for the variation of the Sugar Plum Fairy.

Now that *Nutcracker* Christmas presentations have become annual events throughout the United States, by professional and regional companies alike, it is difficult to remember when this was not a tradition. Balanchine's was not the first full-length production (Lew Christensen's for the San Francisco Ballet preceded it, and in the 1940s the Ballet Russe de Monte Carlo had a shorter two-act version), but since his staging, the ballet has become a habit.

Mounting such a lavish production was a major achievement for the Company, and an encouraging step toward giving ballet, in the words of Kirstein, "some solid basis" in America. But Martin darkly questioned the very idea of the avantgarde New York City Ballet's spending even a penny or a moment on a spectacle that so obviously catered to popular taste.

The Nutcracker was by far the most ambitious project undertaken by the Company at City Center. Besides the tremendous expense involved in rehearsing a cast enlarged by thirty-nine children and the elaborate costumes and sets, there was a particular problem in working the magical transformations: the City Center backstage facilities are cramped and hardly boast the latest equipment. For one thing, the flies are not large enough to hang more than one ballet at a time, so *Nutcracker* had to be prepared on the day of its performance, never beforehand. Then, the wings are so narrow that they quickly filled up with the stagehands who were effecting the miracles; the dancers had to stand outside in the hall awaiting their entrances, and the stagehands themselves needed a network of sound cues because they could not see each other.

With the move to Lincoln Center, all the sets were redesigned to take advantage of the much larger stage space and

The Nutcracker. Above left: **Act I. Christmas Party. Michael Arshansky as Drosselmeyer, Alberta Grant as Clara.** (*Photo Frederick Melton.*) *Left:* **Act I. The Battle between the Nutcracker and the Mouse King.** (*Photo Martha Swope.*) *Above:* **Act I. George Balanchine as Drosselmeyer. NBC-TV, 1958.** (*Photo Fred Fehl.*) *Opposite, above left:* **Act II. Candy Cane. Robert Barnett.** (*Photo Radford Bascome.*) *Opposite, above center:* **Act II. Mother Ginger and her Polichinelles.** (*Photo Martha Swope.*) *Opposite, above right:* **Act II. The Sugar Plum Fairy and her Cavalier. Patricia Wilde, Jonathan Watts.** (*Photo Fred Fehl.*) *Opposite, bottom:* **Act II. Waltz of the Flowers. Marnee Morris as the Dewdrop.** (*Photo Michael Avedon.*)

the more sophisticated backstage machinery. It is possible that more miracles than in the old days now occur, but there are those in the audience who miss the "home-made" effect of the old scenery; in particular, the first Christmas tree, uncurling and wheezing and puffing upward, growing gigantic to some of Tchaikovsky's most glorious music, brought a sense of wonder and excitement that the new slick tree, rising without effort from an ample trap-door, cannot engender.

The ballet was generally well, if not ecstatically, received by the critics, although some, with Martin, found it merely a wonderful treat for children, unworthy of serious critical attention for its dance values. With the passage of years, however, many have discerned artistry within: It's not just a good show, although it is all of that; not just kids running around, with some sensational scenic effects. The snow scene and the role of the Dewdrop contain choreographic magic, and in fact, the audience usually responds to them (and to the growing Christmas tree) with the greatest applause. There are myriad clever details to be discovered—one might start with the mice. In the 1970s, there was a tendency among critics to reanalyze the first act and find Balanchine's most interesting work there; for years it had been dismissed as an excuse for the children to appear on stage—without any "real dancing" in it. One aspect of The Nutcracker has remained unchanged: twenty years later it is still a box-office success.*

Two divergent views of the idea of Nutcracker itself were shown in the 1954 reviews of Martin and Chujoy—Chujoy clearly felt it both a culmination and a brave new beginning; Martin, a dangerous lowering of standards. (As if to underline Martin's argument, most of the critics took up a lot of space on the scenery, little on the dancing.) He wrote: "The work has never before been seen in New York in its entirety, and Balanchine has restored cuts that have been made in practically all the previous productions elsewhere. Even in this full form it is scarcely a full-evening ballet, but rather

a generous three-quarter program.

"But this is quite long enough. Indeed, unless you are one of those who find delight in watching children perform, you may find it advisable to arrive at the City Center along about ten o'clock when the adults take over. Balanchine has seen the ballet as a thing of, by, and for children, and he has the stage alive with them most of the time.

"The whole thing is done in beautiful taste, and with a warm evocation of the drab and leisurely days of 1892 when the piece first came to the stage in Russia. The score is an enchanting one, no matter how familiar it is. The scenery not only reeks of the period, but has a charm of its own which does not depend upon the miraculous transformations he has devised. Karinska's costumes have her usual chic, even in the literal dresses of the children's Christmas party of the first scene, and when she gets into the land of the Sugar Plum Fairy, she achieves some real confections.

"But it is not much of a ballet, and all the genius in the world can never make it one. There is no dancing to speak of until the last scene, there is no story line, and no characters to develop. In the first two scenes, where actual boredom is avoided, it is only through the persuasions of nostalgia. In the first scene, Tobias gives a fine performance of a bit as a toy soldier. In the third scene, the snowflake ensemble is dainty enough, though without outstanding choreographic interest. In the final scene, we come to the series of famous divertissements that have given the ballet whatever popularity it has had in previous productions. These Balanchine has completely re-created, and where they are unencumbered by the children, he has done a fine job of it. The pas de deux has an adagio that is remarkably brilliant, built obviously upon the particular talents of Tallchief. It is quite easy, however, to prefer the familiar old Sugar Plum Fairy's variation to the rather brittle, though rhythmically interesting, one that has replaced it. The coda, as danced on this occasion, was not a notable improvement. The new Arabian dance is a delightful one. A remarkably bouncy little Chinese boy named Li makes a fine bit out of the Chinese dance. Barnett is agile, peppy, and as always a good performer as the leader of the Candy Canes. Reed looks lovely and dances admirably as a Marzipan Shepherdess, and LeClercq does a highly distinguished job as soloist

in the waltz of the flowers, which is choreographed with characteristic Balanchine charm.

"On the whole, it is a loving and imaginative resurrection of a decidedly mediocre work. But it is something to take the children to beyond a shadow of a doubt." [2]

Chujoy: "The New York City Ballet has thrown all its resources, artistic and financial, into the production of The Nutcracker and has come out a winner. The ballet is staged in the grand classic manner, seen in the United States only in the repertoire of the Sadler's Wells Ballet. Almost the entire company is deployed in the ballet, as well as thirty-nine pupils and forty boys of the Choir of St. Thomas Episcopal Church.

"There is sumptuous scenery for each of the scenes, and a transformation in the first act that is little less than wondrous. Unlike European countries, especially France, the visual trimmings of ballet have always been on a modest scale in the United States. Due to financial circumstances, the New York City Ballet, in particular, could not afford the scenic embellishments which ballet requires. For many years the majority of its ballets have been given against a cyclorama. A full stage set was a rare exception and a painted backdrop was considered both an achievement and a financial sacrifice. It was only because Balanchine's prime interest has always been in the actual choreography, not the scenic accouterments to it, that the company could have a repertoire at all.

"In The Nutcracker Balanchine affirmed once again that ballet is not only dance, but is a synthesis of dance, music, poetry, and painting. Balanchine's creation of a classic ballet, in all its well-ordered values, is a reason for hope and joy. If we are willing to accept the dictionary definition of classicism as embodying lucidity, simplicity, dignity, and correctness of style, then Balanchine's Nutcracker is an indication that beyond our limited horizon of the present and the immediate future, there is still a hope for our civilization. From a more limited point of view, Nutcracker is a great achievement for American ballet. That American dancers, stage designers, costume designers, and lighting experts could rise to a level upon which they can create and interpret a classic ballet is a manifestation for which to be grateful."

After praising costumes, sets, lighting,

---

* Due to lack of space, a description of the Balanchine version cannot be included here. The one most filled with the spirit of fantasy was written by Denby for a special *Nutcracker* souvenir booklet for the Company and is reprinted in *Dancers, Buildings and People in the Streets*, pp. 72–74.

and music-making, he concluded, "Above all, of course, stands Balanchine himself, the master magician, who succeeded in presenting a modern version of a children's ballet that means so much to the adult. Without losing a thread of the past he has brought the present a shade closer to the future, when ballet in the United States will assume its proper and rightful place in the scheme of our cultural life." [3]

Martin was positively gloomy by the end of *The Nutcracker*'s initial season: "The greatest peril [was] its box-office success. The indisputable fact is that [it] is an inferior ballet. It denies the very basis of the 'Balanchine revolution,' which has changed the entire art of the ballet by showing it to be an art of dancing—not of miming, spectacle, or story-telling. There is very little dancing in *The Nutcracker*. To make matters no better, it is played largely by children. That it drew a new audience is undeniable, but once it got them there it showed them absolutely nothing to win them to the ballet. It is an outworn superstition that by giving people what is inferior you will ultimately win them to what is superior. The sad and terrible result is usually that they become so much more deeply attached to the inferior that it becomes financially impossible to give them anything else." [4]

The next year (1954–55), a block of time was devoted to *Nutcracker* alone—in that instance, five consecutive weeks during which no other ballet was danced—and thus began the annual tradition of *Nutcracker*s for Christmas. The ballet has also been performed, most often during the summer, in Chicago, Los Angeles, and Saratoga.

The ensuing years have proved that, as far as the New York City Ballet is concerned, the avant-garde and the "rearguard" can coexist happily; and no number of *Nutcracker* performances or new costume ballets seems to deter Balanchine from his *Violin Concertos*, *Duo Concertants*, *Metastaseis and Pithopraktas*, or *Movements*.

All the same Balanchine *is* frequently asked why he choreographed *The Nutcracker*, and this is what he replies: "It's my business to make repertoire. I always say it's like a restaurant—you have to cook, you have to please lots of people. One person wants soup, one wants oysters. My approach to the theater—to ballet—is to entertain the public. Before I couldn't do it because we didn't have a

theater, didn't have musicians, didn't have money. Then, finally, we had a little bigger company—and *Nutcracker Suite* is a million-dollar title in America. So Baum [managing director of City Center] asked me to do it. I said, 'If I do anything, it will be full-length and expensive.' Most important was the tree.

"I knew all about *Nutcracker* because I was in it, and because in Russia Christmas is a German invention. Our Christmas is German. Everything that's on the tree—pfefferkuchen, lebkuchen, everything like that is there. We had German postcards with snow, little deer—very pretty. Also, it's religious. Christ is born, so grown-ups never gave each other any presents out of respect for religion. But children are told beautiful stories about it, and they have to have presents. Our tree was full of food—chocolate, oranges, apples. You just pick up from the tree and eat. It's a tree of plenty. It represents food, plenty, life. We used to sing German songs all night—like 'Tannenbaum.' There was no Russian translation.

"So Baum gave me $40,000. We studied how the tree could grow both up and also out, like an umbrella. The tree cost $25,000, and Baum was angry. 'George,' he said, 'can't you do it without the tree?' I said, '[The ballet] *is* the tree.' It cost $80,000 instead of $40,000. We had lots of beautiful costumes. I used all the music, and I used the story by Hoffmann—not the whole thing, but the prologue of the Hoffmann story. I named the Dewdrop myself—there was no Dewdrop in Leningrad. The Hoop Dance [Candy Canes] is absolutely authentic, from Russia. Yes, I was in it—Mouse, Hoop—everything, just like everybody else."

Although Balanchine's dances were in the Ivanov manner (and, in addition to the Hoop Dance, he quoted the Prince's mime unchanged), the atmosphere was from another era—that of middle-class mid–nineteenth-century Germany. There is a cosy feeling about the Christmas festivities, and in this Balanchine may have been directed by the facilities at his disposal, for he has said, "On the Imperial Russian stage everything was grand. Every room was an imperial room. We couldn't do that here, so I made the ballet closer to the Hoffmann story. It takes place in a bourgeois Biedermeier home."

Denby pointed out several other elements that look back to German sources: "In the pantomime, Balanchine wove sev-

eral new theatrical details, all of them derived from Hoffmann (e.g., the keyhole episode [the prologue, in which Fritz and Clara peek through the keyhole into the living room where their parents are decorating the Christmas tree], the role of a Nephew, the wandering bed). For the apotheosis, originally 'A Hive of Bees' (representing civilization), he substituted a simpler image, but one also derived from the German story [departure in a walnut boat]. He made an old-fashioned Christmas, but kept to actions and manners that his company, including the children, could do naturally. In the group dances he tended to steps and figures of Ivanov's time, one might say to steps that Tchaikovsky had seen." [5]

As for the character of Drosselmeyer, who brings about this enchanted world (and whom he portrayed in a televised *Nutcracker* production), Balanchine says, "He's a strange man who makes toys. They call him 'uncle' because he brings toys every Christmas, and they always expect these mechanical things. And he invented the nutcracker. He gave it to the little girl. Then, when it got sick she saw the dream. Actually, it's not a dream—it's the reality that Mother didn't believe. The story was written by Hoffmann against society. He said that society, the grown-ups, really have no imagination, and that they try to suppress the imagination of children. In Germany, they were very strict—no nonsense. They didn't understand that nonreality is the real thing. Goethe was against him; that's why it was never published in Germany. It was published in Russia and in France, but in Germany it was banned."

Says O'Brien of Drosselmeyer: "He's changed over the years—changed and darkened. In the beginning, he was fat, in a Biedermeier costume. Now he's slim and wears period clothes, more like the original illustrations. I devised a lot of new things with the clock [Drosselmeyer sits on top of the grandfather clock as midnight strikes and seems to conjure up the mice and direct the transformation scene from this perch]. Once Balanchine told me to look a little more like Robespierre. Balanchine himself played the part rather like a very dotty old doctor, with glasses."

Over the years *Nutcracker* has become entrenched, but with Balanchine, things are never static, and he has made many changes from time to time. One of the earliest (1958) was also one of the most controversial: he removed the grand pas de deux, substituting for it a dance for the Sugar Plum Fairy supported not by a cavalier (who disappeared completely) but by four soloists from other divertissements—Chocolate, Coffee, Tea, and Candy Cane. The result of this, according to Terry, "is something like the Rose Adagio from *The Sleeping Beauty* in form, but this new adagio is not nearly as exciting as the Rose Adagio nor is it, to my mind, as stirring as the now absent Grand Pas de Deux, with its entree, adagio, two solos, and coda." [6] Balanchine was reportedly against introducing a romantic element so late in the work; Haggin said, however: "I would think that to the little boy and girl it would seem reasonable for the Fairy, when at last she dances for them, to do so with a Cavalier, who in the children's minds would correspond to the little boy." [7]

In another departure, the Fairy danced her variation in the beginning of the second act, welcoming the children. This feature has remained; by 1959 the Cavalier reappeared as support for the pas de deux, although to this day he is variationless.

The biggest change came with the move to Lincoln Center in 1964, where all-new scenery and many new costumes made their appearance. The sets were generally based on the old idea, although in execution they appeared more substantial, more literal, less flimsy, and less ethereal. In addition, there was a new opening drop showing a village in the snow, presided over by an angel and a star, and a new ending in which the Little Princess (now named Mary) and the Nutcracker Prince exit to the sky in a Christmas sleigh, rather than sailing off in a walnut boat.

Wrote Terry, "No, don't worry! It's still a marvelous Christmas present. It is a brilliantly conceived and executed production. True, it has some pretty corny bits which resemble overblown Christmas cards; but why not? *Nutcracker* is meant to be gaudy as well as gooey, and if you're going to do it in a way to delight and excite the kids, the bigger, the brighter the better." [8]

For the new production, the Coffee variation, which had been performed by a languid male Arab, smoking a hookah and assisted by four tiny birds, became an acrobatic belly dance for an Eastern lady with a diamond in her navel. The background angels, formerly teen-agers, were much younger girls. In 1968, replacing the supported arabesque promenade followed by breathtaking balance, which had been designed especially for Tallchief as the climax of the pas de deux, a mechanical device allowed the Fairy to glide across the stage on a single pointe. And—onward—in 1972, eight tiny white mice were added to the usual adult gray ones.

In the course of its long history at the New York City Ballet, *The Nutcracker* has celebrated its seventy-fifth anniversary (1967) and observed its 500th performance in the Balanchine version (1970). It has seen several generations of children and at least one new generation of critics, who continue to greet it, year in, year out, as "A Christmas Confection," "Sweetmeats," "The Ballet World's Most Famous Christmas Present," "Sweet Sugar Plum," and—only rarely—as "Nutcracker Again."

"Fragment of a conversation heard any December between members of the dance crowd and me:

" 'Shall we go to the New York City Ballet tonight?'

" 'They're into *Nutcracker* already.'

" 'Oh God, that's right. Well, we'll have to wait till January.'

"But this is a very cryptic conversation—a fashionable convention. What it really means is that we are going to go to see *The Nutcracker* as soon as possible." [9]

3

CITY CENTER II

1954–1964

The Company emerged from *Nutcracker* in much better financial shape than before; in fact, it is considered by some that *Nutcracker* "saved" the New York City Ballet. The production was televised at Christmas in 1957 and 1958. The group also had a chance to prove—successfully—that it was not dependent on stars, no matter how illustrious, with the departure of Tallchief in 1954.

Two European tours were undertaken, the first for the spring and summer of 1955, the second for fall, 1956. In both, reception was excellent, but the 1956 tour ended in personal tragedy when Tanaquil LeClercq, at the age of twenty-seven, became permanently paralyzed by polio. Balanchine, who was married to her at the time, stayed at her bedside for a year, first in Copenhagen and then in Warm Springs, Georgia, and the Company faced a long winter season without him. "We felt his presence, though," said one of the dancers, and, indeed, he was kept informed of everything by letter and phone, and continued to run the Company by long distance. Any speculation as to whether his creativity would be impaired was quickly dispelled when he returned in the winter of 1957–58 and choreographed four successful new ballets, including the seminal *Agon.* By then it was time to depart on a different kind of tour, this one to Japan, Australia, and the Philippines—countries which, unlike Europe, had almost no ballet tradition. (*Swan Lake* was the hit of that expedition.) In Japan, Kirstein became interested in the Imperial Gagaku troupe of singers and dancers, which he imported to appear with the ballet in the spring of 1959. On returning from the Orient, the Company celebrated its tenth anniversary.

In 1959 came an event of great importance in the dance world: the first American visit of the Bolshoi. For almost forty years the state of ballet in the Soviet Union had been known only through films. The Bolshoi was greeted then—as now—with praise for its technique and partnering, and condescension for its naive repertory. From a technical point of view, particularly interesting was the "Russian back," which made an acute arc when the dancer's leg was raised high in arabesque and attitude. In Balanchine's classes, legs which had been judiciously placed waist-high in adagio movements, to make a clean right angle with the body, began to rise.

In 1962, the Company had a chance to show the Russians, as they toured parts of Europe and five Soviet cities. The trip was Balanchine's first visit home since he fled Leningrad in 1920. "Welcome to Russia, Mr. Balanchine, home of the classic ballet," said an interviewer, greeting him on his arrival in Moscow. "I beg your pardon, Russia is the home of the romantic ballet; the center of classic ballet is now in America," he replied. The Company was well received, although critics complained that many of the ballets had no heart and were for the intellect only; others were too trivial or "vulgar" for the "lofty and elegant" art of the ballet. Said Balanchine, "That we have 'no soul' merely means that our 'soul' is not like yours."

Also in 1962, John Martin, dance critic of the *Times* since 1927 and the first full-time dance critic on a newspaper in America, retired. His last assignment for the *Times* had been to accompany the New York City Ballet to Russia.

At home, in 1963, came an announcement of stunning impact to the dance world, always the stepchild in the cultural hierarchy: ballet was to be the object of Ford Foundation philanthropy at both the professional and the training levels. Of a grant of more than $7 million (spread over a ten-year period, much of it requiring matching funds), the New York City Ballet received $2 million, the School of American Ballet $3,925,000 (of this, $1.5 million was for scholarships to schools all over the country and for New York teachers and professional dancers to assess the level of training throughout the United States). In the eyes of the Ford Foundation, Balanchine was clearly the most vital force in dance in the country. The grant to the School was to have quite an effect on Company personnel. Such later leading dancers as Mimi Paul and Suzanne Farrell were recipients of Ford scholarships.

Among the top principals of the ten-year period were Diana Adams, Jacques d'Amboise, Herbert Bliss, Todd Bolender, André Eglevsky, Melissa Hayden, Jillana, Allegra Kent, Tanaquil LeClercq, Patricia McBride, Nicholas Magallanes, Francisco Moncion, Yvonne Mounsey, Roy Tobias, Violette Verdy, Edward Villella, Jonathan Watts, and Patricia Wilde. Those who stayed more briefly included Royes Fernandez, Judith Green, Michael Lland, André Prokovsky, Sallie Wilson, and, very briefly, the almost legendary Erik Bruhn. Maria Tallchief returned to the Company for several seasons. Jerome Robbins was mostly busy elsewhere. In 1958, Janet Reed rejoined the troupe from retirement as ballet mistress; in 1960, John Taras became a ballet master. In the spring of 1958, Leon Barzin, principal conductor, who had been associated with Balanchine since Ballet Society, resigned. (The separation was "friendly," but he was disappointed that funds had not been approved for "larger, more ambitious" works.) Six months later, Robert Irving, former principal conductor for the Royal Ballet, was appointed his successor. Hugo Fiorato continued as associate conductor, a post he assumed in 1955.

In 1958, Balanchine, for whom the dance and not the dancer had always been the star, implemented his policy in a graphic manner—by listing his principals and soloists alphabetically. (This practice is now common.) While perhaps accepted by the dancers, it is still resisted by audiences, who continue to have their favorites. "H is for Hayden, Ballerina," began one frustrated journalist.

Meanwhile, ground was broken for the construction of the New York State Theater, to be a part of the complex of artistic buildings at Lincoln Center, which already contained Philharmonic Hall and the Metropolitan Opera, with plans for a legitimate theater and a new home for the Juilliard School of Music. The State Theater was intended for dance and operetta, and the architect, Philip Johnson, was known to have consulted with Kirstein and Balanchine. He later said, "I built it for them." Nevertheless, political and financial problems had to be solved before the Company could move in. By 1963 it had been decided that New York City Ballet would be the resident dance company for at least the first two years of the theater's operation—1964 and 1965.

QUARTET

CHOREOGRAPHY: Jerome Robbins

MUSIC: Sergei Prokofiev (String Quartet No. 2, op. 92, 1941)

COSTUMES: Karinska

LIGHTING, DÉCOR: Jean Rosenthal

PREMIERE: 18 February 1954

STRING QUARTET: Hugo Fiorato, Henry Siegl, Jack Braunstein, Herman Busch

CAST: Patricia Wilde, Herbert Bliss (1st movement); Jillana, Jacques d'Amboise (2nd movement); Yvonne Mounsey, Todd Bolender (3rd movement); 4 couples

This small ballet was unusual in the repertory and marked something of a departure for its choreographer—Terry called it Robbins's first "non-nervous" work: "The impatience of jazz is absent, the fear of conflict is missing, sudden anger and frightened innocence are not to be seen. In place there is serenity." [1] The music was composed while Prokofiev was living in the eastern Caucasus, and he described it as "the combination of the least-known varieties of folk song with the most classical form of the quartet." According to the program note, after the sonata-form first movement came "an adagio based on a Caucasian love song. The final movement derives from a loosely knit series of wild and free Caucasian dances."

Robbins had heard the music and responded to it: "As I went along I saw it more classical and more in what I would call a Doubrovska class costume [knee-length chiffon skirt], but George came in somewhere along the middle and said it had to be Caucasian. Once he put that into my head, the ballet started to go that way more and more. Although I had been in Israel recently (some of the critics knew this), it's not true that there was Israeli material in the ballet."

Herridge wrote that "The choreography suggests folk dance. The ever-changing patterns evoke group interplay in some mountain idyl, [although] it is far richer in invention and more elegant in execution. The first movement is young and joyous; the second tender with love; the third, sharper and more fearful, is darkened ominously—but reasserts itself

triumphantly in the end." [2]

Manchester took issue with just that elegance, feeling that the dancers' obvious mastery made the folk element unconvincing. She found the mixture of folk with ballet "uneasy." [3]

Wrote Martin, "charmingly composed, with its accent chiefly on ensemble formations. The second [section] is far and away the best. This may well be in large part because it is so beautifully danced by Jillana, assisted modestly by d'Amboise. In the final movement, where he is assembling his cast for a recapitulation, Robbins has a bit of difficulty, but otherwise he has made a skillful and expert piece, with a definite flavor. The fact that the music of a string quartet is a trifle thin for so large a group of dancers proves to be helpful rather than otherwise. It gives an air of remoteness, which, in conjunction with the use of the alien medium of the classic dance, makes these folk measures seem like something remembered from afar." [4]

Terry also found charm, but saw no "dramatic center" in the ballet. [5]

Overall, a highly atypical Robbins—although there is probably no man alive who would care to hazard what a "typical" Robbins might be.

WESTERN SYMPHONY

CHOREOGRAPHY: George Balanchine

MUSIC: Hershy Kay (1954; commissioned by the New York City Ballet)

COSTUMES: Karinska (27 February 1955; renewed January 1968)

DÉCOR: John Boyt (27 February 1955)

LIGHTING: Jean Rosenthal

PREMIERE: 7 September 1954

CAST: *Allegro,* Diana Adams, Herbert Bliss; 8 women, 4 men; *Adagio,* Janet Reed, Nicholas Magallanes; 4 women; *Scherzo,** Patricia Wilde, André Eglevsky; 4 women; *Rondo,* Tanaquil LeClercq, Jacques d'Amboise; 4 couples

OTHER CASTS: *Allegro,* Jillana, Yvonne Mounsey, Colleen Neary, Patricia Neary,

* Around 1960, the Scherzo was permanently dropped.

Bettijane Sills, Carol Sumner, Sonja Tyven, Violette Verdy; Robert Lindgren, Arthur Mitchell, John Prinz, Francis Sackett, Michael Steele, Kent Stowell, Roland Vazquez; *Adagio,* Elise Flagg, Melissa Hayden, Allegra Kent, Gelsey Kirkland, Patricia McBride, Mimi Paul, Christine Redpath, Suki Schorer; Robert Maiorano, Richard Rapp, Roy Tobias; *Scherzo,* Carolyn George, Allegra Kent, Dorothy Scott, Barbara Walczak, Sallie Wilson; Robert Barnett, Todd Bolender, Edward Villella; *Rondo,* Adams, Karin von Aroldingen, Penny Dudleston, Suzanne Farrell, Gloria Govrin, Kent; Bill Carter, Jay Jolley, Daniel Levins, Arthur Mitchell, Frank Ohman

While *Western Symphony* is not, contrary to what Denby once wrote, Balanchine's first direct use of American material (*Alma Mater* and then *Jones Beach* came before), it *is* his longest-running American number, and by no means the last. *Stars and Stripes, Who Cares?,* and possibly even *Square Dance* carry on the great tradition. A three-act *Birds of America,* based on Audubon material, has reportedly been in preparation for some time.

According to the program note, "Balanchine's idea was to mount a formal ballet which would derive its flavor from the West, but would move within the framework of the classic school." Kay recalls that Mr. B. commissioned the score after a visit to Wyoming. His first two sketches were refused—the first being "too much like Copland," the second "too complicated." The third—"simple tunes with skeletal, guitarlike accompaniments" —was on the right track. It became a medley of twelve popular tunes—including "Red River Valley" (the unifying theme), "Old Taylor," "Rye Whiskey," "Lolly-Too-Dum," "Good Night, Ladies," "Oh, Dem Golden Slippers," and "The Girl I Left Behind Me"—in the form of a classical symphony.

Balanchine's enthusiasm for the West is known. He likes Westerns on TV. For years his work outfit consisted of bright shirts, often plaid, and frontier pants. For the premiere of the ballet, due to lack of money, the same combination became the stage garb for the men, with multicolored practice clothes for the ladies.

The critics were delighted. Terry wrote: "It may seem hard to believe, but a classical dance technique born in medieval courts and nurtured as an aristocrat

of the theater can speak, through movement, the language of the cowboy and can sing, again through movement, the songs of America's folk. *Western Symphony* has no story to tell, and its Americana is limited to a cowboy hat, western boots, and the pantomimed strumming of a guitar. Nonetheless, it is a completely American ballet not merely in those choreographic patterns which owe something (as far as shape is concerned) to the squares and rounds, the star formations, and the swing-your-partners of our own native dance, but also in the application of classical steps to an evocation of American spirits, humors, rhythms, colors. Here are steps and attitudes and enchainements which you will find in *Swan Lake* or *Coppélia* but they have lost their European accent. Furthermore, Balanchine has found in the vocabulary of the classical ballet movement equivalents for those steps, gestures, antics, and byplays characteristic of American folk and game dancing. So expertly has this been achieved that *Western Symphony* seems just as classical as *Concerto Barocco* and just as American as *Rodeo*. Of equal importance is Kay, who has written a symphony based upon American folk tunes. It is a great score, witty, nostalgic, lovely and lively, and it would be impossible not to dance to it." [1]

Martin: "There is some characteristically ingenious invention in it, and when Balanchine starts getting his dancers tangled up in the twinings and intertwinings of square-dance figures he is even commenting a bit on his own artistic practices. He has contrived a very amusingly sentimental Adagio for Reed and Magallanes, and the final Rondo contains some incredibly funny movement for LeClercq, with d'Amboise bouncing nimbly around her. The Allegro provides beautiful, if less colorful, phrases. The Scherzo seems the least rewarding. There is also a large ensemble that is excellently used, and in the finale it fairly raises the roof. Musically, too, the last movement is the most effective, for here Kay has relaxed a bit from his classic containment and gone in for some wonderful country fiddling." [2]

Lloyd: "A delightful bundle of contradictions, a neoclassic ballet tinged with the folk spirit. The juxtaposition is an incongruity as typical as are the entrechats and tours en l'air to cowboy tunes, or hints of all-hands-around mingled with the balletic port de bras. Fish-dives and fouettés are tossed off in a barn-dance mi-

Western Symphony. Top left: Allegro. **Herbert Bliss, Diana Adams.** *Top Right:* Rondo. **Tanaquil LeClercq.** *(Photo Radford Bascome.)* ***Bottom:*** Adagio. **Melissa Hayden, Nicholas Magallanes.** *(Photo Fred Fehl.)*

lieu. Reed does practically everything, including a half circle of petits tours, in the humorous Adagio. The score, which has more quotations than *Hamlet*, is of course infectious, and to see the rhythms of square dance and round applied to, or subjected to, the courtly elegance of ballet is to the aesthetic sense something like what chocolate-coated pickles might be to the gustatory." [3]

Western has been performed for so many years now that it is easy to forget that at its original unveiling it troubled some as an aesthetic mishmash (as Lloyd implies).

Sabin called it "a paradox. Balanchine veers from a naive suggestion of actual folk dance to forms and figures that are not even remotely western in flavor or connotation." [4]

And Martin: "A somewhat startling hodge-podge of hoe-down and square set sur les pointes and with elegant classic port de bras. Here are no truly characterized Western plainsmen but only a company of strictly classic dancers showing how they would behave if they were plainsmen. Naturally the contrast is enormous and the result incongruous beyond words. After you have got the hang of it however, it is also witty and fairly hilarious. At this juncture, one suspects that [after costuming] it will emerge as a lively choreographic joke." [5]

This seems to be just what happened. Added a year later, the costumes and scenery, so eagerly anticipated as a necessary help in defining the character of the ballet—was it Broadway, movies, imitation music hall, or essentially within the classical tradition?—got reviews of their own. If anything, dressing the ballet reinforced the Western feeling while leaving the classicism intact, and made the whole affair a broader joke, so easier to laugh at and a lot more fun.

Manchester: "Delights its audience even more now that it has a street background, complete with saloons, and costumes which make all the girls look like Marlene Dietrich in *Destry Rides Again* (and very nice, too) and all the boys look like Roy Rogers. The company continues to dance it for about ten times its worth. And of course there is LeClercq's hat." [6]

Haggin also found the hat—"to say nothing of the way she wore it—alone worth the price of admission." [7]

Western has always been an audience favorite and has remained in the repertory since its opening. It is safe to say that every principal dancer with the company has appeared in it at one time or another. Thirteen years after the above reviews were written, it was time to assess another set of new costumes and a—mostly—new cast:

"It seemed like how the West was won all over again. This is, in effect, a home, home on the range version of the many symphonic-style ballets Balanchine has created for his company.

"It is said that when the impresario Serge Diaghilev sought to revive the Fokine ballet *Schéhérazade*, he decided that all the costumes would have to be made brighter to live up to the expectation of the audience's memory. Karinska seems to have taken the same approach, and all her costumes, for the cowpunchers and bright-hued dance-hall girls who make up the cast, are brasher, brighter, and a little more effective. The only major change has been in new and handsome costumes for the leads in the finale, but for the rest Karinska has clearly ordered the mixture as before, but more shiny. It works.

"The only survivor of the ballet's original cast in 1954 is Magallanes, still the cheerfully morose—happiness keeps breaking through his romantic misery—cowboy of the slow movement. Now he is matched by Hayden, who gives the ballet a tongue-in-cheek, world-weary insouciance that no one else can equal. Just as invaluable is Verdy, chic, French, and naughty, dancing up a storm in the first movement, partnered by a flashing Stowell. The only complete newcomer to the ballet was Farrell as the gorgeous Diamond Lil figure of the last scene. Partnered by a more than usually exuberant Ohman, Farrell was superbly snooty and beautifully contained. It put the seal on an exciting performance of an old ballet polished to look like new." [8]

Characteristically, for all the fun, Balanchine did not let down on the technical aspect. In the Adagio, the ballerina throws herself halfway across the stage into (she hopes) her partner's arms; in the Rondo, there are fouettés. Says Verdy, "It's completely exhausting. The only way to get through it is to dance like hell, as though the floor were on fire."

Critics abroad seemed less than thrilled—not angered that classical steps had been wrenched from their natural habitat, not offended or embarrassed by the unabashedly corny humor, but just not very impressed one way or another. It was as if they didn't quite get the point. None of them seemed to have a "rollicking good time," which is the only way truly to enjoy *Western Symphony*.

England:
"It is an unashamed pot-boiler, efficient and craftsmanlike. Balanchine's classic statement of ballet form—the choreographic symphony where the dancing matches or parallels and occasionally even counters the music—is here given, oddly perhaps, with a cowboy hat. The dance-hall girls and cowpunchers go their way quite unconcerned (what would Fokine have thought?), dancing their patterns with carefree simplicity. The ballet is not wearing particularly well." [9]

"It is classical ballet with a cowboy accent. With a flick of his hands, the talented Rapp converts four graceful coryphées into his wagon-team: earlier, this Prince had looked for his Heroine among the assembled corps in the hallowed tradition—with delightfully unexpected results. Parody; but affectionate parody, and first-rate dance invention at the same time. Schorer is a captivating little comedienne, and Govrin a captivating big one." [10]

France:
"The ballet is without plot—which would seem to be the whole point of a 'Western'—and the décor is zero; but, thanks to the gusto of the company, it proceeds in an atmosphere of rather frenzied good humor." [11]

Australia:
"Here, it was hoped, would be a new contribution to ballet, an expression of national America. The dancing itself, however, could have been performed quite effectively in almost any other costumes with almost any other décor." [12]

Russia:
"Is it right that on dance movements of strictly music-hall character are built somewhat bawdy scenes, which, according to their producer, depict the peculiarity of life in the Western states of the U.S.A. with their cowboys and 'girls'? The choice of a motley repertoire of this sort comes rather as a surprise." [13]

"Could have brought a sympathetic smile had it been less vulgar, but this vulgarity eclipsed the humor and possible foundation." [14]

IVESIANA

CHOREOGRAPHY: George Balanchine

MUSIC: Charles Ives (pieces named and dated below; all for chamber orchestra, except as noted)

LIGHTING: Jean Rosenthal

PREMIERE: 14 September 1954

CAST: *Central Park in the Dark* (1906), Janet Reed, Francisco Moncion, 20 women; *Hallowe'en* (1907?, *string quartet and piano*), Patricia Wilde, Jacques d'Amboise, 4 women; *The Unanswered Question* (1906), Allegra Kent, Todd Bolender, 4 men; *Over the Pavements* (1906–13), Diana Adams, Herbert Bliss, 4 men; *In the Inn* (1904–6?), Tanaquil LeClercq, Todd Bolender; *In the Night* (1906), ensemble

OTHER CASTS: *Central Park*, Melissa Hayden; *Question*, LeClercq

REVIVAL (4 movements only): 16 March 1961

LIGHTING: David Hays

CAST: *Central Park*, Patricia McBride, Moncion, 30 women; *Question*, Kent, Deni Lamont, 4 men; *Inn*, Adams, Arthur Mitchell; *Night*, ensemble

OTHER CASTS: *Central Park*, Sara Leland, Virginia Stuart; *Question*, Karen Morell, Suki Schorer; *Inn*, Gloria Govrin, Kent, Leland, Patricia Neary; John Clifford, Richard Rapp

REVIVAL II: 30 April 1975, New York State Theater

CAST: *Central Park*, Leland, Moncion; *Question*, Elise Flagg, Lamont; *Inn*, Suzanne Farrell, Victor Castelli; *Night*
Inn also danced by Jay Jolley

The music of Ives, almost never played during his lifetime (1874–1954), and infrequently heard even today, was a most unusual choice for a ballet, and a choice applauded by serious music critics, who commended Balanchine and Barzin for being more adventurous than most musical societies. Ives's works were called (by Schonberg) a fiendish mixture of "crazy polytonalities and polyrhythms, near-total dissonance, even occasional flights into aleatory. He used tone clusters, unconventional forms, and his music was of unparalleled density, complexity, and technical difficulty. . . . [At the same time], nearly every work is a tone picture of a vanished America . . . a grab-bag of gospel hymns, popular American music, rag-time, jazz, patriotic tunes from 'Yankee Doodle' on, work songs. The ear is jarred by quarter tones, amelodic figurations, microtonalities, wild leaps, brand-new chordal relationships, and a concept of counterpoint that seemed to break every rule in the book." [1]

Said Ives, who was known to despise the work of Mozart, Haydn, Mendelssohn, Tchaikovsky, Stravinsky, Ravel, Debussy, and Wagner (he admired Bach, Beethoven, some Brahms, and Carl Ruggles), "The way I'm constituted, writing soft stuff makes me sore—I sort of hate all music. . . . I hear something else!"

Balanchine's ballet was perhaps as cryptic and unyielding as the music. Of all who wrote about it, Denby came closest to capturing its awesome effect: "*Ivesiana* develops no speed of momentum at all, no beat; it is carried onward as if way below the surface by a force more like that of a tide, and the sharp and quickly shifting rhythms that appear have no firm ground to hold against an uncanny, supernatural drift. *Ivesiana* is a somber suite, not of dances, but of dense and curious theater images. The material [of the music] is noises of nature and scraps of everyday music treated as of equal musical value. The dimensions are compressed, rather than intimate. The wonder of the score lies in the nobility of expression in relation to its subject matter. It [achieves this] with the utmost succinctness but with no meagerness—quite on the contrary, with a kind of eerie grandeur as true and sure as that of an Emily Dickinson lyric.

"This queerly magnificent music is not in our regular concert repertory, and it is worth going to the ballet just to hear it. Watching the ballet, however, one hears it as if with a heightened distinctness, hears its characteristic nuances and its grand expressive coherence as the theater images on stage shockingly confront one.

"Such a theater image is the action on stage [in] 'The Unanswered Question': Out of the darkness a beautiful young girl in white appears aloft, carried by a team of four men, and a shadowy fifth precedes the cluster, turning, crawling, reaching toward her. Carefully, as in a ritual or a circus act, the girl is lowered and lifted, revolved in fantastic and horrifying fashions. In all the shapes her body takes, she is never any less beautiful or less placid. At moments her hair brushes the questioner's face. There is no awareness of his question or of his humiliation on anyone's part but his own. And the cortege moves forward again and disappears—like a great ponderous knot floating about in a shoreless obscurity. This scene, with its casual ghastly incident when the girl falls backward headfirst into space, is the central one of the ballet. As if to heighten the mystery, the spectral white figure never touches the ground.

"[In] 'Central Park in the Dark' a close wedge of girls appears upstage in the dark and oozes forward spreading, covering the stage, kneeling, swaying. A girl runs in searching among them, a boy enters, they meet, and the stage looks like an agitated woods that surges around them as they struggle together, lose and catch one another in the monstrous dark. She drops; instantly with a frantic gesture he rushes off. Slowly the woods shrinks to the far-away clump it first was; much more slowly the girl feels her way with her hands across the deserted forestage. 'Hallowe'en' is a rushing whirl and whirr, a flurry as brittle and spooky as that of leaves at the end of New England October; and leaves too, or with the leaves, a boy and girl whirl and leap forward and away together and are struck down.

"After the hymn-like 'Unanswered Question' comes a noisy city scene, 'Over the Pavements.' Five boys and a girl jump, crawl, intertwine, innocently brutal, while several bands blare at once—a sightless massive energy like that of city streets—then the girl drops her head on a boy's shoulder, he runs off after the others, she skips unpreoccupied in another direction. Next, to a jazz that is small, sour, meticulously insane comes 'In the Inn.' It is the elegant summer 'inn' of New England, and a young couple side by side—with an intoxicated abandon and a miraculous rhythmic edge—invent a dizzy fluctuation of tango, maxixe, charleston, and mambo steps, wander into a horrid combination and out of it, and approach a rough climax, but stop, shake hands, leave each other. After that comes a brief concluding section called 'In the Night,' in which, in a phosphorescent dark light never seen before, a great number of erect figures move on their knees very slowly onward in unconnected directions, and over the nocturnal murmur of the orchestra, as if across invisible meadows, float the smallest and purest notes of bells. Listening for them, it is as if the stage, as if the whole company, had sunk half out of sight into another and slower world.

"It all happens in twenty minutes—painful situations, strokes of wit, local allusions, kinds of movement, shifts of impulse, intertwined rhythms, hallucinating contradictions. There is nothing comfortable to rest on. Details are as cosy as gravel. But the piece in its appalling shifts is steadily expressive. It doesn't waste a note or a motion. There is no vagueness for ear or for eye. *Ivesiana* juxtaposes anguish with innocent fact. It compresses a conflict and drops it into a reach of eternity.

"*Ivesiana* for a critic is as remarkable a novelty as *Four Temperaments* was. At first sight it is more phenomenal, less appealing. Ballets such as both of these are an active part of intellectual life in the United States; they are, it seems to me, among its triumphs. In any case, they are a fight. That is why the spirit, the vitality of the New York City company depend on dancing them. The way the company undertakes the incredible difficulties of *Ivesiana*—no other company in the world would be equal to them—shows it enjoys the battle. It danced *Four Temperaments* several years before it won that one. *Ivesiana* is still a draw." [2]

Terry: "For the most part, *Ivesiana* treats with newly invented movement, strange and unexpected sequences of action, unanticipated body distortions, and an air of eeriness. The difficulties in following either choreographically or in dance performing the rhythmic complexities of Ives's music constitute a challenge and Balanchine has met the challenge brilliantly. In certain episodes, he ignores the beat completely and builds his choreography upon mood and long phrases. Elsewhere, he has created swiftly shifting actions to conform with the metric nature of the accompaniment. In both treatments, he has been strikingly successful in a formal, if not continuously in a theatrical, sense. The most powerful was a nightmarishly beautiful adagio called 'The Unanswered Question.' Excellent also was 'Central Park in the Dark,' macabre, slithery, ominous in its placing of a swift and violent romance between a boy and a girl amid surrounding figures of evil cast." [3]

Martin: "Outstandingly original, astonishingly creative and of almost hyp-

Ivesiana. **The Unanswered Question. Allegra Kent, Todd Bolender.** (*Photo Radford Bascome.*)

notic persuasiveness. It is tinged with morbidity and is couched to a large extent in a quasi-modern-dance idiom that smacks of early Laban. Perhaps both qualities stem in a measure from the music, which is certainly dark in mood and, for all its radical modernism, slightly démodé in air.

"The two sections that seem most successful are 'The Unanswered Question' and the utterly contrasting 'In the Inn.' The 'Question' to which there is no answer is erotic in color, but is kept misty and provocative. It is a lovely piece of choreography, set to a ravishing piece of music. 'In the Inn' is superficially a ragtime episode, but it indulges in grotesque inventions of extraordinary creativeness. It makes a funny and at the same time somewhat awful little composition. The 'Central Park' opening is all mood and eerie unease, and the finale, 'In the Night,' takes it up with genuine daring—thus bringing the work to a sharp and vivid completion.

"Of the other sections, 'Hallowe'en' is tremendously active and energetic, but little of distinctiveness remains in memory, and 'Over the Pavements,' though fascinating in movement and interesting in design, is set to music of forbidding stridency." [4]

Other critics made what they could of it. "The Unanswered Question" was considered the most arresting episode in the ballet. "Central Park in the Dark," "In the Inn," and "In the Night" were also liked; "Over the Pavements" and "Hallowe'en" were not. Balanchine must have felt similarly: On 6 March 1955, he replaced "Hallowe'en" with "Arguments" (2nd movement of string quartet No. 2, 1907), again with Wilde and d'Amboise, and the following 29 November saw "Barn Dance" (from "Washington's Birthday," 1909), with the same principals, instead of "Arguments." (In 1961 this section and "Over the Pavements" were dropped.)

The revival, in which there were a number of changes (including new choreography for "In the Inn"), won over at least one critic who had condemned the piece seven years before—Manchester. She now called it "unlikable but not insignificant." [5]

Haggin described the new version: " 'Central Park,' beginning and ending slowly in a modern idiom that made no coherent musical sense to me, and breaking into ragtime for a few moments, provided the sound-track for the slow entrance and swaying movements of the corps, the powerful metaphors of an episode of sexual violence executed by Mc-Bride and Moncion, and the slow withdrawal of the corps. 'Question'—strings continuing with quiet chords, while at intervals a trumpet repeated the same phrase, and at other intervals flutes broke into agitated exclamations—performed a similar function for a striking episode in which Kent entered standing on the shoulders of four boys who caught her when she fell, passed her around their bodies, and moved her in other ways out of the reach of Lamont, who dragged himself after her. My impression is that in 1954 the boy on the ground never succeeded in touching her; but this time she was delivered once, rolled up in a ball, into his arms for a moment and withdrawn before being raised to the standing position in which she was carried out, with Lamont dragging himself after her. The ragtime of 'In the Inn' was the basis for an episode brilliantly danced by Adams and Mitchell in which the style of Negro jazz dancing was subjected to distortions that seemed to me to have been made even more amusingly eccentric and grotesque, and more erotic, than in 1954. And with 'In the Night,' reminiscent of 'Central Park,' the dancers entered from both sides slowly on their knees, and continued to move across the stage in this strange way until the curtain fell." [6]

Of the ballet's second revival, in 1975, Vaughan wrote, "Still stands as the best of the remarkable avant-garde works Balanchine made during [the mid-fifties], showing his ability to create an atmosphere of menace or mystery by the simplest of dance means only. 'In the Night' still seems pretty audacious after twenty years." [7]

Ivesiana called on new qualities from dancers. Says LeClercq ("In the Inn"), "My part was nice—free and jazzy. The music also was fun. It was like a puzzle trying to get it on time—and the orchestra would goof, and you were never quite sure. There was one part of 'Arguments' where Patty was sort of rocking in a rocking chair, like Whistler's Mother, rocking with Jacques . . . peculiar."

McBride ("Central Park"): "Balanchine told me to close my eyes and pretend I was a blind person. I practiced trying to find something as if I couldn't see. It's very difficult because it's just walking, it's

groping, trying to really feel with your hands."

Schorer ("The Unanswered Question"): "I felt Balanchine wanted mystery, something sphinx-like, Egyptian, endlessly on a pyramid. Yet I think he wanted a sexual woman there."

England:

Reactions from London were particularly interesting, even though the work was not seen there until 1965 and probably did not seem quite so strange as it would have earlier:

"One of Balanchine's searching ballets, strongly influenced by American modern dance, even more strongly influenced by American modern thought. The impetus here comes from the music of Ives, the most interesting of all American native-born composers.

" 'Central Park' is set in the familiar Balanchine territory of love thwarted by an oppressive society, but here the feeling, sounded by Ives's tart Romanticism, is more astringent than nostalgic—a lovely, moving piece. Breath-taking in its technique, 'Question' has a rapt poetry to it that transcends everything but the eerily appealing music of one of Ives's most challenging pieces. 'In the Inn' is a jazzily eccentric game for two self-absorbed players, both happily indulging themselves. The choreography, a grotesque classicism that is deliberately dissociated from naturalistic movement (Gosh!), lacks variety. So, here, does Ives's music. 'In the Night' is fantastic—and the fantasy is a solemn merger between Petipa and Merce Cunningham. For here Balanchine contents himself with his dancers moving across the stage on their knees. This and nothing else—yet the result, so much helped by Hays's perceptive lighting, seems like some dreadful holocaust, with the world maimed and the music lamenting some final resource of a failing human spirit." [8]

"Balanchine matches, illuminates and expands into a further dimension Ives's post-expressionist music with three episodes packed with curious and touching dancing, every bit of which could be adequately performed by dancers trained in the modern dance idiom. It is almost anti-ballet, yet it effortlessly creates three of the four requisite atmospheres. The skittish pas de deux 'In the Inn' holds the only pure balletic episode and is simply a useful review sketch. The impact of 'Central Park in the Dark,' 'The Unanswered

Question' and 'In the Night' is of dream creatures moving in a definitely non-dream world of hopelessness and uncertainty; it is expressed in dancing which holds more slow motion and stasis than any other Balanchine work." [9]

France:

"A manner completely new, but obliquely recalls *Age of Anxiety* or Béjart's *Sacre*. First, a group of dancers, clad in indistinct hues, move in the dusk, victims of a confused imploration, until one couple, joining the collective incantation, turns them into maenads: they attack her. The second piece is even more hermetic and striking: a woman in a pure white leotard is carried about, almost resembling a serpent in her configurations, the constant frustration of a rejected lover. . . . The final piece, a Goyesque nightmare, is the most daring: like crippled creatures, the dancers move on their knees, as if in hallucination, inspiring a nameless secret terror." [10]

ROMA

CHOREOGRAPHY: George Balanchine

MUSIC: Georges Bizet (three movements from *Roma Suite*, 1861–68)

COSTUMES, DÉCOR: Eugene Berman

LIGHTING: Jean Rosenthal

PREMIERE: 23 February 1955

DANCERS: Tanaquil LeClercq, André Eglevsky; Barbara Milberg, Barbara Walczak, Roy Tobias, John Mandia; 12 women, 8 men

I. Scherzo
II. Adagio (pas de deux)
III. Carnaval (Tarantella)

Although for balletomanes *Roma* left a lovely glow, particularly the adagio section, critical reception was mostly tepid, and the work did not remain long in the repertory.

Bizet's music was inspired by a two-year stay in Italy during his early twenties, although he did not manage to complete it for some eight years after returning home ("It drives me crazy," he said about two years before it was finally done). He found Rome, at first, "a city completely lost to art. Rossini, Mozart, Weber, Cimarosa are unknown here." However, soon he was writing "I would scream bloody murder if one single bit of dirt were removed," and when it was time to leave, "I wept for six hours."

As a ballet, *Roma* did not inspire many enthusiastic notices. Denby and Haggin were favorable, but Terry called it "light but highly attractive, far less complex in structure and far more childlike in spirit [than usual]. A ballet of playful innocence." [1] Wrote Hering: "At times quite uninteresting." [2] Martin: "An amiable but unexciting piece choreographically, with a somewhat feeble score by Bizet and somewhat ponderous if handsome setting by Berman. It looks very much like a pièce d'occasion." [3]

Denby lingered over the piece: "Delightfully buoyant and firmly formal. The feeling of buoyancy is like a sense of many fountains splashing; the formality is like that of classic ballet. The grace of it seems modest; but the sense of happiness it gives remains fresh in one's memory in a quite magical way.

"The set [is] like a lofty ruin and like a slum square. The pas de deux [is] magically lit. For the concluding tarantella, a

Roma. **Tanaquil LeClercq, André Eglevsky.**

wreath of bulbs lights up story over story, like at nocturnal illuminations of local Southern saints. Laundry appears, strung up high from wall to wall.

"The long adagio pas de deux for LeClercq and Eglevsky is a most unusual one. It has an equable current and a stillness that do not allow the dancers the relief of a big climax. One can feel the attention of the audience, but also how new the quiet is to them. On stage one notices an astonishing invention—a supported arabesque that slides over the two dancers' linked hands, and as it rests there and the ballerina is turned on pointe, it changes to a renversé extended in first, and the girl looks miraculously cradled as she is slowly spun. In the classic formality of the dancing one may sense the current of a more and more absorbed conversation—from a gentle pleasure in acquaintance, in tentative contact, to a playful ease in intimacy, and then to a sweetly earnest profession of faith. After that there is a mysterious courtesy between the two young people that spins to rest in a still pose swooping like a swallow's flight at dusk. Then the girl withdraws a little, smiling, and returns instinctively to a final pose of trust. The lovers were interrupted by the explosive rush downstage—with their heads down—of two threesomes of tarantella dancers, a wild dash like that of Naples' children.

"*Roma* was not much of a success at its opening. Its modesty turned out to be an extremely avant-garde effect. People went to see what new twist Balanchine had dreamed up and when they were shown the innocent art of dancing they were too bewildered to recognize it." [4]

PAS DE TROIS

CHOREOGRAPHY: George Balanchine

MUSIC: Mikhail Glinka (ballet music from *Ruslan and Ludmila,* 1838–41)

COSTUMES: Karinska

LIGHTING: Jean Rosenthal

PREMIERE: 1 March 1955

CAST: Melissa Hayden, Patricia Wilde, André Eglevsky

OTHER CASTS: Diana Adams, Judith Green, Allegra Kent, Tanaquil LeClercq, Marnee Morris, Violette Verdy; Jacques d'Amboise, Edward Villella

This pas de trois was anything but conventional in form—more like a suite of (mostly) solo dances. "Nobody could dance it, it was so difficult," said Hayden.

Sabin pronounced it "A model of what such a piece should be. Composed in virtuosic style, yet never really flashy or pretentious, enlivened by subtle variety and contrast, and ever-musical in its evolution of phrases and sections." [1]

Wrote Manchester, "A beauty. It is wonderfully planned, beginning with a passage which has all three dancers covering the stage in a succession of small jumps. Arduous though not spectacular, it is rather like the Scarlatti or Bach with which a pianist commences his recital before getting down to the major portion of his program.

"Balanchine has omitted practically nothing from this glittering virtuoso display and has included some dazzling combinations of beaten steps [notably] some wonderful sissonnes battues en arrière for Eglevsky. Yet in spite of all these taxingly difficult feats, the enchaînements are so perfectly arranged that the dancers are able to maintain an air of nonchalance that belies the difficulties; and this slight air of skittishness, which is exemplified in the cheeky little pas de chats with which both girls in turn reject the offered support of Eglevsky, becomes one more of the pleasures of a splendid display piece." [2]

The dancers liked it, too. Eglevsky: "Glinka was a lovely work, a really lovely work. It was unusual—a little adagio, a little slow movement—everything was small, fast, very demanding. I had three variations, and it was so exhausting that I doubt I was much for the girls to hold onto."

Hayden: "I think Mr. B. was tremendously interested in speed at the time, and Patty Wilde had that agility. Her first variation included very fast brisés volés, jetés—jumps, beats, lots of quick relevés, arabesques. My part had bigger jumps and then tiny little things on the floor, stressing pointe work—turns and little bourrées. So there was quite a contrast in movement there, although the music was rather repetitious. Then André came out with big catlike jumps. It had the grand manner, but it was also very charming, like a conversation."

PAS DE DIX

CHOREOGRAPHY: George Balanchine

MUSIC: Alexander Glazounov (from *Raymonda*, 1898)

COSTUMES: Esteban Francés

LIGHTING: Jean Rosenthal

PREMIERE: 9 November 1955

CAST: Maria Tallchief, André Eglevsky; Barbara Fallis, Constance Garfield, Jane Mason, Barbara Walczak, Shaun O'Brien, Roy Tobias, Roland Vazquez, Jonathan Watts

OTHER CASTS: Melissa Hayden, Patricia Wilde; Jacques d'Amboise, Erik Bruhn, Jonathan Watts

Pas de Dix is a set of dances, firmly based on classical ballet technique and mainly an excuse for dazzling technical display with a bit of exotic flavor, in this case, a kind of aristocratic Hungarian. It is good-humored and exciting rather than sophisticated. Here Balanchine chose excerpts from the three-act ballet *Raymonda*, premiered in St. Petersburg in 1898. There is no attempt at authenticity in the character dancing, just suggestions of heel clicking with arms akimbo, performed with broad smiles, in tutus and toe shoes, and interspersed with double air turns and (for Tallchief) turning leaps. Tallchief's sultry solo, in which she assumed the air of a royal Eastern temptress, kicking the back of her head, posing seductively, and plunging her feet like daggers into the floor, was, according to Danilova, based on Petipa's original in mood, but much more difficult. The male pas de quatre, a novelty when it was created, is equally rare in our day. Tallchief's solo and much of the same music with new choreography appeared in Balanchine's *Cortège Hongrois* eighteen years later.

The ballet is essentially a serviceable piece, intended to showcase the abilities of certain dancers and provide the Company with something new. The music is anything but profound, but it is tuneful and dancey.

Wrote Martin, "Simply another of those classic divertissements that Balanchine is continually whipping up to serve the company's needs. There are few

Pas de Dix. Maria Tallchief, Erik Bruhn. *(Photo Fred Fehl.)*

choreographers indeed who can accept what is essentially a hack assignment and turn it into a work of art. The miracle is that Balanchine can do just this year after year."[1] Taken on these terms *Pas de Dix* was a success.

The dancing carried the day. Hering: "Like a grand divertissement at some royal court, yet it bore not the slightest trace of pomposity. The emphasis was on brilliantly incisive dancing with the flavorsome overtones of mazurka and czardas. And although it fragmented into solos, duets, and quartets, there was throughout a feeling of unity and mounting energy that reached its peak in a dashing solo for Tallchief. There was something almost crystalline in the way she moved through space—turning, tossing her head, arching her back. The variations for the other dancers were all beautifully crafted, but it was the solo for Tallchief—and her tantalizing combination of fire and detachment—that made *Pas de Dix* a new jewel in the Balanchine crown."[2]

Martin: "Tallchief's variation is one of the best Balanchine has ever made, and it fits her like a glove."[3]

Manchester was a bit less enthusiastic: "As a last-act divertissement in a full-length ballet with all the trimmings of décor and the background of a full company looking on, this *Pas de Dix*, even though it is not top-drawer Balanchine,

would look very much more effective than it does on a stage which becomes yawningly empty every time the dancers make an exit. Tallchief and Eglevsky have many passages which exist simply for the sake of their extreme technical difficulty. They are not intrinsically either beautiful or interesting. The music is very tuneful with that admixture of pseudo-national idioms characteristic of the divertissement portions of nineteenth-century Russian ballet scores."[4]

Japan:
"An intensely clever pastiche, a kind of free fantasia on Hungarian themes which never pokes its tongue all the way through its check but which comes mighty near it. Essentially a near-parody of the great solemn divertissements of the nineteenth century, it also contained what the audience obviously thought was the finest dancing of the entire evening."[5]

SOUVENIRS

CHOREOGRAPHY: Todd Bolender

MUSIC: Samuel Barber (four-handed piano music, op. 28, 1952; extended and amplified for orchestra, 1955)

COSTUMES, DÉCOR: Rouben Ter-Arutunian

LIGHTING: Jean Rosenthal

PREMIERE: 15 November 1955

CAST: *Three Young Girls (Wallflowers)*, Carolyn George, 2 women; *Attendant*, Arthur Mitchell; *Husband and Wife*, Roberta Meier, Richard Thomas; *A Man About Town*, Todd Bolender; *Another Man About Town*, Roy Tobias; *A Lady and Her Escort*, Jillana, Jonathan Watts; *A Bride and Groom*, Wilma Curley, Robert Barnett; *The Woman*, Irene Larsson; *The Man*, John Mandia; *Maid*, Jane Mason; *Man in Gray*, Herbert Bliss; *Hotel Guests*, 2 women, 3 men; *Attendant (Lifeguard)*, Eugene Tanner

OTHER CASTS: *The Woman*, Marian Horosko, Jillana, Yvonne Mounsey; *The Man*, Roland Vazquez; *Lady and Her Escort*, Lois Bewley, Marian Horosko, Richard Rapp; *Wallflower*, Janice Groman, Allegra Kent, Carol Sumner

The action of the ballet takes place in and

around The Royal Palms Hotel, 1914.
SCENE1—The Lobby
SCENE 2—Third-floor Hallway
SCENE 3—A Corner of the Ballroom ("Wall-flower Waltz")
SCENE 4—Tea in the Palm Court
SCENE 5—A Bedroom Affair
SCENE 6—The Next Afternoon

Both Sides of Footlights Have Fun at 'Souvenirs'

An antic romp in a stylized, old-movie tradition, *Souvenirs* was berated as bad ballet by some, as no ballet at all by others, as lacking in choreography and presenting rather well-worn ideas. ("If we must have pieces in the repertory for people who don't like ballet, this is a great improvement over *Cakewalk*, for instance; but must we have them?" wrote Martin.[1]) It was also considered terribly funny, and many wondered why a delightfully amusing stage spectacle, with a myriad of clever details, was not the perfectly valid province of a ballet company, "even" a serious one. This position was evidently taken by the company management, for *Souvenirs* was performed—and often—for many years.

According to Barber (in a note prefacing the score), "The suite consists of a waltz, schottische, pas de deux, two-step, hesitation tango, and galop. One might imagine a divertissement of the Palm Court of the Hotel Plaza in New York, the year about 1914, epoch of the first tangos; 'Souvenirs'—remembered with affection, not in irony or with tongue in cheek, but in amused tenderness."

Says Bolender of his conception, "I got my idea directly from the music, which I thought was dazzling. The libretto was very long; I threw a lot of stuff out, and it was over a year and a half until I actually got it ready. I found all the costumes at Weyhe art book store, where they showed me some little French pamphlets issued monthly with color pictures of designs from various fashion houses. And so they're real. I was very conscious of the costumes as I worked—the narrow skirts and shoes—and I wanted the movement to fit that. I made the kids do it in rehearsal; even though they were ballet dancers, they were to maintain the look and style of the period. For the finale I wanted a beach scene, but we couldn't afford *anything*; what we got was a string of flags attached to a pole, with a lifeguard standing there, and Jean got a fan to blow on the flags!"

Dancers remembered Bolender's meticulous coaching—"down to the last eyelash," says Mounsey.

Hering provided a concise summary: "Opened with the guests of a resort hotel waltzing decorously about a monstrous velvet-couch-and-potted-palms. Little things began to happen. A Man About Town flirted with a lady and received her calling card, only to have it accidentally knocked out of his hand by a shy debutante. A bride and groom whirled blissfully at their wedding party. And through it all, like a chill wind, stalked 'The Woman.'

Reel two: The Man About Town created havoc in an upstairs hall.

Reel three: With the special feeling he has for the tentativeness of young girls, Bolender sketched three little wallflowers perched expectantly on a settee. One of them conjured up a temporary dream partner.

Reel four: Another Man About Town came between a lady and her not-so-welcome escort.

Reel five: The climax! The Siren and her oily visitor slithered through a cleverly devised tango of mutual conquest.

Reel six: On the beach, with the denizens of bedroom, hallway, and ballroom plunging and squealing in the sun.

"With the exception of its rather loosely choreographed ending, *Souvenirs* was a bright, compact series of images whose atmosphere derived from Bolender's keen sense of timing and from Ter-Arutunian's drape-and-glitter costumes and his witty take-off on the curlicue decor of the period. Barber's lightly sentimental score also added immeasurably." [2]

Others mentioned details. Terry: "The vamp slinks and snarls, uses a tiger-skinned couch as if it were man's most impressive invention, grinds a crimson high heel into the chest of a devasted male victim, and moves as if the ambulatory process were centered in the torso (which indeed it is, technically speaking) rather than in the limbs. Larsson's vamp, listed on the program merely as The Woman—either an understatement or a highly sophisticated commentary—is the most engaging figure in the ballet, and to her and her escort go the funniest movements and the best episodes.

"*Souvenirs*, to be wholly honest, is an extended treatment of an idea suitable for musical comedy. But if it is musical-comedy stuff, it may be noted that other ballets have invaded this area, among

Souvenirs. A Bedroom Affair. Irene Larsson, John Mandia. (Photo Fred Fehl.)

them Ashton's *Façade*. So if there are faults to be found, they lie not so much in its musical-comedy leanings as in choreographic declines. But when *Souvenirs* really moves, it is, in its unpretentious but engaging way, almost a genuine ballet. Not a significant work, but great good fun." [3]

Martin: "It is a mildly merry little spoof of the already fairly thoroughly spoofed mores of the period immediately preceding World War I. It owes a considerable debt to Charles Weidman's 'Flickers' and a lesser one to Jerome Robbins' Mack Sennett ballet. The music has perhaps more wit, if less punch, than the stage action, and its delicate and rather French sophistication are a little lost in horseplay. There are touches of the social dances of the period, but scarcely a nickel's worth of actual choreography. Its funniest moments derive from old-fashioned movie mime and gestures. There are, for example, an amusing scene of silently mouthed dialogue between Jillana and Tobias, and a no-holds-barred vamping scene. But it is the costumes that are most hilarious. Ter-Arutunian has patterned his designs after those of the period and has achieved some superb monstrosities." [4]

Australia:

"A penetrating satire and witty burlesque of leisured American society in which the influences of American dance forms predominate." [5]

JEUX D' ENFANTS

CHOREOGRAPHY: George Balanchine, Barbara Milberg, Francisco Moncion

MUSIC: Georges Bizet (*Jeux d'Enfants*, op. 22, 1871)

COSTUMES, DÉCOR: Esteban Francés

LIGHTING: Jean Rosenthal

PREMIERE: 22 November 1955

CAST: *1. Overture; 2. Badminton*, Barbara Fallis, Richard Thomas, Jonathan Watts; *3. Hobby Horses*, 2 couples; *4. Paper Dolls*, 4 women; *Scissors*, 1 man; *5. The Lion and the Mouse*, Ann Crowell, Eugene Tanner; *6. The Music Box*, Walter Georgov, Una Kai, Roland Vazquez; *7.*

The American Box, 5 women; *8. The Tops*, Robert Barnett, Barbara Walczak; *9. The Soldier*, Roy Tobias; *10. The Doll*, Melissa Hayden; *11. Pas de Deux*, Hayden, Tobias; *12. Galop*, entire cast
Doll also danced by Tanaquil LeClercq

REVIVAL: 8 September 1959

CHOREOGRAPHY: George Balanchine (9–12) and Francisco Moncion (2–8)

CAST: *1. Overture; 2. Pas de Trois*, Susan Borree, Richard Rapp, William Weslow; *3. Tarantella*, 2 couples; *4. Paper Dolls*, 4 women, 1 man; *5. Music Box*, Diane Consoer, Tanner, Vazquez; *6. Jumping Jacks*, 4 men; *7. American Box*, 5 women; *8. Top*, Deni Lamont; *9. March*, Tobias; *10. Doll*, Allegra Kent; *11. Pas de Deux*, Kent, Tobias; *12. Galop*, entire cast

From the program note: "Not a ballet of children at play, but a set of dances of toys children play with. Francés has been inspired by eighteenth- and nineteenth-century wooden toys and some American playthings from our own century."

Few ballets, particularly those so splendidly mounted, have been greeted with such a dearth of enthusiasm. "Pleasantly inconsequential" [1] . . . "indefensible" [2] . . . "too many cooks," [3] said the critics. Among their points of agreement: Bizet's music was as charming as ever; Francés's costumes were delightful and clever;

Jeux d'Enfants. Roy Tobias, Tanaquil Le-Clercq. (*Photo Fred Fehl.*)

choreography was the most negligible element on the stage.

Haggin also mentioned Moncion's Music Box sequence, "an arresting interlude with three figures in magnificent Spanish costumes whose jerky movements, amusing at first, are seen to be enacting a love triangle which ends with the husband stabbing the lover." [4] And Kastendieck referred to the opening moment: "It started off on a wonderful note of fantasy. Between Bizet's music and Rosenthal's lighting, the set emerged from darkness with a certain touch of magic." [5]

The ballet was revived briefly four years later. "The only possible justification [was] the desire to get a little more mileage out of the elaborate and fanciful décor. Still a trivial bore," wrote Manchester, [6] epitomizing the general sentiment.

Balanchine used some of the music and costumes for a newly choreographed pas de deux, *The Steadfast Tin Soldier*, in 1975.

ALLEGRO BRILLANTE

CHOREOGRAPHY: George Balanchine

MUSIC: Peter Ilyitch Tchaikovsky (Piano Concerto No. 3 in E-flat major, op. 75, 1892 [unfinished])

LIGHTING: Jean Rosenthal

PREMIERE: 1 March 1956

PIANO: Nicholas Kopeikine

CAST: Maria Tallchief, Nicholas Magallanes, 4 couples

OTHER CASTS: Diana Adams, Suzanne Farrell, Allegra Kent, Patricia McBride, Violette Verdy, Patricia Wilde; Anthony Blum, Frank Ohman, Peter Martins, André Prokovsky, Jonathan Watts

Allegro Brillante, which began as a last-minute replacement for a canceled work, remains in the repertory after twenty years. It is short and requires few dancers; thus it is useful as a middle ballet. And because it offers a chance for virtuoso display and is at the same time "dancey" and flowing, it is a favorite with both prin-

Allegro Brillante. Above: **Nicholas Magallanes, Maria Tallchief.** *(Photo Fred Fehl.)*
Right: **Patricia McBride.** *(Photo Michael Avedon.)*

cipal dancers and the small corps de ballet (which is usually of soloist caliber). Dancers love to move; and *Allegro Brillante* contains a satisfyingly large number of pure dance steps which follow one after another in a fluid outpouring (as distinct from poses, stretches, technical "impossibilities"). It is not intellectually rigorous, but rather has a comfortable old-fashioned naïveté, with an emotional quality, matching the music, that borders on the sentimental, and it offers opportunity for somewhat exaggerated projection. Skirts fly, heads are thrown back, dancers rush off into the wings. As Manchester put it, "If a Soviet company showed us *Allegro*, we would smile indulgently and think, 'How like them.' " [1] (Indeed, the European critics may be smiling at *us*; they seem to have passed over *Allegro* with barely a comment.)

Says Tallchief, "I loved that business of being lifted into the air with the chiffon skirt, the look and feeling . . . It's extremely nice to dance, it's a little bit different—that expansive Russian romanticism. Of course, some of it is fast, *very* fast." She might have added that the ballerina part can be absolutely dazzling. In addition to Tallchief, Hayden in particular had a great success in the chief role.

According to Balanchine, *Allegro* "contains everything I knew about the classical ballet—in thirteen minutes."

Terry: "The new work is modest in its theatricality but rich in pure dance values. It has no story, no characterization and, actually, no specific mood (other than a general air of pleasantness). Yet it possesses a special kind of fascination as if it were saying, 'Here are some classic dance steps and this is how they look when they are paired with musical notes and phrases.' It is rich in steps, in fresh arrangements of steps, in gesture, and in patterns of movement. And one of its prime virtues is that it presents Tallchief not as an imperious queen, not as a glittering figure of fantasy, but as an exceptionally attractive girl who moves like an angel.

"The very exercise-nature of *Allegro Brillante* permits us to concentrate upon Tallchief as a flawless executant of any movement assigned to her, from a simple raising of the arms through a chain of rapid turns across the stage to perilous actions with her partner requiring split-second timing. One does not have to consider what character she is portraying nor does one have to check up on her command of dramatic coloring. One simply watches her move gloriously, and it is an exciting experience." [2]

Martin: "Though it is certainly not one of his masterpieces, it is put together with all his skill and authority. Its main handicap is its music, which is choreographically unevocative in the extreme. Though the title might suggest otherwise, it is not a ballet of rhinestones and tutus and general glitter. It is more nearly in the family of *Serenade* than that of *Theme and Variations*, romantic in color and lyric in costuming. To be sure, it provides some passages of flashing virtuosity for Tallchief, and nobody knows better than Balanchine how to choreograph for her. Magallanes and the ensemble, too, have some grateful material to work with, and it is not to its discredit that much of it awakens memories of other Balanchine works. If nothing in the nature of history was made, one's hat is off again to Balanchine for his mastery of his craft and of his art." [3]

Manchester: "It is a pity that a master choreographer should so often find himself in the position of having to supply program fillers, but *Allegro Brillante* is a charming one. It suffers from two handicaps: the single existing movement of Tchaikovsky's Concerto is horribly reminiscent of a dozen other pieces of Tchaikovsky and never achieves any real distinction, while the sleazy draperies for the girls with particolored bodices and the gray undershirts of the boys are highly unbecoming. Choreographically, the mood is mainly lyrical, with large, sweeping steps which cover the stage." [4]

Because of the propulsion of the music, *Allegro* looks impossibly difficult. Yet Balanchine placed exits so strategically that most dancers do not find it among their hardest roles. According to Verdy, "There's a lot of strong, broad dancing spaced in very little time. The gestures have to be big, ample, spacious, and they have to look free. Under all that freedom has to be control—the pirouettes, exactness, beats and turns, and, as always with him, the fast work. But if the ballerina is afraid that it will not produce enough of an effect by itself, if she feels she has to compensate by telling the audience that it is hard, a false drama is created. It should be left alone, and one should dance it with passion but with happiness. It's quintessentially Russian in its best possible meaning—a great, romantic, beautiful plastic piece."

THE CONCERT
or,
The Perils of Everybody

A Charade in one act

CHOREOGRAPHY: Jerome Robbins

MUSIC: Frédéric Chopin (Berceuse, op. 57; Prelude, op. 28, no. 18; Prelude, op. 28, no. 16; Waltz in E Minor [posth.]; Prelude, op. 28, no. 7; Waltz, op. 64, no. 1; Prelude, op. 28, no. 4; Mazurka in G Major [posth.]; Mazurka, op. 24, no. 4; Ballade, op. 47, no. 3) *

COSTUMES: Irene Sharaff

LIGHTING, DÉCOR: Jean Rosenthal

PREMIERE: 6 March 1956

PIANO: Nicholas Kopeikine

CAST: Tanaquil LeClercq, Todd Bolender, Yvonne Mounsey; Robert Barnett, Wilma Curley, John Mandia, Shaun O'Brien, Patricia Savoia, Richard Thomas; 7 women, 7 men

REVIVAL: 2 December 1971, New York State Theater

MUSIC: Frédéric Chopin (as above, with Polonaise "Militaire" as overture, and omitting Waltz, op. 64, no. 1, and Mazurka, op. 24, no. 4)

DÉCOR: Saul Steinberg

LIGHTING: Ronald Bates

PIANO: Jerry Zimmerman

CAST: Sara Leland, Anthony Blum, Bettijane Sills; O'Brien, Robert Weiss; Bart Cook, Stephen Caras, Gloriann Hicks, Delia Peters, Christine Redpath; 5 women, 6 men

* Two additional pieces were dropped immediately after opening night.

OTHER CASTS: Merrill Ashley, Allegra Kent, Francisco Moncion, Peters

I don't know exactly what inspired the ballet—maybe a Steinberg drawing, and then listening to the music and thinking how corny it had become from overuse—you hear it in ballet class all the time. I don't think it's possible with any ballet to pinpoint any one source [1974]. . . . My first intention was to denude certain pieces of their banal titles—'Butterflies,' 'Raindrop,' etc.—perhaps restoring them to their purity by destroying the fabricated interpretations. . . . Certain critics, above all Polish ones, insist I have shown a lack of respect toward the Chopin music. Others have, on the contrary, qualified my approach as an 'act of piety.' "—Robbins, 1959

The Concert belongs to that rare species, comedy ballet. The critics laughed loudly, with reservations; audiences mostly just laughed.

Terry: "There were moments which suggested that the New York City Ballet had come up with the comedy hit of the season (or the decade, for that matter) and there were other moments when one felt that a consistently successful and brilliant choreographer had stumbled. Robbins calls his new work a charade, and it is at its feeblest when it is just that and at its most inspired when its jokes are told in dance. Sometimes he has come up with a literal reaction—for instance, the Minute Waltz—and sometimes his own fancies have led him to create a delicious series of anticlimaxes to the little prelude always so popular in *Les Sylphides*.

"It starts with the pianist on stage and a group of varied persons—dreamers, gum-chewers, a bored husband [Bolender], a culture-seeking wife [Mounsey] and the like—as the audience. These figures, augmented by an ensemble from time to time, people the ballet and enact its charades. Things got off to a fine beginning when LeClercq, stirred to the depths by the music, launched herself into a whirlwind of action, with hair lashing, her face and her feet trying desperately to keep pace with the music until complete collapse struck her. Another hilarious sequence had to do with a group of dancers unable to agree on steps and rhythms as they went grimly about the task of destroying choreographic form.

Here was a dance joke, defying literal description, which had the audience shrieking and choking with laughter. Barnett's Minute Waltz, during which he spun wildly around the stage, was also good fun, and there were superb comic moments when the men dancers, picking up the dancing girls in an array of unlikely and unlovely positions, carted them on and off stage. There were some passing humors to the Butterfly Etude, which involved two armies of angry butterflies (a delightful notion), and there were several pleasantly lyrical and nostalgic passages for LeClercq and for the umbrella-carrying dancers in the Raindrop Prelude. But a series of cartoons in which a wife attempted to polish off her husband with gun, poison, and TNT fell flat, and there were other pantomimic gags which were equally lifeless.

"But in spite of its empty episodes, *The Concert* (amusingly costumed) is certainly worth salvaging, for its best scenes are as funny as anything to be found in the theater of dance. Generous cutting, revisions, and complete reworking here and there should find Robbins with another hit to his credit." [1]

Martin headed his review, "A Half Riot": "A completely lunatic fantasy, set to—or perhaps more accurately, set against—twelve short pieces by Chopin. According to the program note, it is a take-off on fanciful sobriquets such as 'The Minute Waltz' and 'The Butterfly Etude,' together with all the other personal 'interpretations' read into music by a concert audience. This is true enough, but actually the piece is a kind of nightmarish revue, in which a series of characters maintains the same relationships through an endless sequence of different situations. It starts out to be quite the funniest ballet that has been seen in modern times, but too much gets to be enough, and before it comes to an end it has knocked itself out by its sheer persistence. There is a hilarious spoof of audiences, and an even more ridiculous one of a ballet ensemble in conflict with rugged individualism, which may be the best sections. A long series of blackouts, set to the prelude that Fokine has made more familiar in *Sylphides*, has a highly amusing idea, but it might be more effective in a Broadway show.

"Many of the jokes are corny, and Balanchine, Fokine, and Robbins himself as choreographers are laid under heavy contribution while they are being kidded.

The Concert. Above: 1956. Tanaquil LeClercq (arms raised). *Right:* 1956. Robert Barnett (far left), Todd Bolender (center), Tanaquil LeClercq. (*Photos Fred Fehl.*)

The real victims, however, are Chopin and Kopeikine. The former, represented in the set by a chaste silhouette, disappears from the scene early, presumably in dudgeon, but Kopeikine is called upon to sit there and play with complete integrity through all the mayhem." [2]

Watt: "Screwy and charming; much of the time, both funny and oddly touching. A pianist, in white tie and tails, appears from the wings, takes his place at a grand piano on one side of the stage, and announces he is going to play the Berceuse, Opus 57. As he begins playing, his audience gradually assembles. A wildly improbable bunch, they carry their own folding chairs and create several minor confusions before they are all in place and reasonably intent on the music. Through the next 11 pieces, they are transported by the music into all sorts of unlikely situations. There is a perfectly idiotic, but somehow charming, sequence with umbrellas to the strains of the 'Raindrop Prelude'; there is an incredible track meet run off with the 'Minute Waltz'; there is a hilarious mazurka danced by three men in pajama tops and a fourth in pajama bottoms, and there are many other diversions, including a kind of fouled-up *Sylphides.*

"Through it all, three familiar people— the bored husband, the outraged wife, and the silly young woman—keep getting tangled up with one another. From the point of view of the piano soloist, it was probably the most unfortunate recital ever offered. For waves of laughter drowned out his performance throughout most of the concert." [3]

Hering mentioned "a lovely introspective Mazurka solo for LeClercq with folding extensions and soft pawings of the floor." [4] Says Robbins of her variation, "The original performance had one dance for Tanny, very near the end, where the pianist was playing and she came in, sort of wandering, and listened to the music and then slowly took off and began to dance. It was a mazurka, and it was just absolutely into the music—it wasn't comic—and to me that was sort of like the beginning of *Dances at a Gathering.* It was a very beautiful dance, sort of a reverie. I took it out when Tanny no longer danced; it was so her."

The Concert remained briefly in the repertory, and in a revised version was later performed by Robbins's company, Ballets U.S.A., for the annual Festival of Two Worlds in Spoleto, where it opened 8 June 1958, with two new drops by Saul Steinberg. Says Robbins of this version (which is close to the one revived by the New York City Ballet in 1971), "There's a lot I cut out—the 'Minute Waltz,' a subway sequence, two more killings. I added other sections. I think I could do another whole ballet along the same track." To those still laughing at jokes created twenty years ago, nothing would be more delicious.

The revival was greeted with great enthusiasm. Goldner, after acknowledging the obvious humor, gave a more penetrating explanation of the ballet's new popularity:

"Occasionally the projections emanate from Robbins rather than the characters. The ballet would be still better, I sup-

pose, if it had stayed with the characters' points of view, but then we would not have had the best episode of all—the umbrella dance, to a Chopin prelude. A person walks on stage and opens his black umbrella. Others appear, see the open umbrella, turn their hands palm up to catch the raindrops, shrug their shoulders in puzzlement because they feel no drops—and open their umbrellas. Soon the stage is filled with open black umbrellas. But that is not the end of it. The group next splits in two, and each crowds under one of two open umbrellas, huddling and herding masses under the tyranny we all know. This is Robbins's 'think piece.'

"I suspect that audiences are riper for comic ballet now than they were in the 1950s. In several ways, that is a good sign. Dance is not as sacred as it used to be. Perhaps many people have grown tired of campy, put-down humor and so find this ballet a tonic. The humor is always straightforward, whether it is being wry in a Thurber-like way or totally rambunctious, silly.

"I also find myself embracing *The Concert* more warmly now than I did fifteen years ago, but mainly for a different reason. In those days Robbins struck me in part as being clever, an idea man, and too imaginative for his own good—what you might call talented. He actually was much, much better than that, but no matter how fine a ballet was, it never (with the exception of *Afternoon of a Faun*) got to the heart of the dance. Perhaps a comic-whimsical viewpoint, which infused much of his work, cannot ever get

The Concert. 1970s. Sara Leland (center, in wide-brimmed hat), Francisco Moncion (with cigar). *(Photo Fred Fehl.)*

to the heart. Indeed, perhaps it is best for a choreographer to have no 'viewpoint.' Upon seeing *The Concert* in 1956, it was obvious that Robbins was very moved by Chopin and in a way personal enough to create something extraordinary. Yet he turned an honest reaction of infinite possibility into a concoction, otherwise known as a concept. The fact that *The Concert* and other ballets were so good only compounded the frustration of knowing that Robbins would be a great choreographer if he decided to go straight.

"He did in 1969, when he created *Dances for a Gathering.* That was quickly followed by *In the Night.* Both are set to Chopin. Both are masterpieces, and I don't think that is an accident. They bear no resemblance to *The Concert* except for one point. All three are projections of Robbins's experience with Chopin. It is not anyone's business to know what the nature of those experiences have been, but they have produced two ballets that are not only beautiful but profound. Unlike *Dances* and *In the Night,* *The Concert* is many times removed from the experience of listening to Chopin. But now that Robbins has had the honesty and courage to face Chopin head-on, inwardly, it is easy to allow him the privilege of fooling around. And I, for one, love it all, knowing that the choreographer who has taken this little holiday is a master." [5]

"An image I treasure is that of Mon-

cion fluttering around like a demented butterfly with a cigar clamped between his teeth, like Broderick Crawford cast as The Queen of the May. Robbins's humor is brilliantly and specifically American . . . and yes, Queen Victoria, it is art." [6]

Moncion: "It's fun to do sometimes, but you have to really work yourself into the mood, break through the reticence. There's a lot of crazy jumping around, but one of the things Jerry said was, 'I don't want this to look like a caricature. This has to be danced, and danced in an attractive fashion—not like some Broadway hoofer who doesn't know how. That isn't what I want. I want clean line, clean steps, real steps.' "

France:

"Chopin making one cry with laughter—scandalous! the purists would say. But what of the dancing-school pianists who massacre him with gusto every day? And how about Clement Doucet, who, in the days of our youthful folly at Le Boeuf sur le Toit, had us dancing to Chopin while beating time—his favorite blues?! With screamingly funny gags, which I'd hate to give away, and a keen sense of observation, Robbins parodies Taglioni ('Butterfly' etudes), Fokine (*Les Sylphides*—the most amusing), Massine (*Le Beau Danube*), and his own master Balanchine (*Serenade*). To the 'Raindrop' prelude he has constructed an umbrella ballet that would make the fortune of a music hall." [7]

THE STILL POINT

CHOREOGRAPHY: Todd Bolender

MUSIC: Claude Debussy (String Quartet, 1893, first three movements), transcribed for orchestra by Frank Black

Title from T. S. Eliot poem "Burnt Norton"

LIGHTING: Jean Rosenthal

PREMIERE: 13 March 1956 (first presented 10 April 1955 as *At the Still Point,* using the complete string quartet, by the Dance Drama Company of Emily Frankel and Mark Ryder, YM-YWHA, New York)

CAST: Melissa Hayden, Jacques d'Amboise; Jillana, Irene Larsson, John Mandia, Roy Tobias

This was perhaps Bolender's most successful ballet and a triumph for Hayden. The choice of music was inspired; in particular, the frequent pizzicati were brilliantly evocative of the heroine's nervous tension and inner torment.

Says Bolender, "I began working very slowly and I simply fashioned it as I went along. I took it somehow from the situation as it existed in their company—there were two of them and then there were four other dancers. I remember the atmosphere at the time—there would be scenes . . . it was like something that was just happening at the time. Ryder never had ballet training, and I loved this; he didn't even know how to lift. Out of that I had to make a whole different kind of relationship between a man and a woman. It's the part Jacques did. It didn't have any ballet steps; in fact, he was wearing heeled shoes. I've always tried to keep it as simple as possible because that was the thing I liked about it: it was just a *man* on stage who moved and didn't dance—that is, he had no variation, he didn't do technical things—but did have the sense of dance. I visualized it as a dialogue between the two, really as though they were speaking to each other—not dancing, but speaking. Technically, I threw the book at Frankel. She had a beautiful modern technique and then she learned ballet, which gave another dimension—another line—to her dancing. It was all dance, really. I tried to evolve it the way I feel Balanchine handles stories—in *Serenade*, *Sonnambula*, *Midsummer*—these are not pantomime things, but the story is there." Bolender accomplished his aims powerfully.

Wrote Hering: "Most memorable of the entire season was a single instant when a young man extended his hand toward a girl, and her hand rose in an arc to meet his. It was the culmination of *The Still Point*. Bolender has uncanny insight into the feelings of young women. His girl in *Mother Goose Suite*, his debutante in *Souvenirs*, and the tortured protagonist of *The Still Point* are all sisters under the skin—poignant sisters seeking fulfillment in romantic love. Of them all, the girl in *The Still Point* is the most touching because she is delineated with the most depth and at the same time with the most simplicity. In fact, simplicity is the prime virtue of this little ballet. Bolender has had the courage and the care to let the dancing speak out honestly without any mimetic overlay.

"The work began in the atmosphere of adolescence—in restlessness, turbulence, and sweetness. Three girls in bright dresses turned and reached in long arabesques. One of them, a slight misfit, touched their hands in a tentative gesture of safety. They forsook her to find two boys who had captured their interest. She gazed after them in confusion; touched the back of her hand to her cheek; and

fled. The others returned to dance playfully with their partners. The lone girl, her confusion and frustration mounting, was tossed between the boys, only to end in flailing solitude. A young man strode in, sank to one knee, and contemplated the girl. He rested his hand on her shoulder as though to quiet her anguish; held his hand out to her, palm upward. And both extended their legs backward along the ground in a gesture of flight. She found his face and stroked it wonderingly. They faced, rising to half toe, and she 'came home' high in his arms. They sank into the final handclasp. Hayden wove endless nuance and pathos into her portrayal, and yet the danced outlines were contained and beautifully clear. D'Amboise communicated the steady masculinity that we have associated heretofore only with Youskevitch." [1]

Martin: "It is a delicate, tenuous poetic piece that makes demands upon its audience. Bolender has composed in remarkable rapport with Hayden, so that it is difficult to tell where choreographer ends and performer takes over. Between them they achieve a curiously Debussyish evocation of inner feeling. It is by no means all clouds and vaporings; there are passion and emotional substance at its center (as there are, indeed, in the music), and Hayden makes it a glowingly beautiful piece of intuitive drama. In the handling of his quartet of assisting figures, Bolender has been less consistently in the right key, but he has got from d'Amboise a simple and admirable performance. He composed it originally for modern dancers, and he himself began as a student of Hanya Holm. It is small wonder, then, that in this new work he has utilized something of the emotional approach of the modern dance. That this approach has awakened so sympathetic a response from Hayden is what is extraordinary." [2]

Manchester: "It is a ballet which means what you happen to feel it means. For me it says something—and says it very movingly—about the uncertainties and agonies of growing up when relationships which had once been so simple suddenly become complex and frightening. It is Hayden's ballet and she is not less than magnificent as the tormented girl who finds spiritual peace and happiness in her acceptance of the security of the love of which she has hitherto been fearful. D'Amboise is impressive in the simplicity of his almost static role as the lover whose gentle certainty resolves the girl's fears.

The Still Point. Melissa Hayden, Jacques d'Amboise. (*Photo Martha Swope*.)

Here he emerges as a fine, serious artist, and an admirable partner in the great pas de deux which is the long, splendid climax of a work which is romantic, lyrical and deeply poignant." [3]

Says Hayden, "Working with Todd, we seemed to build one layer on top of the next; he fed me that way. He was very detailed, very subtle. My whole body was to express my feelings—if I was pained, it should be through my whole body in a physical sense, rather than just on my face, which I would say was physical but very superficial. He noticed shoulders, hands; he was very constructive. I learned when I could be brash and not be brash, when I could be very subtle and still project without feeling that I wasn't coming across. It was at a time when I wasn't doing that kind of ballet . . . I had been through a period of being very classical, and *Still Point* taught me a great deal, which I could also relate to other ballets. For instance, I always wanted to dance *Scotch Symphony* like a breath of air, but not all the choreography is conducive to that. But if you have a concept in mind, you can give this feeling in the movement, without watering it down."

France:
"A lean ballet dealing with extreme human tension, an admirable and subtle treatment of man's essential anguish. Liberation from this anguish of solitude and lack of love is the subject." [4]

Germany:
"Bolender succeeds with a psychologically finely differentiated chamber ballet about the growing up of a young girl, and fully justifies the audacity of using so sensitive a piece as Debussy's string quartet as framework." [5]

DIVERTIMENTO NO. 15

CHOREOGRAPHY: George Balanchine

MUSIC: Wolfgang Amadeus Mozart (Divertimento No. 15 in B-flat major, K. 287, 1777)

COSTUMES: Karinska

DÉCOR: James Stewart Morcom (from *Symphonie Concertante*); David Hays (1966)

Divertimento No. 15. **Early 1960s. Erik Bruhn.** (*Photo Fred Fehl.*)

LIGHTING: Jean Rosenthal; David Hays (1966)

PREMIERE: 31 May 1956, Mozart Festival, American Shakespeare Theater, Stratford, Conn.

CAST: Diana Adams, Melissa Hayden, Allegra Kent, Tanaquil LeClercq, Patricia Wilde; Herbert Bliss, Nicholas Magallanes, Roy Tobias

OTHER CASTS: Merrill Ashley, Susan Borree, Suzanne Farrell, Deborah Flomine, Judith Green, Melissa Hayden, Susan Hendl, Jillana, Sara Leland, Patricia McBride, Marnee Morris, Colleen Neary, Patricia Neary, Mimi Paul, Susan Pilarre, Giselle Roberge, Francia Russell, Suki Schorer, Bettijane Sills, Victoria Simon, Marjorie Spohn, Carol Sumner, Violette Verdy, Barbara Walczak, Lynda Yourth; Herbert Bliss, Anthony Blum, Erik Bruhn, Victor Castelli, Daniel Duell, Conrad Ludlow, Peter Martins, Arthur Mitchell, Frank Ohman, Richard Rapp, Francis Sackett, Earle Sieveling, Kent Stowell, Jonathan Watts

Allegro
Theme and Variations
Minuet
Andante
Finale

This is a ballet of the aristocracy, that world in which cavaliers were never more gallant, ladies never more gracious. There is elegance without ostentation; good breeding does not show off. Cut crystal rather than diamond glitter characterizes the ballet's delicate sparkle. It is one of Balanchine's purest dance creations—a string of dances, solos, ensembles, pas de deux—with muted emotional overtones and little virtuoso display, and words can do it even less justice than is usually the case. (There is no written piece that even attempts this in more than a perfunctory manner.) A dancer once described it as "frosting," which captures something of its prettiness and ornamental nature, but misses its fine, if slight, shadings of sadness and delight.

Most reviewers were ecstatic about the choreography ("exquisite" was the word most frequently used), but few denied that the meandering, unstructured nature of the whole resulted in lengthy stretches from time to time.

The most touching appreciation was written by a music critic (Biancolli), who likened the dancers to the selfless ser-

vants of beauty; its absolute they could never attain, but their lives were sanctified by single-minded pursuit of an ideal: "It is so close to the music that the chances are no company short of a band of dancing Mozarts will ever be able to attain either the perfection of Mozart or the ingenuity of Balanchine; the gap will always remain between what both Mozart and Balanchine have devised and what is humanly possible in the dance. Think of trying to communicate in motion the breathing, soaring line of an Andante that is almost the closest thing to divine grace in music. Suspending the law of gravity would be one way of doing it." [1]

"A carefully wrought projection of the score. If a sameness creeps in, the music is the inhibiting influence. As has happened before, the composer gets in the way occasionally, especially in the final movement. He has, however, inspired some beautiful dance patterns, so there is compensation. As usual Balanchine has followed the notes closely. His art is no better illustrated than in the theme and variations where each one is as well tailored to the music as it is for the dancer. Herein lies his genius." [2] Terry's opinion improved over the years: "Belongs in that category (and a large one it is) of Balanchine's nondramatic compositions inspired exclusively by the form and quality of a given piece of music. It is not, I think,

Divertimento No. 15. **1970s. Peter Martins, Merrill Ashley.** (*Photo Martha Swope.*)

his finest exercise in this field but it has some agreeable designs for the corps de ballet and many gleaming variations for the principals. A whole battery of ballerinas is involved in the work, and each has her own opportunities for display. Perhaps the most exhilarating solo is that given to Wilde, who performs her fleet and complex patterns with a marvelous brio and a beautiful musical sense. But then, there were some stunning sequences provided by the other ballerinas. Three gentlemen were on hand to offer courtesies and assistances to the ladies and, on occasion, to dance on their own. [1956] . . . A ballet which has its very being in the exquisite movement inventions born of the rhythms, phrases, formalities, and colorings of the score itself. [1958] . . . With an elegance of deportment, which would have been familiar to courtiers of the Mozart era, combined with physical virtuosities made possible by the toe shoe (unknown in the composer's day), Balanchine has given beautiful dance duplication to the lovely airs and phrases and graces of the music. [1966]" [3]

Martin considered *Divertimento No. 15* "An extraordinarily brilliant work in the best Balanchine style, an exquisitely imaginative epitome of the flavor of eighteenth-century elegance. Of the five movements of the work, the Theme and Variations section is inevitably the most effective, because of the irresistible invitation of the music. But from beginning to end it is a sequence of exquisite inventions developed with the most transpar-

ent logic. Once or twice Balanchine startles us a bit musically, as at the end of the Andante, but he is so much the complete Mozartean that he can do it with authority. He has given us, indeed, a lovely work.

"It is beautifully danced, also, as it would have to be in order to be danced at all. . . . It is incessantly in motion and teeming with technical demands, but the accent is never upon that kind of bravura that is designed to exploit the dancer. Quite the reverse, the dancers' focus is rather upon the publishing of the vivacious beauty of the choreographer's melodic invention." [4]

Dancers, particularly those who dance the five ballerina parts, have always loved *Divertimento*. Denby wrote that it took the ballet ten years to become popular and that it was the dancers who continually fought to retain it.

THE UNICORN, THE GORGON AND THE MANTICORE
or,
The Three Sundays of A Poet

A Ballet Society Production

CHOREOGRAPHY: John Butler

MUSIC, LIBRETTO: Gian Carlo Menotti (1956)

COSTUMES: Robert Fletcher

DÉCOR, LIGHTING: Jean Rosenthal

PREMIERE: 15 January 1957 (commissioned by the Elizabeth Sprague Coolidge Foundation in the Library of Congress; first presented 21 October 1956 in the Coolidge Auditorium, Washington, D.C.)

CAST: *The Countess,* Janet Reed; *The Count,* Roy Tobias; *Man in the Castle (The Poet),* Nicholas Magallanes; *The Unicorn,* Arthur Mitchell; *The Gorgon,* Eugene Tanner; *The Manticore,* Richard Thomas; *The Mayor and His Wife,* John Mandia, Barbara Milberg; *The Doctor and His Wife,* Jonathan Watts, Lee Becker (guest artist)
The Countess also danced by Allegra Kent

This madrigal-fable tells the story of a Man in the Castle who on successive occasions promenades in turn a Unicorn (Youth), a Gorgon (Manhood), and a Manticore (Old Age) before the townsfolk, and of their reactions to his innovations. The meaning of the fable is contained in the final words of the dying Poet:

'Oh, foolish people
Who feign to feel
What other men have suffered,
You, not I, are the indifferent killers
Of the Poet's dreams.

*Divertimento No. 15. **Left:** Early 1960s. Allegra Kent, Jonathan Watts. (Photo Fred Fehl.) **Right:** Late 1960s. Balanchine rehearsing (left to right)* Melissa Hayden, Suki Schorer, Richard Rapp, Arthur Mitchell, Kent Stowell.

How could I destroy
The pain-wrought children of
    my fancy?
What would my life have been
Without their faithful
And harmonious company?
Unicorn, Unicorn,
My youthful, foolish
Unicorn,
Please do not hide, come close
    to me.
And you, my Gorgon,
Behind whose splendor
I hid the doubts of midday,
You, too, stand by.
And here is my shy and lonely
    Manticore
Who gracefully leads me to
    my grave.
Farewell, farewell.
Equally well I loved you all.
Although the world may not
    suspect it,
All remains intact within
The Poet's heart.
Farewell, farewell.
Not even death do I fear
As in your arms I die.' "

(Program.)

The Unicorn, The Gorgon and the Manticore. **John Mandia, Barbara Milberg, Arthur Mitchell, Nicholas Magallanes, Eugene Tanner, Richard Thomas.** (*Photo Fred Fehl.*)

In this unusual work, the words of the libretto are danced and mimed on stage to the vocal and instrumental accompaniment provided by a chorus of twenty-four (with some solo passages) and chamber orchestra consisting of cello, bass, flute, oboe, clarinet, bassoon, trumpet, percussion, and harp. In his review of the Washington opening, music critic Harrison pointed out that, in form and style, the work derived from late-sixteenth-century prototypes. He found that the antique conventions had been translated—and modified—happily.[1] Sabin, on the other hand, was less convinced of the integrity of Menotti's use of such rich ingredients: "Did Menotti really wish to express the indignation of the artist at the 'indifferent killers of the Poet's dreams' and to reveal the hidden truth that 'all remains intact within the Poet's heart'? Or was he merely having fun, combining satire, allegory, and musical pseudo-classicism in a wild jumble, held together by the sheer brilliance of his improvisational powers?"[2]

As a theater-dance presentation, the work received an unqualified rave from Terry, but a lukewarm dismissal from Martin, who seemed to regard it as an arcane pageant that was a waste of time for the dancers, whatever its other merits might be. All critics praised the execution; Reed's performance was considered a marvel of timing and humor. (Possibly one reason the work did not remain long was that Reed left the Company soon after its premiere.)

Terry: "There is a pale blue Manticore, with droopy spines and a sad, affectionate mien, a fierce and glittering Gorgon, assured of stance, a trifle arrogant, ready for all comers, and the prancing, skittish, endlessly exuberant, unpredictable Unicorn. These are the key, but not necessarily the principal, figures.

"Whether it is a pure ballet (and I happen to think it is) or not, there is no denying that it is pure theater, a brilliantly conceived and faultlessly executed integration of dancing, gesture, poetry, song, instrumental music and visual spectacle. Menotti's music is remarkable in texture, in its ability to make one laugh or cry, in its tunes and in other musical matters. The composer's libretto is equally appealing. Finally, the choreography gives stage image and action to music and words skillfully and vividly.

"In this enchanting allegory-commentary (poetry and satire move side by side), Menotti has presented us with a Poet, a gentle nonconformist, who avoids the society of the townfolk, 'yawns at town meetings' and even refuses to let 'the doctor take his pulse.' Still, he fascinates the villagers, including the local Countess, as he strolls on succeeding Sundays first with a Unicorn, next a Gorgon, and finally a Manticore. The envious Countess must not be bested by the Poet, so she also, and other ladies with her, obtain a like sequence of pets and destroy them in sequence as they presume the Poet has done with his. But when the townspeople rush to the Poet's castle to punish him for his suspected murders, they discover him dying, surrounded by his three devoted monsters, 'the painwrought children of my fancy.'

"In the beautiful setting and stunning costumes, the dancers enact the fable with movements which not only project overt behavior but which also pare the figures down to their petty or noble, their raging or serene, their envious or happy hearts. Butler has seen to it that each of the three mythical pets reveals his specific symbolism clearly in carefree (Unicorn), commanding (Gorgon), and gentle (Manticore) actions, and he has characterized the Poet through pacings (slow and easy), phrasings, and gestures suitable to the dreamer, the pursuer of visions. The Countess is asked to storm and stamp, to gesticulate, to plead, to dissemble as she harries her mild but doting husband, the Count, into submitting to her whims and obtaining duplicates of the Poet's pets for herself. The Mayor and the Doctor are extensions of the troubled Count, and their wives are, for the most part, nervous slaves of the Countess's trend-setting maneuvers. There are splendid moments of movement virtuosity in *The Unicorn, the Gorgon, and the Manticore*, and there are great sweeps of choreographed hilarity for the beautiful but waspish Countess. Indeed, the undefeatable wiles of a willful woman have rarely been so amusingly caricatured in dance as in Mr. Butler's choreography. But there is heart-penetrating sadness also, especially in the ballet's closing passages when the Poet is borne from his castle by his pets to die among these creatures of his fancy, these milestones of his life." [3]

Martin: "Very much off the beaten track, its interest is almost exclusively musical. Menotti is famous for his theatrical sense, but here it has failed him. Instead of working together for a heightened theater effectiveness, the music and the action serve rather to split the attention. To understand the all-important words requires close concentration, with which the movement only interferes.

"The work begins with a slow exposition, and when the issue is actually joined we are given the same essential situation three times over. To Butler has fallen the enormous task of choreographing the action. How anybody could have done more with it is difficult to see, for he has devised ingenious movements and some expert comedy, deriving from that most excellent model, Martha Graham. But in spite of his devotion and his cleverness, it does not come off. The use of mime and gesture only underlines what the words already say. It is an experimental work, and experiments are healthy for the arts of the theater, even if they are not always successful. This one is likely to be of interest only to a highly specialized audience." [4]

THE MASQUERS

A Ballet Society Production sponsored by John McHugh

CHOREOGRAPHY: Todd Bolender

MUSIC: Francis Poulenc (Sextet for Wind Instruments and Piano, 1930–32)

COSTUMES, DÉCOR: David Hays

LIGHTING: Jean Rosenthal

PREMIERE: 29 January 1957 (first presented March 1956 by the Dance Drama Company of Emily Frankel and Mark Ryder)

CAST: *A Young Woman,* Melissa Hayden; *A Soldier,* Jacques d'Amboise; *The Passerby,* Yvonne Mounsey; *A Friend of the Young Woman,* Charlotte Ray; *The Boy She Meets,* Robert Barnett; *Another Soldier,* Jonathan Watts; 3 women, 3 men

The *Masquers* was not a completely satisfactory ballet, even to its choreographer. Bolender spoke of the problems: "I had the beginning of an idea that was really excellent, but I had the wrong score; it drowned me. I should have thrown it out, but I loved the kind of tinny, bangy sound of it—it had a kind of improvised sound, as though it had been written right at the moment and a group of musicians were just playing it right off the tops of their heads. The basic idea was the influence people have over each other and how deadly or how beautiful it can be. I started it out as though everyone were puppets—this is where the commedia dell'arte fit in—and they all respond to something, like puppets, and then it breaks into a real story. That's the problem, and I wanted to keep flashing back to it, and then keep building, but it just seemed to collapse. Even Melissa—you know, she is so dynamic—I wasn't able to shade her into this properly, and she became all one color. The idea I like, and I just might eventually—I might find the right piece of music for it."

Bolender was also very busy that winter with other matters. He had been put in charge of the rehearsal schedule and casting while Balanchine was in Copenhagen; he was still performing, and it was not, he remembers, the best time to be involved in a creative effort as well.

Hayden had difficulty with her role; it was "too undefined as far as what was real and what was unreal." Critics found the choreographic content substantial, but the dramatic idea unclear and the commedia dell'arte aspects gratuitous.

Terry: "Pretty, innocuous and disappointing, although it does have some novel actions, which, as pure movement, invite the concern and the interest of the viewer. But it collapses dramatically. Presumably, the choreographer has extracted characters from the commedia dell'arte and sought to adapt them to the needs of a modern situation fraught with star-crossed romance. But the sweet quaintness of tradition is gone and only stock figures in a stock situation remain. There is the rough, arrogant soldier—contrite too late—around whom the action revolves, and there is the girl who adores him despite his contempt for her and faithlessness. Then we meet the 'other woman,' a completely characterless creature, and another soldier who truly loves the girl. All concerned fight, struggle, love, sorrow, and occasionally gambol and somehow it doesn't seem to matter." [1]

Martin: "It is not a very pretty tale, but there is a certain distinction in its telling. This lies mainly in the notably eloquent movement." [2]

"Offers poor Hayden in still another distressing sexual misadventure," wrote Haggin. [3]

PASTORALE

A Ballet Society Production sponsored by Mrs. Edmundo Lassalle

CHOREOGRAPHY: Francisco Moncion

MUSIC: Charles Turner (1957; commissioned by Ballet Society)

COSTUMES: Ruth Sobotka

DÉCOR: David Hays

LIGHTING: Jean Rosenthal

PREMIERE: 14 February 1957

CAST: Allegra Kent, Moncion, Roy Tobias; 3 couples

Pastorale was Moncion's first full ballet

180

PASTORALE

(he had choreographed sections of *Jeux d'Enfants* in 1955) and the first role created by Kent, newly promoted to principal dancer, with the exception of her haunting "Unanswered Question" in *Ivesiana*. Moncion was encouraged to help fill the void caused by Balanchine's winter-long absence in Copenhagen. "Tender" was the word most used in reviews of *Pastorale*. The set—sun- and shadow-tinged trees—was a particular success. Haggin referred to the music as "luxuriantly nostalgic."

Moncion said, "Everyone had to chip in, and Lincoln suggested I do a ballet—Chuck Turner was a friend of his. We met, and Chuck just played me some tinkly bits that he already had, and I thought of an outdoor setting, and a triangle—something sporty. We started putting things together, and I saw a group entering, then a variation, and then I thought of making one man blind. People didn't like it; they said infirmities on stage were so uncomfortable. But I've seen some blind people who were very much in command of themselves, and that's the way my character was going to be. The story just evolved. I didn't work my part out on anybody else, which made it difficult placing myself in the position of trying to visualize Roy and myself and

Pastorale. **Francisco Moncion, Allegra Kent.** (*Photo William McCracken.*)

Allegra. There was an interesting pas de deux, I think, without being mawkish or overly sentimental. I wanted the blind man completely independent, not evoking sympathy or sorrow, just whatever came. We had a beautiful set."

Critics found the work a stage-worthy first effort.

Manchester: "Small, charming, and touching. There is nothing in the least original about the choreography, but it serves adequately to convey both the atmosphere and the slight story. This tells of a lonely blind boy whose solitude as he sits in the shade of a cluster of trees is interrupted by four young couples who play a game of blind man's buff. The girl who is blind-folded makes contact with the boy without, of course, knowing that he cannot see. Realization is inevitable but her newly awakened emotions are not quite able to cope with the additional complications such a relationship must mean. Moncion is particularly successful in establishing the delicate balance of shifting relationships as the character of the girl develops. He is at his best at the opening of the pas de deux when the blindfolded girl and the boy pass each other repeatedly, separated by no more than a hairbreadth." [1]

Herridge: "Moncion, with a keen sense of projection, makes his characters show what they are feeling and thinking by the way they move or pause, and so there is a surprising amount of drama in an essentially lyrical work." [2]

Lloyd: "Delicately subjective, if not technically exciting." [3]

Martin: "Modest and unpretentious, a touching little idyll. The girl has her inner eyes opened to a disturbing new world, and the oddly romantic color of her revelation separates her from her understanding young lover. The situation ends with three isolated figures all touched with sadness. As a ballet it is too tentative to be effective. Moncion appears to have been more deeply concerned with the dramatic content of his theme, employing choreographic means merely to get it stated. This he has done with fine sensitiveness, and occasionally he has turned a lovely phrase. But the work lacks choreographic substance, choreographic texture, choreographic identity.

"It is his good fortune to have a genuinely sympathetic composer in Turner, whose first ballet score this is. He has a lyric gift and a long phrase and is not afraid of a tune. His score takes the main

structural responsibility for the ballet and carries it frequently over its weaker passages, but composer and choreographer have worked with a real unity of feeling throughout." [4]

SQUARE DANCE

CHOREOGRAPHY: George Balanchine

MUSIC: Antonio Vivaldi (Concerto Grosso in B Minor, op. 3, no. 10; Concerto Grosso in E Major, op. 3, no. 12 [first movement]) and Arcangelo Corelli (*Badinerie* and *Giga* from *Sarabanda, Badinerie, and Giga*)

LIGHTING: Nananne Porcher

PREMIERE: 21 November 1957

CALLER: Elisha C. Keeler

LEADER (on-stage string ensemble): Louis Graeler

CAST: Patricia Wilde, Nicholas Magallanes; 6 couples
Male lead also danced by Robert Lindgren, Michael Lland

REVIVAL: 20 May 1976, staged by Victoria Simon

LIGHTING: Ronald Bates

CAST: Kay Mazzo, Bart Cook, 6 couples

*T*wo little ladies, up the track,
Sashay over, sashay back
In the same old track
Now all you ladies chain
Over once and back again
Over once and away you go
Left hand back and don't be slow
Fly through the air like a bird on the wing
Don't fall down, you pretty little thing
Ladies to the center, back to the bar
Gents go out and stand right thar
Spread out wide, side by side
Spread out wide, like an old cow hide
Right hand around, around you go
Turn around and do-si-do

(Keeler)

Square Dance. Nicholas Magallanes (left), Patricia Wilde (center). (*Photo Fred Fehl.*)

Square Dance was, as Martin observed, "a genuine novelty. Its concept is the most ingenious one of treating the dances of the so-called pre-classic period for their essential relations to the square dances that we know today. . . . With a small group of fiddlers on the stage and a real square-dance caller beside them, calling according to the regular procedure of such social affairs, seven pairs of girls and boys in practice clothes give us a square-dance evening entirely in terms of the standard ballet vocabulary. It is brilliantly conceived, really pointing up the common roots of folk dancing and the academic ballet, with the music that belongs to both. The specific invention is superb, in the use of both floor patterns and steps and it calls for tremendous virtuosity, which is readily supplied." [1]

"Artistry in the vernacular," [2] wrote Biancolli.

Manchester, although she admired the actual steps, found Balanchine's connection between classical ballet and square dance more tenuous: "Pays a little, but not much, lip service to square-dance form with an occasional star figure or ring, and a bit of swing and sway body movement, but most of the time he simply provides some of his most sparkling choreography." [3]

Choreographically speaking, Martin also considered the ballet "a genuine jewel, inventive, vivacious, and rich in the comment of a witty creative mind." [4] He was seconded by Terry: "A fine collection of activities from the vocabulary of the classical ballet which, by some miraculous twist of genius, fit the music and folk-dance demand of the calls [most of the time]." [5]

And Hering: "At first viewing, the work seemed like an arbitrary combining of seemingly disparate elements. But by the second time, all the elements had been buffed into place, with the filigree music and Keeler's homespun square-dance calling synthesized by the swiftly classic dance. And what delightful, demanding, and youthful dancing it was. In Wilde's solos, the batterie was so fiercely fast, the gargouillades so numerous, the turns so profuse, that she was completely absorbed." [6]

The ballet opened with a spirited dance for the ensemble and leads, followed by a pensive pas de deux (the only occasion for sustained movement); there were then separate dances for the women (with Wilde) and the men (with Magallanes), and a rousing finale for all. With its breathless pace and insistent rhythms, *Square Dance* of-

fered meaty opportunities to everyone.

In particular, it provided Wilde, as "ballerina of the barn," with one of her most exhilarating vehicles and exploited to the full her outstanding agility in jumps, turns, beats, and generally vibrant movement, in tempos that could only be called lickety-split. It was "the role of her career. She darts through its intricacies, which are sometimes very intricate indeed, with a smiling nonchalance that indicates that she revels in the surmounting of difficulties." [7]

Not far behind were the ladies and gentlemen of the ensemble, who, lining up for the series of multiple pirouettes that brings down the curtain, after twenty minutes of almost nonstop hoe-downs, promenades, and paler echoes of Wilde's fast footwork, may well have felt that, whatever its other virtues, *Square Dance* offered more steps per minute than any other show in town.

Sooner or later most of the critics complained that the calls did not always accord with the steps, were occasionally inaudible, and sometimes distracted from the dancing. But, as Manchester wrote, "I do not think anyone could possibly be better than Keeler, who deserves his renown as a caller. He has a delightfully earthy personality and seems not in the least fazed at being in such a rarified company as a troupe of ballet dancers." [8]

Said Keeler, who had seen only one ballet in his life before his association with Balanchine, "The only people with bad temper around here are the stagehands. The dancers are wonderful . . . and they sure don't waste any time." He wrote all of the calls himself, after watching rehearsals. ("We asked him to say anything he wanted, as long as he didn't use ballet terms," said Mr. B.)

> *Do-si-do in mountain style*
> *Under the arch, give her a smile*
> *Down the center, lonesome gal*
> *Now she's waiting for her pal*
> *All alone, swing and whirl*
> *Down the center in a butterfly whirl*
> *Lonesome gent, hurry up quick*
> *All right, Pat, here comes Nick!*
> *Now together, away you go*
> *Point your pretty little toe*
> *Sashay to the center, all*
> *How'm I doin' with this old call?*
> *Gents go 'round, come right back*
> *Make your feet go wickety-wack*
> *All the ladies do the same*

Make your feet go wickety-wack
That don't rhyme, but I don't care
Take her out and give her the air!

In the revival, without caller and with orchestra in the pit, the dancing expanded to fill the stage. The catchiness of the square-dance connotation was gone, but the inventive choreography remained, perhaps more brightly polished than before. The ballerina, from a pyrotechnical speed wizard with dashing footwork, became perky, graceful, coltish. And for the man, Balanchine created a new solo, to Corelli's *Sarabanda*, a majestic, stately piece, full of sculptural poses (interspersed with beats and turns) for the beautifully proportioned body of Cook. Wrote Kisselgoff: "Anything but rehash. The correct word is renewal. The spirit behind it is so radically different that it looks deceptively like a new work. Originally Mr. Balanchine had found inspiration in the fact that this 18th-century music had been derived from folk-dance forms that were later refined. Now, it seems, he has chosen to emphasize the refinement." [9]

AGON

CHOREOGRAPHY: George Balanchine

MUSIC: Igor Stravinsky (1953–57; commissioned by George Balanchine and Lincoln Kirstein with funds from the Rockefeller Foundation)

LIGHTING: Nananne Porcher

PREMIERE: 1 December 1957 (preview 27 November 1957)

CAST: PART I: *Pas de quatre*, 4 men; *Double pas de quatre*, 8 women; *Triple pas de quatre*, 8 women, 4 men; PART II: *First pas de trois: Sarabande*, Todd Bolender; *Gailliard*, Barbara Milberg, Barbara Walczak; *Coda*, Bolender, Milberg, Walczak; *Second pas de trois: Bransle simple*, Roy Tobias, Jonathan Watts; *Bransle gay*, Melissa Hayden; *Bransle double (de Poitou)*, Hayden, Tobias, Watts; *Pas de deux*, Diana Adams, Arthur Mitchell; PART III: *Danse des quatre duos*, 4 duos; *Danse des quatre trios*, 4 trios; *Coda*, 4 men

OTHER CASTS: *First pas de trois*, Anthony Blum, John Clifford, Bart Cook, Paul

Mejia, Edward Villella; Renee Estópinal, Susan Hendl, Sara Leland, Colleen Neary, Patricia Neary, Susan Pilarre, Francia Russell, Carol Summer; *Second pas de trois*, Karin von Aroldingen, Gloria Govrin, Violette Verdy; Victor Castelli, Clifford, Richard Rapp, Robert Rodham, Earle Sieveling, Bruce Wells; *Pas de deux*, Suzanne Farrell, Allegra Kent, Kay Mazzo, Patricia McBride; Jean-Pierre Bonnefous, Peter Martins, Frank Ohman

Agon is plainly a masterpiece of our time: Watching it we live more intensely, life becomes more brilliant, more electric. We are forced—or rather, guided—into a tremendous awareness of rhythm and time, and the thrust and rush of the dancers' activity." [1]

"May well be the highest point we have yet reached in manipulating the living anatomy of choreography." [2]

Agon is a dodecaphonic score in twelve movements for twelve dancers, although such symmetry is matter more for the intellect than the sensory perceptions, in the manner of musical retrograde motion. It is one of Balanchine and Stravinsky's most intense constructions, with the logic of perfectly interlocking parts, whose relationship is not always apparent until the last piece is in place, with hindsight illuminating the whole. (This effect is evident not only from section to section, but,

especially in the ensemble dances, from step to step.) Stravinsky at one point said his "subject was figures and the relation of figures" [3]; for Balanchine, the subject was "dancing, just numbers." [4] "Construction," incidentally, would seem to be the appropriate word for this ballet: Said Stravinsky, "The mechanics [of contrapuntal music, the predominant texture of *Agon*] must be adjusted like that of a modern car" [5]; while Balanchine described the "IBM ballet" as "more tight and precise than usual, as if it were controlled by an electronic brain." [6]

In 1968 Balanchine was quoted as saying, "*Agon* is for me the quintessential contemporary ballet. Stravinsky composed it specially for us. . . . In my opinion, it is his—it is *our*—most perfect work, representing a total collaboration between musician and choreographer." [7] Several years later, Balanchine (who is famous for living in the present) may or may not still feel the same, but there is no doubt that the collaboration was extraordinary and profound. A series of famous rehearsal photos shows the grand old musician, always tiny but now bent with age, acutely attentive as the younger master of another art evolves an untried choreographic vocabulary to suit his unheard sounds.* (Balanchine, in the program note: "It is a new piece of diabolical crafts-

---
* By Martha Swope. Many reproduced in Taper, *Balanchine*, pp. 269–76.

Agon. **Balanchine rehearsing Diana Adams (Jonathan Watts watching).** (*Photo Martha Swope.*)

manship; sounds like this have not been heard before; it may take rather developed ears to hear them.") Speaking of his approach to the work, Balanchine said, "Musically, it's complicated. You have to analyze in advance what this music is all about, what kind of a sound it is, why it's written this way, what it represents. Somebody has to analyze this; in this case, I did." [8] Said Stravinsky of the result, "His plastic realization matches my architechtonic music." [9]

Although the music was written specifically as a ballet, only two indications of movement appear in the score: "As the curtain rises, four male dancers are aligned across the rear of the stage with their backs to the audience"; and, near the end: "The female dancers leave the stage. The male dancers take their position as at the beginning—back to the audience." * Within this framework, Balanchine created one of his sparest and most rigorous works. ("There is nothing cheap here. Everything, even at its coolest, is blood," wrote Barnes). [10] Each dancer, clad in severest practice clothes and illuminated by ruthlessly glaring side lights, moves to largely atonal music in distinct and unconventional step combinations ranging from "classical" to "modern," powerful to humorous, from striking to surprising, to (apparently) light-hearted, to—especially in the pas de deux—vulnerable and intimate. (Interestingly, the more "consonant" sections musically, such as the first pas de trois, also contain the most classical dance vocabulary.) If much of the ballet appears to be some kind of vivacious "contest" (the meaning of the Greek *agon*, and not to be taken too literally)—a duel of wits, strength, and agility among the participants, epitomized by the second pas de trois—the pas de deux is more the meshing of two like minds or two like bodies, folding into each other, presupposing a perceptive awareness of their close relationship.

Adams remembers that Balanchine wanted to compose the pas de deux before setting any of the other dances; this implied to her that he felt it would give him the key or approach to the rest of the work. Says Mitchell of that famous part,

"The pas de deux is like seeing live sculpture. Before your eyes, the dancers move from one fantastic pose to another, but you don't know how they got there. Balanchine said, "This is the longest it's ever taken me to choreograph anything [two weeks] . . . because everything has to be *exactly* right.' And that's one of the few, or the only, time I've ever seen him take things and throw them out. Usually, it just flows, but here he experimented, he took out, he changed. Diana's nervous intensity made the whole pas de deux work because it's not so much the difficulty of the steps or how flexible you are, it's the precariousness. The one thing Balanchine kept saying was, 'The girl is like a doll, you're manipulating her, you must lead her. It's one long, long, long, long breath.' And so I always explained to a new partner, 'The secret of this is the less you do the better off we're going to be.' " Haggin referred to the "unimpassioned intensity" of this dance.

Despite the fact that the ballet is "complicated and almost aggressively lacking in conventional ballet allure," and to the surprise of almost everyone, *Agon* was a popular as well as a critical success from the beginning. (Wrote Martin, typically, "It is a work that on the face of it is 'high brow'; the most that could have been expected for it was a succès d'estime." [11]) Nowadays it is simple to call *Agon* a "masterpiece"; everybody does it. Actually, its importance was recognized immediately.

After seeing the preview Martin wrote: "There is no man alive who, after one contact with it, can tell you what there is in it, for it is complex, ingenious, and fantastically off the beaten path formally. But there is nothing fuzzy or turbid about it, and even at first sight you can get from it all you can possibly absorb, and be teased into having a wonderful time while you are at it. Somewhere in the remote subconscious of both the agonists are some court dances of the seventeenth century—branles, sarabandes, galliards—and from time to time when either of them chooses, we are shown whiffs of style and hints of form that are wittily reminiscent of these sources. But they constitute no more than a bare excuse for devious adventures in formal construction. To give a clue as to the style of the work, it is perhaps fair to say that it falls nearest into the Balanchinian department of *Four Temperaments*, though without the problem of essentially romantic music to contend with. Here it is all of a creative piece, sparse, dry—no, rather sec—classic. The bones have been stripped of every bit of flesh and re-articulated into a fresh body, but it is a body that still moves in clean and functional phrases, however irregular in measure, incredible in aural timbre, and inexplicable in relation to normal human movement." [12]

Terry's positive assessment followed: "For sheer invention, for intensive exploitation of the human body and the designs

---

* Before Stravinsky began composing, however, he and Balanchine had determined which combinations of dancers would be used and the approximate length of each section. When he received the finished score, "only the actual sound," says Balanchine, "was a surprise to me."

Agon. **Double pas de quatre. Melissa Hayden, Diana Adams (center front).** (*Photo Fred Fehl.*)

which it can create, *Agon* is quite possibly the most brilliant ballet creation of our day, at least in that area usually described (although not quite accurately) as 'abstract dance.' For *Agon* has no plot, no specific emotional coloring, no dramatic incident. It does, of course, mirror the rhythms, the dynamics, and the witticisms of the music, but it does have a character of its own, for the movements are not only extensions of sound into physical substance but they also comment upon the score, occasionally tease it, race with it, rest with it, play with it. Sometimes [dancers] work in unison, but more often they are called upon to thread their separate and independent movement designs into a larger fabric of choreography encompassing all the dancers.

"Perhaps I have given the impression that *Agon* is primarily an exercise in action, an etude. Nothing could be further from the truth. And if the miracle of skilled and sensitive dance action is not enough for some, let me say that *Agon* is rich in humor. It is not literal humor, but rather movement fun. It comes when a dance step or gesture makes an absurd but somehow pertinent comment on a note or phrase of music, it comes when an involved bit of activity bounces swiftly into an extraordinarily simple resolution, and it comes when we are led to expect a bravura bit and are presented instead with a flippant or gracious gesture.

"Since Balanchine has elected to use classical ballet movements, free-style dance, and swift interjections of gesture in his choreographic plan, the dancers have no easy task, but they fuse these different but related elements so superbly that one is conscious of only a single method of expression." [13]

Manchester compared the taut surface of the work to the timing in a circus act, but where many in the audience were exhilarated by the dancers' continual flirtation with "the edge of risk," as Denby put it, she appeared to be irritated: "They walk a tightrope where the slightest slip will mean disaster; to carry the circus analogy further, watching *Agon* is rather like watching a trapeze performance. The fascination lies in its danger rather than in any aesthetic enjoyment, particularly in the second pas de trois and in the pas de deux. [In the pas de trois, the two men leave the ballerina suspended on a single pointe, then pirouette before taking her hands again; elsewhere they catch her in a split leap.] Audience

Agon. **First Pas de Trois. Carol Sumner, John Clifford, Sara Leland.** (*Photo Donn Matus.*)

anxiety is even more acute in the pas de deux. The convolutions of the two dancers are all but unbelievable, and their timing fantastic. [One of the more tricky movements here is the man supporting the ballerina, who is again on a single pointe, while lying on the ground.]

"There is a less acrobatic, though musically taxing, pas de trois. There is also some fleeting humor—Bolender walking around his own foot, Mitchell leaping with his toes turned up, Hayden walking smugly off after a particularly tricky balance [Verdy mentions the "slight swagger" inherent in this role]. Tobias and Watts dance a two-part canon which is a marvel of timing and speed. It is devilishly ingenious and fiendishly clever. It is not endearing, however." [14]

Denby's impressions caught the dynamics of the movement. He was also quite specific in his description of the action: "Marcel Duchamp said he felt the way he had after the opening of *Le Sacre.* . . . The general effect is an amusing deformation of classic steps due to an unclassic drive or attack; and the drive itself looks like a basic way of moving. . . . The curtain rises on a stage bare and silent. Upstage four boys. . . . They whirl, four at once, to face you. The soundless whirl is a downbeat that starts the action. On the upbeat, fanfare begins like cars honking a block away. . . . The boys' steps have been exploding like pistol shots. The steps seem to come in tough, brief bursts. Dancing in canon, in unison, in and out of sym-

metry, the boys might be trying out their speed of waist, their strength of ankle; no lack of aggressiveness. But already two—no, eight—girls have replaced them. Rapidly they test toe-power, stops on oblique lines, jetlike extensions. . . . Already the boys have re-entered. . . . The energy of it is like that of fifty dancers. By now you have caught the pressure of the action.

"The music starts with a small circusy fanfare. [Three] present themselves as a dance team. Then the boy, left alone, begins to walk a 'Sarabande,' elaborately coiled and circumspect. . . . A moment later one is watching a girls' duet in the air, like flying twins. A trio begins. In triple canon the dancers do idiotic slenderizing exercises, theoretically derived from court gesture, while the music foghorns in the fashion of *musique concrète.*

"The new team begins a little differently. The boys present the girl in feats of balance. . . . Their courage is perfect. The girl's solo is a marvel of dancing at its most transparent. She seems merely to walk forward, to step back and skip, with now and then one arm held high, Spanish style, a gesture that draws attention to the sound of a castanet in the score. As she dances, she keeps calmly 'on top of' two conflicting rhythms that coincide once or twice and join on the last note.

"At this point in *Agon,* about thirteen minutes of dancing have passed. A third specialty team is standing on stage ready to begin. The orchestra begins a third time with the two phrases one recognizes, and once again the dancers find in the same music a quite different rhythm and expression.* As the introduction ends, the girl drops her head with an irrational gesture more caressing than anything one has seen so far. They begin an acrobatic adagio. . . . The absurdity of what they do startles by a grandeur of scale and of sensuousness. Turning pas de deux conventions upside down, the boy with bold grace supports the girl and pivots her on pointe, lying on his back on the floor. At one moment classic movements turned inside out become intimate gestures. At another a pose forced way beyond its classic ending reveals a novel harmony. At still another, the mutual first tremor of an uncertain supported balance is so isolated musically it becomes a dance movement. So does the dangerous scoop out of balance and back into balance of the girl supported on pointe. . . . Earlier in the ballet, the sparse orchestration has made one aware of a faint echo, as if silence were pressing in at the edge of music and dancing. Now the silence interpenetrates the sound itself, as in a Beethoven quartet. After so many complex images, when the boy makes a simple joke, the effect is happy. The audience realizes it 'understands' everything, and it is more and more eager to give them an ovation. There isn't time. . . . The action has reverted to the anonymous energy you saw in the first part. Now all twelve dancers are on stage and everything is very condensed and goes very fast. Now only the four boys are left, you begin to recognize a return to the start of the ballet, you begin to be anxious, and on the same wrestler's gesture of 'on guard' that closed their initial dance . . . the music stops, the boys freeze, and the silence of the beginning returns. Nothing moves." [15]

Kirstein, in one of his most evocative pieces, concentrated on the uncompromising nature of the ballet: "Costumes are black-and-white practice uniforms, near nudity. 'Production' consists of execution alone, determined by the austere complexity of music in the serial method, patterns of cellular structure involving a continuum of variations on a twelve-tone set. No dance work has been more highly organized or is so dense in movement in its bare twenty minutes. Clock time has no reference to visual duration; there is more concentrated movement in *Agon* than in most nineteenth-century full-length ballets. . . . The choreography projects a steel skeleton clad in tightly knit action, lacing a membrane of movement over a transparent net of contrapuntal design, which in shifting concentration on separate dancers gives an impression of intense drama. . . .

"Symmetry, the basis of composition for centuries, focuses on stage center. The new asymmetry broke up the balance of right and left, distributing blocks into shifting cells employing stage periphery equally with a center. New attacks on temporal measure involved new conquest of space. . . .

"Its syntax is the undeformed, uninverted grammar, with shades of courtly behavior and echoes of antique measure. Group numbers assume the well-oiled synchronism of electrical timekeepers. . . . Blocks of units in triads and quartets shift like chess pieces. . . . Dancers are manipulated as irreplaceable spare parts, substituting or alternating on strict beats. . . . Impersonalization of arms and legs into geometrical arrows . . . accentuates dynamics in a field of force. Yet the aura is not mechanistic, but musical, disciplined, witty—offering the epoch's extreme statement of its craft. At a time when experiment had become a necessity for instant novelty, the innovation of *Agon* lay in its naked strength, bare authority, and self-discipline in constructs of stressed extreme movement. Behind its active physical presence there was inherent a philosophy; *Agon* was by no means 'pure' ballet, 'about' dancing only. It was an existential metaphor for tension and anxiety." [16]

England:

"A landmark in modern choreography. Stravinsky's lean and muscular music and

---

* Says Balanchine, "Because Stravinsky's music is so hard on the ear, we decided the ballet should be no more than 20 minutes. With his kind of impact, the audience couldn't follow more. And because it's difficult to get the first time, we repeated it: the introduction to each dance is the same, because you need to hear it several times."

Agon. Left: **Bransle Double (de Poitou). Robert Rodham, Melissa Hayden, Richard Rapp.** (*Photo Martha Swope.*) *Center:* **Pas de Deux. Patricia McBride, Arthur Mitchell.** (*Photo Fred Fehl.*) *Right:* **Pas de Deux. Jean-Pierre Bonnefous, Allegra Kent.** (*Photo Martha Swope.*)

Balanchine's lightly intricate choreography are not so much matched as fused. Together they form a structure in time and space, where the movement is apparently carved out of the music and the sounds seem dependent upon the choreography. This complexity of *Agon* is partly in its architectonics, from its heroic opening where four men are caught in attitudes like athletes in frozen stone through two pas de trois, the first with an offbeat cheekiness and flip humor, the second more mysterious and complex, until one comes to the pas de deux, a strange and strong dance construction, as vivid and as dense as a piece of sculpture.

"Yet all this sounds like too solid flesh —for the essence of *Agon* is that it is a skeleton. Here, or so it seems, is what might happen if you took all the nineteenth-century ballets that ever were, put them into a machine and refined them down to nothing more than this tremendous capsule of dance and music." [17]

Russia:

"Balanchine's choreography, built up on complex and frequently changing counts, is closer to mathematics than to art. The soloists and corps de ballet show amazing cohesion in overcoming the difficulties of the music and choreography, but the composition, addressed as it is to the mind, leaves the heart cold." [18]

GOUNOD SYMPHONY

CHOREOGRAPHY: George Balanchine

MUSIC: Charles Gounod (Symphony No. 1 in D Major, 1855)

SCENERY: Horace Armistead

COSTUMES: Karinska

LIGHTING: Nananne Porcher

PREMIERE: 8 January 1958

CAST: Maria Tallchief, Jacques d'Amboise; 20 women, 10 men

OTHER CASTS: Diana Adams, Melissa Hayden, Allegra Kent, Mimi Paul, Violette Verdy, Patricia Wilde; André Prokovsky, Kent Stowell, Edward Villella, Jonathan Watts

Allegro Molto (full cast)
Allegretto (Tallchief, d'Amboise, 8 women)
Minuetto (6 couples)
Adagio and Allegro Vivace (full cast)

It has often been observed that Balanchine choreographs for particular dancers—that they inspire his choice of steps and that he is able to find and bring out in them qualities of which they themselves are frequently unaware. It is also true that Balanchine responds in a specific way to the music he has chosen, meaning that not only does he suitably fit steps to rhythms and mirror the appropriate mood, but that he captures the more generalized stylistic underpinnings behind a given work or school. A case in point is *Gounod Symphony*, to music by the composer of *Faust*, which, although often beautifully performed, did not look stylistically "right" until more than a year after

its creation, when danced by the French ballerina Violette Verdy, whom Balanchine had not even met when the work was choreographed. Even without a specific dancing instrument, he had captured the "Frenchness" in the music.

Verdy returned the compliment. Says she, "The ballet is like the gardens of Versailles. It has everything we admire there—regularity, invention, diversity, perspectives. It's one of Balanchine's great masterpieces, but went unnoticed, because, like so many things of his, it doesn't spoon-feed you with easy steps, already digested. He asks you to look."

Gounod's symphony, ignored for a century, was written, as he says "to console myself for the disappointment" of the failure of *La Nonne Sanglante*, his opera of the previous year. It was praised by both audience and critics when unveiled in 1855, and special note was taken of the "delicious little fugue."

"A pretty bagatelle," [1] as Manchester

Gounod Symphony. **Top: Violette Verdy (center).** *Bottom:* **Ensemble.** (*Photos Fred Fehl.*)

saw it, was a good summation of the general reaction to the ballet; it was pleasant, a bit pallid, and not about to stir up much audience involvement. "There are sequences which are not especially stirring, but one coasts along," wrote Terry [2]; and others believed that the entire ballet was on this level. Only Martin came down squarely in its favor, championing it through several years of cast changes and rechoreography, complaining only that stylistically the dancers could not do it justice. He remained ever hopeful that time, coaching, different dancers, new steps, and a larger stage would fulfill the potential of the choreography. (This is one of the ballets, along with *Roma* and *Bayou*, whose early demise is especially regretted by Kirstein.)

He wrote: "Entirely fresh. This is not a bravura ballet: it is something far more difficult. It puts a great price on the ability to sustain line and pose, to make non-movement an active element in shaping the continuity of a phrase, to achieve supreme accuracy of tempo and uniformity of attitude throughout the ensemble; and all these things in the face of extremely difficult demands. For once Balanchine has outchoreographed even so accomplished a company as this, and it will take a great deal of dancing before they have mastered what he has given them to do. The second movement may well be its triumph. Its pas de deux is utterly off the beaten track, with deceptively simple evolutions that demand above all else a singing phrase from the ballerina. It is an enchanting [idea], charmingly set off by eight girls in the most delicate bit of fuguing. The minuetto of a third movement is wonderfully conceived, and so is the slow beginning of the final movement, leading into fittingly brilliant passages for the conclusion. There are touches of vivacious fancy throughout, hints of feathery wit, and many flashes of Balanchinian comment on period style. [1958]

"If the stage is too small for it and the company is not fully aware of its particular style, it is nevertheless a delight to watch if only for Balanchine's endlessly rich and essentially exquisite invention. [1959]

"Because of its evocations of the Paris Opéra a century ago and of the 'music covers' of the same period, it has eluded the company's grasp. There still remains something to be desired in the basic awareness of style, but last night's presentation generated a spontaneous and real responsiveness. The reason, on stage and off, is undoubtedly the presence of Verdy, for she is not only a keenly perceptive artist but also a French one. Balanchine's chosen style is in her blood and artistic background, and as she publishes it, it becomes of necessity clear and eloquent. How gratifying to see a notable work come into its own! [1960]" [3]

Terry indicated some specific steps and formations: "With its sylvan scenery and its exquisite pastel costumes, [it] is rather like a very elegant and courtly gambol in a glade. The choreography itself is rich in movement intricacies, all highly polished. In the [minuetto] couples cut through each other's patterns with charming deftness, and in the [finale] Balanchine has come up with one of his elaborate mass interweavings in which the ensemble pursues close-order labyrinthine patterns with regal composure. Over all lies a delicate air of gaiety and therein is the ballet's special charm. Tallchief floated through breathtaking turns (à la seconde), spun swiftly through her pirouettes, made her legs send off electricity in a series of supported entrechats." [4]

In France, where the basic style is more congenial, at least one critic found a different emphasis; he saw the ballet as an ensemble piece. Balanchine mounted the work for the Paris Opéra in 1959—the first ballet he had staged for that once-hallowed hall of dance since *Serenade* had been produced there in 1947: "The ballet revolves around the patterns and dancing of the corps de ballet; the two stars are far less central to the conception. As for the choreography, the Balanchine style is here yet more refined, the designs more delicately intricate than ever before, with sinuous lines stripped of any touch of acrobatics, and marvelous arm movements. . . . A total success." [5]

STARS AND STRIPES

Ballet in five campaigns

CHOREOGRAPHY: George Balanchine

MUSIC: Marches of John Philip Sousa (as below), adapted and orchestrated by Hershy Kay

COSTUMES: Karinska

DÉCOR: David Hays

LIGHTING: Nananne Porcher; David Hays (1964)

PREMIERE: 17 January 1958

CAST: *First Campaign: "Corcoran Cadets,"* Allegra Kent, 12 women; *Second Campaign: "Thunder and Gladiator,"* Robert Barnett, 12 men; *Third Campaign: "Rifle Regiment,"* * Diana Adams, 12 women; *Fourth Campaign: "Liberty Bell"* and *"El Capitan,"* Melissa Hayden, Jacques d'Amboise; *Fifth Campaign: "Stars and Stripes,"* all regiments

OTHER CASTS: *First Campaign,* Carolyn George, Judith Green, Jillana, Patricia McBride, Susan Pilarre, Christine Redpath, Suki Schorer, Carol Sumner, Barbara Walczak; *Second Campaign,* Daniel Duell, Deni Lamont, Edward Villella, Robert Weiss, William Weslow; *Third Campaign,* Karin von Aroldingen, Gloria Govrin, Jillana, Marnee Morris, Sonja Tyven, Violette Verdy, Sallie Wilson; *Fourth Campaign,* Merrill Ashley, Kent, Gelsey Kirkland, Sara Leland, McBride, Colleen Neary, Schorer, Verdy; John Clifford, Arthur Mitchell, André Prokovsky, Kent Stowell, Helgi Tomasson, Villella, Weiss

I like his music," said Balanchine, on being queried why in the world, after probing the depths of Ives and atonal Stravinsky, he had decided to mount a full company ballet to the music of John Philip Sousa. "Does your new work have a story, Mr. Balanchine?" "Oh, yes." "And what is the story?" "The United States."

To note the obvious—the giant flag, the baton-twirling majorettes, the martial music that every American has heard somewhere before, the brass and parade—these are foolproof tactics for a comico-kitsch ballet that the great public cannot fail to adore. *Everybody* will go out humming the melodies.

Or—will they wince when the entire stage is covered with Old Glory, when d'Amboise struts like a rooster and jumps with flat feet, a regiment of girls kicks to their ears in unison, when Hayden runs around the stage on tippy-toe, head coyly cocked to one side, with mock sentimentality?

Balanchine has said that "calculated

---

* Shortly after the opening, the order of the campaigns was switched, with "Rifle Regiment" coming before "Thunder and Gladiator."

Stars and Stripes. **Thunder and Gladiator. William Weslow.** (*Photo Fred Fehl.*)

vulgarity is a useful ingredient" and that he is an old hand at "a big casserole my critics refer to as an applause machine," but what he characteristically omits mentioning is that, in this case, the vulgarity (if he will) is but seasoning for skill, taste, and choreographic substance. Because *Stars and Stripes*, for all its campy posturings, contains more pure dancing, more ingenious—and humorous—dance sequences and dance effects—than the lofty-minded, full-length classics. It may be draped in patriotic clichés, but it "flies Balanchine's irrepressible genius for composition at full staff." [1]

Just a few of the touches: The First Campaign offers a novel variation on Balanchinian labyrinthine design in the form of an interleaving, three-spoked wheel; another regiment paws the ground like horses, shoulders rifles, becomes involved in a whirling circle, and makes a high-stepping exit. On come the men—leaping, turning, marching, saluting, all in triangular formation. A little dynamo jumps higher than the rest and runs crisscross through their formations, ending with a grande pirouette à la seconde, straight from the classical dancing manuals. And for the finish, a stageful of men execute multiple double air turns. So much for the myth that Balanchine doesn't challenge his male dancers. (It's

just possible that before 1958 he never had a group that could perform choreography this difficult.) And finally: An all-American boy, grinning from ear to ear, meets a sweet girl who eyes him tenderly, then lays her head on his shoulder (after a series of finger turns in arabesque). Together they bring down the house with some more-than-energetic dancing—splits, jumps, lifts, multiple turns in a circle for the lady, double bent-knee air turns for her soldier, and then she is carried off, with a longing backward glance, resting daintily on his chest. Of one performance Manchester said, "They piled climax upon climax [in the pas de deux] until the audience was in a state of almost gibbering excitement." [2]

Kirstein has described the ballet as a "musical joke." If so, most critics "got" it: "Shamelessly corny and consistently high-spirited. The first and third 'campaigns' consist of all-girl squads going through some fancy stepping in the manner of the Rockettes, only on pointe. The audience was hugely tickled and went into convulsions when Kent shouldered her leg, which she has been doing every day in class for years. The male troupe really comes into its own as they perform brisk maneuvers in complicated series of turns, beats, and jumps. What gives *Stars* its distinction is its pas de deux. This will

survive long after the audience has ceased to be dazzled by all those gorgeous vivandière costumes and has really taken a look at the choreography. [It] is an amazing creation, staggeringly difficult yet full of both beauty and humor. He asks his dancers for everything from double sauts de basques for d'Amboise to the grand tour en dedans for Hayden. In the adagio, in their solos, and in the coda the dancers were marvelous. They stopped the show. Kay has arranged the scores most cunningly, including some transpositions into waltz time which are a delightful joke in themselves." [3]

"It is the story in movement of [America's] vast energy and exuberance, our love of show, our speed, our rhythm and, perhaps most of all, that sense of humor which makes it possible for us to laugh at ourselves while we are laughing simply because it's great to be alive. There's no telling what non-Americans would think of this glittering, splashy, uninhibited spectacle, but for us, it is a ball. If one finds the marches of Sousa irresistible, then he will be delighted with the score fashioned by Kay on Sousa's music. And if you are one to cheer a simple parade, you will quite probably jump out of your skin at Balanchine's technical fireworks, tricks, and formations. What [he] has devised is nearly indescribable, so much happens so fast. The grand pas de deux is very grand and very classical in its traditional roots, but the cavalier is a handsome officer, his ballerina is really a Liberty Belle, and their activities have the brusqueness and the brilliance of a fabulous maneuver. The choreographer's invention here and in all other sections of the ballet is absolutely stunning, not only with respect to steps and designs but also in its encompassing of humor and enormous vitality." 4

"At first viewing, one noticed the little dance jokes—the allusions to Tiller Girls and Rockettes. But when the jokes had been sifted away, there remained a veritable cascade of brilliant dancing, brilliantly dovetailed. The girls began, like toys massed in a box. Their costumes suggested the colors of the flag, but were never literal. They tossed off a firmament of turns.

"For the Second Campaign, the men formed a counterpoint of cabrioles and brisés. And with a boyish, 'look, no hands' elan, they performed jetés and air turns, all the while saluting jauntily.

"Weakest was the Third Campaign. Its level verged on the popular, with an incongruous rhythmic lapse from march tempo into a soft waltz.

"The Fourth Campaign was a delightfully witty 'soldier's sweetheart' duet for d'Amboise and Hayden. His pompous General Grant stance and her steely imperviousness were bright bits of flavor in spectacular dancing—so spectacular that the concluding ballabile seemed almost anticlimactic.

"There are some who feel that Balanchine merely tosses off this kind of bravura choreography. But is there another choreographer who *could* toss it off?" 5

"In a sense half tongue-in-cheek, yet totally serious. A glorious razzmatazz of Americana, where every girl is a cross between a baton-twirling Rockette and the Statue of Liberty, and every day is the Fourth of July. Only one of those old mail-order catalogues, full of flags and eagles, is as cheerfully, preposterously patriotic." 6

Martin raised questions on the other side of the coin: "A knock-down-and-drag-out riot, costumed in the most elegant concoctions of outrageous star-spangled bad taste, the whole work is actually a glorification of an all-too-familiar vulgarity.

"For all one's desire to believe that it is just a harmless bit of horsing, the terrible fear continues to grow that it is nothing of the sort. It is not the first time Balanchine

has looked carefully at the typical movement he sees around him and translated it into ballet tricks ([think of] *Danses Concertantes* and *Western Symphony*). But here he is dealing with high kicks and circusy lifts, turned-in knees, hammed-up 'performing,' and really reprehensible material, all elegantly taken over as the basic stuff of ballet. Is it as innocent as it seems? Or is it a colossal piece of cynicism?" 7

Fears that *Stars* might prove too gauche for foreign audiences—the ballet was not shown in Europe until 1965—were mostly groundless, at least as far as the local critics were concerned. (The English were the least amused.)

England:
"*Stars* may or may not be the best joke in New York, but here it really failed to make its point." 11

Stars and Stripes. Top: Rifle Regiment. Francia Russell. *Bottom:* Pas de Deux. Melissa Hayden, Jacques d'Amboise. (*Photos Fred Fehl.*)

"Such a classical ballet. The articulation of the structure, the dynamics of the dances, the balance of principals, subsidiary solos, and ensembles, the control of density, are purest Petipa. . . . Balanchine prefers to have fun rather than make fun of. If there are moments which become oddly stirring, that's hardly surprising in a creator whose works always seem to exist on more than one level. The finale presents a marvelous image of how Americans might imagine that Europeans might imagine that two 'typical Americans' would dance a romantic pas de deux." [9]

"Not so exciting as I remembered, although Hayden dancing her solo to a tuba almost gets by. You have to face the fact that Balanchine doesn't care much about program-planning or casting. And he is not very interested in whether the kids keep rigidly in line—which I think is crazy in the Sousa, for instance, because if you're going to imitate the Rockettes you've got to do their stuff better than they do. And Balanchine doesn't care at all if the theater is full or not, and he doesn't give a damn what you think or I write. So there you are, and it's raining too." [10]

France:
"Unanimous success. We have little enough opportunity to applaud majorettes in Paris, still less at the Opéra. . . . The worst banalities become great art when they are expressed with dash. This is true of *Stars*." [11]

Japan:
"*Stars* was a glorified version of Radio City Music Hall, but glorified in good taste." [12]

Australia:
"Has provided [Balanchine] with a glorious opportunity to pander to the flamboyant taste of the audience, to rouse its enthusiasm fully and then really to ridicule public taste. The costumes are blatant. The music makes monstrous, vacuous statements, which the choreography fully exploits." [13]

As for interpretation—well, a hearty smile is a necessity . . . as is a steel technique. Says Hayden of the pas de deux, "Choreographically it's so strong—and difficult. It's so puffy. Nine minutes long and it goes like an instant. At first I did it very seriously, like a *very* grand adagio,

and that was funny in itself. Little by little, mugging started to creep in, depending on who I was dancing with (Jacques began to add funny bits). Most people dance it seriously at first, then begin to 'sell' it a little once they get comfortable. I like to let the audience know that it isn't *so* serious, but you can't disturb the choreography for the mugging. It also depends on where you are. Once in Paris during *Stars*, we were booed, and this was very upsetting. For the next night Mr. B. said to play it straight, so we did—absolutely. And I danced phenomenally—because I was mad. Did you know that in the original rehearsals the pas de deux was *twice* as long?"

WALTZ-SCHERZO

Pas de Deux

CHOREOGRAPHY: George Balanchine

MUSIC: Peter Ilyitch Tchaikovsky (Waltz-Scherzo for violin and orchestra, op. 34, 1877)

COSTUMES: Karinska

LIGHTING: Nananne Porcher

PREMIERE: 9 September 1958

VIOLIN: Louis Graeler

CAST: Patricia Wilde, André Eglevsky

OTHER CASTS: Allegra Kent, Violette Verdy, Edward Villella

REVIVAL: 9 January 1964

CAST: Wilde, Jacques d'Amboise

Balanchine has set two dancers the problem of performing a continuous series of bravura passages and making them look like thistle-down on a gentle spring breeze," [1] was Martin's description of this rather unusual work—unusual in that Balanchine used two of his strongest technicians for a ballet that, despite its many difficult passages, appeared to be essentially lyrical in inspiration. In this it matched the lovely violin music, which, although of a generally lyric cast, lacks a large lyric sweep, consisting instead of tiny, speedy segments. The flow-

ing chiffon costume for the ballerina, rather than the glittering tutu associated with bravura, also underlined the mood.

The result created problems for Manchester, who wrote, "The little work falls rather flat because it has no real point of view, for it is neither truly lyric, classic, nor romantic." [2]

Martin, on the other hand, pronounced it "a gem." [3]

Hering saw it as "an array of brief solos and duets pursuing each other in quicksilver fashion. Gargouillades, fouettés, and arabesque turns all created an image of sophisticated flirtation—of light innuendo and casualness." [4]

Manchester postulated an interesting provenance: "Gives the impression that Balanchine was playing with the idea of creating a dance along the lines of the divertissement numbers of the Bolshoi Ballet, substituting steps of virtuosity wherever the Bolshoi dancers would employ a spectacular lift. There is not a single lift in *Waltz-Scherzo*." [5]

Balanchine, characteristically, hasn't said, but there is no doubt that Bolshoi fever was in the air, with the full company, including Ulanova, scheduled to make its first appearance in America the following spring (1959).

One technical quality possessed by both original dancers, of which Balanchine took particular advantage, was fleetness of foot. Wilde, especially, could skim across the stage, lovely skirts billowing windblown behind her, with something like the speed of light.

When the work was revived in 1964, considerably altered in detail if not in overall impact, Manchester noted that some lifts had been added.

MEDEA

CHOREOGRAPHY: Birgit Cullberg

MUSIC: Béla Bartók (13 piano pieces, including *Allegro Barbaro,* and selections from *14 Bagatelles, Mikrokosmos, Suite: Op. 14, 4 Dirges* orchestrated by Herbert Sandberg)

Inspired by the Greek legend, as dramatized by Euripides

COSTUMES: Lewis Brown

LIGHTING: David Hays

PREMIERE: 26 November 1958 (first presented 31 October 1950, Rikstheatern, Gaevle, Sweden)

CAST: *Medea*, Melissa Hayden; *Jason*, Jacques d'Amboise; *Their Children*, Delia Peters, Susan Pillersdorf; *Creon, King of Corinth*, Shaun O'Brien; *His Daughter, Creusa*, Violette Verdy; *Chorus*, 8 women, 8 men

OTHER CASTS: *Medea*, Verdy; *Jason*, Arthur Mitchell; *Creusa*, Jillana, Allegra Kent

Medea. **Melissa Hayden, Violette Verdy** (*Photo Martha Swope.*)

Medea was welcomed into the repertory as a dramatic ballet with plot and as a splendid vehicle for the dramatic gifts of Hayden (it also revealed unsuspected acting ability on the part of d'Amboise). Fortunately, it was also a good ballet. "Terse, hardhitting," [1] wrote Martin; "a ballet of high dramatic excitement," [2] said Manchester; "taut."

The work was divided into five scenes: Medea and Jason are shown happily with their family, then Jason is seduced by Creusa; Jason discusses marriage with King Creon; Medea learns of Jason's infidelity and confronts him with it; at the marriage ceremony, Medea appears with wedding gifts—a poisoned veil and crown—which kill Creusa as she tries them on and Creon as he embraces her; Medea and Jason again confront each other, but she escapes with the children and kills them.

Martin was the most unreservedly enthusiastic: "A powerful, succinct, extraordinarily direct retelling of the Greek legend, translated into straight narrative form. There is not a superfluous phrase, a meaningless gesture, an item of mere decoration in the choreography from end to end, for Cullberg is of a dramatic mind and bent on driving her theme to its inevitable conclusion. And when she arrives there, she stops with a breathtakingly simple suddenness. It is part of her singular talent to be able to develop in terms of dance, not merely mime, the most vivid emotional transitions, and to develop them with subtlety and perception for all the terseness of their statement. All three of her chief figures are completely credible human beings heightened to the stature of tragic symbolism, but compellingly real.

"And from her three dancers—she has elicited superb performances. Perhaps it would be fairer to say a single superb per-

formance, for their relationships mesh into a unified dramatic projection of wonderful authority. Indeed, it is difficult to separate choreography from performance. Hayden has never given us so richly colored a dramatic characterization, or one so dominated by inner command. Though she reaches levels of tragic fury, she does it without once raising her voice, as it were. And as for d'Amboise, it is not surprising to find him dancing miraculously, but it is a revelation to find him channeling a firm and consistent dramatic stream through his technical skill as a dancer. It is far and away his most mature performance. The chorus of eight men and eight women is beautifully employed both to break and to build the line of the action." [3]

Others also found much to praise: "Everything is of a piece in this choreography, and the work has a relentless drive from the start to the conclusion. There is a stunningly devised opening which depicts Medea and Jason arising from their marriage bed linked together by their children, power and passion in the pas de deux between these two when Medea learns of Jason's infidelity, and a superbly dramatic solo for the tortured Medea. The choreography for [the corps

de ballet, however] seems more decorative than dramatic." [4]

"A fine piece of storytelling. We see [Medea] first as a loving mother and mistress, and it is the contrast between this aspect and that of the fury who wreaks so terrible a vengeance on the usurper of Jason's love which creates the whirlwind of passion to which Hayden brings her tremendous talents as an actress-dancer." [5]

"Cullberg has conceived it as a series of what might be called 'animated tableaux' with the dancers coming alive to act out their parts and then disappearing or falling into quiescence while others take over." [6]

Almost all the critics complained of the absence of scenery and of specified locale, but the harsh costumes, with their serpentine decorations and stiff outlines, the stylized wigs ornamented with metal coils, the brutality of the choreography, and the primitive-rite character of the marriage ceremony (during which the chorus members almost stand on their heads in welcoming obeisance) would seem to set the ballet in some barbaric or pre-Hellenic civilization. One can almost see the open-mouthed peasants of the Minoan Harvester Vase, and some of the friezelike formations assumed by the chorus might have been imbedded in the stones of an Assyrian palace wall.

Cullberg achieved much of her intensity through disconnected segments of fairly traditional steps. Transitions were angular, awkward—or nonexistent. Poses were held insistently long. "An attempt to wed Central European to classical technique, which results in a few bars of expressive dancing and then some classical steps," wrote Williams of an earlier production. [7]

"The very discomfort of the movements in itself conveyed a dramatic tension," says Verdy. Hayden found that some of the steps had no preparation, either in preceding movements or in the music. Though the story was told completely through dance, many of the sequences seemed antidance, or at least antibeauty. Verdy commented on this apparent perversity. "It was difficult to give up the desire to extract a certain beauty, a certain line, a certain feeling of dance from the movements. But it worked well in the sense of drama. It was like an abscess, you were always fighting your material. Cullberg is a very knowledgeable person who knows literature well. She relates a story concisely, clearly, and in no uncertain terms. You can always expect each scene to be well motivated, very relevant to the whole, and the ballet cut into many scenes makes excellent sense from beginning to end. The choreography is not so very inventive and in particular it lacks dancing flow. This is not to say it is bad, but there's never really a moment of dancing that you could detach from the rest and talk muck about its choreographic qualities; it doesn't exist on its own terms, only as material to tell the story.

"The role of Medea went straight to the point. You enter like a furious animal, and you maintain that quality, only with crescendo, until the end. Creusa was a charming part, with sexy, sinuous movement in which you were not always struggling against yourself. Cullberg devised one part—Creusa's dance of death—that was a high point of the ballet. She was being burned by the scarf, and the dancing was like half trying to escape the scarf, and at the same time she was dancing the actual burning. The two things were perfectly expressed together."

Hayden's Medea inspired some of the best reviews of her career: "A gripping study in rebuffed pride and crazed revenge." [8] "A portrayal which squeezed every ounce of drama and melodrama, passion and poignancy, out of a vivid and terrifying role. Not only was Hayden the superb actress here but also a glittering dance technician who stirred the viewer with her physical skill as well as with her dramatic powers." [9] "She fairly makes the place rock." [10] Says she of this role, "It was such a focused work, very direct, and very strongly built on the three characters. And it was a ballet that kind of tore you apart. You couldn't just do it: you had to get yourself terribly immersed in it. My own mother didn't recognize me on the stage when I danced it."

OCTET

CHOREOGRAPHY: Willam Christensen

MUSIC: Igor Stravinsky (Octet for double woodwind quartet, 1922–23)

COSTUMES: Lewis Brown

LIGHTING: David Hays

PREMIERE: 2 December 1958

CAST: Barbara Walczak and Edward Villela; Dido Sayers and William Weslow; Roberta Lubell and Robert Lindgren; Judith Green and Richard Rapp

Octet was placidly received. "Distinctly minor," wrote Terry. "Won't hurt a soul. It is a mildly humorous little piece in which white gloves, black gloves, and gloves of mixed colors, worn at various times by the four couples performing the work, invite minor changes in mood and, hence, slightly different movement qualities." [1] "An unassuming trifle." [2] "Will set no worlds afire, but it is a smart and engaging piece of choreography, [with] very nice invention, fresh manipulation of the group, and general geniality." [3] "Though the novelty lacked any real substance or originality, it had its quiet charm. The steps were mostly classical, with occasional touches of gentle satire and humor." [4]

Some implied that the music was a little "too good" for such use; Martin felt "There may well be more in the score than this choreographic small talk would suggest, for it is young and truly vivacious music, impudently melodic, complex, but almost defiantly clear, and with a wonderful woody timbre to give it its individual character and direction." [5] Manchester had a similar view.

Everybody liked the costumes.

THE SEVEN DEADLY SINS
Sloth, Pride, Anger, Gluttony, Lust, Avarice, Envy

CHOREOGRAPHY: George Balanchine

MUSIC: Kurt Weill

LYRICS: Bertolt Brecht, translated by W. H. Auden and Chester Kallman

COSTUMES, DÉCOR, LIGHTING: Rouben Ter-Arutunian

PREMIERE: 4 December 1958 (first presented June 1933 as Les Sept Péchés Capitaux by Les Ballets 1933, Théâtre des Champs-Élysées, Paris)

CAST: Anna I (singer), Lotte Lenya; Anna II (dancer), Allegra Kent; Family: Mother, Stanley Carlson, bass; Father, Gene Holl-

man, bass; Brother I, Frank Poretta, tenor; Brother II, Grant Williams, tenor; Characters (dancers), 16 women, 15 men

When Les Sept Péchés Capitaux received its world premiere in June 1933, the venerable Genêt, already ensconced at her Paris station, wrote home to the New Yorker that she was the only person in Paris with "an appetite" for it. This slightly overstated the case. An intense young man named Kirstein called it "baffling . . . an important landmark in dancing history" and the theater critic of Marianne considered it "an audacious work, about which I must reserve my opinion until I feel I have completely understood it." Vogue magazine, however, reported that there were hisses (in addition to "loud applause") from certain elements—"Royalists, patriotic Frenchmen, and those who hated the music"—and the most noted dance critic of the time, André Levinson, panned it as "a sardonic cantata, composed with an aggressive monotony."

For whatever reasons—a different production (the work departs in many details from Brecht's published scenario, and the costumes are far removed from the straw boaters and tights worn by the original all-male supporting cast); a better presentation (in 1958, Balanchine starred his golden girl of the moment, Allegra Kent; in 1933, he had been obliged to work with Tilly Losch, wife of the patron of the season, about whom Virgil Thomson could only say, "she has a few defenders"); a datedness that distanced the audience, so that the moralizing and decadent atmosphere were clearly stage phenomena, and not specters from nearby Hitlerian Berlin; a despair and neuroticism that spoke to the nuclear age—when the work was revived in 1958 it was welcomed, and much of the audience even laughed, wisely. There were few expressions of "shocked disapproval," as there had been in Paris; many of wry amusement. (A surprising number of critics commented on the spareness of Kent's costumes, which were no more—or less—revealing than the average leotard, in which she had performed many times.) Some dismissed it as sophomoric, others as too pedantically didactic. Few, however, criticized it for not being a ballet, as had been the case in 1933. It was recognized as "a mixture of cabaret, theater, opera, pantomime, Expressionistic dance, street ballad, jazz ballet, variety show, carnival, circus, and *Singspiel*." [1] In 1933, the paucity of pure dancing steps was considered a shirking of duty by the choreographer; in 1958, as just one more example of his many-sidedness.

"It is a period piece, a mordant musical immorality play. It teaches, in terms of German jazz and German expressionism, the terrible lesson that by indulging in all the cardinal sins a little girl from Louisiana can build a fine house for her pious family and go home to end her days in it. . . . The music is quiet, astringent, almost genial in its insouciant acceptance of human evil. But if music, words, and staging shrug their collective shoulders, they make their purpose cuttingly clear and fairly appalling." [2]

"Presents, with wit and bite, a scroungy, tawdry, bawdy, occasionally degenerate group of characters headed by our girls, who move from low-grade panhandling and pickpocketing through stripteases, love for sale, and similar activities until the funds for the homecoming are earned. It is all brash and evil but it is hearty in the manner of the dance and the musical-theater productions of post-World War I Germany." [3]

The dancing: "There is scarcely any choreography; yet there is a mastery of staging that has a formality comparable to choreography." [4]

Terry described the movement quality: "The masked dancers of the chorus, the action style of the whole work, even most of Kent's patterns hark back to the semi-balletic modern dance of Central Europe some thirty years ago. In fact, the Jooss Ballet's *The Big City* kept coming to mind. But where the Jooss work has aged sadly, *Sins* has succeeded in projecting a nostalgic commentary upon another period, upon a half-forgotten form of theater, sound, and movement." [5]

Todd mentioned that characters in Jooss works were often masked, as here. And Martin noted that "there were still traces of Losch's style, especially of her famous backbend" [6] which Kent reproduced in Envy. The production, however, was mostly new, according to Martin (who had consulted some eyewitnesses) and Manchester, who wrote: "It bears no resemblance to his 1933 version, which anticipated the invention of the word 'chichi' by a number of years. There is nothing chichi here. It is a plunge backward to the Berlin of the

The Seven Deadly Sins. **Pride. Allegra Kent.** *(Photo Fred Fehl.)*

1920s, the most despairing, disillusioning, and decadent of all decades. Brecht and Weill were looking back even then, and what they created was an imagined New World which bore no relation to the real thing but was their own bitter Old World, given the exoticism of strange American placenames which are otherwise meaningless. Balanchine has made the current *Sins* into a period piece which has a startling verisimilitude. It is difficult to believe that this is not a careful revival but an entirely new creation. . . . What [choreography] there is contains little of interest. Weill's score is completely a product of this period, fitting the defeatist philosophy exactly but not lending itself to dancing, which is probably why Balanchine has contented himself with moving his people busily around." [7]

The action: "The opening image had the haunting symbolism of Kokoschka. To the sound of a sad banjo, the curtains parted on a black stage. It was the impenetrable black that is never possible in rooms, only on a stage. Three elements glowed. The first was a family arranged on a platform as though posing for a tintype. A humorously apt fringed lampshade

hung above them. On the opposite side of the stage a street lamp glowed wanly as in the early dawn. And slowly, from deep within the blackness, pale faces emerged side by side.

"In her tantalizing voice (which always reminds us of the slightly mournful off-keyness of a phonograph beginning to run down), Lenya outlined their quest. At the end of each tawdry episode, the family uttered words of pious cant. And one by one, the sections of a house were notched in place before their platform so that they eventually sat staring over the completed roof. In a sense, the cynical Annie and the sentimental Annie reminded one of Brecht and Weill, who wrote their strange fantasy-journey through America before they had ever set foot in the country. Their images of the seamy side of the various cities were uncannily real.

"As Lenya roved the stage with casual command and commented upon every scene, Kent, resembling a sad child, accosted 'prospects' in a park [Sloth]—rode a Valentine-laced horse in Hollywood [Anger]—snuggled on the lap of a 'benefactor' in a Boston bedroom [Lust]. And in one quietly witty scene, she curved her body in a series of exquisite acrobatics on a mat, while her alter ego kept watch over her with a gun and allowed her occasional licks on a coveted ice cream cone [Gluttony]." [8]

"Later, Kent, stripped to legal minimum, is borne in on a cellophane-wrapped platter as the most delectable dish in a night club [Pride]. Still later, she is forced by Anna to divest herself of her finery (all is carefully deposited in a handy sack), for these are earnings [Avarice]." [9]

In Envy, she confronts the faceless crowd of easy livers—G-stringed prostitutes and their tuxedo'd gentlemen—who, although they take no notice of her, drive her to a suicide leap through silver foil. At the end, the family is united in its new home.

The music: "A group of songs sung by Lenya and several hymnlike quartets given by the heroine's platitude-ridden Puritan relatives. A distillation of all the music that floated like blue smoke through the beerhalls, night clubs, and dives of Berlin in the late twenties and Paris of the early thirties. Weill's music [as here] is often honky-tonk with a message. . . . It is a means for sensitizing the text of Brecht, for allowing the words a certain air and lift they might otherwise lack. You do not leave *Sins* with ears

The Seven Deadly Sins. **Top: Anger. Allegra Kent.** *Bottom:* **Lust. Allegra Kent.** (*Photos Fred Fehl.*)

aglow under the fire of memorable tunes; rather, one's recollection consists of the plinking of a banjo, a sudden surge of strings, a syncopated jazz rhythm, the tap of a beat heard far in the distance. It was ever one of Weill's greatest gifts that with a chord he could sum up an era, with a tune bring back an epoch half remembered." [10]

"It is not only the matter but the manner that produces the effect. Brecht and Weill have achieved a superior artistic métier of deliberate cheapness; it is colloquial, thin, a trifle stale. The melodic line is short, its range narrow, its themes tainted with familiarity. The quartet who represent Annie's complacent family back home sing vulgarizations of old German hymns. Similarly, the phrases that Annie sings and the dance tunes that the orchestral score is built upon all echo café music,

as if it were the background of living. In one scene [Pride], a nightclub in Memphis, the managerial Annie complains of her idealistic other half: 'She began talking about art, of all things. About the Art, if you please, of Cabaret.' And—begging their pardons, that is exactly what Brecht and, more especially, Weill have created—an Art of Cabaret." [11]

Décor and costumes: Ter-Arutunian lived in Berlin as a child. His designs were inspired by "the spirit of German Expressionism, and the UFA films, the time of Emil Jannings and the Blue Angel."

"Sometimes his palette was angry, as in the costume for Lenya—an electric blue satin skirt, a brown and orange overblouse, and ridiculous white pumps. Sometimes he launched into the chrome-and-peroxide atmosphere of the period—

as in the final scene with its tinfoil backdrop and rows of pink-fringed, black-booted women. And throughout, there was an air of melancholy isolation, for all the figures (other than Annie) were anonymous behind masks." [12]

"[The costumes] have a kind of horrible beauty about them. They are full of comment as they evoke the style of a stale era with the deliberate intent of telling an ugly story in all blandness. . . . Excruciatingly awful." [13]

Many observers commented on the humor of the piece, despite the sordid subject matter. "Balanchine has achieved a coup-de-théâtre. There is a joyous boldness and vitality about the whole thing and an exhilarated sense of spoofing," wrote Biancolli.[14] This was generated by the exaggerated miming and the oversized, insistently ugly decor, which could only come from those who know what good taste really is. The situations—Kent appearing as the decoration on a platter, a masked man shooting himself out of love for her—were larger than life and a wry comment on it. The family quartet, with its mustachioed mother, singing foursquare homilies, provided another comic touch.

As for the performances, the critics had nothing but praise for Lenya ("whose air of battered wisdom is exactly right for a text which reeks of pessimism," said Manchester), her grasp of period style, her theatrical projection.

For Kent, the role was a triumph. Recently promoted to principal dancer, she was going through the usual trial by fire that accompanies such new responsibilities—dancing two and three parts nightly in every type of ballet. And just while decisively demonstrating her mastery of line, lyric feeling, strong technique, and stage awareness (she had done her first Swan Queen, to much praise, just four months earlier), she was given this chance to dominate a production that was completely unlike anything else in the repertory. To Martin she was "beautiful, innocent, innately expressive . . . truly heartbreaking." [15] Wrote Biancolli, "She gives the role a lurid glamour and a tired poignancy that are truly moving." [16]

Says Kent, "Balanchine trusted my instincts. He demonstrated what he wanted and I embroidered. (A little bit of the Gluttony scene was my own choreography.) I understood the part right away because here was somebody who wasn't allowed to talk. That's perfect for dancers."

NATIVE DANCERS

CHOREOGRAPHY: George Balanchine

MUSIC: Vittorio Rieti (Symphony No. 5, 1945)

WOMEN'S COSTUMES: Peter Larkin

JOCKEY SILKS: H. Kauffman & Sons Saddlery Co.

DÉCOR, LIGHTING: David Hays

PREMIERE: 14 January 1959

CAST: Patricia Wilde, Jacques d'Amboise; 6 women, 6 men

OTHER CASTS: Allegra Kent, Edward Villella

Native Dancers—whose equine namesake was the biggest money-winner of 1953—was mostly an excuse for exploring and exploiting the technical virtuosity of Wilde and d'Amboise. Chujoy mentioned the "spectacular moments for the principals containing jumps, turns, lifts, and supports usually associated with the Soviet ballet." [1] Commentators felt exploitative also, working the horsey subject matter for all the puns it was worth. Headlines such as "NATIVE DANCERS" IN EASY FINISH AT CENTER and BALANCHINE BALLET GOES TO THE POST proved irresistible, and Watt announced that "running five furlongs on a dry track, Wilde and d'Amboise finished lengths ahead of the other starters." [2]

As for the ballet—"Native Dancers has something to do with race horses, but fortunately not too much." [3] It seemed that the horse conceit furnished a bit of humor, but the choreography furnished the interest. "What started out being cute ended by being artistic." [4] The ladies were horses, with pony tails and jingling harnesses, the men their riders. The high spot was the second movement adagio.

Martin found it "only out of Balanchine's second drawer. Nevertheless, it has its virtues. Give Balanchine a gimmick like this and you can trust him to

play with it delightfully, with wit and invention. The second section is quite wonderful. The movement is beautifully and ingeniously equine, and reaches its height when a series of supported leaps through hoops evokes the elegant slow motion of fine horse leaping. The ensemble sections are less rewarding. Like the small and somewhat fussy music, they seem unduly busy." [5]

Terry mentioned Wilde's "leaps and spins, prancings and agile steppings," while noting that Balanchine "has skillfully avoided those equine-like maneuvers which have destroyed several other ballets dealing with fillies, races, and the like. Occasionally, with wit, he makes a closer analogy, as when d'Amboise appears to be shoeing Wilde, or when she, as a free and spirited creature, tries to elude his grasp." [6] Johnson wrote, "[The] ingenious choreography suggests the proverbial jaunty and dare-devil racing tradition; at the same time [Balanchine] includes touches that demonstrate the traditional affection the rider envinces for his high-spirited companion. It is typical of the ballet's tongue-in-cheek wit that our celebrated stallion is, to Balanchine, a filly!" [7]

EPISODES

CHOREOGRAPHY: Martha Graham (I),* George Balanchine (II)

MUSIC: Anton Webern (complete orchestral works, as below)

COSTUMES: Karinska

DÉCOR, LIGHTING: David Hays

PREMIERE: 14 May 1959

I. Passacaglia, op. 1 (1906) and Six Pieces, op. 6 (1910): Mary Queen of Scots, Martha Graham [†]; Bothwell, Bertram Ross [†]; Elizabeth, Queen of England, Sallie Wilson; The Four Marys, 4 women [†]; Darnley, Riccio, Chastelard, 3 men [†]; Executioner; 2 Heralds

II. Symphony, op. 21 (1928): Violette Verdy, Jonathan Watts, 3 couples
Five Pieces, op. 10 (1911–13): Diana Adams, Jacques d'Amboise

* Permanently withdrawn after the Winter 1959–60 season, after which the Balanchine section was presented alone as Episodes II. Since 1961, Part II, without Taylor's solo, has been called Episodes.

Concerto, op. 24 (1934): Allegra Kent, Nicholas Magallanes, 4 women
Variations, op. 30 (1940): Paul Taylor [†]
Ricercata in 6 voices from Bach's Musical Offering (1935): Melissa Hayden, Francisco Moncion, 13 women

OTHER CASTS: Symphony: Sara Leland, Mimi Paul; Anthony Blum, Laurence Matthews; Five Pieces: Karin von Aroldingen, Penny Dudleston, Suzanne Farrell, Wilhelmina Frankfurt, Jillana, Patricia McBride, Marnee Morris, Patricia Neary; Conrad Ludlow, Moncion, Peter Naumann, Frank Ohman; Concerto: Judith Green, Kay Mazzo, McBride, Heather Watts, Lynda Yourth; Bart Cook, Robert Maiorano; Ricercata: Renee Estópinal, Gloria Govrin, Kent, Patricia Wilde; Arthur Mitchell, David Richardson

Doomed to total failure in a deaf world, Webern kept cutting his diamonds, the mines of which he had such a perfect knowledge."—Stravinsky

"Webern's orchestral music fills the air like molecules; it is written for atmosphere. The first time I heard it, I knew it could be danced to. It seemed to me like Mozart and Stravinsky, music that can be danced to because it leaves the mind free to see the dancing. In listening to composers like Beethoven and Brahms, every listener has his own ideas, paints his own picture of what the music represents. How can I, a choreographer, try to squeeze a dancing body into a picture that already exists in someone's mind? It simply won't work. But it will with Webern."—Balanchine [1]

"Webern's talent was such that he needed but ten measures to introduce a situation, comment on it, and resolve it. And this he accomplished through a series of flutters, whispers, sighs, groans, and exultant cries ordered into instrumental patterns that attack at the root of the listener's nerve."—Harrison [2]

"The one thing that disconcerted me at first was to dance with so little sound coming from the pit, but then I realized that what we had to imprint on top of the musical line was making its own time, and was in complete correspondence, and the sound came then as a kind of reward, rather than the expected motivation."—Verdy

† Martha Graham Company.

In advance announcements, *Episodes* was called "historic," both for its use of the little-known Webern's entire symphonic oeuvre (to say the least, this was unusual, probably unprecedented) and for the collaboration it promised between the giants of two warring schools of dance.*

In truth, collaboration was not the perfect description of their joint effort. The idea for the ballet and the choice of music—including which selections Graham was to use—seem to have been Balanchine's (not always with forethought: although he had choreographed a piece to part of Opus 6, "the bells," he withdrew it and gave the music to Graham when she discovered she needed more). The two choreographers created separate works which were presented in sequence (Graham's first) on the same stage on the same evening; further, Graham used four New York City Ballet members (notably Wilson) in her section, while Balanchine interpolated a solo for the Graham dancer Paul Taylor in *his* section. But the two did not act together in a common creative process. And they produced dances which could stand completely alone. The point, already clear, was proven when, after two seasons, Graham's section was withdrawn, and not long thereafter, Taylor's dance disappeared. Even with these excisions, there was quite a lot of ballet left over, and Balanchine's *Episodes* has been fending for itself ever since. (Graham has never performed her section separately, however.)

There were some wry observations at the time to the effect that it was the moderns who used the "traditional" elements of story line and descriptive costumes, while the ballet dancers were stripped to their leotards, devoid of emotion, and sometimes pointed their heels or danced upside down, even though they never took their toe-shoes off. These would seem to be side issues to the actual dance invention, however. Martin felt that Graham had created a powerful work that fit within the personal boundaries she had established for her art. Balanchine, on the other hand, according to Martin, went beyond or outside his already avant-garde vocabulary, and was therefore more forward-looking, more "modern" than the woman who had fought for over forty years to liberate dance from the conven-

* Ballet vs. "modern" was still something of an issue in 1959.

Episodes. **Bertram Ross, Martha Graham.** (*Photo Martha Swope.*)

tions of the ballet.[3] *Here*, perhaps, was a paradox worth pondering.

The two pieces in Graham's section were pre-twelve-tone and more richly orchestrated than the others. She used them as a frame for externalizing the emotions of Mary Queen of Scots in the final moments before her execution. In the story are Bothwell her lover and Elizabeth her murderess. Hering described it: "Graham as Mary stood in stiff black. Her hands rested quietly on the front of her skirt. Above her there extended a horizontal black platform ending on either side in a staircase. Centered on the platform were a black stanchion decorated with heraldic symbols and a vertical black rectangle.

"Mary walked forward in the skittery gait of someone skirting obstacles. She mounted a staircase and, back to the audience, slipped out of her chrysalislike dress. Bothwell awaited her, a crown in his hand. She descended, and the dress remained standing alone—the abandoned vestiture of a queen. A metaphor integral to Graham began to emerge. It was the conflict between love and destiny. In this case, the resolution came quickly, al-

most violently, and Bothwell, dismissed, strode stiffly out. Mary was left in the torment so clearly and rightly expressed in what has become Graham's own personal symbol-movement—the wide leg swirls, the quick, nervous lifting of the knees, the split-fall forward to the floor, the high angling of the arms.

"Four girls encased her in a blood-red gown. As in Graham's *Herodiade*, donning a garment became the symbolical acceptance of destiny. The dance patterns for the girls were devised in sweeping spirals, as though Graham had wished them to draw curves of commentary about the restraint of her own gestures. As they receded, she knelt to cross herself, then stood with her right hand unfolding in resignation.

"The Executioner turned the black rectangle above, and it was the throne, with Elizabeth seated resplendent in gold. Like the image in an old engraving, she descended the staircase with her body facing sideways to the line of descent. Both women hurled themselves into similar sharp extensions, similar arm-positions (as though playing at archery). But Elizabeth's were done with the lavish force of youth. Mary's were tinged with introspection and potential defeat.

"They mounted small platforms, and, to a chiming of bells, engaged in a fateful game of tennis. Like mechanical dolls, they tapped the golden balls while the Four Marys and the four men out of Mary's past surged and fell in anguish.

"The game was over. Elizabeth was lifted high in triumph. Mary zig-zagged among the others, holding out her hand to each. Momentarily she sat upon the throne, then knelt in darkness. A red light suffused the abandoned black dress." [4]

Graham's own performance was described as "tremendous," "powerful," "inimitable," "a moment in eternity." It had quite an effect on the ballet dancers. Hayden went out front each time the ballet was given. "Such magnificent performances! One in particular—I was just choked up. She was fabulous."

Wilson remembers Graham's first words on meeting her: " 'I'm *terrified* of you!' She didn't know whether I'd be able to do anything, and started out trying to make ballet movements for me. She didn't know them very well—it was ridiculous—she would do a movement, gorgeously, and then try to clean it up for me in a ballet fashion. I immediately asked her to teach me to do it her way, and she was delighted. But the whole thing was a struggle in her mind as to whether I would be able to do it or not. The other dancers helped me, and it turned out to be just marvelous. *They* were thrilled that I could actually move my back—they had expected a ramrod. Martha did two versions of my part—the first (in the spring) much less interesting, the second (the following winter) much more in her style, when she realized I could do more.

"In rehearsal, she tried different things to the same music. She stopped and prayed and everyone meditated. You had to be always *with* her—you couldn't just go off and talk in a corner. She talked a lot, referred to history. Even though what she was doing was symbolic, she would explain what the symbol represented. Each thing was weighed carefully. At runthroughs, someone would stand in for her. The part I remember best was when the throne turned around and I had to get up and walk down a flight of stairs sideways without any movement. They said it looked like I was on an elevator."

Graham's section was followed by a five-minute intermission, a "schism" that

Episodes. **Concerto. Allegra Kent, Nicholas Magallanes.** *(Photo Fred Fehl.)*

opened into a world of "logic without reason," where dancers "have become essentially an organization of bones and muscles"—"uniformed instruments for design"—a world without reference to human emotions and barest reference to human bodies (qua bodies). "If only we could locate those five minutes on the universal calendar, we would have the philosophical turning point of human history," wrote Martin. [5]

Obvious antecedents to the Balanchine section were *Four Temperaments*, *Agon*, and *Ivesiana*, but a number of critics talked about new movement thresholds —the present work was but distantly related to anything that had gone before.

For Martin, the implications were cosmic: "What is it all about and why is it so shocking? The work as a whole jolts apart at the couplings more than once (which is perhaps permissible under such a title). . . . If the theme can be reduced to a single word it is manipulability, the susceptibility of human beings to transmutation into monsters—physically, mentally, socially—by forces whose existence they do not suspect. Balanchine shows us the human body moving without the impulsion of human motive, simply as a coordinated assemblage of bones, muscles and nerves, capable of combinations that are numberless because they are without the limitations of function, rationality, or personal responsibility." [6]

Herridge, though puzzled, decided that Balanchine must be poking fun at modern dance. [7] Denby spoke of the

"counter-classic classicism; . . . the lucid abnormality has a wit like Beckett's." [8] Terry considered the sequences to be "marked by the juxtaposition of classical ballet with modern dance, by a fusion of the two, and by an extension of ballet into new areas of design." [9] A number of writers mentioned humor; others saw nothing funny at all.

Each "episode" had a highly individual quality, largely due to the particular dancers on whom Balanchine had fashioned movements that fit more than ordinarily well. As Verdy says, of a role and movement style unlike anything she had ever danced (and which probably did not contain a single "orthodox" step) but which yet was perfect for her:

"That part was congenial because it was really not asking me to go beyond my physical capacities and it had a logic in its own timing that was very natural to me. He was making some technical points about me that were very obvious [clarity and limb articulation]. . . . The part was given to me already free, understood, and fully created."

Symphony: "Suddenly the Webern music sounds quite different—more spare and fragmentary. The dancers, hands joined, formed tight patterns, first an arm, then another arm, then a head, then a leg, then a foot, then a lift with the girl's feet flexing at the peak or on the descent. They all finished with the girls facing to the side, leaning back like ship figureheads against the boys' hands." [10]

"Here and there are hints, echoes, developments of movements Graham has established. Perhaps the most strikingly beautiful passage is a sequence of developpés to a stretched heel. Gradually we become conscious that we have passed into a new dimension of movement. It is unstrained and in a pleasant mood; a trifle disturbing, perhaps, but not ominous." [11]

Five Pieces: This section of tiny spurts of sound and groping movements, punctuated by silence, stimulated the most comment and the most varied interpretations.

"Like little musical gasps, to which Adams and d'Amboise perform fragmentary sequences like tightrope walkers trying to make contact in circumstances of extreme difficulty. One startling moment has Adams hanging around d'Amboise's neck in such a way that her legs, in their flesh-colored tights, seem to spring from his head like giant antlers. The effect is almost awe-inspiring. Some of the tangles border on the ludicrous, and were greeted with little spurts of laughter that were quickly hushed; but since any point the work may have is in association of ideas, such laughter is surely justified if the movements happen to strike a spectator as being humorous at any particular moment." [12]

"An exquisitely grotesque, heartbreaking pas de deux in the briefest of broken graspings. It is two souls struggling for identity, in a realm without orientation, no procedural logic or precedent, no sequence of reaction to action—only snatches of affection. At its close, two long wisps of fabric float down from above and off at either side, like the ghost of a curtain marking some fateful undimensional conclusion." [13]

Concerto: "The choreographer returned to the safety of pure movement. Here Kent resembled a sweetly pliant lay-figure, and Magallanes was the adventurer touching her body lightly to see what shapes it would take. She would dip into an arabesque and at a touch of his fingertips would reverse into a forward extension. She would stand in second. He would tap her leg lightly and watch it fold into a plié. She would bend way over on one leg, and he would fold the free leg through." [14]

"Here we are under the domination of the supreme logic of irrationality. The characteristic muscular phrase of Kent becomes almost the theme, to be exploited to a super-mechanical nonhumanity. Again the stretched heel recurs, and becomes the final capping of a miraculous formal sequence of movement created out of nowhere. In the closing section, Balanchine's well-known 'daisy chains' and 'London Bridges' find themselves in lunatic inversions, and there would seem to be no further to go. . . . But there is." [15]

Variations: "Picks up and identifies flashes and bits and colors from what has gone before, but it is otherwise in an almost totally alien idiom, built of negations and devitalization. Marvelously performed, spiritually hideous, humanly void and null, it gives us the ultimate psycho-electronic pulp." [16]

"The movement was brilliantly inventive and exquisitely performed. Sometimes Taylor flexed his arms like an old-time boxer, sometimes he crawled, catching each foot with his hand as he went, and throughout there was a rhythm of flow-and-halt, as though he were swimming in a secret amniotic fluid." [17]

Episodes. **Five Pieces. Diana Adams, Jacques d'Amboise.** (*Photo Fred Fehl.*)

"It was very spider-like. Paul got into pretzellike positions the likes of which I have never seen before; here was a big boy, so fluid. . . . He would stand up straight and all of a sudden his hands and his neck were all underneath his legs, and his legs were all over his back. Like an octopus. Somehow there was more to him than there really was."—Hayden

Ricercata: In contrapuntal manner, each dance movement—by a block of the ensemble or the soloists—is an equal component of the whole stage picture at any single moment. Most movements are brief, often using only one part of the body at a time. The groups move fugually, in imitation (more or less freely) of the restatements of the musical subject.

"How to end a cycle such as this? Balanchine has clearly known the perilousness of the area into which he has transported us, and he cannot possibly leave us there to drop as we may out of his stratosphere. For our safety and his conscience he must bring us back. [So] here as a finale is a noble restatement of humanity, an orderly collaboration that keeps the essential simplicity of mutual action through all complexities of pattern." [18]

"It was resplendent music, though rather too romantically orchestrated. The choreography was architectural in style. The corps, in groups of three and four, formed levels by standing or kneeling. The soloists were given phrases that emphasized precision, rather than sweep, and that did not truly reflect the music. It

left us with a feeling of inconclusiveness . . . but that seems to be the atmosphere Balanchine wished to convey throughout." [19]

In Europe *Episodes* (the Balanchine section) was generally accepted and admired ("will surely improve upon further acquaintance," wrote one critic who probably felt he should have been more impressed), although there was some mention of unenthusiastic audience reaction. ("Conservative spectators were indignant because they had come to see dances and not complicated gymnastics exercises. Others accused Balanchine of a misunderstanding, feeling that he had tried to translate Webern's music into dance forms that might at best be appropriate for Tchaikovsky music," it was reported from Salzburg.) Five Pieces proved the most provocative section.

England:
"In respect of the work's choreographic unity, the Ricercata makes for a kind of bathos. But to say this is also to acknowledge the extraordinary tension built up by the difficult, unfamiliar, fragmented choreography which has gone before. Five Pieces was particularly effective—a classicism both skeletal and sensual and genuinely enhancing the spare, austere music." [20]

"At its episodic best, it reaches heights. The Five Pieces is a pas de deux of startling honesty. Five fragmented moments, as still as statuary, as cold as print, and as odd as genius, contrive a comment on (stupid, yet here valid, phrase) the human condition, with its loves and hates, or perhaps just all its oxymoronic conditions." [21]

Austria:
"About Five Pieces one could write a whole novel of interpretation: two people of our time, who seek contact and believe they have found it, who live one beside the other without communication. . . . The final part of Concerto, with its entangled girls, reminds one of an amoebalike scattering structure. For the Ricercata, Balanchine sees his own *Concerto Barocco* through the same glasses as Webern sees Bach. But the tracing of thematic connections would be endless if one decided to follow it up." [22]

France:
"To express the telegraphic language of

the soul to the incredibly difficult atonal music of such modern composers as Webern is not given to just anyone. *Episodes* will surely count, in the same way as *Four Temperaments*, as one of the masterpieces of modern ballet. The first piece shows us a dancer, assisted by a partner and framed by three couples, tracing in space, with the precision of a mechanical drawing, lines shattered or cut, with feet often squared and elbows leading. In the second, two acrobats engage in the solitary struggle of attaining and regaining equilibrium as if on a tightrope, surrounded by void. The third, which involves daring interlacings that are never obscene, presents, in effect, a purified version of the frenetic interlockings of Béjart. To conclude, a final mass, inspired by Bach, unfolds like a magnificent musical fresco, bearing the imprint of the best of Balanchine." [23]

Germany:

"One has to be blind not to see the perfect correspondence between the sublime instrumental polyphony of Webern and the counterpoint of dance movements, whose expressive power in the perfect and complicated sequences of Five Pieces reached a wonderful, cold, erotic tension." [24]

The Blackamoors, Suki Schorer, William Weslow; *Harlequin,* Edward Villella; *Acrobats,* 3 women

OTHER CASTS: *Coquette,* Karin von Aroldingen, Marnee Morris, Sallie Wilson; *Baron,* Francisco Moncion, Shaun O'Brien, Roland Vazquez; *Poet,* Victor Castelli, Nicholas Magallanes, Peter Schaufuss, Earle Sieveling; *Sleepwalker,* Suzanne Farrell, Patricia McBride, Kay Mazzo, Violette Verdy; *Harlequin,* Anthony Blum, Deni Lamont

Mystery, passion, drama, period costumes—here was Balanchine being "European" (in respect to the accouterments of illogical plot, décor, shadowy romantic currents) and "operatic" in the nineteenth-century sense (this was borne out by the costumes, which would have been appropriate for something like *Traviata;* specifically, however, aside from the use of the Bellini melodies and the sleepwalker figure, Balanchine's work has no connection with any opera). Denby mentioned Poe: "It gives you a sense—as Poe does—of losing your bearings. . . . When it's over, you don't know what hit you." [1]

Wrote Terry: "The story concerns a Poet who appears at a lavish party, becomes enamored of the Coquette (apparently the host's mistress), sub-sequently (when the guests have retired for supper) meets the mysterious Sleepwalker (the host's wife), is discovered following her to her room by the jealous Coquette and, finally, is stabbed to death by the enraged Baron, the host.

"The choreography itself, though projecting the plot-line clearly, is principally designed to evoke moods and emotions, revelry juxtaposed to fantasy, romance paired with anger. The initial section, with the elegant dancing of the corps of guests, is altogether charming, but the divertissements, provided by the Baron for the entertainment of his friends, leave something to be desired. The core of *Night Shadow* however, is the extended duet of the Poet and the Sleepwalker and here the choreography, though delicate, is hauntingly beautiful. The dance for the two is one of lyrical desperation, for the unseeing Sleepwalker (moving mainly on pointe) eludes the reaching hands of the Poet as he attempts to bring her into his own orbit of reality. She fades from his encircling arms, she steps over the barrier of his prone body, she is but a puppet as he causes her to run or to turn. There is, nonetheless, a sense that she is aware of his presence and in his death, this is realized as she carries his body, alone and unaided, back to the hidden retreat from which she has come." [2]

NIGHT SHADOW
since 1961 called
LA SONNAMBULA

CHOREOGRAPHY: George Balanchine, staged by John Taras

MUSIC: Vittorio Rieti, 1946 (after themes of Vincenzo Bellini from *La Sonnambula, I Puritani, I Capuleti ed i Montecchi*)

SCENARIO: Vittorio Rieti

COSTUMES: André Levasseur

DÉCOR, LIGHTING: Esteban Francés

PREMIERE: 6 January 1960 (first presented 27 February 1946 by Ballet Russe de Monte Carlo, City Center of Music and Drama, New York)

CAST: *The Coquette,* Jillana; *The Baron,* John Taras; *The Poet,* Erik Bruhn; *The Sleepwalker,* Allegra Kent; *The Guests,* 8 couples; *Divertissements: Pastorale,* 2 couples (in 1967 redone for 3 people);

Night Shadow. **Erik Bruhn, Jillana.** *(Photo Fred Fehl.)*

The steps are not particularly demanding (except for some of the divertissements); atmosphere, drama, and "presence" are paramount. With the entrance of the Poet, the company freezes. When the Sleepwalker, unassisted, carries off his corpse, the audience gasps. And as the curtain falls, no one on either side of the footlights can say precisely what has happened. Says Tallchief (the Coquette in the original production), "Balanchine's so mystical, which not many people realize. Look at *Night Shadow*, when all you see is the people looking, heads up, at something—a light. People so often think of him as someone who does steps—mechanical, dry steps—and this is so completely opposite from what he is. To me, his great glory is his wonderful mysticism—he's a poet, really, more than anything else."

The work was "atypical" Balanchine. Wrote Martin, "Though it does not rank with Balanchine's masterpieces by any means, it is a manifestation of his craftsmanship, his taste, and his invention, and deserves to be treated accordingly. Not yet fourteen years old, it is already a period piece, recalling the 'ballet-russe' epoch no less vividly because it was already engaged in breaking away from it. It is a story ballet (somewhat rare for Balanchine), elegantly, perhaps too elegantly, macabre; dealing far more superficially with choreographic matters than we have become accustomed to expect nowadays from the same choreographer.

"Rieti's music is chic (but excellent) and stands up extremely well. The long pas de deux, if such it can be termed, between the Sleepwalker and the Poet is a tour de force and a fascinating one. The somewhat more typically classifiable pas de deux between the Coquette and the Poet is better than one might have remembered. The ensembles demand speed and nimbleness of foot and may quite possibly comprise the best part of the choreography." [3] ("The ballet would be worth keeping if only for the splendid ballroom Polonaise Balanchine has invented for the whole company." [4])

The performances were generally considered excellent, although in Manchester's opinion the Company, so skilled in "the most intricate choreographic convolutions," seemed ill-at-ease with the period and the ever-shifting emotional currents. Balanchine, who verbalizes only about the more prosaic details, com-

Night Shadow **Nicholas Magallanes, Allegra Kent.** (*Photo Martha Swope.*)

plained that his dancers didn't know how to walk like ladies and gentlemen. "But," he said, "that is my fault, because I have never given you those lovely big costumes to wear just to walk across the stage; you have always been counting and in leotards." The divertissements were largely dismissed as filler; it was noted that the variation for the zesty, high-jumping Harlequin, who suddenly gets lumbago, was mostly new (the role had originally been danced by a woman).

The eerie character of the Sleepwalker is central. Who is she? "She symbolizes the beauty denied the poet in life." [5]

"It is the pursuit of the unattainable as symbolized by a woman. Glidingly remote, she makes her way into the Poet's solitude, and she seems half-dream, half-woman as she eludes his every gesture, his every embrace. And yet, in her detachment, she is sensitive almost to the currents of air between them." [6]

"A little figure out of pure melodrama explodes on the pseudo-fantastic scene, showing a curiously fey element in Balanchine's imagination. And we have at once another of his extraordinary episodes in which a woman takes complete possession of a man. At first with childlike wonder, the poet touches, pushes, pokes, spins, and embraces her. Then in unbearable excitement he lies down to encircle her feet. And when she walks over and through and beyond him, he gives himself up exhausted to the unattainable." [7]

Says Kent, "It's elusive . . . I have that candle and my white dress. I don't connect, and that's what's so fantastic—when the Poet does that backbend, I don't see or feel, although something in me does react. It's full of mystery: I'm there and yet I'm not there."

Bruhn commented on the Poet: "An idealist. There is a quite mannered, realistic ball going on, and suddenly the Poet arrives. The people do not know who he is or why he has come. It would seem quite natural that he could not participate completely in this kind of party. One girl, the Mistress, takes a fancy to him but he quickly discards her. Then he is left alone and meets the Sleepwalker who seems quite ideal. This is his life, this is the dream come true. Of course it is not acceptable by this kind of society, which must reject the romantic, intricate jealousies of Mistress, Host, Poet and Sleepwalker. And for this the Poet has to die. . . . There is so short a time to build the character. In this brief ballet you must show the reality and formality and decadence of the society that can be broken only by new ideas, the ideals of the Poet." [8] *

Croce, with her usual pungency, took a plunge into the murky atmosphere: "This is not, like *La Valse*, an easy ballet to get into. It seems chilly and remote. The tone, apart from the melodramatic aura which invests the plot, is edgy and fitful, scraping along an emotional precipice, threatening always to disintegrate into unintentional comedy. But it never loses its balance and it never, even at the end, rewards an audience's curiosity with solid denial of its suspect nature. It just moves to another part of the precipice and hangs there with a frightened smile as the curtain falls.

"The emotion of the ballet comes in a series of nervous shocks, as deeply pleasurable as in a horror story. The ending— is there a finer one in all romantic ballet?—is high traumatic bliss. The pas de deux roles are unthinkably reversed. Now it is the Sleepwalker who claims the inert

---

* This was Bruhn's most congenial and challenging role in his brief career with the Company, although he performed with his accustomed impeccable style in such works as *Divertimento No. 15, Swan Lake, Nutcracker, Pas de Dix,* and *Symphony in C.* Balanchine, for one reason or another, did not find time to create interesting new parts for him, and the Company did not have enough of a premier danseur noble tradition for there to be many suitable roles already in the repertory. He remained only two seasons (winter 1959–60 and winter 1963–64).

body of the Poet, accepts it in her arms and carries it away forever.

"The ideas in *La Sonnambula* are perfectly clear derivations from the romantic ballet of the nineteenth century, but they are forced even beyond the neurotic extremism of *Giselle* and *La Sylphide*. The Poet's character as a hero who engages a divine force is not morally shaded. When he dies he is vindicated, but in a manner that anathematizes not only the explicitly anti-romantic society on the stage but all humanity as well. The ironclad arrogance of the gesture makes the real suffering we've witnessed seem like a personal secret accidentally disclosed. It keeps you at a distance, though you may find yourself in tears." [9]

PANAMERICA

DÉCOR, LIGHTING: David Hays

COSTUMES (except IV): Esteban Francés (IV: Karinska)

PREMIERE: 20 January 1960

I. *Serenata Concertante* (2nd, 3rd, 4th movements) (*Chile*)
Choreography: Gloria Contreras
Music: Juan Orrego Salas
Cast: Allegra Kent, Jonathan Watts, 8 women, 4 men
II. *Preludios Para Percusion* (*Colombia*)
Choreography: George Balanchine
Music: Luis Escobar
Cast: Patricia Wilde, Erik Bruhn
III. *Choros No. 7* (*Brazil*)
Choreography: Francisco Moncion
Music: Heitor Villa-Lobos
Cast: Violette Verdy, Roy Tobias, 4 couples
IV. *Sinfonia No. 5, for String Orchestra*
Choreography: Balanchine
Music: Carlos Chavez
Cast: Diana Adams, Nicholas Magallanes, Moncion, 6 couples
V. *Variaciones Concertantes* (*Argentina*)
Choreography: John Taras
Music: Alberto Ginastera
Cast: Verdy, Wilde, Edward Villella, 8 women
VI. *Ocho por Radio* (*Mexico*)
Choreography: Contreras
Music: Silvestre Revueltas
Cast: Jillana, Deni Lamont, Arthur Mitchell, Roland Vazquez, 5 women
VII. *Sinfonia No. 2, for String Orchestra* (2nd movement) (*Uruguay*)
Choreography: Jacques d'Amboise
Music: Hector Tosar
Cast: Verdy, Bruhn, ensemble of 7

VIII. *Danzas Sinfonicas* (*Cuba*)
Choreography: Balanchine
Music: Julian Orbon

Cast: Maria Tallchief, Conrad Ludlow, Mitchell, Villella, 20 women, 10 men

Panamerica, an evening-long collection of eight short pieces, "coordinated" by Chavez, was—how else to put it?—a great big flop. In fact, it would be hard to think of another such "major effort" (full company, costumes, exotic music) that brought forth such minor fruit, unless it were, coincidentally, another "Pan Am" ballet (*PAMTGG*), some eleven years later, a wildly dressed extravaganza that also sank almost immediately without a trace.

As Hering wrote, "Something atrophied between the plan and the visualization. That something was inspiration." [1] "Tiresome," "dreary," "a worthy experiment," and "a gracious international gesture" were some of the remarks inspired by this salute to Pan-American brotherhood. During the following season, the ballets were presented separately (renamed according to the nationality of their composers), without a much cheerier reception. Only Balanchine's *Colombia* and Taras's *Argentina* found favor. And *Uruguay*, d'Amboise's first choreography, was considered a nice try. *Argentina*, later called *Tender Night*, was the sole ballet to be performed for any length of time.

A few comments:
Colombia: "After a bad start—eccentric

without being very stirring—it built to a stunning coda, . . . but it labors the Latin angle, via loose hips, clenched fists, and a glower or two." [2]

Both Martin and Manchester mentioned its humor.

Brazil: "A stunning beginning, an attractive finale. In between, wispy, perhaps undecided." [3]

"I think we were perhaps parrots in a cage—there was a sort of palm-tree-and-coconut feeling going on."—Verdy

Sinfonia No. 5: "The music seemed endless. Balanchine fairly outdid his past impressive records [in intertwining] with some elaborate choreographic snarls." [4]

Argentina (later *Tender Night*): "A dramatic ballet, not specific in story but suggesting conflict and passion. The two girls, dressed identically, one hard and bright, the other gentle, seemed in many respects like the Odette-Odile arrangement, with the youth as the bewildered suitor and the ensemble of girls serving as a sort of participating chorus." [5]

"If the Marquise de Sévigné or Madame de Lafayette had rewritten a Lorca play according to her own temperament, the result might have been similar. In it were the Lorca-like themes of love overshadowed by jealousy and innocence ensnared by social censure. But the redolence of earth and the heaviness of fate were missing. Instead it was a French salon treatment of a Spanish theme. With a bit more authenticity of character it could have been a moving work, rather than a polished one." [6]

"I used a folk-dance theme that was not, for me, specifically Argentinian. It

Panamerica. **Danzas Sinfonicas** (*Cuba*). (*Photo Fred Fehl.*)

wasn't really a story ballet at all, but a series of variations, although Violette was rather romantic and lyric and Pat was strong, powerful, and aggressive, with Eddie somehow trying to get between them. It begins with a very simple viola theme, where a girl and boy meet. There was a romantic pas de deux. The music lent itself very well to variations. Ginastera was pleased."—Taras

"It was rather sweet, had a nice nostalgia about it. Somewhat undefined, but a nice flavor."—Verdy

Uruguay: "Crams too much in too little time, but d'Amboise does have a real idea and goes steadily about developing it. Truly macabre, and the series of unrelated horrors do have the logical illogicality of all nightmares." [7]

"Somehow," wrote Kastendieck, "the show disintegrated as it progressed." [8]

THEME AND VARIATIONS

CHOREOGRAPHY: George Balanchine

MUSIC: Peter Ilyitch Tchaikovsky (Theme and Variations from Suite No. 3 in G for orchestra, op. 55, 1884)

COSTUMES: Karinska (from *Symphony in C*)

LIGHTING: David Hays

PREMIERE: 5 February 1960 (first presented 27 September 1947 by Ballet Theatre, Richmond, Va.)

CAST: Violette Verdy, Edward Villella; 4 demi-solo couples; 8 women, 8 men
Male role also danced by Jonathan Watts

In an underdressed presentation, *Theme* was given perhaps a half-dozen performances and then disappeared. It would not be seen on the New York City Ballet stage for another ten years, when it was brought back as the last movement of *Suite No. 3.*

The 1960 production was not well received. What Martin referred to as the "formal brilliance, dashing elegance, lift, and sweep" [1] of the original were muted. It had seemed like such a good idea to

have Balanchine's own company dance one of his major works (Verdy recalls a great amount of preparation, during which Balanchine sped up the tempo and changed some of the accents). But "it was something of a letdown when the curtain rose on that over-familiar blue cyclorama and a company dressed in *Symphony in C* costumes. The original décor had revealed the intention of the ballet as a work of great elegance and courtliness culminating in the grandeur of that marvelous final polonaise. All this is lost in the bleakness of the current production. What was left was a series of enchainements, superbly arranged by a master choreographer but remaining fragmentary and isolated." [2]

Martin also faulted it stylistically: "Mild, a trifle gray, without individuality. The girls of the corps wave arms when torsos should be extended. Certainly the splendid Tchaikovsky colors have not been induced, nor has the noble vivacity of Balanchine's composition." [3]

It was further suggested that neither Verdy nor Villella had the maturity for the leading roles, excellent dancers though they were.

Of the superiority of the ballet itself there was no question. When it premiered originally, Chujoy had called it "the great master's greatest work to date." [4]

Terry had written, "Bears an aristocratic lineage, for it stems from the Russian imperial ballet of the later nineteenth century. But let it not be supposed that the choreographer has simply rejuvenated an old and revered balletic ancestor; [he] invigorates traditional movements by forming them into new sequences, by giving them fresh accents and muscular intensities, by extracting for dance coloring the hues of the music being employed, and by freely using movements of his own design. His use of interlacing patterns, of complex body weavings for groups is as much a part of the ballet's elegance and beauty as is the glittering processional which brings the work to a close in a fabulously beautiful and spectacular burst of imperial pomp." [5]

Theme was possibly the first Balanchine ballet that wholly pleased Martin, who had dismissed *Serenade* (1935), been irritated by what he considered the European chichi of *Apollo* (1937), and spoken of Balanchine's style as "meringue and whipped cream" (1940).* In 1947 he wrote, in a tone that still suggested peevishness:

"For once, he has resisted every temptation to treat the music as if it were an exercise in a Dalcroze class, matching semiquaver for semiquaver. Instead, he takes its over-all scheme of development and its broad phrasing as his background for composition, and achieves a succession of ravishing designs, transparent, ingenious, and unforced. He employs virtually every device for which he has been criticized in the past—distortions of classical alignments, intricate inventions, difficult adagio passages, the twining and intertwining of the corps de ballet under each other's arms—yet there is not one of them here that is extraneous or out of key. This is partly because they are used with moderation and partly also because they appear in every case to evolve with their own logic out of the phrases that precede them and to dissolve with similar logic into the phrases that follow. They are all part of a consistent texture instead of being gewgaws set in for bedizenment." [6]

He also reported that he could approach the ballet without "reservations, strains, or subcutaneous antagonisms."

For all its stylistic brilliance and the skilled dovetailing of one movement sequence into another, *Theme* can be looked at as one of Balanchine's most academic works, not for lack of inspiration or reliance on formula, but because so many of the steps are recognizably from the classroom. The ballerina's first dazzling variation is clearly built on pas de chat and pirouette. The man enters with an exciting series of jumps with ronds de jambe. In the adagio section, the ballerina, supported by women, extends her leg in several directions—an exercise every dancer performs daily but one thought to be for practice only. The man is given a really pedagogic dose of double air turns in both directions. And who but Balanchine would think of opening a ballet with a battement tendu, the most "unoriginal" and elementary exercise in the entire ballet lexicon? But in 1947, he actually did it twice—in two of his most inventive (and highly dissimilar) works, *Theme and Variations* and *Symphony in C.*

---

* Haggin observed that "Martin's writing about Balanchine's work for many years was that of someone with an unerring eye for greatness and an unrelenting hatred for it." (*Ballet Chronicle*, p. 11)

PAS DE DEUX

CHOREOGRAPHY: George Balanchine

MUSIC: Peter Ilyitch Tchaikovsky (from *Swan Lake*, 1876)

COSTUMES: Karinska

LIGHTING: Jack Owen Brown; later David Hays

PREMIERE: 29 March 1960

CAST: Violette Verdy, Conrad Ludlow

OTHER CASTS: Suzanne Farrell, Gelsey Kirkland, Allegra Kent, Melissa Hayden, Patricia McBride; Jacques D'Amboise, Jean-Pierre Bonnefous, Peter Martins, André Prokovsky, Helgi Tomasson, Edward Villella

This lovely, bright, small-scale pas de deux has remained in the repertory for many years and is frequently performed in concerts. Manchester called it "a little beauty, a kind of pastiche of a typical Bolshoi concert-program offering. It has all that airiness and sense of flight but done with Western taste and Balanchine's own marvels of intricate enchainements and unexpected lifts." [1] A particularly Bolshoi-like moment (one almost hesitates to make the comparison, for the tone of this work is far removed from *Spring Waters*) has the ballerina leaping across the stage headlong into a fish dive. The music, used in the original Moscow production of *Swan Lake* for the third act pas de deux (in the place now occupied by the Black Swan), was subsequently lost and not heard again until 1953 when it was rediscovered at the Bolshoi. It was, in fact, Tchaikovsky's second attempt at the pas de deux, the first having been rejected by the ballerina as too complex rhythmically.

Terry wrote: "Certainly one of Balanchine's most charming inventions. Although it places innumerable virtuosic demands upon the dancers, its quality does not echo the bright bravura, say, of the same choreographer's *Sylvia*. A wonderful floating lyricism characterizes many of its passages, especially the opening measures, and the entire work is invested with a delightful air of tenderness, romantic but not emotional. Verdy, a sparkling performer, was enchanting, bringing an easy flow of action to the

Pas de Deux. Edward Villella, Patricia McBride. *(Photo Fred Fehl.)*

adagio sections, along with a sweet innocence of manner, and touching the flashy areas of the work with her own French brand of elan." [2]

Martin: "Verdy is obviously the key to its charm. He has built it upon her beautiful phrase, and her capacity for lyrical gaiety. Certainly she has not let him down. She has a remarkable sense of design, and a natural gift for getting the point. What emerges, then, is dainty, tender, wonderfully young and exquisitely danced." [3]

Although obviously designed around the abilities of Verdy, the work was successfully danced by other ballerinas, including Hayden, who brought to it a more legato, flowing line; McBride, with her unforced, youthful ease; and Kirkland, who moved with a liquid daintiness.

THE FIGURE IN THE CARPET

Ballet in five scenes

CHOREOGRAPHY: George Balanchine

MUSIC: George Frederick Handel (*Royal Fireworks Music,* 1749, and *Water Music,* c.1717)

SCENARIO: George Lewis

COSTUMES, DÉCOR, LIGHTING: Esteban Francés

PREMIERE: 13 April 1960

CAST: SCENE I, THE SANDS OF THE DESERT, Violette Verdy, 18 women; SCENE II, THE WEAVING OF THE CARPET (*Pas d'action*), Verdy, 12 women; *Nomad Tribesmen,* Conrad Ludlow, 6 men; SCENE III, THE BUILDING OF THE PALACE, *Entrance of the Iranian Court: Prince and Princess of Persia,* Melissa Hayden, Jacques d'Amboise; *Their Courtiers,* 8 couples; *The Reception of the Foreign Ambassadors: France: The Prince and Princesses of Lorraine,* Susan Borree, Suki Schorer, Edward Villella; *Spain: The Duke and Duchess of Granada,* Judith Green, Francisco Moncion; *America: The Princess of the West Indies,* Francia Russell, 6 women; *China: The Duke and Duchess of L'an L'ing,* Patricia McBride, Nicholas Magallanes, 4 women; *Africa: The Oni of Ife and His Consort,* Mary Hinkson (Martha Graham Company), Arthur Mitchell; *Scotland: The Four Lairds of the Isles and Their Lady,* Diana Adams, 4 men; *Grand Pas de Deux,* Hayden, d'Amboise; SCENE IV, FINALE, THE GARDENS OF PARADISE; SCENE V, APOTHEOSIS, THE FOUNTAINS OF HEAVEN

OTHER CASTS: *Prince and Princess,* Allegra Kent, Jonathan Watts; *France,* Carol Sumner; *Spain,* Jillana; *Scotland,* Gloria Govrin

Figure in the Carpet had a fascinating genesis. Presented in honor of the Fourth International Congress of Iranian Art and Archeology, its title came from Henry James; its pretext was a parallel then recently drawn by the noted Islamic scholar Arthur Upham Pope between the construction of the carpets of Persia (the designs are conceived in layers), which reached its high point in the eighteenth century, and the contrapuntal music contemporary in the West, also composed in blocks, exemplified in the works of Handel. The libretto described the ballet as "a theatrical spectacle which has as its subject the history, construction, and philosophy of the Persian carpet, one of the greatest concepts in the history of world art. In form, it is a court ballet of the early eighteenth century, when Persian patterns first affected the West. The music was composed at the same moment when the greatest Persian carpets were being woven, and it echoes the same principles of interlacing counterpoint and harmony visually apparent in the arabesques of their intricate design."

The scenario devised to accommodate this thesis incorporated other values in the Persian universe, as the ballet progressed from desert aridity to eternal water; from bare earthly subsistence to immortality.

Fascinating, certainly, but excessively literary for an instinctual creator such as Balanchine (and, indeed, *who* could have translated such a program into dance?). As is characteristic of him, he "disposed of the problem by ignoring it. This left him free to allow everything that belongs to Persia to be contained in the scenery while he had a lot of fun devising a court ballet in eighteenth-century style with all the additions that his twentieth-century ingenuity could devise." [1]

The eighteenth-century-court idea presumably was inspired by the music, but here too historicity was (wisely) sacrificed. As Martin pointed out, "To dance so long a divertissement in the manner and the technique of the court ballet would make for incomparable boredom." [2] So Balanchine added Petipa. Not only that, but the long Scene I "had nothing to do with anything [Persia, French courts, historical costume]." It was "merely" a stunning ensemble section, contrapuntal in construction, with interweavings, a sequence of patterns in bourrée that covered the stage (windblown sands?), multiple pirouettes by the entire ensemble on different counts that framed continuous turns by Verdy, with timeless costumes like those from *Serenade*. As ever with Balanchine, the dancing came first.

So it was a mixed bag, with two quite different parts. ("The Sands" sections were quite separate from the court divertissements; Scene III, "The Building of the Palace," marked the break). Overall, it was a big, lavish ballet, to music, as Balanchine remarked, "you're lucky if you get to dance once in a lifetime," costumes (based on historical precedents) and exotic scenery, which culminated in a fountain spouting real water, undeniable beauty. But the format of the second part—a string of divertissements—did not allow for much variety in tone or pacing, and by the end of the evening, there was a certain sameness to the music. The variations, while clever, were sometimes cloying. One dancer compared it to a big meal—with too many rich courses to add up to a satisfying dinner. Martin observed, "Brilliant in detail but

The Figure in the Carpet. Top: **The Building of the Palace. Entrance of the Iranian Court.** (*Photo Martha Swope.*) *Bottom:* **The Gardens of Paradise. Jacques d'Amboise, Melissa Hayden (center).** (*Photo Fred Fehl.*)

not terribly interesting as a whole." [3]

Perhaps tellingly, when the Company attempted to revive the work just a few years later, after it had been rested briefly, no one could remember enough of the choreography to piece it together again (such are the methods still used to

"preserve" works of dance), and the ballet quietly slipped into oblivion.

Scenes I and II: The most sophisticated choreography was in these sections. Terry reported that they contained "some of the most beautiful dance invention we are likely to see in a long time. In the first episode, dancers in sand-colored dress move with swirling restlessness against an ever-moving, softly shimmering backdrop and side panels. And in the second, the dancers, carrying long, multi-colored ribbons [assisted by the Tribesmen], indicate the elemental patterns which will go into the carpet itself. These exquisite scenes are as lovely as anything I have ever seen in abstract dance." [4]

"[After their exit], suddenly the stage was empty. Against a greenish drop, a delicate stencil descended. It fell in layers—first a border, then symmetrical arabesques and birds, and finally a roseate center." [5]

From the libretto: "Layer upon layer, the underlying systems of foliation, as in the great Ardabil carpets, are revealed. First, the prime interlocking tendrils, then interlocking interlace, finally the great lozenge of the red sun blared through the complete design. . . . Patterns of existence displayed in calculated arrangements of meaningful symbols; cloud, mountain, wave, running dog, lion, phoenix, dove, peacock, palm, pool, dragon, set in growing systems of tendril borders, realize a pulsating composition, at once symmetrical but dynamic, which gives the optical illusion of constant movement in depth, color, and chromatic intensity. Perfection is symbolized by the Carpet's plan."

Verdy and twelve "sand creatures" returned, the girls with pink sprigs. Said she of her variations among the sands, "With Handel, the ballet had the absolutely gorgeous, noble intricacies and structure, and yet motion, that gave it identity. I had different entrances among the girls and then I remained alone for a solo which was one of the most beautiful he has ever done. Musically, it was just extraordinary. The material was perhaps not his most original, but the appropriateness of it was unbelievable."

Scene III: "The lights faded. The center of the vertical rug pattern glowed. An unfolding fence-like structure glided on from both sides, forming a courtyard. Behind it bloomed a formal Persian garden. Oriental courtiers filled the enclosure." [6]

From the libretto: "The model of earthly order. The Peacock Throne, a place for Kings. In the Palace Garden, the birds of the sky—which holds rain—nest in willows by man-made streams and pools. Coursing dogs, running hounds are also the first clouds racing across the heavens ahead of thunder. Vegetation, water, animals support the controlled

world of kingship. The signs on ceramic walls, woven in carpets, inlaid in gardens, are also written in the grand calligraphy of Kufic script: 'Oh Man, if there is indeed paradise on earth, it is here, it is here, it is here.' " Fancifully, it continues, the foreign ambassadors here assembled will receive as presents silk carpets which they will take back to their far-off homelands, thus "spreading not only the principles of dyeing, weaving, and design, but the symbols of vegetation, irrigation, and animal life which will dominate decorative art in Asia and the West."

A slow, gliding dance for the courtiers ensues, followed by divertissements "from the four corners of the earth."

France: "Villella, looking and leaping much as the legendary Vestris must have looked and leapt, dances superbly. The ladies are charming but quite overshadowed, as the women of those days must have been." [7] "Fine classical pas de trois." [8] Generally considered overlong and somewhat repetitious, however.

Spain: "A mock-pompous entry which has the most piquant suspicion of Spanish flavor." [9] "Wine velvet costumes trimmed with gold, orange, and saffron especially handsome." [10]

America: "Looked as though they had hopped straight out of the *Indes Galantes.*" [11]

China: "Endearing . . . splendid and witty." [12] This was McBride's first featured part, possibly a little too cute.

Africa: "Striking duet, exceptionally lively but very majestic." [13]

Scotland: "The sauciest variations on a Highland Fling ever devised." [14] The cleverest and most successful number, beautifully costumed.

Scenes IV and V: "The fencelike structure melted away to reveal the garden with its cypresses and soaring phoenixes. The Prince and Princess of Persia appeared in dazzling feather-trimmed white. [This pas de deux was considered long and anticlimactic.] As though influenced by the carpet designs, they performed an intricate terre-à-terre tracery and then took their places, along with the courtiers and guests, to face upstage and watch a fountain of real water send its jets gleaming up into the light. The Persian dream was fulfilled." [15]

From the libretto: "The Moslem paradise. Music-making angels and celestial dancers are stars in their courses. Poor wanderers from the desert wastes find their green home. The desert has flow-

ered. Great fountains gush forth for eternal reward."

VARIATIONS FROM "DON SEBASTIAN"
since fall 1961 called
DONIZETTI VARIATIONS

CHOREOGRAPHY: George Balanchine

MUSIC: Gaetano Donizetti (from *Don Sebastian,* 1843)

WOMEN'S COSTUMES: Karinska

MEN'S COSTUMES: Esteban Francés (from *Panamerica*)

DÉCOR, LIGHTING: David Hays

PREMIERE: 16 November 1960

CAST: Melissa Hayden, Jonathan Watts; 6 women, 3 men

OTHER CASTS: Violette Verdy, Patricia Wilde, Jacques d'Amboise, Edward Villella

REVIVAL (with some new choreography): 29 April 1971, New York State Theater

COSTUMES: Karinska

LIGHTING: Ronald Bates

CAST: Kay Mazzo, Villella; 6 women, 3 men

OTHER CASTS: Patricia McBride, Verdy, Helgi Tomasson, Robert Weiss

If the musical excerpts from Donizetti's opera do it justice, it is easy to understand why it is little known. Certainly, Balanchine understands. Not that he makes fun of it, but rather that he is meticulously fair to it, which can be more deadly in a nicer way. Stylistically, he has hit the nail on the head, as he so frequently does in such cases; and, again according to his custom, he has turned the situation into an excellent opportunity for composing fresh and brilliant bits, from whatever corn-

*Variations from "Don Sebastian." **Left:** **Helgi Tomasson, Patricia McBride.** (Photo Martha Swope.) **Right:** **Jonathan Watts, Melissa Hayden (center).** (Photo Fred Fehl.)*

field, for his dancers to get their teeth into." [1]

Said one dancer, "It's like an endless series of finales." Verdy mentioned circus horses, and, indeed, the character of the ballet could be compared to a perky little circus exhibition, a kind of prancing, show-off piece, with a nod to a traveling opera troupe. There are many small jumps, beats, precision footwork—and hidden technical difficulties. Flourish, jump, hop, smile—the style is easy-going, the accompaniment bouncy and lilting, but virtuoso work is required. Kisselgoff found it Balanchine at his most Bournon-villian.[2] Terry, who called it a "bubbling ballet," described some of the difficulties: "Marvelous inventions, all in the classical idiom, including, for the ballerina, a pir-ouette followed by a supported air-turn into plié on pointes, an extended series of single turns in air for the danseur, an aerial toss in which the ballerina is caught high in air by two cavaliers, and still other surprises. In a delicious tongue-in-cheek aside, there is a brief moment when the company strikes a dramatic pose and one girl wanders around to investigate, as if to say 'What happened to you?'" [3]

Hering: "The dancers engaged in a nimble harlequinade before a pink-and-yellow sea-drop decorated with cherubs. The variations poured forth in breathless succession, building to the pas de deux with its fascinating series of arabesques with the girl grasping her partner's hand and pulling back from it." [4]

The male variation was mostly low beats, and the ballerina had a section,

supported by three men, in which she picked her way about on pointe, with styl-ish shifts of the torso. Balanchine took ad-vantage of Hayden's steely foot work and sharp, thrusting leg motions, which she tempered with charm and dash.

Although the work may have seemed like a utility number, it has had a long life and a major revival, in which there were not only completely new costumes, but some new choreography as well. For the occasion, Barnes wrote, "It has come up smiling." [5]

Hayden describes some of the dif-ferences between the first and second versions: "In a way it's better now, be-cause the costumes are better. But it was much stronger, the colors were more vi-brant—it had more flair, a sort of Spanish air. It had character. The present version is more pastel. Prettier. The intention of the original was not to be lovely, it was supposed to be more bravura. Now there are no more surprises; it's no longer dan-gerous. A certain force is lost."

Says Verdy, "Now it's lighter in feeling, faster, more of a divertissement and less of a marathon."

The ballet was also seen in England, where it was considered as more than a mere bauble—but not too much more: "The choreography, like Donizetti's score, was precise, fluent, clear, admirable in its application of formulae, the obvious work of a master—working well below his most inspired level." [6]

MONUMENTUM PRO GESUALDO

CHOREOGRAPHY: George Balanchine

MUSIC: Igor Stravinsky (three madrigals by Gesualdo of Venosa, "recomposed for instruments," 1960)

DÉCOR, LIGHTING: David Hays

PREMIERE: 16 November 1960

CAST: Diana Adams, Conrad Ludlow, 6 couples

OTHER CASTS: Suzanne Farrell, Susan Hendl, Gelsey Kirkland, Kay Mazzo, Mimi Paul; Tracy Bennett, Arthur Mitchell, Earle Sieveling

Don Carlo Gesualdo, Italian prince, who was contemporary to Shakespeare, Caravaggio, and Monteverdi, was as in-famous during his lifetime for the murder of his wife, her lover, and her child as for his futuristic dissonances. In later years, his companion, one Count Fontanelli, was "likewise a Calabrian nobleman mad-rigalist and murderer of his wife's lover." Gesualdo's music, despite its radical chro-maticism, was popular in his own day, but was then virtually lost for almost 350 years.

As "recomposed" by Stravinsky, his madrigals are softer to the ear; in-struments mute his unexpected vocal harmonics. So too, in Balanchine's choreography, there is no hint of dissonant roughness, but rather, chaste simplicity. Walking is the key movement, clear-cut patterns the motif, and courtly demeanor the tone. In the most robust sequence, the ballerina is thrown three times into the upstretched arms of other partners, but even here it is the suspended image of her full arabesque in flight, rather than the force of her trajectory, that leaves the impression. In the last section, a long still diagonal, backlit in green, takes on an almost dramatic quality.

Most critics found the ballet, in its quiet way, arresting.

Biancolli: "One of Balanchine's happiest inspirations in formal and fluid patterns. Pacing and phrasing were of an austere purity. It is in such ballets that Balanchine best reveals his genius for making time and space his servants rather than his masters, for creating, you might say, movement without motion." [1]

Martin: "It is, indeed, sui generis; not exactly untheatrical but rather extratheatrical, and taken on its own terms, altogether enchanting. Brief as it is, it repays many seeings for the rich variety of its visual musicality." [2]

Barnes: "Just as Stravinsky complied with the music's Renaissance flavor in his adaptation, so Balanchine, while not actually quoting from old dances, has managed with the sketch of a flourish, the hint of a gesture, to convey an impression that, while completely modern, offers, if only in its formal poses, the recollections of a civilization long past." [3]

Herridge: "A quiet, melting, almost melancholy mood, more reflective than showy, more lyric than brilliant, and too short to build any distinct impression." [4]

England:
"The choreography is of a divine clarity and precision: sometimes breathtakingly simple; sometimes as simple in actual sequence as Gesualdo's rising sequence of notes, but as intricately assembled in polyphony as the score itself, with close canons, imitations, and rhythmic displacements." [5]

Germany:
"The madrigals bear an absolutely ceremonial character that supports the structure of the groups. They start, as nearly always with Balanchine, in greatest calm. Nothing looks fidgety. With assurance lines are drawn, with a light hand the so-

loists are disengaged and retained from the exiting groups. A circling through the moving orders is set in motion. Each one of the three pieces develops from a different initial position, but the result is the same: restrained admiration." [6]

LIEBESLIEDER WALZER

Ballet in two parts

CHOREOGRAPHY: George Balanchine

MUSIC: Johannes Brahms (*Liebeslieder*, op. 52, 1869, and *Neue Liebeslieder*, op. 65, 1874, waltzes for piano duet and voices)

COSTUMES: Karinska

DÉCOR, LIGHTING: David Hays

PREMIERE: 22 November 1960

SINGERS: Angeline Rasmussen, Mitzi Wilson, Frank Porretta, Herbert Beattie

PIANISTS: Louise Sherman, Robert Irving

CAST: Diana Adams and Bill Carter; Melissa Hayden and Jonathan Watts; Jillana and Conrad Ludlow; Violette Verdy and Nicholas Magallanes

OTHER CASTS: Karin von Aroldingen, Suzanne Farrell, Gloria Govrin, Susan Hendl, Sara Leland, Patricia McBride, Kay Mazzo, Mimi Paul; Anthony Blum, James de Bolt, Jean-Pierre Bonnefous, Richard Hoskinson, Peter Martins, Frank Ohman, Francis Sackett, Kent Stowell

Balanchine has said that the small-scale silvery delicacy of the Amalienburg in Munich came to mind when he was creating *Liebeslieder*. Brahms, in his two sets of waltzes, was working in the tradition of *Hausmusik*, supplying music for the now-vanished custom of home entertainment among amateur music lovers. The house represented here is probably not a palace, and the guests probably are not royalty, although the women are most elegant in their satin and diamonds and all are the products of impeccable breeding. Pianists and singers share the stage. Thus Part I. In the second half, when chandeliers have become a crown of stars and the ladies have replaced their ballroom slippers with toe shoes and their gleaming gowns

Monumentum. **Diana Adams.** (*Photo Fred Fehl.*)

with tulle, the setting is no longer a drawing room but some celestial place, and the ethereal visions—ballerinas, not women—have become creatures of fantasy.

What unfolds is an hour of dancing in waltz-time, with no plot (although more than a hint of human passions), no change of character, limited possibility of variety in the musical timbre—and ravishing dancing. ("The theatrical scheme is as sparkling as light on water and as endlessly unexpected." [1]) Critics, noting the difficulties of using such music, called the ballet "bold." (A representative comment appeared in the *Times* of London: "A ballet about the waltz that has its dancers, in Goethe's phrase, 'rolling about like spheres.' Of all Balanchine's ballets this is the most daring—skeletal ballroom, two pianists and four singers, together with eight dancers, dancing eternal waltz after eternal waltz." [2])

A few critics complained about the length, but for most, there is no awareness of a problem being surmounted. The dancing flows with inevitability.

Said Martin, "After an hour and five minutes of sheer waltzing, and by only four couples at that, one's major reaction was to wonder if perhaps Brahms had not still another opus hidden away somewhere." [3]

Kennedy: "For all its deliberate sameness, it is never monotonous and not a bit too long. How has he got away with it? I do not know." [4]

Terry described the ballet lovingly: "A gay yet strangely haunting work. In the first act, the four couples move in the style of the social dance. The girls wear heeled slippers and long, gently billowing gowns. But if this is basically simple ballroom waltzing, Balanchine has heightened it ever so subtly, relating the etiquette of the classical ballet to the deportment of the ballroom. Charmingly schooled coquetry, just the hint of an invitation to an amorous but highly refined chase, controlled ardor in becoming embraces, flashes of exuberance, and glimpses of dreams are all contained in these sequences of short, simple, but perfectly modeled dances. And then the dream itself takes command.

"In the second episode, the ballroom candles have been dimmed, the doors have been opened to the night, and the young couples have moved into a world of their own imaginings. The ladies rise on to pointe and, moving to another plane, become the elusive, desirable creatures of

Liebeslieder Walzer. **Part I.** (*Photo Fred Fehl.*)

men's dreams. The ballroom steps and the etiquette of the first scene are also heightened and find their ultimate forms in the sweep, the precision, the physical excitements and stylistic grace of the ballet. The change from one aspect of dance to another is perfectly achieved, for a delectable reality has given way to the ecstasy of the dream. And at the close, in dimness, as if the dancers returned politely but unwillingly from reverie, the stars fade, the lights go up and the ladies are once again in their formal attire.

"A ballet of uncommon beauty. Balanchine has also worked something of a miracle in sustaining and, indeed, developing interest in a storyless theme, patterns and forms which never once hurry toward a climax or rush to make an effect. Naturally, even in the simplest measures, his choreographic invention does not desert him, and the viewer finds himself sighing as contentedly over a delicate touching of hands as over swirling lifts and turns." [5]

Manchester wrote that Balanchine's variations on the waltz "reach into infinity. . . . There is all the prodigality of his invention here. A young choreographer could study it and learn almost everything he would ever need to know about the putting together of an enchainement." [6]

Wrote Martin, "Balanchine has created an endless wealth of variety. It touches shades of sentiment, flashes of emotional color, the most delicate nuances even of

drama, within the frame of the youthful romantic attachment. Nothing at all happens, of course—nothing but the constant revelation of beauty." [7]

Some of the dances in the first part are rather perky, some are sober, some thoughtful, and all are guided by social protocol. There is interaction among the participants.

"Sometimes the couples swiftly circle in unison. A girl [Hayden] progresses diagonally across the floor, with her partner gently nudging her shoulder from behind. Another girl [Verdy] shifts birdlike between two partners. Still another [Jillana] seems to turn intoxicatedly, all the time keeping contact with her partner's outstretched hand. There is flirtation, but it seems to be more in the quality of the movement than in any literal gesture or facial expression. Suddenly eighteen waltzes have gone by. The dancers speed away through the upstage doors." [8]

In Part II, "the ballroom of the imagination," the couples are more isolated, more intimate with each other. The vocabulary is more balletic, and the emotions run deeper. Verdy and Magallanes have a dramatic duet that brings gasps at its sudden configurations: the ballerina ends with a double turn, a quick swivel, and suddenly her head is on his shoulder, before they quickly exit. Haggin has written of the "dark estrangement" of their relationship In an extended, most lyrical group of dances, Adams picks her way across the stage on pointes, then falls backward, as if swooning, into her partner's arms. And Hayden, supported by Watts, glides low along the floor, then extends her leg from under her skirt as if unfolding an expressive hand. Croce: "I have never been able to experience the rise of the second curtain, on those girls now suddenly frozen on toepoint, without a tightening of the heart. The piano ripples in an upward scale, the pose breaks, and the action begins at twice the speed of anything up to that point. The toeshoes, the flying lifts, give everything extra momentum, and the gesture seems redoubled in size and sharpness. What's odd is that the new sweep and scale of movement don't bring a sense of liberation, they bring a sense of anxiety—maybe because the theatrical tension has been heightened. Something conversational in the tone of the ballet has been replaced by something incantatory and solemn, just as the furniture and candlelight have been replaced by wind and stars." [9]

"Gradually another shift takes place. Almost imperceptibly, the sharp little lights fade, and the candelabra glow again. The dancers disappear. The singers begin the last waltz, 'Now, ye Muses, silence! You have sought in vain to portray how joy and sorrow alternate in a lover's heart.' [Goethe] One by one, the couples, in their original attire, stroll in to sit or stand at the far side of the stage and face the singers. The music subsides. The dancers raise their gloved hands to applaud in an ending as exquisitely tasteful and as full of quiet wonder as the entire ballet." [10]

"For Balanchine—or rather for his admirers and critics—Liebeslieder is a stunning confirmation that the great so-called antiromantic of twentieth-century ballet could reveal the depths of human emotions as well as, if not better than, anyone else. For beneath its patina of plotless ballroom dances, it is a study of love and of discreet passions bubbling to the surface. It is this balance between public appearance and personal intimacy that is the formula for the ballet's success. Atmosphere and characterization from the dancers are essential to it." [11]

"Any dancer might yearn for the opportunity to look so beautiful and dance those steps which flow from one to the other with such felicity," wrote Manchester [12]; and, indeed, Liebeslieder has always been a favorite with performers. Says Hayden,

Liebeslieder Walzer. **Part II. Bill Carter, Diana Adams.** (*Photo Martha Swope.*)

"It was a fabulous experience. It seemed to mean something to him. First of all, the dancers found it very difficult to waltz—at one point Balanchine complained we were dancing polkas—and for characterizations to come out with each of the pieces. Here again, the quality of the movement and the pieces related to specific dancers. For instance, Diana Adams—he liked the stateliness of her, her maturity, and he put her with someone (Carter) who was young, blond, looked almost like a child on stage. And not a 'Balanchine' dancer. But perfect for Diana. If you look at the choreography, he's always running after her, running because she was flattered by his attentions. Her movements were so big and luscious. There was a rare moment when Balanchine used a concrete verbal image: during the second part, I have a sequence that is more or less walk, walk, swoop back, turn, then walk and walk. He said, 'You must walk as if you're going through smoke—you know, like a Kool.'"

Says Verdy, "It is so incredibly complete in whatever concerns the business of waltzes forever and the possibilities of relationships between men and women of a particular time in a particular situation. I think that the exploration, the confession, is total. But all this takes place in a time where people did not easily tell things—they were semi-confessing, semi-hiding. That gave all the half nuances, the half colors. Balanchine didn't talk about

these relationships, or the dramatic moments; he *danced* them. My own pas de deux are dreamy for me—romantic in style. When I have the soprano line, it is very legato, thin and light, but when I have bass, I feel another tone—sharper and stronger, maybe angry—resistant and stubborn. Economy and control are very important; a single wrong gesture could destroy the effect of representing the flow of the singing."

"You really work differently in the first half—the second part is much freer," says McBride. "But when you have a ballgown, you don't throw your legs up. You think of yourself as a lady . . . how nice it is to sit in those chairs. In the beginning I thought I'd never learn how to waltz. Now it's become natural. Balanchine's choreography is like that. It takes time to work into a role, but it's rare that you will not feel comfortable in his choreography."

Reaction in Europe—home of the waltz—was quite similar to that at home. Most critics praised Balanchine's supreme inventiveness, and a small number tempered this with the observation that forty minutes would have been better than an hour.

England:
"Plainly one of the subtlest, most delicate, and most beautiful ballets of our age; and I want to discover and see clearly what I just now feel and uncertainly perceive: how the free open dances of the second part spring from the more closed images of the first; and how the flow of waltzes can embrace, without strain or jarring transitions, the classical forms they do. On so many levels this is a bewitching ballet: in the movement; in the varied cadences which close each dance so beautifully. The second part seems to recapture afresh for the twentieth-century audience that breathtaking moment when a woman first rose on pointe, and the poetry of movement acquired a new and more eloquent vocabulary. It is a magical piece, and the close is a quiet miracle." [13]

Germany:
"The waltz has long been a stereotype, especially in Europe, not much given to variation and prone to sentimentality. Balanchine has done away with this, but maybe too definitely. For him the waltz

becomes a trauma, a mania. It is an important work, but the audience did not respond. Why not? Is it that they have gotten so used to audacity that they do not know how to respond to an 'old-fashioned' ballet, even one so obviously exceptional? They don't know what to think—is it outdated? Something new? *Liebeslieder* seems to be a much more American ballet than *Western Symphony,* for all its Wild West costumes. For *Western* comes directly from European academic dance, whereas the longing for 'good old Europe,' with its entertainments and society, as embodied in *Liebeslieder,* has long since faded here, but is still strong in America." [14]

JAZZ CONCERT

PREMIERE: 7 December 1960

This was half an evening's worth of ballets by four different choreographers, and like most works made up of parts artificially brought together (in this case, all the scores had something—but not much—to do with jazz), it had no profile as a whole. The choreographers appeared a bit hamstrung by having to work with preselected material, but the individual ballets were all modest successes. Bolender's and Taras's works lasted the longest; *Ebony Concerto* was revived for the Stravinsky Festival in 1972. Some five and a half years after *Ragtime,* Balanchine choreographed another ballet to the same music, also called *Ragtime.*

As Todd pointed out, all the scores were by Europeans and all were from other periods: "Obviously [they] were inspired by the syncopation inherent in real American jazz, but the basic beat and the results were a thin and arid derivation of the true essentials of our native-born Negro-inspired jazz. Because of this, perhaps, each of these scores sounds dated in a strange, unfashionable way." [1]

Ah, but that was the point, said Martin. In this "high-brow fun piece, three long-hair composers [were] writing under the influence of American jazz." [2]

CREATION OF THE WORLD

CHOREOGRAPHY: Todd Bolender

MUSIC: Darius Milhaud (*La Création du Monde,* 1923)

DÉCOR, LIGHTING: David Hays

CAST: *In the Beginning: Adam,* Conrad Ludlow; *Eve,* Patricia McBride; *Later On:* 10 women, 10 men; *Much Later: Peaches,* Janet Reed; *Sweep,* Edward Villella; *Snake,* Arthur Mitchell; *Bangles,* Lois Bewley; ensemble

OTHER CASTS: *Peaches,* Bewley, Jillana, Sara Leland; *Sweep,* Kent Stowell; *Bangles,* Ellen Shire

Bolender describes the story: "I based it on a Charlie Chaplin film, rather à la *Modern Times.* It was very simplistic: a little girl who's lost and the man with the heart of gold, both of the lower orders, so to speak. Janet was absolutely *perfect.* Lois was the essence of the twenties; I called her Bangles. There were a few Black Bottom movements, some jazzy things, and modified bumps and grinds. It starts with Adam and Eve. After a pas de deux, their guilt comes to the fore, they appear to cover themselves, and the ages pass before them. At the end, he hands her a raincoat. She slips into it, then, before disappearing, takes out a compact and powders her nose. A curtain lifts and you see a twenties cocktail party, then the young girl admonished by her

Jazz Concert. Creation of the World. **Lois Bewley (striped shirt), Arthur Mitchell, Janet Reed (in furs).** (*Photo Martha Swope.*)

parents, leaving home. She meets Sweep in the big city and they have a wonderful time until she gets tempted by Snake, who builds her up to being one of the smartest broads around. Meanwhile, Sweep gets involved with Bangles, but he keeps saying she's not the one he's looking for. Peaches acquires jewels. At that point the graph comes in, and all the people start to pray. The graph goes up, money starts falling, and everybody goes mad, but at the end, the graph explodes, and everybody weaves down with it. Peaches is stripped of her jewels, until she is completely nude, and then a guy runs in and gives her a raincoat. She starts to go home, and Sweep comes by, sweeping up bodies that are rolling along the floor. They meet, and they finish up together."

Terry called it "lively, funny, and occasionally satiric." [1] Martin, bearing in mind the well-known music, wrote: "Bolender has made an entertaining switch. When *Création* was first produced by Rolf de Maré and his Ballets Suédois, it was strongly under the influence of the current revival of interest in primitive African sculpture, and was fairly solemn. Bolender, with a nice sense of mischief, has shifted esthetics from Roger Fry to the Copacabana, and given us an ingenious and generally gay bit of tongue-in-cheek nightclubbery.

"[Although] he reminisces freely over the works of Balanchine and Robbins in the repertory, he manages at the same time to come up with some original bits of comedy, and he has used his people well. But for all the vivacious invention and performance, the total work is little more than a gag." [2]

Manchester urged balletomanes to hurry to see Villella's triple air turns; Reed was loved by everyone; and Bewley was pronounced hilarious.

RAGTIME (I)

CHOREOGRAPHY: George Balanchine

MUSIC: Igor Stravinsky (*Ragtime for Eleven Instruments,* 1918)

COSTUMES: Karinska

DÉCOR: Robert Drew (from *Blackface*)

LIGHTING: David Hays

Jazz Concert. Ragtime. **Diana Adams, Bill Carter.** *(Photo Fred Fehl.)*

CAST: Diana Adams, Bill Carter

This brief work inspired brevity as well in the reviewers, most of whom thought it "a trifle," or something similar. Manchester called it "a few minutes of dancing, which is almost indistinguishable from that in *Western Symphony.*" [1] Others also mentioned Balanchine's borrowing from himself. Only Martin was enthusiastic (in three sentences).

Some years later, Barnes reviewed Balanchine's second dance to this music, making the point that the Stravinsky score is "nothing like a piece of jazz, nor middlebrow showbiz music. Rather it is an autobiographical statement about the jazz-tinctured pop-songs that were rapidly entering the common consciousness just before and during the Great War."

In response, he received a provocative description of the original from a reader, Robert Sealy, who surfaced many years later as a critic for *Ballet Review:* "Carter and Adams in some wreck of a showboat set looked like two elegant, slightly surprised European cabaret 'artistes' dealing gamely with some half-understood craze in the Geneva or the Prague of the time. It was rather cracked and dusty and smeared and sad. It was very nice." [2]

LES BICHES

CHOREOGRAPHY: Francisco Moncion

MUSIC: Francis Poulenc (from *Les Biches,* 1923)

COSTUMES: Ruth Sobotka

DÉCOR, LIGHTING: David Hays

CAST: *Rondeau:* 6 women, 4 men; *Adagietto:* Sara Leland; *Rag Mazurka:* 3 couples, 2 women, 1 man; *Andantino:* Leland, Anthony Blum; *Finale:* ensemble

Says Moncion: "I was originally going to use only the three-minute jazz section of the score, the Rag Mazurka, but the music was so nice that I decided on something fuller. I followed the theme of the original *Les Biches*—a house party, but with little complications. It was essentially a boy-meets-girl story, but I had one more girl than boy, to give myself a problem, and two ladies end up together."

Hering summarized: "It began with a tepid satire on ballroom mores of the twenties. Fending off the competition was a true innocent—fragile, unaspiring. She stood apart and was eventually left alone for a solo of reverie and 'I don't care.' Predictable ending: Nice young man got nice girl. But before this happened, there was a Rag Mazurka with cleanly designed horizontal patterns back and forth across the stage." [1]

Leland, whose first solo part this was, was very well received, as was Blum.

EBONY CONCERTO

CHOREOGRAPHY: John Taras

MUSIC: Igor Stravinsky (*Ebony Concerto,* 1946, for clarinet and jazz band, dedicated to Woody Herman)

DÉCOR, LIGHTING: David Hays

CAST: Patricia McBride, Arthur Mitchell; 4 women, 3 men

OTHER CASTS: Sara Leland, John Clifford

Allegro moderato

Andante
Vivo

The music was described as "a jazz equivalent of a concerto grosso, with a blues slow movement, [in which] the melody of the solo trombone is followed and varied by the solo clarinet." [1]

Manchester called the ballet "slick in the best traditions of the Broadway musical. The first movement, all in silhouette, is very effective. The slow movement is tender and has great charm." [2] Hering mentioned "a staccato finale with the dancers all joining hands to form a grapevine and then falling into a heap." [3] (A moment in the final configuration was choreographed by Balanchine.) Martin was lukewarm; Barnes thought it "familiar, swift, and efficient." [4]

The style was basically that of jazz dancing, in which only Mitchell was trained. Taras, who said he was fascinated by working with a Stravinsky score, found that the dancers were struggling with the movement quality. At the last minute he had the idea to put the first movement in silhouette because "I couldn't stand to see the suffering! It helped immensely."

MODERN JAZZ: VARIANTS

CHOREOGRAPHY: George Balanchine

MUSIC: Gunther Schuller (for orchestra and the Modern Jazz Quartet, commissioned by the New York City Ballet, 1960)

LIGHTING: David Hays

MODERN JAZZ QUARTET: John Lewis (piano), Percy Heath (bass), Milt Jackson (vibraharp), Connie Kay (drums)

CAST: *Introduction* (orchestra): Diana Adams, Melissa Hayden, John Jones (guest artist), Arthur Mitchell; 6 women, 6 men; *Variant 1* (piano): Adams, Jones; *Variant 2* (bass): Adams, 6 men; *Variant 3* (vibraharp): Hayden, Mitchell; *Variant 4* (drums): Hayden; *Variant 5* (quartet): Adams, Hayden, Jones, Mitchell; *Finale*: entire cast

In *Variants*, Balanchine was commended for his continuing interest in experimentation but criticized for having only superficially captured the jazz spirit in his choreography. "[His] ideas go no further than swiveling hips, turning his dancers' toes in instead of out, or up in-

stead of down, and shrugging shoulders and jerking around in general," Manchester wrote. [1] According to Watt, "He borrows his jazz allusions principally from the Lindy." [2] The Harlem strut was mentioned as another source.

In Martin's opinion, the work wasn't very decisive: "With his insatiable curiosity, he could not be expected to leave unexplored the current trend of 'art' jazz. Perhaps in this specific adventure, he has discovered a new direction in which to proceed for evocative theatrical communication, but he has not made clear just what that direction may be. Probably for the first time in his life, he has come up with movement that seems gratuitous." [3]

For Haggin, however, the ballet was "a series of superb pieces in which [Balanchine] combined movements of ballet and movements derived from Negro jazz dancing"; he mentioned "intricate acrobatic and erotic duos; a solo for Jones, with background movements of a group of girls, that worked up from a slow, sinuous beginning to larger, more animated movements and subsided into a slow, sinuous conclusion; a leisurely solo for Adams, with background movements of a line of boys, in which she did more of what she had done so effectively in *Ragtime*; a solo for Hayden whose faster acro-

Modern Jazz: Variants. **Diana Adams.** (*Photo Martha Swope.*)

batic intricacies also were something special." [4]

The music was not exactly what one might have anticipated. Written in Third Stream style (meaning that it combined elements of jazz and of classical music—a concept that never got much beyond Schuller and his adherents), it contained passages for symphonic orchestra and was not permeated by an incisive jazz beat. Parts, in fact, were very, very quiet. The orchestral sections were said to owe something to the sparest Webern. The Modern Jazz Quartet appeared on the stage (with pit orchestra), and, unexpectedly, it was rarely used as a quartet, but mainly as four soloists.

Highlights were considered to be Hayden's solo to the drums, and to a lesser extent, the finale. Terry also admired the ending: "A honey, with the two balleri-nas sagging against each other as if they had had a ball with their partners and were just catching their breath before the next round." [5]

Hayden describes her solo: "Fantastic! We had counts, but the musicians improvised. The sounds weren't always the same, but the underlying timing was there. The solo was tremendous. I entered with a rond de jambe, then a little glide, a very subtle entrance, and then I had very quick twisty steps, then piqué on pointe and then on my heel, lots of extensions with relevé, and fouettés to finish. Very difficult. Quite a climax."

"I work like a dentist," said Balanchine, as he drilled away at this ballet for eight hours at a stretch.

Denby described a rehearsal: "The girl now stood facing center stage, and in a few steps she led the boy there; now they both stood center, facing front; they let go of each other's hand, and began to a 5/8 count a stylized Lindy kick figure, in counter-rhythm to each other, just as the music burst into a 5/4 bar of jitterbug derivation. . . . [Now] everybody's concentration seemed to double. Balanchine invented one novel figure after another. They began and ended within what seemed to be a bar or two. The figures kept the dancers within a hand's reach of each other, and now more, now less, kept the flavor of a Lindy-type couple dance. Very rapid, unexpectedly complex, quite confined, and figures, sharply contrasted, kept changing direction. But in sequence the momentum carried through. When the entire ballet was finished, this turned

out to be a general characteristic it had."

And performance: "The dance fans agreed about the virtuosity, but they found the twelve-tone 'Third Stream' angle more strain than fun. In addition, the piece has been announced as 'New Jazz,' and it wasn't contemporary jazz in its dancing. They objected to the thirties-type jive steps, to the show-biz-type gesture, to the sour night-club look of the staging. As for the dancing, the partners couldn't let each other alone for a minute, the dances couldn't leave out a beat, nobody could dance except on top of the beat. Current jazz separates partners, omits beats; lets the beat pull away, anticipates it, and that elasticity of attack characterizes the gesture, and varies it.

"*Variants* keeps reminding one of conventional Broadway—that sort of jazz plus modern plus ballet. The numbers suggest corny types of stage jazz—the hot number, the ritual-magic one, the snake-hips, the arty, the pert one; the long finale quotes from the show, and ends with a decorative modernistic collapse for the entire cast, capped by a Brigitte Bardot 'beat' pose for the two leading ladies. The dancers suggest that hard-shell type of dance very handsomely. But the rhythm they dance to isn't show-dance rhythm, it isn't quite jazz either. One recognizes jazz-type steps, but one doesn't feel at home." [6]

"In any case, we don't do jazz here; we do ballet, and we try to make it as interesting as possible."—Balanchine

ELECTRONICS

CHOREOGRAPHY: George Balanchine

Electronic tape by Remi Gassmann in collaboration with Oskar Sala

DÉCOR: David Hays

PREMIERE: 22 March 1961

CAST: Diana Adams, Violette Verdy, Jacques d'Amboise, Edward Villella
Also danced by Conrad Ludlow

Electronics was another instance (after *Variants*) of Balanchine's pursuing a topical development in music. Watt described Gassmann's and Sala's score as "a twenty-minute modernistic suite in various tempos, made up of organlike sounds produced by a complex gadget called a Studio Trautonium. The canned sounds are sepulchral, moaning, jingling, piercing, blurry." [1]

Electronics. **Diana Adams.** *(Photo Fred Fehl.)*

The work's reception varied greatly. Some reviews were flatly negative. "Pretty tame," wrote Biancolli, "except the final fade-out in which Adams and d'Amboise went rolling all over the set locked in each other's arms." [2] "The whole idea was one of Balanchine's mistakes." [3] For Denby, usually one of Balanchine's most sympathetic viewers, it was "not a ballet to be proud of. It puts on a highbrow act but what it delivers is middlebrow Radio City corn. . . . It takes place in a cellophane cavern of ice. There are some people in long white underwear with cute horns who are a bit squirmy. Creatures in black underwear, almost invisible, come in; they want to do something to the white ones, but can't think of much, and it's too dark to see, anyway; so everybody leaves. Some cellophane columns jerk around, semi-tumescent. At the end, the chief white-underwear couple make a very odd ball of themselves and roll around awhile." [4]

Watt said it "would make a wonderful World's Fair Industrial Exhibit." Martin, however, was enthusiastic, feeling that Balanchine had found some sort of kinetic equivalent to the music ("definitely a work of art and not just a mechanical gimmick" [5]).

Terry also liked it: "Ethel Merman has been referred to as an 'ear-splitting' delight and the same could be said of *Electronics*. This coldly glittering piece really does play havoc with the eardrums, but this is due to the loudness of its reproduction, for the score is quite musical and not too far out. The ballet, which somehow manages to incorporate both classical Olympian figures, such as Zeus and Hermes, and actions suggestive of science fiction, also combines traditional ballet steps with passing grotesqueries. With its glaring setting and costumes—white, silver, gold, crystal, and a shocking introduction of black—*Electronics* is a thoroughly entertaining piece of stagecraft and inventive action." [6]

Whatever its merits or lack of them, the ballet remained only briefly in the repertory.

Verdy talks about the problems of dancing without a conductor: "We were being bombarded by those sounds that didn't have the usual shape—it was formless. And there was no communication with anybody about it, and that left the dancers often lost and in a sense unsatisfied, because we lost focus about our situation—we didn't know why we were doing what we were doing. Naturally, we had a compulsion to present our bodies in the best way, but without knowing quite why. Actually in that ballet I was never sure whether Balanchine was or was not being serious. (Sometimes I think he feels the audience won't understand what he's doing anyway, so why shouldn't he try pulling people's legs a little?) It was, in fact, a completely 'legal' attempt at the totally so-called abstract science fiction, an otherworldly type of situation in which dancers would be creatures. We wore plastic (which was absolutely à propos for this type of stuff) that used to glue itself in our nose, mouth, and makeup, and we wound up doing all kinds of strange stretches and things. The ballet was like two different tableaux in slightly different moods. One might have been Elysium and the other Hades. My part was rather aggressive because Eddie and I were dancing together, and Balanchine always caught that particular feeling of competition and stamina that exists as a relationship between us on stage."

VALSES ET VARIATIONS
since September 1963 called
RAYMONDA VARIATIONS

CHOREOGRAPHY: George Balanchine

MUSIC: Alexander Glazounov (from *Raymonda*, 1898)

COSTUMES: Karinska

DÉCOR: Horace Armistead (from *Lilac Garden*)

LIGHTING: David Hays

PREMIERE: 7 December 1961

CAST: Patricia Wilde, Jacques d'Amboise; Victoria Simon, Suki Schorer, Gloria Govrin, Carol Sumner, Patricia Neary; 7 women

OTHER CASTS: Suzanne Farrell, Melissa Hayden, Kay Mazzo, Patricia McBride, Violette Verdy; Jean-Pierre Bonnefous, Conrad Ludlow, Peter Martins, André Prokovsky, Peter Schaufuss, Helgi Tomasson, Edward Villella, Jonathan Watts

Valses et Variations. **Patricia Wilde.** (*Photo Fred Fehl.*)

This ballet provided a pretty (pink and blue) frame for some meaty dancing. Frankly a display piece, in form it was a series of solo dances, with a pas de deux and opening and closing ensembles. The music—tuneful, dancy, not in the least profound (with drum rolls here and there at moments of climax and touches of harp and triangle), was the perfect background—or rather, one could say once again that Balanchine had suited his choreographic material perfectly to the music at hand. In so doing, he produced a piece of entertainment, with just enough panache to keep the "jeunes filles" on stage from cloying.

Barnes described this aspect of it best: "With its sickly setting, its pink candy-floss costumes, and its sweetly sweet music, it would win few nominations as Balanchine's best ballet (many of his works have a finer intellectual content, a greater emotional charge, or even a more refined esthetic conception)—yet it is certainly one of those ballets that best show precisely what ballet is about. It is nothing but dancing, but dancing of such indescribable happiness, of such neat aptness, of such simple deftness." [1]

Martin called it "an adorable confection, concocted of marzipan, diamonds, youth, and nostalgia." [2] He was referring in part to the ballet's historical connections; it transmitted some steps probably never seen before outside Russia (or outside the Kirov Theater) and harked back, in style as well as substance, to parts of the three-act Petipa *Raymonda* of 1898, for which the music was written. This milieu is part of Balanchine's heritage.

Manchester described some of the steps: "There is a beautiful variation of the fish dive: Wilde pirouettes, then falls forward, her legs stretched and feet in a tight fifth position, as d'Amboise supports her with his arm. In the variations Balanchine has some fun with one of those problems he loves to set himself. He seems to be exploring the possibilities in performing steps on full pointe which would normally be only partially on pointe. All the girls come in and hop blithely from pointe to pointe, or on one pointe only." [3] She did not happen to mention the mini-fouetté competition between two girls.

The ballerina has two solos, one "lyrical and brilliant at the same time—sustained in feeling but with beats (entrechat-six). The second one has very fast pas de chat and double pirouettes [in some versions, a line of beats]. Because of the steps and the flow of the music, they're both very, very nice to dance," says McBride.

England:

"I would find it hard to disapprove of any ballet that brings the delights of Gla-

zounov's music back into the theater, and when it is Balanchine who uses what the program note calls the 'treasure chest of music titled *Raymonda*,' pleasure is unalloyed. The master at his most ingratiating . . . impeccable classical style. It is almost as if Balanchine were presenting us with the last-act divertissement from some lost St. Petersburg masterpiece, so perfectly is his choreography in harmony with the music. But then one suddenly realizes that he is treating the score with a freedom and a sublety that were unthinkable fifty years ago." [4]

Germany:

"A series of friendly variations and a sugary finale. A small, but effective ballet, a good one to start off the evening, and soon over. Ballet sweets from Balanchine's inexhaustible candy box." [5]

Russia:

"If we brush aside a somewhat overly free treatment of the score of Glazounov's *Raymonda*, we can say that Balanchine staged the waltz, pas de deux, and eight variations with great taste. The festive orchestration of *Raymonda* and its choreography, and the beautiful costumes done in markedly traditional style, with a smile of gentle irony, all produce a radiant impression." [6]

Valses et Variations. Ensemble. (*Photo Martha Swope.*)

A MIDSUMMER NIGHT'S DREAM

Ballet in two acts and six scenes

CHOREOGRAPHY: George Balanchine

MUSIC: Felix Mendelssohn (in order played: Overture and Incidental Music to *A Midsummer Night's Dream*, opp. 21 and 61 [1826, 1842]; Overtures to *Athalie*, op. 74 [1845], *The Fair Melusine*, op. 32 [1833], *The First Walpurgis Night*, op. 60; Symphony No. 9 for strings; Overture to *Son and Stranger*, op. 89 [1829])

COSTUMES: Karinska

DÉCOR, LIGHTING: David Hays, assisted by Peter Harvey

PREMIERE: 17 January 1962

SINGERS: Veronica Tyler (soprano), Marija Kova (mezzo-soprano), 4 women

CAST (in order of appearance): ACT I: *Butterflies,* Suki Schorer, 4 women, 8 children; *Puck,* Arthur Mitchell; *Helena, in love with Demetrius,* Jillana; *Oberon, King of the Fairies,* Edward Villella; *Oberon's Pages; Titania, Queen of the Fairies,* Melissa Hayden; *Titania's Cavalier,* Conrad Ludlow; *Titania's Page; Bottom, a Weaver,* Roland Vazquez; *Bottom's Companions,* 6 men; *Theseus, Duke of Athens,* Francisco Moncion; *Courtiers to Theseus; Hermia, in love with Lysander,* Patricia McBride; *Lysander, beloved of Hermia,* Nicholas Magallanes; *Demetrius, Suitor to Hermia,* Bill Carter; *Titania's Retinue,* 12 women; *Oberon's Kingdom: Butterflies and Fairies,* 13 children; *Hippolyta, Queen of the Amazons,* Gloria Govrin; *Hippolyta's Hounds,* 6 women; ACT II: *Courtiers,* 18 women, 8 men; *Divertissement:* Violette Verdy, Ludlow, 6 couples

OTHER CASTS: *Butterfly,* Elise Flagg, Gelsey Kirkland, Karen Morell, Margaret Wood; *Puck,* John Clifford, Jean-Pierre Frohlich, Deni Lamont, Robert Rodham; *Helena,* Karin von Aroldingen, Penelope Gates, Mimi Paul; *Oberon,* Clifford, Helgi Tomasson, Robert Weiss; *Titania,* von Aroldingen, Suzanne Farrell, Jillana, Kay Mazzo, McBride; *Cavalier,* Anthony Blum, Paul Mejia; *Bottom,* Richard Rapp, Bart Cook; *Hermia,* Susan Hendl, Sara Leland; *Lysander,* Frank Ohman; *Demetrius,* Robert Maiorano, Kent Stowell, Vazquez; *Hippolyta,* Marnee Morris, Colleen Neary, Patricia Neary; *Divertissement;* Hayden, Allegra Kent, McBride, Patricia Wilde;

Jacques d'Amboise, Jean-Pierre Bonnefous, Peter Martins, Stowell, Tomasson

ACT I: A Forest near Athens, on Midsummer Eve
ACT II: At the court of Theseus in Athens: The wedding ceremony of Helena and Demetrius, Hermia and Lysander, and Hippolyta and Theseus

For the first original full-length ballet in America, Balanchine seemed to embrace all those elements he has so often scorned as extrinsic to the best ballet: lavish costumes and scenery, a complicated plot, passages of mime, and majestic walking about. (A glance at his total oeuvre would suggest that he has nothing against any of these, although his most "avant-garde" works do not include them.) The very familiar Mendelssohn music, too, might be considered the lush opposite of the spare dissonances he supposedly loves best.

In fact, however, according to Balanchine, it was as usual his interest in just that music that was the genesis of the ballet. Realizing that the *Midsummer* music alone would not be long enough for his purposes, he spent more than twenty years searching for suitable additions. Much of the extra music he eventually used was obscure—to say the least—including the string symphony to which the second-act divertissement is set, written when Mendelssohn was fourteen. As for familiarity with Shakespeare, Balanchine, despite his foreign birth, had a jump on most of the audience: as a boy he performed as a bug in a St. Petersburg production of the play, with Mendelssohn's music, and claims, "I still know the play better in Russian than a lot of people know it in English." Although he sticks close to the complex plot, he says at once that the work, in basic atmosphere and flow, owes more to Mendelssohn than to Shakespeare. "It is really impossible to dance Shakespeare," he says. "He is a poet. The play in this case does not make a ballet, but the music does. It is *musique dansante.*" [1]

Nevertheless, the first of the two acts follows Shakespeare with amazing fidelity. The Pyramus and Thisbe episode is omitted, and Bottom and his friends have become only minor characters, but the mix-up of the two couples in the forest, the fairy kingdom, the changeling boy, Puck girdling the earth, Titania's bower, "ye spotted snakes," Moth and Mustard-

A Midsummer Night's Dream. Act II, Divertissement. Jacques d'Amboise, Allegra Kent. (*Photo Fred Fehl.*)

seed, Theseus and Hippolyta—all are present. The entire story is told in the first act, by far the most successful part of the ballet. The second act, the wedding celebration, is pure dance.

"Act I [is] the jewel. Here, the great dance master keeps the four lovers, star-crossed and criss-crossed, skimming across the forest scenes in search of solutions to their seemingly insoluble problems while at the same time never losing focus on the fierce fairy fight involving Titania and Oberon. Woven into the bright tapestry of narrative action are the zestful antics of Puck, who moves as if he were Mercury subjected to a hotfoot, and the retinues of adorable butterflies and fairies. It's dreamland, right down to the crimson flower which makes people fall in love, or to Titania's pink, shell-like bower, or to the soft mist which blankets the stage and caresses sleeping lovers." [2]

"To finish off the story; Hippolyta goes hunting at midnight (an odd procedure even for a Queen of the Amazons, but no odder than her hounds, who have horses' tails). A steam screen, through which the lovers rush in and out, allows Puck to unscramble them and pair them off correctly, and finally Theseus enters looking for Hippolyta. Bottom is sent packing, and Titania and Oberon are reconciled." [3]

As for mood, "In his choreography for the distraught lovers, Balanchine has combined romantic action with more than a hint of satire, and the result is delicious. He has done the same for Titania in her magic-induced affair with Bottom in his donkey's head. He has given to Oberon actions which are brilliant indeed and acting passages which clearly define the character of a king who is bent on teaching his wife a lesson, and to Titania, sequences that are at all times exquisite and, with Bottom, delightfully foolish." [4]

Other details: "Certainly one of the wittiest tricks Balanchine employs to move the narrative along is his device of invisible characters from the fairy kingdom. We see Puck, Oberon, and Titania, but the mortals do not, and this enables Puck, for instance, to provide us with several useful asides. Helena, of course, when she plucks a fruit from Puck's hand, thinks he is a tree. We know better." [5]

Puck also has an invisible hand in the swordplay to which Demetrius and Lysander finally resort as they battle for Helena's favor, while the stage becomes clouded with magic fog.

Martin praised the clarity of the plot development, listing his favorite touches: "the opening, for example, with the tiny fairies leading into the action; or the lovely first entrance of the heartbroken Helena, or the scene in which Puck, about to steal the changeling boy from Titania, is beaten away with switches by her handmaidens; or the winning solo by Hermia; or the stunning passage of Hippolyta and her hounds at the hunt; or the mist-enveloped scene in which all the plots are combined and resolved." [6]

Other outstanding moments were the lyrical pas de deux for Titania and her Cavalier; a virtuoso solo (full of brisés volés, among other fast jumps and beats) for Oberon assisted by fairy children and butterflies (a dance Clifford would later refer to as the most difficult in his repertory); and the entire concept of the quicksilver Puck, which was pronounced "a masterstroke" ("We knew it all the time," wrote Hering; "Balanchine is really Puck." [7]). Mitchell, his body glistening with sparkle dust, every step and movement underlining his fleetness and agility, had the role of his career. Barnes saw in Puck, in addition to the "grinning, determined, forgetful" imp, some of the "bluff humanity" of Bottom, "the common man who sees a vision of eternity." [8]

Manchester wrote of Hermia's "lost" solo, "As she drifts distractedly about the stage, blown by her love and fears, Mc-

A Midsummer Night's Dream. Top: Act I. Balanchine as Oberon. Edward Villella (left), Suzanne Farrell, Conrad Ludlow. (*Photo Martha Swope.*) *Above left:* Act I. Oberon's Kingdom. Suki Schorer, Edward Villella. (*Photo Fred Fehl.*) *Below left:* Act I. Lysander, Puck, Demetrius. Nicholas Magallanes, Arthur Mitchell, Bill Carter. (*Photo Fred Fehl.*) *Above:* Act I. Balanchine as Titania, Roland Vasquez (Bottom), Melissa Hayden. (*Photo Fred Fehl.*)

Bride makes this one of the high spots of the evening." [9] Another dancer saw Hermia in the solo as though encased in spider webs, trying to find her way out of them.

Villella as Oberon was considered outstanding; for some, he dominated. "Great leaps with landings soft as snowflakes, and brilliant turns, superbly controlled to each immaculate completion. He is challenging the Russian male dancers on their own terms and he does not come off second best." [10] (Incidentally, the choice of the small Villella fit in with Balanchine's conception of the character, which was based on a German source in which Oberon is an elf and Titania very tall. All subsequent Oberons have been small men.)

Act II, all dance, was rated as a letdown: "Entirely redundant, and, moreover, in a rococo style which is at odds with the Second-Empire-ish first act. It is dragged out to interminable length by courtiers walking about waving garlands, and onslaughts of the corps de ballet." [11]

An exception was the crystalline pas de deux and divertissement, which Martin called "Quite the best bit of the evening. It is shapely, rich in invention, and costumed in matchless elegance and beauty." [12] He felt it was rather lost amid the "ceremonial mass designs" that made up the rest of the act. Verdy calls it "among the most heartbreakingly beautiful pas de deux he has ever done, full of things that were intended for a tall partner delicately to collect a smaller girl."

Act II begins with the Wedding March, and for the end: "At the finale the fairies' forest closes in once more, Puck enters with his broom to sweep the dust behind the door [exiting skyward on wires], and we are left with a sweet reminder of the charms of fantasy that have gone before." [13]

Midsummer did not please any of the reviewers completely. Martin started with the music: "Even if he were twice as gifted, Balanchine could not find in this essentially Biedermeier music anything to evoke the fresh, crisp woodland fragrance of Shakespeare's faërie." [14] Virtually everyone complained about the gaudy décor. Many of the costumes—and all of the wigs—came in for criticism. And most of the reviews mentioned "lulls," "boring spots," and the like.

The ballet has remained in the repertory since its premiere, and it has undergone quite a few changes: the Butterfly is less busy, Oberon's solo is a little less demanding, the divertissement has been shortened (excisions include the men's fugue and final lickety-split coda, plus some solo steps for the corps) and recostumed. In 1966 a film of the entire work was made.

According to the dancers, one of the most rewarding aspects of participating in the ballet was watching Balanchine in rehearsal, acting and dancing all the parts.

BUGAKU

CHOREOGRAPHY: George Balanchine

MUSIC: Toshiro Mayuzumi (1962; commissioned by the New York City Ballet)

COSTUMES: Karinska

DÉCOR, LIGHTING: David Hays

PREMIERE: 20 March 1963

CAST: Allegra Kent, Edward Villella; 4 couples

OTHER CASTS: Suzanne Farrell, Kay Mazzo, Patricia McBride, Mimi Paul; Jean-Pierre Bonnefous, Anthony Blum, John Clifford, Arthur Mitchell

The numerous Japanese envoys to China in the seventh century returned with, among other things, *Bugaku* (literally, dance-music). . . . The *Bugaku* orchestra is composed of wind and percussion instruments exclusively. It is felt that strings and voices are too subtle in their melodies and waverings and would hamper the precision of the dancers' movements. The *Bugaku* orchestra comprises around twenty musicians. The music is harmonic and contrapuntal. More than 500 years before the West had learned to pit two melodies against each other, *Bugaku* music was weaving together two and more strands of musical lines." [1]

Inspired by a visit of the Japanese Gagaku musicians and dancers, an Imperial performing group with a 1000-year history, Balanchine commissioned a Bugaku-type score, but with Western instrumentation. His ballet is in three movements, with a central pas de deux that is highly erotic. It has often been referred to as a "nuptial rite." "It's some kind of ritual that has to take place, like flying fish mating," says Kent. In the sometimes atonal music, the white-lace delicacy/nudity of the woman, and the solid, earth-bound male, *Bugaku* is also highly evocative.

For Cassidy, it had "the subtlety of Japanese painting on silk, the strength of Japanese wrestlers. It could be a ceremonial marriage with the imagined song of the nightingale. It has the look of long-legged, long-necked wading birds in a serene pavilion, the girls in short tutus feather-petaled, with tiny top-knots and no shoulders at all, just that beguiling flow from throat to wrist known to Westerners as Victorian." [2]

According to a program note, "Balanchine has not attempted a direct imitation of the Gagaku gestures or movement, but has transposed the classic Western academic ballet into a style suggested by the music. The costumes are a free fantasy on the traditional Japanese court dress."

A Tokyo correspondent was more specific: "Western strings were made to 'suggest' the *sho* and the *shichiriki*. Japanese court dress was 'suggested' with the girls in chrysanthemum-edged tutus and men in long sleeves and trailing tassels. Balanchine evoked Bugaku effects in the men's steps, for instance, which faced outward to give the sense of postured slow movements 'suggestive' of the hieratic orientality of Bugaku." [3]

The steps, and especially the central pas de deux, were clearly intended as only the most distant echoes of their inspiration (for one thing, all the dancers of the Gagaku are male!). The same applies to the music: "I cannot say that my music is really Japanese-flavored," says Mayuzumi. "But I am a Buddhist and very interested in Zen philosophy, so I hope some kind of Japanese spirit reflects in my work."

Time magazine: "Balanchine proved how right he could be by daring to go wildly wrong." *Time*'s correspondent then gave the following description of the action: "*Bugaku* opens on an empty stage suggestive of a court or an arena. The music begins with atonal violin glissandos so delicately feline that the sight of the first dancer coming on stage is a silent shock—like a slipper thrown at a cat. Five girls dance alone in a ritualistic largo, then five men replace them, moving with the elaborate logic of karate fighters. Each gesture is answered with architectural symmetry, each movement implies a counter-movement.

"What was a ceremony becomes a seduction—or is it a wedding night? The lovers, danced with moody excitement, are circled by their attendants and stripped of their outer robes. In bikini and tights, they dance a pulsing pas de deux that ends in a crouching embrace. Their attendants return, tug them apart and restore their robes, but the partnered dance that follows suggests the first steps of the love duet. The ballet ends—a courtly, exotic, unresolved sexual fantasy.

"Balanchine's notion of the Orient is clearly more erotic than Mayuzumi's. The music is fragmented and ethereal, with no hint of sensuality in rhythm or dynamics. The dance, though, is something else again. The lovers stalk each other with expressionless hunger, and the postures they strike between movements are clear imitations of love." [4]

Biancolli called the ballet "one of Balanchine's noblest ventures" [5]; but Hughes thought it "far from his finest work. Indeed, its pseudo-Japanese mannerisms are rather embarrassing at times." [6]

Manchester liked the ensemble sections, despised the pas de deux as "contortions, uncomely, and unnecessary. The gentle entries of the five girls, coming into sight, as the Gagaku dancers of the Japanese Household did, from behind the raised inner stage—a triumph of lacquer red against a pale cyclorama and white ropes—and the exits just as quiet and gentle; then the similar exits and entries for the five men; these moments are entrancing. As a tribute to Japanese dance, *Bugaku* is superb in these moments of emulation. It is a series of dances, mostly a mixture of classic ballet with some turned-in knees thrown in, culminating in an acrobatic pas de deux for the Samurai-like Villella and Kent. When the curtain rose on that spare, elegant set, and the music, with the intonation of the Japanese court, we expected to be transported into authentic fantasy and for a little while the magic happened. But it did not last." [7]

As is often the case, the ballet gained in effect from repeated performance. In fact, Kent feels that "it took about ten years before it really evolved into something. It's the same now, but better. Something happened. In rehearsal, no Japanese look was stressed. I think of it as ancient Japan

Bugaku. **Edward Villella, Allegra Kent.** (*Photo Martha Swope.*)

. . . the Japanese woman five paces behind the man. I always do it with a face that shows no emotion, with what I feel is a Japanese look. Basically, I avert my eyes. I participate, but my eyes and face are averted from the reality of what's happening."

Says Clifford, "The man's part should really be heavy, it's got to be heavy. Balanchine showed me exactly what he wanted, which was much more vulgar—or exaggerated—than anyone does it. At one point, the man is supposed to really crawl down the woman's leg. Some of the positions are very pretty—but wild. But everything's all right if you do it with a straight face. The whole encounter is *so* cool."

Mitchell recalls that "Mr. Balanchine was always at me to be down, down, down, like a wrestler. He spoke of the girl's movements as a blossom unfolding."

In Europe, critics seemed to be attracted by the ballet's ritual nature and unbothered by the "unseemly" contortions.

England:
"The structure is uncannily beautiful. There is an orchestral prelude, largely a monotone with sliding arabesques spun around it. In the central section, Balanchine resets one of his favorite themes: a lyric, full-hearted hymn to the beauty of the female body. And the Japanese setting provides him with new inspirations, new variations on his theme. The pas de deux is a flow of strange tensions resolved into clearest harmony, of distortions flowering into symmetry. The ballet ends again as ceremony. It is cast as ritual, but ritual fired by a controlled, steady flame of devotion." [8]

"Balanchine's Japanese cultured pearl. The ballet is in essence a couple of pas de deux. Its special fascination is that its language, with apposite Oriental grace notes, is exactly that of the best passages in the austere formative *Agon*, but here the idiom, which in *Agon* seems to be impersonal, has become highly personalized, dramatic, expressive, and indeed, erotic." [9]

France:
"Each 'step,' slowly executed, appears like something taken apart." [10]

Germany:
"Everything is nice and mannered. The delicate slow-motion actions of the girls

are followed by the affected cock walk in the dances of the men. An unintelligible wedding ceremony comes next—soft activities in white. But the rites and groupings of the Japanese are not copied. It is a Japan of Western imagination. In fact, it is only from the continually drawn-out tempos that this glassy, beautiful work gets its East Asian coloring. It is a piece of the most delicate artificiality." [11]

ARCADE

CHOREOGRAPHY: John Taras

MUSIC: Igor Stravinsky (Concerto for Piano and Winds, 1924)

COSTUMES: Ruth Sobotka

DÉCOR, LIGHTING: David Hays

PREMIERE: 28 March 1963

PIANO: Gordon Boelzner

CAST: *The Young Girl*, Suzanne Farrell; *The Dancers*, Arthur Mitchell, 11 men; *The Chaperones*, 8 women

Taras selected a piece which Stravinsky himself was fond of playing. The piano is used as a "percussive instrument" in the first and third movements; "the second movement, with its extremely slow, legato, rather viscous melody accompanied by thick rich chords like folds of stiff drapery, comes as a complete change of mood." [1]

Taras describes his feeling for it: "The first movement suggests to me a strange change of moods—a processional going into a gay dance, which then repeats. Throughout the work there are rather abrupt shifts in emotion and climate. I decided to have girls who are almost like nuns, and one young girl. Boys are brought in to perform for them, and one boy is chosen for a pas de deux with the girl. All the boys come back to dance, and then at the end the nuns return, and the one boy is trapped and kept there. It wasn't a story, really."

This was one of the first roles created for Farrell, who would soon make such an impact in new Balanchine works.

Manchester wrote, "There is so much atmosphere of fantasy here, so many hints of undercurrents, so much in the way of fine dancing, that it is disappointing that *Arcade* has not quite come off.

"[In an area marked by] long red pennants hanging from a square of rods against black curtains stand eight Chaperones, black-clad, with gleaming white foreheads, having the menace of some unexplained auto-da-fé. As they move from the enclosure, the front row of pennants is drawn up, and into the now open space there bound the male dancers in particolored costumes, led by high-jumping De Bolt. Last of all comes Mitchell, and when they are all assembled they kneel with bent heads. The Chaperones return to touch each in turn, until only Mitchell is left. He is the chosen one, and the other men, having assumed a judgelike over-garment, enter in solemn procession surrounding a young girl, Farrell, whose simple dress is covered by a dark cloak with a huge, stiff hood. She and Mitchell dance together, a tender dance of awakening love; but all too soon the Chaperones bear her away. There is a moment of stillness and then, as all the dancers bound forward, the pennants descend. They are trapped." [2]

Hughes felt that "The weakness [might] be caused by the busy-work nature of the choreography for the men. If they are engaged in a competition, the point is not made sufficiently clear. If they are not, why are they there at all?" [3]

Several months later, the costumes and set were removed. At the time, Terry called it "tidy": "It now stands solely on its movements and its patterns. And it stands (even if it doesn't really move) fairly well, for it does possess neat and agreeable patterns, but it has lost, along with its former mood, any real sense of climax." [4]

MOVEMENTS FOR PIANO AND ORCHESTRA

CHOREOGRAPHY: George Balanchine

MUSIC: Igor Stravinsky (1958–59)

LIGHTING: Peter Harvey

PREMIERE: 9 April 1963

PIANO: Gordon Boelzner

CAST: Suzanne Farrell, Jacques d'Amboise; 6 women

OTHER CASTS: Karin von Aroldingen, Allegra Kent, Kay Mazzo; Anthony Blum, Jean-Pierre Bonnefous

The music has been called Stravinsky's most "hermetic": to the layman it appears a series of disconnected sounds—isolated and dissonant, sepulchral noises. The dancing, too, is in very short phrases (sometimes a single step), not always "on" the music.

The ballet was described in the London *Times* as "an essay in suspended motion. Its appeal is at once musical and spatial, and its dancers seem like a mobile caught in the breath of the music. The air is full of pauses." [1]

Pianist Boelzner explained some of the problems: "That's one piece that is very tight, where everything has *got* to be nailed down. To put it somewhat naively, Stravinsky was writing shorthand rhythmic phrases; that is, they're not what you'd call scannable, really, to the ear. But they could be made scannable without the dreariness of following a score because Balanchine can visually clarify the meter. Of course, there's a lot of silence in that score, but Stravinsky never gave up rhythm even though you don't hear it so much in this sort of shattered, twelve-tone music. But you can see it. It's all being ticked away for you on the stage." [2]

The lead couple is identified with the piano. Balanchine selected his tallest, leggiest girls; at times one is aware more of legs than bodies and of outstretched arms like giant bird wings. The accent seems to be on steps that lengthen the limbs—mostly terre-à-terre movements, lunges, crouches, stretches, occasional extensions, particularly by the solo girl. At one point, the six corps girls sink to the floor in splits, while the ballerina does the same movement upside down, held in the air by her partner; more frequently in their movements, the corps and soloists have a less direct relationship to each other, although the corps often presents a friezelike backdrop against which the soloists move. In the powerful ending instant, all the dancers crouch near the floor. In all, very little movement occurs. "Terse," "taut," "compact," "weighty"— these terms describe both music and dancing. Stravinsky is said to have felt that the choreography enlarged his score.

Movements for Piano and Orchestra. **Suzanne Farrell, Jacques d'Amboise.** *(Photo Fred Fehl.)*

He suggested an alternate name for the ballet: *Electric Currents.*

Movements was judged a masterpiece: "Balanchine packs into the work's five epigrammatic movements so much intricate dance that only a person with eight pairs of eyes could take it all in on first acquaintance. What movement! Since there are no tempo contrasts in the work, he sets his dancers ticking away like a swift watch. At times one had the feeling that d'Amboise and the rubber-spined Farrell had solved a geometry theorum or successfully traced through an electrical circuit." [3]

Hughes: "Only prudence keeps me from saying outright that I think it as nearly perfect a work of dance art as I have ever seen. What Balanchine has made is a series of living sculptures, a monument, if you will, of eight figures that rearrange their positions almost constantly. The movement is spare and precisely shaped to the music. For the chorus, it may be their hands alone that move; often they are engaged in successions of poses. The leaders are generally engaged in the kind of Balanchine duet that explores the varieties of poses for two. It is as if Balanchine had examined all the statuary in the world and had summed up all the pose possibilities in this work. Yet the result is not static." [4]

Terry: "The score is spare, devoid of embroidery, romance, emotional indulgence of any sort. The choreography is Spartan, for here perfect discipline, perfect form, perfect control, a cold but won-

derfully bright and pure beauty prevail. Consummate power and meticulous action in a flawlessly trained body are accorded balletic celebration. The style of choreography is, of course, classical. Oh yes, there are occasional examples of flexed feet but they are there simply to remind the eye that the foot can be abrupt as well as graciously extended. The designs and the movements [befit] the Spartan theme, but they are magnificent in their invention for the two trios and for the focal duo. *Movements* challenges the eye and the ear, even the muscle memory, and it wins. It is superb." [5]

Manchester: "Between [the score's] astringent scratchings and squeaks Balanchine has set some of his most astounding choreography. Where his choreography for [*Agon* and *Episodes*], for all its extension into new areas of distortion and acrobatics, was still recognizably based on the classic vocabulary, here there is invention upon invention made possible only by reason of the classically trained bodies on which he builds his movements, yet with no more than a hint here and there of a conventional step. He manipulates the dancers as though they were supremely malleable clay under his fingers. It is extraordinary and fascinating. Farrell and d'Amboise move with supreme confidence through a maze of complicated lifts which are never repeated and are often so subtly and unexpectedly achieved that it will take many viewings even to begin to sort out the gradations which lead to the finished pose." [6]

Movements was Balanchine's first creation for Farrell, whom he continued to choose as his favored interpreter for several years.

England:
"To say that Farrell and d'Amboise 'represent' the keyboard and the six girls the orchestra would be too simple. Rather, the relationship between the leading pair and the others resembles that between the soloist and the other players, and generally their roles run parallel. But so inextricable are sound and sight that one almost has the feeling that at times Farrell, by her movement, calls the piano solo into being; she actually seems to compose it by her dance." [7]

Germany:
"A most delicate walk on and between sparingly set notes—much similar to a pedestrian's effort to avoid puddles on a flooded sidewalk. Everything is possible now for Balanchine: each note and each silence find their corresponding body response. All this reads very nicely, but one sees it with a yawn. Choreographic freedom, buoyed by the music, has become the execution of compulsory figures—figures that contain great mastery, but that could turn into sterility. From this Balanchine is not far distant. He insists on excursions into dance grammar. Where *Agon* was witty and audacious, *Movements* is only an arithmetic exercise of choreographic virtuosity. A ballet computer is fed with steps." [8]

THE CHASE
or,
The Vixen's Choice

CHOREOGRAPHY: Jacques d'Amboise

MUSIC: Wolfgang Amadeus Mozart (Horn Concerto No. 3, K. 447, 1783)

COSTUMES: Karinska

DÉCOR, LIGHTING: David Hays

PREMIERE: 18 September 1963

HORN: Kathleen Wilbur

CAST: *Duke*, André Prokovsky; *A Wealthy Friend*, Shaun O'Brien; *His Wife*, Rosemary Dunleavy; *The Vixen*, Allegra Kent; *Master of the Chase*, Anthony Blum; *Guests*, 4 couples; *4 Footmen*

OTHER CASTS: *Vixen*, Suki Schorer; *Duke*, Roland Vazquez

Is it a good ballet? Oh, come now. Is it that funny? Ah well, Miss Kent is awfully cute," wrote Hughes.[1] He later continued, "About as slight an exercise as a ballet can be and still get by, but the public is obviously amused by it, which means that it serves its purpose."[2] As

such, it "matched" the music, generally considered, along with Mozart's other wind concertos, as "occasional pieces, intended to make a pleasant impression."[3] "Amiable, but very, very minor," was Terry's opinion of the ballet, "won't hurt anyone."[4]

The story was described as follows: "It's a farce. There is this hunting party, you see. It has a Duke, his wealthy friend (with handlebar mustache), the friend's wife, who has a crush on the Duke, a Master of the Chase, and, of course, guests and footmen. The hunt begins and the Vixen finds the Duke. They strike up a friendship at once. The others in the party spy the fox, and the confusion is compounded. The fox leaps on the Duke's friend, and the friend faints. Doubly confounded confusion. The music, oh yes, approaches its end, fox turns into girl, and girl poses with Duke's friend, as the curtain falls. Or, if it isn't exactly like this, it could be."[5]

Details unmentioned above included the friend's allergy to fox fur and the concluding chase. Actually, the fox's tail got the best reviews—it was real fur and of luxuriant length, with choreography of its own. And how do we discover that the fox is really a girl? The final costume is "a see-through suit with a couple of leaves and long hair," says Schorer.

The Chase. Shaun O'Brien, Allegra Kent. (*Photo Martha Swope.*)

FANTASY

CHOREOGRAPHY: John Taras

MUSIC: Franz Schubert ("Fantasy" Piano Duet in F minor, op. 103, 1828, orchestrated by Felix Mottl)

PREMIERE: 24 September 1963

CAST: *First Couple*, Patricia McBride, Edward Villella; 2 couples; *Watchers of the Night*, 10 women
Also danced by Anthony Blum

The ballet was memorable principally for the opportunities it offered to the still-emerging McBride and to the established Villella, who complemented each other in physique and technical ability. Taras admired the music, which lent itself to highly atmospheric stage treatment. There were passages requiring virtuosity and the suggestion of a plot.

According to Taras, "It's the story of two lovers. The girl is affected by the moon and becomes a wolf-lady whenever the moon comes out—it's kind of a Giselle story. The corps resembles Wilis and attacks the man at the end. When the moon goes behind a cloud, the girl returns to herself (she changes her costume slightly). At the end she comes to her senses and he rushes to her, but he dies."

The costumes were uncredited. The Watchers, in addition to their black gowns, wore long artificial fingernails and streaming hair.

Reception was mixed. Terry called it "Evocative . . . uneven, a work which boasts sequences with punch, point, and vividness of dance action but which also suffers from attenuations and phrases which are thin. There are moments of great dramatic impact and pure dance beauties. McBride as the gloriously lovely creature who turns into a witch not only excites the viewer with her powers in projecting the macabre but also dazzles the eye with a series of tours en attitude which are nothing less than fabulous."[1]

For Manchester, "the work relies on atmosphere and exciting dance passages to establish itself as a work of considerable charm, succeeding perfectly in its unpretentious way."[2] Elsewhere, she said, "This is romantic ballet with all that has been added since in the way of a greatly extended technical vocabulary. Taras has not been afraid to mix the romantic flavor with Soviet prowess in the largeness and sweep of the movements for his two principals." [3]

Others felt that this very romanticism—the brooding, the metamorphosis, the unexplained death of the hero—was hackneyed. Hughes complained that the choreography was overly busy.

MEDITATION

CHOREOGRAPHY: George Balanchine

MUSIC: Peter Ilyitch Tchaikovsky (*Méditation,* op. 42, no. 1, from *Souvenir d'un Lieu Cher,* three pieces for piano and violin, 1878, orchestrated by Alexander Glazounov)

COSTUMES: Karinska

PREMIERE: 10 December 1963

VIOLIN: Marilyn Wright

DANCERS: Suzanne Farrell, Jacques d'Amboise

REVIVAL: 10 June 1975, New York State Theater

CAST: Farrell, d'Amboise

A golden-haired woman in flowing white seems to inspire and comfort a troubled poet-figure, to strains of a soaring Tchaikovsky violin—"an exquisite study in mood" [1] ? "a tender pas de deux" [2] ? "an unattainable romance" [3] ? . . . or "dripping" [4] and "syrupy" [5] ? Opinions were divided, except for agreement that Balanchine had produced something quite unlike any of his other works, and one that was at least close to sentimentality. Whether the observer saw it as dreamy or overwrought would depend greatly on his reaction to this kind of music (in the highly romantic style of many Tchaikovsky adagios), for the ballet closely mirrored it. Balanchine called it "contemplative."

"The young man, dressed in black with white flowing-sleeved shirt, is seen brooding on the darkened stage. He falls to the floor and covers his face with his hands as though he were mourning. The girl, young and lovely, in a simple white dress and with hair falling over her shoul-

Meditation. **Suzanne Farrell, Jacques d'Amboise.** (*Photo Martha Swope.*)

ders, enters and begins to comfort him. Their dance is interrupted often by embraces, but these seem to be embraces of despair, perhaps, rather than passion. Eventually the dance ends with the young man kneeling on the floor as at the beginning, the young girl having gone away. A surprise that will touch and gladden the hearts of those who want exteriorized feeling, perhaps even a little suffering, with their dancing." [6]

"Balanchine goes along with both romanticism and sentimentality. In fact he dives in head first. He might well have subtitled the piece 'Homage to Soviet Ballet (Highlights Division),' because that is exactly what it looks like. He keeps his dancers mooning around in a yearning sort of way. They both spend a lot of time kneeling on the floor clutching each other's ankles. There is no development, and we know it is going to end only because we hear the climax in the music." [7]

"To the haunting music, two figures move intensely through sadness, desire, joy, ecstasy, guilt, and melancholy to resignation, acceptance, and peace." [8]

Says Farrell, "Choreographically it is very interesting because in all the technical things we do together, all the partnering, the 'how' of it is camouflaged. This contrasts with something like *Agon,* where the audience sees all the mechanics, where the more your arm shakes when you're holding onto your partner, the greater the suspense. In *Meditation,* you don't want suspense. The hand work is all hidden, and that's the beauty of the

pas de deux. For my first entrance, Mr. B. said just to step out on pointe, with my arms outstretched, and 'hold the air.' "

The ballet was dropped from the repertory when Farrell left the Company in 1969 and revived for her when she returned six years later.

England:
"A mystery. How this trite little pas de deux in early-Soviet style came to be conceived by a master mind is inexplicable." [9]

TARANTELLA

CHOREOGRAPHY: George Balanchine

MUSIC: Louis Moreau Gottschalk (*Grande Tarantelle,* c. 1866), reconstructed and orchestrated by Hershy Kay

COSTUMES: Karinska

PREMIERE: 7 January 1964

PIANO: Jean-Pierre Marty

CAST: Patricia McBride, Edward Villella

OTHER CASTS: Gelsey Kirkland, Sara Leland, Marnee Morris, Suki Schorer; John Clifford, John Prinz, Helgi Tomasson, Robert Weiss

Tarantella: A lively passionate Neapolitan folk dance."

Tarantella demands a nimble foot and good wind. During its five minutes, the dancing is virtually nonstop. Though danced by only two performers, it is not a conventional pas de deux: there is no supported partnering, for instance; the style is demi-caractère rather than grand. The man's role features big leaps covering space (sometimes with both legs thrust in front), beats, and turns; the woman's, quick changes of direction, flexible small footwork; and on the part of both, a knack for the tambourine (which was sounded with hand, toe, and hip), a cheery smile, an air of roguish mischief, and a lot of running around.

The partnership of McBride and Villella, which became celebrated, was here just beginning.

"Vivacious and exciting. It is a classical work balletically but, as its title suggests, it pays homage to the rhythms and some of the steps and conventions (including tambourines) of Italy. Although the choreography does not resemble Bournonville, it is welcomely reminiscent of a genre in which that nineteenth-century Danish ballet master excelled and that was the linking, in the most lilting movement terms, of the elegance of ballet with the buoyant and brisk qualities of folk actions.

"Balanchine has kept matters going at jet speed but with an irresistible airiness of spirit. And, as usual, he has reached into his inexhaustible treasure house of ballet steps, gestures, and patterns and come up with a stunning array of new designs and sequences to delight the eye.

"Villella has many opportunities to display his remarkable elevation and his vir-

tuosic leg-beats, but he is also called upon to move almost constantly at break-neck speed and, in one dazzling section, to replace elevation with steps which barely skim the floor in a way which suggests that gravity is but foolish fancy." [1]

"Almost riotous gaiety and frenzied pacing." [2] "McBride and Villella are as youthful and vigorous as any pair of dancers you could find, but the chances are that even they would not survive if the work lasted much longer than it does." [3]

"The stage is never empty; when one dancer rushes off for a moment's catching of breath, the other rushes on. Separately or together, the pace never slackens. . . . Gay, difficult to a degree but exhilarating and brilliant. Naples was never like this, but who cares?" [4]

Villella once said that for *Tarantella*, the dancer needed bravura technique, the ability to move quickly, and joie de vivre.

Says Clifford, "It's brash, quick; it's really hard. The steps—beats, jumps . . . it's too fast to really jump and that's maddening. The stage is awfully big . . ."

Schorer: "It's tricky in timing and very puffy. But over the years, some of the non-balletic accents have gone. A little turned-in assemblé has become a jump with kick-your-head. Some of the footwork had much more emphasis in the body and the hip. Now there's time for triple pirouettes. The boy rarely touches you; we blow each other kisses and link arms for a kind of circular promenade. I remember Balanchine saying to me about this ballet, 'Dance with everything. When your back is to the audience, your back has to dance.'"

England:
"A jeu d'esprit and the play of a finely cultivated wit. Balanchine comes from St. Petersburg; *Tarantella* is his 'Neapolitan,' the mock-national-dance divertissement of the big old romantic ballets—not mocked by Balanchine, but treated with affectionate good humor that sees the genuine fun as well as the funny side. The music is mock-national too, tuneful, tripping encore-music by a virtuoso pianist. The notes scurry along, but the basic pulse is easy, and much of the piquancy of this pas de deux comes from the extreme rapidity and brilliance of their movement set to a far-from-urgent score. It is witty dance that is *all* dance; the swift, unlabored jokes are made within the choreog-

raphy, by virtuosos. Balanchine's pas de deux are never mere occasional pieces, but real *ballets* for two dancers." [5]

QUATUOR

CHOREOGRAPHY: Jacques d'Amboise

MUSIC: Dmitri Shostakovich (String Quartet No. 1, 1938)

PREMIERE: 16 January 1964

QUARTET: Gerard Kantarjian, Joseph Schor, Caroline Voight, Sterling Hunkins

CAST: Mimi Paul, Jacques d'Amboise, Robert Maiorano, Roland Vazquez
Also danced by Suzanne Farrell

Quatuor seemed to be a ballet about relationships, although unspecified ones.

Wrote Cohen, "First a quartet of musicians entered and seated themselves behind a scrim. Then a quartet of dancers appeared: at one side of the stage three men (apparently a father and two sons); at the other side, a young girl. As the music began, one of the sons broke away, met the girl, and danced tenderly with her. The father (Vazquez) gave his approval. Then the other son was attracted to her. Their relation was lighter, more playful. Jealous, the first son intervened, and the girl—frightened by their quarrelling—ran off. In the end, seeking security, she suddenly fell into the arms of the father." [1]

Sorell called this ending "a twist that was almost farcical," which marred what was otherwise "in pure dance terms, d'Amboise's most mature work." [2]

Manchester found matters far less concrete: "What was the relationship of the three men? Father and sons? Or all friends of rather disparate ages? Was it a ballet of atmosphere evoking memories of youthful love?" After faulting the choice of music, she continued, "For all its weaknesses, it shows that d'Amboise does have the tools for his choreographer's craft. It has so many moments of such sweetness and truth that the faults hardly matter. [There are] movements which speak of the wary testing out of youthful feeling, the dawning awareness of first love. Later, it succeeds very well showing the transference of affection still hardly understood." [3]

Tarantella. **Suki Schorer, Edward Villella.**
(*Photo Fred Fehl.*)

4

"A HOUSE FOR DANCE"
New York State Theater

1964–1976

On 24 April 1964, after Stravinsky's "Fanfare for a New Theater," specially composed for the occasion, the Company opened its inaugural season at Lincoln Center's New York State Theater with its second most opulent production (after *Nutcracker*), *A Midsummer Night's Dream*, completely redesigned for the new space. Shortly thereafter, Tudor restaged his *Dim Lustre*. Very soon Balanchine began to turn out elaborate new works, both one-act and full-length—*Harlequinade*, *Don Quixote*, *Brahms-Schoenberg Quartet*, *Jewels*, a new *Firebird*, and, eventually, a three-act *Coppélia*—which took full advantage of the new facilities, as though he had been just waiting for the beautifully equipped theater to come along. It became apparent that he had nothing against costumes and sets.

In 1965, a subscription plan was announced, following the practice of the Metropolitan Opera—the bane of many discriminating concert-goers' existence. This resulted in the largest advance sale in the Company's history in the first year of operation, so, middle-brow or no, it became a fixture. The Company initiated annual benefit performances to attract society and money, which was also "uncharacteristic" of its former image.

A summer home, the Saratoga Performing Arts Center, to be shared with the Philadelphia Orchestra, opened on 5 July 1966. (The State Theater became a permanent home when, after the initial two-year lease expired, City Center, of which the New York City Ballet continued to be a part, signed a twenty-five-year lease, renewable for another twenty-five.) In 1964 the Company began a series of lecture-demonstrations, sponsored by the New York State Council on the Arts, which took principal dancers and others to schools and towns to talk about and demonstrate their art.

All the new real estate, the signs of permanence, relative affluence, recognition by the Ford Foundation, and the resources to extend itself into the community (that is,

to do more than "merely" scrape a performance season together) pointed to a changed status for the Company: Balanchine the avant-gardist and his selfless dancers were becoming "Establishment." Mr. B. seemed to take it in stride like everything else: he has always risen to—and exploited—prevailing circumstances. Some of his works—to late Stravinsky or Xenakis—continued to be as experimental as ever, even as he revealed a taste for the rich, the lavish, the "traditional" (always with his own refurbishing). Said Kirstein of the Company's new position: "Since being established means having a chance to plan rather than improvise, to enjoy continuity and stability approaching the level of foreign, state-supported institutions, we welcome the epithet. We have always been conservative, in the sense of preserving a traditional dance language, based on the music which most adroitly or capaciously subsumes it."

All of this occurred at a propitious moment, for the dance audience in America was growing in size and enthusiasm at a great rate. What had been an elitist art was becoming a popular one, perhaps the leader in the "culture boom" of the sixties. Little girls, instead of having piano lessons, were sent to ballet school. Dancers were losing their reputations as "oddballs" and "bohemians"; they were also starting to earn a decent living: The status of dancers as well as of dance was changing.

The boom has proved to be no fad (and in the mid-seventies there was a further "dance explosion"). By the seventies, every state had an arts council (the Company received an $800,000 grant from the New York State Council on the Arts in 1974); government subsidy was going directly to the community. Dance departments were established at colleges and universities; some offered a major in dance. Regional ballet companies—professional and amateur—flourished. (Chujoy considered the cross-country tours of the Ballet Caravan to have been a pioneer impetus in the development of regional dance.) All of this activity, this solid network of support, created vast new audiences, which ensured the permanent place of dance throughout the country. (There were rumors that dance aficionados outnumbered baseball fans.)

New York became, as never before, the dance capital of the world, with dance concerts every night of the year. In 1927, John Martin had been the only professional dance critic in the country; by 1970, *The New York Times* alone employed three, with additional guest columnists. In 1966, as chief dance critic, the *Times* imported Clive Barnes, a man of limitless ebullience and enthusiasm (who was also the chief drama critic), with twenty years' experience watching and reviewing dance in England.

The move to Lincoln Center began a new era in many ways: in 1965, Maria Tallchief resigned, soon followed by Patricia Wilde. Neither was "too old" to dance; Balanchine was accused of transferring his attentions to the younger members of the Company. Said he, "They say I abandon dancers at twenty-five. It's not true. But it's my business to start them young. Anyway, if I didn't start them young, there wouldn't be any old dancers." His new protégées were indeed all youthful. They included Patricia McBride, Gloria Govrin, Sara Leland, Mimi Paul, Suki Schorer, Patricia Neary, and his particular favorite of the mid-sixties, Suzanne Farrell.

Possibly because of the spacious new theater, possibly because of Farrell's long-limbed, loose, expansive movement, some discerned a change in Balanchine's attitude. Says Melissa Hayden: "It was hard to hold your own. No one else danced. There was no transition—it was as though he had closed a book of his life and picked up another book, turned to the first page, and there was Suzanne. He loved the new crop of dancers, they had beauty, they had 'bigness'—we were going into a new theater, and he wanted 'bigness.' We were not small fry any more. His classes changed, technically: he wanted large, flowing steps, covering space, where formerly, for instance, he had talked for hours about the articulation of the foot." Balanchine has often said, "The tallest is better because you see more."

In 1969, after six years of prominence, Farrell left the Company. A few of the ballets done for her were retired (*Variations, Metastaseis & Pithoprakta, Meditation*), although many survived a change of cast very well. Of the younger generation, McBride continued her steady as-

cent, and other dancers came to the fore, among them Kay Mazzo and Karin von Aroldingen. By 1970, a new ballerina was on the way: tiny Gelsey Kirkland, whose technique was textbook pure and legendarily strong. The same year, Balanchine imported two male principals from Europe: Peter Martins and Jean-Pierre Bonnefous; and they were soon followed by Peter Schaufuss and Adam Lüders. Helgi Tomasson and Anthony Blum completed the new male roster. Through various upheavals, Hayden had remained; then, in the summer of 1973, in her fifty-first year, she retired. Kirkland, after four busy years, departed for American Ballet Theatre and a newly arrived Russian sensation, Mikhail Baryshnikov. In 1975 Farrell returned to join McBride as leading ballerina. Violette Verdy, after some years of irregular appearances due to injuries, began to dance full-time. Meanwhile, Edward Villella had moved successfully into mature roles such as *Prodigal Son, Watermill, Pulcinella*. Jacques d'Amboise and Allegra Kent performed less frequently. Among those who left the Company were John Clifford, Gloria Govrin, Jillana, Conrad Ludlow, Nicholas Magallanes, Arthur Mitchell, Patricia Neary, Mimi Paul, André Prokovsky, and Suki Schorer.

In 1969, Jerome Robbins came back to the New York City Ballet. His glorious, hour-long *Dances at a Gathering* was the most exciting event of the year, and he followed it with a number of important works, including *In the Night, The Goldberg Variations, Watermill,* and *The Dybbuk Variations*.

Ironically, just about the time of Robbins's reappearance, Balanchine seemed to enter a fallow period. He resurfaced in triumph, however, during his brilliant Stravinsky Festival in 1972, a memorable week in the history of dance during which the Company presented twenty-two new works to honor the man who "made our floor." Of the new ballets, the most meaningful and lasting were all Balanchine's. A second Festival in 1975, in observance of Ravel's one-hundredth birthday, was less successful. Ravel in quantity did not yield the same sense of unending discovery that Stravinsky had.

Just after the Stravinsky week, the Company departed for Russia (also visiting Poland and Munich). A lengthy tour of Europe had been made in 1965, with brief visits in 1967 and 1969; in fall, 1976, the troupe appeared in Paris.

The Company's sixty-fifth New York season opened at the State Theater on 16 November 1976.

CLARINADE

CHOREOGRAPHY: George Balanchine

MUSIC: Morton Gould (*Derivations for Clarinet and Jazz Band*, 1954–55, composed for Benny Goodman)

PREMIERE: 29 April 1964 *

CLARINET: Benny Goodman

CAST: *Warm-up*, Gloria Govrin, Arthur Mitchell, 5 couples; *Contrapuntal Blues*, Suzanne Farrell, Anthony Blum, 2 couples; *Rag*, Gloria Govrin, 4 women; *Ride-Out*, entire company

Gould combines the American jazz vernacular with the traditional form of the concerto grosso, in which trombone, trumpet, or clarinet are solo instruments against a background of an instrumental ensemble" (program).

Clarinade, the first ballet staged in the new theater, was less than worthy of the occasion, despite the presence of Goodman in the pit. In Manchester's words, it "might have served as a filler for a season or two at the less demanding, comfortably homey City Center, but it looks lost and a little ridiculous in its present elegant surroundings. All the clichés of supposed modern jazz are there—the outward thrust of the hip, the forward thrust of the pelvis, the backward rock on the heels." [1]

Hughes was more positive: "Not quite the facile, frivolous exercise you might imagine. The trappings and trademarks of jazz dancing and dancers are there, but they do not constitute the substance of the choreography. Most of the group floor patterns are based on the symmetrical models Balanchine has followed in *Movements* and *Bugaku*, for example, and the intentionally distorted classical ballet style incorporated in these also appears in *Clarinade*, especially in the second movement." [2] Later he wrote:

"It seems to have irritated many observers and it has been dismissed as an embarrassing, unfunny joke by a number of them. After seeing the piece three times, I must dissent from their dissent. [But] to see what there is, you have to

look past the short polka-dot skirts jiggling on hips, and that isn't easy." [3]

"An adolescent romp in which Balanchine demonstrated an unfailing eye for the street-corner attitudes of bemused American youth." [4]

DIM LUSTRE

CHOREOGRAPHY: Antony Tudor

MUSIC: Richard Strauss (*Burlesque*, 1885)

COSTUMES, DÉCOR, LIGHTING: Beni Montresor

PREMIERE: 6 May 1964 (first presented 20 October 1943 by Ballet Theatre, Metropolitan Opera, New York)

CAST: *The Lady with Him*, Patricia McBride; *The Gentleman with Her*, Edward Villella; *A Reflection*, Sara Leland; *Another Reflection*, Ramon Segarra; *It Was Spring*, Robert Rodham; *Who Was She?*, Suki Schorer, 2 women; *She Wore Perfume*, Mimi Paul; *He Wore a White Tie*, Richard Rapp; *Waltzing Ladies and Their Partners*, 5 couples

OTHER CASTS: *Lady*, Karin von Aroldingen, Kay Mazzo, Mimi Paul; *Gentleman*, Frank Ohman

Dim *Lustre* was revived by Tudor personally, at Balanchine's request, in honor of the new theater. Not one of Tudor's masterworks, it nevertheless provided a lush and romantic setting and Tudor's distinctive psychological coloration, thus representing in the Company's repertory one of the major contemporary choreographers, if only imperfectly. Says he of the genesis and creation of the ballet: "I like to start with music and work a story into it. This music was originally played for me by Mary Ann Wells in Seattle, the teacher of Robert Joffrey. She knew it would be perfect for something of mine, and she was exactly right. For Ballet Theatre, I had to do it in about two weeks, much more quickly than I like to work, but I didn't use much variety in the steps (they're mostly chassés). Originally the ballet was to be called 'Sanguine,' because of the color tones of the costumes and because that was the predominant mood."

The steps are rarely the main point in Tudor ballets. What causes this work to

Dim Lustre. Mimi Paul, Frank Ohman. (*Photo Fred Fehl.*)

miss slightly is its rather clichéd pretext, given in a program note: "A whiff of perfume, the touch of a hand, a stolen kiss release whirls of memories which take the rememberers back briefly to other moments and leave them not exactly as they were before." These memories were introduced by a series of blackouts, which, as Barnes wrote, "become both too conventional and too predictable." [1]

Terry: "The new staging is a dream, and well it should be, for the ballet itself is concerned with a series of dreams which come to aristocratic individuals as they dance in an elegant ballroom. The scenery has an airiness about it which lends itself beautifully to the varying moods and memories brought on by the dreams. The costumes too are light and evocative of a social search for chic frothiness. The lighting quickly captures the atmosphere of each scene as well as mirroring brilliantly the linking episodes in which the heroine moves in unison with her own reflection, and the hero does the same, as both pursue visions of their own pasts.

"Using the framework of a happy ball, Tudor introduces the Lady and the Gentleman. They appear to be compatible. But are they? The action of the ball itself is arrested, blackened out as, in suspended time, the man or the woman recalls experiences from the long ago, experiences of youth and innocence, of discovery, of maturity and awakening. At the close, the two part, adding perhaps their own association to their memories. In a sense, it is an elusive ballet, as elusive as its theme. It is not filled with fire-works nor with wildly passionate drama. It is a ballet of moods." [2]

Manchester: "It had and still has a faded Valentine fragrance." [3]

Barnes (who has often called the work Proustian): "The final impression is of a sensitively poetic idea that has evaporated somewhat between its moment of first inspiration and its ultimate execution. The ballet is not quite so good as it occasionally hints it is going to be." [4]

Tudor is fabled for his painstaking rehearsals, in which he explores the characters both technically and psychologically. Says Schorer: "He tells you the background of your character. He's very analytical, the opposite of Balanchine's approach, which is so physical." McBride: "He stopped me once in the middle of a variation and simply said 'Who are you?' I said, 'Audrey Hepburn.' 'Oh yes,' he said. 'It's not too far from *Breakfast at Tiffany's*. That's pretty good.' "

Irish Fantasy. Jacques d'Amboise, Suzanne Farrell. (*Photo Martha Swope.*)

IRISH FANTASY

CHOREOGRAPHY: Jacques d'Amboise

MUSIC: Camille Saint-Saëns (ballet music from *Henry VIII*, 1883)

COSTUMES: Karinska

DÉCOR, LIGHTING: David Hays

PREMIERE: 12 August 1964, Greek Theater, Los Angeles

CAST: Melissa Hayden, André Prokovsky; Anthony Blum, Frank Ohman; 8 women, 4 men

OTHER CASTS: Merrill Ashley, Suzanne Farrell, Deborah Flomine, Allegra Kent, Gelsey Kirkland, Marnee Morris, Kyra Nichols, Violette Verdy; Jacques d'Amboise, Anthony Blum, John Clifford, Conrad Ludlow, Frank Ohman

I*rish Fantasy*, "wittily described as 'campetent,' is a cheerful frolic under a gorgeous puckered bedspread." [1] This light work may well be d'Amboise's best; it is attractive, playful, and avoids pretensions. Manchester had reservations, but also found felicitous moments: "Innocuous, shapeless, deriving rather obviously from *Scotch Symphony*. The beginning is an untidy series of entrances for the

corps, vaguely Irish but not very. It continues with a pas de deux full of awkwardly contrived supports. However, the male variation gives Prokovsky a fine chance to sail around in sustained cabrioles, and Hayden leading the girls in a saucy little heel-and-toe dance is delicious. So is the final jig, with all the dancers letting their arms dangle in the Irish manner while moving only their feet and lower part of the legs." [2]

Barnes: "One of the best of all the many ballets created in the image of Balanchine. . . . [It has] inventiveness and sly touches of humor. One of its most welcome aspects is the stress placed on male dancers." [3] This "frolic" has been in the repertory since its premiere. The lovely canopy (green lace, suspended in swags above the performers' heads) always receives comment.

England:

"It's a merry, likable piece which gives delight and hurts not." [4]

"More notable for its unobtrusive promise than any marked originality. There is a vigorous pas de trois for three men and some prettily Romantic invention in the pas de deux. We have seen many worse ballets by followers of Balanchine, and sadly few better, for Balanchine has had something of the same inadvertently dampening effect upon American classic choreography as Handel once had upon English music or Milton had upon the

English epic. All were followed, but too respectfully and at too great a distance." [5]

PIÈGE DE LUMIÈRE

CHOREOGRAPHY: John Taras

MUSIC: Jean-Michel Damase

SCENARIO: Philippe Hériat

COSTUMES: André Levasseur

DÉCOR: Felix Labisse

SUPERVISION, LIGHTING: David Hays

PREMIERE: 1 October 1964 (first presented 23 December 1952 by the Grand Ballet du Marquis de Cuevas, Théâtre de l'Empire, Paris)

CAST: *The Young Convict,* Arthur Mitchell; *Queen of the Morphides,* Maria Tallchief; *Iphias,* André Prokovsky; *The Leader,* Shaun O'Brien; *The Look-Out,* Deni Lamont; *The Blacksmith,* Roger Pietrucha; *The Men,* 9 men; *Hepiales,* 4 women; *The Ios, Aertheres, Morphides, etc.,* 15 women

OTHER CASTS: *Convict,* Paul Mejia; *Queen,* Patricia McBride, Patricia Neary; *Iphias,* Anthony Blum

Piège de Lumière. **Maria Tallchief aloft.** *(Photo Fred Fehl.)*

A young convict joins a band of runaways [who live permanently in the virgin forest]. As night falls, they build a fire to lure from hiding those butterflies who appear at twilight. Species of every kind swarm through. The most agile, the Iphias, and the most beautiful, the Morphide, linger together; but even love cannot distract them from the fatal flames. Before this trap of light, the massacre begins. The Young Convict snares the Morphide, and the Iphias sacrifices himself to save her. She escapes, leaving with her captor the glittering trace of their encounter: gold pollen from her wings. Now he too becomes a hunted creature" (program).

Piège was a ballet in the French grand manner, in its elaborate literary pretext which hinted at something deeper (by a member of the Académie Goncourt, no less), costumes by a Dior designer, ingenious sets, and in general, the latest in chic. Taras also managed to put some very demanding dancing in it, with a good part for the men. Says he:

"It was an intriguing idea (it could have been just awful)—the idea of convicts and butterflies—but a challenge to see what you could do with butterflies at that time [1952]. I decided not to have any wings, to do everything with arms and legs. I worked out the scenario with the com-

poser—the only time I have ever been able to ask for exactly what I wanted—though the score wasn't very great. It's like movie music, but it was excellent for the purpose."

Some go for this ornate fantasy world, some find it annoyingly arty. Definitely on the positive side was Hughes: "A success. Not a subtle piece, perhaps not a distinguished one, but splendidly theatrical, and it works. There is a little something in the story to think about, in the suggestion that the vicious cycle of the hunter and the hunted cannot be broken. This is not, however, essentially a didactic ballet. It is, rather, a spectacle in which story, sets, costumes, music, and dancing are put together in such a way that each complements the other, and taken altogether, they hold the attention for some forty minutes. The score is almost shameless in its exploitation of pulse-throbbing musical devices—rhythmic ostinatos, facile melodies, Ravelian harmonies, and ascending modulations. But it is wonderful for that very reason—if you are not expecting Mozart or Stravinsky. The music dances superbly, and Taras didn't overlook many tricks in making it dance to the limit. It gets off to a brilliant beginning with a dance for the convicts that includes just about everything the men can do well. Leaps, somersaults, pirouettes, and what-not tumble over each other in the effusion. The Morphide is equal to about

three of the Firebird, which it resembles in many respects. There was no end of darting, fluttering, jumping, and so on, projecting emotional reactions all the while. The leading men had much lively dancing to do, and the Convict also had to project feelings of fatigue, terror and dismay, among other things. With a fine shadowy set, brilliant butterfly costumes to contrast with tattered convict attire, and an imposing funeral procession added to everything already mentioned, it could hardly miss." [1]

Manchester: "The denouement is the weakest part. Up to this point there has been no hint of the supernatural. The convicts are humans, the insects and butterflies exactly that. The Convict is in no sense attracted by the Queen except as an exotic specimen. We are not convinced by the introduction of magic after the drama that has gone before. Nevertheless, the ballet is consistently interesting. The procession of the butterflies through the great shaft of light has a fantastic beauty. The [final] procession is also strange, and beautiful: though gigantic the butterflies may be, they are still all but weightless. The pas de deux of the Queen and the Convict has some obvious difficulties that are not quite compensated for by the achievements." [2]

Terry was negative: "A pretty dreary number, something about convicts and butterflies who are both trapped by the inexorable force of fate (as who isn't?). . . . But if the entire ballet leaves much to be desired, it possesses details of striking choreographic invention and of astute theatricalities." [3]

All noticed the impressive first appearance of the Queen. Says McBride, "It was a stunning, Hollywood entrance. You're borne aloft by the men, with an enormous flowing cape streaming behind. Then the cape comes off, and you start dancing very fast and very technical variations. In those years, it was my most difficult part. (Of course, now—1975— I have *Ballet Imperial* and *Theme and Variations* to worry about.)"

Says Taras of the role, "She has one thing after another. She has an entrance with the boys, a solo variation, another sort of adagio with five boys, another solo variation, then a pas de deux with Iphias which ends up with a coda, a rest, then a kind of berceuse when she comes into the *piège,* then a big pas de deux, followed by a pas de trois with Iphias and the Convict, and a very short coda. I put in gliding turns and turns that go from second into arabesque, and, of course, a lot for the arms. It takes stamina."

Mitchell: "There were some very tricky lifts onto one shoulder and throws. I was nervous, dancing with Tallchief for the first time. Dramatically, my part was very meaty, very enjoyable. John was exact about technical things; dramatically, he let me develop my own interpretation."

Piège was performed for several seasons. Possibly it was dropped because it jarred with the rest of the repertory.

PAS DE DEUX AND DIVERTISSEMENT

CHOREOGRAPHY: George Balanchine

MUSIC: Léo Delibes (excerpts from *La Source* [*Naïla*], 1866, and *Sylvia*, 1876)

COSTUMES: Karinska

LIGHTING: David Hays

PREMIERE: 14 January 1965

CAST: Melissa Hayden, André Prokovsky; Suki Schorer

OTHER CASTS: Suzanne Farrell, Allegra Kent, Mimi Paul; Jacques d'Amboise, Conrad Ludlow, Edward Villella; Carol Sumner

Valse Lente and Pas de Deux: Hayden, Prokovsky
Allegro Vivace: Schorer, 8 women
Variation: Prokovsky
Pizzicati: Hayden
Valse des Fleurs: ensemble

T he ballet was something of a hybrid, with the title more than usually descriptive. It was like two works, with a pas de deux to *Sylvia* music (with some steps remembered from the 1951 *Sylvia: Pas de Deux*) and an unrelated ensemble section, featuring a can-can (to some very familiar music).

This was not one of Balanchine's better efforts. Manchester wrote, "Emerges as little more than a program filler. The best portions are those lifted bodily from the dazzling *Sylvia: Pas de Deux*. The changes minimize rather than heighten the climaxes. His habit of squaring off his

Pas de Deux and Divertissement. Melissa Hayden, André Prokovsky, Suki Schorer (right). (*Photo Martha Swope.*)

corps in fours is used throughout and makes the divertissement look like a stereotype of its kind. Schorer prances in and out and achieves some effective balances with her jetés forward landing in arabesque fondue." [1]

Terry was far less enthusiastic, calling it "tedious, tiresome, and trifling." [2]

Only Barnes found a few saving graces: "The choreography, slight as it is, is remarkably resilient. . . . A tiny French wedding cake of a ballet, all sweet and frosty icing and gorgeous marzipan."

The costumes were universally found "hideous."

SHADOW'D GROUND

Ballet in seven verses

CHOREOGRAPHY: John Taras

MUSIC: Aaron Copland (*Dance Panels*, 1962)

LIBRETTO AND EPITAPHS: Scott Burton

PRODUCTION DESIGN: John Braden

PREMIERE: 21 January 1965

CAST: I. THE DATE: *Caretaker*, Edward Bigelow; *Boy*, Robert Maiorano; *Girl*, Kay Mazzo; II. EPITAPHS: *1895, "As man and wife / they moved through life / of one heart ever / apart never."* Suki Schorer, Richard Rapp; *1922, "Our dear ones perished / in the water, / each a cherished / son or daughter."* 6 women, 4 men; *1847, "Early Bereaved, at length I Grieved /*
Until Another I Believed, / And truly He my grief Relieved." Jillana, Roland Vazquez; *1916, "To the Memory / of / Our Men / Who Flew with Freedom into War / Before their Neighbors Followed. / Their Winged Souls are in God's sky."* 3 women, 10 men; III. CHARON CLAIMS; IV. "FOR THE TRUMPET SHALL SOUND, AND THE DEAD SHALL BE . . ." (I Corinthians XV.20): *1964, "Boy and girl are put to rest, / each upon the other's breast. / Stars cross repeatedly on their rounds, / shadowing memorial ground."*

S hadow'd Ground was completely different in concept and production from anything in the Company's repertory and the first new ballet to make explicit use of the enlarged facilities of the State Theater.

Says Taras, "It is set in a cemetery, which is also a trysting place for a young couple. They meet there rather furtively and, as though they had read the tombstone inscriptions, episodes recall the people buried there. Between these episodes the couples dance again, and in the final pas de deux they immure themselves in the mausoleum and the gates close on them."

The epitaphs were written for the occasion by a young poet; and as each episode was danced, slides related to the events being portrayed were projected.

Despite the unusual ingredients, the work was dismissed by the critics. (Kirstein retains a lingering affection for it, however.) It was felt that the projections overwhelmed the stage action ("The dancers looked so tiny next to the huge pictures, and pretty soon you're not watching the ballet at all," says Taras), and that the work was choreographically "trite." "In addition," says Taras, "a lot of people objected to the poems printed in the program. They didn't add to the ballet, in the sense that you couldn't read them while the action was going on."

Wrote Manchester: "It sounds lugubrious, and it was. It had such an elaborate production that the action was dwarfed beneath it." [1]

Terry: "As Bankhead is supposed to have said, 'There is less to this than meets the eye.' The vastly enlarged photographs indicate locale, suggest mood, or, as in the case of a World War I episode, define an incident of battle. Tombstones are also represented from time to time.

"The epitaphs suggest poignancy or tragedy or other moods, but the choreography rarely does. Listening to the wonderfully danceable music, one wished for choreography which would capture folk energies, and dramatic actions which would reveal the very hearts of those who had lived and were now at rest beneath the stones. True, Taras used some freestyle movement, such as the game he choreographed for the young men before they leave for war [1916]; and in the episode involving a bereaved woman who finds a new love [1847], he created a few gestures which mirrored inner conflict. In the main, however, the choreography fell short of its mark. Perhaps this genre of ballet were better left to a de Mille, a Lor-

ing, or perhaps to a Graham or another modern choreographer. Taras was just not at home with this type of Americana." [2]

Hughes: "The music sounds as though it could have been created much earlier [than 1962], for it is akin to the style Copland used as far back as 1940 for *Our Town* or a few years later for *Appalachian Spring*. This makes it just about right for what [the collaborators] must have had in mind when they conceived [the ballet]. They began with a cemetery on a hill, a boy and a girl in love, and nineteenth-century costumes. By the time they got to the end, where the lovers— Romeo and Juliet, probably—walked into their tomb, they had covered quite a bit of ground—including Paris and the Eiffel Tower—and illustrated a number of epitaphs. But that American feeling had not been lost. The idea probably seemed novel and good when it was conceived, but it did not work out very well. The combination of black-and-white and colored slides was not satisfying esthetically, the pictures chosen seldom seemed pertinent to the dancing or literary idea. The seven verses [scenes] provided for dancing by duos and trios that tended to be lost beneath the big pictures. But Taras managed to give the decoration strong competition in his choreography of a basketball game and a kind of battle situation involving aviators. These sequences for male dancers had the strength

of numbers and vigorous activity.

"For the City Ballet, *Shadow'd Ground* represents a fresh approach to ballet production, and for that reason the idea, if not the result, must be encouraged. It is true, however, that the experiments of the Judson Dance Theater have proved that far more of interest can be done with multiple-screen projection (using motion pictures), and it cannot be said that *Shadow'd Ground* is adventurous compared to all that has been done in dance theater." [3]

Says Taras, "I tried to break it up so that there weren't all pas de deux—for the boating party, where everyone was drowned, I had ten people, and then there was an all-male sequence, which was like the Lafayette Squadron of World War I, so that had projections with bombardments and planes. One of the problems was that the mechanics worked badly—there wasn't one performance when all the slides came on at the right times (they were shifted on musical cues). The music was originally written for Robbins and Ballets: U.S.A., but not used then. I think it's rather attractive. There was a great deal of opposition to Copland at the time—it was fashionable not to like him. I think the audience was interested in the ballet visually, but the idea that it was set in a cemetery and full of dead people was not appealing. *Giselle* is the only cemetery ballet that works."

Shadow'd Ground. **Epitaphs: 1916.** (*Photo Martha Swope.*)

HARLEQUINADE

Ballet in two acts

CHOREOGRAPHY: George Balanchine

MUSIC: Riccardo Drigo (*Les Millions d'Ar-lequin*, 1900)

COSTUMES, DÉCOR, LIGHTING: Rouben Ter-Arutunian

PREMIERE: 4 February 1965

CAST: *Harlequin*, Edward Villella; *Colombine*, Patricia McBride; *Pierrot, servant to Cassandre*, Deni Lamont; *Pierrette, wife of Pierrot*, Suki Schorer; *Cassandre, father of Colombine*, Michael Arshansky; *Léandre, wealthy suitor to Colombine*, Shaun O'Brien; *La Bonne Fée*, Gloria Govrin; *Les Scaramouches, friends to Harlequin*, 4 couples; *Les Sbires, hired by Cassandre to capture Harlequin*, 3 men; *La Patrouille*, 5 men; *Le Laquais; Alouettes*, Carol Sumner, 8 women; *Les Petits Harlequins*, 8 children

OTHER CASTS: *Harlequin*, Jean-Pierre Bonnefous, John Clifford; *Colombine*, Nicol Hlinka, Gelsey Kirkland; *Pierrette*, Elise Flagg; *La Bonne Fée*, Renee Estópinal, Nina Fedorova

Lengthened version, using complete score and adding 12 couples and 24 children to the cast, premiered 9 January 1973

ACT I: House of Cassandre
ACT II: An Enchanted Park

Harlequinade. **Act I. Edward Villella. (Background, Scaramouches.)** (*Photo Martha Swope.*)

As a boy, Balanchine appeared with other children in Petipa's *Harlequinade* (which had premiered 10 February 1900, St. Petersburg); on the ballet's sixty-fifth birthday, he made a version of his own. Balanchine used the same story, followed the action as marked in the score (says Schorer, "where the score says 'Pierrot takes key,' for example, he is guided by that exactly") and, presumably, caught the spirit, if he did not reproduce all the choreography, of the original. (He has said that this was precisely his intent.)

The characters, of course, are not Russian, but creations of the Italian commedia dell'arte, here with a touch of English influence, particularly in the décor, which is reminiscent of Pollock toy theaters in London. The wispy (and stan-dard) plot, which concerns the efforts of Colombine's father to keep her from Harlequin and marry her off to a rich old suitor, is mostly disposed of in Act I, with Act II given over to danced divertissements (a procedure Balanchine also followed in *Midsummer Night's Dream*). Cassandre's attempts to separate Colombine and Harlequin are abetted by Pierrot and thwarted by Pierrette, who is Colombine's maid. At one point, it appears that Harlequin has been killed, but the Good Fairy, who materializes on the far side of a convenient Greek statue, brings him back to life, then covers him with money, which makes him, at last, an acceptable suitor. Thus Act I contains all the spice and characterization—again, in the same manner as *Midsummer Night's Dream*; both second acts leave something to be desired, despite some dance interest. There is also a problem with the music, cheerfully described as "hack," although it provides an ever-tuneful background. In the main, it was felt that Balanchine had created a felicitous—if occasionally cloying—confection, full of

"toy-theater stylizations and bright-spangled simplifications."

Kisselgoff wrote, "A ballet that takes place on a large-scale puppet stage and whose score incorporates a French song about the first duke of Marlborough is obviously a work of charm and cheer." [1] Barnes: "It is Balanchine's sheer, discon-certing genius to have produced an old ballet so that it looks like a new ballet pretending to be an old ballet." [2] And Kis-selgoff again: "Balanchine's ballet is not quite as old-fashioned as it looks. It has some very modern choreography: the classical choreography for the leads goes beyond the technical capacities of nine-teenth-century dancers. And its cruel message of 'Love [with money] conquers all' is conveyed with contemporary cool." [3]

Manchester: "The plot runs out very early, but the music, unfortunately, does not, and nearly an hour of it is almost more than flesh and blood can stand. The result is that *Harlequinade*, which would have been a lively half-hour of nonsense, runs rapidly downhill from the moment, early in the second act, when the Good Fairy bestows upon him the 'millions' which win for him the hand of Colombine. It is an enchanting moment as she pours the golden coins out of a cornucopia she just happens to have by her. After that all that is needed is a brief, gay passage for the united lovers and a finale for the whole company. Instead we have innumerable entries for a flock of skylarks, and all kinds of dances for everyone.

"There is one little typically Petipa joke which Balanchine has retained in the score. Petipa liked to interpolate a popular song, and Drigo was willing to oblige. Everyone will recognize a tune in the second act; it is known in English as 'For He's a Jolly Good Fellow,' but what Petipa and Drigo were actually using is the old French song 'Marlbrouck s'en va t'en guerre.'

"The setting's 'tuppence colored' children's theater look is perfect for its present purpose. The best of *Harlequinade*, and it is a dazzling best, is in the individual dances arranged for the principals. McBride has a real triumph, especially in her first variation, which contains some glorious développés melting into attitudes en tournant on pointe. Villella is a marvelous Harlequin, all quicksilver and laughing triumph as he overcomes his enemies with his magic bat and dances with a flourish that puts an exclamation point at the end of every phrase." [4]

Kastendieck: "It starts out as a story ballet, but this soon disintegrates into divertissements strung together with so flimsy a thread that it disappears altogether. Before all this happens, the work has already become the kissingest ballet on record. Its musical-comedy finale, however, is just airy dance, introduced with a 'flutter' number to cause a ripple of amusement. Laughter comes early when the original Harlequin is torn limb from limb by the police and thrown dismembered from the house balcony. It continues when some inebriated soldiers (the night watch?) perform their duty in choreographic pattern. Then it fades away. There's some hocus-pocus involving 'La Bonne Fée.' In a sense, anything is likely to happen, but it may not happen soon enough. In being a pretty ballet, *Harlequinade* gets pretty tame at times." [5]

Herridge: "Don't be misled into thinking this is a story ballet. Its substance is in its ballet virtuosity. The atmosphere is of

Harlequinade. Top: **Act II. The Marriage Ceremony. Edward Villella, Gloria Govrin (La Bonne Fée disguised as a Magistrate), Patricia McBride, Suki Schorer, Deni Lamont.** *(Photo Martha Swope.)* *Bottom:* **Act II. Patricia McBride, Edward Villella, Michael Arshansky, Shaun O'Brien.** *(Photo Fred Fehl.)*

use mainly in the incidental humor, which is delicately sly, gently spoofing. There is a droll number with five drunken dragoons, tottering and uncertain but somehow on tempo. A fatuous lute player [Léandre] gets stuck on one note. A group of Alouettes flutter delightfully. A willowy group, ominously dressed in black, are more silly than frightening. And the Scaramouches, chicly dressed, fill out the scene with their striking ensemble dancing. There is something for everyone. Even a few children are added at the end, as tiny Harlequins." [6]

In 1973, Balanchine restored some

music that he had previously omitted, now using the complete score. This time, instead of "a few children," there was a "ballabile des enfants" in the second act, with the parts of miniature Scaramouches, Polichinelles, petits Harlequins, and Pierrots et Pierrettes taken by thirty-two small students. Balanchine made a new polonaise for them, as well as a new tarantella in the first act for some adults, who were described as the "cortège des invités."

Rather unusually, for a work in this repertory, the ballet offers a gallery of portrait roles. There is a wonderful part for

Villella, a blend of comedy and virtuosity, a good soubrette role for tiny blonde Schorer, and a superb part for the droopy, rubbery Lamont.

O'Brien, too, created a delightful, foppish characterization. Says he, "Balanchine showed me the steps exactly, and the concept of the character. I had an idea that it should be younger and sillier, sort of ridiculous, a cream-puffy type male. But he wanted it more of an old fool. So I do it more that way. After a while, he changed the wig and some of the movements. I had added some very florid, baroque gestures, and he said, 'No, I wouldn't.' He never says 'Don't,' just something like 'Maybe you shouldn't.' I devised the make-up, and he studied it. I had done a turned-up nose and lots of curls; I was thinking of a Regency macaroni type, but he wanted a hook nose and older and more foolish; maybe senile almost. I do it that way now. And I've never known him to have such a good time with a costume! He supervised every inch of it; we were there for hours while he shaped that stomach [this judiciously placed belly gives Léandre hilarious problems in walking through a doorway]. He was extremely meticulous about the appearance.

"Incidentally, I remember a version of the ballet Romanov [a contemporary of Balanchine, also Russian-born] staged for the Ballet Russe de Monte Carlo, and there are many similarities, even some of the same steps. Romanov was also remembering things from his childhood. What I mean is that Balanchine has probably reproduced the sense and the essential points of the original, while filling in the rest with new material."

Says Schorer, "My part was really fun. Hop, hop, hop, running around on pointe, blowing kisses, getting mad at Pierrot, even though he's my husband, because he's always trying to keep the lovers apart. I keep trying to get them together. I'm mad because he won't give me the key—I have to sneak it away. I tie his sleeves together. At one point, when he tries to get into the house, I come running out with the broom and hit him with it. Then at the end of the first act I help Colombine and Harlequin escape, and Pierrot's left hanging out of the house. At the beginning of the second act, I'm still running after Colombine, trying to put her cape on. They finally sign the marriage license. Then I forgive Pierrot."

McBride: "Colombine's very mischie-vous, but she doesn't have as much character as the other three. It's mostly dancing. My variation is extremely difficult, and the pas de deux is very fast, never stops moving. There's very little pantomime for me. There's not much time for it. But wonderful, beautiful dancing."

DON QUIXOTE

Ballet in three acts

CHOREOGRAPHY: George Balanchine

MUSIC: Nicolas Nabokov (commissioned by the New York City Ballet)

COSTUMES, DÉCOR, LIGHTING: Esteban Francés, assisted by Peter Harvey

PREMIERE: 28 May 1965 (gala benefit preview 27 May 1965, with Balanchine as Don Quixote)

CAST: *Don Quixote*, Richard Rapp; *Dulcinea*, Suzanne Farrell; *Sancho Panza*, Deni Lamont

PROLOGUE (*Don Quixote's Study*): *Don Quixote*; *Dulcinea*; *Sancho Panza*; *Fantasies*, 6 children
ACT I, SCENE 1 (*La Mancha*): *Don Quixote*; *Sancho Panza*; *A Peasant*; *A Boy*; 6 *Slaves*; 2 *Guards*; SCENE 2 (*A Village Square*): 3 *Market Vendors*; 2 *Waitresses*; *Café Proprietor*; *Townspeople*, 16 women, 8 men; *Dead Poet*; *His Friend*; 2 *Pallbearers*; *Marcela*, Farrell; 2 *Policemen*; *Organ Grinder*; *Puppeteer*; *Puppets* (children): 5 *Saracens*, *Christian Girl*, *Christian Boy*; 4 *Palace Guards*; 2 *Ladies in Waiting*; 2 *Gentlemen in Waiting*; *Duke*, Nicholas Magallanes; *Duchess*, Jillana
ACT II (*The Palace*): *Don Quixote*; *Sancho Panza*; *Vision of Dulcinea*; *Duke*; *Duchess*; 2 *Ladies in Waiting*; 2 *Gentlemen in Waiting*; *Major Domo*; *Ladies and Gentlemen of the Court*, 8 couples; *Merlin*, Francisco Moncion; *Divertissements*: *Danza della Caccia*, Patricia Neary, Conrad Ludlow, Kent Stowell; *Pas de deux Mauresque*, Suki Schorer, John Prinz; *Courante Sicilienne*, Sara Leland, Kay Mazzo, Carol Sumner, Frank Ohman, Robert Rodham, Earle Sieveling; *Rigaudon Flamenco*, Gloria Govrin, Arthur Mitchell; *Ritornel*, Patricia McBride, child
ACT III, SCENE 1 (*A Garden of the Palace*): *Don Quixote*; *Sancho Panza*; *Pas d'Action: Knight of the Silver Moon*, Ludlow; *Maidens*, Marnee Morris, Mimi Paul, 16 women; *Cavaliers*, Anthony

Blum, Ohman; *Variation I*, Paul; *Variation II*, Morris; *Variation III*, Blum; *Variation IV*, Farrell; *Merlin*; *Night Spirit*, Govrin; SCENE 2 (*La Mancha*): *Don Quixote*; *Sancho Panza*; *Pigs*; 4 *Bearers*; SCENE 3 (*Don Quixote's Study*): *Don Quixote*; *Sancho Panza*; *Housekeeper*; *Priest*; and entire company.

OTHER CASTS: *Don Quixote*, Jacques d'Amboise, George Balanchine, Jean-Pierre Bonnefous, Moncion; *Dulcinea*, Leland, Mazzo; *Pas Classique Espagnol* (added 1972), Karin von Aroldingen, Merrill Ashley; Tracy Bennett, Blum, Peter Martins; *Pas de Deux Mauresque*, Muriel Aasen, Elise Flagg, Gelsey Kirkland, Christine Redpath; Victor Castelli, John Clifford, Bart Cook

PROLOGUE and ACT I
In which Don Quixote reads—Dreams and Fantasies—Vision of Dulcinea—The attainment of knighthood and beginning of the quest—Incident of the boy and the peasant—Adventure of the slaves—Sancho's adventure in the market place—Marcela and the murdered poet—Performance at the puppet theater—Arrival of the Duke and Duchess
ACT II
In which Don Quixote and Sancho Panza come to Court—Entertainment at Court—A Masque and other diversions—Merlin makes magic—Vision of Dulcinea
ACT III
Of knights, ladies, and sorcery—Further adventures and a stampede—How Don Quixote comes home—Apotheosis and death

The ambitious *Don Quixote*, now more than ten years old, is a problem ballet. Kisselgoff put it aptly: "Boring is what some persons will think of [*Don Quixote*]. Stimulating is what this rich and very personal work of art can prove to be to those who watch it very closely." [1]
Other views:
"It's big. It's expensive. It's eye-filling. But it isn't a very good ballet. The solid virtues cannot fill vast expanses of choreographic inaction. The art of ballet dancing is the weakest ingredient in this staging of the Don's sad tale."—Terry [2]
"The embroidery was exciting. As dance-theater, however, it was much less than exciting."—Campbell [3]
"Do not expect to be superficially entertained by a comic romp, by a bag of theatrical tricks, or by a costume show, for it is a serious work. It is also, I think, a success."—Hughes [4]

"Too much is danceless mime. Even reducing the story to its essentials required excessive time, and in those simple line sketches Balanchine took up too much of it. Worse, he seemed at a loss in doing it, and although these periods were not terribly long, they seemed that way. Surely, more than half of the work is dance and yet it hardly appears it." [5]

"Balanchine's three-act work tells the famous history of the Don's madness related to its social background—the Spain of Philip II. It is also a sumptuous spectacle, the handsomest in international repertory. It offers an enormous amount to look at—sets, indoors and outdoors, hundreds of costumes, props, beards, small children, a thirty-foot giant, animals, a penitential procession, a traveling marionette show, a village festival, a court ball, a divertissement, a masque, a long classic pas d'action, lots of pantomime—the way to watch shifts unpredictably. Rich and strange, bitter, delicate and tragic, the piece gathers in one's imagination. When it is finished, it seems to have become a somber story of alienation. Its dramatic force has been an increasing pathos."—Denby [6]

"It is a grand ballet, but also, with its personal theme of a man's soul on the way to salvation, it is a strangely intimate ballet, and it is this particular quality of a small true voice set against a large orchestra that gives the ballet its immeasurably touching quality."—Barnes [7]

"This is a big, lavish, adventurous [work] I for one will never think of in such terms. What will stay with me is the darkling look of it, the melancholy mood, the knightly quest, the madman's courtesy to put sanity in disrepute, the glory of striving, the rue of rejection, the gently mocked absurdity of reaching too far, the enriching reminder that true poverty of spirit lies in not reaching far enough."—Cassidy [8]

"The flaws are immediately apparent. There is little dancing. The village scene in Act I is dismal. The episodes in which the Don learns—or does he?—that people are masochists and that they prefer slavery to freedom are poorly delineated. The Don is a static figure; he is a martyr from first to last. He is a visionary, but he is also a sleep-walker. And then there is the music, banal and at times trivial.

"I also happen to think *Don Quixote* is a great ballet. It is a statement about life, it is a true restatement of a literary masterpiece, and it is Balanchine's most personal

Don Quixote. Prologue. **Richard Rapp, Suzanne Farrell.** (*Photo Michael Avedon.*)

ballet. Going beyond the novel, the ballet captures the darkness and neuroticism peculiar to Spanish culture. Like a poem, the work is also supremely rich in associative images, bringing to mind the Spanish inquisition, the black mass, and Hieronymus Bosch. In short, the world of Don Quixote is upside down and immoral. The sarabande of Act II is the essence of cruelty and decadence, and the following variations, particularly the Pas de Deux Mauresque, contain undercurrents of violence, false gaiety, and narcissism. The dances in Act III are not quite lyrical, but rather mournful and desperate in their twists and turns, especially the passages for Dulcinea. Choreographically, *Don Quixote* is one of Balanchine's thinnest ballets, yet its dramatic and literary texture deepens and thickens with each viewing."—Goldner [9]

There are two principal reactions to *Don Quixote:* those who want complete satisfaction from the aural and visual spectacle, who want the entire "story" to unfold as they sit, are usually disappointed, and, yes, often bored. As a dance (or theater) presentation, it has static moments. Others, however, taking into account the ballet's literary and philosophical background, see it as an intellectually stimu-

lating commentary on important themes of pride, humility, integrity, faith (the ballet is replete with Christian symbolism), romantic vision, artistic vision, the nature of truth, the ideal, human nature, mysticism, the artist as outsider, and very probably, some of Balanchine's personal feelings about art, death, and the reasons for existence. (Says he, "The theme is the hero's finding an ideal, something to live for and sacrifice and serve. For the Don it was Dulcinea, a woman he sought in many guises. He gave his whole life for her—although he never even saw her. I myself think that everything a man does, he does for his ideal woman.") Others enjoyed it as an interpretation of Cervantes.

This is a very rare case of a Balanchine ballet that reveals itself most fully in recollection, not in immediate kinetic impact. It hints at a great many themes, but it does not spell out very much. So much of the Don's character is internalized that it cannot be realized either in dance or in any visual way at all; says Balanchine, "His specific search for truth is more philosophic than physical." So the audience works very hard and is not immediately rewarded. Meanwhile, the dance surface of the work is uneven. Barnes wrote, "It is a ballet for connoisseurs in a generous mood." [10]

There are additional frustrations. Don Quixote is not a dancing role. Opera and ballet, which depend on physical virtuosity for expression, have the same dilemma in depicting old people, and in almost no case is an old person more than an ancillary eccentric or clown. Not here. This creates acute problems for the interpreter. ("It is difficult to give a choreographic characterization when there is no choreography.") On the other hand, a dancing Don (wrote Barnes) would be as inappropriate as a dancing Lear.

The second major drawback is the music. Music critics found it derivative of Stravinsky, Hindemith, and others, and completely undistinguished on its own ("moovie musick"). The only sections that are original and expressive are the passages for Dulcinea (or Don Quixote's vision of "all the aspects of woman, the cord on which the beads of his life are strung, the unifying element of his precarious existence"), which occur in each act, and isolated moments in the Act II divertissements, notably the Renaissance-style Sarabande for the court couples and the Pas de Deux Mauresque. For the rest, Porter found it a "wretched score, which lays a deadening hand on the evening. It is short-breathed, repetitive, feeble in its little attempts to achieve vivacity by recourse to a trumpet solo or a gong stroke." [11] Musical support of this nature puts an enormous strain on an evening-long entertainment.

It seems clear that Balanchine has never been completely satisfied with the work, since he changes parts of it continually. A major addition is the Pas Classique Espagnol in Act I (an episode with a belly dancer is also new here), while a second solo for Marcela and a Juggler variation have departed. Nabokov has written a great deal of new music, which is not more inspired than the old.

This is not the first time the Don Quixote story has been treated as a ballet. In fact, Balanchine danced in the Petipa production at the Maryinsky when he was twelve, a version, with revisions, that is still in the Bolshoi repertory. However, there is virtually no connection (Don Quixote, wearing a very similar costume, also enters on horseback in the Russian Act I—that is about the only resemblance). The Bolshoi work is an energetic, good-natured affair, with bright costumes, zesty dancing, a Minkus score, and no room for an aging idealist; the Don is a cardboard figure. Balanchine and

Nabokov had been discussing a new interpretation for about thirty years.

Says Balanchine, "The ballet at the Maryinsky had nothing to do with Don Quixote. Now, *we* are doing *Cervantes*. It is a very serious subject. Don Quixote is a true knight errant; Sancho Panza is all the people in the world. We're all riding donkeys and we think we're on horses. It is a very serious idea—almost like the second coming of Christ. Cervantes was jailed for it, you know."

Wrote Hughes, "Don Quixote, the Spaniard who lost his reason from too much reading about knights errant and chivalric romance, was a comic character in many respects, and there are many episodes in this production that are comic, at least on the surface. But Balanchine has not been deceived by the surface of the story and its befuddled hero. He has recognized the Knight of La Mancha as a kind of Walter Mitty, a man whose fantasies may be foolish, but whose rejection of reality shows a desire to see the world in a brighter light than is visible to the naked, rational eye. His Don Quixote therefore is a wistful, touching figure from the moment he commands Sancho Panza, his foolish, goodhearted squire, to knight him properly with the accolade of sword to shoulder. From that moment the Knight of La Mancha is headed for nothing but trouble until, having seen a final vision of the adored Dulcinea, he dies—peacefully, if sadly—in his bed." [12]

One is hard put to recall any really comical episodes. Sancho Panza is a slightly amusing character, and there is a puppet-show sequence (in which the puppets are little children) that makes one briefly smile. But there is not much that is funny about the ballet.

As Cassidy wrote, "The whole has a wry and salty, sometimes alum, taste, a darkness of texture, a mocking, lacerating wit, a rueful pride of spirit often noblest in defeat. And it has terror, sheer, stark terror. Observe the Don, pig-snouted, the Don enmeshed, the Don caught and caged and carried off by the recurrent horror, the mockery of the masks." [13]

Denby also discussed this aspect: "Balanchine has reinterpreted comic details of the book in a wider tragic sense—the hooded penitents transporting a statue of the Virgin become the Inquisition; the burning of books by his best friends becomes an *auto da fé*; ordinary pigs become half-human; the Don's cage becomes an image of horror; a buxom

country girl becomes a delicate ballerina. Similarly, the masked hazing of Don Quixote at the Duke's, gracefully as it moves, by the shock of its pauses —particularly the last pause, the face blinded by whipped cream, turned immobile to the public—becomes a bitter denunciation of society's meanness. The ballet is not only gloomily lit, but also somber in ideas it suggests. Even if the Inquisition is shown as an hallucination, one recognizes the social fact it represents in a contemporary sense, and remembers the Inquisitor in Dostoevski." [14]

There are two roles around which the ballet revolves—Don Quixote and Dulcinea. The Don, as mentioned, is a difficult character for the stage. Francés, who was actively involved in the creation of the ballet and whose designs were widely praised, confirmed the collaborators' view of Don Quixote as "a hero of Christianity, even a Christ figure, condemned to mockery. The people he meets know he is crazy, and yet they treat him with a certain respect. In some way he is illuminated to them, though they eventually mock him. His search for purity and ideal love, his efforts to conquer evil, his heroism—all ends in ridicule." [15] Balanchine has referred to him as a "secular saint."

Barnes saw in the character "a Christ-like sufferer, always turning the other cheek, something in the mold of St. Sebastian"; Manchester wrote of his "sweet patience."

Terry found "he has done it entirely in terms of mime but he has designed it, molded it, enkindled it with poignancy and deeply felt comic tragedy." [16]

Gottfried: "Wisely avoiding detail, he concentrated on the idealist in a world where idealism is not merely passé but where humanity has become so twisted one would have to be mad to be an idealist." [17]

Cassidy: "Balanchine's Don is straight out of the old Doré illustrations obsessed by heaven and hell, whose very burr of Spanish sun suggests the nimbus of the Host. [In Act II] for an instant the Don is scarlet-robed, crowned with thorns." [18]

Balanchine, who has performed the role several times, has never found a completely satisfactory interpreter, it seems. "No one is *tall* enough to play Don Quixote," he told Moncion, who says, "I think he means 'tall' with inner dignity and

Don Quixote. Above left: **Act I. Francisco Moncion,
Kay Mazzo.** *Top above:* **Act II. Suzanne Farrell,
George Balanchine.** *Left:* **Act III. Kay Mazzo (center).**
Above: **Act III. Apotheosis. George Balanchine.**
(Photos Fred Fehl.)

237

without negativism." Rapp says that "when I got the armor on, I was playing him very stiff and decrepit. Balanchine said, 'No, no—it's an old man but it's young in feeling and vigorous in movement.' I found the part exceedingly difficult. You're afraid you're going to make a fool of yourself, but if you're going into a part like that, you have to go in absolutely all the way. It's like diving into cold water, but you just have to do it. Of course Balanchine shows everything, fantastically. We didn't discuss the character. He doesn't *say* specifically what he wants, but he demonstrates everything. Much of the part is reacting to circumstances. Physically, the role is difficult because you really get beaten up! I used to come out with a bloody nose. I got kicked. The armor was built over a wire frame and that would stick into me. Then you're whipped, you crawl all over the stage. It used to be an absolute pleasure to get into that net. [Don Quixote spends much of Act III lying in a corner in a magic sleep, trapped in a net.]"

Moncion: "It's an exhausting part. I don't know how Balanchine ever did it. The last scene is difficult—to make something out of that procession. Just getting up slowly, coming to, and watching a vision. But I feel it misses being the big dramatic role it might be. The ballet was geared for Dulcinea."

Indeed, the undisputed glory of the work, both dramatically and choreographically, is the role of Dulcinea. She appears first as the servant girl and a vision of the Virgin (nondancing sections), then as the shepherdess Marcela, mourning the dead poet, with a tricky, clipped variation requiring precision in the use of pointes and body direction, and dizzying little spins. In Act II, she is on only at the very end, after Don Quixote has been thoroughly humiliated, a dream figure of comfort in flowing chiffon. In Act III, as the captive maiden, comes her most demanding and thrilling variation, with its ominous overtones—she covers her eyes, looks lost and tormented. It is a long series of falls, shifts, and extreme yet flowing movements of the torso, perfect for what has been referred to as the "fearless" movement of Farrell.

Wrote Hughes, "Bravo! Farrell is absolutely glorious throughout the work. She has the beauty of health and unforced radiance, an easy, natural femininity, and a dance technique that is dazzling. Just how dazzling is revealed in the Act III solo.

***Don Quixote.* Balanchine rehearsing Richard Rapp.** (*Photo Martha Swope.*)

This dance is characterized by unexpected accents and changes of direction and step that make it a tour de force of body control." [19]

It was believed that Farrell, whom Balanchine had referred to as an "alabaster princess," was the closest earthly embodiment of his ideal, and this gave added poignancy to the entire role, particularly when he performed as Don Quixote.

Says Farrell, "I've done more performances crying simply because it's really beautiful. I love it. Choreographically, it's well suited; it builds. You have time to get used to being on stage before you have to do anything demanding. The third act solo—I never knew I danced like that until Mr. B. choreographed that for me. Then as I did it, I saw, and I felt that these movements were what I did well. It took him to see those movements for me. Oddly enough, though, despite all the wonderful dancing, many people have said they especially remember me in the first and last scenes, with my bare feet and hair down. He didn't work much on characterization. If you follow Mr. B.—do what he wants the way he wants—the story and the emotion come through. But he gives you a lot of opportunity to bring something to it yourself. Most of the acting and the mannerisms were mine."

There is other dancing besides Dulcinea's, of course. The Prologue is all pan-

tomime; in Act I, for the past several years, there has been a Pas de Deux Espagnol, replacing the original *jota* for the ensemble. Porter found this to be "a wonderful set of dances, superbly fashioned—a suite in which the soloists and a concertante group of twelve girls are deployed in ever-varied textures. One is dazzled, as always, by the prodigality of Balanchine's invention and shares the evident delight with which he created new, surprising sequences and patterns while limiting himself to the formal language of 'classical-ballet Spanish,' as established by Petipa. [The dance] 'speaks for itself'—though it does not really speak about *Don Quixote.*" [20]

The dances in the second act are more integral to the story. Porter wrote, "These quirky divertissements—entertainment at the ducal party—fall more naturally into the dramatic structure of the piece, and are framed by court dances in which elegance and cruelty are combined. The black-and-gold scene, the black-and-gold costumes, and these cold, precise dances in which aristocratic formality suddenly takes on accents of menace conspire to suggest the Spain of Philip II. The dances are not irrelevant, for Don Quixote is present, and finally shamed, during them; through the chilly glitter of a chivalry that has become a mere code of manners, his true, warmhearted chivalry moves like a steady flame amid flickering agate." [21]

The dancing highlight of his act is the Pas de Deux Mauresque. Says Schorer, "It was a very easy dance, but effective. Slow, undulating, very soft, on and off pointe, sometimes with flexed foot. I always felt it was kind of Slavic, and John [Prinz] had a few jumps where he touched his feet to his head. It was one of the few places in the score where there was any melody. I liked it particularly because I didn't have to move fast, hop around, or 'be cute.' It was as if Balanchine looked at me in a new way." The divertissements all have an Eastern flavor.

Act III has the most extended dance sequence, which includes an entire corps in long chiffon, drenched in moonlight, with silvery-toned music. There is a dreamy quality to their dancing, but the solos for the two women are constricted for lack of musical flow. Then come Dulcinea's brilliant moments. Porter calls it "A vision scene, a dream that turns to nightmare, a whirl of knightly exploits, romance, and sorcery, in which reminiscences of the adventures we have seen mingle with those we know that the knight has read about. It is Don Quixote's dream; the poetic sequence of enchanted dance images portrays his reeling fancies." [22]

Something interesting happens to the narrative line here—the point of view switches during this scene only from Don Quixote's to Dulcinea's. The final scene has no dancing, as Don Quixote, on his deathbed, stares at a relentless procession of menacing hooded figures and other men of religion—the cruel religion of Spain.

Denby, with his usual eloquence, described the unfolding of the ballet: "It starts with mime, as the novel does with Don Quixote among his books of chivalry. He falls asleep. A great monster swoops down. A tiny blond girl perched on a book implores his help; tiny knights in armor and tiny armed monsters attack. He is sound asleep in his chair when a young servant girl enters, quietly goes across the room to raise a curtain and let in the sunrise light. Her quietness tells she has often done this before. He wakes and sees her waiting by his chair. Now she washes his feet and loosens her hair to dry them. She gives him his shoes and he kisses her forehead. He walks forward, thinking about chivalry. She runs after him, drops on her knees, and with a swift movement offers him his sword, pretending to be the page of an imaginary knight. Then she rises and goes out to work without looking back. The room disappears and he is standing sword in hand facing an immense arid plain. On a cart the image of the Virgin appears. It is the same dancer who a moment before was the servant. To the Virgin Don Quixote, as if entranced, dedicates his sword. Sancho runs in, the armor and spear in his hand clattering, and takes a pratfall.

"So one discovers at the start who Dulcinea is—the Virgin, a shy country girl, and a tiny blond princess in a nightmare. The gesture of drying his feet with her hair suggests the Magdalen; more than that it is an ancient gesture that belongs to washing a child. Dulcinea is both very close and very far off. From then on, one is ready to see her through his eyes.

"After Don Quixote has made Sancho knight him, they don't find adventures right away. Then grisly projections appear in the sky; two incidents from the novel leave the Knight and Sancho badly beaten up but beginning to recover. The scene changes to the ancient plaza of a remote small town, with loungers and three village girls dancing. More girls and boys join in. Sancho runs in hugging a stolen fish. Two Guardia Civil grab him and turn him over to the loungers, who enjoy manhandling him. Arriving on horseback, Don Quixote rescues him. A further comic scene is interrupted by a man who drags in a shepherdess—Marcela. He points to a dead man on a bier; the villagers threaten to kill her. The Knight rescues her, and she dances. Her dance is amazing, so transparent, so distinct, so unforeseeable in its invention. It is about virginal freedom. A curtained cart appears. Its small curtain rises on a puppet show, adorable in action and in decor—a perfect pleasure. The tiny blond heroine of it is captured by the Moors. With drawn sword Don Quixote madly rushes to her rescue, the puppet theater collapses on his head and knocks him out. The local Duke and Duchess come onto the plaza and invite him to their palace at once. Barely conscious, he is lifted on Rozinante; Sancho follows on Dapple.

"[Act II.] A vast black and gold throne room in the Duke's palace. Our friends [are seated] near the throne; the aristocratic guests welcome the knight with exaggerated deference. He and Sancho watch a court dance which the Duke and Duchess soon join. The Spanish arm gestures are amusingly elaborate. A divertissement of five numbers follow, performed by hired entertainers. Suddenly one, then more masked aristocrats point to Don Quixote; in a swirl of ironic masked figures [the Duchess] whispers to the Duke, and then returns to the courteous Don. It is a prearranged hazing. Master and man are blindfolded, are made sport of. Brave Don Quixote is crowned Emperor and whipped and left exhausted. A vision of Dulcinea appears, and he stumbles after her. A masked lady taps him on the shoulder, he turns to her, another taps him, you hear a soft thud and see his face blinded by whipped cream. He pauses, then turns blindly toward the disappearing vision of Dulcinea.

"[Act III.] An immensely high gate fences in a moonlit forest—the most mysteriously beautiful setting of the evening. Sancho leaves his exhausted master asleep by the trunk of a tree. A moment later filmy girls appear. Dulcinea and her friends are supported by three bold knights. Though Dulcinea's dazzling pas de deux ends on a hint of menace, miraculous variations follow, one girl boldly striding and turning, another at top speed resting utterly still for an eighth note, then dancing at top speed again. Like a dream, these dances remind you of something recent. Is it perhaps the divertissement, perhaps the shepherdess? The man's powerful variation has arm gestures from the court dance. Dulcinea's variation—marvelous in the feet, in the novel and unorthodox épaulements— carries the hidden secret to its climax. Dancing faster and faster, more and more desperate, opposed by a woman in black like the Duchess, tortured by the enchanter Merlin, Dulcinea at last appeals to the sleeping Knight—he starts up—the horror has vanished, faithful Sancho takes off the encumbering net. But the garden has turned into a landscape of windmills. He is challenged by a giant who grows as big as a windmill. Unappalled, the Don charges him; his lance caught in the windmill fan, he rises high in the air, drops, crawls still alive toward Sancho. Sancho binds his bleeding head. A charging herd of swine stampede him. Masked courtiers of the Duke carry on a cage and open the door. The Knight on all fours feebly crawls away. They move the cage to catch him. Sadly Sancho heads him into it, and they shut it. Like a beast, he is carried to his own home. There Sancho helps him out. The old curate and the old housekeeper undress him and put him to bed. In a fever he sees the Inquisition approach. He sees the burning of his books. He is humble but does not recant. A vision of the Virgin on a cart appears —the image with which the ballet began—after a long pause she raises her head and looks at him. He is lifted in ecstasy, as mystics are by levitation. She vanishes, he collapses sobbing to his bed. His friends return with the shy servant girl. He dies and they mourn him. The servant girl picks up two small sticks, she goes very slowly to the corpse and lays them on his chest to form a cross." [23]

Don Quixote. George Balanchine as Don Quixote. *(Photo Martha Swope.)*

VARIATIONS

CHOREOGRAPHY: George Balanchine

MUSIC: Igor Stravinsky (Variations in Memory of Aldous Huxley, 1965)

LIGHTING: Ronald Bates

PREMIERE: 31 March 1966

CAST: 12 women; 6 men; Suzanne Farrell

Variations, another product of the splendid collaboration (although Stravinsky was not actually on hand for the choreography), received decidedly mixed notices, depending on whether the viewer considered this essay in "lean geometricism" to be "arid, sterile, curiously remote," or of "chaste, crystalline clarity." The difficult music was described by a professional listener (Kerner) as "an eight-minute set of manipulations of a twelve-note theme consisting of all the tones in the chromatic scale. . . . [It is] scored for various interplays among string, woodwind, and brass choirs with more than occasional solo punctuation. The theme is a down-up-down-up-down series that first appears in small-span chords. There follow twelve variations. . . . It is perhaps Stravinsky's most com-municative since he first took up serialism nine years ago"; [1] by a dancer as "difficult; strange sounds; not music, really, just violins squeaking around."

Stravinsky: "The density of the twelve-part variations is the main innovation in the work. One might think of these constructions as musical mobiles, in that the patterns within them will seem to change perspective with repeated hearings. They are relieved and offset by music of contrasting starkness. . . . I do not know how to guide listeners other than to advise them to listen not once but repeatedly." [2] Balanchine took him at his word. In his ballet the piece was played three times.

Barnes described the work in detail: "It is in three parts, each choreographed to the complete score, and all given a kind of unity by a few movement motifs—a certain casual crisscrossing or putting one leg before the other, or a certain nonchalant wrist-flap of the hands. The first part is for twelve girls, dressed in simple black. The movements are natural, and the abruptly flowing convoluted patterns suggest such things as unfolding flowers, the symmetrical groupings of aquacades, or, then again, the sharp impinging lines of natural forces, lovely geometrical explosions as the dancers coalesce and evanesce. This is the click of Geiger counters, the tick of the computers, and, most important, the music of the spheres.

"Now Balanchine changes his position. Having shown us Stravinsky's energy, he moves on to Stravinsky's structure. Six men take the stage. The mood is athletic, even with a few adagio-pyramidal groupings. Balanchine now seems to go at the music with a scalpel. Down the middle of the stage he puts an imaginary line, and divides his athletes into two mirror groupings. The dancers swing from center to side to center, whizzing and dangling on the unbreakable elastic of Stravinsky's imagination. The music sounds completely different.

"But those heroic battles are not the entire story. Balanchine shifts ground once more. He takes one girl and comments upon the music, without particularly expressing it. He makes a few friendly jokes about the score, contrasting surprise sonorities with equally surprising dislocated movements. Zoom like an exploding chorus-girl, Farrell's leg hits the sky in a super-high kick, and with a series of pelvic thrusts she glides, through Stravinsky's—or rather, through Stravinsky's and Balanchine's—music. [The ballet] is, at first glance, a masterpiece—uneven, for the last episode is less well contrived. [Hearing the music] is like walking around a piece of modern sculpture—first one aspect catches the heart, then another. Balanchine has walked around this

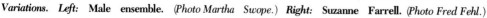

Variations. **Left: Male ensemble.** *(Photo Martha Swope.)* **Right: Suzanne Farrell.** *(Photo Fred Fehl.)*

new score, and *Variations* is the story of that walk." [3]

Terry: "Minor Balanchine, modest Balanchine, and I don't believe the great choreographer intended it to be much more than the agreeable study in form that it is. [It] is not without interest. It holds the eye, but it is dry, dry except for a brief phrase or two for the men dancers, an interweaving mass design for the women, and the always fluid dancing of Farrell." [4]

Manchester: "The first two [settings] make an effect as of watching a kaleidoscope, one all black and white as the girls fall from one sudden pose to another, the second in grisaille, as six young men in gray perform some minor acrobatics. [In the third], Farrell, in white tunic, pony-tail flying, struts, drags her elegant feet, juts out a hip and prances about the stage. The music arrives at no climax, so each variation stops rather than comes to an end." [5]

"Perspiration would clearly be out of place—and that is meant as something of a criticism, for while the work is inventive and beautiful, its beauty is austere and its inventiveness mathematical. It leaves its viewer uninvolved." [6]

Says Farrell, "It was a wonderful idea to play it three times; I think it would be fun if we could split the stage into three levels and see everything going on at once. It's amazing how he could create so many different steps to the same music. This was one ballet I was not crazy about at the beginning—the music was hard to hear, and my variation long; eight minutes is a long time to make something interesting all alone. After I started to see what he had done for the others and what he had done for me, and to get used to the music, it became a lot easier. My variation started out very fast, very, very fast, with something on practically every note. Then all of a sudden it stopped; then it would just pick up in spurts. Lots of times I would 'stagger,' fall off balance, and he left that in. A lot of it was personal mannerisms. Then, after frantic dancing, it stopped, and the next steps were not really set. They were there, but a lot depended on the tempo, whether I held my balance, did my pirouettes—it would be different every time. It was sort of set and not set. In a way it was a challenge. And I began to have more fun with it after a while. Parts were difficult, parts not so difficult, and parts were made to look in-

teresting and let you rest at the same time. People don't always take as readily to that sort of choreography as they would to someone in a tutu, or the kind of music they can move with and identify with. At the end I finished with a walk-over. That variation had just about everything in it."

Said Balanchine, "Without her, there would have been no *Variations*." [7]

SUMMERSPACE

A Lyric Dance

CHOREOGRAPHY: Merce Cunningham

MUSIC: Morton Feldman (*Ixion*)

COSTUMES, DÉCOR: Robert Rauschenberg

PRODUCTION SUPERVISION: John Braden

LIGHTING: Ronald Bates

PREMIERE: 14 April 1966 (first presented August 1958 by Merce Cunningham and Dance Company, American Dance Festival, New London, Conn.)

CAST: Anthony Blum, Deni Lamont, Sara Leland, Kay Mazzo, Patricia Neary, Carol Sumner
Also danced by Teena McConnell

Summerspace was a very unusual work for the Company to undertake. Cunningham had done nothing for the New York City Ballet since *The Seasons* (1947), which, unlike *Summerspace*, was created for what he considered the capabilities of ballet dancers (the performers at the time found it neither difficult nor avant-garde).

Summerspace was done originally on his own company and, although basically the same work, it looked quite different on the bodies of ballet dancers. By training, ballet dancers seek lightness, and pointe shoes accentuate this; so a feeling of weight, of "floor-groundedness" was lost with the transfer to pointe. Further, the impulses of the movements in ballet and modern dance are completely dissimilar. The ballet dancers found the many sustained things "painful." Manchester: "Cunningham's magic was to create space out of small stages. Here his magic is taken away from him because he already had all the space in the world." [1]

Preoccupation with space was also revealed in Cunningham's notes on the original creation of *Summerspace*, which, to his delight and constant awe, he was able to rehearse in its entirety in a large living room (referred to as a ballroom): "The summer part of the title came after the dance was finished, but the notion of space was always present. I fumbled

Summerspace. **Kay Mazzo, Patricia Neary.** (*Photo Martha Swope.*)

SUMMERSPACE

around with steps and written notes about steps, as I often do, but the principal momentum was a concern for steps that carry one through a space, and not only into it, like the passage of birds, stopping for moments on the ground and then going on, or automobiles more relentlessly throbbing along turnpikes and under and over cloverleaves. This led to the idea of using kinds of movement that would be continuous, and carry the dancer into the playing area and out of it. [Some of the steps mapped out in the space] were turning, leaps, runs, walks, skips in repetition, a complex whirling phrase. The dance came out to have a great deal of turning in it. To this gamut of movement in given space-directions was applied a chance procedure. . . . As much as possible I worked with a single dancer all the way through his actions except where a movement came directly in contact with another dancer. Perhaps this is what gives the dance its sense of beings in isolation in their motion, along with the sense of continuous appearing and vanishing. When we began to put the dance together in the ballroom, it was both difficult and exhilarating. Difficult with the abrupt demands in changes of speed, physical coordination, and the learning of the continuity, and exhilarating, too, having such a large free space to do large movement in. (Even with a large area, it is astonishing how often six people can find themselves on top of each other.) We presented it in the spot-costumes, against the pointillist backdrop, and with the music. The audience was puzzled." [2]

The work was taken in stride by the ballet dancers. Critics found it novel and admirable. It did not remain long in the repertory, however, possibly because it was difficult to maintain.

Barnes wrote: "A shimmer of light, a flash of dance, an instant of looking back on some experience of summer, of shaking, hazy heat, and eyeballs pressed red against the sun, of cool shade, and cooler lemonade, of dappled leaves, of innocent and fugitive summer love—the ballet is as nonstop as that sentence. The music is firmly in the area of chance. Feldman neglects conventional musical notation and indicates his musical preferences loosely on graph-paper by means of numbers. The players are permitted to play any notes they take a fancy to, with Feldman dictating only the tonal range, number, and rhythmic timing of the notes played. The resulting squiggles of sound are

[very] pretty and arresting. The decor is Seurat abstracted (like cool orange juice out of a hot orange) into the most beautiful wallpaper the world has ever known.

"The choreography is one with the music and decoration. In a way Cunningham's dancing is as pointillistic as the backcloth. He uses a series of repetitive steps, like the repetition of a musical phrase, to give a spot, a single dominant spot, of movement color. For this he utilizes especially big, searching jumps or tight, toplike little turns, as if he were a painter dabbing on reds or yellows. He [also] uses classical steps, yet often the arms will be tied to the dancers' sides, so that the familiar movements look oddly aberrated. Also, there is the lack of conscious continuity, for when the dancers stop, they stop with a certain flair—a certain awareness that white also has a place in the spectrum, and that nonmovement can also be a positive statement. This askance kind of dancing, quirky, unexpected, and suddenly beautiful, is typical of Cunningham." [3]

Gale: "I saw a greensward by a river under a hot sun, with dragonflies, fishes, horses on the path, and dancing notes on the water. This pointillistic skyscape setting is carried through in color in the costumes and laps over the footlights into the equally pointillistic and cruelly complicated score. Against this nervous background, the dancers whirl, spin, slide, posture, kick, and patter in unending and seemingly unrelated patterns scarcely touching or noticing one another. Yet the movements have continuity and cohesion. It is fascinating to watch Cunningham's sensitivity in planning whatever it is he is playing, for even if *Summerspace* is an abstraction, it shines like the classical parabola of a sonata." [4]

Says Gordon Boelzner, the rehearsal pianist, of Cunningham's methods: "He has of course no need for music at rehearsals, in fact no need for music. When he staged *Summerspace*, those rehearsals were silent except for the sounds of his clapping or counting, but once in a while I'd come in and insist on tinkling through Feldman's score just because I wanted to work with him. I rather liked watching him rehearse without music because you see, for example, one person doing something in a different time from another person, and it rubs together in a very interesting way." [5]

BRAHMS-SCHOENBERG QUARTET

CHOREOGRAPHY: George Balanchine

MUSIC: Johannes Brahms (First Piano Quartet in G minor, op. 25, 1861, orchestrated by Arnold Schoenberg, 1937)

COSTUMES: Karinska

DÉCOR: Peter Harvey

LIGHTING: Ronald Bates

PREMIERE: 21 April 1966 (gala benefit preview 19 April 1966)

CAST: *Allegro*, Melissa Hayden, André Prokovsky, Gloria Govrin; 8 women, 4 men; *Intermezzo*, Patricia McBride, Kent Stowell; 3 women; *Andante*, Allegra Kent, Edward Villella; 3 female demi-soloists, 12 women; *Rondo alla Zingarese*, Suzanne Farrell, Jacques d'Amboise; 8 couples

OTHER CASTS: *Allegro*, Gelsey Kirkland, Kay Mazzo, Violette Verdy, Lynda Yourth; Anthony Blum, Peter Martins, Earle Sieveling, Robert Weiss; Karin von Aroldingen, Nina Fedorova, Colleen Neary; *Intermezzo*, Kent, Sara Leland; Bart Cook, Conrad Ludlow, Nolan T'Sani; *Andante*, Elise Flagg, Kirkland, Neary, Christine Redpath, Suki Schorer; John Clifford, Adam Lüders, Stowell, Peter Schaufuss, Weiss; *Rondo*, von Aroldingen, Merrill Ashley, Marnee Morris; Martins, Paul Mejia, John Prinz

A large, almost over-lush work in dusky ballgowns, mirroring the exultant music with its sweeping, yet thick and heavy melodies. Balanchine, who always seems to know precisely what aesthetic level he is working at, said the scene was like a television ballroom—just a few too many voluminous drapes and off-rose satins. Some found in it a hint of old Vienna.

The work is actually four separate sections (therefore called by some "symphonic ballet"), and full of dancing. Yet it is not quite the most distinguished Balanchine, with the exception of the Intermezzo. This is a melting adagio, full of dippings, swoopings, lyrical backbends, with the woman transported over the stage in the most graceful of positions, appearing willowy, weightless, beautiful, dreamy, soulful. The man is her solicitous

Brahms-Schoenberg Quartet. Above: Allegro. Earle Sieveling, Melissa Hayden. *Right:* Intermezzo. Conrad Ludlow, Allegra Kent. (*Photos Martha Swope.*)

and protective partner. It seems almost more about impeccable good breeding than about dancing, for all that the dance images are exquisite. Elsewhere, the work is drawn out, with the fourth movement very broad (following the gustiness of the music).

Wrote Terry: "A beauty, knowingly balanced and shrewdly built, for it balances classical ballet action with flights into demi-caractère spirit, sweeping lyricism with bright bravura, and it builds through steps which are lively but elegant to a Hungarian gypsy finale which warrants the straight-from-the-shoulder description 'socko.' True, not every phrase nor even every segment is top-drawer Balanchine, but the majority of the passages represents [him] at his inventive best in the classical idiom. The weakest section was the opening Allegro, for the choreography was more routine by far than that of the rest. In the Intermezzo, McBride was radiance itself in some of the most exquisitely wrought designs that Balanchine has created. The third movement, supported by a stunning ensemble, lifted the ballet still higher, and the last section exploded into a dazzling gypsy finish." [1]

Barnes: "A powerful but uneven ballet. At times Balanchine is creating at full pressure, but elsewhere he seems to be filling in time. . . . Its craftsmanship is evident, but so is its solidity. It is a ballet weighted down by its music, yet it undeniably offers spectacular opportunities to its dancers." [2]

Miller: "Has all the ballet-ballet con-

ventions: pretty-pretty costumes of mossy hues, tulle and ribbons, pretty-pretty draperies of the boudoir or mortuary variety, ballerina and cavalier roles in each of the four movements, and a 'big' score. For all its trappings, this Balanchine is as inward and personal as his other Brahms, *Liebeslieder Walzer.* Example: Ludlow wrapped up with Kent and utterly embraced by the Intermezzo." [3]

As Kirstein notes, this was the first big plotless work in which the full large new stage was explored.

Most agree that the first movement was a disappointment. Hayden says that

"it was one of the few things Balanchine ever created for me in which I did not feel comfortable. He started out with fantastic steps that required very intricate partnering, which he could do but others could not. It was going to be like the best of *Liebeslieder* on pointe, very difficult, but it had to be watered down and watered down. I lost my identity in it."

It has a flamboyant part for female soloist, however, usually danced by a big girl, complete with leaps and almost bacchanalian backbends.

Of the second movement, the acknowledged jewel, McBride remembers, "He started it, but seemed to be having problems, practically the only time. He took a few days off, went away. When he came back, it went so fast; he finished the movement in about an hour. It was as though everything had formulated itself in his head while he was away, then just melted into place. One step flowed into another. It's such a beautiful thing, very difficult with timing. But the partner does it all. I'm off-balance all the time, mostly bending back; I actually have a special arc for Brahms."

In the third movement, it is the corps groupings that are the most interesting, although the ballerina, usually a small girl, has some dainty beating footwork, with a touch of perky march rhythm, and there are some swift and athletic passages for the man, with beats and air turns, also for the small and the fleet.

For those who like such things, in the

Brahms-Schoenberg Quartet. **Rondo alla Zingarese. Karin von Aroldingen.** (*Photo Martha Swope.*)

Rondo there are tambourines, ribbons, stomping, kicking, and enormous smiles: "Here Balanchine is surely having a high old time making fun of all the tzigane conventions that ever were." [4]

JEUX

CHOREOGRAPHY: John Taras

MUSIC: Claude Debussy (1912)

Libretto after Vaslav Nijinsky

COSTUMES, DÉCOR: Raoul Pene Du Bois

LIGHTING: Jules Fisher

PREMIERE: 28 April 1966

CAST: *The Young Man,* Edward Villella; *First Young Girl,* Allegra Kent; *Second Young Girl,* Melissa Hayden

OTHER CASTS: Karin von Aroldingen, Sara Leland

*J*eux, originally choreographed in 1913, has an important place in dance history. According to Kirstein, this was the "first ballet in our time to capitalize on a contemporary theme—visually, musically, and in its narrative pretext. While sport was its ostensible subject, tennis was but a metaphor for psychological patterns in modern manners." [1] It is also said to be the first ballet in modern dress, choreographed to a score commissioned by Diaghilev from Debussy, and one of three "dangerous experiments"—strangely original, sexually absorbed works by the enigmatic, half-adolescent Nijinsky. While not so overtly erotic as his first ballet, *L'Après-midi d'un Faune* (which caused a scandal), *Jeux* dealt with a subject potentially more volatile than the sexual intercourse explicitly suggested in *Faune: Jeux* involved an uncomfortable—and unresolved—triangle, with overtones of lesbianism. (His later *Sacre du Printemps* concerned puberty and ritual sacrifice.)

Nijinsky was innovative choreographically as well. In *Faune* his dancers turned sideways, in stylized imitation of the Greek dancing seen on Attic vases. Of *Jeux,* Lydia Sokolova has written: "The novelty of *Jeux* was that it was danced on three-quarter point: That is to say, the dancers neither stood on their

Jeux. Melissa Hayden, Edward Villella, Allegra Kent. (*Photo Fred Fehl.*)

points nor on the ball of the foot. Instead of wearing the usual, padded toe-shoes, the girls and Nijinsky had slippers which were just slightly hardened at the tips. It was not really very effective; it looked as if they were trying to dance on their points and not doing it properly. It must have been the first ballet inspired by the modern craze for sport. *Jeux* had some pretty and original groupings, but there wasn't much to it. Nijinsky's idea must have been to turn his dancers into puppets by inventing a stiff and angular choreography, and to suggest that in the twentieth century, love was just another game, like tennis." [2]

Kirstein has for many years been intrigued by Nijinsky, and it would not be surprising one day to see a Kirstein study asserting the primacy of Nijinsky the choreographer over Nijinsky the legendary dancer.* In any case, it was Kirstein who suggested that Taras mount a new version of the work.

The scenario is simplicity itself; the homosexual innuendoes are so oblique as to be easily ignored. What occurs on stage is, in fact, merely an interlude; at the end, as Kent says, "nobody gets anybody."

Says Taras, "The libretto is the libretto, and I followed it religiously. I always feel that if something is written as a ballet, you have to try to work with it as it was meant to be—if you can't, if you can't find a way,

* This has now appeared, with the title *Nijinsky Dancing* (New York: Knopf, 1975).

then you shouldn't do it. With *Jeux* it's all very clearly marked—I did a lot of research on Debussy and looked at reviews of the time to see what had been done. As the two girls start out, it's perhaps innocent, but it's a very intimate relationship. There is a great deal of nervousness—they're always looking to see if someone's watching. This doesn't have to be lesbian; it could be just terribly girlish, kissing each other, playing with each other. It's all there in the music. It's playful, it exudes freedom, and it suddenly gets tense and nervous, and I think they certainly were very friendly. When the boy comes, one of them becomes interested in him immediately; the other runs away. When she sees the first girl involved with him she gets angry with both, and has a sort of tantrum with them. He gets interested in her, and then there's sort of a wave, and all three are involved. It becomes not a nightmare but, well, almost like a dream. That's why I suddenly made them all do everything in slow motion, because it's so unreal. And then something so perfectly commonplace, like the return of the ball, breaks it up."

Taras made no attempt to copy Nijinsky's three-quarter point style (the original choreography has been lost).

Jeux was quite well received; however, it is not a robust work on the surface, and the reviews implied that there was a lack of substance in it.

Barnes wrote, "A ballet of great charm and atmosphere. The choreography is slight but effective and full of grace and craftsmanship. Most important, Taras has managed to suggest and sustain the mood of a hot summer evening, where secrets are told and emotional corners turned, one of those evenings with thunder in the air, after which, for these three, nothing can ever be the same again. In addition to the apt sensitivity of choreography and production, the ballet was considerably helped by the lushly overpowering scenery, which, with its verdant lakeside setting, was perfect in suggesting summer languor and just those muffled undertones that are at the heart of the ballet. Interestingly, a major change [has been] to make the relationship between the two girls more serious than in the original. Nijinsky was trying to produce a twentieth-century ballet where love has become a game of flirtation no more serious than tennis. Taras, correctly I think, has found a deeper tone in the music, and the relationship of the girls is no longer merely flippant." [3]

Terry: "Although there are poignant, sensitive, troubled, and even near-violent (emotionally, that is) moments, it is a curiously thin, fragmentary, formally unresolved bit of choreography." [4]

Manchester: "Continues to fascinate as an exploration into relationships which Proust's 'jeunes filles en fleur' would have understood very well." [5]

Says Hayden, "Even with movement, music, story one can be completely lost without good direction. This John provided. The movement may imply certain things, but the story was just what you saw. Two girls were involved, but childishly, and the distraction was the boy, who caused a sense of rift between the two. The boy was unconcerned, not terribly involved with anyone. John always has such wonderful taste. The look of the whole thing was terrific—especially the scenery, and Allegra's outfit."

NARKISSOS

CHOREOGRAPHY: Edward Villella

MUSIC: Robert Prince

From an idea by William D. Roberts

COSTUMES, DÉCOR, LIGHTING: John Braden

PREMIERE: 21 July 1966, Performing Arts Center, Saratoga Springs, New York

CAST: *Narkissos*, Edward Villella; *Echo Figure*, Patricia McBride; *Image-Nemesis Figure*, Michael Steele; *Figures*, 11 women, 9 men

OTHER CASTS: *Narkissos*, Paul Mejia; *Echo Figure*, Kay Mazzo

Narkissos, Villella's first full-scale ballet, turned out to be too ambitious for his level of development at the time (he had previously only set concert numbers). He was also burdened by a difficult libretto, "raucous" music, and costumes that were "store-window chic."

Manchester: "The obsessive self-love of Narkissos, the punishment of Nemesis which dooms him to fall in love with his own reflection, and the unrequited love of the nymph Echo who pines away until

nothing remains but her voice, is a slight enough subject for a ballet. By dragging in all kinds of Freudian implications, Villella creates difficulties for himself which he is never able to surmount. His own dance passages have a dark, violent beauty, and he has devised some interesting new movements for himself. The trouble is that his dancing exists in isolation; it does not grow out of the action, or forward such story as there may be." [1]

Barnes: "The usual legend has been changed, it seems. Narcissus is now a simple loner—we see him crouched, in typical fetal position, examining his reflection. The world proceeds around him, but he can only express himself in exhibitionistic bursts of energy. Apparently Villella is implying that the back-to-the-womb infantilism that may lead to narcissism may also lead to homosexuality. The choreography was dull. It was classical in style, but lacked a creative spark. The ensemble work was both repetitive and unimaginative. The best passages were the male pas de deux for Narcissus and his Nemesis and those Villella had created for himself. Remains a first ballet that makes you anxious to see his second rather than discuss this first." [2]

Despite announcements from time to time of a new Villella ballet, none has yet been presented by the Company.

LA GUIRLANDE DE CAMPRA

CHOREOGRAPHY: John Taras

MUSIC: Georges Auric, Arthur Honnegger, Daniel Lesur, Alexis Roland-Manuel, Francis Poulenc, Henri Sauguet, Germaine Tailleferre (1954), after a theme by André Campra (1717)

COSTUMES: Peter Harvey, Esteban Francés (from *Figure in the Carpet*)

DÉCOR: Peter Harvey

PREMIERE: 1 December 1966 (gala benefit preview 19 April 1966)

CAST: *Theme (Campra) and 1st variation (Honnegger)*, 8 couples; *2nd variation (Lesur)*, Violette Verdy, 4 women; *3rd variation (Roland-Manuel)*, 3 women; *4th variation (Tailleferre)*, Mimi Paul, 8 women; *5th variation (Poulenc)*, Marnee Morris, Patricia Neary; *6th variation*

(Sauguet), Melissa Hayden, Arthur Mitchell; *7th variation (Auric)*, entire cast

OTHER CASTS: *4th:* Karin von Aroldingen; *6th:* Kay Mazzo, Conrad Ludlow

The ballet was a pièce d'occasion that mistakenly found itself in the repertory. Says Taras, "They're tiny pieces, written for a festival at Aix-en-Provence (Campra was a Provençal composer). It was perfect for a gala function, presenting everyone with ceremony."

It was clearly not durable enough for repeated showings. The ballet's chief backstage interest was that it marked the return of Verdy after a long absence following an injury.

From the audience's point of view, there was very little of interest at all.

Barnes found it "A feeble ballet. The music, elegantly artsy-craftsy, is perfect testimony to the fact that, whatever their immediate generation imagined, when the musical chips are down, 'Les Six' and their followers hardly string up to a row of beans. Decoratively, the work combines the chic with the nasty in an almost shuddering fashion. The choreography never rises above its circumstances. A pas de deux for two girls (Poulenc), the best in the piece, has a perky brilliance. Taras is clearly demonstrating first his craftsmanship and second that he is nobody's fool. Yet the ballet glitters like black on black in a fog." [1]

Herridge: "Only a classroom effort. The period is pseudo–Louis XIV; the style is abstract; the vocabulary is simple; the steps are predictable." [2]

PROLOGUE

CHOREOGRAPHY: Jacques d'Amboise

MUSIC: William Byrd, Giles Farnaby, and others (keyboard works, selected, arranged, and orchestrated by Robert Irving)

COSTUMES, DÉCOR, LIGHTING: Peter Larkin

PREMIERE: 12 January 1967

CAST: *Othello*, Arthur Mitchell; *Desdemona*, Mimi Paul; *Iago*, John Prinz; *Cassio*, Frank Ohman; *Her Friends*, Emelia, Kay Mazzo, Allegra, Marnee Morris; *Guardian*, Deni Lamont; *4 Youths*; *2*

Prologue. **Mimi Paul, Arthur Mitchell (center).** *(Photo Martha Swope.)*

Courtesans; Mother and Children; Merchant; Moneylender; Beggar; Carabiniere; 8 Monks; 2 Maids; Footman; Musician; 2 Students

OTHER CASTS: *Othello,* Francisco Moncion; *Iago,* Ohman; *Cassio,* Michael Steele; *Allegra,* Lynne Stetson

Variations:
1st duet: Allegra, Cassio
1st solo: Emelia
2nd solo: Iago
2nd duet: Othello, Iago
3rd solo: Guardian and Youths
Pas de deux: Othello, Desdemona, ensemble

A fantasy on elements of 'Il Moro di Venezia,' taken from the *Hecatommithi* of Giraldi Cinthio, one of Shakespeare's sources. The action occurs before Shakespeare's play begins" (program).

D'Amboise's fifth ballet, in a complete departure for him, concerned the first meeting of Othello and Desdemona. Lavishly mounted, with potentially fascinating literary pretext, it was not a success. The costumes and settings were criticized as "campily efficient" and expensive-looking, the program note was considered pretentious, and some of the dance invention was called thin.

Wrote Barnes: "A disappointing ballet—but one not without compensations. Here is something that is little more than a classical divertissement tricked out with trappings to make a pseudo-dramatic ballet. . . . Unfortunately, instead of the good things having been brought out, they have been obscured with a deep layer of silly chi-chi. Unquestionably the characters are taken from Shakespeare rather than Cinthio—and one presumes the only reason to mention the almost unknown Italian novelist is to provide the work with a spurious literary gloss of intellectual chic. The choreography seems to come in two sizes, and the dichotomy here represents yet another booby trap along the primrose path of its artistic direction. All of the dances for the background figures are conceived along the waggish, fussy style that Massine seemed to find suitable for most situations. The remainder is more inventive and, while coming directly from Balanchine, also shows distinct signs of individuality, [for instance] the solo for Iago." [1]

Terry: "On top of the dramatic nothingness, there is dance nothingness." [2]

Herridge: "The intention is to set the scene for the later tragedy, to show the beginning of Othello's and Desdemona's love, and the cause of Iago's hate. [But] very little of this gets across in the choreography itself. The smitten pair sit in the background for the most part, and stare at each other. Their final pas de deux is pleasant but undistinguished. Emelia and Cassio are seen in other nice little divertissements. But you can't really be sure what has happened. The whole scene is played without an impelling emotion and with scarcely a hint of things to come." [3]

In a minority report, Hering found effective characterization, particularly of Othello and Iago. In addition she noted: "The pas de deux between Othello and Desdemona is the most sensitively wrought piece of pure dance that d'Amboise has made to date. If he could be encouraged to make the ballet longer, or to retain its present length and delete some of the secondary variations in favor of penetrating more deeply into his principal characters, it could be a moving vignette." [4]

RAGTIME (II)

CHOREOGRAPHY: George Balanchine

MUSIC: Igor Stravinsky (*Ragtime for 11 instruments,* 1918)

LIGHTING: Ronald Bates

PREMIERE: 17 January 1967 (first presented at the Stravinsky Festival of the New York Philharmonic, Philharmonic Hall, Lincoln Center, 15 July 1966)

CAST: Suzanne Farrell, Arthur Mitchell
Also danced by Richard Rapp

A reworking of the 1960 *Ragtime* for *Jazz Concert,* this version had no more staying power.

Wrote Terry, "It would be better as 'after theater' than theater. Farrell's high kick and her coltish high spirits constitute the main attraction." [1]

Hering: "There are exaggerated extensions; little circling promenades, one foot flat, the other on pointe or half toe; there are finger-snappings and hands circling at the wrist. But a trifle is a trifle." [2]

Barnes: "Oddly enough, one of the most effective stage décors is a small orchestral ensemble [as here]. Perhaps the idea of a sort of artistic simulacrum of a cabaret number appealed to Balanchine, for *Ragtime* has many of the externals of the form. Possibly too many. This doh-de-oh-do dancing, with its jazzy struts, high kicks, hands circling in palsy-walsy gestures appeared to lack something that might be called an attitude. Stravinsky's jazz is jazz with a difference, and it is a difference that Balanchine seems to have taken too little note of. Too banal for comfort." [3]

Ragtime. **Suzanne Farrell, Arthur Mitchell.** (*Photo Fred Fehl.*)

TROIS VALSES ROMANTIQUES

CHOREOGRAPHY: George Balanchine

MUSIC: Emmanuel Chabrier

COSTUMES: Karinska (some from *Bourrée Fantasque,* with additions)

LIGHTING: Ronald Bates

PREMIERE: 6 April 1967

DANCERS: Melissa Hayden, Arthur Mitchell; Gloria Govrin and Frank Ohman, Marnee Morris and Kent Stowell; 6 couples

OTHER CASTS: Patricia McBride, Conrad Ludlow, Paul Mejia

Trois Valses was called a "throwaway," a "trifle," "champagne," "froth," and so forth. Created at the last minute (to replace a projected Taras staging of Satie's historic *Parade,* which was abandoned due to copyright problems), it was undeniably light and bright, but, as so often with Balanchine, there was a shadow more than meets the eye—here a touch of nostalgia amidst the harmless fun.

For several critics, the ballet was too reminiscent—or not reminiscent enough—of *Bourrée Fantasque* (the same

costumes, though refurbished) or the hallowed *Cotillon* (some of the same music), both earlier Balanchine works to Chabrier.

Wrote Barnes, "A boy and a girl are dancing; lightly and affectionately they kiss. They part, look back at each other, and the girl, with more affection than flirtation but a hint of both, blows her lover a kiss. The curtain falls. Somehow this incident, happy and uncomplicated, sums up the feathery and fluttery *Trois Valses,* a piece of gorgeous trivia. Spins and embroidery are at its heart." [1]

Gale: "Three brief little dance movements—the first for the ensemble, the second a pas de deux, the third a frieze for the girls joined by their swains, and segue into a breathless finale. A clever, bubbly bauble of absolutely no importance." [2]

Hering: "The highlight was a solo for Hayden in which the yielding back-dips of her upper body and the suppleness of her shoulders reflected a languor all the more provocative because it was surrounded by her natural drive. But Balanchine did not seem to find the point of the music—perhaps there was none to find." [3]

About a year later the ballet was scaled down, performed by fewer dancers with two stage pianos replacing the orchestra. Soon thereafter it disappeared.

JEWELS

CHOREOGRAPHY: George Balanchine

MUSIC: "Emeralds": Gabriel Fauré (from *Pelléas et Mélisande,* 1898, and *Shylock,* 1889); "Rubies": Igor Stravinsky (*Capriccio* for piano and orchestra, 1929); "Diamonds": Peter Ilyitch Tchaikovsky (from Symphony No. 3 in D major, op. 29, 1875)

COSTUMES: Karinska

DÉCOR: Peter Harvey

LIGHTING: Ronald Bates

PREMIERE: 13 April 1967

PIANO: Gordon Boelzner

CAST: *Emeralds:* Violette Verdy and Conrad Ludlow; Mimi Paul and Francisco Moncion; Sara Leland, Suki Schorer, John Prinz; 10 women; *Rubies:* Patricia McBride, Edward Villella; Patricia Neary; 4 women, 8 men; *Diamonds:* Suzanne

Farrell, Jacques d'Amboise; 4 demi-solo couples; 12 women, 12 men

OTHER CASTS: *Emeralds:* Melissa Hayden, Susan Hendl, Allegra Kent, Leland, Kay Mazzo, Christine Redpath, Schorer; Anthony Blum, Frank Ohman, Earle Sieveling; *Rubies:* Gelsey Kirkland, Leland, Schorer; John Clifford, Paul Mejia, Robert Weiss; Karin von Aroldingen, Renee Estópinal, Marnee Morris; *Diamonds:* Merrill Ashley, Kent, Mazzo; Jean-Pierre Bonnefous, Peter Martins

Jewels was a box-office sensation. Barnes's contention that "it is open to doubt whether even Balanchine has ever created a work in which the inspiration was so sustained, the invention so imaginative, or the concept so magnificent" [1] certainly helped. There were other rave reviews. The ballet arrived on the crest of increased public enthusiasm for dance. Word got around, and for a while *Jewels* was, in the language of Broadway, a real "hot ticket."

This unusual brouhaha was engendered by a work that was not popularly oriented: its designation as the first three-act plotless work—set to unknown Fauré, percussive Stravinsky, and less than compelling Tchaikovsky—might mean something to historians but was hardly geared to win the battle for dance. And, if the truth were told, despite many moments of great beauty and ingenuity, it was not the very best of Balanchine: "Emeralds" was a bit bland; "Rubies" could grate on the nerves; "Diamonds" had stretches of the commonplace. Yet people came. Wrote Kirstein dryly: "The very title sounded expensive before any step was taken."

The story goes that Balanchine was inspired to create the work by a visit to the jeweler Van Cleef and Arpels. Said he, "The whole thing was—I like jewels. I'm an Oriental—from Georgia in the Caucasus, and a Russian. I would cover myself with jewels." But then he added, characteristically, "The ballet had nothing to do with jewels. The dancers are just dressed like jewels."

According to *Time,* "When most men visit Van Cleef and Arpels, the result is likely to be an overdrawn bank account. When Balanchine visits, the result is a—gem dandy—ballet." [2]

Manchester evoked the ballet's special glow: " 'Emeralds' takes place in floods of gentle green light in which the dancers move in Romantic ballabiles as though they were part of an 1840 ballet whose plot had been lost. It is all low-keyed and lovely.

"Then comes 'Rubies.' It is brilliant but a little too hectic. Whereas I never tire of all that goes with classic technique, I tire fairly quickly of its deliberate distortions, the throwing out of the hip, the turning in of thigh and knee, which Balanchine uses as the visualization of certain kinds of Stravinsky.

"['Diamonds'], sparkling white every-where, suggests the late-nineteenth-century ballet of the Maryinsky Theater, St. Petersburg. The nobility and elegance of every pas, the sense that we might be watching the final divertissement of a fa-vorite classic, permeates the whole glorious work. Surely here Balanchine is recalling his own days in that same the-ater and paying it homage prompted by his affection and his genius.

"The finale is a great polonaise, and it is a sight to see as all the dancers come sweeping on. National dances do not come easily to American dancers—they did not quite have the measure of it—but it is all there and Balanchine, who has al-ready given us wonderful polonaises in *Theme and Variations* and *La Son-nambula*, has surpassed himself here." [3]

Barnes added more detail: "Balanchine seems to have chosen music that provides a deliberate contrast between one act and the next. This has, of course, imposed its own individual flavor upon each of the dif-ferent acts, so the work becomes a three-angled view of classic dancing. It is probably fanciful, yet I found myself struck with the idea that Balanchine was offering some kind of choreographic homage to the three countries nearest to his heart and life—France, the United States, and Russia. 'Emeralds' is the 'French' ballet of the trio—and Balanchine has created some gracious and graceful dances that are seamless in their flow with the music and that flit across the stage like beautiful birds on a summer night. The movements are complex, with convoluted gestures and held like tendrils, in a style that seemed the peak of lyrical romanticism, all the more intense for being set to the soft-toned voice of Fauré.

"*Capriccio* has that not-quite-echt-jazz feel that Stravinsky utilized at the time, and 'Rubies' seemed the 'American' part of the trilogy. The dancing is sharply ac-cented, with a quirky yet quite unforced kind of invention. Legs fly out at high and

Jewels. Emeralds. Violette Verdy, Conrad Ludlow. (*Photo Fred Fehl.*)

unexpected angles, feet that you expected pointed are made flat, and flirtation is given an edge of delicate and even urbane malice. This is Balanchine's most sophis-ticated vein of choreography, and the dances pour out of him—so that at one moment a girl with India-rubber legs is diverting the attention of four suitors, while a little later a boy is bouncing across the stage, keeping just in front of a quar-tet apparently chasing him. This is genu-ine dance humor, understated, witty, and yet always deriving its wit from the jux-taposition of the dances.

"In the last act, the mood is Russian. We are at once in the atmosphere of 'Dia-monds,' for Balanchine has gone back to his Imperial Russian childhood, and here is the glitter and brilliance of the old Maryinsky. Balanchine has taken us to this territory before, but never with more confidence or more high-style panache, truly classic grandeur." [4]

Garis took a long and measured look: "Unquestionably a major work, but I ad-mire it also because it is a big hit and was meant to be: I like being reminded again of the supreme theatrical instinct that links Balanchine with Shakespeare and Mozart as the kind of genius who can obey and even enjoy and want the neces-sity of pleasing an audience. *Jewels* is a work of genius both as a work of art and as show-business. Though there's no impor-tant meaning in the fact that *Jewels* is the 'first abstract three-act ballet,' there's a lot of good copy in the phrase. The unity of *Jewels* is a matter of surface, of appear-

ance; what is being unified, in fact, is your attention during an evening at the the-ater. But then that's the aim of all theatri-cal art. And underneath the expert packaging are three superb new Balan-chine ballets.

"I wondered why Balanchine, who loves music with a strong beat and solid theatrical power, wanted to use this lux-uriously silky score [Fauré] with almost no beat. 'Emeralds' turned out to be un-like anything [he] has done before. To suit the slow, even flow of the Prelude he has invented a paradise of motionless motion; it is a *mondaine* and elegant paradise, ap-propriate to the music; the movements, like the music, are pure the way expen-sive things are pure; yet the ballet is far nobler in feeling and scale than Fauré, without disrespect for Fauré's meanings. This gleaming shadowless green world is nature methodized, an artifact. But the people are real. The memory of Baude-laire's 'L'Invitation au Voyage' is ines-capable: 'Là, tout n'est qu'ordre et beauté, / Luxe, calme et volupté.'

"Many brilliant dances follow the Pre-lude: the sweep of Paul's long-limbed solo and the pas de trois. But the bright, still, unimpassioned clarity of the Prelude gov-erns the dimensions and dynamics of these quicker dances, and motionless mo-tion is recaptured, deepened, and mo-mentarily darkened by the pas de deux for Paul and Moncion, which seems to represent the private life of this paradise. Balanchine derives the whole dance from the quiet andante beat of the music, con-

Jewels. **Rubies. Patricia McBride, Edward Villella.** (*Photo Fred Fehl.*)

triving not a dance so much as an evenly measured walk, interrupted at unemphatically unpredictable intervals by extensions and lifts. In this intricate and arbitrary pattern the lovers seem to be obeying a difficult foreign code, quite unlike what we think of as convention in classical adagio. At the emotional climax Balanchine uses one of those distorted configurations we are accustomed to in *Agon, Epsiodes,* or *Movements,* but he has subtly modified it into a kind of Byzantine civility. And then with Verdy the social world returns.

"'Rubies' reminds us of other Stravinsky works and of what Balanchine has done with them. For the parts of the *Capriccio* that most resemble the overtly entertaining show-music of *Jeu de Cartes,* Balanchine has devised movements in the spirit of *Card Game;* but the *Capriccio* is reminiscent too of Stravinsky's more serious music, and accordingly we see in 'Rubies' elements of Balanchine's serious work: *Four Temperaments,* in particular, but also *Prodigal Son, Movements,* and *Variations.* The recombination makes a new work, and a new feeling. Morris's provocative poses in the opening section are like sexy show-dancing of the twenties and thirties, but more static and weighty. Near the end of the first movement, when her limbs are manipulated by four men, the effect is funnier than similar things in *Agon,* but the quiet music keeps it from being openly comic. In the second movement, the distorted accents are seriously witty, with the impersonality and power-

ful thrust down toward the floor that Denby has called attention to in *Four Temperaments;* but Villella's solo has an explosive animal force that isn't like anything in *Four Temperaments;* and McBride's solo has a corresponding nervous drive. The last movement would be as lighthearted as *Card Game* but for the irregular phrase-lengths. The high point of this movement, Villella circling the stage with his gang, crystallized the period nostalgia and parody you sense throughout the whole ballet—it looks like a trickcyclist's act. But the basically loose carefree charm is fiercely charged up by Villella's brilliant virtuosity, and the spins as he leaves are just this side of violence. Everybody feels happy about 'Rubies.'

"That there is less to say about 'Diamonds' is a fact about the ballet's meaning, not about its value. 'Diamonds' is not a newly invented world, like 'Emeralds,' nor an inspired new combination of familiar materials, like 'Rubies'; its impulse is toward radical purification, distillation, abstraction. When Farrell is at her best, 'Diamonds' is one of the largest, most intense, most uncluttered experiences in ballet." [5]

Everyone had a favorite section: Manchester clearly preferred "Diamonds"; by

1975, Barnes was coming down on the side of "Rubies." For some, "Emeralds," the least enthusiastically welcomed at the beginning, turned out to be not only the most beautiful but the most enduring part of the composition.* "Rubies" came off as rather vulgar, if "cute." And "Diamonds," except for its poignant and gracious pas de deux, was, in its ensemble work, less than startlingly original.

Wrote Kirstein, in this mood, " 'Diamonds' used two scherzi, a grand adagio, and a gorgeous polonaise, seeming to employ the entire company of ninety and fill the stage to the point of surfeit. This is one of the prime examples of Balanchine's applause-machine. Minutes before the end, the fluid collective organism drives

---

* As a token, perhaps, of his own lasting interest in this part, Balanchine created an additional pas de deux for Verdy and Blum (to more *Shylock* music) in the spring of 1976 as well as another new dance—a pas de sept for all the principals (to *Pelléas*). As Kisselgoff described it, "[The pas de deux] is totally in tune with the opening duet, [with] the same stress on back-to-back partnering. Verdy and Blum enter from opposite wings. They leave by walking backward, she leaning quietly against his side. It is a pas de deux one yearns to see again. [In the pas de sept] there is again the air of the promenade, but there are new chain formations and patterns. But nothing is more startling than the last noble image. The four women leave, the three men drop to one knee." (*NYT,* 2 May 76.)

Jewels. **Diamonds. Jacques d'Amboise, Suzanne Farrell.** (*Photo Martha Swope.*)

toward a sumptuous climax. The audience's empathy and instinctive appetite for block-busting muscular effects devour a big crescendo, gulping at a stage crammed with uniform, symmetrical, head-on movement and firm primary gesture while the big orchestra builds to smashing curtain tableau. *Jewels* has been an unequivocal and rapturous 'success' since its introduction. But some who watch it frequently find that 'Emeralds' rather than the bouncier 'Rubies' or the panache of 'Diamonds' are indeed the most exquisitely set gems in this particular parure." [6]

Says Verdy, " 'Emeralds' is a difficult way to begin. The audience does not warm up. They can't, because it's reserved, proportioned, elegant, and it has a social coldness and restraint. There's no climate, only beautiful, dreamy moments of underwater quality. Naturally, the audience reacts with appreciation and politeness, but never with any kind of warmth or spontaneity. My beautiful solo, with those arms—almost a pantomime—he did in an hour, he had me fill in the steps between the main movements. I think that 'Emeralds' could only be the good, slow start; that 'Rubies,' being a little bit outrageous, had to be sandwiched in between, and that you would extinguish that kind of provocation with a monumental return to full company. 'Diamonds' is possibly not top-drawer Tchaikovsky, not the best constructed. But if a piece is ever so slightly secondary, you will never see Balanchine compensating at any price. You will see him confining himself to the existing limitations rather than forcing a sensation or effect, superimposing it on an unsatisfactory support. He is too honest a musician for that."

Schorer: "The whole of 'Emeralds' has that smooth quality. I ran on pointe very levelly. 'Rubies' was tricky. One of the steps is in a count of ten—triple turn back, double piqués, double en dedans. It's half jazz, half elegant."

Farrell: " 'Diamonds' is hard because you're out there in white and there's no hiding. 'Diamonds' you can't sell. It's too dignified to sell. And you can't cover anything up."

"Rubies," under the title *Capriccio*, was performed during the Stravinsky Festival in June, 1972.

Jewels had a mixed reception in Europe.

England:
"Turned out to be paste. This was disappointing in every way, as it was just three typically Balanchine opening ballets strung together to fill—well, almost fill—an evening." [7]

France:
"It is a minor masterpiece of dance for its own sake, presented without décor in the resplendent costumes of that old magician Karinska. It is crammed with invention and incredible difficulty. The first part, 'Emeralds' is a 'festival de port de bras' in which one sees clearly that the ballerinas of Balanchine are not merely Rockettes with spines of steel. The second part is by far the most brilliant. In it Balanchine resorts to such fabulous acrobatics that he seems to be parodying himself, stopping movements abruptly and letting his dancers freeze." [8]

Germany:
"At the beginning one is delighted, but the longer the performance lasts, the more one is disillusioned. Balanchine had already exploited to the full the finesse of his figures and patterns of movement, his clever combinations and enchainements; now he repeats himself. These *Jewels*—the very title indicates an untimely 'l'art pour l'art'—only glitter dimly. And there are, formerly impossible with Balanchine, repeats and conventions. Balanchine, considered to be the most musical of all great choreographers, seems to have become uncertain even in this field." [9]

Russia:
"In the 'Rubies' section, the ballet master succeeded in 'interweaving' with finesse the classic technique and complexly patterned movements corresponding to the musical inflections of the composer. The glitter and pomp of Tchaikovsky's music have been mounted like finely polished gems in 'Diamonds.' " [10]

GLINKIANA
later, second movement only, called
VALSE FANTAISIE

CHOREOGRAPHY: George Balanchine

MUSIC: Mikhail Glinka

COSTUMES, DÉCOR, LIGHTING: Esteban Francés

PREMIERE: 23 November 1967

CAST: *Polka*, Violette Verdy, Paul Mejia; 3 couples; *Valse Fantaisie*, Mimi Paul, John Clifford; 4 women; *Jota Aragonese*, Melissa Hayden; 6 women, 8 men; *Divertimento Brillante (Pas de Deux)*, Patricia McBride, Edward Villella

OTHER CASTS: *Polka*, Sara Leland; *Valse*, Merrill Ashley, Judith Fugate, Allegra Kent, Gelsey Kirkland, Leland, Kay Mazzo, Suki Schorer; Daniel Duell, John Prinz, Robert Weiss; *Jota*, Suzanne Farrell

This piece was four individual numbers under one infelicitous title (later changed to *Glinkaiana*). The first and third sections were comic, the second and fourth were straight; this jarred some spectators, as did the lowering of the curtain, bows, and change of scenery after each dance. The music was not a unifying factor. Just how disconnected the pieces were, presumably even in the mind of their creator, became clear when the ballet was often staged with at least one of them missing. Within little more than a year, the ballet was pared down to a single episode, *Valse Fantaisie*, and eventually it took that title.

Wrote Barnes, "These four pieces move Balanchine to sweetly tongue-in-cheek variations on national dance styles that are far too beguiling to be satirical and yet retain something of the objectivity that a satire would demand. He takes Glinka's dance forms and makes fun of them in a way that is so wholeheartedly affectionate that the results are both funny and adorable." [1]

Each section had a most individual flavor, and critics could not resist describing them. Barnes:

" 'Light' hearted and light-fingered, delicate and imaginative, superb, puff-pastrylike trifles. The Polka has four dizzy French girls and their even dizzier, mustachioed French swains, nimbly polka-dotting across the scene. Here Verdy is wooed by a dashing Mejia, and both do wonders to the music that itself has enormous wit and charm. One of Balanchine's qualities is the speed with which he makes his effects. This same speed is even more notable in the second episode, Valse Fantaisie, the choreo-

Glinkiana. **Left:** **Polka. Paul Mejia, Violette Verdy.** (*Photo Fred Fehl.*) **Right:** **Valse Fantaisie. Mimi Paul.** (*Photo Martha Swope.*)

graphic highlight of the work. Here, to a waltz of gossamer beauty, dancers whirl and sway in a misty yet still buoyant abandon. Just as in the Polka, Balanchine has deliberately limited his range of steps. He uses the waltz rhythm to support very free patterns, with constant ebbs and flows, entrances and exits. Russian-Spanish is an idiom in itself. In flamboyant red, and as flouncy as a fiesta, dancers belt out ballet Spanish until at the back Hayden strolls on, swinging her hips and twirling her shoulders. The pace hottens. Balanchine uses Spanish dance with a nice affection, neither stressing it nor torturing it, but letting it ride with the music as frothily as the shake of a flamenco skirt. Hayden dances the style with an inbred aristocratic authority. The ballet ends with a glittering showpiece pas de deux." [2]

Marks: "All ingenious invention, it was either perfectly choreographed for its principals or its principals were perfectly matched to its choreography. Verdy is the deliciously Gallic protagonist, always ahead of everybody, irrepressibly insouciant [Balanchine called this a femme-de-chambre-and-valet polka]. The scene changes to a moonscape with silhouetted tree and far-off dream pavilion. The dancers are in shades of lavender. [It is] beautifully danced by Paul, whose eloquent phrasing sometimes gives the impression of suspended movement, as if she were with each step discovering the inner rhythms of the

waltz and relishing them. Holding her own under a hot Mediterranean sun, Hayden puts in a virtuoso performance of the Jota that is three parts *duende* to three parts prima ballerina. It is all done with great crackling flair and immense authority. Following the Jota's flash of red-hot temperament is the quiet cool green of the Divertimento, against a backdrop dominated by a prancing horse statue. The choreography rests lightly on the music, a piano solo, in almost casual understatement. The two dancers share movements that are gracious, balanced, completely unforced, often performed in unison." [3]

Says Verdy, "It was my first soubrette role since *Con Amore.* I had a lot of fun."

Schorer: "The Valse is so lovely. The steps flow from one another and the music. Everything is pretty. There are many jumps and running steps, but nothing awkward, and at the end, when you're exhausted, it's not difficult, just tiny fast steps. You feel beautiful."

METASTASEIS & PITHOPRAKTA

CHOREOGRAPHY: George Balanchine

MUSIC: Iannis Xenakis (*Metastaseis,* 1953–54; *Pithoprakta,* 1955–56)

LIGHTING: Ronald Bates

PREMIERE: 18 January 1968

CAST: I. *Metastaseis,* 22 women, 6 men; II. *Pithoprakta,* Suzanne Farrell, Arthur Mitchell; 7 women, 5 men

Metastasies & Pithoprakta, a ballet with a difficult name, was brief (eight minutes and ten minutes) and intense: for McDonagh, it was "in essence a microscopic view of the human eye" [1]; Manchester found *Metastaseis* "one of the most awe-inspiring theatrical conceptions I can remember." [2]

Xenakis's ideas (the composer is an architect as well as Associate Professor of Mathematical and Automated Music) were described in the program note: "From 1955, he introduced into his music the concept of 'clouds' and 'galaxies' of events in sound, calculus, and the theory of Probability, under the name of Stochastic music. Stochastic is now a rare or obsolete word, derived from the Greek for 'aim at the mark,' or pertaining to conjecture. In Xenakis's usage, it means the calculus of chance, the determination of probabilities—the calculation of accident. From 1958, he made use of the mathematical theory of Games, which he called Strategic music (as in chess), and finally the theory of Sets and mathematical logic, called Symbolic music. 'Metastaseis' is a Greek word meaning 'a state of standstill.' The 'metastases' are a hinge between classical music (which also includes serial composition) and 'formalized' music, used by Xenakis. 'Pithoprakta' means 'action by probabilities.' "

Barnes, Terry, and others not professionally concerned with music claimed to find it listenable.

Terry: "Falls most sweetly, though unconventionally, on the ear through throbbings, pulsations, and a sort of circulatory rushing—perhaps like the bloodstream itself—which seems to echo the hidden rhythms of the inner man." [3]

Manchester described the ballet in detail: "The miracle Balanchine has performed here is to take two pieces of exceptional complexity and aural difficulty and make them such perfect servants of his dance that henceforth they will live in perfect oneness with the ballet.

"[In Metastaseis], a great mass of figures lie in a giant wheel formation in the middle of the stage. As beams of light play across them, [picking] out the white leotards and tights, the mass gradually moves. It heaves, it undulates, until slowly figures assume their full height. Girls are lifted into the air, to fall forward, to be swung round and up again, as the light catches them. Then the figures disperse, as mercury breaks from its phial to spill and roll in little globules. The dancers leap, they paw the ground, they form and re-form. Then they rush across the stage in diagonals, the men catching the girls as they jump past them. Slowly we realize that something extraordinary is happening. Where the diagonals began from downstage right to upstage left, they have now been reversed; the leaping, the pawing continues but the mass is little by little becoming more and more compressed. With the shafts of light still stabbing at them, the figures have drawn together, the girls are being lifted again, they fall, are swung and lifted to fall again, and at last the great mass has returned to its original form. Inert, prone, they lie there as we first saw them, and the light fades and dies. We have watched a gigantic and complex dance palindrome. It is like the heartbeat of some mighty machine which reaches its full intensity of action and then slowly runs down again.

"Where Metastaseis makes an impersonal use of the dancers, Pithoprakta is built around the possibilities of the male and female body. A corps, now all in black, counterpoint the movements of Farrell and Mitchell, caught separately or together in a blazing spotlight. The emphasis is on the extremes to which that other marvelous machine, the body, can be pushed and still retain its grace. For all the contortions, the spasmodic gestures, there is never harshness or ugliness. At the climax, the corps falls, one after the other, to the ground, and it is like some majestic, winter-naked tree falling, its branches cutting through air." [4]

Metastaseis: "The music [for both parts] deals not with melody but with shapes, weights, and sonorities, and both it and the choreography imply the existence of some kind of order, a mathematical or logical principle perhaps, which lies concealed, just below the surface. In the first section, a large number of dancers is used as a featureless mass, a lump of clay forming itself into a moving, changing sculp-

Metastaseis & Pithoprakta. **Pithoprakta.** Suzanne Farrell, Arthur Mitchell. (*Photo Martha Swope.*)

ture. [Later,] when the girls are lifted one by one up out of the mass only to fold over and fall slowly back again, the picture brought to mind was that of a slow-motion film of lava being flung out of the mouth of a volcano." [5]

"As full of cold whorls of movement as ice floes in Antarctica. A movement, and a sound, seem to break all over the stage in kinetic chain reaction. The dancing is either violently explosive or softly swirling, and you feel yourself to be looking upon matter rather than upon people." [6]

Pithoprakta: "Here, a smaller blackclad corps reminded one of the veins in a Tchelitchew painting. Hovering in the upstage shadows or now and then reflected in ovals of light flashed on the backdrop, they seemed to create an ambiance both internal and external for the principals. The two danced side by side, but not in contact. The movement for Farrell was cool, yet tense. That for Mitchell became more and more frantic, with disjointed head rolls, hip gyrations, a jiggling, puppetlike anger. Farrell became isolated in a spotlight while the black creatures rolled past her feet like so much dust. They disappeared, as did Mitchell, leaving her kneeling, folding her arms over her head and placing her palms against each side of it." [7]

"The movements of the corps give great prominence to elbows—thrown out—and hands—patting the floor, held up, groping and wobbling. There is something of the puppet, and something of the

Metastaseis & Pithoprakta. **Metastaseis.** Ensemble. (*Photo Martha Swope.*)

insect, in what Balanchine has given them to do. Farrell performs a strange solo. Her pointe shoes are used to test and probe the earth as if it were thin ice. Her body, constantly rippling, pulls away from the earth, but her focus is down. The movement, both for her and Mitchell, is the loosest I've ever seen Balanchine create. Sometimes the two of them look almost like rag dolls being flung about the stage." [8]

The general feeling seemed to be that *Metastaseis* was the more compelling of the two sections.

Farrell: "It was probably the most different thing I had ever done. Crazy sounds, no counts, very vague choreography, crazy costume. The lighting—spotlight on a black stage—made it difficult. So did my hair all over the place. Mr. B would say, 'It's very effective,' so, of course, I was willing to do it. My steps were backbends, turning, on the floor; Arthur did a lot of shaking. We were rarely supposed to touch. Most of it was done with parallel palms a few inches apart. This made it very interesting. I always felt a little sloppy, though. And when I came offstage I never had the least idea how I had danced or what effect I had made."

Mitchell: "Balanchine would say, 'Oh, he's too dressed. Take something off him.' He never liked me to have a lot of clothes on in that ballet."

Farrell wore a bikini outfit with fringe on the bottom; Mitchell wore gold pants.

HAYDN CONCERTO

CHOREOGRAPHY: John Taras

MUSIC: Franz Joseph Haydn (Concerto No. 1 in C major for flute, oboe, and orchestra, 1786)

COSTUMES, DÉCOR: Raoul Pene Du Bois

LIGHTING: Jules Fisher

PREMIERE: 25 January 1968

SOLOISTS: George Haas (oboe), Andrew Loyola (flute)

CAST: *1st movement:* Kay Mazzo, Patricia McBride, John Prinz; 6 couples; *2nd movement:* McBride, Earle Sieveling; 6

Haydn Concerto. **Patricia McBride, Earle Sieveling.** (*Photo Fred Fehl.*)

women; *3rd movement:* entire company

OTHER CASTS: Deborah Flomine, Sara Leland, Violette Verdy

Haydn Concerto was a light, easy-going divertissement, "an attractive neoclassical ballet that will always find a place in the repertory, if only for its great charm and the opportunity it offers for good dancing." [1] Taras decided to create a work for two principal couples, and as music he chose a piece originally for hurdy-gurdy (a somewhat different instrument in Haydn's day than in our own)—or, in truth, for two hurdy-gurdies—here, refinedly rescored for flute and oboe. In a casting switch, languorous Mazzo was given the allegro section (with Prinz); while McBride, so fleet of foot, did the adagio (with Sieveling); later, Verdy, allegro dancer par excellence, also did the adagio. (The men were cast less unexpectedly.)

Wrote Herridge: "There were no surprises, but there were charm and taste and admirable skill. The mood, following the music, is courtly, romantic, and sprightly, like playtime in an eighteenth-century palace. Adding to that effect are a backdrop that suggests a tapestry from a court music room and ever-so-chic period costumes." [2]

Hering: "Like the music, the ballet had an air of lively composure. In addition, it was extremely well made. The setting and the rather elaborate conception of eighteenth-century livery made one look upon the dancers as servants in a royal

household, perhaps that of Prince Esterhazy. [There was] a lovely flirtation pas de deux." [3]

Barnes: "The first movement opens with a youthful couple, full of the joys of spring. [Hering mentioned 'flashing batterie.'] The mood has something of the eighteenth-century pastoral to it, with courtiers dressed as peasants, and gentry eating cake rather than bread. The choreography is extraordinarily unaffected and ungimmicky, yet it has a pulse and an appropriateness. Toward the end [of the first movement], McBride enters, as if looking for her suitor. The ensemble indicate that he is nowhere to be found, and she, tinged with disappointment, dances a somewhat plaintive solo. In the slow movement, she finds her lover and they dance a leisurely, lyric pas de deux that matches the grave formality of the music, yet also catches the music's freshness and charm. The last is a typical romplike finale, full of cheerful dancing and dashing entrances, in which the two couples lead the ensemble in a last burst of Haydn-like jollity." [4]

SLAUGHTER ON TENTH AVENUE

CHOREOGRAPHY: George Balanchine

MUSIC: Richard Rodgers (from *On Your Toes,* 1936, with new orchestration by Hershy Kay)

COSTUMES: Irene Sharaff

DÉCOR, LIGHTING: Jo Mielziner

PREMIERE: 2 May 1968 (gala benefit preview, 30 April 1968)

CAST: *Hoofer,* Arthur Mitchell; *Strip Tease Girl,* Suzanne Farrell; *Big Boss,* Michael Steele; *2 Bartenders; Thug; 3 Policemen; Morosine, premier danseur noble,* Earle Sieveling; *Gangster; 7 Ladies of the Ballet; 4 Gentlemen of the Ballet*

OTHER CASTS: *Hoofer,* Frank Ohman, Richard Rapp; *Strip Tease,* Susan Hendl, Linda Merrill

In 1936, *Slaughter* was a lively and innovative Broadway-musical ballet; innovative because Balanchine was using really good dancers—Ray Bolger and Ta-

Slaughter on Tenth Avenue. Left: **Arthur Mitchell, Suzanne Farrell.** *(Photo Martha Swope.)* ***Above:*** **Balanchine with Arthur Mitchell, Suzanne Farrell.** *(Photo Fred Fehl.)*

mara Geva—and also because *Slaughter* was the first full-scale ballet in a musical (with a cast of characters and a plot all its own), and the first to advance the action of the show and thus be thoroughly "integrated." It was a take-off on mobsters, the Russian ballet world, and show-biz practices, and it introduced the word "choreography" to Broadway (at Balanchine's request). *On Your Toes* was characterized by Brooks Atkinson as "tip-toe with talent."

Thirty years later, *Slaughter* fell somewhere between a campy amusement and a has-been. Anderson described the story: "A jealous premier danseur (who spoke his lines with a thick Ruritanian accent) hires a thug to kill a rival during the premiere of a new ballet. This ballet—*Slaughter on Tenth Avenue* itself—concerns the seedy types who patronize a strip joint near the waterfront where tempers are so short and life so cheap that brawls occur almost hourly and the bartenders complacently sweep the corpses out the door with a broom. Against the shabby barroom setting, all in shades of red, the habitués of the dive cavort like figures in a Reginald Marsh painting of Manhattan low life. One of the customers falls in love with a Stripper who meets him for an after-hours tryst. They are discovered by the 'Big Boss' who, enraged

at the girl's faithlessness, shoots her. The 'corpse' of the Stripper manages to pass a note to the dancer warning him of the real murder plot. At last, the police arrest the thug, who has been sitting in one of the theater's boxes perusing the racing form." [1]

Anderson did not say that the end of the Hoofer's dance would be the signal for the shooting; knowing this, the Hoofer keeps repeating the would-be closing phrase "one more time," until the police arrive.

Balanchine created new choreography for the 1968 production. Said he, "It is not really a revival of the old *Slaughter*, just that we are using the same music to make something with new dancers. It will be old-new. I am not trying to make it look like the old one, like years ago. Some people and some critics will probably say it's not like the old one. I don't know that anyone remembers it exactly. The steps? Steps are what? It will be the same type of thing, but it will probably be better— prettier and more interesting."

Critics were less than overwhelmed: "thin" was the word most often used. The ballet became quite an audience favorite, however, and provided two juicy—and unusual—roles for the dancers.

Jowitt wrote: "Although *Slaughter* is as theatrical as it ever was, some of the

movement seems dated. Balanchine was working with a very simple vocabulary. The girl's part consists largely of abandoned backbends and sensuously uncoiling développés of the leg. The man sticks to admiring lunges, embraces, and a desperate tap routine. The movement for the corps is what I'd call rinky-tink. It's the lusciousness of the performances and the production that put it across." [2]

Barnes: "In 1936 it must have seemed fresh and splendid. I suppose even now it has a certain historical value. But it is certainly an oddly puerile work to put into a ballet repertory. It is rather as if, with the kind of inverted snobbery afflicting so many organizations, the Metropolitan Opera settled for a sumptuous staging of *Show Boat*. If it were to be amusing, it would be amusing for the wrong reasons—and this is precisely the case with *Slaughter*. It was a joke ballet to start with; a ballet to be laughed at by people knowing nothing about dance, rather than appreciated by ordinarily sophisticated audiences. And the strange thing is that today—whatever it was when it was first created—it is not even good of its kind. The score might be quite pleasing in an old-fashioned musical, and the same is probably true of the impressively vulgar setting in nightclub baroque and brothel red. Balanchine's choreography is musical but here very dated. It is a pastiche sanctioned by nostalgia and sanctioned by history, but it remains a perfunctory, feeble work. If the magic name of Balanchine were not attached to it, it would be very properly mocked off the stage." [3]

Kisselgoff: "Demands some voluntary suspension of disbelief from its present-day audience." [4]

Says Mitchell, "*Slaughter* was quite a trip. Mr. Balanchine told me to make up some tap dancing, 'You know, like Ray Bolger.' We even got Ray Bolger in there, but he couldn't remember a thing. So then he'd say, 'Okay, you have sixteen bars. I'll be back in an hour, and you have something.' When we got to the part with the gun and 'one more time,' he was very specific about what he wanted. It's a good, fun piece. Balanchine often said to me, of this and others, 'You know, Arthur, when you're serving a meal, you can't give all meat. You have your appetizer, your main course, your dessert, and your coffee.' This ballet was not a main course."

REQUIEM CANTICLES (I)

Arranged by George Balanchine

MUSIC: Igor Stravinsky (1966; for contralto, bass, chorus, and orchestra)

IN MEMORIAM: Martin Luther King (1929–1968)

COSTUMES AND PROPS: Rouben Ter-Arutunian

LIGHTING: Ronald Bates

PREMIERE: 2 May 1968 (single performance)

SINGERS: Margaret Wilson (contralto), John Ostendorf (bass); chorus

CAST: Suzanne Farrell, Arthur Mitchell; ensemble

Kirstein had marched in Alabama; for Mitchell, King's death would be the impetus for forming, in Harlem, the first black classical ballet company and large attendant school; Stravinsky had written, "I am honored that my music is to be played in memory of a man of God, a man of the poor, a man of peace."

Herridge described the work (which came at the end of the evening): "The choreography not only visualizes the music on stage, but greatly enhances the original. It brings out the exultantly lyric aspects of the complex threnody and the solemn voices singing the words of a Requiem service. A chorus of dancers, clothed in long white tulle, each bear candelabras of three lights. Balanchine is able to create with them a multiple design. Sometimes you can see only the lights moving on a darkened stage. Sometimes you see the dancers too as they form ever-changing groupings, with a lone dancer (Farrell) searching among them for something not yet there. Sometimes the lights are placed on stage as the chorus circles

them. And in the center, in contrasting purple, is Mitchell as the King figure for whom the Requiem is celebrated. At the end he is raised aloft by the group against a back scrim of light streaks shooting skyward." [1]

When the ballet was over, the audience departed in silence.

STRAVINSKY: SYMPHONY IN C

CHOREOGRAPHY: John Clifford

MUSIC: Igor Stravinsky (1940)

COSTUMES, LIGHTING: John Braden

PREMIERE: 9 May 1968 (first presented May 1967 by the Workshop of the School of American Ballet)

CAST: *1. Moderato alla Breve:* Marnee Morris, Anthony Blum; 8 women, 8 men; *2. Larghetto Concertante:* Kay Mazzo; 8 men; *3. Allegretto:* John Prinz; 3 women, 3 men; *4. Largo—Tempo Giusto alla Breve,* Renee Estópinal and company

OTHER CASTS: Karin von Aroldingen, Deborah Flomine, Gloria Govrin, Lynne Stetson; John Clifford, Conrad Ludlow, Frank Ohman

This first work of the twenty-year-old Clifford to be mounted by professionals was difficult to review definitively, because, says the choreographer, "It had a hundred versions—every performance

Requiem Canticles. **Suzanne Farrell (center), Arthur Mitchell (above).** (*Photo Martha Swope.*)

was different, even the costumes were changed constantly. A real baptism by fire. Mr. B. kept asking for changes and more changes. I guess he was right—he was pulling out as much as he could. But I started to hate the music. Sometimes the choreography worked, sometimes it didn't. Balanchine, you know, sometimes makes his own piano reductions. He did that in this case. That's really nerve-wracking, because it means he knows *every* note!"

Barnes wrote that it was "at first promisingly disastrous, although later amended into something more than respectable." [1]

Hering: "Produces an inconsistent effect. Sometimes its animation is refreshing. At other times it seems merely cluttered. . . . Last year, it looked like frantic Balanchine. This year, with revisions, the ballet bristled with the tempestuousness of a creative mind that almost has to be forcibly harnessed." [2]

The main problem seemed to be the difficult music—called "rhythmically devilish"—as well as the fact that Clifford "has tried literally and punctiliously to match the concertante style of the orchestration with individual movements and flurries of movements—quite forgetting that the ear and eye take in stimuli at a different time scale, so that what may sound fine to the ear, if put slavishly onto the stage, looks muddled, and fussy." [3]

Said Denby, "What I liked was that there was no meanness in the ballet when there was so much possibility of getting angry at the score and the trouble it makes." [4]

Anderson described the initial version: "The first movement was set for a large corps—perhaps too large—and soloists. There were quirky touches, as when the corps repeatedly made a gesture akin to drawing a bow (but with palms held out flat) and when a line of girls entered paddling with their hands as though swimming in a pool of air. Yet the overall effect was one of fussiness. The second movement began and ended with Mazzo moving amongst silhouetted boys who sinuously undulated their arms; in the middle section, they tossed her about in a rough-and-tumble fashion. The third found Prinz dashing assertively, and the finale again utilized a rather helter-skelter large corps, with Estópinal ['rotating bravely in a pool of light'] as focal point. Clifford seems determined to put every step he knows—and he knows lots—into his ballet." [5]

LA SOURCE

CHOREOGRAPHY: George Balanchine

MUSIC: Léo Delibes (*La Source* [*Naïla*], 1866; after 5 February 1969, more music from *La Source* added)

COSTUMES: Karinska

LIGHTING: Ronald Bates

PREMIERE: 23 November 1968

CAST: Violette Verdy, John Prinz

OTHER CASTS: Gelsey Kirkland, Kay Mazzo; John Clifford, Peter Martins, Helgi Tomasson, Edward Villella

Ensemble section added 5 February 1969, with Carol Sumner, 8 women; also danced by Susan Pilarre, Suki Schorer

La Source was something a bit different in a pas de deux—and it was not an immediate success. For one thing, it did not represent Balanchine at his finest; for another, stylistically it was foreign, and not dedicated to the moment of high climax. On its own terms—as a showcase of nineteenth-century French dancing, to nineteenth-century French dance music—it was perfectly on target ("dainty workmanship and nineteenth-century jokes," said one observer; "quaint pretty old tunes," said another).

Says Verdy, "Clearly it is not Balanchine's greatest, but it is a moment of incredibly refined French dancing—ornamented, very detailed, with a lot of subtle nuances of charm, femininity, coquetry. There is a certain use of sophistication in the sense of a civilized social encounter with the audience."

In form, *La Source* was also unexpected. Some called it more a miniature ballet than a pas de deux: the man has a long variation before the ballerina even appears; in all, each has two solos and there are two adagios (usually, there is one of each), plus the normal coda (finale). The ballet may have been too taxing; about a year later, Balanchine inserted the ensemble sections from his earlier

Stravinsky: Symphony in C. **Marnee Morris, Anthony Blum.** (*Photo Fred Fehl.*)

La Source. **Edward Villella, Violette Verdy.** (*Photo Martha Swope.*)

Pas de Deux and Divertissement (1965), perhaps to rest the principals.

Wrote Barnes of the original: "Although only a duet, it is nearly twenty minutes long and has the feel and importance of a full-scale ballet. It is certainly a strange work, and perhaps strangest of all, the work ends, very gently, with a waltz for the two rather than with the usually accepted flash-bang coda. It becomes obvious that Balanchine's intention here is deliberately to avoid the classic structure. It is almost axiomatic that any pas de deux in ballet has the characteristics of a love duet; but whereas most of them represent love in the blaze of the sun, this is rather love in the afternoon, a delicately autumnal love full of soft and fading falls. Part of this is the music, as sweet and yielding as fondants, as outrageously ornate as art nouveau and, above all, mindlessly sensual. Balanchine has choreographed his piece in the French manner, very fluffy, very sophisticated, and very chic." [1]

Manchester: "It ripples along like its title. There are all kinds of felicitous enchainements but somehow they never build to a climax; and the waltz finale slows the work down just as one begins to long for a little excitement. Balanchine must have planned it this way but it is rather like waiting with a pleasant sense of expectation for a party and then hearing that there isn't going to be one." [2]

The ensemble parts introduced a new and jarring stylistic element. Says Verdy, "These parts are like French operetta, very light, frolicky, a little bit of a take-off on French dancing: the pas de deux is more serious, refined, and tender."

Barnes: "The sudden introduction of the ensemble does not add much to the total strength of the piece. On the other hand, it is still extraordinarily craftsmanlike." [3]

Kisselgoff: "There is something of the Paris Opéra Ballet about the ensembles, but if there is a touch of decadence, decadence is not the essence of *La Source*. There is more than decorative dancing by a chorus line here. There is also an unconventionally structured pas de deux, quite unlike anything choreographed by Balanchine before. It is this duet, interwoven with the more chic, weaker ensemble passages, that rescues it from triviality. [In the material for Verdy,] there is a perfect entente cordiale between a choreographer and a dancer. She brings the Parisian piquancy and pizzicato that Balanchine requires in the ballerina's solos

Tchaikovsky Suite. **Marnee Morris, John Prinz.** *(Photo Martha Swope.)*

to differentiate them from the more formal classicism of his 'Russian' style." [4]

The piece, of course, took advantage of Verdy's special abilities. Balanchine also intended it to launch Prinz into orbit as a danseur noble in the making. ("People think he cares only about the ballerinas. They should only know the care he takes with the men," says Verdy.) Prinz did not remain with the Company, however. Possibly because the ballet was not wholly in the grand manner, being less imperious and more perky, it beautifully displayed the darting dancing of the small-boned Clifford and the petite Kirkland in later performances.

TCHAIKOVSKY SUITE
later called
TCHAIKOVSKY SUITE NO. 2

CHOREOGRAPHY: Jacques d'Amboise

MUSIC: Peter Ilyitch Tchaikovsky (Suite No. 2 for Orchestra, op. 53, 1883)

Production designed by John Braden

PREMIERE: 9 January 1969

CAST: *1st Movement,* Marnee Morris, John Prinz; 6 couples, *2nd Movement,* Allegra Kent, Francisco Moncion; 6 couples; *3rd Movement,* Linda Merrill, John Clifford; 4 couples; entire company

OTHER CASTS: *1st,* Deborah Flomine, Melissa Hayden, Gelsey Kirkland; Jacques d'Amboise, Clifford, Helgi Tomasson; *2nd,* Kay Mazzo, Christine Redpath; Anthony Blum; *3rd,* Merrill Ashley, Kirkland, Redpath; Bart Cook, Deni Lamont, Bruce Wells

An attractive work, without strong distinctive personality. *Tchaikovsky Suite* evokes Russia, but a Russia of villages, not of court. The men wear Georgian dress, with black leather boots, the girls have Ukrainian ribbon clusters on their headdresses. As usual with works of d'Amboise, it was remarked that he followed his illustrious model with taste, but without daring.

Wrote Barnes, "An essentially unpretentious and essentially agreeable work, a kind of light-hearted peasant wooing ritual, in which classical choreography is given an ethnic coloration. D'Amboise has learned from Balanchine the value of craftsmanship, and while his ballet may rarely make you gasp with astonishment, it is always honest and workmanlike. It would be nice to see something a little more startling in his next effort." [1]

The most resonant section was the second movement, which struck a note of mystery and somberness. (Moncion was compared to a feudal lord.) In the lively first, a "false ending," and a later moment when the ballerina was handed down a lineup of men, were criticized. The third was a good-humored, bouncy finale.

Belt wrote, "Each of his works has demonstrated considerable merit without being of unusual distinction. There is, however, a welcome earthiness and wry sense of humor that seems to be his trademark. The choreography for the principals is quite splendid, providing ample opportunities for display in the brilliant outer movements, and some languid designs for the rather sentimental slow middle section. The failure to achieve a genuine triumph seems to come from the cluttered work for the six supporting couples." [2] He noted that the repertory already had a full complement of works of this type—mostly by Balanchine.

Manchester: "Full of good things, especially its use of the male dancers. The kind of ballet that makes an audience feel warm and happy. Although somewhat disjointed, each movement has its own charms." [3]

The ballet remained in the repertory for several years.

FANTASIES

CHOREOGRAPHY: John Clifford

MUSIC: Ralph Vaughan Williams (*Fantasia on a Theme of Thomas Tallis*, 1910)

COSTUMES: Robert O'Hearn

LIGHTING: Ronald Bates

PREMIERE: 23 January 1969

CAST: Sara Leland, Kay Mazzo, Anthony Blum, Conrad Ludlow

OTHER CASTS: Allegra Kent, Johnna Kirkland, Polly Shelton, Lynne Stetson, Richard Dryden, Robert Maiorano

*F*antasies was a departure both for the twenty-one-year-old Clifford and for the Company. The music of English composers is barely represented in the repertory, and unabashed romanticism, complete with ideal visions, is equally rare. Says Clifford of the challenge: "I wanted to do something romantic, after the *Stravinsky Symphony*, but at first the Vaughan Williams seemed unballetic, too big, too mushy. Then I saw it as very religious—a Druid wedding, Stonehenge. This led me to ghosts and toward real re-

Fantasies. **Conrad Ludlow, Sara Leland, Kay Mazzo, Anthony Blum.** (*Photo Martha Swope.*)

lationships between the characters—a man and a woman with their own dreams. Along the way, the religious aspect was lost; I find the music also very sensuous. I saw the real woman as a spinster-type, the real man as older. The ghosts are invisible to the others, while they see everything. But I intended only a hint of a story. Sometimes it seems to me a very juvenile work. But it's probably the most secure thing I did for the Company."

Hering described the action: "He has created a bittersweet pas de quatre about dream love and real love. It begins with an enraptured duet for Ludlow and his dream-love (Mazzo). She is by turns elusive, then playful (as when she does a handspring which lands her on his shoulder). As their counterparts, Leland is enveloped in the glow of nascent womanhood; Blum is the dream boy. The couples intermingle in a choreographic structure as lucid as it is restless. The dream lovers constantly push the others together until they cling spontaneously. In the distance, Mazzo and Blum, in silhouette, walk slowly toward each other, perhaps letting us know that in mature love one does not necessarily relinquish

one's fantasies. They are simply absorbed." [1]

Barnes: "Stands on its own. It is a very good piece—derivative more in spirit than substance, and reveals a choreographer of far more than usual interest. We have our loves and our ideal loves— we have the girls we meet and the girls we dream about. The man is happy in the dream aspirations of an imaginary beloved. Then he encounters a girl, equally happy with another man. All four meet— the dreams and the realities intermingle. Dramatically, it is a subtle ballet, much more in the mood of Tudor than Balanchine, with typically sudden shifts of emotions carried forward on a wave of dance. [Occasionally] Clifford appears concerned with choreographic originality, but most of the time his business is with choreographic aptness. He combines Soviet-style partnering with a very Tudoresque awareness of the psychological motivation of movement. A good work, arresting and moving. The music proved perfect." [2]

Kisselgoff: "There is a modern psychological thread in his view. In a literal but inventive use of [Bolshoi-style] lifts, Clifford sums up the moral of his story in a highly dramatic moment: at one point the woman sails over the shoulder of her dream lover to land unexpectedly in the arms of the man, while his own dream figure ducks out of the way." [3]

This maneuver drew much comment. Denby elaborated on some of the idea: "That one lift is very fine. It happens so suddenly; it's not as though the whole ballet had been planned around it but as though the idea crystallized at that moment. The only trouble with the ballet is that those large, open movements imply so much psychologically. Tudor's are much more limited—how shall I say?—in space. While the dream people could very well have that large, open gesture, that classic-type gesture, the real people have too much of it to make a strong contrast. On the other hand, since it's the same person in a quandary, it's a problem what to do, how to make the same person so different. What's very interesting about the whole ballet is that the ideal people get the real people together, and they retire into a distance where you can barely see them but where they still exist, and the real people are left together the way they are. That's a remarkable idea for a young man to have, and the fact that he carried the idea through to the end is remarkable. So my criticism, that the real people are too much like the others, is an objection not to his idea, but to his experience of gesture, not an objection as far as the general verve and continuity of the piece go. There is not enough difference for [his] really interesting Tudor-type idea. The piece turned a bit into *Spring Waters*." [4]

PRELUDE, FUGUE AND RIFFS

CHOREOGRAPHY: John Clifford

MUSIC: Leonard Bernstein (1949)

LIGHTING: Ronald Bates

PREMIERE: 15 May 1969 (gala benefit preview 8 May 1969)

CAST: Allegra Kent, John Clifford; 3 couples (preview: Linda Merrill)

OTHER CASTS: Marnee Morris, Delia Peters; Anthony Blum, James Bogan

Riffs are those little virtuoso displays that rock guitarists are fond of throwing out to their listeners when they perform. The jazzy score lends itself to such virtuosity on the dance floor, but the displays are little ones." [1]

Says Clifford, "It was a trifle, intentionally—in fact, at the beginning, it was supposed to be only for the benefit preview. (Later there were other performances.) I wanted to do something zappy

and crazy, with bell bottoms and silly pantomime, to take advantage of Allegra's sense of humor."

Wrote Marks, "A jazz dance with a thirties look, [despite] its contemporary look." [2]

Sargent, "The score seemed awfully old-fashioned. This sort of thing ought nowadays to be accompanied by rock music." [3]

DANCES AT A GATHERING

CHOREOGRAPHY: Jerome Robbins

MUSIC: Frédéric Chopin (Mazurka, op. 63, no. 3; Waltz, op. 69, no. 2; Mazurka, op. 33, no. 3; Mazurkas, op. 6, nos. 2 and 4, op. 7, nos. 4 and 5, op. 24, no. 2; Waltz, op. 42; Waltz, op. 34, no. 2; Mazurka, op. 56, no. 2; Etude, op. 25, no. 4; Waltz, op. 34, no. 1; Waltz, op. 70, no. 2; Etude, op. 25, no. 5; Etude, op. 10, no. 2; Scherzo, op. 20, no. 1; Nocturne, op. 15, no. 1)

COSTUMES: Joe Eula

LIGHTING: Thomas Skelton

PREMIERE: 22 May 1969 (gala benefit preview 8 May 1969)

PIANO: Gordon Boelzner

CAST: Allegra Kent, Sara Leland, Kay Mazzo, Patricia McBride, Violette Verdy; Anthony Blum, John Clifford, Robert Maiorano, John Prinz, Edward Villella

OTHER CASTS: Muriel Aasen, Merrill Ashley, Melissa Hayden, Susan Hendl, Gelsey Kirkland, Delia Peters, Susan Pilarre, Stephanie Saland; Jean-Pierre Bonnefous, Victor Castelli, Bart Cook, Peter Martins, Earle Sieveling Helgi Tomasson, Robert Weiss, Bruce Wells

Dances was unquestionably the critical and popular success of 1969, and it also marked Jerome Robbins's return to the Company after an absence of twelve years. The work was almost unanimously praised by the reviewers, who particularly singled out its radiant outpouring of pure dance—endless in variety, endless in invention—and the glowing comradeship projected by the participants. Much was also made of the folk elements in the essentially classical dance vocabulary, the gesture of a dancer bending down to touch the stage—was this a peasant's contact with the soil? the dancer's reaching for the security of the floor?—and of the closing episode, which contained no dancing at all.

Said Robbins, before the opening: "I'm doing a fairly classical ballet to very old-fashioned and romantic music, but there is a point to it. In a way it is a revolt from the faddism of today. In the period since my last ballet I have been around looking at dance—seeing a lot of the stuff at Judson Church and the rest of the avant-garde. And I find myself feeling just what is the matter with connecting, what's the matter with love, what's the matter with celebrating positive things?" [1]

Dances at a Gathering was a celebration of dance.

Robbins, usually reluctant to talk about his work, discussed *Dances* at some length with Denby. The interview is prefaced with Denby's own thoughts about the ballet:

"It wasn't planned as a surefire piece; it wasn't planned at all beforehand, and began by chance. . . . The ballet is set to Chopin piano pieces and the program lists ten dancers but tells you little more. [Rejecting any programmatic intent, Robbins said his inspiration was "Chopin's music."] The curtain goes up in silence on an empty stage. It looks enormous. The back is all sky—some kind of changeable late afternoon in summer. Both sides of the stage are black. Forestage right, a man enters slowly, deep in thought. He is wearing a loose white shirt, brown tights, and boots. He turns to the sky and walks

Prelude, Fugue and Riffs. **Linda Merrill.** (*Photo Martha Swope.*)

slowly away from you towards center stage. You think of a man alone in a meadow. As he walks you notice the odd tilt of his head—like a man listening, inside himself. In the silence the piano begins as if he were remembering the music. He marks a dance step, he sketches a mazurka gesture, with a kind of pensive vigor he begins to improvise and now he is dancing marvelously and, in a burst of freedom he is running all over the meadow. Suddenly he subsides and, more mysterious than ever, slides into the woods and is gone. Upstage a girl and boy enter. At once they are off full speed in a double improvisation, a complexly fragmented waltz, the number Robbins speaks of as the 'wind dance' [op. 69, no. 2]. . . . The music and the dance seem to be inventing each other. For a dance fan, the fluid shifts of momentum are a special delight. For the general theater public, Robbins's genius in focusing on a decisive momentary movement—almost like a zoom lens—makes vivid the special quality of each dance, and all the charming jokes.

"[Robbins] thought he would like to do a pas de deux for [McBride and Villella]—perhaps to Chopin music. As he listened to records it occurred to him to add two more couples. In the course of rehearsals, however, all the six dancers he had chosen were not always free, so he went on choreographing with four others, using those who happened to be free. Gradually he made more and more dances, but without a definite plan for the whole piece. When about two-thirds of the ballet was done, he invited Balanchine to rehearsal. At the end of it he turned to Mr. B. and said, 'Don't you think it's a bit long?' Mr. B. answered, 'More. Make more!' He did.

"Robbins said to me, 'As you see, there are still never more than six dancers dancing at once.' He told me that as the dances and relationships kept coming out of the different pieces of music and the particular dancers available, he began to feel that they were all connected by some underlying sense of community and by a sense of open air and sunlight and sudden nostalgia perhaps.

"We spoke of the many lovely lifts—one at the end of Eddie's pas de deux with Pat where it looks as though he were lifting a sack onto his shoulder and the sack suddenly changes into a beautiful mermaid. Robbins explained how it came out of a sudden metamorphosis in the music.

"We were talking of Villella's gesture of touching the floor in the final minutes of the ballet, and Robbins mentioned that he was perhaps thinking of the dancers' world—the floor below, the space around and above."

ROBBINS: "The ballet will seem different in almost every performance, not vastly, but shades will happen, depending on the dancers. The dancers read [in a review] what the ballet is about, then they change because now they *know* it; before they just *did* it. I don't know what to do about that except to ask them not to. I always tell them to do it for themselves, and to think of 'marking' it—don't think of doing it full out. I like watching ballets, anyway, best of all at rehearsals when a dancer is just working for himself, really just working. They are beautiful to watch then. I love to watch George work that way. Just love to.

"I *would* like to see the Bolshoi or Kirov dance this. It might finally turn out to be a peasant parody! That folk part of it—I was surprised. At first I thought [the dancers] were very elegant people, maybe at a picnic, maybe doing something—their own thing. And then also to me the boys and the whole period are very hippyish. The boys still had [beards] at rehearsal because of the long layoff. It really affected what I was doing. I like the boots. There is something in the nature of knowing who they are and having love and confidence in them, confidence, which I feel is in the work, finally. Loving confidence in themselves and the other people. It has some strangenesses in it too; every now and then I look at a step and think, That is a very odd step.

"There are hardly any liberties [with the music] taken at all—only one where at the end of Eddie's first dance it's marked *fortissimo*. I didn't like it, it was a little obvious, like I was trying for a hand. I thought there was something else there, so I took it on retard and soft. There are no sentimentalities. I got worried for a while; I thought when people come to this big theater and they have just seen a big ballet with a lot of marvelous sounds, the piano is going to sound like a little rehearsal piano. But it doesn't. It seems to fill the house.

"I didn't mean [the lighting] to look ominous, but I suppose that vast sky is almost like nature changing on you. I originally thought, We'll do it using the wings and cyclorama because it's just going to be

a pas de deux. I don't know if I want a set, or anything softer around the edges. That's a very hard line, those black wings. But once it starts, I don't suppose you are particularly aware of it any more.

"It is funny how [woods, meadow, and trees] were evoked. My names for the dances themselves, for instance, the second dance—I call it the 'wind dance' because to me the dancers are like two things that are on the wind that catch up with each other. There is something about air—breezes which are clawing them and pushing them almost like two kites. And the 'walk waltz' [op. 70, no. 2] or 'the three girls' to me is somehow in the woods. On a Chekhov evening.

"They must do [the looking around at the end] very softly. It is very hard for them to just walk on and look at something without starting to make it dramatic. I keep telling them, 'Relax, don't be sad, don't get upset, just see it, just whatever you want to pick, just see. It's a cloud passing, if you want. Take it easy on it, don't get gloomy.'

"If I had to talk about it all, I would say that they are looking at—all right—clouds on the horizon which possibly could be threatening, but then, that's life, so afterwards you just pick up and go right on again. It doesn't destroy them. They don't lament. They accept.

"That last two weeks I spent in arranging, trying to get the right order. Not only who danced what, but also that sense of something happening—making the dances have some continuity, some structure, whether I knew specifically what it was or not. At one point I had the scherzo finishing the ballet and the grand waltz [op. 34, no. 1] opening it. It was a marvelous sort of puzzle. Here I have all these people and these situations and I know they belong to each other—now let me see how. I was originally going to call it *Some Dances*. I was going to say *Dances: Chopin, in Open Air*, but that isn't the right title. In French, *Quelques Danses* is nice, but in English, *Some Dances* is sort of flat. If you say *Eighteen Dances* or *Nineteen Dances*, it divides them into compartments.

"The end had to come out of the scherzo, that very restless piece which ends with them all sort of *whoosh* running out—disappearing like cinders falling out into the night, and it couldn't end there. That's not how I feel about these people—that they went *whoosh* and disappeared. They are still here and they still move like dancers. They take . . . a 'passeggiata'—they take a stroll, like in an Italian town, around the town's square at sundown [Nocturne]. They may have felt a threat, but they don't panic, they stay. So coming back after the scherzo to the stage and the floor that we dance on, and putting your hand on it—if it's the earth or a ballet dancer's relationship to a wood floor—*that* somehow is the ending I knew I had to get to somewhere.

"I didn't know how my hand would be. It's almost like an artist who has not been drawing for a long time. I was so surprised that the dances began to come out and began to come out so gushing, in a way. And I worked in a way I hadn't worked before. Whether I knew the details or not, I pushed through to the end of the dance. I sort of knew where it was going, and then I'd go back and clean it up and fill it up. Quite often the dancers weren't even sure how they got through the steps to the next step. But they went with me. I was pleased to be choreographing again and to have it coming out. I want to go on and see if I can work a little bit more the way I've worked this time—that sort of trusting the intuition more than self-controlling the intuition. . . .

"At so many rehearsals [the dancers] didn't dance all out. They sort of walked.

[Eddie] came into rehearsal and had to save himself for the performance and just marked through it. I ran back and said, 'Now, that's what I want.' I don't think they realize how trained they are—so clear. Like someone with a great voice who can whisper and you hear it." [2]

The reception was almost universally ecstatic; "If necessity is the mother of invention, the necessity Robbins felt must have been nothing less than the urgent demands of beauty itself," wrote Belt, capturing the widespread spirit of euphoria. [3]

Goldner was more specific: "Shortly after Chopin's piano music begins, a man wanders into the scene, his back to the audience. He gazes at the sky, listens to the music for a few seconds, and finds himself being drawn into a dance. At first he dances in private, as though humming, but then his movements become more expansive and formal, so that when a couple appear they do not seem to be intruding.*

---

* It is interesting that Goldner describes the man entering after the music has begun, Denby before; Goldner has the couple coming on while he's there, Denby after he's gone. It is quite possible that Robbins changed these details from one performance to the next (he often does this); more probable, however, that reviewers remember differently. In any case, the lack of "score" or record to consult points up a major difficulty for dance critics: their starting point—the primary material—is elusive in a way that works of painting, music, and literature are not.

Partners change as quickly as mood, but the impulse to move to the beautiful music is constant. And although the dancers begin to interest us as individuals through their expression of melancholy, playful, whimsical, or daring moods, glorious dancing is really the point.

"Each variation is a miniature but rich portrait of social behavior. The lovers are coy, hesitant, or rapturous, and the ménage-à-trois arrangements are exactly that, arranged and touchy. In one solo, a shy girl seems to be glad to have the stage to herself, while a few variations later, a flirtatious girl can't find anyone to flirt with and so leaves with a final, desperately gay wave. At one point, six dancers abandon themselves to group play with a virtuoso display of ballet's fancier supported leaps, which coincides with Chopin's own bravura display of piano technique. At other times, the Polish in Chopin is underscored by dances lightly salted with folk movement.

"Robbins's choreographic and thematic ideas flow with such variety and spontaneity (to the point of having an improvisational quality) that the ballet's unusually long length of one hour does not seem long at all. When the ballet does end, it is hard to find one's land legs, but then it is also difficult for the dancers, who, in the last variation, gaze at each other and the

Dances at a Gathering. Peter Martins, Anthony Blum, Patricia McBride, Robert Maiorano, Gelsey Kirkland. (*Photo Martha Swope*.)

sky as though wondering where they have been. One began to wonder where Robbins himself had been. It is as though he had been incubating for years and then suddenly burst forth with invention." [4]

Barnes: "It is as honest as breathing, and in some special way more a thing to be experienced than merely just another ballet to be seen. It is also one of the most significant evenings in American theater since O'Neill. Chopin is all daggers and velvet, all poet and peasant. This Robbins has accepted. And then Chopin's feel for place, his need for belonging, for that peasant assurance of the earth beneath him and the sky above. This Robbins has captured.

"Who are they? A community certainly. They gesture to one another with the affection of friends, and they share life together. They own land in the sense of belonging [to it]. The earth is theirs, the sky is theirs, and they can face nightfall with a friendly embrace. They sketch out a domestic, humanly-scaled poetry in the air. Robbins is never afraid to be different: He will put his girls into extravagant slides, for example, and have them thrown crazily—almost—over the boys' shoulders. Yet he is different with naturalness. His dances have the feel and weight of people about them. They are loving, youthful and real. . . .

"I think I would have suggested a cross between *Liebeslieder Walzer* and Tudor's *Dark Elegies*. The judgment would have been far too superficial—yet there is something of that dazzling virtuoso ease of the Balanchine and equally there is the feeling for the community, life, and the earth that is so characteristic of the Tudor work. In atmosphere it seems both European and non-European—looking back with nostalgia on European roots, yet gazing with a very American steadiness at the pioneer horizon. Yet for all its ethnic shading, *Dances* remains a classic ballet—and a classic ballet of incredible diversity. There is a pas de six in which the dancers keep on striking postures and grouping themselves for all the world like eminent Victorians having their photos taken, or there is a contest dance for [two men], each whirling around the other like airborne acrobats, or there is a terribly tender scene for three girls, walking with innocence and tenderness under a warm night sky. In such moments the dancing and the emotions, the dancers and the people, are fused in an expression as natural as birdsong. As natural and as naked." [5]

Battey wrote: "Almost every moment of Robbins's ballet is one to treasure, but if I could choose just one moment to relive it would be the marvelous opening, when Villella enters, unrecognized at the first instant, his back to the audience, and starts to move in designs so sensitive and ravishing that notice is instantly served of dance inspiration of the highest order." [6].

Jowitt: "It is so transparent that through this one dance's complex simplicity you seem to understand what Dance is all about. The dancing is Polish only in the way that the music is: a suggested rhythm, fragment of melody, a quick gesture transformed by an individual creative intellect. You see a pair of hands on hips or behind the head, male hands, clasping arms, feet stamping—but they are gone almost before you notice them. The vocabulary is balletic, rich and immensely clever, but made to look simple by Robbins's beautiful way of shaping phrases. Preparations are never obtrusive; girls rise almost invisibly onto pointe, as if such an action were the natural consequence of drawing breath. Contemporary ideas about art have freed Robbins to be romantic in a way that choreographers contemporary with Chopin were not ready to be. Not for them the irregularities, asymmetries, open forms that give *Dances at a Gathering* its air of naturalness and inevitability. There seems almost to be an invisible wind on stage—one of those gentle, but exhilarating winds—that pushes the dance along. One of the most memorable movement motifs is just a smooth run, forward or backward.

"*Dances* is very long, and I like that. It has the exhausting beauty of certain celebrations. At the end, the dancers all gather to watch something moving far in the distance behind the audience. A falling star? A bird? It doesn't matter." [7]

Goldner described a few of the passages: "In one of the dances three girls stroll and casually fall into dances as they might fall into thoughts. One raises an arm, as though saying 'Ah,' then another lifts her arm more formally. The third picks up that stylization and adds a theatrical torso movement to her arm movement. Before you know it, they're dancing. Just as casually, they peter out. Men enter. The girls dance with them, but they do not come out of their reverie. The men might be like thoughts; certainly, they disappear as quickly as thoughts do.

"In another dance two girls are pursued by three men with dazzling speed, lightness, and variations on the odd man out. They are like five water fountains playing together on a breezy day. At the very last moment, a third girl runs on and joins the single man. After a split-second pause, she and the other two women curtsy, their heads lowered. The men lower their heads too, and each looks intently at his partner. In an instant, the bubbling and sashaying turn into a tremendous hush. For a second the dancers are caught in midair, and just as quickly they find their repose. Each now has a partner; they are men and women, whereas a few seconds ago they were water bubbles.

"One of the most exciting dances of all [op. 34, no. 1] takes place about midway through. Six people dash on, spread themselves far and wide, raise their arms above their heads, and gently but persistently mark time to a waltz. You know something is up. They begin to dance. The steps get bigger, covering more ground, and the jumps get higher. Next, they line up and the girls leap into the men's arms. And finally, at the climax of the last series of jumps, a girl positively catapults herself with multiple turns in the air into the man's waiting arms. He catches her and quickly swings her around, letting her head drop to the floor. Her head misses the floor by an inch or so. This is some joy ride!

"In one of the duets, a man lifts his partner sideways so that her body is almost parallel to the floor. She spreads her legs, one pointing toward the ceiling and one toward the floor. She then bends each leg and draws them in so that her feet touch. Then she straightens her legs again. In itself, it is a fantastic movement, because it is extremely difficult for the man to hold the woman high in the air horizontally, while the woman's leg movement only stresses her incredible position. McBride flung open her legs, brought them together slowly and then opened them with such deliberate slowness that they created a muscular tension like that felt when pulling taffy. The image of her floating at that crazy angle and then feeling the taffy effect will be indelible. That is what dancing is about." [8]

Haggin, one of the few who was not completely satisfied, mentioned "Robbins's gift for comedy in the amusing piece in which Kent kept on dancing charmingly and hopefully as one boy after

Dances at a Gathering. Top left: Sara Leland, Anthony Blum. (*Photo Martha Swope.*) *Top right:* Bruce Wells, Helgi Tomasson. (*Photo Martha Swope.*)
Bottom left: John Prinz, Patricia McBride, Robert Maiorano. (*Photo Fred Fehl.*) *Bottom right* (counterclockwise from left, rear): Kay Mazzo and Anthony Blum, Violette Verdy and John Clifford, John Prinz and Sara Leland, Allegra Kent and Edward Villella, Robert Maiorano and Patricia McBride. (*Photo Fred Fehl.*)

another showed interest and began to walk beside her, but then lost interest and drifted off; [and] the perceptive Robbins eye in the étude [op. 25, no. 4] made of Verdy's striking manner of pointing up the movements a choreographer gives her to do. But my eye saw in some places the Robbins gift for applause-getting show-biz tricks and stunts." [9]

Verdy's solo, in which she "almost" dances (but instead merely indicates steps in an extremely telling manner) was considered one of the most unusual and striking in the ballet. Says she, in admiration: "For all the praise I get now for dancing this solo, I always answer, 'You should have seen Jerry create that and dance

it—he was unbelievable.' I couldn't begin to copy. When the ballet was mounted in London, Nureyev wanted to dance that part, because there is something that even a man can find there, and that is complete self-absorption in a dance and a rhythm."

Leland talked about working on the ballet: "The scherzo [op. 20, no. 1] is the hardest part of the ballet. It's the last dance, with a lot of entrances and exits and a pas de deux in the middle. A slow pas de deux. Then it gets fast again. And it's all very vague. We have to take our cues from each other. It's not just doing steps to music, it's having to relate to the mood of how the thing is swinging.'And it's very hard on the dancers. Jerry would

say, 'I just want you all to mush and then I want you to go like *this*. I want to just— go!' Like, burst apart. And then come together."

"*What about the use of gesture in the opening and in the closing section when Eddie touches the ground? What sort of coaching is required for that?*"

LELAND: "The thing that made it easiest for me was that [Jerry] used to tell us this: It's in the evening and it's probably after dinner and you all come out of your homes. And you look at your land. It's a very peaceful feeling. He would say, It's *not* sad, walk like—and he would carry himself so beautifully. And just look as if you're looking over the horizon at all you own. Then a storm begins but it doesn't frighten you, it just happens to be there. And so you turn and you watch it. And then you do the gestures, walk to the back, girls bow and boys bow, and then you come to the center and you're all just—accepting, and when you take the boys' arms and you're walking around just before the curtain comes down, he would say, It's not greeting, it's just accepting, and you acknowledge each one as you pass them. You just look at each other as if these are your comrades and your friends."

"So that passing look is at a storm."

LELAND: "Yes. We call it 'the storm' when we rehearse it."

"I've always assumed it was a bird or something in the sky."

LELAND: "It could be. But we call it 'the storm' because the music sounds stormy. . . . [Jerry] explains [the opening] by saying, You're alone and you're back in a ballroom. He sometimes says ballroom and sometimes says rehearsal studio because he thinks it's easier for the dancers to think of it that way. But I like the other approach better. He says it's a place that you're coming back to years later that you danced in once. And you go in, and you're recalling. It's a dance of recall, a dance of remembrance. And you're thinking, Oh yes, I used to dance here at one time. And I did this step. Oh yes. Dee-dum. Oh yes, that's the way it was. Then you start to dance. Then you dance dance dance and you jump jump jump, at the end you stop—you turn—and the gesture, it's like, Oh I remember. The whole ballet is self-centered. You should never dance anything for the audience. It ruins it if you do. You should dance only to each other. As if the audience weren't there. It's very hard."

"Do these characters, these people in the ballet, know one another very well?"

LELAND: "I would say that they're very good friends."

"Is anybody in love with anybody else?"

LELAND: "I feel that we're not. I feel that we all love each other in a very loyal way, and we all get along very well and we never fight. I feel that we're aristocrats; we're peasants, but we're very well-bred peasants. There's a story behind [the male duet], too. Jerry says that the dance is two dogs. He really likes to have it done by a big boy and a small boy. He says that Tony [Blum] is the big dog of the neighborhood and Eddie [Villella] is a little fox terrier yapping at his heels and getting a

little dizzy. The giggle dance is just fun. It's the most fun dance of all, like children playing. When I first did it I was just trying to do steps. And eventually Jerry got me to forget about steps and just enjoy it. And now I really do."

"And the story behind Violette's solo?"

LELAND: "Violette is the mistress of the house, her big manor house. It's a suggestion of a dance. When she first comes on it's like, I own this house and you're all my guests, and did you know I used to dance? I used to do this step. I used to do a grand jeté. But Robbins says it's a marked grand jeté, a suggestion of one. And then she bows. The idea is that she's showing how she used to dance. And she says, 'Oh, I'll do one more step.' "

"It's like the feeling that's set by the opening solo."

LELAND: "Yes, in a sense. And he does like that dance, Violette's dance, done by an older dancer. There's [another] part in the ballet for a young girl, Kay's part." [10]

Says Robbins, six years later (1975): "I get annoyed when people see stories in it; for instance, we gave some pieces nicknames—'giggle dance,' 'three women'—not because they were descriptive of the music, but merely as identification points. I don't like the audience to fix on it one way. I don't want to call it 'dancers coming into rehearsals'—although that's what I see. The ballet is about dancers and love of dancing. I don't see them as peasants, although there are folk elements in the music. I see them as very elegant. Dancers are very elegant. I see now also a feeling, an infusion of European nostalgia that I didn't recognize when I was working on it. It's changed, of course."

The ballet was just as enthusiastically welcomed abroad. Amusingly, where most American critics saw the participants as Europeans, most Europeans saw them as Americans.

England:

"A creation so moving could only come out of deep personal feeling. The dance arrangement itself is simple, being a fast flowing sequence of variations for every possible combination of the ten soloists. I heard more than one sigh of relief that Robbins should have brought back good, straightforward dancing, and to have said so much while doing so. As one would expect, he has added touches of his own, so subtle that they evade notice or even description while still making the most tell-

ing effect. The solos are inventive, the double work sparklingly original and in places fiendishly difficult, but all so finely wrought that one was only aware of mood and effect. The choreography for the men is particularly notable, as he has completely broken away from the very limited range of steps men are usually given. The mood or theme of the work is almost impossible to describe in words, so linked are they with the dance—indeed, they *are* the dance! The quietly serious ending, after so much gaiety and freshness, leaves one with the curious, inexplicable, theatrical emotion. I make no apologies for saying that it made me want to cry." [11]

Germany:

"Robbins has given amnesty to emotions. Choreography returns from its autocracy to men. It enters their service once again. This happens in *Dances* with a sigh of relief, as if some long-denied liberty had been given back to the dance, and on this breath the piece is carried along. It seems inexhaustible. This 'gathering,' this being together, of which the title most modestly speaks, fundamentally is a new sociability in which the formal principles of dance and its humanitarian will of expression meet in unanimity. A ballet of mutual understanding and cordiality, of mutual confidence. Never does Robbins pull the net of his choreography ashore empty or filled with shallow phrases. Never does he throw it out with over-meaningful gesture." [12]

"An evocation of stillness determines the choreography, a glance, a turn of the head, an ascending hand movement, a resigned drop of the shoulders: in these moments are manifested the poetry of this ballet.

"It is, if you like, an affectionate 'old-fashioned' ballet, an exquisite danced elegy, with a wonderful economy and simplicity that come not from lack but from wisdom. This is the first ballet Robbins has choreographed since he became fifty. And so this ballet has become a farewell to youth, not only his own, but also to that of American ballet. An unmeasurable amount of melancholy and resignation hang on the movements of the dancers; though they give themselves happily and unconquered, the ballet ends quietly, pensively, and a little sad, that now all must be over." [13]

France:

"[Robbins] demonstrated that the purest

classical balletic language is capable of being a perfect vehicle for contemporary thought and feeling. All remains unpretentious and direct. Robbins has responded to Chopin with an immediacy that musical tradition has too often veiled. To the charm he has added gaiety; to the grace, humor. In all of it there is a radiant nobility; romanticism becomes a healthy game, intensely dynamic. One is delighted by the subtle movement of hands that can suggest in seemingly casual flutter the involvement of a lover's heart; or marvels at the leaps that end each episode, the sort to which any Russian specialist in balletic lifts would aspire." [14]

Russia:

"Contemporary plastic movement culled from everyday life seems to underscore the democratic character of [Robbins's] scenic images. Classical ballet movements combine with traditional gesture and elements of folk dancing. This is especially noticeable in *Dances at a Gathering*, to Chopin's music, whose choreography brings out both the acting and the dancing mastery of the artists." [15]

REVERIES
in 1971 called
TCHAIKOVSKY SUITE NO. 1

CHOREOGRAPHY: John Clifford

MUSIC: Peter Ilyitch Tchaikovsky (Suite No. 1 for orchestra, op. 43, 1878)

COSTUMES: Joe Eula (after revision, performed in practice clothes)

LIGHTING: Ronald Bates

PREMIERE: 4 December 1969

CAST: *Introduction and Fugue*, Anthony Blum, 12 woman; *Intermezzo*, Johnna Kirkland, Conrad Ludlow, 4 couples; *Marche Miniature*, Gelsey Kirkland, 4 women; *Gavotte*, entire cast

REVISION: 21 November 1971, with the title *Tchaikovsky Suite No. 1*

CAST: *Introduction and Fugue*, Blum, 12 women; *Divertimento*, Gloria Govrin; Susan Pilarre, Christine Redpath; *Intermezzo*, Elise Flagg, Ludlow, 4 couples; *Marche Miniature*, Gelsey Kirkland;

Scherzo, Flagg, Govrin, Gelsey Kirkland, Blum, Ludlow; Pilarre, Redpath, James Bogan, Bruce Wells; 4 women; *Gavotte*, entire cast

OTHER CASTS: Renee Estópinal, Susan Hendl, Robert Maiorano, David Richardson

Reveries was, in Barnes's opinion, "a lovely piece of choreography," and a favorite of Clifford himself. It was also memorable for providing the young Gelsey Kirkland with one of her first solo roles, a perky and amusing Marche Miniature, which brilliantly revealed the sharpness and speed of her attack. It would not be long before Balanchine would cast her as his new golden Firebird.

Barnes continued: "Set to four movements of the suite, a rag-bag of music, with scholastic figures and almost indecently urgent romanticism. But Clifford has used it with a telling and economic sensibility. Almost nothing is exaggerated. The first movement has one poetic male youth and serried ranks of female veils, coquettishly playing in the wind. Yet it is not the normal cliché. The rest of the ballet ignores these fast-spinning, vulgarly pink-skirted girls [until] the finale. This is a cardinal error of construction [but] Clifford gets away with it. There is a sumptuous and love-rapt pas de deux and beautiful solos for Blum and Gelsey Kirkland. The entire piece is elegant yet fun." [1]

Hering: "He found in the music not Slavic shadows but even-tempered sunniness. The décor was the starry sky. Running from one girl to another, Blum seemed to set them all in a swirl of motion like the little figures on a magic mirror. Then he took over the stage. On a diagonal path of light, Johnna Kirkland slowly glided, looking like a moonbeam guided by a voice heard only by herself. Ludlow partnered her gently, then led her away with a kiss. Then four girls bounced in rhythm as Gelsey Kirkland turned cartwheels before them. For the finale, Clifford became rather safely conventional." [2]

Says he, "I was proudest of the fugue in the first movement, manipulating groups of three, four, and five girls. [Several critics mentioned the skill displayed in this.] After the starry-night lighting was dropped, I felt the piece lost its whole

Reveries. **Johnna Kirkland, Conrad Ludlow.** *(Photo Martha Swope.)*

candy glitter, so I choreographed the remaining two movements, put everyone into leotards, and made the whole thing more abstract. I liked the first version best. *Reveries* was not my name; I intended the piece as a homage to Petipa, and I think I did achieve the Petipa style (except the fugue—that's my style). Also, I've always been curious to see what my ballets would look like in other repertories—say, Ballet Theatre. This one would look slightly Balanchine, of course, but not as much as it does when it's next to Balanchine."

The enlarged version added the Scherzo and the Divertimento (a solo for Govrin), as well as other changes. Goldner wrote: "Now that Clifford has removed the small ensemble from the Marche Miniature, the variation is even more effective—a lovely, gentle variation on doll-like dancing. The Divertimento begins with Govrin kneeling, a carry-over from the start of the first movement [in which the man knelt]. She waves her arms as though pleasurably biding time before a party. The rest of the dance is like a party, with Govrin a self-confident hostess as she waltzes and darts among her guests. The new Scherzo is like a finale, with the lead couples constantly appearing and disappearing. Because the Scherzo is followed by the actual finale, the Gavotte, the ballet's ending is prolonged over two movements. The expanded work could be pruned." [3]

Barnes: "Clifford tends to improve his ballets. His work here is intentionally rhapsodic, and sighing is a way of life. He has a strict regard for Balanchinian symmetry, and for the most part he likes architectural patterns, and he also has an intelligent fondness for metachronal patterns, where movements are repeated sequentially, adding visual interest to the music's own contrapuntal statement." [4]

IN THE NIGHT

CHOREOGRAPHY: Jerome Robbins

MUSIC: Frédéric Chopin (Nocturnes: op. 27, no. 1; op. 55, nos. 1 and 2; op. 9, no. 2)

COSTUMES: Joe Eula

LIGHTING: Thomas Skelton

PREMIERE: 29 January 1970

PIANO: Gordon Boelzner

CAST: Kay Mazzo and Anthony Blum; Violette Verdy and Peter Martins; Patricia McBride and Francisco Moncion

OTHER CASTS: Suzanne Farrell, Melissa Hayden, Allegra Kent, Gelsey Kirkland, Sara Leland; Jean-Pierre Bonnefous, Conrad Ludlow, Earle Sieveling

I'm still fascinated by the music of Chopin. It keeps opening up further avenues for me, so there is more to come. I may do another work first, but I'll be back to Chopin. There will be another Chopin ballet from me and then, I hope, a whole evening of Chopin [1970] [1] . . . Someday I'd like to do a Chopin ballet called *Other Waltzes, Other Mazurkas* [1975] * . . . You see, the thing is, I can never say what a dance means. I can't concern myself with anything that's not movement. The trouble with interviews is that they pin you down to verbal formulations when what really matters is on the stage. Talking once about *Dances at a Gathering*, we got into a deep conversation about nature. I found myself saying that certain things in *Dances* were like the wind, like clouds or leaves. But that isn't true. *Dances* is about relationships. I can't describe it more definitely than that [1971]." [2]
—Robbins

Robbins would undoubtedly say the same about *In the Night*. He also prefers

* In 1976 Robbins choreographed *Other Dances*, to Chopin, for American Ballet Theatre.

In the Night. Anthony Blum, Kay Mazzo, Francisco Moncion, Peter Martins, Patricia McBride, Violette Verdy. (*Photo Fred Fehl.*)

that each of his ballets be experienced as separate entities, without reference to other works. Most observers, however, considered *In the Night*, a pure-dance work to piano music of Chopin, an exquisite small-scale sequel to *Dances at a Gathering* and drew parallels between the sunny atmosphere in one, the darkness in the other; the peasants in *Dances*, the aristocrats in *Night*; the youthful carefree companionship in *Dances*, the young, but adult love relationships in *Night*. And, strictly on its own, most found *In the Night* a rapturous mood piece, deeply emotional, and with some sumptuous partnering.

Sealy: "With *In the Night*, Jerome Robbins has solved all the problems of dancing to Chopin. The music is well-chosen but dangerous. Chopin is the quickest to invite us into the dance and the quickest to step on our toes. His music for the piano is silk, as strong as hemp, woven into thousand-knotted, miniature dramas so complex that an attentive, really keyed-up listening to one waltz, one nocturne, one scherzo, one mazurka is hard intellectual labor. One is exhilarated by one's exhaustion. In the way that the essence of a five-act tragedy can be distilled into a sonnet or a three-hour opera into *lieder*, so is it with Chopin's piano music; it is music so concentrated that the playing of a few minutes of it is, in reality, an hours-long experience. That's why, finally, I was defeated by *Dances at a Gathering*: I couldn't continuously rise to so many brilliant occasions. Without

question, *In the Night* is the right length, but it is so much more than being the 'right' length: it is an entire success.

"As always, the music is muscular and demanding. It could never be background music or 'floor' music, so Robbins has worked out the miraculous means for a co-existence. He never dances *on* the music—he dances in it; he inhabits it. Within each second of the piece, he separates the dance from the music, then the drama from the dance. When they are divided—equal to each other in dominance and power—he puts them back together again: quick; they commingle. It is much the same with the technique and innovation of the actual choreography. A Robbins ballet is always fully rooted in a classical ground yet at the same time it is difficult to 'call' the dance figures (there are no 'thirty-two fouettés'). A tough nut, diamond-hard, a sheer cliff impossible to scale, yet, at the same time, easy, inviting, instantly welcoming, a Robbins work is like nothing else in the theater. He is busy making universes.

"The ballet has no scenario and it may be a mistake to assign a story too closely to the dances, but *In the Night* seems (to me) to be a serious, reflective comedy about husbands and wives, communicating troubled and tender secrets by lightning-flash as from the eyes. After the curtain, Mazzo and Blum enter upstage left with raised arms as if leaving a brightly lit room. Two lavish backbends seem to indicate an open, trusting arrangement. Mazzo's wild turns and evasions announce the deeper feeling. A supliant mood as the two embrace. With gentle mastery, Blum turns Mazzo topsyturvy. Afterwards, face to face, a restrained bow and a big lift off right. In the second dance, a chandelier is projected in the sky. Verdy and Martins walk arm in arm about the stage. A lift backward, a lift front. Pretty falls and turns. A more superficial relationship than the other, perhaps, but sexually secure. The woman is aloft on the man's chest in a startled exit. In the third dance, McBride, immediately preceding Moncion, makes a flaring, frenzied entrance stage left to stage right. Anger. An imperious stomp from the lady, a quick departure and return. 'Talking' pantomime. Intense throws and slides. Moncion exits melodramatically to return at once. Gestures. An enraged double exit. McBride returns, subdued, and in a moment of intense and delicate irony, makes a supremely witty gesture: Lightly but searchingly, she touches Moncion all over his body and curls up at his feet. She is lifted up to pointe. It is a very great passage of theatrical genius. In the fourth part, the couples dance separately and together. The women meet, the men bow. The social scale is balanced, the contract is re-confirmed. Queen Mab has had her moment and has flown away." [3]

Terry: "Have you ever *seen* a nocturne? *I* have, courtesy of the choreographic magic of Robbins. The movements that he has designed for his dancers do more than give body-shape to the melodic lines, the rhythms, the textures, the sonorities, the 'breathings' of the music. Relationships and incidents are indicated by the nocturnal figures as they travel their musical pathways in shadows or in shafts of moonlight, tenderly, and shyly or eagerly, reflectively or almost rhapsodically. The touchings, the pressings, the embracings of bodies are exquisitely conceived so that the whole emerges as a poem to the most natural aspects of romance.

"What is especially lovely is the gallantry displayed by the gentlemen for the gentlewomen, and the etiquette that governs the enchanting patterns when the couples meet. There are moments, too, when the purest dance imageries prevail, such as when Verdy is held in an upsidedown position by her partner and her legs, held tightly together, reach to the skies; slowly a tremor comes to the legs in the most delicate batterie, and, as they descend slowly to the floor, one seems to see a cascade of moonbeams drifting to earth.

"Two hundred years ago, Jean-Georges Noverre, choreographer, innovator, reformer, set out to restore meaningfulness, expressivity, even truth to an art that had become almost acrobatic. He wrote in his historic *Lettres sur la danse et les ballets* that 'this art has remained in its infancy only because its effects have been limited, like those of fireworks designed simply to gratify the eyes. . . . No one has suspected its power of speaking to the heart.' Today Noverre would be awed by the 'fireworks' of ballet technique, but he would also have been amazed at the emergence of a theater dance that would 'speak to the heart.' Perhaps *In the Night* would have affected him most, even more than modern dance masterpieces, for he would see a vocabulary of movement rooted in his own classical traditions, and he would experience physical fireworks used to illumine the fires of the heart." [4]

Barnes: "Here the dancers are aristocrats of that emotional Ruritania known best by poets and choreographers. Robbins has found a rich vein of choreography in the classic adagio. He has developed it from fairly conventional sources—Soviet ballet is one—and humanized it. He is a choreographer who seems never to remark, 'Oh, that's beautiful,' but rather, 'What does that beautiful movement say?'

In the Night. **Patricia McBride, Francisco Moncion.** (*Photo Martha Swope.*)

A lovely work. The ballet was danced with just the correct sense of rhapsodic skill, the right touch of an abandon never quite abandoned." [5]

"*Dances* is flawless and complete, an indisputable masterpiece. *In the Night*, for technical reasons, is somewhat less, but otherwise is just as beautiful, just as expressive of one's secret response to the inner passion of the music. In at least one respect, *In the Night* is startlingly more dramatic, and that is in its lighting, as when, in the third nocturne, the most ardent of the three couples fly from the wings down a blinding column of white light thrown diagonally across the stage. Touches such as these are so right, so like one imagines they were meant to be that communication is instant and profound. The ballets pierce the psyche like a needle, and inflame and drug the mind with their beauty." [6]

Moncion: "Of our part, Jerry definitely said we were having an argument: 'It's one of those on-again, off-again affairs; they might get together, they come, they go.' The first section is a mood piece. It has birdlike gestures; it floats. The second section is a very elegant polonaise. Jerry has always used lots of lifts, even in the fifties."

Croce observed that "*In the Night* is Robbins's first ballet to deal with mature people. McBride and Moncion recall the lovers in such poems of John Crowe Ransom's as 'Two in August' and 'The Equilibrists.'" [7] Elsewhere, interviewing Robbins, she wrote:

"Both [*Dances* and *Night*] are based on the music of Chopin, and both, like Fokine's classic Chopin ballet *Les Sylphides*, are essentially dance suites without a plot. Yet Robbins has managed to convey even more strongly than Fokine the effect of a dramatic web and of a continuous dramatic action behind the scenes. I couldn't recall that happening in any other Robbins ballet that I had seen, and I asked him whether he had set out to do something new. Robbins shook his head. 'I never think about things like that. That effect is there, if it is there, because it's in the music. I had no idea about some drama happening offstage and I'm not even sure Fokine invented it. What would we know if we found out that he had? It's not such a new idea anymore. Think of the second movement of Balanchine's *Serenade* or *Symphony in C*. Those girls who come on are certainly coming from somewhere.'" [8]

WHO CARES?

CHOREOGRAPHY: George Balanchine

MUSIC: George Gershwin (songs as below), orchestrated by Hershy Kay

COSTUMES: Karinska

DÉCOR: Jo Mielziner (November 1970)

LIGHTING: Ronald Bates

PREMIERE: 5 February 1970

PIANO: Gordon Boelzner

"Clap Yo' Hands" played by George Gershwin

CAST: Karin von Aroldingen, Patricia McBride, Marnee Morris, Jacques d'Amboise; 15 women, 5 men

"Strike Up the Band" (1927): ensemble
"Sweet and Low Down" (1925): ensemble
"Somebody Loves Me" (1924): Deborah Flomine, Susan Hendl, Linda Merrill, Susan Pilarre, Bettijane Sills
"Bidin' My Time" (1930): Deni Lamont, Robert Maiorano, Frank Ohman, Richard Rapp, Earle Sieveling
" 'S Wonderful" (1927): couple
"That Certain Feeling" (1925): 2 couples
"Do Do Do" (1926): couple
"Lady Be Good" (1924): couple
"The Man I Love" (1924): McBride, d'Amboise
"I'll Build a Stairway to Paradise" (1922): von Aroldingen
"Embraceable You" (1930): Morris, d'Amboise
"Fascinatin' Rhythm" (1924): McBride
"Who Cares?" (1931): von Aroldingen, d'Amboise
"My One and Only" (1927): Morris
"Liza" (1929): d'Amboise
"Clap Yo' Hands" (1926): von Aroldingen, McBride, Morris, d'Amboise
"I Got Rhythm" (1930): entire cast

OTHER CASTS: Merrill Ashley, Suzanne Farrell, Sara Leland, Kay Mazzo, Jean-Pierre Bonnefous, Peter Martins

Gershwin and Balanchine—was this a strange combination? Wrote Goldner, "What are we to make of choreographer Balanchine, who creates quintessential classic ballets (*Symphony in C*, *Ballet Imperial*, *Agon*) side by side with *Western Symphony*, *Stars and Stripes*, or a square dance set to Vivaldi and Corelli? A man who [dresses] his dancers in white tutus and black mesh stockings with equal conviction; who himself sports a heavy Russian accent and dude clothing, the tight but well-tailored pants and shirts and string bow ties that movie cowboys fancy; who has said that his favorite dancer is Ray Bolger; who advises one of his dancers to read Tolstoy and Pushkin, and then goes home to watch Westerns on television?

"The point is that Balanchine is not a snob or a 'character,' despite his string bow ties. He is not a reverse snob, either. He talks about Bob Hope and Westerns and has used Gershwin's songs for his newest ballet simply because he loves them all. He loves America. The unfurling of the American flag at the end of *Stars* is meant to be funny, but the humor is mixed with affection. It is not camp; nor is Balanchine going slumming or being whimsical when he choreographs to cowboy tunes and Gershwin." [1]

So much for the unlikeliness of it all. Moreover, Balanchine had had plenty of experience in the commercial theater, mostly in the thirties and forties; and he had worked with Gershwin previously (*Goldwyn Follies*, Hollywood, 1938). (Just about that time, Martin decided that Balanchine had found his true calling not in leading abortive ballet enterprises but in putting together dances for musicals.) The unprecedented part came in mounting a dance work to Gershwin on a classical ballet company.

It happened this way: Balanchine had a book of Gershwin songs, arranged as Gershwin played them in concert and given to him by the composer. "I played one and thought, 'beautiful,' " says he, " 'I'll make a pas de deux.' I played another, just as beautiful, I thought, 'a variation.' And then another and another, and there was no end to how beautiful they were." [2] At the premiere all but the first and last songs were piano solos. Later all were orchestrated with the exception of Gershwin on tape in "Clap Yo' Hands."

That some of Balanchine's works are classics is unquestioned. In a wry program note, Kirstein "elevated" Gershwin songs to the same level:

"The dictionary says 'classic' means standard, leading, belonging to the highest rank or authority. Once it applied mainly to masterpieces from Graeco-Roman antiquity; now we have boxing and horse-racing classics, classic cocktail-dresses and classic cocktails. Among classic American composers we number Stephen Foster, John Philip Sousa, and George Gershwin. First heard fifty years ago, the best of the Gershwin songs maintain their classic freshness, as of an eternal martini—dry, frank, refreshing, tailor-made, with an invisible kick from its slightest hint of citron. Nostalgia has not syruped their sentiment nor robbed them of immediate piquancy."

Hering described the ballet: "It is bright with afternoon as the orchestra launches into 'Strike Up the Band.' The strutting corps which opened *Who Cares?* seemed momentarily to be trying to inject a campy flavor Balanchine had not asked of them. Soon, however, they relaxed into the easygoing lines of 'Sweet and Low Down' and the more specifically balletic shapes of 'Somebody Loves Me.' Five boys swaggering to 'Bidin' My Time' resembled soft-shoe dancers endowed with a higher body line and a look of more precisely molded energy. Three duets were backed by a frieze of girls in period poses. Was Balanchine affectionately remembering the eager but still rough-hewn dancers he first had to work with in this country? Was he trying to make the superbly sleek children of his today-company sense some of this in their own bodies?

"So much for the ragtime Gershwin. Night washed over the skyline. Gershwin the sophisticate took over. Here was the world of long cigarette holders and penthouses with white rugs symbolized by McBride offering to d'Amboise all the poignancy of a woman who dares not speak lest she weep. Their duet to 'The Man I Love' may well endure long after audiences have become fickle about the rest of the ballet.

"D'Amboise slipped smoothly from being loving with McBride to reckless with Morris to cool with von Aroldingen. Alone he was the never-to-grow-up male so often apotheosized in Broadway musicals. He twirled his forearms from the elbow or did carefree turns with his arms spread straight out. And when, like some Manhattan Island Apollo, he brought the three girls together, all radiated that 'angelic unconcern for emotion' which Balanchine has always felt to be characteristic of American dancers." [3]

The ballet could be divided into two parts: the rather brassy numbers for the corps and the seemingly more deeply felt sections for the principals (starting with "The Man I Love").

Who Cares? Above: Karin von Aroldingen. *Right:* Jean-Pierre Bonnefous. *(Photos Donn Matus.)*

Barnes wrote: "The ballet is not likely to be regarded as one of Balanchine's major works although it does, not unexpectedly, have some extraordinarily lovely passages in it. In both the ensembles and the double work the choreography is too conventional to do anything but dance admiringly alongside the music. To be sure, the duets are occasionally enlivened by the quickflash of an inspired lift, but for the most part they are show business of a show that has already been closed for one or two decades. But the four main solos, and perhaps the final quartet to the Gershwin recording, are different things again. Balanchine's choreography for 'Fascinatin' Rhythm,' dazzlingly danced by McBride, is a perfect gem of musicality and invention: marvelous in its stops, starts, and emotional swirls. D'Amboise danced with that charming friendliness that characterized all of the great prewar hoofers, and yet with an unforced brilliance far beyond their technical capacities. . . .

"There are many beautiful things in *Who Cares?* But when it is all over, well, you remember the good pieces, but you also remember the show-biz feel of the total enterprise. Balanchine is trying to evoke the lively spirits of Fred and Adele Astaire, and the thirties. Yet, revealingly, he is at his best when he is at his most contemporary and most true to his own canons of classic ballet."[4]

Sealy was more favorable: "*Who Cares?* is wonderful. We have a New York ballet in two parts: *Raymonda on Fifth Avenue* [first eight songs] and *Apollo in Central Park*. It is brilliant high-wire act, and it must have been difficult to keep it from becoming what it most definitely is *not:* nostalgia, show biz, Broadway, dear old Busby, or anything to do with the past. What it's really about is the inherent joy of being a man or woman with a healthy body and the ability to *dance, dance, dance.*

"As usual, Balanchine has walked the wire over the falls. Like all strong, self-assured artists, [he] makes his intention clear right at the beginning; to emphasize that it is a classical ballet, eight songs have been made into a suite of classical dances, by turns dainty, humorous, robust and romantic, and given to the ensemble. [Next] a Gershwin *Apollon Musagète*. This memorable quartet dances to eight songs. Never in a theater have I wanted so much to jump the moat and join in. It is pure, unmitigated, uncut joy, an open, palpitating, vulnerable heart on the sleeve. [McBride and d'Amboise] together in 'The Man I Love,' angular, cat-wary, in and out of each other's arms, alternately aloof and impassioned, alert to the rising and falling sounds from the piano, have the memory-burning dance of

a lifetime. It is finally Gershwin's music itself, with its slight pretentiousness, that jells the ballet, preserves Balanchine's fast-stepping, high-breasted, cheeky, slightly put-on attitudes. Warning: Sample *Who Cares?* sparingly. It is a late Balanchine goody, a narcotic liqueur that might make one sick if taken in great quantities."[5]

But Goldner thought two masters met and clashed: "Balanchine's sense of humor is essentially dark, often bordering on the fantastic and gothic, while Gershwin's is dry and sophisticated. With that incompatibility, *Who Cares?* became a humorless ballet, although some dancers brought their own easygoing charm to it. Balanchine's choreographic style is intensely lyrical, while Gershwin is lilting and hummable. There were times when the choreography was actually too beautiful for the music, for Gershwin's wit involves undercutting would-be love songs with knowing, sexy melodies.

"For 'The Man I Love' Balanchine staged an innocent and ethereal love duet for McBride and d'Amboise. An elegant pas de deux for Hendl and Ohman sat uneasily next to 'Do Do Do.' These dances would be magnificent set to another composer.

"In his other American ballets, Balanchine could bend the music to a purely classic style. Gershwin's music is too potent with association and too rich musically to be handled in that way. He must be reckoned with on his own terms. The problem is that Balanchine has never been able to treat the jazz style authentically and comfortably. In some numbers of *Who Cares?* he resorted to high kicks, flailing arms, and tap-dance stances that we associate with third-rate musicals rather than with Gershwin. Other times, we saw a variation on soft-shoe routines, which also does not 'get' Gershwin. Generally, Balanchine was either running way ahead of Gershwin in lyricism and subtle musicality, or Gershwin was in the lead in humor and in his conception of popular American culture. [It] was a relay race, and because each man is a giant in his own way, the race could not conclude in a draw, much less with a winner." [6]

The work was criticized by some for the "Mantovani" orchestrations; for its tendency to gaudiness, particularly in the backdrop and the costumes of the female corps, as well as in some of their steps; and for the difficulty experienced by the female ensemble in performing the casual, loose-limbed Broadway-type movements with the proper style (the boys managed it better). Highlights were the roles for McBride (especially her solo, with its extremely tricky rhythms); for von Aroldingen; and, above all, for d'Amboise, whose perfect throw-away virtuosity infused his entire body. Some called it his greatest role.

Says von Aroldingen: "It was very gay, just floated out of him. You think it's so unlike Balanchine, it's so jazzy. One would think he'd just make a jazz ballet out of it, like everyone else, a dance like Broadway, but he put it on pointe—it's sort of like a tap dance on pointe. It's hard; my variation is a killer—lots of high jumps—yet it looks like a gay nothing. Balanchine would sing, even the words, at rehearsals. You were just carried along."

Says McBride, "We started 'Fascinatin' Rhythm.' He played it on the piano. Then he choreographed it so fast—and danced it so well, much better than I ever could. The middle section, especially, I could never do the way he did. There are intricacies in the variation from beginning to end. It's a brilliant thing. I come out looking cute; then it goes into something else, where you're another person. In the middle, you're slow and sexy. You should have seen Mr. B. doing that! He was di-

vine! I did it many, many times with the tape recorder so eventually I didn't have to think about counting. Now I really have fun with it. The duet was also put together very fast. There's one part where he has me moving like a snake. We practiced many things that I couldn't do right away, like a very tricky jump onto Jacques's back. I think Mr. B. had a good time choreographing that ballet."

The ballet was taken on the Company's Russian tour in 1972. Yuri Slonimsky, Soviet ballet historian and critic, wrote: "The musical arrangement and orchestration have deprived it of many appealing qualities. In a theater which shows such respect for the highest examples of music, it is more than strange to listen to music which is reduced in places to mere sound accompaniment for the dancing. Often deprived of any support from the music, Balanchine nevertheless unfolds a large, almost traditional grand pas in the famous Petipa style. Apart from a rather ordinary beginning and ending, the work contains much that is interesting, inventive, and unexpected in the vocabulary of dance. This is especially true of the pas de deux, although I must admit that sometimes one could do with less 'parade-allez' and more spiritual depth, concentration, and if one may say so, stillness on the part of the performers.

"In this work the ballet master introduces us to American youth. His portrayals may lack individuality and at times these young people resemble too closely the image of youth created by the movies of the forties. The artfully free combination of almost traditional ballet classicism (in this respect the costumes of the corps de ballet girls are too balletic and not in the best of taste) with contemporary dance movement gives a genuine flavor to the performance, although much of it is of slight value. The three soloists dance inspiredly, with moments of virtuosity.

"But the real hero of the piece is a simple, good-natured, fun-loving fellow portrayed by d'Amboise—an artist of exceptional charm who renders the varying moods of his personage to perfection. This role, in which Balanchine wittily mixes classicism with everyday life and popular dancing, contributed the major success of the performance. In this portrayal both the ballet master and the dancer restored to the dance its most important and precious attribute—inspiration."

SARABANDE AND DANSE (I)

CHOREOGRAPHY: John Clifford

MUSIC: Claude Debussy (*Sarabande*, 1901; *Danse*, c. 1890; orchestrated by Maurice Ravel, 1923)

COSTUMES: Joe Eula

LIGHTING: Ronald Bates

PREMIERE: 21 May 1970

CAST: *Sarabande:* Johnna Kirkland, Earle Sieveling; *Danse:* Violette Verdy, John Clifford
Danse also performed by Gelsey Kirkland

The ballet received wildly divergent reviews.

Barnes: "It is a modest yet imaginative little work, not shatteringly important yet effective on its own terms. The first duet is markedly the more interesting. What is important about the ballet is its perfect acceptability as a choreographic novelty. It will last a few seasons and then be forgotten. But Clifford has learned something, a gap in the schedule has been filled, and everyone is happy." [1]

Kisselgoff, however, saw something different: "*Sarabande* is so truly extraordinary that its originality is startling. It is that rare thing in American choreography—the completely acrobatic pas de deux. There is here, as in his *Fantasies*, a suggestion of Soviet-style lifts. Yet it is free of the spectacular toss-in-the-air kind of lift. Rather, it is imbued with lyricism. It is the combination of styles that makes the pas de deux so remarkable. It is completely new, neither in the old plastique mode nor the modern-dance sculptural style." [2]

For Anderson, it "had the air of something concocted in a hurry." [3]

Says Clifford, "This was intended for one-time-only performance, for a gala that was never held. It's not a full ballet. The first movement was the better one choreographically. *Danse* was hard, because I was performing that myself. As I look back, it wasn't bad, but not as original as *Sarabande*. I wanted the ballet dropped. I didn't want to put myself into a position where the audience would think that I think I'm just as good as Balanchine by turning out trivia. And it *was* trivia."

Sarabande and Danse. **Earle Sieveling, Johnna Kirkland.** *(Photo Martha Swope.)*

Suite No. 3. **Valse Mélancholique. Kay Mazzo, Conrad Ludlow (right).** *(Photo Martha Swope.)*

SUITE NO. 3
later called
TCHAIKOVSKY SUITE NO. 3

CHOREOGRAPHY: George Balanchine

MUSIC: Peter Ilyitch Tchaikovsky (Suite No. 3 in G Minor, op. 55, 1884)

COSTUMES, DÉCOR: Nicolas Benois

LIGHTING: Ronald Bates

PREMIERE: 3 December 1970

CAST: *1. Élégie,* Karin von Aroldingen, Anthony Blum; 6 women; *2. Valse Mélancholique,* Kay Mazzo, Conrad Ludlow; 6 women; *3. Scherzo,* Marnee Morris, John Clifford; 8 women; *4. Tema con Variazioni,* Gelsey Kirkland, Edward Villella; 4 demi-solo couples, 8 women, 8 men

OTHER CASTS: *1.* Frank Ohman, Nolan T'Sani; *2.* Sara Leland, Christine Redpath; Bart Cook; *3.* Colleen Neary; Robert Weiss; *4.* Merrill Ashley, Patricia McBride, Mazzo; Jean-Pierre Bonnefous, Peter Martins, Peter Schaufuss, Helgi Tomasson

In *Suite No. 3,* Balanchine grafted new material onto an already existing work. *Theme and Variations* was created as an independent entity in 1947; musically it was the fourth movement of Tchaikovsky's suite. In 1970 Balanchine supplied steps for the first three movements.

Odd as this procedure might have seemed (*Theme* by itself is a full-scale ballet of some twenty minutes in length, a highly esteemed work), the results were even stranger, for Balanchine appeared not to have attempted any stylistic integration between the old and the new. To the crisp and exacting *Theme*, with its sparkling tutus and tiaras, he added three movements of moonlit girls in strapless ballgowns, hair flowing long, some of them in bare feet, and all dreamily bathed in subdued lighting, and removed from the audience by a scrim.

Goldner had the ingenious idea that he was showing an evolution from romanticism to classicism—that each movement was more classical than the last. The lighting grows brighter, the steps become more difficult, the soloists emerge from the shadows that first almost hid them, and begin to dance as couples rather than as lost souls. She wrote:

"[First] he gives us extreme romanticism. We see the dancers behind a scrim, a scrim suggesting whirlpools of water, no less. The girls wear their long hair loose, and in the first section they are not even wearing toe shoes. The costumes are long, in blues and lavender. The lighting is thick with atmosphere.

"In the first part, the choreography is completely complementary to the scenic aspects. Without any defined steps, the girls and one man run and leap freely and with abandon. There are no patterns to their groupings, and although there is a female soloist, her role is only vaguely defined. In such fluidity, she easily merges with the corps. The second part is built

around a couple, but the pas de deux as such is still in a nascent stage of development. Yet there is less free movement, and there is a greater distinction between the ensemble and the couple. Balanchine is pulling in, but he really begins to tighten the reins in the third section. This is an allegro, which necessitates denser choreography. Not only are there more steps to the beat and greater speed and precision but some exploitation of technical skill. The female lead does quick turns and the man high jumps. The ensemble is definitely in a supportive role. In fact, we have now moved so far from the spirit of the first two sections that the girls' long hair and the scrim seem out of place. The faint lights of chandeliers, which begin to glow behind the scrim, are much more in keeping with the choreography. And thus, when the scrim rises on the fourth and final movement, revealing a grand ballroom and ladies and a gentleman in formal ballet attire, we should not gasp with surprise. After all, wasn't Balanchine working up to the St. Petersburg court all the time? Forget the romantic ambiance for a minute, for weren't those woodland sylphs *dancing* differently from section to section?

"Well, yes, Balanchine did pull off a great tour de force. He did bring us to the classical style entirely within the framework of romanticism. Yet I was still thrown off balance when that scrim ascended. When I saw those dancers in their tutus, at first poised for action, and then gliding into the opening ports de bras, my reaction was: at last, now we get down to business. Not that classicism is more satisfying than romanticism, but it so happens that the very first seconds of *Theme and Variations* are infinitely superior to what is seen in the preceding parts." [1]

Saal had other thoughts about the split personality of this ballet: "Balanchine poses the timeless metaphysical question of 'What is reality?' The first movement is distilled romanticism, danced behind scrims which shroud the dancers in a mysterious blue mist. A Byronesque man is visited by a bevy of muses. He dances [with one], hardly touching, in a delicate swirl of arms and trailing fingers, she elusive, he slow to pursue, as though in a dream or else fearful of sullying that disembodied feminine spirit with his masculine passion. If it's a dream of love, the second movement is flesh and not spirit. But it's a loveless ceremonial intercourse, like the performance of a harem dancer before a sultan, artificial in gaiety, sly in abandon, heartlessly seductive. The brief scherzo is healthily carnal, a nonstop bacchanale. And then the scrims rise. The stage is ablaze with light from giant chandeliers, the dancers posed prettily. It's an idealized tsarist Russia. The harmony of these dancers, finally, is the ideal mixture of flesh and spirit. But this finale is no longer merely an evocation of imperial Russia. It's the culmination of a series of dreams. It's reality. Or is it? Is it perhaps the heart of the dream itself, the pure clear vision of a never-never land? Well, reality for Balanchine is not in conclusions but in action. This is how bodies move to music, he's saying, and that is our reality." [2]

The scrim was abandoned after the first performance; it is now clear that all four episodes take place in the same ballroom.

For all the interesting theory, however, it was felt that in mood and tone Balanchine's work was dangerously close to the banal.

Micklin began his review with a definition of *camp*, then: "Balanchine's newest ballet is about as pure camp as I have seen in dance in a long while. Calling an artistic endeavor camp is not necessarily a putdown. Yet I found the first two of its movements grim; the third mildly satisfying, and the finale finally enjoyable. Think of any one of a dozen old-fashioned movie musicals—with Gene Kelly, Rita Hayworth, or anyone—where the male and female partners drift through a misty romantic duet accompanied by a few ethereal chorus girls. Abstract scenery

Suite No. 3. **Tema con Variazioni. Gelsey Kirkland, Edward Villella.** (*Photo Martha Swope.*)

and lavender lighting are present here in Hollywood style, while two stars flow through an endless series of yearning, innocent gestures of love. That's the first movement. A 1940s movie musical in living color. 'Camp rests on innocence.' (Sontag) It also rests on nostalgia, and this work is heavy with nostalgia for the traditional virtues of ballet: glamour, sheer romanticism, and bravura displays of neoclassicism. Yet, except for the final movement, in which Villella and Kirkland dance an absorbing and very beautiful series of duets and solos in the grand ballet manner, *Suite No. 3* is devoted to a misplaced fondness for the sentimental charms of Hollywood's yesteryears." [3]

In similar vein, Goldner wrote: "The [new] choreography is limp rather than limpid. It strives for a breathlessness and ecstasy, but is actually an exaggeration of those aspects of romanticism. Was Balanchine simply uninspired, or was he making a satirical statement about romanticism? Was he being excessive on purpose? Experimenting with romanticism to the *n*th degree and then killing it with marshmallow topping? If Balanchine was in fact playing with parody, then the new part is an interesting failure, but a failure nevertheless because parody should not yield dull choreography." [4]

At the opening, Barnes accepted the work happily and without questions, but he later called it a "dextrously mixed bag": "Here is the Tchaikovsky-Petipa style of the imperial ballet, but also an

Isadora Duncan-like hint of the fresh Romanticism that was to have such an effect on Michel Fokine and the new ballet. It works well enough, although by far the better part of the work is the original *Theme and Variations.*" [5]

This last remained basically as it was when created, except that some new and harder moments—gargouillades, tiny swift beating and jumping movements— were added to challenge and introduce Kirkland, a wonder-child whose technique was described as "porcelain-coated steel." Physically tiny, she had a lightness and speed that few could approach, as well as a technical command that was extraordinary. For some time, other ballerinas shied away from the role. However, says McBride, "It looks breathtakingly fast, but it's no faster than other Balanchine ballets."

The Benois costumes and setting were roundly panned.

Germany:
"A relapse into dusty neo-romanticism that mistakes mannerism for poetry. In a ballroom, girls with flowing long hair and floating long veil dresses à la Edvard Munch try once more to evoke Jugenstil emotions, but choreographically this is so dull and dim that even the completely unmotivated abrupt change of style for the finale, presenting a full-company entree in tutus, cannot diminish the impression that the ballet had come from an old storage chest." [6]

Russia:
"In the last movement we not only admire the choreographic inventiveness and inexhaustible fantasy of the ballet master and his ability to discover the most subtle and true plastic tonalities, but we are captivated by the poetic atmosphere born of the true alliance of music and movement. Plastic movement becomes music made visible." [7]

KODÁLY DANCES

CHOREOGRAPHY: John Clifford

MUSIC: Zoltán Kodály (*Marosszék Dances*, 1930; *Dances of Galánta*, 1933)

COSTUMES: Stanley Simmons

LIGHTING: Ronald Bates

Kodály Dances. **Anthony Blum, Johnna Kirkland.** (*Photo Martha Swope.*)

PREMIERE: 14 January 1971

CAST: Johnna Kirkland, Anthony Blum, Colleen Neary; 8 women, 8 men
Also danced by Sara Leland

Says Clifford, "This was my least successful ballet. It started out as an abstract ballet—two pas de deux, no gypsies, no campfire, no comedy. The one pas de deux that remained was the best part. When the tambourines came out, some people loved it because they saw it as a real take-off on the Bolshoi. After we went to Russia, I realized that it was more of a take-off than I had thought!"

Goldner wrote: "Not a divertissement, but it does not seem to make a full entry either. One reason is that the choreography is neither Hungarian nor à la mode of that style, not even in the most free sense. Perhaps it was intended to be a vulgarization, as all those panting chests, arched backs, leering faces, and rumpled manes would suggest. But it was not funny; rather, it seems an adolescent misinterpretation of the Hungarian ethos and, incidentally, of the music. Whereas the music's rapid changes in tempo and texture are dynamic and, yes, Hungarian, Clifford's choreography follows Kodály in fits and starts, producing a disjointed rather than temperamental quality." [1]

Siegel: "A gypsy camp. Center stage is a giant bonfire exuding an inordinate amount of smoke. Neary is artistically crumpled on the floor in front of the fire

as the ballet begins. She rises and stretches and does a solo with a lot of flinging around of arms and legs, a lot of ribbons and hair streaming out in all directions. Couples come on and carry out some arm-waving, thigh-slapping, heel-stamping, and similar balkanisms. Blum dances with Kirkland, and after their duet the sky turns magenta. Neary dances with two boys. Finally everybody dances in unison, shaking tambourines at the audience." [2]

CONCERTO FOR TWO SOLO PIANOS

CHOREOGRAPHY: Richard Tanner

MUSIC: Igor Stravinsky (1935)

COSTUMES: Stanley Simmons

LIGHTING: Ronald Bates

PREMIERE: 21 January 1971 (first presented 1970 by the Workshop of the School of American Ballet)

PIANISTS: Gordon Boelzner, Jerry Zimmerman

I. CON MOTO, Gelsey Kirkland, John Clifford; Christine Redpath, Giselle Roberge, 6 women; II. NOTTURNO, Colleen Neary, James Bogan; III. QUATTRO VARIAZIONI,

Variation 1, David Richardson, 6 women; *Variation 2,* Kirkland, Clifford; *Variation 3,* Redpath, Roberge; *Variation 4,* Bogan, Clifford, Richardson; IV. PRELUDIO E FUGA, entire cast

OTHER CASTS: I. Sara Leland, Redpath, Bart Cook; II. Lynne Stetson, Bonita Borne; III. Tracy Bennett

Considered a nice student try, but out of its depth on a large professional stage. It was probably pushed out in the open prematurely because the anticipated Robbins *Goldberg Variations* had not been completed.

Wrote Barnes: "Attempted to slavishly follow both the music and the choreography of Balanchine. It is a common failing for a young choreographer to imagine that if he matches every note on the run he produces musical choreography. The style owes a great deal to Balanchine's *Variations*—with pelvic thrusts, alarmed glances, and waving legs." [1]

Herridge: "A creditable work with striking moments, but too often a conventional copy of Balanchine. It is well organized and has an exceptionally difficult pas de deux in Part II." [2]

Belt: "A rather decorous farrago more appealing than significant." [3]

Everyone remarked on the length of Neary's legs. The ballet was presented at the Stravinsky Festival, June 1972.

FOUR LAST SONGS

CHOREOGRAPHY: Lorca Massine

MUSIC: Richard Strauss (1946–48)

COSTUMES: Joe Eula

DÉCOR: John Braden

LIGHTING: Ronald Bates

PREMIERE: 21 January 1971 (first presented 1970 by the Workshop of the School of American Ballet)

SOPRANO: Joyce Mathis

CAST: Robert Maiorano, Susan Pilarre, Bonnie Moore, Meg Gordon, Johnna Kirkland, Bryan Pitts, Lisa de Ribere, Bonita Borne, Nolan T'Sani

Four Last Songs. Robert Maiorano, Bryan Pitts. *(Photo Martha Swope.)*

OTHER CASTS: Susan Hendl, Deborah Koolish, Polly Shelton, Heather Watts; Stephen Caras, Bart Cook, Earle Sieveling

Four *Last Songs* had a surprisingly mixed reception. The score was, of course, undeniably beautiful, rich, evocative, poignant. It was clear that Massine was after mood, not an interpretation of the song texts, which dealt mostly with farewells and endings. Massine's studio was inhabited by nine young dancers, sensing their bodies; only some of their movements matched a weighted quality in the music. Although Barnes could think of nothing good to say about the ballet, complaining particularly that the choreography was unrelated to the music, Goldner found something positive in precisely this characteristic: "A striking parallel relationship (separate but equal) between dancers and music develops, making the texture of the work more complex than if Massine had faced Strauss head on. Because he had no rhythmic structure to work with and might have destroyed the music's continuous flow had he worked phrase by phrase, Massine swallowed the score in one gulp and treated it impressionistically rather than literally. Once committed to that approach, he went the whole way. Instead of interpreting the score, he recreated it by having the dancers move as a polyphonic base to both the singer and orchestra. It is such a quiet, odd, and loose

kind of dream that one can easily imagine a slight ping causing the work to shatter into a thousand pieces, as quietly as it was born. And yet it grows stronger and bolder in memory, deriving its resilience, I suspect, from its very fragility. However slowly its spell goes to work, it does finally grip the imagination." [1]

Siegel: "The dance, set in a ballet studio, opens as soprano Mathis walks across the stage. She begins to sing and Maiorano starts a solo while the other dancers exercise at the barre. Gradually the dancers become more involved with each other, drifting almost without volition into duets and groups, then wandering away in meditation. Maiorano and Pitts have a rather sexual duet; two girls wrap themselves around each boy. All at once we are aware that the singing has ended. The dancers look at the audience as if they have been caught dreaming in public; embarrassed, they go back to the barre. Slowly Maiorano walks to the singer and embraces her. Massine's idea is effective, and it doesn't sink into sentimentality. But his movement idiom is unclear. The small ensemble of nine is frequently doing nine things at once. It's hard to decide which one to look at, and the group as a whole isn't designed for harmonious viewing, so the proper mood doesn't quite get established." [2]

Herridge: "A find, different from anything in the repertory, a new way of moving for the Company which allows breathing space for individual prowess among the dancers. Nine dancers move

about as though at barre in a studio. Occasionally they group in some organized pattern but more often each seems on his own. The same phrase may start them, but each develops his own thing. They seem to improvise, but of course they don't. Lyrical ecstasy is everywhere until the last song is ended and the group comes to rest. It has been less a class than exultation in the sheer joy of stretching one's body." [3]

CONCERTO FOR JAZZ BAND AND ORCHESTRA

CHOREOGRAPHY: George Balanchine and Arthur Mitchell

MUSIC: Rolf Lieberman (1954), performed by "Doc" Severinsen and the *Tonight Show* orchestra

LIGHTING: Ronald Bates

PREMIERE: 6 May 1971 (single performance for gala benefit)

CAST: 21 dancers of the New York City Ballet and 23 from the Dance Theater of Harlem

I. Introduction and Jump
II. Scherzo I
III. Blues
IV. Scherzo II
V. Boogie Woogie
VI. Interludium
VII. Mambo

Black dancers en masse on the stage of the New York State Theater for the first time ever; "Doc" Severinsen and the *Tonight Show* orchestra; French champagne at the reception following; a score by the prestigious director of the Hamburg Opera (with, as overture, a medley of Beatles music); collaborative choreography by Balanchine and Mitchell; a boost for the Dance Theater of Harlem— *Concerto* had a little bit of everything. While not much of a ballet, as a drawing card for the benefit evening it was eminently suited to the occasion. As Goldner wrote, it had "a thrown-together look. The nicest part of the gala was the party that came after the performance." [1]

Barnes: "Lieberman's idea of jazz is somewhat less than sophisticated, and his

Concerto for Jazz Band and Orchestra. **Members of the Dance Theater of Harlem and the New York City Ballet. "Doc" Severinson and the Tonight Show orchestra** (rear). *(Photo Martha Swope.)*

LIGHTING: Thomas Skelton

PREMIERE: 27 May 1971 (open working rehearsal 24 July 1970, Performing Arts Center, Saratoga Springs, New York)

PIANO: Gordon Boelzner

CAST: PART I: *Theme,* Renee Estópinal, Michael Steele; *Variations,* Gelsey Kirkland, Sara Leland; John Clifford, Robert Maiorano, Robert Weiss, Bruce Wells; 6 women, 6 men; PART II: *Variations,* Karin von Aroldingen and Peter Martins; Susan Hendl and Anthony Blum; Patricia McBride and Helgi Tomasson; 14 women, 9 men

OTHER CASTS: *Theme,* Kathleen Haigney, Francisco Moncion, Francis Sackett; *Variations I,* Elise Flagg, Delia Peters, Christine Redpath; Bart Cook, Daniel Duell, Bryan Pitts, Nolan T'Sani; *Variations II,* Allegra Kent, Heather Watts; Daniel Duell, Frank Ohman, Wells

idea of classical music is more than conventional. [The music] was a well-intentioned, if patronizing, attempt to bring what he quaintly calls 'the current dance forms of today into "art" music.' The two companies flash on in jolly sequence, and while the choreography was far from deathless, it was always happy." [2]

OCTANDRE

CHOREOGRAPHY: Richard Tanner

MUSIC: Edgar Varèse (*Octandre,* 1924, and *Intégrales,* 1925)

LIGHTING: Ronald Bates

PREMIERE: 13 May 1971

CAST: Johnna Kirkland, Bryan Pitts, Christine Redpath; 12 women, 8 men

In *Octandre,* Tanner did not "imitate" Balanchine, as he was accused of doing in his previous ballet, *Concerto for Two Solo Pianos.* If anything, he (possibly) borrowed an idea from Robbins's *Cage*—that of the predatory female. With this notion, a décor of silver tendrils, and perhaps a nod at the title of the piece (*octandria* = monoclinous or hermaphroditic plants, having eight distinct stamens), "it was natural," wrote Kisselgoff, "that sex should be all over the stage. And it was. [Yet it

seems] not the subject of the ballet, but a metaphor for loss of innocence and ensuing corruption." [1]

A female is raped by a gang of men, then helps lure a second female into the men's clutches. The same is more or less repeated in reverse—a group of women, led by the first female, attack a male, who in turn prepares to capture a second male and deliver him to the harpie group. "In all," continued Kisselgoff, "an unsuccessful ballet but a good unpleasant idea." Herridge: "At this stage, unsettling and unsatisfying." [2] The music was called "unconventional and unmelodious."

Wrote Siegel, "The ballet approximates the music's mysterious textures and tensions, and its unemphatic stresses. The movement was earthbound and sexually suggestive, yet lyrical, without urgency or thrust." [3]

In all, a ballet that shouldn't have gotten out of the workshop.

THE GOLDBERG VARIATIONS

CHOREOGRAPHY: Jerome Robbins

MUSIC: Johann Sebastian Bach (Aria with Variations in G, BWV 988, 1742, "The Goldberg Variations")

COSTUMES: Joe Eula

Robbins's exhibition of the composer's formal patterns is exhaustive instruction in hearing and seeing."—Kirstein

Said Robbins, "I guess, after the Chopin, I just wanted to get away from romantic music. I wanted to see what would happen if I got hold of something that didn't give me any easy finger ledge to climb. It seemed to me that in the *Goldberg Variations* Bach was describing something very big and architectural, and so I thought I'd try that and see how I could do. The piece was really spread over a long period [more than a year], which in a way I'm grateful for because it gave me a lot of time to think. It was like approaching a beautiful marble wall. I could get no toehold, no leverage to get inside that building. The first weeks of rehearsal were as if I were hitting it and falling down, and having to start over. Chopin wasn't that hard, because of the emotional and romantic line of the music. Bach throws you back on yourself a lot more." [1]

"Biggest? No, the monster scene in *Firebird* was the biggest! The number of dancers has nothing to do with the size of the challenge. The challenge of *Goldberg* is that it's thirty variations all in the same key and formally all alike. Yet the possibilities of interpretation are endlessly rich. The theme [of the ballet] is the music, baroque music, and perhaps also my involvement with the dancers. The ballet represents weeks of work with these specific dancers and it's nothing that I can talk about." [2]

Says Violette Verdy (who worked on the ballet but never performed it, due to injury): "I think that his own personal, intellectual complexity does not allow him to content himself with a simple solution—he looks for something more inventive, more original, more intricate. Mr. B. will choose *not* to use a piece of music for as good a reason as he will decide *to* use something else. Where he will stop, Jerry will not stop. Jerry has not hesitated to use *Goldberg,* and that kind of challenge is the kind of challenge a Balanchine will not need, will not want, and will dismiss for very judicious reasons. A Jerry will decide that *there* is a challenge for him. For Jerry, it was fascinating to 'solve' *Goldberg.*"

There can be little doubt that Robbins selected a score that almost defied realization in dance. Not only was it restricted to one key but also to a single instrumental texture (after experimenting with the harpsichord, Robbins settled on piano accompaniment); it was also about an hour and twenty minutes long (Robbins observed *every* repeat), and, as a well-known piece, it already had established associations that had nothing to do with dance. In attempting to operate within such limitations, it was as though Robbins had taken a cue from the composer of this "Keyboard Practice, consisting in an Aria with Divers Variations . . . Composed for Music Lovers, to Refresh their Spirits":* "The problem of incorporating the same bassline into thirty effectively contrasting variations did not seem big enough to Bach. Without deviating from the variation form he presents in his set nine different kinds of canon. There is also a *Fughetta,* a French *Ouverture,* and a roguish *Quodlibet.* In between these contrapuntally elaborate variations are a number of highly diversified character pieces: gay and vigorous, . . . gracefully skipping, . . . brilliant, . . . light, in the manner of Scarlatti, deeply moving chromatic, . . . and magnificent, containing passages which vigorously contradict the traditional conception of the conservative Bach." [3]

_____

* Although it is popularly believed that *Goldberg Variations* were written to help Count Kaiserling fall asleep, the impression left by Forkel is that they were intended to *entertain* him during his sleepless nights.

For Robbins, it was not enough "merely" to choreograph this famous work: he also avoided any narrative implications and, in all but a decorative sense, costumes as well. He took the restrictions and made them integral to his solution: the work is all the more powerful for the sense of resistance it conveys and for its obvious length. As in the music, one is aware of the effort and ingenuity involved; in both, for all the lovely details, it is the cumulative effect that is so exciting. According to a music critic, Robbins's impressive achievement consisted in "casting new light on a great piece of music. Everything he demands of his dancers seems to be an artistic and imaginative approach to the problem of how to get from one place to another and look very beautiful while doing it. And while this is all happening, the inner nature of Bach's own genius is also being laid bare by the visual patterns on the stage." [4]

Wrote Goldner, "Robbins and Bach achieve the same kind and degree of intensity, so that both your eyes and ears burn." [5]

The work is dense the way Bach's contrapuntal writing is dense: there is a great deal going on at once, but everything is concentrated toward a single end, so the mind/eye/ear are not fatigued by confusion, even as they are almost surfeited with sensations. "Like the score, the dance reveals itself with reserve, suggesting other meanings and possibilities, playing with the several meanings of 'variation' and offering variations in several dimensions." [6]

Barnes called it "full of amplitude and grandeur" [7]; Goldner "an epic and very beautiful journey" [8]; Jowitt "a sumptuous banquet." [9]

Says Robbins, "I felt, when I first heard [Rosalyn Tureck] play the *Variations,* that it was a journey, a trip, that it took you in a tremendous arc through a whole cycle of life and then, as it were, back to the beginning." [10]

The ballet also traces such a journey. Says Robbins in 1975: "I don't have much to say about *Goldberg.* I'm proud of what I did."

Goldner's critique reflected something of the ballet's own sinewy texture: "It is monumental in scope, [and] probably the longest ballet without a story ever created. When the ballet is over, you have witnessed the classical ballet vocabulary expanded to its outermost limits and then some. The ballet feels as long as it

really is, which also contributes to its monumental effect. It is magnetically fascinating in its variety, lucidity, and ease, [and] it is deliciously exhausting not because it is long but because there is so much to see. And because Robbins has created such clear choreographic lines—they are simultaneously extraordinarily inventive and as naked as classroom exercises—one cannot help but see into the core of technique and choreography. *Goldberg* is a virtual education in dance. What do we see? Quartets, duets, trios, octets. Acrobatic stunts. A grand polonaise. Some baroque flourishes. A little bebop. A fugue for choreographic themes. A dance where people fill the stage and stroll. Arcing over the dance suite is a structure that gives the ballet just the right amount of shape, neither oppressive nor trivial.

"The first part is more open and personal. The beginnings and ends of variations seem relatively undefined. No one has an exclusive partner, and the ensemble is actually many soloists. In this section most of the wit, pathos, and ambiguous human situations emerge, especially in the quartet in which the couples are of the same sex. Then comes the polonaise, and we enter the formal arena. There are three explicitly leading couples who embark on three self-contained pas de deux, interspersed with solos, one of which is unabashedly virtuosic. The ensemble functions quite conventionally, at one point standing in a semicircle at the back of the stage while the soloists hold stage center during their dazzling codas. The duets themselves are full of daring, intricate leaps and turns, perhaps a development of the comparatively pristine first part. The solos too are self-contained and formal in comparison with the community spirit of the preceding section." [11]

Jowitt: "There are hints of actual baroque dance in [the opening Sarabande], the gently rotating wrists, the flexed-footed gestures, the progressions from turned-in to turned-out legs. The first variations are direct, clean-lined, athletic; they have the look of the best contemporary ballet. There is a cheerfully competitive air about what the men do. Little flashes of ballroom dance styles, of Broadway, spurt out of the dancing from time to time. You have the sense of a constant process of replacement, rearrangement, growth, as duets are absorbed into brief sextets, which in turn vanish from the stage so that a solo may begin. Some-

The Goldberg Variations. Top left: **Part I. Gelsey Kirkland, Robert Weiss.** (*Photo Fred Fehl.*) *Top right:* **Part II. Anthony Blum, Susan Hendl.** (*Photo Martha Swope.*) *Center left:* **Part II. Helgi Tomasson.** (*Photo Martha Swope.*) *Left:* **Part II. Final tableau before restatement of Theme.** (*Photo Fred Fehl.*) *Above:* **Robbins rehearsing Peter Martins, Karin von Aroldingen (Part II).** (*Photo Martha Swope.*)

where along the line, the movement begins to become more attenuated, more flowing, more romantic in character. Then impetuous but intricate and startling kinds of things happen. The climax of this occurs in a duet for Blum and Hendl, which seems to be constantly turning back upon itself (once he spins her down into some exaggeratedly low turns—the kind skaters do). The dancers begin to add things to their costumes— jackets, skirts. Unison passages, virtuoso stunts by the soloists. For the first time, the audience applauds in the middle of variations. All the dancers parade onto the stage. But the dancing turns quieter and graver, and the last image of the ballet is of the original couple moving into the restatement of the theme." [12]

Gelles: "The choreography is compact and has a vital and concentrated energy. It's musicality of the highest intelligence, and weaves a wonderfully lyrical counterpoint to the rather more austere score. It's also full of funny liberties that Robbins allows himself. As the piece progresses, the company works its way from a state of theatrical innocence to a full-fledged maturity. Robbins has made the first half of his abstract scenario in some sense exploratory, the second more modern and formalized. Up to the mid-point, each section of the score is choreographed for an always-changing ensemble, and this gives a marvelous kaleidoscopic quality to the weight and texture of the dance. Usually there is an overlap in the various casts. One member will remain the constant between every two segments, binding them with a special sense of continuity and growth. It's the ballet I'd most like to see from the flies of the theater, because from the auditorium one senses that the floor patterns made by the dancers are as rich and intricate as the designs seen from out front. *Goldberg* touches mind and heart." [13]

Barnes: "What do the costumes mean? Nothing—they are merely an attempt to give formal visual shape to the musical form, to mark out the work's structure and to give it an artificial but necessary dramatic progression. Robbins shares with Balanchine the ability to let music color his dancing. There is never a mistake. [With Chopin] Robbins was all remembered emotion; here [he] is structure and form and radiantly confident. It reminds us that the eighteenth century was the very first and the very last era that really thought it knew everything.

"The forms are lovely. Robbins can use a diagonal as if no one had ever used that structural form before. And always there is the dance movement—movement that looks as if it has been discovered, never invented. Any choreographer can show lovers—Robbins can show people. Even in this lean and classic exposition of dance, supported by Bach's same yet infinite variety, you feel the presence of dancers at a celebration. What can one say about *Goldberg* after one has said thank you?" [14]

Bivona: "It adds up to no grand philosophy and that is also part of the beauty of Robbins's tone, which persistently maintains its matter-of-factness. He has taken 'classical' to mean sanity and the capacity for relationships, and above all the capacity to create and use disorientation rather than to become its victim. The ballet is not an interpretation of Bach; it is a reflection on a certain kind of world Bach suggests." [15]

The first section (in practice clothes) has been called an "ideal class," a "dancing manual." Steps are short, precise, like Bach's clipped notes. Goldner noted that Robbins had a "step-by-step" approach, "rather than phrase by phrase. Three passés, glissade, arabesque. [An entire variation is based on rond de jambe par terre, with a man leading and the small mixed corps following one beat behind.] As when hearing the notes of Bach, you are seeing the most basic component of choreography, the step. It shows us the raw stuff of movement. It draws us to the essential technique, undistorted, simple but not simplified or simplistic, and as interesting as any elaborate choreography. The plié, passé, glissade, and arabesque function like the new modern dancers' breathing, running, and leaning. How lucky it is for Robbins that he can make those steps ends in themselves, without having to abandon the medium and willfully tear down mountains—that he can make a bloodless revolution."

She also mentioned "a solo [for Kirkland] about rubato. Each balance in arabesque is held a fraction longer than the beat allows; she makes up for time lost in the little glissades that take her from one balance to the next. Interestingly, the dance reaches its climax when rubato yields to the straight beat of the music, as Kirkland makes big jumps toward the back of the stage. The restored steady rhythm is deliciously luxurious, like the calm after the storm. [Croce referred to "Kirkland's ex-

quisite solo." [16]] The dancers also swallow space. Leland's first solo, in which she covers lots of ground in a variety of diagonals is almost a tour de force use of space, mostly because we see her full-face although her line of direction is on an angle with us. Her wide, open jumps make a stirring contrast with her complicated route and, more delightful, they seem to take her almost magically on that route. Within a few moments she has covered the entire territory and, in contrast with most movement on the diagonal, we hardly know where she's going until she gets there. This solo opens up the diagonal to previously unforeseen and infinite possibilities." [17]

Other memorable sections include men's dances with pushups, a "flying angel," a quote from *Concerto Barocco*, cartwheels, lying down and tracing circles on the floor, and numerous double sauts de basques, double air turns, and other challenging male steps, often completed with a courtly flourish. Elsewhere the men and women perform the same steps (often on different beats or with different accents), as in an adagio for girl and two boys: she is promenaded in arabesque, then one boy promenades the other in arabesque, and finally, a lone boy does an unsupported arabesque turn. Then there is a quartet, in which the girls partner girls, boys partner boys, before switching to the more conventional double work. Wrote Patricia Barnes, "The variations have been conceived in a very free manner, coloring the fabric and character of the music rather than providing any strong architectural structure for the ballet. There seems no particular reason, for instance, why a choreographic sequence for boys, playfully, lightheartedly indulging in a display of calisthenics, should be followed by a baroque and stately sextet, but it doesn't matter, for the contrast keeps us interested and it all seems so right." [18]

Several reviewers mentioned the irregularity of spacing. Bivona wrote: "The asymmetry of form is particularly insistent in the first half, part of the youthfulness and spontaneity of its mood. This is Robbins's most adult handling of his perpetual children-at-play theme, and his most moving awareness of the daring and limitations of childhood. The spacing tends to tilt groups towards stage left, for instance, and Robbins freely allows such events as eight corps members—four boys and four girls—suddenly reducing to four boys and three girls with barely a pause to their dance, only a fluid regrouping as beautiful as the original symmetry. And that fourth corps girl is lost because she suddenly, for no given reason or signal, stops and joins Clifford, whose solo has been weaving through the group, and dances with him for a while until they depart together. It is a striking discord, and yet done naturally, with a baroque complexity of event and love of irregularity—that passion for many voices being heard—that Robbins exploits beautifully throughout the work." [19]

Adding to the youthful abandon, there is a good deal of running, stomping (in the manner of a social dance, perhaps a gigue, no longer really "folk"), kicking up the heels, and a great feeling of freedom, especially in the boys' big jumping passages. There is potential for flirtation, too. And for other pursuits of adolescence: "[In Part I], the dancers tend to be portrayed as children. They play London Bridge, engage in gymnastic tumbling and general playfulness. Yet it soon becomes obvious that this camaraderie is really a euphemism for the statements on sexuality that Robbins has made overtly elsewhere in some of his other ballets. There are many options, we are told here. Yet because the dancers are consistently asked to appear juvenile while executing the most exacting adult virtuosity, there is an affectation to this section that is absent from Part II." [20]

In the second half, the components of the "dancing manual" are put together in statements that are both more extended and frequently so far removed from the basics that the steps have no names. And, if Part I is full of playful children, Part II is peopled with young adults, refined but not aristocratic, full of enthusiasm still, but with stylistic flourishes and possibly even a hint of romantic attachment.

The initial pas de deux (Hendl-Blum) is highly complicated yet lyrical, and, interestingly, consists of sustained movements against a bouncy accompaniment. From plié on one leg near the floor, she is suddenly aloft, held in arabesque; she flips over his back; he turns her inside out; she comes out of one complicated position by somersaulting forward onto the floor.

The second duet (von Aroldingen-Martins) features big lifts which might be called contrived. (Goldner found this "moody, weighty, and vaguely sad." [21])

The girl finishes one sequence raised on her pointes but almost sitting on her heels. Her partner has a small solo in which his arms and legs are moved by outside forces—like a puppet's.

The third, and, if any can be so called, the star couple (McBride-Tomasson) have the most humorous and lightest steps, those that play most with—and against—the rhythms, and the most "conventional" technical flourishes—as when she finishes a sequence with fouettés and he goes from multiple pirouettes to grande pirouette à la seconde. Patricia Barnes thought their section together was reflective of "the bucolic humors of the eighteenth century, as hands on hips, backs to the audience, their bodies seem to shake with merriment, but this humor is touched with a twentieth-century jazziness that perfectly fits the music's rhythms." [22]

This couple is the first to appear fully costumed—the man wears a period jacket, the woman, a little dress with ruffles, pearls, and low square neckline. Soon they are joined by an entire corps so attired, then by the other soloists, including those from Part I. In one of Robbins's masterstrokes, suddenly all are in a circle (without anyone's having seen how it happened) and soon the full stage is performing the boisterous rhythms of the closing Quodlibet (in which Bach incorporated two popular tunes, "Long Have I Been Away from Thee" and "Cabbage and Turnips") in a kind of gentlefolk style, with hand-clapping and low steps using the whole foot. For a moment they pause in a group downstage—a perfect closing figure, one might think, but then the stage darkens and thins and only the opening couple is visible, now in practice clothes, performing the Sarabande.

Goldner remarked that, although beautiful, the dances of Part II were not as "special" (unusual) as those in Part I. She found the solos for Martins and von Aroldingen "the most personal parts of this section, eccentric, dealing with bizarre bodily placement and changes in weight." [23]

Bivona wrote of this section: "There is nothing especially quirky about the young people of the first half, except perhaps their freedom; the actual steps they dance are pure-water classicism, with only occasional experiments in the grotesque. In the second half, the people are themselves odd, and one misses the un-self-conscious beauty of the children almost with irritation—but that is the point. The

grotesque is now possible and the choreography is often very peculiar indeed.

"The acrobatic duet for Hendl and Blum is as strange as Martins's solo, for while they are presented as lovers, in their sureness of one another and their mutual, careless pride, their dance is hardly a declaration of love. It is an exhibition of will, stretching itself slowly against vivid, racing music. Only toward the end of the dance does the music's excitement force them into stunts of arrogant beauty. But they never really give in; they retain, even in their most explosive acrobatics, a drag against the sound, and the opposition is cool and willful, detached and quite implacable altogether.

"Von Aroldingen's ugly, plié squats have made earlier appearances before her solo makes them prominent, but only she presents them as a bravura joke. [There is] a wickedly funny duet for McBride and Tomasson which lets fly at every target in sight—the courtly propriety of the theme-dancers, the jazz implications of Bach, Robbins's own propensity for corner-lot kids' games, and even a near-Rabelaisian burst of stomach-shaking mock laughter. What is interesting is that this pair have a questioning and sad duet which comes closest to an internal realization of the limits of [Goldberg's] world. It is the slowest and most thoughtful of the dances, directly emotional as the pair continually appeal to each other as none of the other couples do.

"Nowhere else is Robbins's tone so subtle. Its stillness, its restrained acrobatics, its relentless heaviness, its unsettling pauses and unanswered questions disturb; and when the duet is followed by a great burst of classical virtuosity in the coda solos, one's relief is almost physical. [But] the coda is not the finale, and in one of his simplest and most perfect insights, Robbins brings the ballet to what appears to be a crashing finale. The audience begins to scream applause. But the dancers pick themselves up and begin to repeat the theme which opened the ballet, the simple ideal which they have all exhausted." [24]

A work as insistent and ambitious as this one was bound to stimulate some negative responses as well. Croce felt Robbins to be "fatally attracted to pretentious enterprises," that Goldberg was "ninety minutes at hard labor," and "Robbins working under great and obvious strain." [25] Some found the gymnastic, acrobatic touches kitschy, the lying-on-the-floor sequence forced. Kisselgoff complained of the "mannered" first section and, although she admired the choreography in Part II, characterized the Hendl-Blum duet as "ungratefully manipulative." A very few complained of boredom—or, at least, of battle fatigue—by the second half. There is no doubt that *Goldberg* makes extraordinary demands on its audience—which would seem to make it right at home in the repertory of the New York City Ballet.

Germany:

"Too complex, too artful to be tossed off as mere fashion. In an admirable way Robbins has here united old ballet and modern movement, historic material and a touch of carefree youth that distinguishes the American way in its best moments. What is reflected under a mask of understatement is a repressed resignation—'That's the way we are today, past are the times of forceful gestures, of gorgeous costumes, of grand entrees. We, too, have a desire to reflect ourselves in art, to grow beyond the moment.' Robbins has now left far behind the foreman furioso of *West Side Story*. He now works with calmer means, makes what has been scrupulously rehearsed seem improvised, presents highest precision with a gesture of apparent casualness." [26]

Russia:

"One may not always agree with a certain stylistic gaudiness of Robbins's treatment, but one also notes that all the sections of this composition are inwardly connected." [27]

PAMTGG

CHOREOGRAPHY: George Balanchine

MUSIC: Roger Kellaway (based on themes by Stan Applebaum and Sid Woloshin)

COSTUMES: Irene Sharaff

DÉCOR, LIGHTING: Jo Mielziner

PREMIERE: 17 June 1971

CAST: Kay Mazzo, Victor Castelli, 24 women, 16 men; Karin von Aroldingen, Frank Ohman, 6 women, 6 men; Sara Leland, John Clifford, 16 women, 12 men

OTHER CASTS: Gelsey Kirkland, Jean-Pierre Bonnefous, Earle Sieveling

Pan **A**m **M**akes **T**he **G**oing **G**reat was an expensive disaster. Or perhaps it didn't aim high enough to attain disaster proportions. (Kirstein referred to it as a "plastic souvenir.") Expensive it unquestionably was. It is said that Balanchine was disappointed in the music, having originally envisaged something of "great strangeness, bordering on the metaphysical," but one wonders what he could have expected from an amplified version of a television commercial (elsewhere called "junque, pure and simple"). The chief novelty—aside from the idea itself—was the costumes, many of which had parts made not of fabric but of plastic, which had to be sawed, nailed, and glued together. There were over a hundred of these. The resulting work was overdressed and over-

populated. The fact that it so clearly cost a lot of money made the blatant exhibition of banality harder to take.

The action revolved around three couples—young marrieds, a pair of hippies, and some jet-setters. There was a mixup of luggage at the end. The ensemble took the roles of stars, clouds, passengers, and airline personnel. The second movement, in which the hippies performed slinky steps to blues music, was considered the best.

Wrote Barnes, "Not a ballet worth reviewing. Its music, based on this idiotic commercial jingle, is almost too trivial for elevator noise. I am positive that [such a Broadway choreographer as Donald Saddler] would have done a much better job, even though I doubt that anyone, burdened with that awful music, could ever have got it airborne." [1]

Marks: "Broadway Balanchine, and for all its attempts to look like tomorrow, only the lucite luggage really convinces. Mielziner's swept-wing silhouettes, runway lights, cloud formations, etc., are handsome but square. Sharaff's mod outfits were in *Women's Wear Daily* yesterday—and that's a long way from tomorrow. Balanchine's paste job of jazz, jive, and whatall (forms from the past) descends to a catalog of bumps and grinds, flapping arms and hands, swooping airplane lifts, and endless spins. It's an SST-sized flop." [2]

Since the ballet was quickly withdrawn, perhaps it should be left without further elaboration to RIP. Balanchine, however, must have had the last laugh. At the time of *PAMTGG*, which followed a succession of less than distinguished Balanchine works (*Slaughter on Tenth Avenue*, *Firebird* revival, *Tchaikovsky Suite No. 3*) and inferior ballets by younger choreographers which Balanchine, as artistic director, was chided for having allowed to appear on stage, discreet—and not so discreet—suggestions began to appear in print that Balanchine was losing his touch. Critics did not know at the time that he was already planning his monumental Stravinsky Festival, at which, of the twenty-two new ballets presented, the top four, by everybody's estimation, were Balanchine creations and could rank with or near some of the greatest he had ever done.

PAMTGG. **Karin von Aroldingen, Frank Ohman.** (*Photo Martha Swope.*)

PRINTEMPS

CHOREOGRAPHY: Lorca Massine

MUSIC: Claude Debussy (1887)

COSTUMES: Irene Sharaff

LIGHTING: Ronald Bates

PREMIERE: 13 January 1972

CAST: Violette Verdy; Christine Redpath, Virginia Stuart; 7 women

Debussy wrote that his symphonic suite *Printemps* was intended to embrace "the slow and miserable birth of beings and all other forms of life in Nature, their gradual blossoming, and finally the joy in being reborn." Possibly the ballet also dealt with this theme; and there were poses reminiscent of Botticelli, as were the costumes.

Few ballets have been so quickly and completely dismissed. Barnes wrote: "Looks like an autumnal homage to Isadora Duncan by an enthusiastic but ill-advised disciple. To say it doesn't work is to be more than generous." [1]

Goldner: "Similar in touch to *Four Last Songs*, except that this one is very bad. Debussy was a mist far off in the distance; the choreography like a thick fog pressing in. Only images of girls rushing about remain. Total shapelessness and a dulling sameness of dynamics." [2]

Hering: "All that resulted was a look of massive pregnancy and the chartless wandering that also marred Massine's previous ballet." [3]

Barnes criticized the management for allowing the work on stage. It was soon withdrawn.

CHOPINIANA

Staged by Alexandra Danilova, after Michel Fokine

MUSIC: Frédéric Chopin (Nocturne in A-flat Major, op. 32, no. 2; Waltz in G-flat Major, op. 70, no. 1; Mazurka in D Major, op. 33, no. 2; Mazurka in C Major, op. 67, no. 3; Prelude in A Major, op. 28, no. 7; Waltz in C-sharp Minor, op. 64, no. 2; Waltz in E-flat Major, op. 18, no. 1)

LIGHTING: Ronald Bates

PREMIERE: 20 January 1972

PIANO: Gordon Boelzner

CAST: Karin von Aroldingen, Susan Hendl, Kay Mazzo, Peter Martins; 16 women

OTHER CASTS: Susan Pilarre, Lynda Yourth

Chopiniana was a daring experiment. To take so well known a work as *Les Sylphides*, an acknowledged masterpiece (a very old one, in the context of ballet history), which has remained almost unchanged since it was first presented in the West in 1909—and to take, what is more, a "breakthrough" work, seminal in twentieth-century choreography, whose steps are taught to aspiring ballet students around the world—and streamline it can only be called daring. As Kisselgoff noted, Shakespeare is often presented with success in other than its period costume, but this has not been tried before with a ballet chestnut. It was a provocative move.

Actual steps were not changed, but pantomimic allusions (the original had no actual pantomime) were dropped. The music was played on the piano, not by the orchestra, with the overture deleted. The most startling difference was that the traditional long tulle dresses and woodland grove backdrop were exchanged for white practice clothes and blue cyclorama. And dancers schooled in the Romantic tradition were replaced by acolytes of Balanchine.

Danilova defended the lack of costumes: "It was [first] done [in Russia, 1908] for an annual school performance, and they probably, like we have, just had that white wardrobe tutu past the knee"; and the use of the piano: "From the beginning it was done with the piano. Chopin never orchestrated. And in Paris people said it was illogical to orchestrate Chopin when he wrote strictly for the piano."

The title was changed back to *Chopiniana* (as the work was known before 1909) to stress the musical roots of the piece and the nonreferential nature of the choreography. It is probable that Diaghilev had adopted the name *Les Sylphides* for extra-artistic—that is, theatrical and commercial—reasons: An evocation of Taglioni would not be lost on the Paris audiences that first saw *Les Sylphides*; it was chiefly France where Romantic ballet had flowered more than a half-century before.

Reaction to the new *Chopiniana* was divided, with more weight—and heat—on the negative side. Some observers felt that removing the costumes destroyed the Romantic atmosphere integral to the steps themselves, while others believed that for the first time the steps were clearly visible. For some, the solo piano further changed the mood, and, in addition, it was too soft to mask the footsteps of the ensemble. On the ineffable matter of Romantic style, however, there was more agreement: New York City Ballet dancers, race-horse ready and eager though they were, didn't have it. Only Mazzo and Martins were considered partial exceptions.

Kisselgoff wrote: "The most sensational event of the dance season so far. There is no question that this reinterpretation—for that is what it is—of a classic in the international repertory will be considered an outrage by those who keep in mind Fokine's intentions. Yet this production must be viewed almost as completely new ballet. On its own terms, the concept behind it proved a daring success. There has been no rechoreography. The steps, like the text of a play, have been preserved. In an interview, Kirstein expressed the wish that this first plotless ballet, which he saw as 'the last classic ballet' before *Serenade* (1934), be done for the Company. It would, he said, show the continuity between Fokine's and Balanchine's classicism. In effect, this practice-clothes production has revealed the pure-dance aspect of Fokine's choreography at its strongest. [This] was the ballet in which Fokine himself set out to prove that he had not turned away from classic dance to 'theater.' Although the accuracy of the reproduction must probably be credited to Danilova, the complete restylization of the ballet suggests the influence of Balanchine. Its Romantic imagery has been abolished. The mimetic suggestions of the sylphides' gestures have disappeared. No one harkens or listens. Fokine did strive for an expressiveness in his movement; the ballet has been robbed of its poetry. Yet it has gained a new dimension, thanks partly to a speeding up of the musical tempi." [1]

Herridge: "Danilova, discarding the filmy skirts and restoring the exact tempo throughout, has given us a mere skeleton of the Romantic choreography we associate with the piece. Gone is the ethereal

Chopiniana. **Kay Mazzo, Peter Martins** (*Photo Michael Truppin.*)

Balanchine dancers, von Aroldingen says, "I like—I'm used to—dancing very open, very big; this seemed smaller, in a way. It's the one thing of Balanchine's I couldn't accept—the way he's done it. It's true that now it's stripped down and it's beautiful, but there was a costume made for me, three layers, white, lovely. Balanchine asked me to try it out with little runs and jetés. I did, and all of a sudden I felt that I was flying, that I *could* be a sylphide. There wasn't enough money, but this is one case where a costume could have helped a little. All those slow landings, with nothing on, were very disturbing!"

The ballet in this version had a brief life.

quality, the airborne spirit of Taglioni. In their place is a studio rehearsal of the classic, without benefit of floating costumes or woodland setting or even full orchestra—just a lone pianist making music as lean and spare as the dancing. The girls performed neatly as though by rote." [2]

Goldner: "Will strike some as cantankerous and perverse; others, like myself, as a stroke of genius. Now we can more clearly see *Chopiniana* for great choreography. On the most obvious level, we can see what choreography is in the legs. It is easier to see that Fokine has been brilliantly economical. Danilova's staging has also brought out the choreography's precision and deliberateness. The ensemble looks more vivid, more important. The placement of dancers now looks more linear, lending to the pretty formations a welcome touch of austerity. One also becomes more aware of the lovely repetitions and the fact that *Chopiniana* is in one aspect a study in entrances and exits. The ballet is as beautiful as ever, but it is not of a genre. The production in other words, does not preclude style, just stylization. In its reinterpretation, it restores and preserves. This is useful." [3]

Dale Harris: "*Les Sylphides* pointed the way to the future, since, as its creator realized, it was the first internationally seen abstract ballet, the first to dispense with narrative motivation in favor of musical inspiration. In this respect, it leads inevitably to the work of Balanchine. It is hard not to believe that the Company is using this production to make the lineage clear, even to draw our attention to it forcibly. The ballet presented is more like an act of arrogation than a job of restoration. What this production offers is not at all an 'academic masterpiece,' as the program has it, whose 'force, logic, and ingenuity' have been dulled by 'layers of sentiment and sentimentality.' The opinions here are unexceptionable, but the theatrical results have very little to do with them. You do not destroy a ballet's intentions and somehow reveal a masterpiece. [This production] does not so much tell as embody a falsehood. It lies in the management's disingenuous belief that the choreography can somehow be separated from style and style from connotation. The notion that this particular choreography could ever be presented without regard for its emotional ramifications is patently absurd. Without tenderness and an air of evanescence the ballet is not so much plotless as pointless.

"Without long skirts, moreover, it is immodest. The businesslike little tunics dispel the nocturnal atmosphere and impose logic on dream, but they also reveal what should be obscured or left in a state of incomplete disclosure. The famous moment in the pas deux when the danseuse is lifted up to the man's chest and leans back against his shoulder while performing entrechats now has an air of indiscreet revelation. The raised leg of the soloist on the floor in the opening and closing tableaux looks inappropriate and provocative. This *Chopiniana* is entirely consonant with Balanchine's view that ballet ought to be clean, spare and devoid of all overt emotionality. [And] in many ways, [its] real failure is that the dancers could not transform Fokine into Balanchine." [4]

Of the Romantic style, seldom asked of

WATERMILL

CHOREOGRAPHY: Jerome Robbins

MUSIC: Teiji Ito (1971)

COSTUMES: Patricia Zipprodt

DÉCOR: Jerome Robbins in association with David Reppa

LIGHTING: Ronald Bates

PREMIERE: 3 February 1972

MUSICIANS: Dari Erkkila, Genji Ito, Teiji Ito, Kensuke Kawase, Mara Purl, Terry White

CAST: Edward Villella; Penny Dudleston, Colleen Neary, Tracy Bennett, Victor Castelli, Hermes Condé, Bart Cook, Jean-Pierre Frohlich, Deni Lamont, Robert Maiorano; 10 women, 9 men

Watermill, "that ballet with no dancing in it," was another substantial work from Robbins (following *Dances at a Gathering* and *Goldberg Variations*), by virtue of its length (more than an hour) and its complexity. In its deliberateness, also, it had the feel of a "major statement." It is a work to music using primarily Oriental elements and with a distinctly Eastern feeling, although it is not, according to the program note, "to be construed as Oriental." It is easily described—or perhaps uneasily so—for although "little" happens, a retelling of what aurally and visually occurs stops far short of accounting for the resonances in the ballet.

For "what happens" is the least of it. Goldner posed the relevant question: "Nothing is happening. On the other hand, everything is happening . . . or is it?" Is *Watermill*, in its suspended world, "a masterpiece or a bore?"[1] Reaction was definitely mixed, although generally favorable, with reservations. The piece was seen as compelling theater, if not exactly dance, and, so far as movement was concerned, a highly interesting involvement with slow motion. Barnes wrote that "Robbins is here experimenting with theatrical time. We expect theatrical time to be condensed—we see a man's career compressed into a few hours' traffic on stage. In dance the speed can be even faster—a love affair becomes a fleeting thing of looks, glances, sudden embraces, and swift farewells. Robbins has had the idea of extending time in the theater rather than compressing it."[2]

In this and the sparseness of the action, the work could be seen as almost defiantly "untheatrical." And in another act of seeming defiance, Robbins cast the virtuoso Villella for the leading role, a part in which he doesn't dance a step. The very unexpectedness of this casting accounted for some of the fascination in Villella's undeniably superior performance.

The subject as well as the substance of the work was probably time itself, or perhaps time as it pertains to one man, to the present in which he exists and the past that he reflects on—his lifespan. Meanwhile, as a background, the seasons pass. Art critic Genauer, who had just covered a Japanese Nanga painting show, related *Watermill* to an Oriental painting: "A visit to Asia House should be a prerequisite for viewing [it]. As it happens, just the title of a single painting in the Nanga show, Buson's 'Autumn Moon on Lake Tung-t'ing,' along with its catalog description, 'Scene of a fisherman in his boat playing a flute, with wave lines subtly curving in partial accommodation to the curve of the shape, and somehow echoing the sound of the flute,' serve as an accurate description of the scene and the mood for *Watermill*. There is, in fact, almost as little action in *Watermill* as in a Japanese or Chinese painting. A moon slowly waxes, then wanes again. A robed figure enters, very slowly removes his clothes, lies down. Young people drift on stage, carrying brightly colored paper lanterns on bamboo rods waving in lazy calligraphic patterns. Lovers all but transfixed slip through the motions of sexual meeting, silent and ineluctable as rippling waves in a stream. Yet it all makes for an experience of such dramatic intensity, requiring and rewarding such concentration, as to be unmatched in dance repertory.

"[Although the program warns otherwise], it's as Oriental as an ancient scroll painting by a Zen master. I remember seeing one once inscribed, as so many of them are, with a poem. Its translation was 'I am moving all day and not moving at all. I am like the moon underneath the waves that ever go rolling.' *Watermill* moves—or doesn't move at all—for a full hour. During that hour, time as we think of it stops. Only the movements of nature matter—a sexual pas de deux is as unhurried and far removed from violence as the moon's rising—and its sounds. The instruments, like the flute and the horizontal harp called the koto, simulate soft natural noises like insects and night birds. Sometimes they come in random tones that suggest nothing, and sometimes they give way to silence. Throughout the entire work I was, like the figure played by Villella (a monk, perhaps?), in a sort of dream, coming out of it, at the end, intensely moved, aware I had experienced something strange and transfiguring."[3]

Further details—and it is a ballet of fine-honed details—were noted by Goldner: "*Watermill* is the *dernier cri* of productions. Consider first, technology, stage machinery. Snow usually comes in quantity, a blizzard; in this work it falls gently, evenly, thinly, laying a blanket of quiet over the landscape. The wind machine [usually] sends chiffon dresses heaving and dry ice billowing. In *Watermill* it creates only the faintest rustle in the three wheat stalks that dominate the stage. In the autumn section, it sends a few leaves to drift onto the stage. In the final moments of *Giselle*, the Wili Giselle drops two lilies from her hand just before entering her grave. The flowers fall sadly and reluctantly, like an ebbing pulse. The leaves of autumn fall that way. It is a breathtaking moment. The falling snow and leaves and rustling wheat capture the Oriental delicacy, subtlety, precision and suggestiveness. It is his quest for, and achievement of, perfection and Robbins's exquisite sensibility that makes *Watermill* so enthralling.

"A sound of wind before the nightmare is at just the right sound level to suggest the very beginning of a (psychological) storm. The contrast between the love-making picnic and the nightmare picnic is a beautiful physical realization of perception that is psychologically determined. The love picnic takes place at the front of the stage in a relatively bright light (the lighting is quite dim throughout). The picnic blanket is bright purple and yellow; the girl's long hair is a glistening gold, an idealization of the color of wheat. During the nightmare the picnic takes place at the back of the stage, in an area so dark one can barely make out the shapes of the people. Their blanket is dark, an old army one perhaps? Then there are compositional details. For example, each of the Japanese lanterns and small kites that some boys carry on two separate occasions hovers and bobs in the air at different altitudes. Four of the lanterns are large and of primary colors, but two of them (one on each side) are small and white. These are small points, but they are immensely satisfying visually and emotionally, because it is obvious that it has all been done with extreme deliberation and painstaking care."

But the details, like the action, are only part of the story. Goldner continued, "No matter how apparent is the fact that this rarified aesthetic sense is intrinsically bound up with the Japanese sensibility, the other fact is that that is not what *Watermill* is about. The crux is the creation of a certain state of consciousness that has come to be associated with Oriental meditation, with Zen. The ballet is long. The dancers do move, but slowly. Very slowly. Recently, many choreographers have been slowing up dance movement so as to intensify and magnify it. Robbins's people do even less and take longer about it. As a result, not only is there a kinetic intensification but an intensification of time itself. This is further heightened by the reedy, sparse score, which falls like droplets into a pool of water. The central figure, a kind of Everyman, is the stillest of all. He observes, remembers, and perhaps sleeps. His movements and those of the tillers, harvesters, and boys who carry lanterns and kites are measured, ceremonial and self-aware, though not self-conscious. One begins to feel time, feel the muscles that enable a person to stand erect. Likewise, one must meditate on the moon that is going through its phases and ascending and descending, and on the wheat that moves ever so slightly.

"The meditational climax occurs when each of several women separates one stalk of wheat from the composite stalk, slowly walks with it a few steps, looks at the stalk in her hands, watches her hand let go of the stalk, and then watches the stalk as it falls to the ground. One woman, however, does not release her stalk. She waves it back and forth. She looks at this pendulum motion. The other women and the Everyman slowly shift their attention to it. Then they watch it. If you, the audience, cannot look at that pendulum motion long and hard enough so that you simultaneously lose yourself yet feel a greater self-consciousness than you've ever felt, so that you can feel your eyeballs seeing, than you are not 'with' *Watermill*. If you try to do it because you know that Robbins has set up perfect conditions, you'll experience frustration and a touch of insanity. The aesthetic pleasure afforded by the myriad details is quite different from responding to its choreography and the state of mind it embodies. Appreciating that the wheat moves, but barely, is not the same as meditating upon its motion. Objectively speaking, in terms of the relationship between mode of presentation, choreography, and content, *Watermill* is perfect. But I could not participate in the Zen experience." [4]

Barnes called the work "a new theater of ritual. There is also a certain influence here of Noh drama and Kabuki. But the relevancies and indications are specifically nonoriental. This is a great work—a ballet that attempts to question the art of ballet and, indeed, our concept of the theater: At first sight [it] seems to be trying to make a new statement about dance, rather in the way that Nijinsky tried in *L'Après-midi d'un Faune* many, many years ago. It is very possible that Robbins sees this work as an essay in autobiography. (I hasten to add that this is nothing but a guess.) Certainly *Watermill* has a man of mature years looking back on the patterns of his life and the shadows of his destiny.

"The structure, or at least [the] form, owes much to Noh drama, [but] the ballet itself embraces a concept of humanity that cannot be constrained by national or ethnic boundaries. The stage is dominated by three enormous sheaves of wheat. A changing moon indicates the seasons of [the man's] fulfillment. The music at times will be languorous flute, sweeping upward in simple, half-remembered love-songs, while at other times it will be counterpoised by the barking of dogs, a harsh

remembrance of times past. The man sees all. He stands in the sun and in the snow. He plays with the ritual ears of wheat, he watches balloons of destiny float off into his future. And he contemplates life from the still center of his dream." [5]

As for the music, the program notes, "the score stems mainly from the religious ceremonial and theatrical music of the Orient. It employs numerous percussion instruments including cymbals, gongs, drums, bells, and maracas; also the Sho Koto, Shichiriki, whistles, various flutes, and Shakuhachi (a bamboo flute used in Japan in the thirteenth century, played mainly by Zen Buddhist priests, whose compositions for it still survive). These musical-religious works usually are comtemplative evocations of nature and the seasons."

The composer says that most of the score is pentatonic—"there is kind of an African scale in the summer section, a Japanese-Irish feeling in the fall, and so on. I suppose [the ballet] is autobiographical to some extent, but for us [the six instrumentalists] it's a mood —or four variations on a mood. We try to present a feeling—intense, very

Watermill. **Edward Villella (far right).** *(Photo Martha Swope.)*

slow, precise, with many important si-
lences—silent sounds." The silent sounds
"come when a musician begins a melody
in his head but does not make it audible
immediately. The first four or five notes,
for instance, may be 'played' inwardly and
yet are intended to be felt in some way by
dancers and audience." [6]

Said one of the musicians, "Actually,
we have no conductor. Nobody leads, nobody follows. I can get very high watching
the dancers and playing for them."

The music was composed after the ballet had been set. Says Robbins, "When
Ito played the tapes, I mentioned that I
heard a dog barking. He said, 'Dog barking?' We discovered that there had been
something wrong with his machine."

The ballet was greeted with boos as
well as cheers, in addition to inappropriate noises—such as talking—during
the performance. (Audience reaction was
reported as a story in itself, although most
of the critics who mentioned the booing
defended the ballet.) There were also
negative reviews. Most detractors found
the work pretentious, arty, or superficial.
A few found it unoriginal. Wrote Barnes:
"Is *Watermill*, as some people have suggested, including a young choreographer
and quite a few young dancers, a gigantic
hoax, a work of solemn pretensions but
empty achievement, naive symbolism
and hollow poetry? I think the answer is
obvious: No." [7]

Some, however, said Yes. Gelles:
"Theatrically cunning and stylishly conceived, it is fundamentally an artificial,
stagey work whose attitudes have already
atrophied and lost their zest. Robbins has
written a Haiku in movement, a wispy,
wistful lyric etched in gestures that are
lean and spare. Two stylistic streams con-
verge. From the East comes the atmosphere of Japanese theater, and from the
West comes both a self-consciously poetic
posing, its mythic overtones echoing
Martha Graham, and the actual language
of the dance itself.

"Robbins hasn't rested with a simple
series of flashbacks, but has overstruc-
tured the work and overweighted it with a
heavy symbolism. Boyhood, for instance,
is recalled by the faintest of crescent [of
the moon], adolescence as the golden
sliver grows, and manhood at the ripest
moment.

"His hero is in a sense outside time, ru-
minating in solitude, and what we see is
supposedly the life of his mind. But now

Watermill. **Edward Villella.** (*Photo Martha Swope.*)

and then Robbins has him cross the temporal divide, bringing him in contact with
the objects of his fantasies. This has a double effect. First, it creates a state of dramatic entropy, a self-defeating standstill
that robs *Watermill* of impetus and force.
Secondly, this indecisiveness sets Robbins at a tremendous distance from the
heartbeat of the piece. Despite its aura of
autobiography, the work is impersonal in
a way rare for [him]." [8]

O'Connor: "An exercise in what one
perceptive student of the form calls 'fake
deep.' " [9]

Croce: "What is clear to me is that
whatever Robbins is 'into,' he is not into
it very far. The question of where we are
if *not* in medieval Japan is as naive as the
symbolism that runs through it. We are
where Robbins thinks he should be just
now. We are keeping up with the
Zeitgeist, in Cross-Culture Land; and in-
sofar as *Watermill* perpetuates and plays
up to the semi-conscious snobbery that is
reflected in the values, tastes, and 'life-
style' of so many fashionable New Yorkers, it is a perfectly disgusting piece of
work. If there were anything to the tedious hokum there might be some point
in raising questions about the less obvious
goings-on. Who is the second runner
(Maiorano) and why is it he who returns
toward the end rather than the victim of
rape-castration (Castelli)? Who are the
creatures with plumes (Lamont, Neary)
dancing through the snow? But these occasional obscurities arise only in contrast
to the predictability of everything else.
The Christian-Freudian symbols, the
Graham-style props and frame-of-

memory format are so facile and familiar
that one's curiosity isn't even aroused.
The only novelty is that, except for one or
two sequences, it all happens in slow motion." [10]

Even Kirstein, who responded favorably to the ballet, wrote, "The tempo of
the work is, in all truth, diabolically
slow."

In fact, Kirstein had been supportive
from the very beginning. Says Robbins,
"It grew out of experiments I did at the
American Theater Lab. When I outlined
the idea to Lincoln, he immediately said,
'go with it.' I put the whole thing together
in eight hours; I was surprised. (It was
done in sections; then we had a
runthrough for the cast, in the studio, so
they could see what it looked like all
together. They were amazed. I found that
it ran over an hour.) Then I went back and
refined it. The company was wonderful;
they were into it right away. It goes so
against their training. And Eddie was fabulous. Almost no one else could do it. I
must admit I was a little thrown by the
reception . . . I was sitting next to a
friend on opening night, and about halfway through, when people started to
giggle, I whispered, 'They're going to boo
at the end,' but then I was surprised
when they *did.*"

STRAVINSKY FESTIVAL 18–25 June 1972

When Balanchine first proposed the Stravinsky Festival, it sounded like less than an inspired idea. After all, he had been celebrating his own festival for fifty years, as *Apollo, Agon, Firebird, Orpheus, Movements,* and others attested. What could he possibly add? And why was the idea so exciting to him, after all he had already done?

As it turned out, Balanchine's demonstration of "how sound traveled through [Stravinsky's] life" was one of the memorable experiences of a lifetime. Twenty-two new works were presented, in a single week, along with performances of Stravinsky ballets already in the repertory and a few purely musical pieces as well. Robert Craft conducted on several occasions, and the French pianist Madeleine Malraux, who had memorized the *Lost Sonata* (the score was unavailable), made two appearances. No new *Agons* were unveiled, but Balanchine enriched the repertory with *Violin Concerto, Duo Concertant, Divertimento from "Le Baiser de la Fée,"* and *Symphony in Three Movements,* and provided six other delightful though more transitory entertainments. (The remaining choreographers fared somewhat less well.)

Although regular performances were suspended for a week during the season so the Company could prepare the Stravinsky onslaught, the logistics of rehearsing and mounting the Festival were staggering, the energy expenditure enormous. How was so ambitious a plan ever realized? As Goldner wrote, "The New York City Ballet did it by doing it." [1] Says Robbins, "George opened a window and said we were going to fly. We just followed him." For despite the spirited collaboration of many, it was Balanchine's festival, his personal tribute to a fellow-artist and friend. On opening night he made a speech: "Today *is* Stravinsky's ninetieth birthday and he *is* here. (Actually, he took

a leave of absence.)" This living presence made the proceedings joyous instead of lugubrious. Even the final ballet of the Festival, *Requiem Canticles,* a celebration of death, invited less grief than awe, while the close of the evening (after the undanced *Symphony of Psalms*) was quite unusual. Kirstein requested that there be no applause. Spectators left the auditorium in silence, then were offered thimblefuls of vodka on the way out. "In Russia," Balanchine had said, "we don't mourn; we drink the health of the guy that died."

Looking back, Gellen wrote, "For me the week held much to be grateful for: the chance to hear so many fine scores; the spectacle of the NYCB dancers rising to glory night after night from what must certainly have been nerve-deadening fatigue; the air of supercharged excitement in the theater. Above all, I thank the Festival for dispelling the notion that Balanchine would never again make the kind of dances that had once made him a legend. I drink the health of the guy that died and rose again." [2]

THE PROGRAMS

18 June:
Fanfare for a New Theater
Greeting Prelude (Happy Birthday)
Fireworks
(first three works not danced)
Lost Sonata
Scherzo Fantastique
Symphony in Three Movements
(conductor: Robert Craft)
Violin Concerto
Firebird

20 June:
Symphony in E-flat
The Cage
Concerto for Piano and Winds
Danses Concertantes

Kirstein and Balanchine pay tribute to Stravinsky. (*Photo Martha Swope.*)

21 June:
Octuor
Serenade in A
The Faun and the Shepherdess (*not danced*)
(mezzo-soprano: Frances Bible)
Divertimento from "Le Baiser de la Fée"
Ebony Concerto
Scherzo à la Russe
Circus Polka

22 June:
Scènes de Ballet
Duo Concertant
The Song of the Nightingale
Capriccio for Piano and Orchestra ("Rubies" from Jewels)

23 June:
Concerto for Two Solo Pianos
Piano-Rag-Music
Ode
(conductor: Robert Craft)
Dumbarton Oaks
(conductor: Robert Craft)
Pulcinella

24 June:
Apollo
Orpheus
Agon

25 June:
Choral Variations on Bach's "Vom Him-
    mel Hoch"
Monumentum pro Gesualdo
Movements for Piano and Orchestra
Requiem Canticles
    (conductor: Robert Craft)
Symphony of Psalms (*not danced*)
    (conductor: Robert Craft; The Gregg
    Smith Singers)

LOST SONATA

CHOREOGRAPHY: George Balanchine

MUSIC: Igor Stravinsky (scherzo from Sonata in F-sharp Minor, 1903–4)

PREMIERE: 18 June 1972 (Stravinsky Festival)

PIANO: Madeleine Malraux

CAST: Sara Leland, John Clifford

Lost Sonata was not listed on any program; it was sprung on the opening night
audience at the last minute by Balanchine. After the expected speeches, he
said, "Oh, I have a little surprise for you
all! We found a little sonata, written before I was born, but I know Stravinsky
wrote it for me."

Says Clifford, "It was a very pleasant
little character dance—about a minute
and a half—rather casual, his way of getting the festival off to an unpretentious
start, sort of like a party. He choreographed it in an hour. I think we were
supposed to be very young. Sally wore little heels and a white skirt; I had on knick-
ers, white tights and shoes. We couldn't
believe we were starting the festival—just
the two of us on stage and a piano."

Wrote Lewis, "A charming wisp of a
pas de deux, danced with artless exuberance." [1]

Stravinsky had written, some sixty
years after composing the music: "The
lost—fortunately lost—piano sonata: it
was, I suppose, an inept imitation of late
Beethoven."

SCHERZO FANTASTIQUE

CHOREOGRAPHY: Jerome Robbins

MUSIC: Igor Stravinsky (Op. 3, 1908)

LIGHTING: Ronald Bates

PREMIERE: 18 June 1972 (Stravinsky Festival)

CAST: Gelsey Kirkland, Bart Cook; Stephen Caras, Victor Castelli, Bryan Pitts

OTHER CASTS: Susan Hendl, Sara Leland,
Heather Watts, Daniel Duell

In approaching the music, Robbins must
have been largely guided by the fleet,
hummingbird-like qualities of Kirkland;
he composed a "fluttery bit of woodland
frolicking," "a brilliant skimming dance,"
"fluid and feathery and ever-inventive."
Wrote McDonagh, "It's pleasant and just
keeps floating along" [1]; but the dance was
not highly inflected, and the work
seemed to lack a definite character.

Wrote Gellen, "The whole ballet skims
along quickly enough, but it ends up
gasping for a climax that never really
comes off. The difficult and faultlessly executed bravura isn't convincing because
there are no breathers and the audience
doesn't have a chance to enjoy itself. Robbins has made a speedy, breathless ballet.
The music is bright and hard with a kind
of insistent buzzing quality. [But] the timing is off and the piece lacks drama. The
opening section for the three boys gives
them good, dancey steps. But it goes on
too long and they don't seem to fill the
time or the stage. When the lead couple
finally arrive, they aren't really introduced effectively; they seem central
only by virtue of their 'togetherness.' The
ballet isn't unpleasant; it just isn't very interesting." [2]

Lewis: "Has a breathless rapture. Not
in the vein of major ore Robbins has been
mining the past few years, it still has a
glistening radiance. The dance matches
the romantic fantasy of the music with a
lilting glow of movement, using arching
bodies that swoop low to the floor and sail
or spin through the air." [3]

All of the men's parts were very demanding and displayed beautifully a new
crop of male dancers who were not yet

Scherzo Fantastique. Gelsey Kirkland, Bart
Cook. (*Photo Fred Fehl.*)

soloists but undoubtedly on their way
(Cook was promoted not long afterward).

The men were compared to Puck; Kirkland to a wood sprite.

SYMPHONY IN THREE MOVEMENTS

CHOREOGRAPHY: George Balanchine

MUSIC: Igor Stravinsky (1942–45)

LIGHTING: Ronald Bates

PREMIERE: 18 June 1972 (Stravinsky Festival)

CAST: I. Sara Leland, Marnee Morris,
Lynda Yourth, Helgi Tomasson, Edward
Villella, Robert Weiss; 5 demi-solo
women; 5 demi-solo men; 16 women; II.
Leland, Villella; III. Entire cast

OTHER CASTS: I. Merrill Ashley, Christine
Redpath, Victor Castelli (Tomasson role);
II. Jean-Pierre Bonnefous, John Clifford

Originally a large, raw, sprawling
work, a complex ballet of unwieldy
power, *Symphony in Three Movements*,
with the passage of time, has settled into a
large and still hugely complex work, but
one of power harnessed. Undoubtedly, it
is better rehearsed than when it was originally presented; it is also clearly one of
those Balanchine creations that are not
fully assimilable after one or even several
viewings. In this case, a coherence has
emerged that was not evident in the
beginning.

Symphony in Three Movements. Left: **II. Sara Le-land, John Clifford.** *Right:* **III. Final pose.** (*Photos Martha Swope.*)

The score has a distinctly 1940s-movie flavor (in fact, one movement, in another version, was originally intended as film accompaniment; another was a response to newsreel footage of Nazi soldiers). Balanchine matched this "dated" quality with his opening long diagonal lineup of girls in pony tails (in Boardwalk formation?) and recurrent "cute" jumps with feet drawn up under the body. And he translated the stressful character of the music, the "shock tactics," the "explosions of sound" into an overfull stage, spilling with dancers, and sudden roars of virtuosity.

The match between music and dance was a close one; wrote Goldner, "As in all Balanchine masterpieces, one is never sure if the music sounds the way it does because of the choreography or if the choreography feels a certain way because of the music." [1]

Particularly arresting details of choreography are Tomasson's pyrotechnical outbursts and the strange "Eastern" duet for Leland and Villella.

Kisselgoff called it "one of the most exciting works in the entire international repertory" [2]; Barnes compared it to "open-heart surgery." [3] To Goldner, it was "dangerous" [4]; for Gellen, "gut-chilling": "[Not] easy to watch. Dancers crowd the stage. They knife in violent diagonals through the space. They shift into massive blocks that pound forward and then suddenly shatter, sending whip-spinning bodies in all directions. When they exit, it's never on the downbeat; it's as if they are always off toward another arena to

fight and explode all over again. Like someone twisting a rubber band into tortured knots, Balanchine builds the tension to mind-blitzing proportions. The pauses merely let him gather more force as he presses harder and harder toward a moment when the work threatens to rip itself into shreds, and then at the height of the final raw paroxysm, he cuts the current and freezes the work in mid-spasm.

"What a ballet! Balanchine didn't start off the easy way, and the gamble paid off. The dramatic force of *Symphony* had something to do with an irrational fear that it would never come together, that it was apocalyptic and would keep us waiting forever to find our release." [5]

At the least, this was one of Balanchine's most unusual, "uncharacteristic" works. It was premiered the same night as the rich, driving, acerbic *Violin Concerto*, and the combination was, in all senses, stunning.

The best way to evaluate the ballet seemed to be to approach it as straightforwardly as possible, step by step, and to that end, Goldner and Gellen provided detailed descriptions. Goldner wrote: "It is difficult to locate the nucleus of action, and the placement of dancers is not so much asymmetrical as dislocated. It is, I think, the most raw and unleashed ballet Balanchine has done.

"The curtain rises on a long diagonal of girls in leotards with pony tails. Stravinsky's chords blare out and the girls swing their arms violently in big circles, fling them upward and plunge forward, their heads lowered and arms thrown in

front of them. It seems a demoniac invocation, to which Tomasson responds, it seems, by leaping from the wings onto the stage. He leaps at a slight angle to their diagonal, and for the rest of the dance his plane of movement is jarringly different from that of the group. He does big but disconnected movements—pow, silence; pow, silence. Soon, he is joined by Yourth, and they continue the leap-halt sequence. Meanwhile, the ensemble walks on pointe, their backs in a slight crouch, their pony tails swinging, their arms flailing. Their dancing is too cool and mechanized to be Amazonian; it is more scary. Their little side-to-side shuffles, studies in insouciance, turn the Broadway chorus line into a menacing army.

"Next Leland dances in the middle of a small corps. The group begins to circle, in a rolling walk step; Leland circles in the opposite direction. Walking accelerates to running and Leland breaks into a series of turns. She charges through the girls, who are rushing headlong at her. After a few big circles, the girls run off and Leland spins off with even faster turns into . . . outer space. No sooner is she off than [Clifford] and entourage bound on. Their steps are smaller and form more of a matrix, but this dance too gobbles up space. Due to the constantly changing patterns and drive of the corps, the ballet's overall momentum parallels and finally runs ahead of the music.

"In the final part of this first movement, the original ensemble of sixteen rushes on and again lines up in a diagonal. Again, Tomasson jumps in front of them.

But this time he jumps from the front instead of the back wing, and he is angled slightly differently. Too, the girls' diagonal subsequently splits in two by a pace, so that you are not sure if the line is jagged by intent or mistake. The outline is the same as the beginning: the inner details 'off-key.' This quasi-resolution is perhaps the most unsettling moment of the ballet so far. After Tomasson's last jump, one by one the girls suck in their outflung arms and legs and unfurl them into an open position, their backs arched forward and their faces uplifted toward the audience.

"The duet [Leland and Clifford] is strangely quiet, sensuous and meditative, with a pronounced Eastern tingle. Much of the movement is on bent knees. Elbows are bent and the hands are flattened, palms out. The couple cuts exotic poses, but langorously and with sexual passivity. They separate and come together, separate and come together as in a trance. They move with feline cool, but underneath is a feeling of suppressed energy—perhaps barbarism.

"As the two dancers leave the stage others leap on, so as to sever the interlude by a stroke of the whip. The ballet resumes its headlong course. There are two moments of relative stasis: when the three female soloists and three male soloists engage in canonic interplay. But Balanchine finds in them, or imposes on them, an agitation that links to the rest of the ballet. In front and in capital letters is the soloists' choreography—aggressive but quickly executed leaps, plunges and socking arabesques. In contrast, the large ensemble does small foot steps but large and energetic arm motions. Its rhythm is steady, while that of the soloists is syncopated. Because of this and sheer number, the ensemble looks-sounds like a drone, carrying its oppressive foreboding. This quality crystallizes when eight girls place themselves in the wings right and left so that only half their bodies are visible. They are half-seen but keenly felt. Then they make big and deliberate side steps on bent knees and on pointe onto the stage and half off, onto the stage and half off. In exact rhythm with the walk, their arms sweep back and forth across their faces, like slow windshield wipers.

"The ballet ends with a brief spell of unison dancing for the entire cast of thirty-two. The men then run forward and fall to the floor, poised to spring into the audience. The others space themselves across the stage. A few raise their arms upward or to the side. The effect is like a stripped-down and flattened totem pole, recalling the figurations of the pas de deux section. The dancers stand immobile." [6]

Gellen: "The ballet begins with Tomasson's urgent, percussive solo that takes place in front of a diagonal line of forbidding girls whose arms stretch up and out from their arching bodies, clawing through the air. Immediately there is a frustrating wildness in the air that shifts to watchful attention as Youth enters. She and Tomasson have a very fast gymnasts' duet that suggests nothing so much as a need to use their bodies violently. They bend and stretch and pull each other off center, exorcising the tension from their spirits. They exit. Leland enters alone, rather calm. She dances her solo before a corps of girls. Her dance becomes increasingly driven. She seems a prisoner on the stage, and at the end of her solo she turns around the stage in a series of brilliant, compulsive piqué turns that describe a line between pairs of girls skipping in a circle. As Leland exits you feel that the force and momentum of her turns have mercifully propelled her off the stage, spun her free from a lethal marathon, and as the music doesn't end or breathe, you can imagine her twirling on until she finds an open space to be *alone* with her brilliance.

"On surges Villella with a group of boys. The dance here is not unlike the section of 'Rubies' where Villella initiates a kind of follow-the-leader dance game. But in that piece the spirit is all good-natured fun. Here, Villella jets about the stage trying to shrug off his companions, really ditch them. The music keeps thrusting forward with really merciless aggression until there is this curious brief interval for Morris and Weiss that is sweet and relaxed. Their moment of peace is curtailed as the rest of the cast comes whooshing out again. The first movement ends with Tomasson again solo on stage in front of that line-up of girls who, at the last moment, strike their clawing pose, and as the music dies they wilt against the last notes in a sinister, rather perverse curl that leaves them in a fixed, hostile tableau. The piece has been on only a short while, but I feel as if I've been in the theater for an hour, and I'm exhausted.

"Balanchine has made us feel the chilling, harsh tensions of some future universe where privacy and community have been irrevocably polarized. The second movement exploits a kind of lyric but unromantic notion of exile. The whole movement is a pas de deux that relishes the quiet, still sanctum they inhabit. They move deliberately, and the dance is curious because they seem to communicate more expressively when they are apart. Balanchine has given them a kind of nonreferential mime, a series of angled, space-age mudras that draws them closer to each other. But when they dance together, it's as if they never make contact, like two magnets joined at the wrong poles. The dance isn't combative, but they never appear to give in to each other with total weight and harmony; they've forgotten how to make love. The air around them is all oxygen, cold and clear. Too pure. The pas de deux ends with Leland posed against her partner's side, arms uplifted like frozen snakes—a modern Siva.

"The closing movement returns to the oppressive, surging tension and release of the first section. The dance has a pounding, pulverizing shape that pits kaleidoscopic wheels against diagonals that shift to boxes and triangles. At one moment the corps of white-clad women suddenly leave the stage to line up from the edge of the black sidecloths back into the wings, and you know there must be thousands of them stretching all around the globe. The ballet ends with the principal dancers and soloists giving way to strange disjointed shapes mirrored in those girls behind them—breathing antennae, science-fiction angels or devils. The final image is powerful and frightening—an open gridded cube, harsh white and black, and a petrified forest of robots." [7]

VIOLIN CONCERTO
since 1973 called
STRAVINSKY VIOLIN CONCERTO

CHOREOGRAPHY: George Balanchine

MUSIC: Igor Stravinsky (1931)

LIGHTING: Ronald Bates

VIOLIN CONCERTO

PREMIERE: 18 June 1972 (Stravinsky Festival)

VIOLIN: Joseph Silverstein

CAST: *Toccata*, Karin von Aroldingen, Kay Mazzo, Jean-Pierre Bonnefous, Peter Martins; 8 women, 8 men; *Aria I*, von Aroldingen, Bonnefous; *Aria II*, Mazzo, Martins; *Capriccio*, entire cast
Bonnefous role also danced by Bart Cook

Violin Concerto was one of the outstanding works of the Stravinsky Festival. Its nearest relative is *Agon*. (Wrote Kisselgoff: "*Agon* is a series of *separate* dances, each ending with a kinetic epigram. *Violin Concerto* is a *succession* of dances, each different but flowing into another." [1]) Balanchine craftily disguises the flow, however, which comes as a last-minute surprise. The music moves with the relentless, scratching energy of a buzzsaw in the outer movements and is lyrical but still sharply accented in the center sections; the ballet seems made up of disconnected steps of every variety, the many threads of which do not recognizably come together until the last movement—also the only time the full company is on stage together. This disconnectedness is reinforced by the primacy of the largely staccato rhythmic pulse over the the melodic line, by Balanchine's having at least a part of the body (sometimes as small as an elbow or toe) seeming to move on every note, and by the dancers' performing mostly alone (even when they are dancing together).

The four soloists dance individually in the opening movement (each supported by a corps of four), each with perky measures: the boys are airplanes, they Charleston; girls trot with knees raised; Martins performs a few classical steps—saut de basque, pirouette; Mazzo picks her way on pointe, turns in her attitude. In Aria I, von Aroldingen does a crab step around the feet of her partner, movements seem arbitrary, there is much reaching, crawling, bending, with little resolution. At the end, she lies on the floor. Mazzo and Martins, whose music is the sweetest in the work (Aria II), are more tender; they touch with an awareness of touching; they are mutually solicitous, where von Aroldingen and Bonnefous were competitors. Delicately they take hands. At the end, he kneels and she leans back on him, his arm drawn across

***Violin Concerto*. Aria I. Karin von Aroldingen, Jean-Pierre Bonnefous.** (*Photo Martha Swope.*)

her forehead. This is the only "mood piece" in the work. In the final section, a sort of "hoedown" that never stops moving, there are hints of mazurkas, with hops and shuffles, as one group feeds into another until all are involved.

Goldner wrote in some detail: "The setup [of the first movement] is orderly and controlled, even a little starched. In contrast is choreography that at times threatens to explode through sheer momentum and cumulative impact of entrances and exits.

"Tension, due in part to this contrast, is felt from the start. The curtain rises and the music begins. Mazzo and group stand alertly in stage center but do not move a muscle, while Stravinsky is off and running. You sit poised, then anxious: when will they begin to dance to music that begs for dancing? In a few seconds (which did not grow shorter on second viewing), Mazzo does begin, by kicking her legs a little to the back of her while her arms fly up above her head. The movement is done with great care, yet there is something casual, even haphazard, about the kick. It is beyond the encased shape of a classical pas, yet it has equal stature. That kick is a forecast for the rest of the ballet. *Violin Concerto* is without formal steps, while the superstructure is quite formal.

"Instead of making a series of pas, even the most flowing of series, the dancers literally move. They kick and prance. Jumps are primarily functional rather than feats of elevation; they are a way to cover a lot of territory, quickly. One of the most exciting moments in the first part occurs when four boys elongate a usually small jump so that they travel across the stage in one leap. It is repeated

four times, the men making a square on the edges of the stage with incredible speed. Most of the dancing, however, is tight and small. For in counterpoint to the gustlike speed and momentum of entrances and exits is a persistent tick, tick, tick. They move obviously on counts, very fast counts, like the smallest, most sophisticated parts of a machine.

"The final section, for the entire cast, has even fewer steps and is squeezed down to only the ticks. It is done practically in place. The idea, I think, was to create the appearance of movement or energy through the dancers' syncopation with the music and each other. Groups of limbs move against each other. While the soloists are sliding, prancing, and two-stepping up front, the ensemble shifts weight from one leg to another, turns one knee inward and outward, raises the arm up and back to over the heart, rotates the wrist palm outward, palm inward. It is the most visual music composition Balanchine has ever choreographed, and to do it he had to discombobulate bodies and manipulate the ensemble to a degree he has never attempted before.

"To orchestrate the score literally, with arms and legs and shifting masses of material (bodies), was a bold and successful experiment. But the idea was sometimes carried out in folk motif, and this I found a bit coy. Perhaps Balanchine was making a joke about Stravinsky's Russianisms. He would have done better to let the folk bit slip by, finding instead less evident analogies, as when the group breaks into a kind of Indian war dance for a moment at the end. Now *that* was unexpected, showed a wonderfully whacky imagination, and was entirely appropriate to the music. The first duet is unhappy and tortuous. Never has so much bodily contact been achieved so unnaturally, against the laws of simplicity, against the will of the dancers, and even against standards of good taste (von Aroldingen does a handstand to disengage from one embrace). As their limbs interlock, their faces are turned in opposite directions. They struggle to unlock at the very moments when they are going through contortions to embrace. These dancers choose not to look at each other, though the positions of their bodies demand it. As a result, they are always out of kilter and under a certain amount of physical strain.

"The duet for Mazzo and Martins has some inward turns of the legs, full turnings away, and agitated interweavings of the hands, yet it is supple and supremely graceful. The dance now strikes me as being 'about' a choreographer and a ballerina. Martins rotates Mazzo, walks her, activates her. She leans back against him and ever so carefully moves one foot in front of the other, while he turns her body so that she is moving toward us, always at a striking angle. When he is not by her, she is still, waiting but unworried. The unorthodox, 'unharmonious' aspects of her movements—flexed feet, sudden collapses in the legs and torso, and the like—are smoothly resolved. . . . Martins rolls Mazzo from one foot to another. In this little air voyage, she starts out with one foot pointed and the other flexed. With great deliberation and yet speed, she simultaneously points the flexed foot and flexes the pointed one. We can almost see each dot along the arced paths her feet trace. As the trip ends, she lands on one foot and whips her flexed foot along the floor into a point. This is an exclamation point to a juicy five-second game. Many choreographers have played with flexed feet in classical ballet, but Balanchine's version is now the definitive one." [2]

Gale: "The ballet is dazzlingly complex and uninterrupted by shifting groupings that eddy and flow about a counterpoint of dance laid on, and often against, the music. Balanchine uses little movement that is new, but he uses it in ways that are disarming and revelatory. The flip of a hand here, the slow draw of an arm there, a sudden inward thrust of thigh, an outward encompass of legs—all, in his endlessly fecund intellect, assume original meaning. In the opening Toccata and closing Capriccio the dancers are like leaves that scud gaily before the wind. Balanchine has built two fantastically fine pas de deux. One is swift and feral; the second is sweetly sad." [3]

Mazo: "At second glance, the work is even more stunning than it was at first. Balanchine has created a flowing, unrelenting series of tensions, playing off entrances against exits, spins against straight lines, diagonals against horizontals, and one part of a dancer against the others. The piece begins in free, almost jazzy movement and finishes in a free Capriccio that is as joyous as a houseful of puppies. The duets contrast brilliantly with one another. The first is feline, sharp-focused, and detached. The solo violin at times becomes a third, active partner to the dancers, now leading them on, now playing the contrary flirt. The second is softer, full of warm yielding, yet making full use of the angular movements we have come to associate with Balanchine's Stravinsky." [4]

As usual, but, if anything, more so than usual, Balanchine created movements that perfectly suited the four quite different bodies and temperaments of the soloists he had chosen. Says von Aroldingen, "It's so rewarding to dance you forget the difficulties."

In 1941, Balanchine choreographed a completely different work to the same score, called *Balustrade*, for the Original Ballet Russe.

Russia:

"We derived great pleasure from the ballet master's interesting choreographic inventiveness and original fantasy in *Violin Concerto*. Within the restricted means of Aria I, the artists succeeded in being both expressive and convincing. We were delighted by the ballet technique of the American dancers: by their purity of movement, correct 'fifth position,' rapid gyrations, exceptional balance and precise musical rhythm, practiced mastery, exactitude in every movement, and that coordination and smoothness which are completely indispensable not only to the soloists but to the whole art of ensemble dancing. Nevertheless we would like to see more expressive plastic motion, more melodiousness—for they also contribute to the dance, to the beautiful aspect which we call its poetry and soul. Everything is literature, to the last period, comma, and even ellipses. . . . But it occasionally lacks that 'life of the human spirit' without which any technique grows dim." [5]

Violin Concerto. **Aria II. Kay Mazzo, Peter Martins.** (*Photo Martha Swope.*)

SYMPHONY IN E-FLAT

CHOREOGRAPHY: John Clifford

MUSIC: Igor Stravinsky (Symphony in E-flat, op. 1, 1908, dedicated "to my dear teacher N. A. Rimsky-Korsakov")

COSTUMES: Stanley Simmons

LIGHTING: Ronald Bates

PREMIERE: 20 June 1972 (Stravinsky Festival)

CAST: Gelsey Kirkland, Peter Martins; 22 women, 10 men

Allegro moderato
Scherzo
Largo

Allegro molto

"Call it very minor Balanchine." [1]

Says Clifford, "I already wanted to do a ballet to this music, because it's so unusual. No one would guess it's Stravinsky. It's big, and that's a problem. But it was difficult doing it for the Festival. I had planned to use a different lead couple for each movement, but everyone already had too much to do. Mr. B. wryly said it would be a challenge to choreograph a forty-minute ballet with just two soloists. It *was* a challenge! I had to be careful not to make the steps too hard, especially at the end. I wish it had had more time to settle into the repertory. Maybe sometime I'll get to do it as I originally had in mind."

Barnes: "The work, for all its faults, had a sure and useful zest. The choreography lacks something in focus, but then so perhaps does the music. Admittedly the ensemble work here was ordinary, to say the most, yet there were some elements that had the grace of a true choreographer." [2]

Gellen: "Great gobs of fast, furious rushings-about by a huge corps, and a quasi-dramatic structure very tenuously based on the idea that Kirkland and Martins were meant for each other but just couldn't manage to get it all together. Strained my patience and my stamina." [3]

CONCERTO FOR PIANO AND WINDS

CHOREOGRAPHY: John Taras

MUSIC: Igor Stravinsky (1924)

COSTUMES: Rouben Ter-Arutunian

LIGHTING: Ronald Bates

PREMIERE: 20 June 1972 (Stravinsky Festival)

PIANO: Gordon Boelzner

CAST: Bruce Wells; Robert Maiorano, Frank Ohman; Tracy Bennett, Victor Castelli, Peter Naumann; 8 men

This was the same music Taras used for his earlier ballet *Arcade* (1963), but, says

he, "so much time had elapsed between the two that I couldn't remember anything, so it didn't bother me, and, anyway, I treated it completely differently. It's one of Balanchine's favorite pieces, and he's always trying to find some way to keep it in the repertory."

Taras was not particularly pleased with the results, nor were the critics. It should be remembered that some of the many new ballets were included in the Festival to round out the aural picture, and were put together "on demand," without too much inspiration on the part of their creators.

Wrote Barnes, "Not especially successful. A ballet composed entirely for male dancers is an interesting idea, but somehow [here] it is left just as an idea. The work has an air of achievement to it. But it never makes the best of its opportunities. The music has a certain feminine grace that sounds ill-fitted for this all-male fiesta, and in following the accent of the music, Taras has betrayed his own original conception of masculine olympics." [1]

Kisselgoff: "The choreography is based on the daring premise that an all-male cast can get away with adagio movement. This idea has a certain fascination in the first of three sections, where the fourteen men are occasionally given the swagger of acrobats. Yet in the second movement, the steps are simply too delicate for the trio of dancers." [2]

The costumes, originally in shades of red, were changed to black-and-white practice outfits. Says Taras, "Balanchine wanted them in what the boys wore at the Imperial School, which was tight britches, white socks, and white shoes. It does make the steps look more interesting."

DANSES CONCERTANTES

NEW CHOREOGRAPHY: George Balanchine

MUSIC: Igor Stravinsky (*Danses Concertantes,* for chamber orchestra, 1941–42)

COSTUMES, DÉCOR: Eugene Berman (courtesy The Ballet Foundation)

PREMIERE: 20 June 1972 (Stravinsky Festival) (first presented 10 September 1944 by the Ballet Russe de Monte Carlo, City Center of Music and Drama, New York)

CAST: Lynda Yourth, John Clifford; 8 women, 4 men

OTHER CASTS: Sara Leland, Christine Redpath; Daniel Duell

Marche
Pas d'Action
Thème varié (4 variations)
Pas de Deux
Marche

The reputation of *Danses Concertantes* preceded it. Historians and balletomanes remembered, or remembered hearing about, the original Ballet Russe production, Balanchine's first new work for that company, smartly costumed by Berman in his usual mode of ornate elegance (which, for once, did not encumber the figures). The whole was tart, clever, sophisticated—the latest in chic by three masters of style. Denby had called it "brilliantly animated and brilliantly civilized, a highly artificial, a very exact, and a delicately adjusted entertainment." [1] Martin, who was far from won over to Balanchine's position in those days, found it "vacuum and soda, vintage 1925" [2]; Lederman, "mocking and allusive." [3]

But the work had been allowed to languish, and Balanchine never revived it for another company, so it remained more talked about than seen. For the Stravinsky Festival, the Berman mounting was still available, and, although Balanchine completely redid the choreography, it is said that in form and effect, the work resembles the original.

The heart of the ballet is a series of pas de trois—in this version, showing yards of long legs—each rather quirky and individual, deliberately odd, and a lengthy pas de deux for a small couple, in which, says Clifford, "Balanchine put every trick of mine in the book. That meant quick movements, jumps, high kicks, penché arabesque [extremely rare for a man], and other extensions, lots of exuberant jumps and beats. Whenever I warmed up for the part, I had to make sure *everything* was working. The pas de deux is very long, hard, puffy."

Despite such a background, the ballet promised somewhat more than it delivered. Effects were made, but they quickly evaporated, generating a feeling of unease or inconclusiveness. And yet, inherent in the restless musical surface itself is a lack of substance, so once again, it seemed, Balanchine had accurately re-

Danses Concertantes. Renee Estópinal, Tracy Bennett, Delia Peters, John Clifford, Christine Redpath. *(Photo Martha Swope.)*

flected his accompaniment. Adding to the unsettled feeling, the piece flirted with humor, but never gave itself over to it. In such a cocktail-party world, one twitters archly; one does not laugh out loud.

Barnes, however, found it a "gem": "Completely charming. The costumes, baroque and handsome, with strangely veined decorations, have all the air of commedia dell'arte with none of its implications. The dances are formal. The music, with its acid charm, dissonant harmonies, and faintly dislocated rhythms, has a pungent mood of its own. There is a sense of hothouse jazz here that Balanchine has perfectly captured. His dances are almost purposely perverse, they triumph in oddity. The style and color of the piece—its bright costumes clashing impudently with one another—were enchanting. Clifford had all the finesse the part needed, and a certain cheekiness, an insouciance, that went naughtily and joyously with the acerbic music." [4]

Gellen: "A delight. It begins with each group passing briefly before the front curtain with a commedia dell'arte flourish, making little dance jokes to the audience. The tone is one of friendly irony, very knowing, and not unpleasantly brittle. Personalities are sketched. Swift and tantalizing, this device makes its point very quickly as the front curtain rises to reveal the entire cast assembled in the more formalized area behind it. The following sec-

tion, with four pas de trois, is truly breathtaking. The dance images and styles are as varied as the dancers on the stage. But every dance is a world unto itself—hard, perfect. One is a languidly flowing, very funny dance based on the endlessly long legs of Neary and Estópinal, with Sackett a willing pivot to their plunging penchés and boundary-less arabesques balancées. The last is a hot, twisty rhythmic hopscotch. The not-so-grandly-danced pas de deux was much more difficult to 'see.' " [5]

Gale: "The music becomes a taut, lean Italianate circus, broadly mischievous yet tightly constructed, with sudden shifts of temperament and steps—trotting, prancing, a classical Charleston, a fling at heresy—and he gets away with everything. There is a curiously unbecoming part in it for the leading girl—unheard-of for Balanchine." [6]

Most critics complained about the casting of the leading roles, finding the dancers not sufficiently artful. Wrote Gellen, longing for "raffinement suprême": "Clifford's role called for equal parts of Harlequin and Fred Astaire; he gave us equal parts Marge and Gower Champion." [7]

Kisselgoff: "If [Clifford and Leland] would choose to tone down what the choreography itself already stresses, the results might be rather different. Throwing away lines in a joke requires a certain

talent, and in this case the scriptwriter's material stands on its own." [8]

Says Clifford, simply, "He said it should be like vaudeville, that I should perform Hollywood-style. The pas de deux he wanted very classical until the finger-snapping, then go into a soft shoe . . ."

Balanchine, as is so often remarked, choreographs for the particular dancers at hand. His original ballerina (Danilova) had been in her forties when the ballet was done; it is more than possible that he was looking for something different then. In 1972, however, critics seemed to expect a reproduction of her role and style. Says Clifford, "A similar thing happened in *Agon;* I did the first pas de trois. Balanchine wanted a big kick—'Slap your foot up at the side,' he said; 'I want it like a circus, that step—big and vulgar—fan kick, step, kick, step, slap.' I was afraid—I always thought *Agon* was so serious—but the truth was that it hadn't been done that way previously because the other men who danced the part didn't *have* a big kick. The critics thought I had taken it upon myself to change the steps! But it was what Balanchine asked for."

OCTUOR

CHOREOGRAPHY: Richard Tanner

MUSIC: Igor Stravinsky (*Octuor,* for winds, 1923)

LIGHTING: Ronald Bates

PREMIERE: 21 June 1972 (Stravinsky Festival)

CAST: Elise Flagg, Deborah Flomine, Delia Peters, Lisa de Ribere; Tracy Bennett, James Brogan, Daniel Duell, Jean-Pierre Frohlich

Sinfonia
Tema con variazioni
Finale

This occasional piece, presented during the Stravinsky Festival only, was considered a nice try. Wrote Micklin, "Achieved what Balanchine regularly accomplishes—getting inside of the Stravinsky music and rhythm flow." [1]

Barnes: "The music has a jazzy infor-

OCTUOR

mality. There are four couples, with movements that have a certain synchronized chic. But it does not really work. However, Tanner is working with more confidence than in the past, and he did give a certain accent to this now evocative score of Paris, jazz, and architecture." [2]

Gellen: "Tanner is the first choreographer who seems to have understood that the Balanchine vocabulary of movement is technically intrinsic to the choreographic style. He has a certain comprehension of Balanchine's Stravinsky mode. He knows how to make his dancers move, but he doesn't know where to move them. The use of space isn't energetic enough, so that the dancers seem constricted. Everything is very tight and small and desiccated. The opening sections are nervous and unnecessarily quirky. But the ballet seems to come together a bit. Not very good, but it's an honest, intelligent effort." [3]

The same score was used for William Christensen's *Octet*, presented by the Company in 1958.

SERENADE IN A

CHOREOGRAPHY: Todd Bolender

MUSIC: Igor Stravinsky (1925; for solo piano)

COSTUMES: Stanley Simmons

LIGHTING: Ronald Bates

PREMIERE: 21 June 1972 (Stravinsky Festival)

PIANO: Madeleine Malraux

CAST: Susan Hendl, Robert Maiorano, Robert Weiss; 4 couples
Also danced by Bruce Wells

Says Bolender, "Balanchine assigned me the music. Anything Stravinsky writes is stimulating, he's such a master craftsman. The ballet was based on a pas de trois. The main couple move among, then away from, the group; by the end of the first movement, these people had established a relationship sufficiently strong that they always returned to the same partners. All leave, the girl stops, she pulls away, and it's like a mælstrom, a blackout—it swirls and swirls and she winds up facing quite a different man. At the end of their long pas de deux, the same swirl happens again, and she winds up between the two men. By the end of the third movement, and another swirl, she's left with the first man. It ends on a tentative note—all repeat a statement made at the opening, they touch hands, then everybody starts to walk away, along a different path."

Wrote Barnes, "Not too much inspiration. . . . There is a blandness here.

Bolender was shrewd in his casting." [1]

Micklin: "Deliberately unspectacular but imaginatively organized." [2]

Gellen: "Obviously Bolender chose a current safe style. A neo-*Dances at a Gathering* that moves gently about the stage, the work is pleasant to the eyes. There is a bit of abstract narrative with two males in conflict over the woman, but it isn't too important or too obtrusive. The work is a lot of simple things, soft and genial and unimportant." [3]

DIVERTIMENTO FROM "LE BAISER DE LA FÉE"

CHOREOGRAPHY: George Balanchine

MUSIC: Igor Stravinsky (excerpt from concert suite "Divertimento," 1934 [full-length ballet, 1928])

COSTUMES: Eugene Berman (from *Roma*)

LIGHTING: Ronald Bates

PREMIERE: 21 June 1972 (Stravinsky Festival)

CAST: Patricia McBride, Helgi Tomasson; Bettijane Sills, Carol Sumner; 10 women

OTHER CASTS: Gelsey Kirkland, Christine Redpath, Jean-Pierre Bonnefous

One of the acknowledged gems of the Stravinsky Festival, *Baiser* may not have the immediacy of the forceful *Violin Concerto*, the dynamic *Symphony in Three Movements*, or even the poignant *Duo Concertant*, but it leaves its own mysterious reverberations. Some saw in its dark foreboding and its troubled gaiety echoes of the fateful story upon which the complete ballet was based, but in the *Divertimento* there is no hint of narrative, and only a single step remains from the Company's 1950 staging of *Baiser* (the girl's long penché arabesque to the low arm of the man, kneeling on the floor—"like falling off a mountain"). Along these lines, some found in the girl the embodiment of both the Bride and the Fairy, and in the prominent male role a reflection of the original, in which the Bridegroom was the protagonist.

Balanchine's gift for choreographing to

Serenade in A. Susan Hendl, Robert Weiss. (Photo Martha Swope.)

Divertimento from "Le Baiser de la Fée." Left: **Patricia McBride, Helgi Tomasson.** (*Photo Fred Fehl.*) *Below:* **Patricia McBride, Helgi Tomasson.** (*Photo Martha Swope.*)

the strength of his dancers was brilliantly in evidence. McBride's delicacy, particularly her baroquely eloquent and assertive yet filigree arm movements, were memorably used in a variation that produced a kind of silvery tone. (Wrote Barnes, "At times her multifaceted dancing has the unexpected twists and turns of a Calder mobile." [1]) Tomasson's perfect placement and purity of technique served in one of Balanchine's most unusual male variations—dark and pensive—which for full effect demanded exact off-balance jumps and landings, "shuffle" turns on quarter-point, a strange paddling motion of the hands; Tomasson finished with a turn with head thrown back, as if hearing a distant call. Again, McBride's graceful torso was used in an adagio (added later), to lowered blue lights, where the ballerina is supported in a backbend, walking on pointe.

Barnes, "Quietly and yet also deafeningly entrancing. Just as Stravinsky gives

us Tchaikovsky with a vital tinge of acid, so Balanchine provides us a Petipa far more sophisticated than we might have expected." [2]

Gellen: "McBride's [first] entrance is a bit mysterious; she glides suddenly into the midst of the dancing girls, is feted and danced about, made 'special'; and then she exits. The pas de deux is neither erotic nor peaceful. It looks terribly difficult, a grand pas d'amour—supple, intricate, 'off-center.' It is with Tomasson's solo that the heart of the piece reveals itself. His variation, which begins with joyous leaps, suddenly suggests his lack of freedom. In a series of croisés assemblés élancés that cleave the air, he falls in a broken motion to the knee. It's as if he flies into the sky only to be struck by an intimation of doom. But that fall is no release, no resolution. His weight never relaxes into the floor. He springs up again, over and over. Tomasson performs the solo with tremendous restraint, and yet

there is an extraordinary texture here. He is a brilliant technician and musician; but that is nothing new. Here he seems to have grasped a necessary and very special timing that projects in the space of a few moments a whole world of contradictory emotions. He is half the free mortal, half the creature of another dimension." [3]

Kisselgoff commented: "In this bright joyful, and tender pas de deux, backed by an ensemble, Balanchine has reserved the most inventive sequence for Tomasson. The man's variation, with its unexpected changes of direction, suggestions of swoons, and a series of jumps followed by falls to the knee, appears totally original. In the coda, the extraordinary way Tomasson seems to be off balance when he is not is a tribute to both the imagination of the choreographer and the rockfirm technique of the dancer." [4]

In November 1974, Balanchine added another pas de deux, to music that incorporates the theme "None But the Lonely Heart." McDonagh was satisfied: "The ballet, which previously ended with the principals united in front of the gaily costumed corps, now proceeds with a new pas de deux that has something of the moody magic of the previous male 'arm gathering' solo. This now appears to be developing the tragic side of the story. The procession of the corps between the kneeling couple was hauntingly beautiful, as was the final separation of the two partners. This addition helps to clarify some of the ambiguities of the piece." [5]

Croce: "Balanchine has taken McBride's signature attitudes and distorted them slightly to reveal their dark implications. In the earlier duet, she dipped and turned in different directions, pirouetting with a powerful swing of her leg to lock him behind her. Now, in the new scene, she freezes in low-slung arabesque and, as he turns her, gradually knots herself about him until the two are fused. The bride of the original tale becomes the fairy, and this, too, recalls a traditional Balanchine theme—the heroine whose aspect flickers between vampire and goddess. The sinister-sweet elements in McBride's nature are perfect for the role. The *Divertimento* is one of the most superbly crafted pieces to have come from Balanchine in recent years—but it's basically footnote material, a collection of thoughts about a lost work of art." [6]

Says McBride, "*Baiser* is very difficult; it looks so easy. The new pas de deux is so different from anything he's done. It's very passionate and lyrical, and very moving—the way they end. They separate and go off in different directions. It's the same spirit as one of the most beautiful variations Mr. B. has ever done for a man, very dramatic.

"There are tricks in it. My 'arm' variation is very fast. One has to be on top of the music. Oddly, Mr. B. didn't set any arms, although he gave me some suggestions. You have freedom to do what's most natural with the arms, but, of course, the variations are very classical, so that's a guide. Then there's a final pirouette, not facing the audience but on the diagonal. He wants a double turn on pointe, with the third on half-toe—much harder than three on pointe. In the first pas de deux, there are so many bourrées, then that low penché arabesque (this always seems so impossible)—Mr. B. stops that in rehearsal and we do it over and over. There's one place where she bourrées past him. He lifts her and she continues, 'as if walking on air.' He wants it to look as if she's just gliding by—'just ignore him; he's not there.' Then when he puts me down, the effect is very unusual. That's another thing we've practiced over and over again; he tries to find the smoothest possible way of doing it."

SCHERZO À LA RUSSE

CHOREOGRAPHY: George Balanchine

MUSIC: Igor Stravinsky (1925)

COSTUMES: Karinska

LIGHTING: Ronald Bates

PREMIERE: 21 June 1972 (Stravinsky Festival)

CAST: Karin von Aroldingen, Kay Mazzo; 16 women
Also danced by Christine Redpath

The briefest (four minutes) of trifles, amusing for both dancers and audience. The all-female cast wore Russian "nightgowns" or "nursemaid outfits"— calf-length, waistless white dresses— with aristocratic crown-like headdresses and long ribbons. There were dainty

Scherzo à la Russe. **Karin von Aroldingen, Kay Mazzo (front row).** *(Photo Martha Swope.)*

heel-and-toe folk suggestions, and in its completely unstrenuous nature, the piece was reminiscent of Russian female folk ensembles, which depend for their effect on charm and the glow of health, always leaving trepaks, split leaps, and other "typically" Russian folk steps to the men. Of course, Stravinsky called his music "in the Russian *manner*," which is not precisely the same thing as being Russian. In this, Balanchine matched him.

Says von Aroldingen, "You feel like a child or a doll when you do it. The whole thing is a smile. It's over so fast. That surprise short ending—it just stops dead— shows Stravinsky's humor."

Wrote Barnes: "A slight joke but a warm one. Balanchine has made, slightly irreverently, the kind of Nursemaids' Dance that he feels Fokine should have contributed to *Petrushka*. Brief, clever, and lightly bewitching. . . . A meringue, a clockwork Easter egg by Fabergé. The choreography counterpoints two bouncing bands of Russian virgins smiling saucily through their rites of spring." [1]

Gellen: "Over almost as soon as it began, it probably didn't amount to very much. But it had a lot of style and wit." [2]

Goldner: "A spicy music-box number led by two figurines. Each dancer follows her little groove, and together they make a pretty and orderly picture. One might not want to spend a lifetime in a Swiss village, but a visit is immensely satisfying, and so is this little ballet. No one is hiding an intention to charm. Balanchine throws in a small monkey wrench to the just-so proceedings and the girlish manners: he

brings the ballet to a proper, conventional 'ending' before the actual ending. After the false finish nothing is predictable. When the ballet *does* end, it does so in mid-note and mid-step. The girls raise one arm toward the center of the stage, but there is nothing final about the gesture. Stravinsky wrote notes that take four minutes to hear, and Balanchine choreographed steps that take four minutes to see. Their work defies labels, whether it be 'magnum opus,' 'little gem,' or 'incidental' [the music was originally incidental music for a film]. They approach their assignments straight on. You could call their attitude innocence, or the quintessence of sophistication." [3]

CIRCUS POLKA

CHOREOGRAPHY: Jerome Robbins

MUSIC: Igor Stravinsky (1942; dedication: "for a young elephant")

LIGHTING: Ronald Bates

PREMIERE: 21 June 1972 (Stravinsky Festival)

CAST: *Ringmaster,* Jerome Robbins; 48 students of the School of American Ballet

Ringmaster also performed by David Richardson

Circus Polka was a lark, done to the music Balanchine had requested for his famous "ballet of the elephants" for Ring-

Above: Circus Polka. Little girls from School of American Ballet with Robbins (right) as Ringmaster. *Right: Scènes de Ballet.* Patricia McBride, Jean-Pierre Bonnefous. (*Photos Fred Fehl.*)

ling Brothers. This time around, Robbins did the choreography. Wrote Gellen, "Out popped Robbins in a ringmaster's getup, and for eight minutes we were treated to everything he does best. The work was made for thousands of little girls who twinkled in lines and circles and carousels of movement, all very bright and—most importantly—childlike. They ended up forming Stravinsky's monogram, I.S., and it was over in a splash of color and sweetness." [1]

Among the children was Hayden's daughter. Contrary to expectations, the ballet was performed subsequently. In 1974, one of d'Amboise's daughters was the right size for it.

SCÈNES DE BALLET

CHOREOGRAPHY: John Taras

MUSIC: Igor Stravinsky (1944)

COSTUMES: Karinska

LIGHTING: Ronald Bates

PREMIERE: 22 June 1972 (Stravinsky Festival)

CAST: Patricia McBride, Jean-Pierre Bonnefous; 6 female demi-soloists; 12 women

OTHER CASTS: Merrill Ashley, Peter Martins

In *Scènes de Ballet*, Stravinsky produced a prototype ballet score that did not allude to any ballet in particular. He wrote, "This music is patterned after the forms of the classical dance, free of any given literary or dramatic argument." [1] The score contains the following indications: Introduction: Andante; Danses (corps de ballet): Moderato; Variation (ballerina): Con moto; Pantomime: Lento, Andantino, Più Mosso; Pas de Deux: Adagio; Pantomime: Agitato ma tempo giusto; Variation (dancer): Risoluto; Variation (ballerina): Andantino; Danses (corps de ballet): Con moto; Apothéose: Poco meno mosso.

Taras himself felt that the music was "a digest version of a romantic ballet." To flesh out this non-scenario, Taras set his ballet in an unreal woodland and populated it with chiffon-clad creatures who look indigenous. Frustratingly, he hinted at emotions and situations that did not materialize. Thus, happy meetings, sad partings, ominous warnings, and the like were presented, without, however, resolution or development (some reviewers saw touches of *Giselle, Swan Lake,* or *Sylphide*—but this seems a bit of an overreaction to the quasi-narrative aspects of the work). Choreographically, the ballet was highly skillful; Taras was particularly adept at handling groups. In character and point of view it was weak— wrote Barnes, "Taras creates classic choreography with an enviable grace and ease, but grace and ease are all there is" [2]—but in atmosphere and movement invention, it was compelling.

Wrote McDonagh, "Set in a moonlit glade of bare trees with a spooky glamour to them. Six girls are seen dancing in the foreground, seemingly unconcerned with their vaguely old setting and enjoying themselves for the sheer pleasure of being there. Subsequently they are joined by two groups of other girls, similarly clothed in light flowing dresses, participating in the same mysterious celebration. It is like a witches' sabbath without malice, or a macabre meeting of campfire girls, waiting for something or someone.

"The something and the reason for the ballet is the encounter in this romantic glade of McBride and Bonnefous. The remainder of the ballet is an extended pas de deux for them with interludes of dancing by the corps girls, who function as decorative guardians of McBride. Their patterns and formations are very tasteful and pretty and the dancing of the lead couple is wonderfully light and strong. The core of the ballet is in the flow and athletic vigor of their partnership. It is a work of clear limits but within them exerts an assured charm. . . .

"Though not working with the most original of situations, Taras has crafted a ballet that has an eerie energy and nicely defined work for the corps in its decorous defense of McBride. It is her special grace to irradiate the stage with an aura of excitement through the tasteful impetuousness of her entrances. Taras has wisely provided her with lots of opportunities to dash to and from the pursuing Bonnefous to allow that vitality to be felt. It works well for the ballet, and the patterns for the corps frame and contain it skillfully." [3]

DUO CONCERTANT

DUO CONCERTANT

CHOREOGRAPHY: George Balanchine

MUSIC: Igor Stravinsky (1939; for violin and piano)

LIGHTING: Ronald Bates

PREMIERE: 22 June 1972 (Stravinsky Festival)

SOLOISTS: Lamar Alsop (violin), Gordon Boelzner (piano)

CAST: Kay Mazzo, Peter Martins

I. Cantilène
II. Eclogue I
III. Eclogue II
IV. Gigue
V. Dithyrambe

Duo Concertant. Gordon Boelzner (piano), Lamar Alsop (violin), Peter Martins, Kay Mazzo. (*Photo Fred Fehl.*)

Duo Concertant was seen as the essence of what the Festival was all about: it was not only a close union of dance with music, dancers with musicians (pianist and violinist were on the stage); here, the music actually penetrated the dancing, and did not merely accompany it: the dancers stood still at times and visibly listened. And in its intimacy, the ballet recalled the very personal nature of the fifty-year collaboration that the festival both celebrated and prolonged.

It was also seen as a ballet "about" putting a dance together (captured beautifully in a remarkable series of Swope photographs showing Balanchine demonstrating with one partner, then the other): when the dancers begin, she moves first only her arms, then only her legs; he moves only his arms, then only his legs. Though clearly a most tender love duet, there is often little difference between the male and female steps (except when he supports her); only the look is different— she small and "lost," he protective. The dance seems both intensely felt and theatrically calculated: an artful casualness— and moody response—is affected within a clearly structured format. And the "heavy," passionate lighting scheme— spotlights, blue tints—is at odds with the small-scale, frolicsome movement and the playfulness of the performers. Duo Concertant has scratchy, curt, dissonant moments and seems constantly to be strain-

ing at its imposed limitations; yet its lasting impression is one of sweetest beauty.

The choreography is unusual, with few, if any "dance steps." Rather, there are articulated segments in a movement design. Balanchine provided the elegant, small-boned, wistful Mazzo with her most fitting role. As for Martins, Gellen wrote: "Balanchine has understood that there is another part of [him] that is not Apollo, not that large, glamor-boy, space-filling dancer. He has given him steps and movements that are very small, and he has made Martins articulate in a way we have never seen before. Balanchine has made him a role that lets him be fast and delicate, and he is brilliant." [1]

Porter wrote, "In Stravinsky's career, Duo Concertant followed directly on the Violin Concerto and continued, with chamber forces, that vein of rhythmicized lyricism. Formally, Balanchine's Duo Concertant is a different sort of work: not so much a fusion with the score as a commentary on it—and perhaps also a description, unusually frank and confiding, of his way of assembling a ballet. To the first movement, the dancers just listen. In the second, they try out some steps. He invites her to initiate moves to the third, follows her lead, tries her ideas, modifies them, checks her once, and, after her gentle insistence, checks her again with courteous determination to impose his own pattern. (Something similar has happened between the instrumentalists.) Music akin to Violin Concerto has led to some movements, in this different context, recalling the manner of their pas de

deux in that ballet. In the final Dithyrambe, it is as if some new spell has been cast. The light fades. The dancers disappear, are found again. Some phrases can take visual shape, others are left to the musicians alone. It is a small ballet that is mysterious, satisfying, and perfect." [2]

Hering: "Had the dancers wandered accidentally into a music rehearsal and decided to stay for a while? As the violin took over, they experimented with some lifts and some snakey arm patterns. They became more serious about the music and about each other as their arms interlocked or as they watched each other in solos. Then they were transfixed by the music. They were no longer dancers but symbols of a force deeper and more impersonal. Martins stood in the semi-dark and watched Mazzo as her face was caught in a circle of light. He came forward. She offered her hand. It became lost in his two hands and then tenderly, reverently, he turned one of her hands around so that the fingers faced upward. He kissed the back of her hand. Later in the finale, the entire sequence was repeated. I am certain that in the context of the Festival, this vulnerable gesture must have been as touching and as serious in its attitude about art as in the meeting of fingers in *Apollo.*" [3]

Gellen: "If *Symphony in Three Movements* was the most explosive new ballet of the Festival, *Duo Concertant* was the most moving. It's difficult to write about this pas de deux. It made me apprehensive at first—oh, another lurking-around-the-piano ballet. But then I was really swept away as this grave and sweet work unfolded. The two dancers begin and the style is modern, with chopped rhythms, stops and starts. They pause to listen once again.

"It doesn't really matter if you believe the pretext involved. As a piece of theater it has breathtaking invention, for your attention is forced away from the dancers to the musicians. I don't think [Balanchine] wants us to 'believe' in the spontaneity of the action as much as he wants to force us into an awareness of the sound. Musicality in choreography, or rather, the lack of it, is a complex matter. I think most people are unaware or unobservant of the way ballet coexists with music. It seems that music is taken for granted unless it obtrudes. Balanchine has made it obtrude on purpose.

"The closing section takes place on a darkened stage with only a harsh circle of spotlight. Everything is very still, and Mazzo stretches out her arms into the darkness. The dancers touch, briefly. They don't so much dance as just make contact. Martins slides away. She makes a gesture of despair. Then he is alone in the light and finally they are together in an embrace that is part reverence, part adolescent romanticism. I wept, I think." [4]

Goldner: "Watching them listen is a theatrical experience in itself. Their faces speak a multitude of unknown thoughts, but the intensity and sweet concentration with which they listen suggest that the notes are running through their bodies. Finally, they are moved to dance. At first they stick closely to the music's beat, almost 'conducting' it with arms and legs; torsos are still.

Duo Concertant. **Kay Mazzo, Peter Martins.** (*Photo Martha Swope.*)

"Becoming more free, the dance turns into a melting duet, each phrase winding down on slightly bent knees, as in a whisper. They dance with seeming spontaneity. Even when Balanchine arranges an unusual means of partnering—as when he scoops her from the floor holding only the underside of her thigh—the movement spins off them with utter simplicity and naturalness. In other sections, they occasionally stop dancing to listen. At those times, Martins firmly takes hold of her hand or slips his arm around her waist. She is shy, but the music pleases her and so does he. She does not move away. They listen in repose, arm in arm. . . .

"In the last part dancers and musicians go their separate ways. The stage darkens. A spotlight falls on the pianist and violinist. Another one lights a small area in which the dancers will play out their final drama. Mazzo places her arm in the light, so that it seems to exist independently of her body. Martins hastens to the arm and links his with it. He then embraces her, sinks to his knees, and feels her face with his hands. She steps out of the light; then he does. She comes back and again extends her arm into the light. He rushes back, kisses the back of her hand with hushed passion, and sinks to the floor like a supplicant before a goddess. The jump from youthful hand-clasping to ceremonial hand-kissing is brazen for its staginess and unexpectedness. But out of that staginess come certain truths; in fact, the ending is an exquisite confession of them. It intimates that music transports Balanchine into a fantasy experience. It declares that to Balanchine the female dancer is an image of love, a Muse-ballerina who inspires but is unreachable. The worshiper is the male, whose fate is to be indelibly inspired, possessed but not possessing. It is the story of Balanchine's art." [5]

THE SONG OF THE NIGHTINGALE

CHOREOGRAPHY: John Taras

MUSIC: Igor Stravinsky (*Song of the Nightingale,* symphonic poem for orchestra in three parts, 1917; adapted from the 1913 opera)

COSTUMES, PROPS: Rouben Ter-Arutunian

LIGHTING: Ronald Bates

PREMIERE: 22 June 1972 (Stravinsky Festival)

CAST: *Nightingale,* Gelsey Kirkland; *Mechanical Nightingale,* Elise Flagg; *Emperor,* Francisco Moncion; *Death,* Penny Dudleston; *Fisherman,* Peter Naumann; *Members of the Court,* 14 women, 20 men; *Japanese Ambassadors,* 4 men

Nightingale also danced by Elise Flagg

The inclusion of *Song of the Nightingale* in the festival sounded a note for history. It was one of the earlier scores presented, but, more than that, like *Firebird* it harked back to another era of the ballet (the title roles in both were originally danced by Karsavina). In addition, as his first professional work to Stravinsky's music (he had created a student composition to *Pulcinella* in 1920), Balanchine's 1925 dances to the *Nightingale* score, though not a collaboration, may be considered the beginning of the illustrious partnership.

In 1972 he was not the choreographer, however. Perhaps once was enough, for the score presents a number of problems. Basically, it calls for a lavish costume parade in which a complicated story has to unfold in a limited amount of time. And despite the fact that this is clearly a fairy-tale story and setting, the music is not sweet to the ear, and the ballet is essentially "downbeat." Stravinsky appended the following synopsis to his piano reduction (the quotes are from Hans Christian Andersen):

"1. *The Fête in the Emperor of China's Palace.* In honour of the Nightingale that sang so sweetly 'the palace was festively adorned. The walls and the flooring, which were of porcelain, gleamed in the rays of thousands of golden lamps. The most glorious flowers, which could ring clearly, had been placed in the passages. There was a running to and fro, and a thorough draught, so that all the bells rang loudly. . . .' The Nightingale is placed on a golden perch; and a CHINESE MARCH signals the entrance of the Emperor.

"2. *The Two Nightingales.* 'The Nightingale sang so gloriously that the tears came into the Emperor's eyes. . . .' The

The Song of the Nightingale. **Francisco Moncion as the Emperor (second from left), Gelsey Kirkland.** *(Photo Martha Swope.)*

lackeys and chambermaids reported that they were satisfied too; and that was saying a good deal, for they are the most difficult to please. . . .' Envoys arrive from the Emperor of Japan with the gift of a mechanical nightingale. 'So soon as the artificial bird was wound up, he could sing a piece, and then his tail moved up and down, and shone with silver and gold. . . . He had just as much success as the real one, and then it was much handsomer to look at. . . . But where was the living Nightingale? No one had noticed that it had flown away out of the open window. . . .' The fisherman is heard out-of-doors, singing for joy because his friend has returned.

"3. *Illness and Recovery of the Emperor of China.* 'The poor Emperor could scarcely breathe. He opened his eyes and saw that it was Death who sat upon his chest, and had put on his golden crown, and held in one hand the Emperor's sword, and in the other his beautiful banner. And all around, from among the folds of the splendid velvet curtains, strange heads peered forth . . . these were all the Emperor's bad and good deeds. . . . They told him so much that the perspiration ran from his forehead.' The mechanical bird refused to sing. Then the little live Nightingale was heard singing outside the window. 'And as it sang the spectres grew paler and paler. . . . Even

Death listened and said, "Go on, little Nightingale, go on!" . . . And Death gave up each of its treasures for a song . . . and floated out at the window in the form of a cold white mist. . . . The Emperor fell into a sweet slumber. The sun shone upon him through the window when he awoke refreshed and restored.'

"FUNERAL MARCH. 'The courtiers came in to look at their dead Emperor, and—yes, there they stood astounded, and the Emperor said "Good morning!" ' Meanwhile, the friendly Nightingale has flown back to the fisherman who is heard singing his song once more." [1]

Taras: "It has the same problem that most Stravinsky story ballets have—there's never enough time to tell the story, not everything is taken care of, and the story is not very satisfactory. You have to rush all the time (originally the same events were contained within a whole opera). Stravinsky does not really follow the Andersen—I looked at that. For a time, there was talk about doing a combination of the ballet and the opera, to make it more important. I liked the look of it. The big skirts for the men gave a style to their movements. The costumes for the Nightingale was a problem, because nightingales are not pretty birds—drab and ugly. (Karsavina wore a Greek tunic when she did it!) Balanchine said he

had set Markova all sorts of air turns and things in his version. I gave Gelsey very difficult steps, but, of course, she could do anything. I just wish I'd had more music. The story is very hard to express. The Nightingale represents two conflicts—between the real and the fake bird, and between life and death. There are really two dramas. The mechanical bird, for example, is almost unimportant, except to give the real nightingale an excuse to escape."

A major criticism was that the story was not clearly told (and there were no program notes to help out). Mainly, however, it was felt that no one could have done much, balletically, with the material at hand.

Wrote Barnes, "This is a ballet that has suffered many versions. The costumes, almost all of them primary shades of arrogance, are exquisite. The dance moves with finesse through the landscape of its style. Yet even this is finally insufficient. I was perfectly happy to see this work, yet had it not been part of this grandiosely comprehensive Stravinsky retrospective I would have been even more disappointed by its blandness. The theme—frankly a difficult one to handle—all but disappeared in an abstraction that the graces of the choreography could hardly justify. The work has a certain credibility, [and] unquestionably it uses Kirkland with a kind of resourceful humor." [2] After the ballet's performance during the following season, Barnes wrote further: "I doubt whether the ballet's insubstantial charms will prove enduring in the repertory. There are some evanescent things that should be allowed to evanesce." [3]

Gellen: "This kind of work just isn't possible any more. All that costuming, all that bejeweled nonsense, end up as just so much time filled in. Taras has set this fragile tale in a kind of fractured narrative style that unfortunately wasn't even reasonably clear. The range of color was fantastic, [but] Kirkland's costume in gray and light nudes tended [to make her] disappear on stage. Obviously a heavy point was being made about the virtues of the pure and perfect power of nature vs. the useless, sterile power of artifice. I enjoyed the St. Christopher section, where the nightingale is borne across on the back of a loinclothed Fisherman with a staff, still blowing bubbles." [4]

Clearly, the ballet served its purpose in the context of the festival.

PIANO-RAG-MUSIC

CHOREOGRAPHY: Todd Bolender

MUSIC: Igor Stravinsky (1919; for solo piano)

COSTUMES: Stanley Simmons

LIGHTING: Ronald Bates

PREMIERE: 23 June 1972 (Stravinsky Festival)

PIANO: Madeleine Malraux

CAST: Gloria Govrin, John Clifford

A "jeu d'esprit" about a man and a woman who are very competitive, says Bolender, and of quite disparate sizes. A one-joke number not intended for long life.

Stravinsky said that in the music he was "stressing the percussion possibilities of the piano." The piece was dedicated to Arthur Rubinstein.

Wrote Barnes, "It is a slight joke about a large ballerina and her small partner. The choreography is bright and breezy. Its humor lies largely, of course, in the discrepancy in his dancers' sizes, but there are some bright passages, such as when Clifford gets involved in a series of neck locks, and his acrobatic fancy of jumping over Govrin's surprised body." [1]

Gale: "The rhythmic violence of the music emerges from a rearrangement of jazz elements that make for turbulence. The male-female roles are intentionally reversed. Both dancers have a natural bent for jazz." [2]

ODE

CHOREOGRAPHY: Lorca Massine

MUSIC: Igor Stravinsky (1943)

LIGHTING: Ronald Bates

PREMIERE: 23 June 1972 (Stravinsky Festival)

CAST: Colleen Neary, Christine Redpath, Robert Maiorano, Earle Sieveling; 3 women, 3 men

Ode was Massine's final work for the Company, at least as resident member. His tenure had been brief. Imported as a soloist, he had danced few roles, and his three ballets were not very well received, with the exception of *Four Last Songs*, which drew mixed reviews. More importantly, his approach to choreography (and use of music) was completely foreign to the style and sensibility of the Company. He did not fit.

In *Ode* he was working in the same impressionistic manner that characterized his earlier ballets. Gellen observed that "Massine continues to experiment with a kind of personal, private musicality that just leaves me out. I'm sure that Rupert Brooke would have loved it: strange voices in the trees and wondrous depressive sunsets. His *Ode* is another one of those random, Romantic pieces that fills the stage with deeply meaningful little moments of passion, pain, and panic, but although the style is not offensive, in this piece as in his others he fragments the stage in a way that makes the piece unseeable. There are pockets of space in which many groups of dancers work simultaneously, but each group is involved in some very heavy stuff, so that you are uncomfortably aware that you should be seeing it all even though you know you can't. For me at least, this produces a kind of frustration that makes me angry. This type of thing is properly referred to as self-indulgent. Are audiences necessary?" [1]

Barnes was slightly more encouraging: "Has its statuesque moments of sculptural identity, moments out of time when, Béjart-like, the choreographer ignores the music and creates a certain dramatic effect. This is perhaps the best thing we have seen from Massine, but there is a lack of vital energy here." [2]

Robert Craft honored the work at its premiere by his presence as conductor, but it did not remain in the repertory.

DUMBARTON OAKS

CHOREOGRAPHY: Jerome Robbins

MUSIC: Igor Stravinsky (Concerto in E-flat for chamber orchestra, 1938)

COSTUMES: Patricia Zipprodt

LIGHTING: Ronald Bates

PREMIERE: 23 June 1972 (Stravinsky Festival)

CAST: Allegra Kent, Anthony Blum; 6 couples

Dumbarton Oaks. Anthony Blum, Allegra Kent. (*Photo Martha Swope.*)

OTHER CASTS: Christine Redpath, Jean-Pierre Bonnefous

Dumbarton Oaks was a work in search of a personality. Says Kent, "I couldn't find anything to latch on to, and I suspect Jerry couldn't, either." It was given in "tennis, anyone?" 1920s sporting outfits; later, it was given in a ballet studio setting; finally, it settled on tennis.

Theatrically speaking, it didn't have a "point." But in its details, its dance invention, it was full of grace and cleverness. Kent's duet was "ravishing." Said Barnes, "A total charmer, full of the subtlest reverberations, matching happily with the music and taking the structure of the score and finding the comedy that lurks dangerously—as so often with Stravinsky—beneath the surface. Balanchine is subjective with Stravinsky; Robbins is objective. Balanchine feels these scores; Robbins observes them. [In this] tennis party, everyone says 'Yes, Yes, Nanette.' Robbins laughs at tennis players, Busby Berkeley chorus lines, Tchaikovsky's dance of the Little Swans, and so much else. It is all twenties tea-and-tennis campery but done with such sensibility and such profound understanding of what this music is all about." [1]

Jowitt: "Robbins's setting surprised everyone—horrified some—with its irreverent treatment of the music. The curtain went up on an elegantly trellised garden tennis court. The corps of six-and-six skipped on, looking ready to do *The Boyfriend*, but with a sweetness and modesty that kept the ballet from being just another clever twenties parody. Robbins shaped the ensemble passages into meticulous unison phalanxes with an occasional impetuous solo twist, or clear-cut antiphonal contests between the sexes. There were even a couple of high-kicking chorus lines. Kent and Blum circled the stage in a light busy-footed couple dance full of silly, suddenly-we're-in-love charm, which ended with a sportsmanlike handshake and a retrieval of tennis rackets.

"For their second entrance, the men and women put on soft-heeled shoes so that they could patter out intrepid little rhythms, emphasizing crannies in Stravinsky that we might have missed. I sometimes feel that Balanchine is excited mainly by creating, but Robbins, I think, is excited by the process of direction, by being able to make a step look a certain

way. The dancers looked especially stylish, well-rehearsed, and—considering the idea of the piece—remarkably free from overt camp or aggressive performing." [2]

Gellen: "Many seemed to find the mood and style of the piece peculiar in view of the nature of the music. That didn't bother me in the least. But somehow the whole thing was terribly trivial and thin. The work is set as a kind of tennis/tea-dance amidst paper lanterns and rattan lawn furniture. The time is not very clear, although the dancers are dressed in flapper and jelly-bean outfits. The corps work has chorus-line kicks to the audience and Charleston steps and a lot of flirtatious half-comedy routines. But Robbins is slumming and it never jells. It isn't funny enough, or outrageous enough, or anything enough." [3]

Says Kent, "The costume was divine."

PULCINELLA

CHOREOGRAPHY: George Balanchine and Jerome Robbins

MUSIC: Igor Stravinsky (1919–20)

COSTUMES, DÉCOR: Eugene Berman

LIGHTING: Ronald Bates

PREMIERE: 23 June 1972 (Stravinsky Festival)

SINGERS: Elaine Bonazzi (soprano), Robert White (tenor), William Metcalf (bass)

CAST: *Pulcinella*, Edward Villella; *Girl*,

Violette Verdy; *Pulcinella's Father*, Michael Arshansky; *Devil*, Francisco Moncion, Shaun O'Brien; *Beggars*, George Balanchine, Jerome Robbins; *Concubines*, 2 men; *2 Policemen*; *Little Boy*; *6 Musicians*; *Townspeople*, 7 women, 5 men; *Pulcinellas*, Deni Lamont, Robert Weiss, 10 men, 12 children

OTHER CASTS: *Girl*, Carol Sumner; *Devil*, John Clifford; *Father*, O'Brien

Pulcinella, the big "production number" of the Festival, had so many versions that the Company choreologist gave up trying to notate it.* (From the look of the opening-night performance and the many revisions that were later made, it was clear that the ballet was still in rehearsal when it was first presented.) Broadly speaking, however, the story line remained constant. Robbins elaborates: "The story is mostly George's. His Pulcinella combines the traditional commedia dell'arte character with Goethe's *Faust*. He's a terrible, stupid man with a marvelous voracity for life. He steals and gives his loot away. He beats up people and becomes a victim. He has a great instinct for survival."

---

* The Company had a resident choreologist (dance notator) for only a few years. From time to time, for a particularly difficult ballet, a choreologist has been hired, but in addition to the expense and time this requires—extra rehearsals are necessary—there is a practical difficulty: very few can decipher the score. Moreover, like music notation, dance notation (in which symbols are equivalent to movements) cannot give a very precise notion of dynamics. For this, videotape or film is helpful (the Company has some videotapes, for rehearsal purposes only).

Pulcinella. **Violette Verdy, Edward Villella (right).** (*Photo Fred Fehl.*)

Pulcinella. **Left:** **The Spaghetti Orgy.** *(Photo Fred Fehl.)* **Right:** **Edward Villella, Carol Sumner.** *(Photo Martha Swope.)*

Balanchine: "In the Punch-and-Judy shows I saw as a child, the Devil always took Punch—or Pulcinella—to Hell at the end for his bad behavior. In our version, Pulcinella dies at the *beginning* and then sells his soul to the Devil in order to be resurrected. When the Devil tries to make him live up to the contract, he tries all sorts of tricks to keep from going to Hell. Finally, Pulcinella and his friends pretend to hang the Devil, and force him to tear up the contract. We're using the characters but not the plot of the original Diaghilev production. The story is funny, a bit dirty, and quite cruel—more like the real commedia dell'arte plots of the early sixteenth century." [1] Goldner augmented this sketch with details:

"Pulcinella has died. His corpse (skeleton) is borne by his friends, who are so busy weeping crocodile tears over death that they abandon the coffin, which then must proceed on its own (magical) way to the grave. No sooner is the skeleton dumped into the casket than the Devil appears. The skeletal arm signs the contract, the bones ascend from the casket, and out pops the resurrected Pulcinella, swinging his arms like the winning champ and taking bows for his miraculous performance. He resumes his career of mockery, petty crime, and debauchery, in the latter assisted by two Concubines (men in drag) sent by the Devil. Later, the Devil comes to collect the rent, threatening Pulcinella with a vision of his second funeral. Pulcinella, naturally, is recalcitrant. Despite the scorn Pulcinella heaps upon his sweetheart, she has a plan to save him from death. She thrusts a young, golden-haired boy in front of the Devil. He lasciviously follows the decoy

and Pulcinella is off the hook. He thanks the girl with a kick and celebrates his new lease on life with a spaghetti orgy. The Devil, after doing a striptease around the spaghetti pot, is unmasked (rather, untailed) and thrown into the pot. Celebration by dancing follows." [2]

This does not cover *all* of the action. As the program explained, this was not the story used by Massine in the original ballet for Diaghilev. (Among other things, Balanchine felt that Picasso had "taken over" that one.) The ballet was a collaborative effort ("Two people work faster than one," said Balanchine, during the frantic preparations for the festival). Says Robbins of their working together: "The *Pulcinella* collaboration was somewhat similar to *Jones Beach*, except that I worked on whole sections, and he did other whole sections. I did a variation, he did the second variation; the finale I think we did together—he did some of the steps and I did some of the steps. The dance we performed together he did. He originally did the theme of Violette's variation, and I think I did the second two variations on it. I did most of the boys' group dances.

"Every ballet I do with George is essentially George's conception; I am really more of an assistant than a cochoreographer. It's his program, he knows where he wants to go, although occasionally he would ask me what we should do here or there. It was his idea to do the spaghetti—which is delightful. He gave me that whole section, saying only that here they do a show and then there should be a chase. That's all he'd say—so I did a show and then a chase. When I work with him, I try absolutely to under-

stand what it is he wants and what he's after and to do that. I only try to fulfill myself as an extension of him."

The production was elaborate. Balanchine had requested from Berman lavish costumes and sets (with many moving pieces, to change scenes) in the style of the younger Tiepolo's Puncinello drawings. The music, originally written as a ballet, required three singers (whose songs, randomly selected from Neapolitan sources, bear no relationship to any plot).

It was remarked that *Pulcinella* was directed, not choreographed. There was little "ballet dancing" in it, with the exception of the final variations and a long solo for Verdy, but plenty of gutsy movement. The ballet was, in fact, a series of broadly played mime scenes.

Problems began as the scenery and costumes, beautiful as they were, appeared to overwhelm the dancers. Although Villella received great praise for his interpretation, it was clear that behind his half-mask and huge pantaloons much was being lost. Then, the "story line" was quite unclear, if not "impossible to follow." The score is lengthy; the ballet, with its huge cast, started to get out of hand; there was a great deal of running, chasing, mugging to no discernible end.

The chief difficulty, perhaps, was that the work was so clearly unfinished and bore the marks of a slapdash creation. Wrote Goldner, "There is no telling what it will evolve into." [3] Gellen: "We'll have to wait a few seasons and then maybe its intentions will be clearer." [4]

Wrote Barnes, "[Balanchine and Robbins] have decided to concentrate on the style of the ballet rather than to become lost in its content, and have sought to re-create the entire scurrilous, nose-thumbing, urchin spirit of commedia dell'arte. Berman has designed the ballet with chic, gusto, and authenticity. At times he goes too far, but for the most part he has caught the right rapscallion Bergamasque spirit. So, too, does the choreography, which is nervy and boisterous. The ballet reminds me of *Tyl Ulenspiegel*, in both the spurting vigorousness of its conception and also in the picaresque development of its story. Villella is raffish, Rabelaisian, and altogether delightful. How long this will wear outside the Festival is open to doubt. . . . On second sight, [Villella, Verdy, Berman are] not enough. Balanchine and Robbins have not provided the ballet with any proper story line, and the choreographic style has more energy than taste." [5]

Jowitt: "A great sloppy, bawdy concoction. There seemed to be hundreds of Pulcinellas, roistering around in red caps, white floppy suits, beaked-nosed masks. Villella lumbered splendidly. The escapades appeared to involve a welching on a contract with the Devil (Moncion) who kept appearing in drag (O'Brien) but with horns showing. Verdy appeared as a kickable peasant girl and reappeared later looking very spicy and did a long sprightly solo. I liked a funeral procession of pall-bearing Pulcinellas who abandoned their job by twos and threes, returning just before the corpse crashed to the ground. I also like an insane surfeit of spaghetti that threatened to cover the stage. Oh, and in the middle of an elaborate final celebration, Robbins and Balanchine marched on as two beggars, pretended to thwack each other with big sticks, did a fumbly dance, and generally thrilled the fans." [6]

Gellen: "A wildly disorganized work with lots of people, lots of costumes, and lots of sets that didn't make too much sense. I'm confident that this piece will go through a lot of rethinking and see a history of changes." [7]

It has, including a new pas de deux, but the basic problems remain. The ballet has been filmed for television (as yet unreleased in the United States), and the use of close-ups and various "angle" shots, usually so distracting in the filming of dance, may work in its favor by clarifying the story line, making the pantomime more legible, and reducing the sense of clutter.

An additional point was raised by Goldner: Was this merely a series of amusing skits, or something more? "Vision is the first problem in need of resolve. Is Pulcinella to be dark comedy or a frolic?" [8] Says Verdy, "I think he put into the libretto a great many of his own philosophical conclusions about the great issues of life—good, bad, death, evil, devil, etc." Goldner mentioned "the possibility of reading into the ballet an allegorical statement about the Stravinsky Festival and a revolt against solemnity." [9]

As usual, some of Balanchine's finest moments have been lost—those occurring in rehearsal when he was demonstrating the part for Villella. Says Verdy, "One day I was there watching with Lincoln Kirstein. We turned to each other, practically with tears in our eyes because it was so touching. I said, 'It's incredible—it's everything that one knows about the theater.' And Lincoln said, 'Yes, it's not only the commedia dell'arte that you see there, it's also the French theater and the early modern Russian theater.' All this—everything—went into *Pulcinella*." Some of the moments have been preserved by Swope in a splendid series of photographs.*

CHORAL VARIATIONS ON BACH'S "VOM HIMMEL HOCH"

CHOREOGRAPHY: George Balanchine

MUSIC: Igor Stravinsky (for mixed chorus and orchestra, 1956; variations on Bach's treatment of "Vom Himmel Hocn" in his *Christmas Oratorio* [1734] and his *Canonic Variations on "Vom Himmel Hoch"* for organ [1748])

DÉCOR: Rouben Ter-Arutunian

LIGHTING: Ronald Bates

PREMIERE: 25 June 1972 (Stravinsky Festival)

CHORUS: Gregg Smith Singers

CAST: Karin von Aroldingen, Melissa Hayden, Sara Leland, Violette Verdy, Anthony Blum, Peter Martins; 15 women, 13 men; 12 children

* Reproduced in Goldner, *Stravinsky Festival*, and Taper, *Balanchine*.

Choral Variations on Bach's "Vom Himmel hoch." Balanchine with children at rehearsal. (*Photo Michael Avedon.*)

A ceremonial piece, given once, referred to by Kirstein as a "grand défilé" of several generations of dancers, ranging from Hayden, the Company's senior ballerina, to little girls who were students at the School. It echoed, in a sense, the aging Bach's parade of his musical tools (his canonic variations were written as a demonstration piece to gain admission to a "Society of Musical Knowledge" about three years before his death). The dancers were all in white; the stage was decorated with "an arrangement of shining tubes, suggesting the vaulting architecture of organ pipes."

Wrote Barnes: "To this heavily Stravinsky-accented Bach, the dancers came together for a formal and uncluttered suite of dances." [1]

Goldner: "The adults are assembled around the perimeters of the stage and the children pose in the middle. First the children do port de bras. When they are finished they stay in place and Leland dances among them. Her steps are basic exercises with slight twists, and her dance is like an improvisation at the barre. Then Hayden dances. Her steps are also simple—échappés, bourrées, entrechats, and passés. But the musical accents are catchier, and one of the combinations (échappés with port de bras) is a veritable tonguetwister for feet. Verdy and Blum [then] cover the ground in soft lunges and move in mostly éffacé, or an open position. The next duet, for von Aroldingen and Martins, covers the most ground but is not as spacious as the preceding one. In fact, it is relatively convoluted and so seems out of place. Now the ballet gathers and swells. The entire cast weaves its way around the stage. It is a giant processional.

"*Vom Himmel Hoch* is didactic in its staging and choice of steps and personnel. It is self-consciously pristine, the only Balanchine ballet in which dancers stand on stage without moving. Presence is enough. Tribute is writ large. Of course, Balanchine has been showing us the past/present all the time, but in *Vom Himmel Hoch* he wanted to make a speech about it and wanted his dancers literally to bow before the principle. [The ballet] is simple and beautiful. When the procession begins, it is like the faint rumblings before the sky opens." [2]

The piece ends, wrote Gellen, with "a kind of reel and a final 'grand reverence.'" Homage was in the air.

REQUIEM CANTICLES (II)

CHOREOGRAPHY: Jerome Robbins

MUSIC: Igor Stravinsky (1966; for contralto, bass, chorus, and orchestra)

LIGHTING: Ronald Bates

PREMIERE: 25 June 1972 (Stravinsky Festival)

SINGERS: Elaine Bonazzi (contralto), William Metcalf (bass), chorus

CAST: Merrill Ashley, Susan Hendl; Robert Maiorano, Bruce Wells; 7 women, 8 men

Requiem Canticles, clearly relevant to the occasion (Stravinsky called it a "celebration of death"), was Stravinsky's last major composition. Balanchine had used the same music for a memorial to Martin Luther King, which received a single performance, in 1968. When the idea of the Stravinsky Festival was still forming, Robbins expressed immediate interest in the score. The work was performed once, on the last evening of the festival, and in all probability will not be seen again (although it is in the repertory of England's Royal Ballet).

"Stark" and "strong" were the words most often used to characterize Robbins's treatment of the music. Wrote Barnes: "Seemed to be an attempt to formalize grief. It was cool, but at once unemotional and agonized. It seemed a distillation from many choreographic sources—many of Robbins's own ballets and perhaps shades of Tudor's *Dark Elegies* and Balanchine's *Ivesiana*. The ensemble, dressed in black leotards, entered to the urgent, rushing music. They grouped across the stage in stylized pain, with one arm lurched forward and the hand fluttering with an insectile anguish. The soloists came in dancing to the music's slower cross rhythm. It was remarkable how well Robbins realized this almost abstract and transfigured view of death. From its mo-

ments of mechanized frenzy, to the softer graver dancing of the soloists, to the flickering hands, clenching and unclenching in agonized unison, right to the final silent shouts of grief that seemed like the tears on a stone monument, Robbins depicted an anatomy of loss and an anguish controlled with an objective artist's eye." [1]

Lewis: "Robbins has created a taut work that gains power from the alternation of stasis and quivering, convulsive movement." [2]

Gellen: "The piece is all solid grieving and no corpse. Well managed and clever. It has a solid and consistently pleasing shade. But for all its clarity, it is empty at the center." [3]

Some felt the treatment was overwrought. Kisselgoff mentioned "pretentious pieties." [4]

Wrote Goldner: "Self-conscious attempts at gravity and ritualism. Most of the movements and patterns are mannered and manipulative. For example, when the last chimes of the score ring, the dancers huddle and look soulfully outward and upward. In exact time to the droplets of music, each moves his head slightly and in a slightly different direction from the others. It is ever so carefully planned and ever so corny." [5]

The Festival closed with *Symphony of Psalms*, a choral work without dancing, in which the dancers (and students) sat on stage, listening.

Requiem Canticles II. (Photo Martha Swope.)

CORTÈGE HONGROIS

CHOREOGRAPHY: George Balanchine

MUSIC: Alexander Glazounov (from *Raymonda*, 1898)

COSTUMES, DÉCOR: Rouben Ter-Arutunian

LIGHTING: Ronald Bates

PREMIERE: 17 May 1973 (gala benefit preview, 16 May 1973)

CAST: Melissa Hayden and Jacques d'Amboise (classical); Karin von Aroldingen and Jean-Pierre Bonnefous (character); 16 couples

Czardas: von Aroldingen, Bonnefous
Pas de Quatre: 4 women
Variation I: Colleen Neary
Variation II: 4 men
Variation III: Merrill Ashley
Pas de Deux (with solos): Hayden, d'Amboise

OTHER CASTS: *Classical,* Suzanne Farrell, Kay Mazzo, Patricia McBride; Bonnefous, John Clifford, Peter Martins, Peter Schaufuss; *Character,* Bart Cook

A "grand, imperial farewell" to the Company's senior ballerina, Melissa Hayden, who was a charter member of the organization and probably the first Balanchine principal (with the exception of Eglevsky) to stop dancing because of

age. (Her contemporaries from the Company's "first generation"—Tallchief, Wilde, Adams, Reed, Jillana, Marie-Jeanne—had all retired early for other reasons.) Only d'Amboise could match her tenure, and he had not been dancing leading parts the entire time.

Hayden had a native store of temperament and energy; articulation and refinement had come later. It was in the late fifties that she began to be recognized as exceptional even with Balanchine's rarified circle of exceptional dancers, an outstanding artist in both dramatic and classical roles. In a company most of whose principal dancers were in their twenties, she had long been unique; in a company of "no stars," a true star. At the age of fifty she decided "Why not stop before you begin making excuses? Why not stop when you're still enjoying everything?"

As a farewell present, Balanchine gave Hayden a ballet. "Conceived in the late style of Petipa," (according to the program), this *corteggio,* or courtly parade, of both classical and character dances was said to contain what Balanchine and his Imperial School colleagues Danilova and Doubrovska remembered of the original *Raymonda.* As always, there was much choreography of Balanchine's own, including a ballerina solo that he lifted intact from one of his previous ballets, *Pas de Dix,* based on, but much more difficult than, the original Russian. (Sexy, sultry, "Oriental," and brilliant, it was eminently suited to Hayden, although its familiarity to New York audiences somewhat muted its effect as a personal tribute to her.) Although properly ceremonial and festive,

Cortège Hongrois. Above: Jean-Pierre Bonnefous (left), Jacques d'Amboise and Melissa Hayden (center), Karin von Aroldingen (right). (*Photo Martha Swope.*) *Below:* Balanchine as flower boy, Melissa Hayden. (*Photo Fred Fehl.*)

the ballet could not be called one of Balanchine's most artistic or interesting; it appeared to be more a series of flashy—yet pallid—entrées than a cohesive work. Costuming was gaudy; and the music, after *Pas de Dix* and *Raymonda Variations,* seemed tired.

Wrote Goldner, "If any choreography could match the sentiment [of the occasion], it would be Balanchine's. But, alas, the choreography per se does not match the thought behind it. This is one of the few Balanchine ballets that does not quite fulfill the grandeur of the music or the Imperial Russian spirit in which it was conceived (perhaps the only one). With the exception of a properly grand Grand Pas de Deux and two delectable variations for fledgling soloists, the choreography verges on the hackneyed.

"Perhaps Balanchine could not come to the music fresh. Performance is another problem. The choreography is laden with Grand Promenades, a style and spirit from which the City Ballet dancers are temperamentally alienated. Too, there are several Hungarian-style dances, but traditional character dancing has never been taught to the dancers." [1]

Siegel: "You don't think of Hayden in the same way as other NYCB stars: she's more assertive, she plays full-out to the audience and for every ounce of excitement that's in the dance. And *Cortège Hongrois* is very like her somehow. It is huge and high style. There was a prodigality, a sense of spectacle about [the "olden"] days that the Company ordinarily renounces, but once he makes up his mind, Balanchine doesn't just dabble in reminiscence. You might easily call *Cortège* downright ostentatious. The work boasts two complete corps de ballet, one classical, led by Hayden and d'Amboise, and one 'character,' led by von Aroldingen and Bonnefous.

"*Cortège* is quite extraordinary in form. After an opening processional, it goes into a giant adagio, except this adagio is done by eight couples simultaneously, without principals. Then there's a big czardas, followed by [variations]. At last, Hayden and d'Amboise appear for their pas de deux, which is very traditional and exacting [lots of shoulder lifts and the full-scale treatment of variation for each, plus coda]. And slowly the dance unwinds, with a big waltz by the ballet corps, another czardas, and a finale by everyone.

"Then comes the apotheosis of all time. After the last break-neck sequence and split-second pose, Hayden stands center stage, gazing into the top balconies of her triumphant past, and the dancers parade by her into new positions of homage. Something dramatic happens with the lighting, and people begin bringing huge baskets of flowers onto the stage. The audience, naturally, goes wild. There is no word for the exquisite vulgarity of the costumes." [2]

Jowitt: "There are a few fine dance passages in the ballet for both corps and soloists. The czardas has the requisite sensual vehemence. There are two wonderful solos, the first full of sly, fast footwork, the second [with] many sudden changes of direction and intricate, questioning little perches. The big pas de deux is decidedly odd. In the beginning, Hayden is very grand, melodramatic almost; d'Amboise supports her in slow twisting balances that yearn toward something in the wings. Her solo is fraught with imperious melancholy. Later she becomes gayer. She looks splendid, regal, a little out of place; it's as if some Bolshoi ballerina had wandered in by mistake and started to do the real *Raymonda*." [3]

Kisselgoff: "Balanchine's least inventive musing on the original version of the Petipa-Glazounov *Raymonda*." [4]

At the benefit preview, the night on which Hayden officially announced her retirement, Mayor Lindsay presented her with the Handel Medallion. At the end of the ballet, as clouds began to form in the background sky, baskets and baskets of flowers were carried on to the stage. Balanchine was among the "flower boys." Says Hayden, "The tribute was glorious—very theatrical. It just goes to show you can shake up an audience despite everything. It was a beautiful gift."

After Hayden was gone, one might have expected that the apotheosis would be cut—there is a slam-bang ending to the dancing, with full company on stage just before it—but no. It has remained, as perhaps one more of Balanchine's numberless tributes to the ballerina, his eternal star. Fittingly, the first to inherit Hayden's role was the Company's prime candidate for new first ballerina, McBride.

An Evening's Waltzes. **Jean-Pierre Bonnefous, Patricia McBride.** (*Photo Martha Swope.*)

AN EVENING'S WALTZES

CHOREOGRAPHY: Jerome Robbins

MUSIC: Sergei Prokofiev (*Suite of Waltzes,* op. 110, 1946 [waltzes from *Cinderella, War and Peace, Lermontov*])

COSTUMES, DÉCOR: Rouben Ter-Arutunian

LIGHTING: Ronald Bates

PREMIERE: 24 May 1973

CAST: *1.* 8 couples; *2.* Patricia McBride, Jean-Pierre Bonnefous, 4 couples; *3.* Christine Redpath,* John Clifford; *4.* Sara Leland, Bart Cook, 4 couples; *5.* Entire cast

OTHER CASTS: *2.* Susan Hendl; Peter Schaufuss, Bruce Wells; *3.* Gelsey Kirkland; Peter Martins, Helgi Tomasson

An *Evening's Waltzes* was a pure-dance piece, full of invention, but despite dazzling individual steps, one which did not have a great deal of impact. The rather noisy, tired-sounding music may have been to blame.

The ballet has some virtuoso partnering, which requires perfect timing, and when properly performed, some of the feats are breathtaking. It thus presents the dancers in a most effective and rather different way. Outstanding are the second waltz, in which McBride and Bonnefous search for each other across a ballroom, and execute some tricky and unconventional turns and lifts (in one, McBride in almost a flying angel position, is supported above Bonnefous's head; her performance was described as "radiant"); the third waltz, with slides across the floor and more acrobatic lifts (in one "Bolshoi" moment the ballerina, parallel to the floor but high above her partner's head, is flipped in the air); and the fourth, mostly runs, unsupported leaps, and compelling large arm movements, which ends in an unusual manner, with the leading dancers

---

* Originally designed for Gelsey Kirkland, who suffered an injury before the opening.

sitting on the floor, arms almost outstretched and palms cupped upward. All the dances are marked by beautifully refined arm and shoulder positions.

The ballet was considered a "useful" rather than a "significant" addition to the Company's repertory. Goldner wrote: "*An Evening's Waltzes* is not an evening long, but the title is descriptive of its essential formality and of a place inhabited by aristocrats, which are what dancers—especially the City Ballet dancers—are.

"Taking a cue from the music, Robbins has attempted to devise what may be called the Dark Waltz. The first and third principal couples especially are remote, while the ensemble is a somewhat menacing element. The accent is down, the high lifts heady. One notices that the drapes hang at a strange tilt. The dancing too is a little off-keel, but not enough. For all its suggestion of hidden danger, the dancing does not really explore that theme as deeply as it might. Musically, Robbins was out to discover, I suspect, the underside of Prokofiev, most notably the waltz from *Cinderella*, which in the context of that ballet certainly has no dark connotations. He heard something new in the music, which is about the best reason for choreographing, and yet the overall effect lacks the depth of feeling that a true musical reinterpretation should evince. In fact, by virtue of a certain staginess and overdramatic lighting, the ballet looks at times like one of those old-fashioned surreal dream sequences in a movie. The dancers were absolutely magnificent." [1]

Barnes: "Perhaps the lack of any strong music inspiration has led to a work that is quite attractive but also somewhat bland. It does not have the strength, vigor, and incisiveness that have characterized Robbins's choreography of late. One interesting thing is that Robbins uses a rather larger ensemble than is his custom, and he uses it with considerable skill. Incidentally, the choreography at times, in its fleetness and energy, recalls the *Scherzo Fantastique*, but the earlier work has a more dazzling quality. This is far more muted." [2]

"What it lacks is depth. Robbins's newest ballet concerns itself with surfaces: the contrasting of romantic movement with the vinegary, discordant lyricism of Prokofiev's music, the attractiveness of elegant simplicity. Robbins is very good at this sort of thing, at making stylishness seem significant. *An Evening's Waltzes* is not an exuberant ballet, nor is it ap-

parently meant to be so. It emphasizes the sweet directness of fluid, graceful motion." [3]

Says Robbins: "The Company needed a new ballet. That's what happens in a repertory. Balanchine always says, 'Just keep working, keep doing things. Some of them are bound to be good.' But it's a hard thing to do—to keep plunging ahead when your instinct is to polish and hone. It's hard to live with the reactions. I think the expectations in this Company are so high. Because some of the works are masterpieces, the audience expects all works to be masterpieces."

FOUR BAGATELLES

CHOREOGRAPHY: Jerome Robbins

MUSIC: Ludwig van Beethoven (Bagatelles, op. 33, nos. 4, 5, 2, published 1823; op. 126, no. 4, published 1825)

COSTUMES: Florence Klotz

LIGHTING: Ronald Bates

PREMIERE: 10 January 1974 (gala benefit preview as *A Beethoven Pas de Deux*, 16 May 1973, with Violette Verdy, Jean-Pierre Bonnefous)

PIANO SOLO: Jerry Zimmerman

CAST: Gelsey Kirkland, Jean-Pierre Bonnefous
Also danced by Helgi Tomasson

In selecting these Beethoven bagatelles, Robbins appeared to choose music that resisted choreography, whose syncopations and suspensions fought with dancing sweep at every turn. The resulting dainty dance seemed filled with tiny awkwardnesses, like a continual stubbing of toes; or perhaps, as Jowitt pointed out, "his musicality has become more subtle—so subtle, in fact, that several critics dislike his recent duet, *Four Bagatelles*, on the grounds that it was abrupt and tricky and violated the music's flow; but musicians point out that the little Beethoven pieces are actually as perverse and packed with 'what-if-I-tried-this?' as the ballet." [1] (Croce found it "unmusical, choreographed for two dancers who don't exist;

Four Bagatelles. Jean-Pierre Bonnefous, Violette Verdy. (*Photo Martha Swope.*)

the driving idea behind the choreography seems to be that it's unperformable." [2])

Others detected a disingenuous note—as Goldner pointed out, the duet vacillated between the effect of an intimate improvisation (in this, an echo of the music) and a grand-style pas de deux: "Robbins makes such a point of achieving a trifle that he achieves a Trifle. The dance begins *au naturel*, as a dance for two, but when one person runs off so that the other may do a solo, we are in the world of convention, the world of a pas de deux. Accordingly, the solos exhibit certain technical accomplishments for the sake of the audience's pleasure. Resort to convention is a perfectly legitimate solution to practical problems, while exhibitionism is the natural stance in dance for the theater. But Robbins seems to be disturbingly ambivalent about theatrical machinery and persona, and in the process of making dancing more 'real,' he makes it unbelievable. Overriding the whole ballet is a tone of modest quiet and charm which spells trifle. *Four Bagatelles* insists that something is nothing much, and that because it is nothing much, it is something. What you feel, right from the beginning, when Kirkland and Tomasson execute a series of curlicue strolls and poses, is friendliness. We see two very friendly friends doing little nothings (by way of a grand développé à la seconde in promenade, enough to give an accomplished dancer pause, let alone one's chum) and taking in some country air (by way of a duet, two solo variations, and a coda)." [3]

Kisselgoff called it "deliberately 'naïf.'" [4]

There was also the matter of interpretation. The ballet was created for the highly inflected styles of Verdy and Bonnefous, both of whom invested each little wrinkle with nuance. When Kirkland and Tomasson took over, with their pure, unshowy technique and modest demeanor, many of the impediments were smoothed over, appearing only to lend a choppiness to the larger movements.

Some found, however, that *Four Bagatelles was* a sparkling little bauble. Terry: "Unpretentious but substantial. Exquisitely fashioned. Robbins sees to it that his dancers emerge as warm, almost radiant human beings whether the mood is frolicsome or romantic, poetic or spiced with bravura." [5]

Maskey: "Fresh as a new leaf and sturdy as a sequoia. I expect to be encountering it for some time to come. There is an air of mutual concern and compatibility between the two dancers which is more companionable than lover-like; the vocabulary is classical, lightly laced with folk references. The choreography is technically taxing and the partnering allotted to the man complex, but Kirkland and Tomasson soften the shock of virtuosity with an irresistible and cosy charm." [6]

Of the choreography, Kisselgoff wrote: "It becomes apparent that Robbins is paying a capsule tribute to the nineteenth-century classic ballets. In the first part, [he] throws out almost subliminal quotes from three styles. A fleeting reminder of Denmark's Bournonville school, as in *Flower Festival at Genzano*, occurs in the beginning with the girl's penchées arabesques, head tilting, and the man's leaps. Later, as Kirkland slowly extends her leg to the side from on-toe position, while Bonnefous supports her in an image directly culled from the grand pas de deux of *The Sleeping Beauty*, there is a flashing allusion to the Russian style of Petipa. The adagio ends with Kirkland down on one knee and Bonnefous behind her, in a reversal of the traditional pose that closes the adagio of Act II of *Giselle*— a nod toward French Romantic ballet. These are, of course, whiffs of history wafting through a contemporary work, and the allusions are absent from the solos. The male variation has folk touches that are echoed in the coda and some interesting experiments in phrasing. It is a tricky solo somewhat short on transitional steps. The ballet-peasant costumes suggest that the man is en route to the flower festival, while his partner may be Giselle's second cousin." [7]

VARIATIONS POUR UNE PORTE ET UN SOUPIR

CHOREOGRAPHY: George Balanchine

SONORITY: Pierre Henry

COSTUMES, DÉCOR: Rouben Ter-Arutunian

LIGHTING: Ronald Bates

PREMIERE: 17 February 1974

CAST: Karin von Aroldingen, John Clifford
Also danced by Victor Castelli

Porte et Soupir was a calculated "avant-garde" novelty destined for short life. Its accompaniment was sound, not music—more precisely, that arrangement of recorded sounds called musique concrète. In the original score there were twenty-five variations on the first theme ("Sommeil"); of these, Balanchine choreographed fourteen, with such titles as "Stretching," "Gestures," "Yawning," "Snoring; Humming," "Death." According to the description in the program, "Balanchine used the variations as a pas de deux, the patterns rigidly indicated by notations in the score. The duet of the female Door and the male Sigh depends upon measured vibrations of sound removed from the usual eight- or twelve-tone scale. The manipulation of the décor is also on a strict metrical count, the rhythms of which are elastic but precisely indicated."

This "décor" ("designed in creep-camp") was a tremendous, stage-full cape or skirt, attached to the Door and controlled with strings by a number of stagehands. According to Clifford, despite the incidental fact that one of the protagonists was male, the other female, Balanchine intended at least the "male" role as sexless. In any case, each performs independently of the other, with no reference to the other, and almost never at the same time.

The gimmicky nature of the piece was not lost on Balanchine: "They say I have created a *psychological* ballet," says he, with a gleam in his eye. "They call it avant-garde. But thirty years ago I did the same thing in *Errante*."

Since at the end the Sigh disappears in the skirts of the Door, the ballet lent itself to such interpretations as a predatory female devouring a male; Death and Man; the womb claiming the male; "an enlarged picture of the episode between the Siren and the Prodigal Son." It was variously seen as grotesque, humorous, merciless, and intellectually cruel. The Sigh was even considered (by Hering) a projection of Balanchine's personality.

The black silk billowed with great style, but the sounds seemed to go on endlessly. *Porte et Soupir* yielded most of its secrets on first viewing.

Goldner wrote, "Following the score creak by creak and breath by breath, Balanchine sets up a physical juxtaposition between door and sigh. The door is tall. Her body does not bend, but breaks at the joints. Her motions, particularly those of her arms and neck, stop in midcourse, and her body parts move independently of one another. In the first part of the ballet she barely moves from stage center. Later on she does move, but only to set her cape in motion. As she moves to the left and right, a sliding white panel at the back of the stage follows her, to reinforce the idea of a mechanistic universe. She is frightening because she is a robot. With her black cape fluttering, then engulfing the back and sides of the stage, she is obviously fate, death, or simply the inevitable. When the curtain first rises one sees the sigh only. But as soon as a spotlight falls in back of the sigh to illuminate the door and her cape, the outcome is known. The door-cape apparatus will envelop the sigh.

"The sigh's response to this situation is what constitutes the ballet's comic character. In contrast to the door, the sigh is short and slight. He is a quivering mass, seemingly without joints. His arms dangle, his back hunches over, his head bobs. He is not old; his white hair connotes lifelessness, not age. He moves all over and everywhere, but with the driving randomness of panic or hysteria. Futility, and the ballet's comic sense, are encapsulated when one of his arms bangs at the air in fury or protest while the other arm encircles his throat in self-strangulation. If the door is terrifying, the sigh is

Variations pour une Porte et un Soupir. Victor Castelli (far left, floor), Karin von Aroldingen. (*Photo Martha Swope.*)

grotesque. The central image of his dances is a deep squat; he looks like a frog. Given the fact that the sigh's fate is sealed or that, in Balanchinian terms, he is trying to waltz to a march, his struggle is comic. The ugliness and desperation of his struggle make the comedy terrifying and at times vicious, but no less absurd.

"If it does anything, Balanchine's choreography illuminates the silliness of this musique concrète, but I cannot believe that he would raise it from the grave just to give it another funeral. If that be the case, then *Variations for a Door and a Sigh* reaches into a blacker humor than I wish to acknowledge." [1]

Barnes: "Balanchine has staged his novelty with considerable and adroit theatricality. The major theatrical device seems to have been adapted from Alwin Nikolais's work *Tent*, but it is nonetheless effective for that. There seems to be some kind of sphinxlike confrontation, which ends when the man is swallowed alive by the woman's voluminous cloak.

"At one level, it can be seen as simply the sigh entering the door, but at another it seems to suggest a rather curious relationship between men and women, but then that may be just the sad result of having an anthropomorphic male sigh and an anthropomorphic female door. With his costume and make-up, this sigh looks like a fallen angel from Blake, and his dance images are sinuously twisted, like snakily undulating question marks that so often suggest fetal crouchings. This is a sigh almost in embryo. The door is a

Theda Bara-style sexpot, with slinky black hair and a Folies Bergère manner. Balanchine's choreography for his siren door was stabbing, predatory but minimal. His choreography for that cloak was sensational. [But] *Porte et Soupir*, for all its fun and modishness, is never surprising." [2]

"Repulsive, funny and nastily attractive. Everything about it partakes of the pop-art sensibility, [but] exploitative and sensational as the ballet's concept is, it does what it sets out to do more successfully than any of its models." [3]

"Too long to be parody and too anchored to its monotonous electronic score to be fluent." [4]

Says von Aroldingen, "You really have to memorize the timing of the sounds. It's impossible to work with counts. The most difficult part was handling the skirt. We had a small model in the practice room, but it didn't have the same tension. People say it's odd that a woman is the door and a man the sigh, but both in French and in my own language [German], it's that way. And, in a sense, women are stronger, at least on the inside."

Clifford: "I felt Balanchine wanted my part limp, like the Melancholic in *Four Temperaments*, although someone said the part reminded him of the Paul Taylor solo in *Episodes*. It's all very contorted and distorted. Balanchine demonstrated everything, on his knees, in the studio. And, as done by an older man, the most frightening quality is injected into it. He wanted me very unenergetic, and not reacting to the door at all."

DYBBUK
since November 1974 called
THE DYBBUK VARIATIONS

CHOREOGRAPHY: Jerome Robbins

MUSIC: Leonard Bernstein (*The Dybbuk Variations*, 1974)

COSTUMES: Patricia Zipprodt

DÉCOR: Rouben Ter-Arutunian

LIGHTING: Jennifer Tipton

PREMIERE: 16 May 1974 (gala benefit preview, 15 May 1974)

SINGERS: David Johnson (baritone), John Ostendorf (bass)

CAST: *The Young Woman* (*Leah*), Patricia McBride; *The Young Man* (*Chanon*), Helgi Tomasson; Bart Cook, Victor Castelli, Tracy Bennett, Hermes Condé; 8 women, 6 men

OTHER CASTS: *Young Woman,* Gelsey Kirkland, Deborah Koolish; *Young Man,* Cook

1. In the Holy Place: 7 men
2. The Pledge: male duet (fathers); 2 couples, 3 couples (including McBride, Tomasson)
3. Angelic Messengers: variations for 3 men
4. The Dream: pas de deux (McBride, Tomasson)
5. Invocation of the Kabbalah: The Quest for Secret Powers: Tomasson, 6 men
6. Passage: 7 men
7. Maidens' Dance: McBride, 4 women
8. Transition: McBride
9. Possession: pas de deux (McBride, Tomasson)
10. Exorcism: entire cast
11. Reprise and coda: entire cast *

The ballet was inspired by the dybbuk of Central-European Jewish folklore, a spirit that inhabits the body of another person. Robbins's specific source was S. Ansky's Yiddish play, *The Dybbuk,* first produced in 1920. However, as he

---

* There have been a number of changes since opening night: principally, the Angelic Messengers and Transition sections have been deleted, then restored; Passage and Pledge have been dropped. There is no indication that the last changes have been made.

has stated several times, "Anyone expecting to see *The Dybbuk* will be disappointed." According to the program note, "The ballet is not a retelling of Ansky's play, but uses it only as a point of departure for a series of related dances concerning rituals and hallucinations which are present in the dark magico-religious ambience of the play and in the obsessions of its characters."

A synopsis of the play appeared in the first programs, but was soon omitted. However, the ballet alludes to certain particulars in the play, and a knowledge of its general plot is a necessity. (Robbins gave his dancers the play to read.) Briefly, the story concerns a young couple, Chanon and Leah, pledged to each other years before by their fathers. Subsequently, however, the girl's father has arranged her marriage to a much richer suitor. "Chanon desperately turns to the Kabbalah to help him win Leah for himself, and as a last resort, he invokes the powerful but dangerous other-worldly formulae of ancient usage. At the supreme moment of discovering the secret words that unleash the dark forces, he is overwhelmed by the fierce ecstasy of the enlightenment and dies. Chanon returns to Leah as a dybbuk and, claiming her as his rightful bride, clings ferociously to his beloved." The elders exorcise the dybbuk, but Leah, "unable to exist without her predestined bridegroom, leaves her life to join him in oblivion" (excerpts from program).

The dance rendition was described by Buckle: "In a ritualistic dance, seven holy, hatted young men set the scene. Two devoted friends [pledge]. The children are born (this is all part of the same dance, which ends as it began with the friends linked and swinging slowly around each other) and fall in love (pas de deux). But (it is implied) the girl's father has arranged a more ambitious marriage for her. We see her reject a veil; that's all the narrative we are bothered with. In the Invocation of the Kabbalah, there are mysterious solos for the boy and six men, which are spells. The boy dies of this most potent magic, and is wrapped up. By a clever trick another body has been substituted and the boy suddenly emerges on the opposite side of the stage, wearing a transparent white gown like the girl, to enter and possess her. He is now a Dybbuk. In the strangest of dances they become one person. There follows the terrible Exorcism. In a tender group, the

Dybbuk. **Invocation of the Kabbalah. Helgi Tomasson aloft.** (*Photo Fred Fehl.*)

lovers are united in death. I have not mentioned the Angel. He appears twice, and his second entry is a stroke of theater so simple that only an angel like Robbins or Cocteau could have thought of it. He takes one step downstage left, and stands for a couple of seconds looking at the girl's dead body. Then he courses gently in a horseshoe curve and exits upstage left." [1]

In the play, the Angel—a character suggested to the playwright by Stanislavsky—"serves as chorus and as mysterious suggestion of the interplay of natural and supernatural that constitutes the very texture of the play. [His speeches are] rarely without ambiguity and foreshadow overtones of meaning." [2]

Such a figure might be seen as a metaphor for Robbins's abstracted treatment of his whole theme.

The work was a collaboration between Robbins and Bernstein, and the composer conducted both the benefit preview and the official opening night. The score, inspired by the numerology of the

Kabbalah, was described by Henahan as "prevailingly tonal, full of traditional triadic harmonies and simple metrical patterns. Bernstein frequently adds spice with the sort of agogic accents and exaggerated dotted rhythms characteristic of Hassidic music and dance. The function of Hassidic music is to enable the listener to lose himself in religious ecstasy, and the score approximates this at many points. There are insistent reminders of Prokofiev's *Romeo and Juliet* and a strong Russian flavor throughout." [3]

Most critics thought it highly serviceable as a ballet score. In all, *Dybbuk* had the look and feel of a substantial work, and this was reinforced by its length.

The ballet, however, was seen as "oddly unexciting for so emotional a subject." [4] Goldner found it "a dramatic ballet without drama" [5]; Barnes mentioned the "unstressed dramatic personas." [6] In seeking to free himself of plot, Robbins became almost completely nondenotative. Emotions and incidents seemed to be presented at several removes; this left the audience also removed. Goldner: "Robbins's decision to treat the play as an abstract fantasy is legitimate, but what is so disappointing is the absence of abstract emotion, idea, or even point of view. Major events happen—love, separation, death, spiritual possession, exorcism—but they are so heavily veiled by Robbins's desire to be nonspecific that they became nonevents." [7]

These "nonevents" projected an even, low-keyed emotional tone, which was responsible for some impression of monotony.

Jowitt commented, "I can't say what Robbins had in mind, and for once I'd like to know, because there's something vexingly slippery about the work as a whole. It's a suite of dances pervaded by a gloom of Jewish ritual and punctuated by traces of drama from S. Ansky's famous play. I find myself imagining it as footage for an eerily pallid film of the play, which some gifted cinematographer has had to abandon. Key scenes are missing; those that remain happen fugitively, in a limbo of time and space. Yet the dramatic element is so powerful that it's impossible to think of *Dybbuk* simply as a ballet with a suffocatingly sinister atmosphere. Since Robbins easily could have produced either a striking ballet or a dance drama, I assume he intended neither." [8]

In the same vein, Kisselgoff remarked, "Proves disconcerting in sections, [and] it is not simply because the plot is present only by implication. Rather, it is because Robbins has refused to use movement and gesture literally to express emotion. Much of the atmosphere is created by sequences of steps that have no dramatic meaning in themselves. How Robbins tells his story in pure dance is his secret, and it is when he does so that he is most startling and successful." [9]

Buckle felt some of the same characteristics were virtues: "I bless him for abolishing narrative links. There is no expressionist violence—in fact, hardly any facial expression—and not much narrative, but [it is] a work blazing with imagination and genius. No, 'blazing' is the wrong word. [It] smolders darkly. It is so odd, so unexpected, so original, and so quiet that there is a danger that many people will miss the point altogether: many *have* missed it." [10]

In a few cases, Robbins's dance steps or motifs were allusive of something specific: The elders in the first dance pattern themselves in the shape of a Menorah. The dybbuk enters Leah's body in an explicit manner: Leah, when possessed, adopts particular movements of Chanon's—a one-sided, "jagged" jump, a kind of lurching walk, straight-kneed, from one toe to the other (in the play, she speaks with masculine voice). And the costumes and backdrops bear Jewish references (the men wear phylacteries). But in general, the dance movement is not only nonallusive but nongestural: it is somewhat modern-dance in feeling, particularly in its low, terre-à-terre quality and absence of "ballet" vocabulary, but it lacks the dynamic use of the torso associated with much modern dance. The slow, heavy impression, the high stylization, and the infrequent use of technically demanding steps give the movement a ritualistic quality, which is reinforced by repetition—the men holding hands, stalking low, for example. Several reviewers saw reflections of Graham and Israeli folk dance in the choreography.

Barnes. "The heart of the ballet [is] the running duets for the hero and heroine, both in white caftans, both set apart, emotionally, spiritually, and often physically from the rest of the work." (For Goldner, "Even the love duets are nothing but passionate runs and flying lifts." [11]) He mentioned the "dramatic use of the floor," and considered that Robbins had "caught the intense spiritual incan-

Dybbuk. **Possession. Patricia McBride, Helgi Tomasson.** (*Photo Martha Swope.*)

descence of both his leading dancers. The ensemble dances for the Hassidic chorus and the mysterious, interweaving entrances of the messengers are [also] very well done. Elsewhere, Robbins adopts the showbiz padding of his composer." [12] Herridge mentioned the "ethereal purity, an innocence blessed by attendant angers" of the Dream pas de deux and "a beautiful solo for Leah when she quietly denies her father's wishes. I liked best the Possession, a duet marked by clasping of Chanon's arms around Leah's body—not so much in passion or love as in a melding of the two bodies into one. The Exorcism itself is far from violent." [13]

Jowitt: "In the beginning seven men execute a somber line dance. The steps are not very Hassidic, nor entirely balletic. The men's costumes are possibly meant to invoke the atmosphere of dreams, of eroticism repressed by austerity. The dancing looks strangely cramped, unalive in space: it emphasizes the slow march rhythms of Bernstein's score. A fine, brusquely friendly male duet introduces a brief ceremonious encounter between two couples and their two children—the betrothal, in a dream. The two [lovers] dance together. The next thing we see is a frantic, pulsing solo for Tomasson and very interesting tortuous ones for the six men who crouch in a watchful semi-circle. The scene culminates in the hero's collapse. Then McBride, dancing with her bridal veil and

her maiden friends, suddenly begins to execute movements from Tomasson's solo. He enters in a white robe like hers; he shadows her, keeping close, twisting and lifting her. The duet is a metaphor for his spirit entering her body. The exorcism is another formal dance for the group of men. In a wonderful touch of theatrical sleight-of-hand, the veiled bride crumples to the floor while her spirit (McBride) rushes to her lover's arms. The men are left staring at a huddled white shape—a chrysalis whose tenant has flown." [14]

Lewis mentioned two episodes: "The pact between the two fathers is suggested with a curving male duet, hands linked and circular patterns repeated. Then the young men and woman are brought forward, with the same kind of submission to parental authority and ritual that the bride and bridegroom have in Robbins's *Les Noces.* One of the most effective passages is Invocation of the Kabbalah. Tomasson dances with six men followed by several striking male solos. As the progression into mystical secrets proceeds, the dancing becomes sharper and more impassioned. One solo ends with the dancer lying on the floor, one foot pointed heavenward, as Tomasson echoes this with a hand pointed high." [15]

Says McBride of *Dybbuk,* so different from the other parts Robbins has created for her, "He gave us the book and talked a great deal about the characters, but from the beginning he said he didn't want to follow the story, so I never expected a 'story ballet.' I only expected hints. In fact, it's gotten more and more abstract (he's changed things since the opening). It's not a technical display; in Jerry's later works that I've done, even *Dances at a Gathering,* it's the movement that's really important. You need a strong technique to do them, but you don't do feats. It's a whole different style of dancing, a kind of free style, and yet firmly based on classical technique.

"Mr. B., you know, often seems inspired by a particular body, but Jerry has an idea first, and he tries to follow that. Much of *Dybbuk* wasn't actually worked out on me, but on another dancer (although he let me know I was going to perform it). Jerry has so many possibilities; he comes up with steps and they're often so beautiful. Then he'll say he doesn't want to use them. Frequently, you could use his discarded steps for a whole other ballet, they're so good. People say he's unsure, but I don't think it's that at all: he can afford to throw away a lot of ideas because he's got so many other good ones—it's amazing—especially lifts, with great rushing preparations. (Mr. B. doesn't use this kind of thing too much.) They go about things so differently; you could write a book about the differences between Mr. B. and Jerry. With Jerry, you

Bartók No 3. **Debra Austin.** (*Photo Martha Swope.*)

The Postal Rate Commission still has to pass on this proposal, to charge businesses 16 cents a letter while retaining the 13-cent rate for personal letters (among other expected increases). But there is little reason to doubt that the commission will go along with a procedure that has come to seem like a ritual.

The law that created the Postal Service condemned it to a course very much like the one that has proved almost fatal to the railroads. The service was to make itself "financially independent" by 1985, with inadequate Congressional subsidies until then. Lacking both the will and the means to exploit electronic breakthroughs in communications, the Postal Service has had no alternative to boosting rates while reducing services.

The predictable result has been a reduction in business. A commission appointed by Congress last year concluded that the service would lose 23 percent of its first-class mail to electronic message systems by 1985.

COSTUMES: Ardith Haddow

LIGHTING: Ronald Bates

PREMIERE: 23 May 1974 (first presented 27 March 1974 by Los Angeles Ballet Theater)

CAST: *I:* Debra Austin; Muriel Aasen, Wilhelmina Frankfurt; 4 women, 4 men; *II:* Sara Leland, Anthony Blum; 6 women; *III:* entire cast

Says Clifford, "I knew I was doing a Balanchine ballet—I *like* Balanchine ballets. Of course, anything that's 'abstract' is im-

mediately labeled 'Balanchine.' In that sense, Ashton has done Balanchine ballets, Macmillan has done Balanchine ballets. At any rate, with this one, working in Los Angeles, I had a chance to do something in the Balanchine manner without his looking over my shoulder. Not that he's an ogre—but my knees buckle when he walks into a rehearsal room and I'm doing choreography."

Bartók No. 3, the last ballet of Clifford's to be mounted by the Company, was, predictably, received as a pleasant exercise in the Balanchine style. (Soon after its New York premiere, Clifford left the Company to head his own group in Los Angeles.)

The work was notable for its easy flow. Barnes wrote: "He still perhaps has not fulfilled himself, but I felt hints of a new originality. The first movement was the most impressive. The dancers invaded the space and kept it as their territory. The second movement was more conventional. Clifford used [the dancers] rather than extended them, revealed them rather than exposed them. With the last movement, Clifford recaptured something of the first movement's spontaneity and fluency. The dancers grabbed their way through the music with a surging authority, and the movement rounded out the ballet with a definite dynamic impetus." [1]

Herridge: "[The music] is a pleasantly

tinkling sort of work, as effervescent as a cluster of sparklers and just about as substantial. In that sense, the dance truly matches the score. It's all pleasant enough, and adeptly fashioned, but you forget it as soon as you've seen it." [2]

Micklin: "The diagonal lines of attack; the crisp, bright interplay between soloist and ensemble dancers; the confident, punctuating gestures which emphasize rhythmic pulse; the patterns which fearlessly go against the grain of the music—all these are Balanchine trademarks. In short, nothing is truly original, but [Clifford] has, much like an extremely talented musical arranger, put together elements of proven virtuosity with remarkable skill. A second movement pas de deux has all the fluidity and nonspecific gravity of Balanchine at his tart, yet romantic, best. Most of all, there is a demanding first-movement solo for Austin which sings of the joy of balletic movement." [3]

SALTARELLI

CHOREOGRAPHY: Jacques d'Amboise

MUSIC: Antonio Vivaldi (Concerto in D minor; Concerto Grosso in D minor, op. 3, no. 11)

COSTUMES, DÉCOR: John Braden

LIGHTING: Ronald Bates

PREMIERE: 30 May 1974

CAST: Merrill Ashley, Christine Redpath, Francis Sackett; 4 women

OTHER CASTS: Marnee Morris, Colleen Neary

D'Amboise's work was considered one of his best—perky and attractive, if still rather timid. As Micklin wrote, "I only wish that he would take more chances; that he would infuse his choreography with the confidence and magnificent ease which distinguish his own dancing." [1] Herridge: "It is charming and sunny, but all too familiar, with no attempt to break new ground." [2]

Within these limitations, however, the ballet was considered to be skillfully done: "It alternates lively ensemble-with-leader sections and slow duets. The two group numbers suggest Italian folk-dance rhythms. As the title suggests, they sparkle with tiny hopping steps, accented with kicks and leaps. The adagio sections are romantic with flowing movements. The entire work is short, which is doubtless in its favor." [3]

Kisselgoff was quite impressed: "D'Amboise is at his simplest—that is, his strongest—here. The saltarello was an Italian court dance, in a sense the Roman counterpart of the southern tarantella. D'Amboise has not given us an Italian ballet, but he has translated the Italianate pulse of the music into movement themes of lively balletic variations on hopping, leaping, and kicking. A welcome and effective respite of tranquility occurs in the two adagio duets that come near the end of each concerto. In the [second] duet, for Redpath and Sackett, d'Amboise is at his most original and best. The image is of quiet emotion behind the glamour of performance: The woman leans her head against the man's chest. Her leg 'paws' the ground. He leads her as she walks on toe. They entwine their arms in an echo of the original embrace. One feels a definite circus mood to *Saltarelli*—of the tent circus rather than the three-ring spectacular." [4]

One of the nice features of the ballet was that it used all the dancers virtually as soloists.

COPPÉLIA

CHOREOGRAPHY: George Balanchine and Alexandra Danilova, after Marius Petipa (1884)

MUSIC: Léo Delibes (1869–70)

SCENARIO: Charles Nuitter, after E.T.A. Hoffmann's *Der Sandmann* (1815)

COSTUMES, DÉCOR: Rouben Ter-Arutunian

LIGHTING: Ronald Bates

PREMIERE: 17 July 1974, Performing Arts Center, Saratoga Springs, New York (gala New York benefit preview 20 November 1974)

CAST: *Swanilda/Coppélia*, Patricia McBride; *Frantz*, Helgi Tomasson; *Dr. Coppélius*, Shaun O'Brien; ACT I: *The doll Coppélia, Villagers*, 8 couples; *Mayor*, Michael Arshansky; *Swanilda's Friends*, 8 women; ACT II: *Swanilda and her friends; The Automatons: Astrologer, Juggler, Acrobat, Chinaman*; ACT III: *Burgomaster; Villagers, Brides, Grooms, and Friends*, 8 women, 6 men; DEDICATION OF THE BELLS: *Waltz of the Golden Hours*, Marnee Morris, 24 children; *Dawn*, Merrill Ashley; *Prayer*, Christine Redpath; *Spinner*, Susan Hendl; *Jesterettes*, 4 women; *Discord and War*, Colleen Neary, Robert Weiss, 8 couples; *Peace (pas de deux)*, Patricia McBride, Helgi Tomasson; *Finale*

OTHER CASTS: *Swanilda*, Muriel Aasen, Stephanie Saland; *Frantz*, Jean-Pierre Bonnefous, Peter Martins, Peter Schaufuss

ACT I: A Village Square in Galicia
ACT II: Dr. Coppelius's Secret Workshop
ACT III: A Village Wedding and Festival of Bells

Coppélia, a jewel of the French ballet, was actually created in an age of decadence. The Romantic movement, epitomized by Taglioni, with France in the forefront, had run its course. Artistically, the Opéra of Paris was in extreme decline; its entertainments served a clientele that as frequently as not strolled in late, after finishing brandy and cigars, and spent a good part of the evening looking at others in the audience. According to Kirstein, "Ballet was the sink of bad taste"; Guest remarked that, on the occasion of *Coppélia*'s premiere, in 1870, "the Emperor stayed awake for the entire performance." [1] The role of the male in ballet was almost nonexistent at the time: usually, women *en travesti* briefly dressed the stage, but, understandably, for them there were no "male" solos and no supported partnering. Then, as if to assist art, life intervened in the form of the Franco-Prussian War, closing the Opéra for more than a year. Supremacy in ballet passed to Russia, where *Coppélia* was staged with choreography by Petipa in 1884 (revised by Cecchetti in 1894).

The ballet as it is known in most of the Western world derives from Russian sources, specifically from Petipa's last régisseur, Sergeev, who took voluminous notes with him when he fled to Europe after the revolution. Another emigré was Danilova, who as a young girl in Russia danced Prayer and in the West became a legendary Swanilda, performing the role (in a Sergeev reconstruction) for fifteen years.

Why did Balanchine, whose most recent works had been *Porte et Soupir*, *Violin Concerto*, and *Symphony in Three Movements*, choose to do *Coppélia* at this stage in his career? He is known to admire Delibes, Stravinsky, and Tchaikovsky preeminently among ballet composers, although his ballets to Delibes have been few (*La Source* and *Sylvia*, both pas de deux). Surely the resources for mounting *Coppélia* could have been acquired long ago. Says he, "Everybody asks why I waited so long. I cannot answer. Why should I do it at all? For many years I wasn't interested in *Coppélia*. So I didn't do it. I was doing something else that seemed much, much more important. This was not the Ballet Russe. I couldn't do a full-length *Swan Lake*, *Giselle*, *Sleeping Beauty*. First of all, they are absolutely impossible [to put on]. And for a long time, *Coppélia* wasn't a title [that would attract an audience]. *Now* it is. And now we need a *Coppélia*, especially for Saratoga, for children, for the 'masses.' I thought that if all the children in the ballet brought their brothers and sisters and parents—already we would have one audience. Saratoga needed something. . . . I said, 'What can I do? I don't know . . . let's take *Coppélia*; it's the least *harmful*.' Another problem—it wasn't written for male dancers. There are no pas de deux. You have to put things in. A new third act. That makes you think—'Should we do, or shouldn't we?' Finally I said, 'All right.' It's beautiful music."

Coppélia. Above: Act I. Shaun O'Brien (Dr. Coppélius), Terri Lee Port (the doll Coppélia). *Top right:* Act I. "Ear of Wheat" adagio. Helgi Tomasson, Patricia McBride. (Background, Swanilda's Friends.) *Right:* Act II. Patricia McBride (Swanilda dressed in Coppélia's clothes), Shaun O'Brien, Helgi Tomasson (seated, wrapped in blanket). (*Photos Martha Swope.*)

Says McBride, "Years ago, I told Mr. B. I was going to do *Coppélia* in a concert with Eddie Villella. He seemed so excited, and said immediately, 'Oh, ask Mme. Danilova to show you. She was such an incredible Swanilda. She remembers all the steps. She was marvelous.' "

The New York City *Coppélia* is a restaging of the version Danilova danced, with some exceptions. The czardas and marzuka of Act I are new (interestingly, Delibes studied in Hungary, which may have prompted this music). All of Act III is also Balanchine's, since the Russian Act III is lost (the French Act III was dropped permanently as early as 1872; and to this day at the Opéra Frantz is still played by a woman). Balanchine followed the Delibes-Nuitter scenario, in which the final act, the Festival of the Bells, takes the form of a masque. Additionally, using

music from *Sylvia*, Balanchine created a male variation in Act I and a full-scale pas de deux (complete with another male solo) in Act III.

The story of *Coppélia* is well known. Frantz and Swanilda love each other; but then Frantz spies another pretty girl, Coppélia, sitting in a window and loves her as well. (Says Danilova, "The whole story hinges on his indecisiveness.") When night falls, Frantz sneaks into Coppélia's room, which is actually the workshop of the strange old eccentric, Dr. Coppélius. Meanwhile, Swanilda, miffed, decides to poke around Coppélius's house. When she hears him returning, she dresses in the clothes of Coppélia, who is revealed as a life-size doll. Frantz, caught by Coppélius, is put to sleep with a drug, while the old man attempts to bring his beloved doll to life. As Swanilda goes along with his fantasies, he grows more

and more excited, throwing her props to make her dance a Scottish reel and a Spanish fandango. When Frantz awakens, Swanilda scornfully shows him the naked doll whom he was blind enough to love, while Coppélius, realizing he has been tricked, is a broken man. In the last act, the young couple unite to celebrate their marriage.

Much was made of the characterizations, which differed significantly from tradition. Swanilda, usually highly exuberant, charming, and pouty, is all of these in this production; but, in addition, she exhibits an almost nasty glee as she wreaks havoc in Coppélius's toyshop and shows a streak of cruelty as she mocks both the gullible fuddy-duddy Coppélius (who truly believed he had given life to Coppélia) and the equally gullible and lightweight Frantz (unable to distinguish between a pretty doll and a pretty *and* human girl). (Why she marries such a shallow creature is open to question—but characterization breaks down completely in Act III.) In addition, Swanilda's traditional mime in Act I and her doll-like behavior in Act II—stiff, mechanical, and complete with national dances—provided McBride with opportunities not offered by other works in the repertory. Says she, "Our company is not used to doing this type of ballet, and I'm glad I had other experiences first. It was such a joy to watch Danilova. The first-act mime is all hers. In the second act both she and Mr. B. were very strict with me. They wanted it very doll-like. She's not really a person. It's almost like fooling the audience too. In other versions, she is more obviously a girl from the beginning; when he's looking the other way, she'll joke around. Here, she doesn't move. She's really the doll. And she's serious. They didn't want me doing anything with my face."

As for Coppélius, O'Brien won an ovation with his dark Hoffmanesque portrayal, which gained its share of laughs but was also unexpectedly touching. Most Coppéliuses are doddering, silly old fools; O'Brien found more sinister hues and also human passion. Coppelius's world *is* that workshop; the mechanical toys are truly his offspring (Croce mentions his " 'speech' to Coppélia, delivered in a paroxysm of joy, 'I have made you and you are beautiful.' "); and his later disappointment is heart-tugging. The program notes, "Staging of *Coppélia* forsook its source in Hoffmann's tale of the lass over whom rival inventors battled until they dashed out her enamel eyes. [Offenbach used the same inspiration for the doll Olympia in *Tales of Hoffmann*.] It was forgotten that Dr. Coppélius, who deludes himself by imagining he has created a breathing organism, is a grotesque or quasi-tragic figure, rather than a clown. He could stand for the alienated artist-genius victimized by a provincial society of bumpkins or philistines."

Elsewhere Kirstein has written, "Automata are metaphors for unguessed possibility in raw material, whether metal machine or flesh-and-blood ballerina. A choreographer of mannequins (the magician Coppélius) is archetype of ballet masters. In succeeding versions, sinister elements became diluted. The essential subject—the artist responsible for creating work with independent or eternal life—remained." [2] (Curiously, after his memorable and comic appearances in Act

I and his tour de force characterization dominating Act II, Coppélius is given but a perfunctory appearance in Act III, doing less than in the original libretto.)

Goldner wrote of Coppélius: "In most contemporary productions, [he] is batty and senile, easily consigned to the status of a fall guy for Swanilda's heartless trick. Balanchine and O'Brien conspired to make the doctor and therefore the whole story more complex. Coppélius was as mocking of the villagers as they were of him. Frantz's belief that the doll Coppélia is real was proof of his stupidity, as far as Dr. Coppélius is concerned. The revelation that, at bottom, Coppélius was also deeply in love with Coppélia was a rigorous lesson on the power of will and the conflict between rational and irrational instincts. O'Brien's exquisite mime and acting unearthed all of Coppélius's gentleness, pride, and vulnerability as well as cynicism and alienation, and he damn near stole the show." [3]

O'Brien, who had been turning in brilliant cameos for years, was revealed as a virtuoso character actor. Says he, "Coppélius was a magnificent, tragic failure. His dolls were not meant to be sold; their creation fulfilled emotional needs. I think each of the dolls represents some romantic ideal of himself, with the ultimate creation being Coppélia. Although he loves each in a special way, it's like having the perfect child after trying many times. In his room, he is the center of the universe, and she is its epitome. Danilova kept saying his character was 'funny,' but I knew she didn't mean funny in the usual sense. She didn't show it in a way that was really funny. There was a certain element of mystery, and when she showed, she emphasized a very serious, somber thing.

"The 'Gothic quality' that the critics saw is mine, I think, starting from her outline. She and Balanchine gave me the go-ahead signal to develop it on my own; I had their tacit approval. (When Balanchine doesn't like something, you'll know it.) All of the classical mime was Danilova's, but there are many parts in between; certain points, musical and choreographical, had to be adhered to, but in much of it I was unrestricted. Then Balanchine would touch it up a little. He might say, 'It's not necessary to be so old.' And if I were doing something a little bit different, he would say, 'Well, all right, but maybe do something like this so it will look right with what you're doing.' You know, relate it to the rest.

"The music is extremely helpful, almost operatic. You can almost put words to it. In fact, there are moments when there are words in the mime.

"The relationship that occurs between me and Patricia on stage—I've never had that happen with anyone. It's a particular excitement that is worked up between us as opposing personalities. It didn't happen so much in rehearsals; she doesn't come together one-hundred percent until the performance. Danilova, for instance, shows every part as authentically as possible, but I think she also realizes that she was unique and that what she is showing is very much herself as well. And she's perfectly willing to permit a person to take what she gives and use it in relation to his or her own personality, ability, technique, and body. That's what she did with Patricia. And Patricia absorbs everything, of course, but she doesn't show it right away. And then this wonderful theatrical intelligence comes to the fore on stage."

Says Danilova of the pantomime, "We sped it up. Everything is so fast today, especially in New York. If you put on one of those old ballets unchanged, everyone would fall asleep. Instead of always explaining your next move, you just move." She recounted how she and Balanchine together evolved the dotty, halting walk Coppélius uses in the first act: " 'This is how an old man walks. He takes little steps and his body tilts forward slightly, a bit off balance. He is afraid of falling.' 'Yes,' said Balanchine, 'But he also does this,' and he would take little mincing steps, his body tilted forward slightly, and then he would stop suddenly and veer in another direction. 'Old men are always forgetting things.' "

The third leading character, Frantz, has the least personality, perhaps reflecting his humble origins as a girl. He is basically a pretty light-headed country boy and certainly fickle. He is also good-natured. He mainly exists as a dancer, with comic and demi-caractère moments, mixed, of course, with that purest classicism of which Tomasson is a master.

Dancing. . . . Says McBride, "There's so much dancing in it." Her divertissement with eight friends, in which she concludes with a series of brisés across the stage and a backbend, is a highlight of Act I; there are also the folk dances, solos for the leads, and the mournful "ear of wheat" adagio, in which Swanilda, following an old custom, shakes the wheat to

Coppélia. Above: Act III. Merrill Ashley (Dawn) with children from the Waltz of the Golden Hours. *Left: Act III.* Peace pas de deux. Patricia McBride, Helgi Tomasson. (Background, Jesterettes, Swanilda's Friends, Villagers.) *(Photos Martha Swope.)*

discover whether Frantz loves her. Hearing no sound, she concludes that he does not. Act II is given over to the stylized movement of Swanilda and the mechanical toys. Act III is a series of dances: for the Golden Hours (a soloist and many children); for three women, Dawn, Spinner, and Prayer, of which the first is outstanding—a difficult combination of fast footwork and large movements, with changing directions, ending with a daring leap onto a single pointe (Goldner wrote, "Balanchine has found a new way to suggest the hummingbird's mid-flight pause. She alights from a jump on pointe and on bent knee, but instead of hopping off pointe on the rebound, she perches for a split second, freezing an ephemeral moment." [4]); a kitsch number for a horde of Valkyries (which Herridge saw as a spoof of Wagner); a grand pas de deux; and a giant finale.

The critical reception of the new *Coppélia* was most favorable. "Coppelia shines . . . sparkles and zips along like no other version of this ballet. The dramatic points are well taken [and] the dances hold their own interest," wrote Kisselgoff. [5]

Barnes: "Ever since the fifties, the ballet has been seen more and more in purely rustic terms—as a kind of genre piece. What Balanchine has done is to return it to a kind of fairyland. This is not a realistic peasant ballet—from beginning to end it is a fantasy, largely for children and with children. Because Balanchine has seen this as a children's ballet (if I read his mind right), he understands the child's need for horror. Coppélius is made into a serious Hoffmannesque characterization, full of Gothic creepy horror. The setting, with its oblique angles and odd lines, suggests a children's Dr. Caligari.

. . . This *Coppélia* is so different from almost all others that it is bound to be controversial, all the more so because its differences may not be particularly apparent to the unwary. This is a child's picture-book *Coppélia*, from its childlike paintbox settings and costumes to its Gothic villain, and even its cheerfully irrelevant final masque. And, for the first time, Balanchine has used children to pleasing and credible effect." [6]

Croce: "Swanilda's valse lente is the [ballet's] opening dance. By custom, it's a straight classical solo, and it gives us the ballerina in full flight almost as soon as the curtain has gone up. But in [this] version, McBride runs down to the footlights and, on the first notes of the waltz, addresses the audience in a passage of mime. 'This one up here,' she says, pointing to Coppélia on her balcony, 'she sits and reads all day long. That one, who lives over there, is in love with her, but she never notices him. Me, I just play.' And she plays (dances), first for her own pleasure, then for Coppélia's, with enticing steps that seem to say, 'Come down and play with me. See how nicely I play.' The structure of the waltz is mime, dance, dance-mime; in one stroke the means by which the story will be told are laid before us.

"Balanchine's hand is evident in that first-act entrance of Swanilda, and in the mazurka and czardas, which surely have never before been so thick and busy with (musical) repeats, so fertile with invention. Their one weakness is that they are isolated from the action and don't serve any purpose. [Another problem] is the sudden unmotivated shift to a sunnier mood that follows Swanilda's solemn 'ear-of-wheat' dance.

"The part of the ballet that is just about perfect is Act II. Here again, Balanchine has been at work; you can almost feel him assuming command of the action the moment Coppélius enters his workshop to find it overrun by Swanilda and her friends. Coppélius is not a buffoon, and Swanilda is not a zany. He's a misanthrope, a tyrant, believably a genius who can create dolls everyone thinks are alive. She is a shrewd, fearless girl who grows into womanhood by accepting as her responsibility the destruction of Coppélius. She must break his power over Frantz, who has chosen the perfect woman, the doll Coppélia, over the natural woman, herself. The conflict between idealism and realism, or art and life, is embedded in the libretto, and Coppelius's passion is in the music. I enjoy burlesque versions of Act II, but the heart of the music isn't in them. Balanchine's Coppélius is kin to other Balanchine artist-heroes—not only Drosselmeyer but Don Quixote and Orpheus and the Poet of *La Sonnambula*. When he raises Swanilda-Coppélia onto her pointes and she remains locked there, upright or jack-knifed over them, he's the strangest of all alchemists, seeking to transform his beloved twice over: doll into woman, woman into ballerina. Swanilda must become as totally manipulatable, totally perfectible, as a Balanchine ballerina. She must be a work of art, and then burst out of her mold.

"Balanchine's dances are not uniformly masterpieces, but, taken all together, they ought to extend the life of this ballet another hundred years. In their unique blend of light irony and ingenuousness,

they are a mirror of the music—serious music that was not meant to be taken too seriously. For the third act, Delibes envisioned a village wedding, with the villagers putting on an allegorical pageant of man's works and days. Most productions get through Dawn and Prayer and then give up. Balanchine uses all the music Delibes wrote, and he does not mistake its spirit. His choreography really does present a plausible village pageant stuck together with metallic threads and parchment and candlewax, but noble nonetheless, with an anti-grand-manner grandeur. The Waltz of the Hours, that sublime gushing fountain of melody, is danced by twenty-four grinning little girls [and soloist], who form choral borders for the solos that follow. The entrance of the three graces—posed motionless as beauty queens in a carriage that circles the stage twice—is one of the most piercing visions in the ballet. And the solos for Dawn and Spinner are outstanding. Discord and War is a romp for boys and girls in horned helmets, a flourish of capes and spears waved as idly as picket signs—a witty number. Then, after the bridal pas de deux, comes an exhilarating finale, with climax piled on smashing climax. Best of all is the ballerina's fish dive into her partner's arms, instantly followed by the only thing that could top it—the return of the twenty-four golden tinies cakewalking on in a wide curve, with Morris in the lead tearing off piqué-fouetté turns." [7]

Greskovic wrote about the ending: "The *grand fête finale* that closes the ballet seems to utilize every device that Balanchine knows about a 'big' finish. The 'cast of thousands' surges, snakes, circles and explodes the stage with that unique energy commonly called the New York City Ballet." Greskovic also noted that "mime is seemingly being deleted daily from various story ballets in an effort to prove that 'every good choreographer can tell everything with inventive classroom steps,' [but] Balanchine and Danilova have remembered that they are telling us a story with their ballet—not illustrating extensive program notes. What a refreshing and rewarding thrill it is to 'watch' Swanilda and Frantz's opening monologues, aimed at us. From the start it's 'Here's who I am and why I'm here and what's happening'—all silently enunciated and straightforwardly delivered. [And], if I found this a dancing-filled story before, now its a dancing-fuller story." [8]

The "ice-cream" décor, an integral part

of the proceedings, drew mixed reactions. Barnes admired the first two acts, "enclosed with a kind of valentine border," but found in the third, "the bell motif is just too much, and the sugary nature of the setting seems too bland." [9] * Kisselgoff remarked on its "gingerbread" look. Maskey called it "a mixture of styles ranging from Second Empire French to contemporary Hallmark Card"; Croce devoted several paragraphs to complaining about the designs; the costumes for Dawn, Prayer, and Spinner have since been redone.

Coppélia, in its success, reinforced, although the point needed no underlining, the position of McBride as first ballerina of the company. (Verdy and Kent were at the time making infrequent appearances.) She was called "luminous," "the heroine of the occasion."

Wrote Belt, "McBride grows more radiant and astonishing technically with every performance. Her Swanilda is the role of a lifetime and she carries if off with superstar glitter, charm, and shameless bravado. As the winsome lass she is adorable, as the doll and various Spanish and Scottish types she is superb, and as Patricia McBride she dominates the spectacle every single moment." [10]

Croce: "The role comes as a climax to the present and most exciting phase of her career. She has not sacrificed any of her speed or sharp-edged rhythm or subtlety of intonation. And although the role gives her plenty of unaccustomed material, she sweeps through it without ever once looking like anyone but herself. She persuades you that Swanilda is Patricia McBride and always has been. This is a remarkable triumph for an artist whom the world knows as the flag-bearer of the New York City Ballet, the embodiment of its egoless star system. McBride doesn't throw us cues to let us know how we ought to take her; she doesn't comment, doesn't cast herself as an observer of life. All she knows about life she seems to have learned through dancing, and all she has to tell she tells through dancing." [11]

Says McBride, "It's an honor to do the role, the experience of being in the same room with Balanchine and Danilova. It's very special to dance. And it's a wonderful

---

* Several painted bells, marking the "Fête de Carillon," bore the initials of the inventors—C.N., L.D., E.T.A.H., A.St.L. (Arthur Saint-Léon, choreographer of the original)—and of our indispensable contemporaries, G.B. and L.K. Another was dedicated to the ballet itself, with the inscription "J'étais créé par Léo Delibes, 25 mai 1870."

role for a ballerina—the whole ballet is built around her. It's such a juicy challenge, to completely lose yourself, completely lose your identity, who you are. In a way you become something other. And you know, compared to dancing *Ballet Imperial*, it's a snap."

SINFONIETTA

CHOREOGRAPHY: Jacques d'Amboise

MUSIC: Paul Hindemith (Sinfonietta in E, premiered 1950)

PRODUCTION DESIGN: John Braden

LIGHTING: Ronald Bates

PREMIERE: 9 January 1975

CAST: Christine Redpath, Colleen Neary, Bart Cook, Francis Sackett; 2 demi-solo couples; 12 women, 4 men
Also danced by Debra Austin

Presto
Adagio and Fugato
Intermezzo Ostinato (Presto)
Recitative and Rondo (Energico)

Sinfonietta was worlds apart in mood and style from the d'Amboise ballet that immediately preceded it, the sprightly *Saltarelli*. Although some reviewers found it a step forward for the choreographer, most were not impressed.

Wrote Kisselgoff: "Perhaps its chief interest is that it is his least Balanchinian exercise. Not only does he not echo the music's structure, but even gives it an unexpected programmatic interpretation. The setting is a sort of primeval forest; however, this is not the primeval forest where history has not yet recorded the felling of the first tree. Unfortunately, it is a scene that has been revisited too often. *Sinfonietta* is still another pagan-rite ballet concerned with mythic ceremonies that are never specifically defined but are replete with allusions. The choreography is in a deliberately nonvirtuosic style and conventionally balletic for the soloists. A sizable ensemble, often locked into chain formations, made up the congregation of worshippers." [1]

"His boldest, most concentrated, and interesting statement as a choreographer." [2]

RAVEL FESTIVAL 14–31 May 1975

As focus for the Company's second festival, Balanchine selected the centennial of Ravel. "Why Ravel?" everybody asked. "Why not Ravel?" said Balanchine. It seemed, however, a strange choice, particularly since Balanchine himself had never shown a special affinity for Ravel's music as support for his ballets (creating only two for his company in forty years), although it appears that in his student days, along with *Pulcinella*, he staged a version of *Valses Nobles et Sentimentales*.

The Company decided that to honor Ravel was also to honor France. Said Balanchine in a curtain speech at the gala benefit, "La Belle France gave us La Danse. But another thing, one absolutely important thing—why I am still alive—it's because of the wine. . . ." Mme. Giscard d'Estaing, wife of the President of France, attended the opening night; Manuel Rosenthal, one of Ravel's few pupils and protégés, was invited to conduct the first program; French pianist Madeleine Malraux also performed. The format was slightly different from that of the Stravinsky Festival: The new Ravel ballets were unveiled on three successive Thursdays, and repeated through Saturday. During the rest of the week, other repertory was performed.

Many questions were raised as to the suitability of Ravel's music for dancing and indeed the quality of some of the music itself. There was also the consideration of audience stamina (one program contained eight new works) and motive: Was the Company trying to capitalize on the festival idea, which had paid such dividends in the case of Stravinsky three years before? It goes without saying that only a choreographer's company, such as this one, could even entertain the idea of presenting sixteen new works in a period of three weeks; but just because it could be done, did that mean it should be done? The most crucial factor, however, had nothing to do with these things, and yet colored the Ravel Festival more than any of them: Ravel, it could be said after the festivities were over, had not inspired Balanchine. He produced only one major work of outstanding merit (*Le Tombeau de Couperin*), along with several serviceable pieces and a few disasters. Robbins, by contrast, was somewhat more successful than he had been with Stravinsky.

The magic was missing.

THE PROGRAMS:

14 May (gala benefit)
Sonatine
Concerto in G
L'Enfant et les Sortilèges
(conductor: Manuel Rosenthal)

15–17 May
Sonatine
La Valse
L'Enfant et les Sortilèges
Concerto in G
(conductor: Manuel Rosenthal)

22–24 May
Introduction and Allegro for Harp
Shéhérazade
Alborado del Gracioso
Ma Mère l'Oye
Daphnis and Chloe

29–31 May
Le Tombeau de Couperin
Pavane
Un Barque sur l'Océan
Tzigane
Gaspard de la Nuit
Sarabande and Danse
Chansons Madécasses
Rapsodie Espagnole

SONATINE

CHOREOGRAPHY: George Balanchine

MUSIC: Maurice Ravel (1906)

Sonatine. **Violette Verdy, Jean-Pierre Bonnefous.** (*Photo Fred Fehl.*)

Concerto in G. **Peter Martins, Suzanne Farrell.** (*Photo Fred Fehl.*)

LIGHTING: Ronald Bates

PREMIERE: 15 May 1975 (Ravel Festival) (gala benefit preview 14 May 1975)

PIANO: Madeleine Malraux

CAST: Violette Verdy, Jean-Pierre Bonnefous

The benefit night of the Festival was attended by several French dignitaries; in the intermission Balanchine was invested with the Order of the Légion d'Honneur. *Sonatine*, played on stage by French pianist Malraux, starring the Company's two French-born principals, Verdy and Bonnefous, and with the stage backlit by a none-too-subtle reference to the *tricouleur*, * was clearly a civilized gesture appropriate to the occasion. Its overall flavor was playful, wispy, and slightly windblown; it was also a piece in which formal courtesies—bows and promenades —were not out of place.

The ballet proved to be something more than the throwaway curtain-raiser probably intended, for all that the music was brief (seventy-seven measures) and

* Since removed.

small-scale, and the dance steps more like punctuation marks than of real substance in themselves. Possibly the difference was Verdy; she invested the delicate inflections and slightly quirky steps with just the right amount of presence. This was the first work Balanchine had choreographed for her in some years, and she made the most of it. As Garis wrote, "It was almost as if [he] had deliberately made it a slight piece, knowing that Verdy's mastery would make something important of it and knowing that this combination would produce a winner." [1]

Croce: "[It's] about the French virtue of making much out of little. Verdy's role is a small masterpiece. Balanchine is still able to make a part for her that's unlike any she has done, and [she] dances it as if she knew exactly how great a gift this is." [2]

To Steinberg, it was "subtly and enchantingly responsive to the harmonic comings and goings of the music." [3]

Wrote Barnes, "The mood is light and rhapsodic, but there are a few happy moments of unaffected originality—such as the end of the first movement when Verdy leads Bonnefous offstage backward, or the czardaslike touches that the choreographer has surprisingly introduced." [4]

Vaughan commented, however, that

Bonnefous's choreography was "Lifaresque, with its parallel leg positions." [5]

Goldner wrote in somewhat more detail: "Delicious and skillful. All *Sonatine* is, is a stroll for two. Verdy walks on pointe; Bonnefous is her escort. Occasionally he turns her under his arm or skims her off the ground, so that her feet can prick the air as a continuum of the ground—and that's it. What I admire most is Balanchine's decision and ability to sustain [the] small scale within a formal context, to be unpretentious without being pretentious about it. *Sonatine* ends with what is usually a climax, a manège of turns around the stage and into the wings, but in this ballet the device has the effect of making dancers and dance go poof into thin air. In ending on the sly, *Sonatine* sticks to its guns." [6]

CONCERTO IN G
since fall 1975 called
IN G MAJOR

CHOREOGRAPHY: Jerome Robbins

MUSIC: Maurice Ravel (Piano Concerto in G Major, 1928–31)

COSTUMES, DÉCOR: Rouben Ter-Arutunian

LIGHTING: Ronald Bates

PREMIERE: 15 May 1975 (Ravel Festival); (gala benefit preview 14 May 1975)

PIANO: Gordon Boelzner

CAST: Suzanne Farrell, Peter Martins; 6 couples

OTHER CASTS: Sara Leland, Bart Cook

In *Concerto in G*, matching in spirit Ravel's unaccustomed "borrowings" from jazz (as the composer called them), Robbins produced a rather clichéd but nonetheless skillful and entertaining work, with a creamy-smooth central pas de deux. Particularly in the outer movements, both music and dance gave the impression of having been seen or heard somewhere before. In Robbins's extensive quotations of Broadway-style material—coy poses, rambunctious youthful hijinks such as bicycle-pedaling motions, beach-type activities, twenties-flapper broken wrists—he seemed often to reach for the too-obvious solution, possibly in keeping with Ravel's idea that a concerto should be "light-hearted and brilliant and not aim at profundity or dramatic effects."

Ravel modeled his center movement, an adagio, after the Larghetto of Mozart's Clarinet Quintet, K. 581; to this Robbins made a "lovely, bluesy duet" (Barnes) for the physically well-matched Farrell and Martins (his first choreography for Farrell, who after her long absence had returned to the Company the preceding January). Garris commented that "he didn't show you something new about them, but he didn't hide their talents and he didn't abuse them. That quiet and steady slow movement doesn't go deep or far, but it really goes." [1] The duet ended with a beautiful lift, Martins carrying Farrell off high above his head as she looked down at him.

Barnes, who felt the music sounded a bit like Gershwin, wrote that ballet "here and there suggests an updated version of *Interplay*. Where Robbins has been especially adroit is in fitting the dances to the weight and mass of the music . . . sportive choreography." The pas de deux he found "casual and yet careful, making beautiful use of pauses." [2]

Steinberg: "Farrell's extensions soar as elegantly as [the] endless melody, and the duet unfolds to become a fascinating dialogue, loving but cautious, guarded, full of retreats and backings off. It catches with almost painfully exact perception the elusive, cool, untouchable quality that makes Ravel at his best so haunting." [3]

Goldner found this coolness more of a coldness: "It turns out that the nub isn't jazzy insouciance but a dreamy walking-on-air duet. Martins floats Farrell around the stage so that her body collapses and recovers without a ruffle, without any hint of exertion and hence of passion. Robbins's proposal that dancing be literally effortless I find particularly inhumane and misrepresentative of the art. [His] duet is an adolescent fantasy of what dancing, and romance, should feel like." For the rest, she found it "one of Robbins's Sunday outings. Many of the sleight-of-hand devices feel contrived—and there goes everything. Why, in the opening tableau, does one girl face the back of the stage when everyone else is facing front? Why does he try to twist an ungainly squatting position—a plié in second position with the legs far apart—into a perky image? [The ballet] relaxes into pleasantness as it progresses, with one or two moments of genuine humor, but the credibility gaps rising out of the first few moments make it difficult for [it] to be as disarming as it is supposed to be." [4]

INTRODUCTION AND ALLEGRO FOR HARP

CHOREOGRAPHY: Jerome Robbins

MUSIC: Maurice Ravel (*Introduction and Allegro* for harp, string quartet, flute, clarinet, 1905)

COSTUMES: Arnold Scaasi

LIGHTING: Ronald Bates

PREMIERE: 22 May 1975 (Ravel Festival)

HARP SOLO: Cynthia Otis

CAST: Patricia McBride, Helgi Tomasson; 3 couples

To Ravel's opulent, lush, heavy-summer-evening harp arpeggios, Robbins made a pretty work whose principal virtues were the stylish phrasing of McBride and her elegant and flowing red Scaasi gown. Robbins himself considered it "an assignment," undertaken merely to fulfill the requirements of the Festival and not seen afterwards. He used touches of gypsy and Spanish and many running and floating steps.

Herridge: "Limpid choreography danced with ever-flowing grace." [1]

Barnes: "The mood is suggestive of leaves and breezes. McBride and Tomasson dance in a drifting series of pas de bourrées and arabesques, often gently swaying together." [2]

SHÉHÉRAZADE

CHOREOGRAPHY: George Balanchine

MUSIC: Maurice Ravel (*Shéhérazade* overture, 1898)

LIGHTING: Ronald Bates

PREMIERE: 22 May 1975 (Ravel Festival)

CAST: Kay Mazzo, Edward Villella; 2 couples; 8 women
Also danced by Peter Schaufuss

Balanchine's treatment of Ravel's first orchestral score (rich with exotic coloration, à la Rimsky-Korsakov) was an innocuous disappointment. Among other things, it contained almost every pseudo-Eastern reference one could think of, including undulating arms for the women, Buddha-like poses (arms joined above the head, fingers to the ceiling, heads jutting abruptly from side to side), men glowering like warriors.

Barnes: "Ended up looking a little like a Serge Lifar ballet of the late forties. The superficial Orientalisms consist of bent knees and elbows." [1]

ALBORADA DEL GRACIOSO

CHOREOGRAPHY: Jacques d'Amboise

MUSIC: Maurice Ravel (orchestral version of piece originally for piano, both 1905)

COSTUMES: John Braden

LIGHTING: Ronald Bates

PREMIERE: 22 May 1975 (Ravel Festival)

CAST: Suzanne Farrell, Jacques d'Amboise; 4 couples

This work, called by Croce a "Spanish supper-club adagio," seemed entirely appropriate to the music, of which the musicologist Stuckenschmidt wrote, "It makes the line between serious thought and parody difficult to discern." [1] Croce continued, "It had a few raw thrills. D'Amboise made [Farrell] look hot, twisty, and alive. [She] has a wonderful way of complying with all the broad effects a choreographer may dream up and swerving just in time to avoid their grosser implications," [2] which is one way of saying the choreography verged on the vulgar. Farrell wore a brief costume; d'Amboise threw her around hair-raisingly.

MA MÈRE L'OYE

Fairy Tales for Dancers

CHOREOGRAPHY: Jerome Robbins

MUSIC: Maurice Ravel (5 pieces for piano 4-hands, 1908; enlarged to 7, with interludes, and orchestrated, 1912)

SCENARIO: Maurice Ravel, based on fairy tales by Charles Perrault and others

COSTUMES: Stanley Simmons

LIGHTING: Ronald Bates

PREMIERE: 22 May 1975 (Ravel Festival)

CAST: *Story Teller; Princess Florine,* Muriel Aasen; *Good Fairy,* Delia Peters; *Bad Fairy,* Tracy Bennett; *Beauty,* Deborah Koolish; *Beast,* Richard Hoskinson; *Hop o' My Thumb,* Matthew Giordano; *Laideronette,* Colleen Neary; *Green Serpent,* Jay Jolley; *Prince Charming,* Daniel Duell; *Cupid; Blackamoors,* 2 couples; *Pagodines,* 2 couples; *Courrier;* 5 women, 8 men
Beauty also danced by Judith Fugate

Robbins went back to Ravel's own ballet scenario for his treatment of the music, except that his participants were clearly dancers acting out fairy tales, not Ravel's fairy-tale characters themselves. In the prologue, dancers are shown sitting backstage listening to a story teller. Then they begin to put on a little skit about the Sleeping Beauty. After pricking her finger and falling asleep for a hundred years, the Princess dreams other fairy tales, which the dancers enact: Beauty and the Beast, Hop o' My Thumb, and Laderonette, the ugly Empress of the Pagodas. Prince Charming arrives and wakes her; the ballet ends with their marriage. Robbins dressed his dancers in pastel practice clothes; "costumes" were suggested sketchily by various props—boots, hats, and so forth.

Ma Mère l'Oye generated mixed reactions. Some saw it as heavy-handed and self-consciously cute; others found it a well-crafted piece that charmed without cloying, despite the dainty sweetness of the music. Some found the pale, light look of the costumes perfect for improvisation; to others, the ballet was mounted in a raggedy and sparse manner. Robbins observed all of Ravel's directions (written into the score), even to the Princess skipping rope and the Good Fairy whistling through her teeth. Broad gestures such as these bothered some spectators, as did Robbins's quotations of well-known mime passages from *Sleeping Beauty* and other traditional ballets. Some sheaves of wheat that appeared for the Laideronette section were seen as an in-joke about his own *Watermill*. It was suggested that he was making fun of these ballets and playing down to his dancers. Says he, "I love *Sleeping Beauty* and all the ballets presented there. Some people said my treatment wasn't worthy of Ravel, but I followed his libretto exactly."

Ma Mère l'Oye. **Ensemble.** (*Photo Martha Swope.*)

Croce, who liked the ballet, wrote about it at some length: "A peculiarly shrewd and touching rendition of the power of theatrical fantasy; by adding one element to [Ravel's scenario, Robbins] colors the whole ballet to such an extent that it appears, from first to last, to be his own creation. He surrounds Ravel's frame [the story of *Sleeping Beauty*] with another frame, making the ballet a charade put on by dancers, whom he sees as the scamps of the theater. He succeeds in turning *Ma Mère l'Oye* into a typical Robbins kid-style ballet. Impudences specified by Ravel [skip rope, whistling] seem like Robbins's inventions. When he throws in chunks of classical mime out of *Sleeping Beauty*, the satire fits right in. So does the general satire of the New York City Ballet and its uncommendable habit of mounting new ballets in the fittings of old ones. Here is that Armistead garden drop yet again, pieces of *A Midsummer Night's Dream*, *Nutcracker* bed, the French doors from *Liebeslieder*, lanterns and grass stalks from *Watermill*. The whole company and its repertory are jumbled together in a salute to Ravel; it's also a more serious conception of Ravel's ballet, coming from Robbins, than a reverent incense-and-gossamer production would have been.

"In the poetic style of *Ma Mère l'Oye*, Robbins returns to those qualities which first defined him as a unique theater artist. [It] is bound to be underestimated because it looks so easy and hasn't a lot of dancing, but it's a New York artifact of wide significance. It catches up the beloved Robbins myth about dancers as children and relocates it in our current world of young dancers' workshops, professional children's schools, and incubators of the performing arts.

"The fantasy rolls: theater trunks are thrown open, hats with plumes come out, the scenery moves, the traffic rumbles. These dancers aren't wistful dreamers; they're sober technicians, as systematic as circus acrobats. They do not try to cajole you with an illusion of spontaneity; everything is mechanical, deadpan, precise, and twice as funny because of it." [1]

Herridge: "Robbins shows how aptly one can apply humor to Ravel's romanticism. Here he has told several fairy tales with immense charm and sophisticated tongue-in-cheek. The tone is marvelously funny in a quietly subtle way. There is Beauty and the Beast with a Beauty so busy admiring her mirror image that she almost doesn't see the Beast. There is Hop o' My Thumb who is so much more clever than his frightened big brothers. And there is the ugly Empress of the Pagodas who becomes beautiful once more after bathing in the magic waters—the latter danced in Robbins's humorous Oriental style of 'The Small House of Uncle Thomas.' " [2]

Barnes: "The obviousness of the humor is quite remote from the shaded subtlety of the music, and most of the jokes are quite extraneous to the score's purpose. Robbins has adroitly told the story, but for the most part the choreography itself looked banal. [His] production sense never fails him; nor does it prevent the ballet's seeming peculiarly hollow." [3]

Vaughan: "Both [the dancers] and Ravel deserve something more dignified." [4]

Goldner: "Charming and darned clever on the surface. The dancers wear practice outfits with only emblematic relationships to the fairy-tale characters they portray. The princess, for instance, wears a big gold cardboard crown and a rehearsal tutu. Overriding all the intra-ballet references is of course the reference to *The Sleeping Beauty* itself, one of the most famous of all ballets. And naturally, Robbins has a jolly good time with that coincidence. The princess not only pricks her finger on the spinning wheel but vigorously sucks it. At the end, the bridal trains of the wedded couple are literally never-ending. They are still trailing out of the wings when the curtain falls.

"Robbins's continual train of gentle and not-so-gentle jokes is endearing, but there is also something not quite honest about it all. His *Ma Mère l'Oye* is rather like an adult children's book. For children, it is too sophisticated (or not sophisticated enough, depending on your view of children). For adults, it is too fey in its childlike charm." [5]

DAPHNIS AND CHLOE

CHOREOGRAPHY: John Taras

MUSIC: Maurice Ravel (1910–12)

COSTUMES, PRODUCTION DESIGN: Joe Eula

LIGHTING: Ronald Bates

PREMIERE: 22 May 1975 (Ravel Festival)

CAST: I: A SPRING AFTERNOON: *Daphnis*, Peter Martins; *Chloe*, Nina Fedorova; *Lyceion*, Karin von Aroldingen; *3 Nymphs*; *12 Maidens*; *Abductors*, 4 men; II: EVENING: *Leader*, Peter Schaufuss; *Companions*, 2 women; *The Gang*, 8 women, 8 men; *Chloe*; *3 Nymphs*; III: DAWN: *Daphnis*; *Chloe*; *Lyceion*; *Bacchantes*, 2 women; *20 Maidens*; *20 Youths*

OTHER CASTS: *Daphnis*, Daniel Duell, Bryan Pitts; *Chloe*, Merrill Ashley, Suzanne Farrell, Judith Fugate; *Leader*, Bart Cook

Taras's treatment of Ravel's most famous ballet score (commissioned by Diaghilev and an indifferent success in its own day) was perhaps the most acutely disliked work of the festival. Costumes—motorcycle-gang leather for the pirates, Grecian-type tunics in neon colors for the maidens—were ridiculed; the back projections, of a proto-Kline nature, had a few defenders who found them effective rather than pretentious. Taras displayed the lack of dramatic instinct that has marked many of his works: while a number of the individual steps were nicely put together, much was very bland, and the story was not quite told, leaving irritating ambiguities (but without enough hints to make things engrossingly mysterious). Traditionalists noticed that one of the characters, Dorkon, had been omitted (as had the vocal chorus); Vaughan suggested that Taras would have done better to use one of the *Daphnis* orchestral suites, without reference to the story, which he found "reduced to utter confusion." This would have had the additional advantage of shortening the work.

Vaughan continued: "The pirates were turned into a band of Hell's Angels and their molls, while the finale, led by the spurned seductress (Lyceion) in the guise of a bacchante, made no sense at all, especially when the lovers came on for an obligatory final embrace, ignoring the surrounding orgy." [1]

Garis: "[To begin with,] the silk-underwear music lacks interesting pulse for dancing and the story is empty. [Here,] the characterization of Daphnis had a degree of sheer sappiness you don't ordinarily see on the professional stage, and Chloe was an uncreated thing." [2]

Barnes: "Generally a disaster area." [3]

It is probable that the complaints wouldn't have been nearly so heated had not Ashton's ballet to the well-loved score been so fondly remembered.

LE TOMBEAU DE COUPERIN

CHOREOGRAPHY: George Balanchine

MUSIC: Maurice Ravel (four movements orchestrated from 6-part suite originally [1919] written for piano)

LIGHTING: Ronald Bates

PREMIERE: 29 May 1974 (Ravel Festival)

CAST: *Left Quadrille:* Judith Fugate, Jean-Pierre Frohlich; Wilhelmina Frankfurt, Victor Castelli; Muriel Aasen, Francis Sackett; Susan Hendl, David Richardson; *Right Quadrille:* Marjorie Spohn, Hermes Condé; Delia Peters, Richard Hoskinson; Susan Pilarre, Richard Dryden; Carol Sumner. Laurence Matthews

Prélude
Forlane
Rigaudon
Menuet

Le Tombeau de Couperin. **Ensemble.** (*Photo Martha Swope.*)

Tombeau was the uncontested highlight of the Festival and a little jewel on any terms. The score was intended by Ravel as an homage to eighteenth-century French music (not Couperin alone) as well as a memorial ("tombeau") to some of his departed friends (each movement is dedicated to a friend who died in World War I). In form it is a suite of dances in baroque and classical style, which Ravel transformed into mournful plaints, primarily through the use of modes, in contrast to the more restful diatonicism of his models. (The modal idioms sound an antique or archaic note, while the compressed chromaticism is distinctly modern.) Ravel invested with a new darkness forms originally intended for inconsequent socializing.

Balanchine's work, which did not observe the overtones of lament, retained the aura of formal dances with the use of couples, the formations of square, diamond, and so forth, and the ritualized courtesies between partners; he embellished and reaccented basic steps. The period aspect of the work, both in the etiquette of the performers and in the open acknowledgment of specific dance forms (not to mention the crisp geometry of the patterns—like a parquet floor) was so inescapable that the ballet might have been

enhanced by elegant costuming. For once, practice clothes belied the content. (Garis argued, however, that costumes would have made the period feeling too literal.)

Interestingly, in addition to smiling all over, several critics found that this work, unusual for Balanchine in its preset outline, had connections with several of his other ballets. (*Agon* was most frequently cited.)

Vaughan: "Deeply satisfying. Stravinsky is quoted as saying that Ravel composed 'with the finesse of a Swiss watchmaker,' and nowhere is this quality more apparent than in this suite of dances in early eighteenth-century style. Choreography matched the music in the precision and delicacy of its symmetry; simply on the level of musical analysis made visible, the ballet held one totally absorbed. More important was the fact that it set off profound and complex resonances, referring as it did not only to the origin of ballet in social dances of the past, both courtly and common, but to so many of Balanchine's own works that have drawn on this kind of material, works as various as *Concerto Barocco*, *Agon*, *Square Dance*, and even *Who Cares?*" [1]

Garis: "The style that *Tombeau* is 'about' is the court dancing suggested by the music. We all know a little bit about this style from square dancing, from seventeenth- and eighteenth-century French and Italian paintings, from what gets done on stage when Congreve is revived, and so on. And I think I'm right in saying

that we all have thought of it as not involving much 'real' dancing, so it was at first very interesting and then intensely moving to see what happened when the dance genius of Balanchine set out to show us the real dancing in this genre. Nothing was forced; it was quite intelligent revelation; and *Tombeau* isn't perhaps what one could call a piece of high creativity. It isn't *Agon*. Yet there's a real relation between the two, not only in style but also in procedure. *Agon*, too, takes off from court dances. It goes miles further than *Tombeau* into Balanchine's own personal vision, partly because it wants to, intends to, but at least partly because—thanks perhaps to the collaboration with Stravinsky—it naturally turned into a great work and became airborne and couldn't avoid going all that way. But in *Agon* as in the much smaller *Tombeau*, Balanchine strips things down to show the basic dance impulse of the genre." [2]

Barnes: "Balanchine uses [the ensemble] with such grace and sensibility that it is itself a star. The ballet looks so handsome and its movements are so extraordinarily well aligned and well attuned to the music that the entire work from beginning to end absolutely sings." [3]

Gelles: "Balanchine has given [the two quadrilles] identical steps and gestures for virtually the entire piece, and it is fascinating to feel how the simplest movement is reinforced emotionally by being performed by two instead of one. It's a very subtle business, a matter of weight and texture, but perceptible nonetheless. In general, the movements are as clean and economical as the movements in *Agon* and *Four Temperaments*. In working with Ravel, however, Balanchine has flavored his steps and gestures with inflections that are courtly and quintessentially French." [4]

Goldner: "Just as one was about to toss the Ravel Festival into the drink, along came a Balanchine ballet that looks like a masterpiece. It is one of those marvels of complicated simplicity, set for two quadrilles that remain politely yet firmly discrete until the last dance, the Menuet. The first dance becomes the tonic chord for the next three. It is done in the square formation typical of barn dances, and anyone who has ever spent an evening square-dancing would have no trouble calling out the figures (ladies' and men's chains, four-hand stars, promenades) or recognizing the etiquette unique to the form—the endless curtsies and little sashays acknowledging neighbors. The formation of the second dance is a line of sixteen which is divided into eights, maintaining the original quadrilles, and then again into fours, and then again, sometimes, into twos. The dancers always move on the diagonal, so as to reshape what is basically a brutally horizontal field of action into a delicious carousal of angles. The steps of the last two dances are enlarged versions of the first, but now we see them performed as a reel instead of a square. The reel itself is exposed from two perspectives: on diagonals and, at the beginning of the last dance, in a straight line perpendicular to the audience.

"Many of Balanchine's ballets define their boundaries and rules of play as they are being played, but *Tombeau* presents them to us as a prearranged story. How [he] arranges the groupings so that each has a different weight and how he arranges the multitude of promenades and ladies' chains so as to make each one unique are as much of the story as are the dancers' exquisite manners and the ballet's ambience of graciousness and high spirits.

"*Tombeau* poses and answers questions relating to the very core of form. The ballet compels one to recognize that the first dance would look flatter and feel heavier if the squares were not tilted into diamonds; to see that, in the second dance, the difference between parallel diagonals and crossing diagonals is the difference between the public and the domestic.

One must marvel at Balanchine's ability to juggle between those worlds without snagging the ballet's fleet pace. Similarly, one must notice the delicate balance between vernacular and classical language.

"One must notice all these things, if only on a subconscious level, because Balanchine presents them as transparently and persistently and rationally as do many of the better conceptual, minimalist choreographers of the latest avant-garde. *Tombeau* sets itself tasks (to borrow the lingo of the New Dance) and follows along quite rigid procedural lines. One could diagram it, perhaps computerize it. But oh the differences: it's entertaining; it's complicated, *very* complicated. If *Agon* smiles, *Tombeau* laughs. A yet more telling difference, I think, is that one of *Tombeau*'s key formal characteristics is also its great dramatic thread: when will the two quadrilles become one? In the second and third dances Balanchine works them acrobatic touches kitschy, the lying-on-the-floor sequence forced. Kisselgoff comacross the dividing line, the ballet suddenly pops into full bloom. The welding of formal and expressive elements is one of Balanchine's great gifts to all people for whom Humanism is still an ideal. Where, except in Balanchineland, can one experience circles and lines as moods?

"*Le Tombeau* is also full of irrational pleasures, and I love it for that too. Somewhere in the middle of the last dance everybody lines up again for a reel, and Judith Fugate, at the head, walks down between the rows to meet her partner at the other end. She walks on pointe, daintily yet with a piquant sting in her legs. Perhaps that moment connects with Ravel in a particularly insightful way. Perhaps it encapsules in two seconds flat why ballet is done on pointe and why Balanchine's contra dances are so much spicier than their models. Or perhaps it's wonderful because Fugate's strut is a charming apologia for exhibitionist dancing. One imagines hearing a raucous caller, or thigh-slapping from her peers, as accompaniment to her little journey down the path, and the strange mingle between court and country, Fugate's modesty and pride, is irresistible. It's easy to see how that moment fits into the entire ballet, but just how Balanchine infiltrates an intimation of twang into such an elegant figure is a mystery. The mystery of that moment, the intangible thrill of it, will keep me coming back fresh to *Tombeau* time after time after time." [5]

CHOREOGRAPHY: George Balanchine

MUSIC: Maurice Ravel (*Pavane pour une Infante Défunte*, orchestral version of 1899 piano piece, 1911)

LIGHTING: Ronald Bates

PREMIERE: 29 May 1975 (Ravel Festival)

CAST: Patricia McBride

PAVANE

Pavane, to one of Ravel's best-known pieces, was considered by Croce "curiously, a miss." [1] Others concurred (Barnes: "Contemplative but unmemorable" [2]). It contained very little dancing, or, at least, almost no ballet technique. There were walking, running, backbends; but much of the movement was reserved for the long scarf or cape, which McBride swirled, threw, wrapped around herself, and, at the end used as a veil and possibly a handkerchief for weeping. Many of the configurations were reminiscent of Loïe Fuller pictures; the ballet's Eastern/Spanish feeling (Moorish, perhaps) also recalled Ruth St. Denis.

Wrote Vaughan: "A complete surprise; it's unlike anything Balanchine has done in recent memory. I never saw *Errante*, but my guess is that it might have been something like this. Mostly it was all plastique, with sorrowing gestures: At the beginning, McBride stood and slowly raised her hands to her eyes, which were covered by a veil—an unforgettable image." [3]

Garis: "*Pavane*, while truly awful, never turns to camp. It is an étude in a dance genre that at first I wanted—contemptuously—to call Radio City Large Scarf until it occurred to me that this was exactly what it was. You can't really say what went wrong with *Pavane*—[but] you did think of the silent movies and it all turned out to be banal and vulgar but oddly sincere." [4]

UNE BARQUE SUR L'OCÉAN

CHOREOGRAPHY: Jerome Robbins

MUSIC: Maurice Ravel (orchestral version

of piece originally [1906] for piano, 1907)

COSTUMES: Parmelee Welles

LIGHTING: Ronald Bates

PREMIERE: 29 May 1975 (Ravel Festival)

CAST: Victor Castelli; Daniel Duell, Laurence Matthews, Jay Jolley, Nolan T'Sani

In this brief work, the dancers gave the feeling of being on the ocean, swaying slightly and moving in a slow, smooth way, like molasses. They assumed poses reminiscent of antique statues: standing in Praxitelean contrapposto, kneeling with drawn bow, or momentarily evoking the Roman Mercury. The work seemed an essay in music, with the dance elements distracting, or perhaps a study of bodies. Many of the movements recalled eurythmics. The ballet was shown during the festival only.

Vaughan: "A bit of music visualization, negligible except for Castelli's line in arabesque." [1]

Croce: "Made five boys look sweetly pretty." [2]

Jowitt: "[The music] seems to have beguiled Robbins with its impressionistic qualities, so his dance tilts and sails and rocks, and sometimes the men are like sailors, and sometimes like billows." [3]

TZIGANE

CHOREOGRAPHY: George Balanchine

MUSIC: Maurice Ravel (1924)

COSTUMES: Joe Eula

LIGHTING: Ronald Bates

PREMIERE: 29 May 1975 (Ravel Festival)

VIOLIN: Lamar Alsop

CAST: Suzanne Farrell, Peter Martins; 3 couples

Tzigane brought Farrell back to the audience of the New York City Ballet. Not that this marked her first performance since returning to the Company; she had danced often during the preceding season. But this was Balanchine's first work

Tzigane. **Suzanne Farrell, Peter Martins.** *(Photo Fred Fehl.)*

for her in six years, and for most critics and spectators, that was enough. (Although Martins was listed as her partner, he did not appear till halfway through the ballet, and his role was perfunctory.)

As a dance, *Tzigane*, with its nightclub-gypsy atmosphere, poses that would look appropriate on technicolor postcards, and hackneyed movements (giant backbends, broken wrists, turned-in knees, hip undulations, clapping, strutting, stomping) came close to a parody of the gypsy fire and drama one might expect in low-budget movies. In keeping with it all, Balanchine instructed the violinist not to try for beauty but for "gypsy" feeling. The violin part is fiendishly hard; according to Stuckenschmidt, "all the difficulties of virtuoso violin music of the nineteenth century were exceeded by it." [1] The study of Paganini's *Études* had been Ravel's starting point.

As ever, Balanchine suited his dance to the musical style. Wrote Gillespie: "The choreography includes elements of visual kitsch and virtuoso turns but they are present in the brilliant violin solo." [2]

In a vein of admiration, Croce wrote: "In *Tzigane*, there was and there can only be Farrell. With no one else could this florid gypsy-violin rhapsody find so comfortable a home in the theater. The first half, for violin solo, becomes a five-minute dance solo that touches a new height in contemporary virtuoso performance. Farrell's dancing is a seamless flow, [but] there were moments that stopped my breath: a high, motionless

piqué balance lightly stepped into from nowhere, a headlong plunge into arabesque penchée effortlessly held as she turned over to face the sky, chaîné turns changing speed, [triple] pirouettes slowing to an insolent balance-finish, which she executed with her hands cupping her head." [3]

Vaughan: "Made to measure for the mature and wonderful dancer Farrell has become, a collaboration between choreographer and dancer in which both knew exactly how far they could go in ironic comment on the music's evocation of smoldering gypsy passion; [for instance,] the moment when Farrell ran on pointe in a full backbend over Martins' arm—it was satirical, perhaps, but a breathtaking dance moment too." [4]

Garis: "In this exhilarating etude for foot positions in the gypsy genre, there are more intricacies and subtleties of choice than you'd believe possible. It is exciting not only for the rapidity and range of its choices of position and direction and balance but for its rapid and sensitive changes of tone and level of intensity, from the directly passionate and rhapsodic to the wittily self-mocking and then on to open joking. *Tzigane* is probably only minor Balanchine. But to have him choreographing for Farrell again was worth the whole Festival—or so I think right now." [5]

Jowitt: "The long strange solo for Farrell [was] slow, loose-jointed, and not altogether pleasant, like an elegant drawing of an awkward child." [6]

THE TORONTO SCENE

by Michael Crabb

How many times can you say farewell and say it with class? Well, if you are Veronica Tennant, twice for sure. In February, 1989, the veteran National Ballet star gave what many people thought was a farewell performance when she danced the full-length *Romeo and Juliet* for hometown fans. It was a nostalgic moment since Juliet was the very Cranko role that had launched Tennant on her path to fame 24 years before. It was not, however, quite what National Ballet manage-

Curtain call at the Veronica Tennant Gala on
November 21, 1989   Photo: David Street

ment had in mind. All along they had been planning to hold a November gala to mark Tennant's 25th anniversary with the company, and her unexpected decision to retire threw carefully laid financial projections into disarray. Galas are big fund-raising opportunities, and the National Ballet hoped to make a $100,000-plus killing from Tennant's 25th.

Rumour has it that Tennant had to be persuaded to return for another farewell performance but, being the loyal trouper she is, the 43-year-old ballerina finally consented, and the event went ahead on November 21. As it turned out, the two farewell performances, just nine months apart, dovetailed very nicely. Tennant's 25th anniversary gala was an opportunity to celebrate her remarkable range as a dancer — not just, to use the late critic Nathan Cohen's words, "the brooding Miss Tennant", but Tennant the comedienne and Tennant the pure classicist.

As the lady of the moment herself pointed out in an eloquent though seemingly impromptu commentary, if she was starting out today she would be lucky to gain admittance to her alma mater, the National Ballet School. Her body has never been the perfect ballet physique and her triumph has been one of artistry and theatricality over flesh and bone.

Live portions of the programme reminded us of Tennant's gifts as a dramatic actress, while a collection of excerpts from works by National Ballet-bred choreographers such as Constantin Patsalas, James Kudelka and David Allan showed how Tennant was always willing to put her dancing talent

and prestige behind indigenous creativity. But it was the collection of film and video clips, particularly of Tennant with Nureyev in *The Sleeping Beauty* from 1972, which re-established her claim to have been one of the National Ballet's strongest and most dynamic classicists.

The biggest thrill of the gala was the surprise guest appearance of Stuttgart Ballet star Richard Cragun to partner Tennant in a role she had long coveted, that of Katherine in Cranko's *Taming of the Shrew*. Cragun, with his technical power apparently unabated at age 45, drew a suitably pugilistic performance from Tennant in the famous "Fight" pas de deux — a pyrotechnical display that brought the audience to its feet.

Appropriately, however, Tennant chose to leave her audience with a more emotionally-charged finale, the complete last act of Cranko's *Onegin*. Her final scene with partner Raymond Smith, when Tatiana must bid a tearful goodbye to the man she still loves, was filled with irony — the ballerina making her last exit.

Yet the tone of the evening was celebratory and not regretful. Tennant chose to leave at a time when she obviously could have gone on dancing; so much better than fading away.

Tennant's 25th unfortunately coincided with the nearby opening of a one-week Toronto engagement by the touring Ballet British Columbia. With the Tennant gala followed by two appearances by Evelyn Hart in *Giselle*, Ballet B.C. had tough competition but, despite smaller audiences than it has enjoyed on its two previous Premiere Dance Theatre visits and several dancer injuries to contend with, the Vancouver-

based company still managed to show why it has become so popular in Canada's largest and reputedly most fastidious city. *The Globe and Mail* and *The Toronto Star* praised both the dancing and repertoire, although the two major dailies were split on the merits of Laszlo Seregi's *Variations on a Nursery Song*, the one work on the programme put there by Ballet B.C.'s new artistic director, Pat Neary. One clear impression that almost all local followers of the west coast troupe took away was of a stronger dancing company. The men particularly looked cleaner and more assured.

Meanwhile, Reid Anderson, in his new post at the National Ballet, seems to be having his own impact on the dancing there. When the company's lengthy fall season opened it looked as if someone had given them a lecture on earning their keep. There was a new animation to the big classics especially. Instead of bored villagers lurking round the fringes of Giselle's cottage we got to see real characters, each clearly delineated and with a personal history to bring to the action. It made each night's Mad Scene absolutely gripping, and the effect spilled over into subsequent performances of the full-length *Napoli*, first staged after Bournonville's traditional version by Peter Schaufuss in 1981. Schaufuss was back to dance in two performances with Karen Kain who, despite an injured foot which cost her several shows during the season, gave an exceptionally buoyant, effervescent reading of Terasina.

The modern dance scene got off to a lively start with a selection of guests from the Montreal International Festival of New Dance showing up at Harbourfront, to be followed later in the season with a ten-year retrospective of work by Robert Desrosièrs. The locally-based Desrosièrs company opted for a retrospective when plans for a new full-evening work had to be shelved because of an injury to one of the choreographer's key dancers. Ironically, the programme, titled *Avalanche*, gave a stronger impression of Desrosièrs as choreographer than many of his full works have done. Stripped of much of their special effects and lavish, playful sets and decors, the works on view inevitably focused on movement and showed how Desrosièrs's vocabulary and fluency in creating group dances have evolved over the years.

Dancemakers also chose to look back in their fall performances by presenting a revival of a four-year-old site-specific work, *Atlas Moves Watching* by artistic director Bill James. The audience sat looking out across 600 square feet of fresh sod through a storefront window onto Toronto's King Street West. Passersby unintentionally became part of the action outside the store, while the audience found itself turned into performers as people stared in from the street. The piece itself carries a quasi-apocalyptic message about a world out of balance — a message that got lost in the sheer delight of the piece's unusual and amusing situation in a former print shop. ▼

On November 26, 1989, Suzanne Farrell retired from dancing and from the New York City Ballet. Many people in the audience, in the packed New York State Theatre, had been attracted to ballet through Farrell, through her beauty, captured in photographs, and through the legend of her relationship and interaction with George Balanchine. You did not even have to have seen her dance to be enticed and entranced by her image and story, for these things traveled in magazines and in Bernard Taper's biography, *Balanchine*. You could even say that the New York State Theater itself was built in part by Farrell, for her work with Balanchine and the ballets he made for her — *Meditation, Movements for Piano and Orchestra, Don Quixote, Diamonds, Chaconne* — are among those that were the first to reach a wide and expanding audience for

Ohio, to New York and the School of American Ballet. Once in the New York City Ballet, Farrell was first noticed by Jacques d'Amboise (who would later spot the talent in Merrill Ashley and Kyra Nichols), and d'Amboise invited her on little touring groups and gave her her first chances to dance big parts; it was he who suggested Farrell when, in 1963, Diana Adams was unable to perform the premiere of *Movements for Piano and Orchestra* and needed to be replaced. The rest is history, and pretty

NEW YORK DANCE

by Anita Finkel

ballet in the 1960s.

Farrell's career, 1961-1989, is an entire history of an era of ballet in this country. She came from the midwest and presumably indifferent training; a Ford Foundation fellowship, her mother's ambition and her own iron will directed her from Cincinnati,

overfamiliar, too — the ballets, the marriage, the tag-lines ("it's all in the programmes"). In Farrell's 28 years on the stage, there were three careers — the unicorn years leading to her departure in 1969; the return under Balanchine (1975-1983); and the last lonely years on what became enemy territory. By the time she stood centre stage with her arm clutched in Lincoln Kirstein's and a carpet of white roses tied in green and silver at her feet, Farrell was more than a ballerina making her farewell, and more than the last verdant symbol of an era. She was the beacon and token of an ideal of art that seems to be setting with the millenium. It's not too much to say that everything European art achieved between the years 1000 and 2000 a.d. stood in front of us taking a last bow in Farrell's gracious, lonely, satin-clad posture. Whatever we confront in 2001, it will owe little to the dynasties of empire that gave birth to ballet and ballerinas, to ideals of virtue, femininity, honour and suffering that culminated in the writing of the romantic poets who invented ballet; new formalisms will have to be invented for the art of the 21st century, and they won't owe much to Vestris, Taglioni, Cecchetti and Petipa. For one night, November 26, beauty had its last stand as an ideal in New York City, and it wasn't old-fashioned. But beauty like this won't be back. As the company grouped around Farrell at the end of *Vienna Waltzes*, you could see it on many faces onstage as well as off. Farrell's own visage cracked at the very end of the dance, which ended in a sob — anyway she was looking up far too much, and her partner, Adam Luders, had to struggle to engage her gaze. Maria Calegari, to her right, dissolved in tears, which also struck Judith Fugate, Carole Divet, Florence Fitzgerald, and Deborah Wingert;

in the middle of it, Kyra Nichols smiled a sunny, unbroken, unbreaking smile. In a way, the formality that was meant to underlie the occasion, and which was unbroken for the farewells of Martins and of Balanchine himself, cracked apart for the tribute to Suzanne Farrell, which just could not uphold the courtly and composed veneer.

Like Martins in 1983, Farrell left in *Nutcracker* season. As time has gone by, *Nutcracker* has taken an ever-increasing hold on this city. Now, you *really* can't get into NYCB's 38 performances if you don't have a ticket by the first week in November; at City Center, a few blocks away, the Joffrey Ballet's third run of their production sold every seat in the house including the seldon-used second balcony. As it happens, the Joffrey's production is in much better shape than NYCB's, though as a conception it is not as glorious or fine. But so much is in the playing. NYCB's first night was afflicted with some unforeseen difficulties — Peter Frame was an emergency replacement for Luders in the pas de deux, and had trouble handling Merrill Ashley, the Sugarplum Fairy — the two have seldom danced together, so this was a little like a rehearsal in public. For the first time, Darci Kistler was opening-night Dewdrop, in a performance marked by good pirouettes but a tentative attack and some real uncertainty in foot work when it came from moving from place to place or holding a balance or position. Stacy Caddell was especially weak as leader of the Marzipan Shepherdesses. Only two of the adult cast made an artistic mark — Helene Alexopoulos as Coffee, and Damian Woetzel in Candy Canes. It was the children who held the piece together and shone for both individual and ensemble artistry — for the second or third year, the "corps" of Polichinelles that come bounding out from under Mother Ginger's skirt firmly,

GASPARD DE LA NUIT

CHOREOGRAPHY: George Balanchine

MUSIC: Maurice Ravel (three poems for piano solo, 1908; inspired by *Gaspard de la Nuit,* a book of poems by Aloysius Bertrand [d. 1841]

COSTUMES, DÉCOR: Bernard Daydé (execution supervised by David Mitchell)

LIGHTING: Bernard Daydé (in association with Ronald Bates)

PREMIERE: 29 May 1975 (Ravel Festival)

PIANO: Jerry Zimmerman

CAST: *Ondine,* Colleen Neary, Victor Castelli; 5 women; *Le Gibet,* Karin von Aroldingen, Nolan T'Sani; 8 women, 3 men; *Scarbo,* Sara Leland, Robert Weiss; 3 men

Gaspard de la Nuit, pieces for piano, are three romantic poems of transcendent virtuosity." So wrote Ravel about one of his most famous, provocative, and technically difficult works. In truth, the pieces are somewhat more. Ravel was attracted to the refined miniature prose-poems of a "goldsmith in verse" (whose perfection in detail would have appealed to him); the author, Bertrand, had been influenced by the fantastical and morbid tales of E.T.A. Hoffmann, which in turn owed something to the war-horror engravings of Callot. In gothic manner, Bertrand wrote of a certain Gaspard, "a manifestation of the evils of the night." The pieces were only the first of Ravel's fascinations with the sepulchral world of the supernatural. Of the composition, he wrote, "The devil has had a hand in it. No wonder, for the devil himself is indeed the author of the poems." [1]

Balanchine's treatment, elaborate in production, alluded to the words of the poems (given in the program, as they were in the score, although Ravel wrote no vocal line): "Ondine" had a watery feeling (mostly conveyed by lighting); in "Le Gibet," dark figures hung from rings; "Scarbo," who "pirouette[s] on one foot and roll[s] about the room," was easy to approximate in dance; his "nail scratching the silk of my bedcurtains" perhaps accounted for the discomfiting noise of

Gaspard de la Nuit. *(Photo Martha Swope.)*

fingernails scraping the surfaces of mirrors. For the most part, however, *Gaspard* was a mood piece, whose tone was set by the murky lighting throughout and the use of mirrors in each section, rather than by dance images. Figures were mostly half-hidden in darkness; the women wore their hair long, like old hags.

Barnes dismissed the ballet as a "gimmick-strewn wasteland, a surprising essay at a Roland Petit ballet during the fifties." [2]

To Croce it was "a taste of Les Ballets 1933, but Balanchine now seems beyond the steadfast chic of Paris and its appetite for morbid pleasures." [3] Garis called it a "mess." Others found more to say but scarcely more to like. A few impressions lingered (Jowitt wrote of a "delicate, almost voluptuous sense of horror" [4]) but of choreographic substance there was little.

Goldner: "Dancing and décor swamped each other so thoroughly that no dramatic statement was made. The most successful was 'Le Gibet' because it was the most outrageous. The dancers, wearing wigs that blot out their faces, dangle on ropes. Others, carrying mirrors and draped in black, slowly crisscross the stage. [Croce

mentioned that "two of them struggle in a tortuous and obscure way to make love." [5]] [In 'Scarbo'] had the choreography been even more nervous, the stage could have looked like a hard, glittery black diamond. But instead we got 'plot,' as the dancers tried to scratch their images off the mirrors." [6]

Vaughan: "The décor was appropriately elegant and mysterious. In 'Ondine' Castelli entered carrying a piece of black glass in the shape of a hand, gazing at it with total absorption, and only when Neary took it from him did he become aware of her presence; at the end he regained possession of it, as Neary reached after him with one hand and pressed the other to her lips. 'Le Gibet' was a necrophilic pas de deux [in which] eight dancers passed across the stage in a diagonal procession carrying what looked at first like mirrors but proved to be glass death's heads—it was like something out of a Cocteau movie. 'Scarbo' was lighter in feeling but still gallows humor. Two grotesque, mercurial creatures appeared and disappeared behind oval mirrors manipulated by three men.* [Some] found [*Gaspard*] an unfathomable piece: I found it fascinating to see Balanchine going deeply into his imaginative resources to find equivalent dance or theatrical imagery for this most elusive of Ravel's scores." [7]

SARABANDE AND DANSE (II)

CHOREOGRAPHY: Jacques d'Amboise

MUSIC: Claude Debussy (1901; c. 1890, orchestrated by Maurice Ravel, 1923)

COSTUMES: John Braden

LIGHTING: Ronald Bates

PREMIERE: 29 May 1975 (Ravel Festival)

CAST: *Danse,* Colleen Neary, Bart Cook; 3 men; *Sarabande,* Kyra Nichols, Francis Sackett

Despite the order in the title, *Danse* was performed first, a sprightly number

---

* Balanchine used more than mirrors in his seemingly perverse pursuit of optical illusion by substituting uncredited dancers in black for the silver-clad principals in "Scarbo" at moments when the silvers had no time to change outfits.

SARABANDE AND DANSE (II)

with some "horsy" steps for Neary's coltish looks and jumping ability. *Sarabande* was a period piece, recalling court manners and decorum of another age, although more energetic. The movements might be considered stylized Elizabethan. Everything was very long and elegant; the participants were very much a courtier and his lady.

Jowitt: "[*Danse*] looks like a tribute to opening day at the races at Saratoga— elegant but vigorous and very American. That's okay: he's given Neary some marvelous syncopated gallops and skips." [1]

Goldner: "We all know that Neary can jump. So what else is new? *Sarabande*, however, is surprising for its control, stateliness, and consistency, the best work [d'Amboise] has done since *Irish Fantasy*." [2]

Chansons Madécasses. **Helgi Tomasson, Patricia McBride, Debra Austin, Hermes Condé.** (*Photo Martha Swope.*)

CHANSONS MADÉCASSES

Songs of the Madegasque (Madagascar)

CHOREOGRAPHY: Jerome Robbins

MUSIC: Maurice Ravel (*Chansons Madécasses: Nahandove, Aoua, Il est doux,* settings for voice, piano, violoncello, and flute of poems by Evariste Parney [1787], 1925–26; commissioned by Elizabeth Sprague Coolidge)

LIGHTING: Ronald Bates

PREMIERE: 29 May 1975 (Ravel Festival)

MEZZO-SOPRANO: Gwendolyn Killebrew

CAST: Patricia McBride, Helgi Tomasson; Debra Austin, Hermes Condé

This unusual work was found compelling and mysterious by some, empty and boring by others. The music was undeniably arty—the recherché instrumentation was stipulated in the commission—while full of ravishing colors; the same could be said of the ballet. Robbins was intrigued by the anomaly of refined French art music supporting prose poems on folk rhythms and imagery. In his words, "One of the most striking aspects is the earthiness and immediacy of the content of the source material and, by contrast,

Ravel's use of such cool, elegant, and minimum musical means to transform it into the art-song form."

The poems are erotic and voluptuous, exuding a tropical languor. But Ravel concentrated on exoticism (although the dark rich tones demanded in the vocal line—which, according to Ravel, was treated as the "principal instrument" in the quartet—are of the most sensuous nature).

Similarly, there were no lovers in Robbins's ballet—his movements were odd, angular, sculptural. Some of the poses were reminiscent of Gauguin's Tahitians; some movements were like slow gymnastics; there was a sense of stillness (Tomasson like an alert animal waiting and watching); much of the dancing was terreà-terre (few jumps or lifts); the women sat on their feet like servants; a man lay on the floor; a woman snapped her fingers; sometimes all four danced in unison, in one section with their arms about each others' waists; the men walked; the ballet ended. Robbins's movements were nonvirtuosic. Perhaps he was seeking the same simplicity Ravel also felt paramount in this work, and also did not fully achieve.

A principal source of irritation among spectators was Robbins's use of a white couple (dressed in white) and a dark couple (in black), which, presumably, was inspired by the opening line of the second poem: "Place not your trust in the white man, inhabitants of these shores." Says

he, "It hasn't a big 'significance,' but it's somewhere there in the sources." Most critics, however, felt it was a rather too-obvious ploy.

Croce: "Bad conscience, sexual hypocrisy, racial guilt? Robbins's mirror images don't come from the world of the ballet or of Ravel; they come from the world of Edward Albee. In the ballet, there's no way to think even if one wants to. The only reason one can't formulate a meaning for what he has put on stage is that there isn't any." [1]

Goldner: "The black couple do one 'African phrase,' and that's it for race relations." [2]

Garis: "In general, the piece just didn't register. Perhaps fortunately—the theme about race relations would probably have been truly offensive in effect if it had any effect at all." [3]

As for the rest, wrote Barnes, "Cool, couth, and interesting. Robbins, with nothing more than two pairs of dancers and a few potted palms, redolent of a slightly seedy once-grand hotel, suggested a strange and languorous world. Note the small nuances he introduces into this realm of the classical duet—with little finger snaps and hands held soft behind the neck—or watch his use of stasis, or the men resting on the ground in Michelangelo poses while the women dance in canon. McBride and Tomasson demonstrated how well they understood that silver core of stillness that runs through much of Robbins's choreography. The other couple [was] presumably an intentionally black mirror image which perhaps had some relationship with the literary content of these Madagascan songs." [4]

Jowitt: "Lovely in parts but unclear in approach. McBride and Tomasson twine around each other, but then after sinking to the floor, she circles him with demure little bourrées. It's as if Robbins has followed the words a little way and then pulled back. [Then] he seems about to pick up on words of the second song ('white man') but instead produces a strange and quite beautiful, warily companionable dance for four." [5]

Goldner: "Robbins's most interesting piece for the [festival], if only because [of] the easygoing nobility with which Mc-Bride and, above all, Tomasson negotiate [his] self-conscious notions of simplicity. Robbins [is] a veritable genie for being able to persuade a convincing anti-Balanchine style out of two of Balanchine's most sympathetic instruments. *Chansons* is quintessential Robbins, beautifully paced and spaced, terribly manipulative. It's another of Robbins's diddlings with contemplative movement. Its stillnesses and queer haiku gestures are always handsome, but the ballet is more bloated than pregnant with meaning. Alienation between the spectator and the action sets in sooner or later; sooner or later one begins to ponder how long it took Robbins to arrange the groupings of potted palms." [6]

RAPSODIE ESPAGNOLE

CHOREOGRAPHY: George Balanchine

MUSIC: Maurice Ravel (1907)

COSTUMES: Michael Avedon

LIGHTING: Ronald Bates

PREMIERE: 29 May 1975 (Ravel Festival)

CAST: Karin von Aroldingen, Peter Schaufuss, Nolan T'Sani; 12 couples

Prélude de la nuit
Malagueña
Habañera (pas de deux)
Feria

Rapsodie Espagnole was a hard ballet

Rapsodie Espagnole. **Karin von Aroldingen (right front).** (*Photo Martha Swope.*)

to like. Even those who admired it (and this opinion was by no means unanimous) found difficulty in making it sound appealing. Croce, reacting favorably, wrote: "With music this familiar the decision to make the ballet not high serious art but wittily ersatz art seems entirely appropriate. The *Rapsodie* is pop Balanchine—Hollywood Spanish; spectral and glamorous, it looks like the most expensive entertainment available at some oasis of a resort hotel." [1]

Goldner reserved judgment on the whole, but wrote of "an incipiently vicious tango duet in the vein of *La Valse*, some good moments of what has been called 'organized chaos,' and moments of driving momentum." [2]

Gelles, an admirer, found that Balanchine "used boys like chorus girls." [3]

For the large ensemble, there were undulating, slithering movements; men did gypsy steps to castanets; women did high, slow kicks. The aura of a nightclub floorshow was unmistakable. Saddled with such baggage—to which might be added mention that the costumes, rhumba outfits, were panned—the ballet, it would seem, barely had a chance.

For Croce, it was the compositional technique that made the difference: "Although it is pictorial music of the most imaginative kind, its images are impractically paced for choreography. Until Balanchine staged it. I wouldn't have believed it could be made into a ballet. Even Balanchine doesn't quite bring it off, but he is at his most insistent and re-

sourceful; he works at the piece as if it were the first one he'd ever made, and just because the material is so recalcitrant his superb craftsmanship is the more exposed—you can see him preparing his effects, hovering in discreet withdrawals or holding actions, then pouncing in a massed attack. The fun of the ballet is in watching Balanchine maneuver. The marvel of it is that so much of it works as a *stage* fantasy; even the edginess becomes at times wonderfully suspenseful. He loads the stage with those long-stemmed nymphs of his and arrays them in open, steady poses, balances, and splits to the floor. The opening sequence, with them all spread out in diagonals and one by one converting écarté positions into closed and then open croisés, is like a redoing of the opening of *Symphony in Three Movements*." [4]

Others were very definitely not entranced with any aspect of the ballet. Wrote Barnes: "Very ballet-Spanish and mildly boring." [5] Vaughan: "Had all the vulgarity that *Tzigane* so carefully avoided and exploited the most grotesque qualities of those female dancers who seem to have been bred for speed rather than line—sway backs, retracted pelvises, splayed fingers, turned-in legs." [6]

THE STEADFAST TIN SOLDIER

CHOREOGRAPHY: George Balanchine

MUSIC: Georges Bizet (March, Berceuse, Duo, Galop from *Jeux d'Enfants*, op. 22, 1871)

COSTUMES, DÉCOR: David Mitchell

LIGHTING: Ronald Bates

PREMIERE: 30 July 1975, Performing Arts Center, Saratoga Springs, New York

CAST: Patricia McBride, Peter Schaufuss

Soldier also danced by Robert Weiss

Commissioned by the Saratoga management, this slight work concerning the love between a paper doll and a toy soldier was considered something of a "non-event" (by Barnes), particularly coming so soon after *Coppélia*, which, of course, also centered on a doll (also played by McBride).[1] The ten-minute pas de deux was suggested by a Hans Christian Andersen story of the same name, in which a one-legged soldier is attracted to a ballerina paper doll because, with one of her legs high in the air, she too is standing on one leg only; after adventures, including his ingestion by a fish, he melts and she turns to cinders on a tile stove, where a thoughtless child has dropped him and she has been blown by a gust of wind. Only his heart remains. Balanchine neglected (or changed) most of these details and concentrated on the love story.

The situation, and McBride's variation, were found also in the Company's *Jeux d'Enfants* (1955); the choreography for Schaufuss was new, although some thought it reminiscent of the soldier's variation in *Nutcracker*, and, as in *Jeux d'Enfants*, he led an amusing regiment of (painted) wooden soldiers. This was Schaufuss's first custom-made Balanchine role, a grateful circumstance for any dancer, but one particularly welcome to a performer of alien background, stylistically speaking, who was taking a while to find the Balanchine way. (Verdy and Martins have commented on the difficulty of the breaking-in period for a developed dancer; it is less a matter of technique than of phrasing, nuance, quality of movement, and speed in musical and muscular response.)

Barnes complained that the ballet contained "typical toy choreography. Everything is jerky, jokey, and uncoordinated, and also rather sad."[2] Others were more pleased.

As Tobias wrote, "Nobody is pretending this is a major work. The soldier's marching variation is first, with the awkward angles and umptitump arms of mechanical playthings. [Then] McBride flexes her pink-satin feet back into an arch, flipping them over into precise, pointed struts, with the jerky charm of an animated doll. [Her solo] ends with her applauding her own feats. The consequent courtship pas de deux is kept within its doll character (promenades with the leg extended à la seconde, foot flexed, for example), as is the entire piece, which is both its deft novelty and its limitation. The tin soldier is so enticed even by the circumscribed range of beauty and virtuosity, he offers the ballerina his heart, literally. Next a fast sec-

The Steadfast Tin Soldier. **Patricia McBride, Peter Schaufuss.** (*Photo Martha Swope.*)

tion is built up of different kinds of turns—a theme and variations of centrifugal force, with Balanchine exercising his dancers in their vocabulary, the way the trainers do their thoroughbreds at Saratoga's race courses. Midway in this movement, the ballerina rushes aside, thrusts open the window-doors, and, although her pantomime tells us it's because she's hot, there seems to be a daring mischievousness about her action too. Wind billows the curtains out, threatening the fragile toys. The dancer-doll spins in uncontrollable, circling piqués; it's supposed to be the wind that drives her into the flames, but it looks as if it's as much her own wilful motion. She is consumed by the fire, leaving only the steadfast heart; the soldier picks it up, and weeps. Balanchine has given the toy-ballerina a personality; that perfect charm of heartless doll-like beauty, and a temperament that is capricious, energy-filled, ardent and free. The piece is very small in scope and it's managed with the delicacy and wit with which Balanchine can shape even trifles."[3]

Croce found that "although it's only an excuse for a pas de deux, the story might be stronger than it is. I think Balanchine means to tell it earnestly but blithely, without sentiment. However, it isn't clear that the doll runs into the fireplace because she's blown there; nor is it clear that she's incinerated. The music (the galop from Bizet's *Jeux d'Enfants*) contains no motive for the doll's death, but, properly staged, it could sound the exact note of heartless whimsey the piece is aiming at.

Doll dances have a perennial fascination. The overt simulation is a release from the conventions of theatre; it plays upon our need to judge empirically, rather than through a tolerance of fiction, what is "real." And every doll-dancer invents her own pseudo-personhood. Patricia McBride has invented one pseudo-person called Coppélia. She now invents another, without a name, warmer and sillier than Coppélia. The mechanics of the part are not undertaken as a great feat (unlike those mannequins in store windows which really set out to fool you), and they soon vanish into conventional fiction: we must take flesh and bone for wood and sawdust, when a moment ago we were mesmerized by the proposition that wood and sawdust were plausibly there. *The Steadfast Tin Soldier* is a dance and not a puppet show. The dance is continuously absorbing, stringent even in its moments of coyness, and McBride brings an ageless vitality to the doll's character. She has the sparkle of an experienced soubrette." Playing opposite the relatively inexperienced and still tentative Robert Weiss, she resists the temptation she often yields to when her partner is not a match for her—the temptation to compensate for him by exaggerating her own authority. It is a beautifully tempered performance."[4]

CHACONNE

CHOREOGRAPHY: George Balanchine, staged by Brigette Thom

MUSIC: Christoph Willibald von Gluck (ballet music from *Orpheus and Eurydice*, first produced 1762)

COSTUMES: Karinska (Spring, 1976)

LIGHTING: Ronald Bates

PREMIERE: 22 January 1976

CAST: Suzanne Farrell, Peter Martins; Susan Hendl, Jean-Pierre Frohlich; 4 soloists; 2 demi-solo couples; 13 women, 6 men

Ensemble (added spring, 1976)
Duet (flute solo from Dance of the Blessed Spirits): Farrell, Martins
Pas de Trois: Renee Estópinal, Wilhelmina Frankfurt, Jay Jolley
Pas de Deux: Hendl, Frohlich

Pas de Cinq: Elise Flagg, 4 women
Pas de Deux (minuet, gavotte): Farrell,
  Martins
Chaconne: Farrell, Martins, demi-
  soloists, ensemble

Named for the ballet's (and the opera's) final movement, *Chaconne* was a lovely work, a "late-blooming Balanchine masterpiece,"[1] that was warmly received and showed to perfection the crystalline contours and unostentatious elegance of the Company's dancers. But it was of singular construction, both stylistically and formally: Kriegsman called it an "enigma,"[2] Goldner a "two-minded masterpiece."[3] Wrote Croce: "The two-sidedness is a problem."[4]

Perhaps it was two ballets, imperfectly integrated; some identified the elements, rather too superficially, as the Martins-Farrell sections on one side, and all the other parts on the other. In form the ballet was a series of more or less unrelated divertissements, interspersed with dances for the two principals, followed by what promised to be a grand finale but was in fact a large movement in which some new demi-soloists were introduced and previous soloists never appeared. As if to reflect this unexpected choice of dancers, this final movement was diffuse; for once, Balanchine did not clearly tell the eye where to look.

Balanchine choreographed the dances in 1963 for a Hamburg production of the entire opera (repeated in Paris in 1973); for the New York unveiling, he opened the ballet with a new supported duet for Farrell and Martins; then in spring, 1976, when the work was outfitted with costumes, he added a new ensemble section as an opening, to precede the duet. The work's stylistic discrepancies may stem from this construction over several years, or perhaps the ensemble parts were re-created exactly as in 1963, while Balanchine reaccented the Farrell-Martins sections to suit the idiosyncratic style of his ballerina. Moreover, the dances were created originally as interludes between parts of the vocal drama and not intended to be seen one after the other; continuity was not then a concern. Whatever the reasons, the movements for the principals (and the opening ensemble) are more lyrical and flowing, expansive, romantic, and elegiac than the sections for soloists and ensemble. These have the look of court entertainments, with rather clipped, pre-cise movements and stylized positions. The parts sit discordantly with each other, and the finale is unresolved (Croce complained of "loose ends"). Within each section, however, are choreographic gems. And as Goldner wrote, "One can't presume that internal links [between the dissimilar parts] will never be discovered. Nor can one make too much of this disparity, given the absolutely gorgeous dances Balanchine has given the world's two most gorgeous dancers."[5]

The opening ensemble, with the corps in flowing beige, has frieze-like connotations, with the corps, mostly walking and in bourrée, moving in profile to soft flute measures.

The principals' soulful first encounter was described by Kendall: "To a flute solo, Martins walks slowly from an upstage wing and Farrell from a downstage one toward each other. They meet, they join hands in an arc, but they keep their gazes down. They seem to be sensing each other in the darkness. Martins simply walks Farrell; he turns her as she dips underneath his outstretched arm; he lifts her slightly by the waist; finally he carries her off as her front leg reaches again and again for the ground. The episode could be a distillation of the Orpheus and Eurydice myth. Or just a dream prelude. It is also a profoundly subtle piece of partnering."[6] Goldner mentioned "slow lifts and haunting walks through the universe. The

Chaconne. **Peter Martins, Suzanne Farrell.** (*Photo Martha Swope.*)

duet relies more heavily on lifts than usual, but this love dance is nevertheless one of mutual effort and will. For, one of Farrell's legs is always lapping the ground and swimming forward, and who's to know whether it's her leg (so alive it could be the encasement for her brain) or Martins' arms that are doing the most propelling?"[7]

Then begins the body of the ballet: "Dancers in simple white costumes enter in lines, like courtiers gathering about a throne: given the social circumstances of Gluck's day, it may be a king's throne; given the ballet's spirit, it may be the throne of the king of love; and given the proscenium theater, the dancers' frontality suggests that their king may be the audience itself."[8] "The variations following the entree are as translucent and simple and profound. Banking on the inherent strength of ballet technique, as a composer banks on scales, Balanchine shows us how baby talk may be eased into singing, supple sentences. Avoiding didactic simplicity, he drops dabs of color into the dances without subverting the whiteness. In the Pas de Trois, Jolley carries his arms as though they held a lute; sometimes he plucks imaginary strings. Estópinal and Frankfurt swish their tunics as though they were long taffeta dresses. Hendl and Frohlich remind one of clever court jesters via the broken lines of their arms and her attitudes perched on bent knee. Whereas the Pas de Trois is nothing but transitional steps, their duet darts and spins with no transitional movements (a technical challenge). Next comes a Pas de Cinq for cygnets, crisp and adorable. And then the big swan and consort return for a duet and variations."[9] In this fuller pas de deux, with partnering, then "labyrinthine" variations for each, the dancers seem to skim. The man moves in light beats in a circle, the woman in off-accents making magnificent use of fluid body changes. "As in their first duet, the prevailing mode of white classicism switches to a lacier, more convoluted texture [than the preceding dances]. The tone is more personal. Yet vestiges of impersonal nobility exist in the utterly noncompetitive nature of their solos."[10]

Wrote Croce: "But then Martins and Farrell return, and the court ballet fades away, to be continued by other means. Farrell (now with hair classically knotted) is high-rococo expression in every limb and joint. Architecturally and ornamentally, her dancing is the music's mirror, an immaculate reflection of its sweep and buoyancy, with no loss of detail. Farrell's response to music is not to its moment-by-moment impulse but to its broad beat, its overarching rhythm and completeness of scale. When people speak of her as the perfect Balanchine dancer, this is probably what they mean. The blurriness I complained of is not in what she does. The trouble is simply that such poise, such angelic transparency, is a law unto itself. What happens in the middle of *Chaconne* is that a whole new ballet crystallizes, a new style in rococo dancing appears, which in 1963 was unknown. Balanchine turns the clock ahead so suddenly that if it weren't for Farrell's and Martins' steadiness we'd lose our bearings. Their first pas de deux gave no hint of what was to come. Now, in a minuet, they present a solemn façade or gateway to the variations for them both that follow in a gavotte. These are like sinuous corridors leading one on and on. It is excess, but it is controlled excess—never more than one's senses can encompass yet never less. Farrell's steps are full of surprising new twists; her aplomb is sublime. And Martins achieves a rhythmic plangency that is independently thrilling. (When people speak of him as the perfect partner for Farrell, this is not all they mean, but it's part of it.) Together, from the gavotte onward into the concluding chaconne these two dancers are a force that all but obliterates what remains of the divertissement. Balanchine's ensemble choreography here is musically focussed, but visually unrhymed. His yokes and garlands and summary groupings don't quite manage to gather and contain the new material for Farrell and Martins within the shell that remains from Hamburg-Paris. Evidently, Balanchine has restored the musical repeats he cut in Paris, but instead of giving them back to the corps (or, as seems more likely, to the demi-soloists), he assigned them, with new choreography, to Farrell and Martins."[11]

Goldner found the finale "reminiscent of *Symphony in C* but smaller and softer—an extravaganza minus the sheen. Pearls, not diamonds."[12]

Amidst others' superlatives Kriegsman demurred: "At first sight it seemed merely an interesting anomaly—beautiful in a decorative sense, but distinctly chilly and remote."[13]

UNION JACK

CHOREOGRAPHY: George Balanchine

MUSIC: Hershy Kay (adapted from traditional British sources, as detailed below, commissioned by the New York City Ballet, 1976)

COSTUMES, DÉCOR: Rouben Ter-Arutunian

LIGHTING: Ronald Bates

PREMIERE: 13 May 1976 (gala benefit preview 12 May 1976)

CAST (in order of appearance): I, SCOTTISH AND CANADIAN GUARDS REGIMENTS: *Lennox*, Helgi Tomasson, 9 men; *Dress MacLeod*, Jacques d'Amboise, 9 men ("Keel Row"); *Green Montgomerie*, Sara Leland, 9 women ("Caledonian Hunt's Delight"); *Dress MacDonald*, Kay Mazzo, 9 women; *Menzies*, Peter Martins, 9 men ("Dance wi' My Daddy"); *MacDonald of Sleat*, Karin von Aroldingen, 9 women ("Regimental Drum Variations"); *R.C.A.F. (Royal Canadian Air Force)*; Suzanne Farrell, 9 women (Scottish theme from the *Water Music* by George Frederick Handel); *Finale*, entire company ("Amazing Grace," "A Hundred Pipers") II, COSTERMONGER PAS DE DEUX: *Pearly King*, Jean-Pierre Bonnefous; *Pearly Queen*, Patricia McBride; 2 little girls (music hall songs, ca. 1890–1914: "The Sunshine of Your Smile," "The Night the Floor Fell In," "Our Lodger's Such a Naice Young Man," "Following in Father's Footsteps," "A Tavern in the Town") III, ROYAL NAVY (traditional hornpipe melodies, "Rule Britannia"): Victor Castelli, von Aroldingen, Bart Cook; d'Amboise, 8 women, 8 men; Leland, Tomasson, Mazzo; Martins, 8 women, 8 men; WRENS (*Women's Royal Naval Service*), Farrell, 8 women

The hand flag signaling in the finale is a marine semaphore code spelling "God Save the Queen"

What's in a flag? To Balanchine, [it] stands for the ritualistic, pride-bearing side of a nation. How and why the repetitious pace of ritual should be transformed into dance are questions that [he] alone seems able to answer.[1]

"It's Balanchine once again launched on a seemingly undanceable idea, through which he succeeds in showing us new things about dance."[2]

"In all the Bicentennial, no one seems

to feel any obligation to our sources in the United Kingdom. We share the language of Milton and Shakespeare. This [ballet] is our tribute to tradition. [In 1776] we declared independence, but we also declared a permanent connection to Britain."—Kirstein[3]

"The British invented democracy and a way to behave."—Balanchine[4]

Writing of the Company's giant Bicentennial offering, which, rather perversely, honored the land of George III, Kirstein related those notions of judicious behavior to the civilized control required for an organizational rhythm in art as well as life, the formal restraints that make possible the utmost in expressive freedom, yielding universal rather than particular meanings. Such conventions are as unquestioned as the components of ritual; ritual is epitomized by the eternal Changing of the Guard, which as surely as anything spells "British Empire." Kirstein postulated a parallel between the artful meter of verse and the rhythm of theatrical dance; between the meter of verse and the meter of marching; feet in marching, feet of soldiers; metric as a metaphor for the order and tradition that cement society. Soldiers uphold this order by defending the country and thus its institutions. (Hymns are also governed by meter, and Christian soldiers also march; soldiers have a "sacerdotal mission," preserving country, flag, roots, faith, in a profession that, like the monarchy, transcends the individual who practices it.) In conclusion, Kirstein wrote: "Syllables spelling *Union Jack* are steps, not words. Yet it can be claimed that these steps rhyme, can be scanned (as well as seen) in a galaxy of meters. [What's new in art?] What seems, strangely enough, to be new is the need to organize (metrical) feet, which are both measured and mnemonic. [There are no] substitutes for the strict muscular exercise in prosody which ruled Chaucer and Milton. Balanchine's *Union Jack* is visual, aural, metrical versification by an expert. And who indeed (happens to be) today's Shakespeare of the dance?"[5] (This equation of the two masters, not for their command of material, universality of expression, inventiveness, insight, or discipline—such connections have been made before—but as equally inspired creators of steps with scansion was a delightful new conceit.)

The ballet had antecedents other than Kirstein's Anglophilia. In 1926, Balan-

Union Jack. Top left: **Scottish and Canadian Guards Regiment, MacDonald of Sleat. Karin von Aroldingen.** *Above:* **Royal Navy, finale. (l. to r.), Bart Cook, Sara Leland, Helgi Tomasson, Kay Mazzo, Jacques d'Amboise, Suzanne Farrell, Peter Martins, Karin von Aroldingen, Victor Castelli.** *Top right:* **Costermonger Pas de Deux. Jean-Pierre Bonnefous, Patricia McBride.** *(Photos Martha Swope.)*

chine choreographed for the Ballets Russes *The Triumph of Neptune,* a series of tableaux in the style of a Victorian Christmas pantomime, with a score by Lord Berners. Balanchine performed in blackface as a tipsy Snowball, Sokolova as the Goddess danced a memorable hornpipe, and Geva jigged as the incarnation of Britannia herself. (Wrote the *Daily Express* reviewer at the time: "We saw at the Lyceum last night the beginnings of a British ballet.") After Diaghilev's death, Balanchine spent some time in England between 1929 and 1933 ("It was a very dignified life there," says he); there, among other things, he first met Kirstein. At some point during his London stay, he must have visited the music halls, where, Croce suggests, lacking much English, he was forced to grasp the essence of the songs through a close observation of gesture.[6] He also has a long-standing interest in the Scottish tattoo, which he claims as

an inspiration for his *Scotch Symphony* of 1952 (although he did not specifically allude to it in that ballet).

Subliminal influences aside, *Union Jack* had been in preparation for about three years. Research into musical sources and costumes came first (which authentic tartans were chosen depended on their color); as usual, the choreography took the least amount of time.

Kay describes the method for fleshing out the score: "The dancers are not doing real Scottish dances; it's an abstraction of those dances. And I am doing the same, an abstraction of the music. In the first part I am composing a score based on traditional Scottish music, with variations and embellishments. Otherwise you would end up with eight-bar tunes that are repeated."[7] The Navy section presented the same problems—a lack of variety in the sources: "The basic tune for a pas de trois was a hornpipe played by

pianist Boelzner at rehearsal. The tune was in two sections, which Boelzner played over and over. Before Kay 'covered up' this tune in his final score, it provided a skeleton of beats upon which Balanchine choreographed. Kay and Boelzner wrote down the number of counts needed for each sequence. Boelzner played the tune repeatedly for the duration of the just-created dance as Kay tape-recorded the music for tempo."[8] Then Kay worked seventeen hours a day for seven weeks to complete the score. "It was rough," says he; "I do it because of Balanchine's musicianship."[9] Dancers could not recall when Balanchine seemed to have more fun choreographing a ballet. An unforgettable picture was the master in rehearsal, nimbly hornpiping away while smiling to himself, and finishing one particularly toe-twisting sequence with a double pirouette, to a burst of applause.

Union Jack, with *Stars and Stripes* and the projected *Tricolore,* will eventually provide a full evening's entertainment to be entitled "Entente Cordiale."

Part I, which is about twice as long as the other two combined (the ballet runs 70 minutes), was awesome for its extended treatment of the march. Balanchine set himself some of the strictest formal limitations imaginable, and within them achieved a tour de force. Dancers —row after row—were expressionless and perfectly in step; the music was mainly drum-roll, with light-textured melodic overlays. Says Balanchine, "I've seen the military tattoos in Scotland. It's fantastic—200 pipers coming straight at you, the way they sway." [10] Bender called the massing "ominous."

Goldner described it: "The first ten minutes of *Union Jack* is marching. Each regiment parades through a frivolously conceived London Bridge toward the center of the stage. It halts for four drum rolls, marches in a maneuver, halts again for four beats, and parades to the side of the stage. As one regiment is moving to the side, the next is already entering through the bridge. A galaxy of blues, reds, green, yellows, black and white swell the stage in great waves, while the four-beat halts freeze each wave at its crest. The momentum is incredibly lush; the colors glorious; the number of personnel overwhelming, and the variations in marching pattern delightful. The crux of this ceremony, though, is those four-beat halts. They tilt the extravaganza into something austere, perhaps a little barbaric. They beam a glimmer of light onto the ritual underlying the ceremony, but rather than deny the splashy glamour of ceremony or the gleeful skill with which Balanchine arranges hordes in a limited space, they suggest a continuum of time between the Celts and the Rockettes." [11] (Interestingly, the instruments corresponded in weight to the size of the dancers: the tall d'Amboise entered to the tuba; the slight Leland to the piccolo; the larger Mazzo to a trumpet; the tallest woman, von Aroldingen, to a bassoon; the six-foot Martins to a trombone).

The regiments then leave the stage, returning separately or in pairs for variations, again with musical weight approximating physical size. Lennox and Dress MacLeod (all men) jig together, interweaving and clapping. Green Montgomerie (smallest women) perform delicate steps on pointe to a soulful bal-

lad, feigning sorrowful yearning by covering their faces. Menzies and Dress MacDonald dance a jaunty reel to music alternating between march-drum and melody-orchestra, with "London Bridge" formations and spirited trotting steps. To unaccompanied drums, the Amazons of the group (MacDonald of Sleat) move in agitated, soldierly manner. Finally, to Handel (music used previously by Balanchine for a beguiling divertissement in *The Figure in the Carpet*), the R.C.A.F. have a dainty variation, more "ballet Scottish" than those preceding. The march-drone of the beginning—brass and drums—accompanies the exit. The men leave last, in silhouette.

Part II takes place on the stage of a music hall. The Costermonger Pas de Deux struck Goldner as an "entre'acte": "He carries a red rose and large handkerchief; she carries a flask. Together they enact for the audience's pleasure and, presumably for the benefit of their own wallets, a soap opera about courtship. Balanchine uncomfortably jiggles between vaudeville and ballet. Bonnefous does a pure soft-shoe routine, and the delight of the dance is not only its transparent treatment of style but Bonnefous's amazing feel for it. Here a Russian-born choreographer designs English music-hall paces for a Frenchman, with native-tongue results and without the strained tongue in cheek that marks the first duet. But at present, I do not see how the Bonnefous phenomenon justifies [the section]." [12]

For the Royal Navy, the lights go up on "coloring book" ships at sea and the most strictly entertaining, just-plain-fun part of the show. (Part I had solemnity and measured tread; Part II was tinged with cynicism—these were small-time entertainers, after all, and one sees a million one-night stands ahead of them; but Part III wasn't a commentary on anything—just unadulterated hi-jinks.)

Saal described it: "Here, Balanchine invents a cascade of variations on the hornpipe and unleashes a succession of rollicksome tars who manage to show off the entire alphabet of naval gesture, from one-footed shuffles to falling overboard. The exuberant hilarity was infectious, the various combinations of seafarers endless—from the rubbery-legged bosun of d'Amboise to Farrell leading a bevy of hip-swiveling Betty Grable pinups. At the end, signal flags appeared miraculously in hand and the entire company semaphored 'God Save the Queen' (or so

the program said)." [13] Croce called it, "an extended hornpipe festival in the form of a musical-comedy revue." [14] Herridge was reminded of *H.M.S. Pinafore.* [15]

Croce wrote a lengthy piece about the ballet: "Although he's used Scottish folk dances and musical-comedy dances and military marches in other ballets, Balanchine has never done anything like *Union Jack* before. He's 'classicized' many of the steps in his customary fashion, but it would be difficult to call *Union Jack* a classical ballet in the same sense as *Scotch Symphony* or *Who Cares?* or *Stars and Stripes.* It has the impact of a forthright character ballet. Working with traditional folk and popular dance forms, Balanchine has this time exalted them through a process of scrutiny rather than of adaptation. We have the feeling of seeing things in deep focus, and of only now and then seeing double: two dance forms, classical and vernacular, in mutual exploitation. In the first section Balanchine, through devices of isolation and repetition, fastens our attention to certain fixed formal values: the hypnotic drag-step walk, the suddenly struck pose with a foot profiled in piqué position and balanced by one upflung arm, the drag step resumed, or taken up by the entrance of another regiment. The values are not Balanchine's invention, but the emphasis on them is. He extracts the essence of a form and gives it expansion. He prepares us for its expression in dance. Scottish dancing opposes the liveliness of the feet to squared shoulders and 'dead' arms, but when Balanchine gives us the flashing, slicing footwork of a Highland fling executed by two competing male regiments, Scottish feet seem livelier than ever before.

"Everybody wears kilts in 'Scottish and Canadian Guards Regiments,' and at the outset—a succession of long, slow entries to a sustained tattoo—everybody does the same steps. But the women, who wear toeshoes, do them very differently from the men, in their character shoes and regulation gaiters. With wider turnout and flexed arches, the women's feet look more selectively placed, more cultivated, than the men's; they're like a feminine melody set against a masculine drone bass. The distinction, absolutely mesmerizing, is something you will see on no parade ground in the world. So is the calculated difference between the swaying walk of the women and the massive tilt of the men. Another difference is that the men are in their evenly measured tread only somewhat the same, while the women are precisely the same. (An extra-calculated sway in Farrell's movements underlines the fact.)

"Such rudimentary elegancies make the close-order drills of the seven regiments spellbinding, and the drills themselves—the marching and countermarching—are as magical as card tricks. Balanchine has anatomized the mythological power of parades. His changing of the guard, which happens differently each time, is like a series of incantations. There is some obligatory taskmasterishness in what he changes it *for*; the individual dances that the regiments do once they're on are not of equal strength. The weakest is the 'ballet' of Leland's regiment, the first of the women's dances. After the modulated thunder and flash of the marches and flings, the wispy toesteps look like a retraction of graven testimony. Theoretically, they build on what we've seen, but in reality they niggle and spread false sentiment. Balanchine goes doggedly through all the changes of rhythm, but the variety accumulates no drive of its own, and the stylistic unity of the piece is impaired. (So is the unison of the ensembles, which the girls, on pointe, can't hold to strictly.) What should have looked like *Scotch Symphony* turns out more like *Irish Fantasy*. The mixed ensemble that follows, a combination of the Martins and Mazzo regiments in an elaborate Scottish reel and running set, is a partial recovery, a return to folkloristic roots. The dance has a droll formality, and, as a sample of ballroom etiquette, it reminds us of the intrinsic variety of the folk material. But the next dance, which is sheer invention, is the most persuasively folklike of all. 'Regimental Drum Variations' is the wild-warrior number, and Balanchine has set it for von Aroldingen's group —entirely for women. A mélange of hammering points and thunderbolt leaps, it takes the house by storm, stops dead, and adds one more tornado twist before a final dead stop. After this, a more sedately girlish number, full of large shapely hops and kicks, can only be anticlimactic, even if the music is by Handel and the dance led by Farrell.

" 'Scottish and Canadian Guards Regiments' has a formula Balanchine ending for which the State Theatre stage is too small: all clans but one melding, composing themselves into male-female couples, and steadying themselves for a mass

grand adagio to the anthemic 'Amazing Grace.' The excluded clan joins in time for one last fling; first the seven principals dance it alone, then they're echoed by the chorus ('A Hundred Pipers'). The recessional, set to a reprise of the opening tattoo, looks as stately as the grand défilé of the introduction, but it is accomplished in about half the time, with rank upon rank half-stepping to the footlights, swerving, and moving off row between row. The stage blacks out into silhouette.

"The 'Costermonger Pas de Deux' is danced through an implied reek of tobacco and stale beer. Patricia McBride and Jean-Pierre Bonnefous mimic a couple of music-hall entertainers, a husband-and-wife team (it is further implied) who have immortalized themselves playing the Pearly King and Queen on the stage. The pearlies were the legendary street people of Cockney London who covered their clothes with pearl buttons, and Ter-Arutunian's costumes, suitably decorated, are the baggy street clothes, in satin, of the Edwardian era. McBride wears a large feathered hat, Bonnefous a cap. . . . There's a bustle-on entrance with plenty of time for greeting friends in the audience. (It looks ad lib.) There's a sentimental adagio in which much is made of three props—a rose, a hanky, and a bottle of gin. Bonnefous's eager, imploring mime is all staccato bursts (an extension of his performance last season in *Harlequinade*); McBride doesn't believe a word of it. There are two soft-shoe solos: one for Bonnefous, with his brolly (which sprays buttons when opened), the other for McBride, with 'talking' mime that is like a hail of patter. The coda brings on the children of the act and a real donkey and a cart and anything that may ensue from donkeys on the stage. As yet, the act is too loose. The gag material needs some filling out, and both of McBride's exits should be repaced. But this chummy limelit interlude, unlike anything ever seen before on the New York City Ballet stage, is so quick to establish its own highly particularized world that we're immersed before we know it, and by the time it's over we've become part of it. 'Good old Mavis and Alfie,' we say. 'They've done it again.'

"Part III, 'Royal Navy,' is yet another set of customs, curiously reflective of the first two. It combines anecdote and spectacle in a stream of pell-mell motion. The first dance, a hornpipe trio, sets the pattern: chattering, razor-like feet, vivid

splashes of pantomime (swimming, hauling rope, tying rope, peering through spyglasses—the lot). While the band bangs along with 'We'll Go No More A-Roving' and 'The British Grenadiers' and 'Colonel Bogey,' the dancers keep hurdling the four-bar phrase, landing on different beats, so that the pattern never grows monotonous. From toytown scale, a few simple dance shapes billow to a flood of hilarious images. In 'British Grenadiers,' sailors swarm in the shape of a Navy bean; then they link hands and make waves. Somewhere in the backwash, Martins appears as a matey bos'n, a pipe between his teeth, Farrell leads a flock of Wrens in yachting caps and shorts. Balanchine polishes clichés till they shine like certitudes, and he's economical, too. For the finale, which has the full company wigwagging 'God Save the Queen' in maritime semaphore, he uses the hand-over-hand rope-hauling gesture as a way of equipping the dancers with hand flags without having them leave the stage; the flags are just spirited on from the wings with a few rhythmic heave-hos. The semaphore is set, a letter a bar, to 'Rule, Britannia!' The sixteenth bar is a salute. *Union Jack* is that kind of show—grand, foolish, and full of beans."[16]

For so ambitious an offering, much of the critical response was muted. Many critics, indeed, acted surprised—as if they could hardly believe that a Balanchine work, to which so much time had clearly been devoted, could be theatrically uneven. In this vein, Mazo wrote: "The dance contains episodes in which the humor is a bit strained and others which are more repetitious than they should be, but at its best, *Union Jack* is Balanchine's best."[17] Herridge: "It is more a staging feat, a cross between parade maneuvers and the Rockettes, with superior personnel. The choreography is a balletic distillation of the highland fling and other such dances, spiced with bouncy turns and toe precision. But the abstraction is not far enough removed from the source to be interesting."[18] (She reacted more positively to parts II and III.) Micklin: "Don't go expecting to be thrilled by the choreography."[19]

Barnes analyzed more closely what some considered the ballet's sometime lack of impact: "It seems that Balanchine has gone rather more deeply than usual into his dance sources with not altogether happy results. In [Parts I and III], he

[has] taken an uncommonly—for him—authentic view of the dances. The Scottish episode (which is probably, at first glance, the best) is an extraordinary exercise in slow-motion, counter-wheeling choreography. Yet for all his skills in deployment—and they are literally legion—there is a lack of variety. There is also a lack of variety in the hornpipe section. The dancers, again, are brilliant, yet the effect is charming but bland. As for the cockney music-hall numbers, these are really supported, so far as I know, by no surviving dance tradition at all. Balanchine, I think for him with absolute rightness, is a tincture-nationalist in the tradition of Petipa. The claymore-banging authenticity and the sporran-swinging tedium of the Scottish number are far more Scottish than *Scotch Symphony*. But, somehow, also less so. *Scotch Symphony* gave the spirit of the glens. This only gives an exploitive grandeur to the marches. It is different. It would never have done for Petipa, or, I suspect, for the Balanchine of the irreverent and unabashed—and also underrated—*Western Symphony*. . . . [*Union Jack*] does have its charms and merits—but it is not, at least at first glance, top-drawer Balanchine, or even second-drawer Balanchine for that matter. It is ceremonial Balanchine, which is something quite different." [20] Goldner: "The problem with the highland flings is not their lack of grandeur but of snappy dazzle." [21]

Apart from questions of choreographic texture, there is a difference in approach among the three sections—weighty in Part I; gently mocking in Part II; carefree and silly in Part III. Ideas underlying Part I, as verbalized by Kirstein, pertain not a whit to the Navy (Farrell's sexy sailorette and Martin's comic deckhand aren't conceivably "tributes" to anything). This may or may not be bothersome. Goldner explained: "The difference between Scotland and Britannia is that the first is real fake and the second, fake fake. In its not so innocent innocence, the sailor section both undercuts and reinforces the majesty of the Scottish tattoo. Balanchine perpetrates a giant attitudinal flip that in some deep way isn't a flip at all and in another way is a grosser flip than one dare imagine. How he can have it both ways is *Union Jack*'s marvelous paradox. My delayed and still tentative recognition of this feat is what leaves me in mid-flip.

"Whereas costumes in the Scottish section are authentic-looking and authentically glamorous, the sailor outfits are almost indecently cute. Whereas the jigs are quick, the hornpipes skitter. The Scottish dancers are buoyant; the sailors goofy. Martins, in his towering hat of fur, is the most resplendent of the Scots; he's the dopiest of the sailors, an oversized clod who doesn't know aft from a girlie sailor's behind. He and d'Amboise's sailors make broad mimetic gestures spelling boat; other sailors' smiles spell cute. Farrell becomes an outright sassy tart as the leader of WRENS; their strutting dance is a veritable unleashing of the chorus-line metaphor that's been simmering all along. Finally, the deeply felt pomp of the military maneuvers is turned upside down in the ballet's departing tribute to Great Britain. The sailors signal in marine code 'God Save the Queen.' They could just as well be spelling 'authentic,' so outlandish is this piece of realism.

"The tattoo comes across as a personal interpretation of a public theatrical spectacle; the [Navy] throws a predigested myth back on itself. Strangely, they neither cancel each out nor follow the conventional argument on the one hand, on the other. Rather, *Union Jack* presents the beautiful and the ridiculous through a bifocal lens, united by joyous brio." [22]

It seemed clear the work as a whole did not match what must have been the grandeur of the conception. There was the feeling of a major statement incompletely uttered. Goldner wrote: "The crucial point about *Union Jack* is that somewhere in it is a [single] ballet with important themes. This question is what and where." [23] With typical industry, Balanchine went to work at once making changes. At the time of writing—June 1976—*Union Jack* is barely three weeks old, and it is too early to say what it may eventually become. A widespread reaction, however, among critics (including Barnes) as well as non-professional observers, is that by the second performance the ballet had already become a lot more fun.

POSTSCRIPT

At the end of forty years a company exists, acclaimed throughout the world wherever ballet is considered art. As in the beginning, there is Balanchine, commanding center stage, faithful still to principles formulated from what must have seemed thin air forty years ago: the primacy of pure dance, the ensemble as star (more precisely, the choreography as star), distinguished musical support, the classical academy revitalized, enlarged, reseen, reborn, and yet existing side by side with "modern" movement of little apparent classical connection. He has lived to see the complete vindication of his personal vision. This is not to say that his way pleases everyone, only that he seems to have realized his own dreams on his own terms.

The story continues. . . . Balanchine's choreography has been discussed throughout this book, and it would seem fitting to close with some of his own infrequent remarks on the subject: "Steps are easy. It's why you do them that's important. By 'why' I mean a visual reason for moving in a certain way. The eyes accept only a certain amount, so the problem is to put the images that you become aware of into time. I encourage young choreographers, but sometimes they say, 'Why don't you like my work?' and I tell them it's not skillful enough. 'Skillful' means not only that you know the basic grammar of dance; you have to have a flair for putting steps together in some design that will provoke an appetite in people. And then you must apply these steps, these gestures, to bodies—you take out of people what they look like. . . . You know what the problem is? A skillful dancer who has perfected and trained her body for twenty years can just stand there and *confuse* a choreographer. He gets so fascinated by this trained body that he looks at it and says, 'Would you bend, please?' and then the person bends, and he says, 'Would you turn, please?' and the person turns. And then he signs his name. It's not his. It took twenty years for that boy or girl to learn these steps! Ninety per cent of the people who call themselves choreographers are amateurs! If they were doctors treating patients, everybody would be dead by now. Here, it is not quite so serious. Only the public dies if we produce a bad ballet.

. . . [So] the dancer really makes the dance, not the choreographer. It's important to recognize a dancer, like a jewel. You faint from its beauty." *

Says Robbins, "His choreography for a Tchaikovsky piece or a Gershwin piece or whatever is so *those* worlds and no others. . . . The Mozartean world of *Divertimento No. 15* is so exquisitely Mozartean—it could only be that. I've heard him say to the dancers, 'You are snow. Haven't you ever seen snow?' Or, with Bizet he'll say, 'Listen to the music; dance to *that* music.' People think I'm exact, but look at his classes! He's teaching and he wants it a certain way, and *exactly* that way. It is a very special instrument, that company."

It is not merely Balanchine's masterpieces, or even his extraordinary fecundity, that make him the lifeblood of the Company today. Kirstein says, "Balanchine is ballet master, teacher, choreographer, impresario"; he is also guidance counselor, mentor, and solicitous guardian of the young. It is his inspiring daily presence in these guises that make him the Company's driving force. Many choreographers set their works and go away; Balanchine probably spends more hours at the theater than any of his dancers.

His continuing concern and involvement, his faith in the present, past, and future of his own company and of dancing itself are expressed, for one, in his devotion to teaching. He conducts classes almost daily, training the dancers of today and tomorrow to provide a continuity that keeps time always in the present, one generation flowing into the next, the material of dance continuously alive. He builds on a foundation of classical technique—which has shaped dancers for 400 years—then derives from this base related but new movement, to prepare his dancers to do things that dancers have never done before. It is in the studio that he may be closer than on stage to the living stream of dance itself: he actually creates dance (as distinguished from creating dances) by giving his "an-

---

* *New Yorker*, 22 May 1971 and *Newsweek*, 2 May 1966.

gelic messengers" new instruments for the eventual projection of an unimagined vocabulary. He is said to feel that his teaching, more than his ballets, is his chief legacy, the only part of his work he might be eager to preserve (on film or in some other way); he is notoriously uncaring about what posterity—or even the near future—does with his ballets, essentially believing that they die with him.

Balanchine is a man of few words, especially where dancing is concerned, but perhaps significantly, it is in class that his conversation is peppered with some of his most telling images. Says Violette Verdy, "There are things that I find absolutely unforgettable. Very often in class he comes through, apparently out of nowhere, with some of his most meaningful statements about dancing, undoubtedly distilled from his own experiences and philosophy. For instance, one of them was: 'Just do it—what does it matter if you're going to die in the next minute, then you will have done something full out before you die!' Or another: 'Look at a flower in the woods. Nobody is going to see that flower, nobody is going to take that flower, nobody is going to do anything about that flower—yet there it is being a flower, for nobody, for no reason other than that of being what it is supposed to be.' In those moments, when he reminds us of those things, there is the whole mystery, right there, you see."

SOURCES

The following authors and printed works are quoted in the text, sometimes in abbreviated form. Full names of dancers, choreographers, and others quoted directly are given either in the catalogue listing or elsewhere within the text of the ballet to which their remarks refer.

AUTHORS

Anderson, Jack
Avila, Juan de
Baccaro, Mario
Baignères, Claude
Baker, Robb
Balanchine, George
Barnes, Clive
Barnes, Patricia
Battey, Jean (also writes as Jean Battey Lewis)
Beaumont, Cyril
Belt, Byron
Bender, William
Bennett, Grena
Berger, Arthur V.
Biancolli, Louis
Bivona, Elena
Bland, Alexander
Bohm, Jerome D.
Bowers, Faubion
Bradley, L. J. H.
Browse, Lillian
Brunner, Gerhard
Buckle, Richard
Buonincontro, Maurizio
Campbell, Mary
Carter, Elliott
Cassidy, Claudia
Chapman, John
Chotzinoff, Samuel
Chujoy, Anatole
Cohen, Selma Jeanne
Coleman, Emily
Coton, A. V.
Crisp, Clement
Croce, Arlene
Denby, Edwin
Diamond, David
Dodd, Craig
Dorris, George
Downes, Edward
Downes, Olin
Eguchi
Engel, Lehman
Frangini, Gualtiero
Frankenstein, Alfred
Freedley, George
Gale, Joseph
Garis, Robert
Geiringer, Karl
Geitel, Klaus
Gellen, Paul
Gelles, George
Genauer, Emily
Gianoli, Luigi
Gillespie, Noel
Goldner, Nancy
Golea, Antoine
Gottfried, Martin
Greskovic, Robert
Guest, Ivor
Haggin, B. H.
Harris, Dale
Harris, Leonard
Harrison, Jay S.
Hastings, Baird
Henahan, Donal J.
Hering, Doris
Herridge, Frances
Hinton, James, Jr.
Hughes, Allen
Ilupina, Anna
Johnson, Harriet
Jowitt, Deborah
Kastendieck, Miles
Kendall, Elizabeth
Kennedy, James
Kerner, Leighton
Khachaturian, Aram
Kimball, Robert
Kirstein, Lincoln
Kisselgoff, Anna
Koegler, Horst
Kolodin, Irving
Krevitsky, Nik
Krieger, Victoriana
Kriegsman, Alan M.
Krokover, Rosalyn
Laciar, Samuel L.
Lawrence, Robert
Lederman, Minna
Lewis, Jean Battey
Liepa, Maris
Lloyd, Margaret
Lombardi, Michael
McDonagh, Don
Manchester, P. W.
Marks, Marcia
Martin, John
Maskey, Jacqueline

Mazo, Joseph H.
Merlin, Olivier
Micklin, Bob
Miller, Margo
Mishkin, Leo
Monahan, James
Moore, Lillian
Norton, Elliot
O'Connor, John J.
Osins, Witaly
Parente, Alfredo
Perkins, Francis D.
Porter, Andrew
Purchet, Maurice
Rauschning, Hans
Rich, Alan
Robinson, Roland
Rosenfield, John
Ruppel, K. H.
Saal, Hubert
Sabin, Robert
Sanborn, Pitts
Sargent, Winthrop
Schmidt-Garre, Helmut
Schonberg, Harold C.
Sealy, Robert

Sergeev, Konstantin
Siegel, Marcia B.
Sirvin, René
Slonimsky, Yuri
Smith, Cecil
Sokolova, Lydia
Sorell, Walter
Steinberg, Michael
Stewart, Malcolm
Stuckenschmidt, H. H.
Sylvester, Robert
Terry, Walter
Tobias, Tobi
Todd, Arthur
Vaughan, David
Vecheslova, Tatiana
Vitak, Albertina
Watt, Douglas
Webster, Daniel
White, Eric Walter
Williams, Peter
Willis, Thomas
Zakharov, Rostislav
Zivier, Georg
Zoete, Beryl de

NEWSPAPERS AND PERIODICALS

Der Abend, Berlin
AmDancer
    American Dancer (combined with *Dance* in 1942)
Art News
L'Aurore, Nice
Avanti, Milan
Ballet, London
Ballet Review
Boston Globe
Boston Herald
Boston Post
Brooklyn Eagle
Center
Chicago Daily News
Chicago Tribune
Monitor
    Christian Science Monitor
Chrysalis
Corriere della Sera, Milan
La Critica, Buenos Aires
La Cronica, Lima
Daily Telegraph, London
Dallas Times Herald
Dallas News
D&D
    Dance and Dancers, London
DL
    Dance Life
DM
    Dance Magazine

DN
    Dance News
DO
    Dance Observer
DP
    Dance Perspectives
DT
    Dancing Times, London
L'Express, Paris
Express, Vienna
Le Figaro, Paris
Le Figaro Littéraire, Paris
Financial Times, London
Guardian Weekly, Manchester
Harper's Magazine
HiFi/MusAm
    High Fidelity/Musical America
    Informations et Documents, Paris
L'Italia, Milan
Izvestia, Moscow
Jersey Journal
Literaturnaia Gazeta, Moscow
LI Press
    Long Island Press
    Mainichi Daily News, Tokyo
Guardian
    Manchester Guardian
Il Mattino
    Il Mattino d'Italia, Naples
ModMus
    Modern Music
    Le Monde, Paris
    Moscow News
    Münchner Merkur, Munich
MusAm
    Musical America
    Musical Courier
    Nation
    La Nazione Italiana, Florence
    Die Neue Zeitung, Berlin
    Newark News
    Newsday
    Newsweek
NYA
    New York American
Compass
    New York Compass
NYN
    New York Daily News
    New Yorker
NYP
    New York Post
NYHT
    New York Herald Tribune
NYJA
    New York Journal-American
    New York Magazine
    New York Morning Telegraph
    New York Staats-Zeitung und Herold
Star
    New York Star

NYS
New York Sun
NYT
New York Times
NYWJT
New York World Journal Tribune
NYWT
New York World-Telegram
NYWTS
New York World-Telegram and Sun
Observer, London
Observer WR
Observer Weekend Review, London
Ongaku Shimbun, Tokyo
El Pampero, Buenos Aires
Partisan Review
Philadelphia Inquirer
Ledger
Philadelphia Evening Public Ledger
Playbill
Pravda, Leningrad (*Leningradskaia Pravda*)
Pravda, Moscow
Providence Sunday Journal
El Pueblo, Buenos Aires
Roma, Naples
Chronicle
San Francisco Chronicle
SR
Saturday Review
SR/W
Saturday Review/World
The Scotsman, Edinburgh
Soho Weekly News
Sovetskaia Kultura, Moscow
Spectator, London
Süddeutsche Zeitung, Munich
Sunday Times, London
Sydney (Australia) *Morning Herald*
Syracuse Post Standard

Tempo
Il Tempo di Milano
Theatre Guild Magazine
Time Magazine
Times, London
El Universal, Lima
WSJ
Wall Street Journal
Washington Post
Washington Star
Die Welt, Berlin
WWD
Women's Wear Daily
VV
Village Voice
Voce
La Voce Repubblicana, Rome
Yomiuri Japan News

BOOKS

Only books on music and dance are listed. The few others to which reference is made are fully cited in the Notes.

Balanchine, George. *Balanchine's New Complete Stories of the Great Ballets.* Edited by Francis Mason. Garden City, N.Y.: Doubleday, 1968.

Beaumont, Cyril. *Supplement to the Complete Book of Ballets.* London: Beaumont, 1945.

Biancolli, Louis. *The Mozart Handbook.* Cleveland and New York: World, 1954.

Chujoy, Anatole. *The New York City Ballet.* New York: Knopf, 1953.

Denby, Edwin. *Dancers, Buildings and People in the Streets.* New York: Horizon, 1965; paper, Curtis, 1965. (Note: all page references to paperback edition)

————. *Looking at the Dance.* New York: Pellegrini & Cudahy, 1949; paper, Curtis, 1968. (Note: all page references to paperback edition)

Geiringer, Karl. *The Bach Family: Seven Generations of Creative Genius.* New York: Oxford University Press, 1954.

Goldner, Nancy. *The Stravinsky Festival of the New York City Ballet.* New York: Eakins Press, 1973.

Haggin, B. H. *Ballet Chronicle.* New York: Horizon, 1970.

Kirstein, Lincoln. *Movement and Metaphor: Four Centuries of Ballet.* New York: Praeger, 1970.

————. *The New York City Ballet.* With photographs by Martha Swope and George Platt Lynes. New York: Knopf, 1973.

Lederman, Minna (ed. and intro.). *Stravinsky in the Theatre.* New York: Pellegrini & Cudahy, 1949.

Merlin, Olivier, et al. *Stravinsky.* Paris: Hachette, 1968.

Sokolova, Lydia. *Dancing with Diaghilev.* Edited by Richard Buckle. New York: Macmillan, 1961.

Stuckenschmidt, H. H. *Maurice Ravel: Variations on His Life and Work.* Philadelphia: Chilton, 1968.

Taper, Bernard. *Balanchine.* New York: Harper & Row, 1963; paper, rev. and updated, Collier, 1974.

Terry, Walter. *Ballet: A New Guide to the Liveliest Art.* New York: Dell, 1959.

White, Eric Walter. *Stravinsky: The Composer and His Work.* Berkeley and Los Angeles: University of California Press, 1966.

NOTES

Note: The number preceding each title refers to the page on which that ballet appears.

36 SERENADE

1. Kisselgoff, *NYT*, 15 Nov. 74. 2. Terry, *Ballet: A New Guide*, p. 265. 3. *Ongaku Shimbun*, 23 Mar. 58. 4. *DT*, Mar. 35. 5. *NYT*, 18 Oct. 40. 6. *DM*, Jan. 49. 7. *MusAm*, 15 Dec. 50. 8. *DM*, Mar. 53. 9. *NYHT*, 3 Sept. 54. 10. *NYT*, 3 Sept. 54. 11. Monahan, *Ballet*, Sept.–Oct. 50. 12. Buckle, *Observer*, 16 July 50. 13. O.V., *Corriere della Sera*, 10 Sept. 53. 14. Rauschning, *Der Abend*, Oct. 56. 15. Khachaturian, *Izvestia*, 10 Oct. 62. 16. Slonimsky, 72.

39 ALMA MATER

1. R.E.R., *Washington Post*, 7 Dec. 34. 2. *NYT*, 2 Mar. 35.

40 ERRANTE

1. *DT*, Aug. 33. 2. *NYHT*, 2 Mar. 35. 3. Avila, *El Universal*, 13 Sept. 41.

41 REMINISCENCE

1. *NYT*, 2 and 10 Mar. 35. 2. *DT*, Apr. 35. 3. *ModMus*, Mar.–Apr. 35.

42 DREAMS

1. *NYT*, 6 Mar. 35. 2. *DT*, Apr. 35.

42 TRANSCENDENCE

1. *NYT*, 6 Mar. 35. 2. R.E.R., *Washington Post*, 7 Dec. 34. 3. *DT*, Apr. 35.

43 MOZARTIANA

1. *DT*, Aug. 33. 2. *ModMus*, Mar.–Apr. 37. 3. *NYHT*, 8 Mar. 45. 4. *NYT*, 8 Mar. 45.

44 CONCERTO

1. *ModMus*, Mar.–Apr. 37.

44 THE BAT

1. Bennett, *NYA*, 21 May 36. 2. Perkins, *NYHT*, 21 May 36. 3. *NYWT*, 21 May 36.

45 ORPHEUS AND EURYDICE

1. O. Downes, *NYT*, 23 May 36. 2. P.S., *NYWT*, 23 May 36. 3. Chotzinoff, *NYP*, 23 May 36. 4. *Time*, 30 May 36.

46 APOLLON MUSAGÈTE

1. Porter, *New Yorker*, 9 Dec. 72. 2. In Lederman, ed., *Stravinsky*. 3. *DN*, Dec. 51. 4. In Lederman, ed., *Stravinsky*. 5.

NYT, 2 May 37. 6. *NYT*, 9 Sept. 51. 7. *MusAm*, 1 Dec. 51. 8. *DM*, Jan. 52. 9. *NYHT*, 23 and 28 Oct. 45; repr. Denby, *Looking at the Dance*, pp. 114, 117. 10. *NYT*, 8 Dec. 57. 11. Buckle, *Sunday Times*, 5 Sept. 65. 12. Brunner (reporting from Germany), *Express*, 24 Aug. 65.

50 THE CARD PARTY

1. *ModMus*, Mar.–Apr. 37. 2. *NYT*, 2 May 37. 3. *DN*, Mar. 51. 4. *DM*, Apr. 51. 5. *NYT*, 10 Sept. 51.

51 LE BAISER DE LA FÉE

1. *ModMus*, Nov.–Dec. 40, repr. Denby, *Looking at the Dance*, p. 186. 2. *DM*, Feb. 51. 3. Lederman, *ModMus*, Spring 46. 4. *NYT*, 2 May 37. 5. *NYT*, 2 May 37. 6. *NYT*, 18 Feb. 46. 7. *NYT*, 29 Nov. 50. 8. *MusAm*, 15 Dec. 50.

53 ENCOUNTER

1. *Boston Post*, 22 Jan. 38. 2. Dec. 36. 3. *Monitor*, 10 Nov. 36.

54 HARLEQUIN FOR PRESIDENT

1. *Variety*, 26 Aug. 36. 2. *Boston Herald*, 23 Jan. 38.

54 PROMENADE

1. *NYWT*, 2 Nov. 36.

55 POCAHONTAS

1. Beaumont, *Supplement to Complete Book of Ballets*. 2. *NYT*, 25 May 39. 3. *NYN*, 25 May 39.

55 THE SOLDIER AND THE GYPSY

1. *Monitor*, 10 Nov. 36. 2. 2 Nov. 36. 3. *NYWT*, 2 Nov. 36.

56 YANKEE CLIPPER

1. *Boston Herald*, 23 Jan. 38. 2. *NYT*, 29 May 38.

56 FOLK DANCE

1. *Boston Herald*, 23 Jan. 38.

57 SHOW PIECE

1. *NYT*, 24 May 38. 2. *ModMus*, Jan.–Feb. 38. 3. *Boston Post*, 22 Jan. 38.

58 FILLING STATION

1. *Dallas Times Herald*, 30 Nov. 38. 2. Rosenfeld, *Dallas News*, 30 Dec. 38. 3. *Chronicle*, 8 Nov. 38. 4. Norton, *Boston Post*, 22 Jan. 38. 5. *El Pampero*, 21 July 41. 6. *NYHT*, 13 May 53.

59 AIR AND VARIATIONS

1. Bohm, *NYHT*, 26 May 39. 2. Terry, *NYHT*, 29 Dec. 39. 3. Frankenstein, *Chronicle*, 8 Dec. 38.

60 BILLY THE KID

1. *NYT*, 28 May 39. 2. *NYT*, 28 May 39. 3. *AmDancer*, July 39. 4. *NYHT*, 29 Dec. 39. 5. *NYHT*, 28 May 39. 6. *DO*, Oct. 38. 7. *NYHT*, 10 Oct. 43.

61 CHARADE

1. *NYT*, 27 Dec. 39. 2. *NYHT*, 27 Dec. 39. 3. *DM*, Mar. 40. 4. *NYS*, 27 Dec. 39.

62 CITY PORTRAIT

1. *Time*, 8 Jan. 40. 2. *ModMus*, Jan.–Feb. 40. 3. *MusAm*, May 42. 4. *NYS*, 29 Dec. 39. 5. *NYT*, 29 Dec. 39. 6. *NYHT*, 29 Dec. 39. 7. Diamond, *ModMus*, Jan.–Feb. 40.

63 TIME TABLE

1. *MusAm*, Feb. 49. 2. *DM*, Mar. 49. 3. *NYHT*, 14 Jan. 49. 4. *NYT*, 14 Jan. 49.

64 BALLET IMPERIAL

1. *NYT*, 21 Feb. 45. 2. *NYHT*, 21 Feb. 47. 3. *ModMus*, Mar.–Apr. 45. 4. *NYHT*, 21 Feb. 45; repr. Denby, *Looking at the Dance*, p. 93. 5. *ModMus*, Mar.–Apr. 45. 6. *NYT*, 14 Jan. 73.

66 CONCERTO BAROCCO

1. *Chicago Tribune*, 16 Aug. 67. 2. *NYHT*, 1 Nov. 43. 3. *NYT*, 11 Jan. 67. 4. *NYHT*, 16 Sept. 45; repr. Denby, *Looking at the Dance*, pp. 108–109. 5. *DM*, Jan. 49. 6. Coton, *Ballet*, Sept.–Oct. 50. 7. Zivier, *Die Neue Zeitung*, Sept. 52.

69 PASTORELA

1. Avila, *El Universal*, 13 Sept. 41. 2. *DN*, Feb. 47. 3. *NYHT*, 19 Jan. 47.

70 DIVERTIMENTO

1. *El Pueblo*, 18 July 41. 2. *El Pampero*, 21 July 41.

70 JUKE BOX

1. 23 July 41.

71 FANTASIA BRASILEIRA

1. *La Cronica*, 14 Sept. 41.

71 THE SPELLBOUND CHILD

1. *NYT*, 16 Feb. 47. **2.** *NYHT*, 21 Nov. 47. **3.** Haggin, *Nation*, 11 Jan. 47. **4.** Krevitsky, *DO*, Jan. 47. **5.** *NYP*, 16 May 75. **6.** *NYT*, 16 May 75.

72 THE FOUR TEMPERAMENTS

1. Denby, *Looking at the Dance*, p. 54. **2.** *Boston Globe*, 14 and 28 Jan. 68. **3.** *DN*, Dec. 46. **4.** *DN*, Dec. 48. **5.** *DM*, Jan. 49. **6.** *NYHT*, 16 Oct. 65. **7.** *NYHT*, 23 Nov. 51; 25 Feb. and 7 May 53. **8.** *NYT*, 11 Oct. 65. **9.** *New Yorker*, 8 Dec. 75. **10.** *NYT*, 2 Feb. 47. **11.** *NYT*, 23 Nov. 51. **12.** *NYT*, 7 Jan. 59. **13.** *Times*, 14 Aug. 50. **14.** Zivier, *Die Neue Zeitung*, Sept. 52. **15.** Merlin, *Le Figaro Littéraire*, Dec. 63.

76 RENARD

1. *NYT*, 16 Feb. 47. **2.** *DN*, 1 Feb. 47. **3.** *New York City Ballet*, p. 164. **4.** *NYHT*, 19 Jan. 47.

77 DIVERTIMENTO

1. *NYHT*, 23 Feb. 50 and 3 Nov. 48. **2.** *DN*, 1 Feb. 47. **3.** *NYT*, 3 Nov. 48. **4.** *DM*, Jan. 49. **5.** *Sunday Times*, 6 Aug. 50. **6.** *Times*, 4 Aug. 50.

78 THE MINOTAUR

1. *NYT*, 6 Apr. 47. **2.** *NYHT*, 6 Apr. 47. **3.** *DN*, May 47.

79 ZODIAC

1. *Chrysalis*, III, 5–6, 50. **2.** *DN*, May 47. **3.** *NYT*, 6 Apr. 47. **4.** *NYHT*, 6 Apr. 47.

79 HIGHLAND FLING

1. *NYHT*, 6 Apr. 47. **2.** *DM*, May 47.

80 THE SEASONS

1. *NYT*, 15 Jan. 49. **2.** *MusAm*, Feb. 49. **3.** *NYHT*, 16 Jan. 49. **4.** *Nation*, 19 Feb. 49.

81 BLACKFACE

1. *NYHT*, 19 May 47.

81 PUNCH AND THE CHILD

1. *DM*, Jan. 49. **2.** *Star*, 20 Oct. 48. **3.** *NYT*, 19 Oct. 48. **4.** *NYHT*, 19 Oct. 48.

82 SYMPHONIE CONCERTANTE

1. *NYHT*, 11 Nov. 45. **2.** *NYT*, 19 Oct. 48 and 23 Feb. 50. **3.** *MusAm*, Mar. 50. **4.** *NYHT*, 23 Nov. 49. **5.** *Nation*, 2 Feb. 46. **6.** Denby, *Dancers, Buildings and People*, p. 68. **7.** Balanchine, *New Complete Stories*, p. 430. **8.** Manchester, *Ballet*, Sept.–Oct. 50. **9.** *Times*, 19 July 50.

83 THE TRIUMPH OF BACCHUS AND ARIADNE

1. *Musical Courier*, 15 Nov. 48. **2.** *NYHT*, 2 Nov. 48. **3.** *NYT*, 2 Nov. 48. **4.** *DN*, Mar. 48.

84 CAPRICORN CONCERTO

1. *NYT*, 23 Mar. 48. **2.** *DN*, Apr. 48.

84 SYMPHONY IN C

1. *New Yorker*, 9 Dec. 72. **2.** Aug. 47. **3.** *DN*, Apr. 48. **4.** *NYHT*, 23 Mar. 48. **5.** *NYT*, 23 Mar. 48. **6.** *Ballet*, Sept.–Oct. 50. **7.** Buckle, *Sunday Times*, 5 Sept. 65. **8.** Buonincontro, *Il Mattino*, 11 Oct. 53. **9.** Rauschning, *Der Abend*, Sept. 56. **10.** Sergeev, *Izvestia*, 14 Oct. 72.

87 ÉLÉGIE

1. *DN*, June 48. **2.** *NYHT*, 6 Nov. 45. **3.** June–July 48.

87 ORPHEUS

1. *DN*, June 62. **2.** *NYT*, 29 Apr. 48. **3.** White, *Stravinsky*, p. 402. **4.** White, *Stravinsky*, p. 406. **5.** *NYT*, 29 Apr. and 17 Oct. 48. **6.** *DN*, June 48. **7.** *MusAm*, Mar. 50. **8.** *NYHT*, 23 Feb. 50. **9.** *Times*, 19 July 50. **10.** Beaumont, *Sunday Times*, 30 July 50. **11.** *Times*, 29 July 52. **12.** Monahan, *Guardian*, 30 July 52.

93 MOTHER GOOSE SUITE

1. *NYHT*, 2 Nov. 48. **2.** *DN*, Dec. 48. **3.** *NYT*, 2 Nov. 48. **4.** *NYHT*, 2 Nov. 48. **5.** *NYHT*, 21 Nov. 43. **6.** *Times*, 28 July 50. **7.** Monahan, *Guardian*, 30 July 50.

93 THE GUESTS

1. *Star*, 17 Jan. 49. **2.** *DM*, Mar. 49. **3.** *MusAm*, Feb. 49. **4.** *NYT*, 12 Jan. 49. **5.** *NYT*, 27 Nov. 49. **6.** *NYHT*, 26 Nov. 49. **7.** Smith, *MusAm*, Feb. 49. **8.** Monahan, *Guardian*, 2 Aug. 50. **9.** Bradley, *Ballet*, Sept.–Oct. 50.

95 JINX

1. *DM*, Jan. 50. **2.** *DN*, Jan. 50. **3.** Hering, *DM*, Jan. 50. **4.** *NYHT*, 23 Nov. 49. **5.** Martin, *NYT*, 25 Feb. 50. **6.** Monahan, *Guard-*

ian, 15 July 50. **7.** *Times*, 11 July 50. **8.** Bradley, *Ballet*, Sept.–Oct. 50.

96 FIREBIRD

1. White, *Stravinsky*, p. 48. **2.** *Time*, 12 Dec. 49. **3.** *NYHT*, 4 Dec. 49. **4.** *NYT*, 4 Dec. 49. **5.** *DN*, Jan. 50. **6.** *DM*, Jan. 50. **7.** *Nation*, 21 Jan. 50; repr. Haggin, *Ballet Chronicle*, p. 17. **8.** *DT*, Feb. 50. **9.** *NYHT*, 4 Dec. 49. **10.** *DM*, Jan. 50. **11.** *Times*, 21 July 50. **12.** Monahan, *Guardian*, 21 July 50. **13.** Buckle, *Observer*, 23 July 50. **14.** Buckle, *Observer*, 13 July 52. **15.** Stuckenschmidt, *Die Neue Zeitung*, 6 Sept. 52. **16.** L.P., *Avanti*, 23 Sept. 53. **17.** *Newsweek*, 8 June 70. **18.** Manchester, *Monitor*. **19.** *Ballet Review*, 70. **20.** *Jersey Journal*, 1 June 70. **21.** *NYT*, 23 Jan. 74.

100 BOURRÉE FANTASQUE

1. *DN*, Jan. 50. **2.** *NYHT*, 2 Dec. 49. **3.** *NYT*, 2 Dec. 49. **4.** *Compass*, 4 Dec. 49. **5.** Monahan, *Guardian*, 15 July 50. **6.** *Times*, 28 July 52. **7.** *Il Mattino*, 9 Oct. 53. **8.** *Voce*, 17 Oct. 53.

102 ONDINE

1. *NYT*, 10 Dec. 49. **2.** *NYHT*, 10 Dec. 49.

102 PRODIGAL SON

1. Alexander Pushkin, *The Queen of Spades and Other Stories*, trans. Ivy and Tatiana Litvinov (New York: Signet, 1961), p. 85. **2.** *Newsweek*, 30 June 69. **3.** *DT*, Jan. 73. **4.** *DN*, Apr. 50. **5.** *NYT*, 24 Feb. 50. **6.** *NYHT*, 24 Feb. 50. **7.** *NYT*, 24 Feb. 50. **8.** *DT*, Apr. 50. **9.** *MusAm*, Mar. 50. **10.** *NYT*, 11 Nov. 60. **11.** *DN*, Oct. 61. **12.** Interview with Croce, Dorris, McDonagh in *Ballet Review*, II, 5, 69. **13.** "Acrobatics and the New Choreography," *Theatre Guild Magazine*, Jan. 30. **14.** *Spectator*, 11 Aug. 50. **15.** Kennedy, *Guardian*, 3 Sept. 65. **16.** *Times*, 3 Sept. 65. **17.** Sirvin, *L'Aurore*, 24 June 69. **18.** Stuckenschmidt, *Die Neue Zeitung*, 6 Sept. 52.

107 THE DUEL

1. *NYHT*, 25 Feb. 50. **2.** *NYT*, 25 Feb. 50. **3.** *DT*, Apr. 50. **4.** *DN*, Apr. 50. **5.** *Times*, 9 Aug. 50. **6.** Buckle, *Observer*, 13 Aug. 50.

108 AGE OF ANXIETY

1. Martin, *NYT*, 28 Feb. 50. **2.** *NYHT*, 27 Feb. 50. **3.** *NYHT*, 12 Mar. and 28 Feb. 50. **4.** *NYT*, 19 Mar. 50. **5.** *NYHT*, 27 Feb. and 12 Mar. 50, 14 Nov. 51. **6.** *DM*, Apr. 50. **7.** *MusAm*, Mar. 50. **8.** *DM*, Apr. 50. **9.** Sabin, *MusAm*, Mar. 50. **10.** Martin, *NYT*, 28 Feb. 50. **11.** *Musical Courier*, 15 Mar. 50. **12.** *NYT*, 3 Sept. 54. **13.** *Times*, 11 July 50. **14.** Bradley, *Ballet*, Sept.–Oct.

50. **15.** O.V., *Corriere della Sera*, 10 Sept. 53.

110 ILLUMINATIONS

1. *NYHT*, 19 Mar. 50. **2.** *New York City Ballet*, p. 241. **3.** *NYT*, 8 Apr. 67. **4.** *NYT*, 3 and 26 Mar. 50. **5.** *NYHT*, 3 Mar. 50. **6.** *NYT*, 8 Apr. 67. **7.** *NYN*, 3 Mar. 50. **8.** De Zoete, *Ballet*, Sept.–Oct. 50. **9.** *Times*, 21 July 50. **10.** Beaumont, *Sunday Times*, 23 July 50. **11.** Buckle, *Observer*, 23 July 50.

114 PAS DE DEUX ROMANTIQUE

1. *NYT*, 19 Mar. and 4 Mar. 50. **2.** *NYHT*, 4 Mar. 50. **3.** Buckle, *Observer*, 13 Aug. 50.

114 JONES BEACH

1. *DN*, Apr. 50. **2.** *Compass*, 12 Mar. 50. **3.** *Times*, 25 July 50.

115 THE WITCH

1. *Observer*, 20 Aug. 50.

116 SYLVIA: PAS DE DEUX

1. *DM*, Feb. 51. **2.** *NYHT*, 2 Dec. 50. **3.** Baccaro, *Roma*, 6 Oct. 53.

117 PAS DE TROIS

1. Terry, *NYHT*, 14 Nov. 51. **2.** Chujoy, *DN*, Apr. 51. **3.** Hinton, *MusAm*, 1 Dec. 51.

117 LA VALSE

1. *DN*, Apr. 51. **2.** *NYT*, 6 June 51. **3.** *DM*, Apr. 51. **4.** *Playbill*, Jan.–Feb. 70. **5.** Interview with Croce, Dorris, McDonagh in *Ballet Review*, II, 5, 69. **6.** *Nation*, 24 Mar. 51; repr. Haggin, *Ballet Chronicle*, p. 22. **7.** *Times*, 8 July 52. **8.** Frangini, *La Nazione*, 21 Oct. 53. **9.** Ruppel, *Süddeutsche Zeitung*, 24 Aug. 65.

119 LADY OF THE CAMELIAS

1. *NYT*, 1 Mar. 51. **2.** *NYHT*, 1 Mar. 51. **3.** *NYT*, 1 Mar. 51.

120 CAPRICCIO BRILLANTE

1. *NYT*, 8 June 51. **2.** *NYHT*, 8 June 51. **3.** *DN*, July 51.

120 CAKEWALK

1. *NYHT*, 13 June 51. **2.** *DM*, Aug. 51. **3.** *Times*, 22 July 52. **4.** Beaumont, *Sunday Times*, 27 July 52.

122 THE CAGE

1. *DN*, July 51. **2.** *NYT*, 24 June 51. **3.** *NYHT*, 15 June 51. **4.** *Morning Telegraph*, 31 Mar. 66. **5.** unsigned, *DM*, Aug. 55. **6.** Monahan, *Guardian*, 9 July 52. **7.** *Scotsman*, 26 Aug. 52. **8.** Merlin, *Le Monde*, 15 June 55. **9.** Gianoli, *L'Italia*, 9 Sept. 53. **10.** Yomiuri, *Japan News*, 1 Apr. 58.

125 THE MIRACULOUS MANDARIN

1. *NYT*, 16 Sept. 51. **2.** *NYT*, 7 Sept. 51. **3.** *NYHT*, 7 Sept. 51. **4.** *DM*, Nov. 51. **5.** *New York City Ballet*, p. 300.

126 À LA FRANÇAIX

1. *NYHT*, 12 Sept. 51. **2.** *DO*, Nov. 51.

127 TYL ULENSPIEGEL

1. *New York City Ballet*, p. 305. **2.** *NYT*, 15 Nov. 51. **3.** *NYHT*, 15 Nov. 51. **4.** *MusAm*, 1 Dec. 51. **5.** M.S., *Art News*, Feb. 52. **6.** *NYHT*, 2 Dec. 51. **7.** *Scotsman*, 29 Aug. 52.

129 SWAN LAKE

1. *DN*, Dec. 51. **2.** *NYHT*, 21 Nov. 51. **3.** *NYT*, 21 Nov. and 5 Dec. 51. **4.** Manchester, *DN*, Jan. 57. **5.** Kisselgoff, *NYT*, 20 May 70. **6.** Barnes, *NYT*, 28 Nov. 66. **7.** Lewis, *Washington Post*, 31 Aug. 72. **8.** Beaumont, *Sunday Times*, 20 July 52. **9.** Monahan, *Guardian*, 12 July 52. **10.** Parente, *Il Mattino*, 7 Oct. 53. **11.** Gianoli, *L'Italia*, 9 Sept. 53. **12.** Zivier, *Die Neue Zeitung*, 4 Sept. 52. **13.** Robinson, *Sydney Morning Herald*, May 58.

132 LILAC GARDEN

1. Manchester, *DN*, Jan. 52. **2.** *NYT*, 21 July 40. **3.** *NYHT*, 4 May 43. **4.** *NYT*, 1 Dec. 51. **5.** *NYHT*, 1 Dec. 51. **6.** *DN*, Jan. 52. **7.** *DM*, Jan. 52. **8.** *NYHT*, 1 Dec. 51. **9.** *MusAm*, 15 Dec. 51. **10.** *Times*, 22 July 52. **11.** L.P., *Avanti*, 23 Sept. 53.

134 THE PIED PIPER

1. *NYHT*, 9 Dec. 51. **2.** *NYT*, 5 and 9 Dec. 51. **3.** Monahan, *Guardian*, 12 July 52. **4.** Zivier, *Die Neue Zeitung*, 6 Sept. 52. **5.** C.S., *Tempo*, 23 Sept. 53.

135 BALLADE

1. *DN*, Apr. 52. **2.** *NYT*, 15 Feb. 52. **3.** *DM*, May 52. **4.** *NYHT*, 15 Feb. 52.

136 BAYOU

1. *NYT*, 16 Mar. 52. **2.** *NYHT*, 22 Feb. 52.

137 CARACOLE

1. *Time*, 3 Mar. 52. **2.** Denby, *Dancers, Buildings and People*, pp. 59–61. **3.** *NYT*, 16 Mar. 52. **4.** *NYHT*, 20 Feb. 52. **5.** *Times*, 28 July 52. **6.** Beaumont, *Sunday Times*, 20 July 52.

138 LA GLOIRE

1. *NYT*, 16 Mar. 52. **2.** *NYHT*, 27 Feb. 52. **3.** *DM*, May 52. **4.** *Times*, 28 July 52.

138 PICNIC AT TINTAGEL

1. *New York City Ballet*, pp. 332–333. **2.** *NYT*, 29 Feb. 52. **3.** *NYHT*, 29 Feb. and 16 Mar. 52.

140 SCOTCH SYMPHONY

1. *NYHT*, 13 Nov. 52. **2.** *DN*, Dec. 52. **3.** *DM*, Jan. 53. **4.** *NYT*, 13 Oct. 68. **5.** *NYHT*, 30 Nov. 57. **6.** *NYT*, 13 Nov. 52. **7.** Merlin, *Le Monde*, 10 July 55. **8.** Parente, *Il Mattino*, 9 Oct. 53.

141 METAMORPHOSES

1. *NYT*, 26 Nov. 52. **2.** *DM*, Jan. 53. **3.** *NYHT*, 26 Nov. 52.

143 HARLEQUINADE PAS DE DEUX

1. *NYT*, 17 Dec. 52. **2.** *NYHT*, 17 Dec. 52. **3.** *NYT*, 17 Dec. 52 and 1 Feb. 53.

143 KALEIDOSCOPE

1. *NYHT*, 19 Dec. 52. **2.** *DM*, Feb. 53.

144 INTERPLAY

1. *NYT*, 18 Oct. 45. **2.** *NYHT*, 4 Nov. 45; repr. Denby, *Looking at the Dance*, pp. 117, 119. **3.** Martin, *NYT*, 24 Dec. 52. **4.** Hering, *DM*, Feb. 53. **5.** Terry, *NYHT*, 1 Mar. 56.

144 CONCERTINO

1. *NYT*, 31 Dec. 52. **2.** *NYHT*, 31 Dec. 52.

145 VALSE FANTAISIE

1. Sabin, *MusAm*, Feb. 53. **2.** *NYT*, 7 Jan. 53.

146 WILL O' THE WISP

1. *DM*, Mar. 53.

146 THE FIVE GIFTS

1. *DN*, Mar. 53. **2.** *NYT*, 7 May 53. **3.** *NYHT*, 21 Jan. 53. **4.** *DM*, Mar. 53.

147 AFTERNOON OF A FAUN

1. *DM*, July 53. **2.** *DO*, June–July 53. **3.** *NYHT*, 24 May 53. **4.** *DN*, June 53. **5.** *NYT*, 15 May 53. **6.** *L'Express*, 18 June 55. **7.** Merlin, *Le Monde*, 15 June 55. **8.** Frangini, *La Nazione*, 9 May 55.

149 THE FILLY

1. *NYT*, 20 May 53. 2. *NYHT*, 24 May 53. 3. *MusAm*, June 53.

149 FANFARE

1. *DN*, Sept. 53. 2. *NYHT*, 3 June 53. 3. *NYT*, 3 June 53. 4. *DM*, July–Aug. 53. 5. Manchester, *DN*, Sept. 53. 6. Hering, *DM*, July–Aug. 53. 7. *Times*, 4 Sept. 65. 8. Porter, *Financial Times*, 4 Sept. 65. 9. Frangini, *La Nazione*, 21 Oct. 53.

150 CON AMORE

1. *NYT*, 10 June 53 and 4 May 62. 2. *NYHT*, 10 June 53. 3. *DN*, Sept. 53.

151 OPUS 34

1. *NYN*, 22 Jan. 54. 2. 6 Feb. 54; repr. Haggin, *Ballet Chronicle*, pp. 31–32. 3. *NYT*, 21 Jan. 54.

153 THE NUTCRACKER

1. *DN*, Feb. 54. 2. *NYT*, 3 Feb. 54. 3. *DN*, Mar. 54. 4. *NYT*, 28 Mar. 54. 5. *Center*, Feb. 54; repr. Denby, *Dancers, Buildings and People*, p. 76. 6. *NYHT*, 30 Dec. 58. 7. *Hudson Review*, Apr. 59. 8. *NYHT*, 13 Dec. 64 and 23 Dec. 65. 9. Jowitt, *VV*, 2 Jan. 69.

161 QUARTET

1. *NYHT*, 20 Feb. 54. 2. *NYP*, 23 Feb. 54. 3. *DN*, Apr. 54. 4. *NYT*, 20 Feb. 54. 5. *NYHT*, 20 Feb. 54.

161 WESTERN SYMPHONY

1. *NYHT*, 8 Sept. 54. 2. *NYT*, 8 Sept. 54. 3. *Monitor*, 25 Sept. 54. 4. *MusAm*, Oct. 54. 5. *NYT*, 8 Sept. 54. 6. Manchester, *DN*, Apr. 55. 7. 26 Mar. 55; repr. Haggin, *Ballet Chronicle*, p. 34. 8. Barnes, *NYT*, 24 Jan. 68. 9. *Times*, 1 Sept. 65. 10. Porter, *Financial Times*, 1 Sept. 65. 11. Merlin, *Le Monde*, 10 June 55. 12. Robinson, *Sydney Morning Herald*, 18 Apr. 58. 13. Khachaturian, *Izvestia*, 10 Oct. 62. 14. Ilupina, *Moscow News*, 19 Oct. 62.

164 IVESIANA

1. *NYT*, 21 Apr. 74. 2. *Center*, Oct. 54; repr. Denby, *Dancers, Buildings and People*, pp. 105–110. 3. *NYHT*, 15 Sept. 54. 4. *NYT*, 3 Oct. 54. 5. *DN*, May 61. 6. *Hudson Review*, July 61; repr. Haggin, *Ballet Chronicle*, p. 56. 7. *DM*, Oct. 75. 8. *Times*, 8 Sept. 65. 9. Coton, *Daily Telegraph*, 8 Sept. 65. 10. Merlin (reporting from London), *Le Figaro Littéraire*, 13 Sept. 65.

166 ROMA

1. *NYHT*, 24 Feb. 55. 2. *DM*, Apr. 55. 3. *NYT*, 20 Mar. 55. 4. *Center*, Apr. 55; repr. Denby, *Dancers, Buildings and People*, pp. 91–93.

167 PAS DE TROIS

1. *MusAm*, Mar. 55. 2. *DN*, Apr. 55.

168 PAS DE DIX

1. *NYT*, 4 Dec. 55. 2. *DM*, Jan. 56. 3. *NYT*, 4 Dec. 55. 4. *DN*, Dec. 55. 5. *Japan Times*, 19 Mar. 58.

168 SOUVENIRS

1. *NYT*, 12 Dec. 55. 2. *DM*, Jan. 56. 3. *NYHT*, 16 Nov. 55. 4. *NYT*, 16 Nov. 55. 5. Robinson, *Sydney Morning Herald*, May 58.

170 JEUX D' ENFANTS

1. Haggin, *Nation*, 7 Jan. 56; repr. Haggin, *Ballet Chronicle*, p. 36. 2. Martin, *NYT*, 4 Dec. 55. 3. Kastendieck, *NYJA*, 23 Nov. 55. 4. *Nation*, 7 Jan. 56; repr. Haggin, *Ballet Chronicle*, p. 36. 5. *NYJA*, 23 Nov. 55. 6. *DN*, Oct. 59.

170 ALLEGRO BRILLANTE

1. *DN*, Apr. 56. 2. *NYHT*, 2 Mar. 56. 3. *NYT*, 2 Mar 56. 4. *DN*, Apr. 56.

172 THE CONCERT

1. *NYHT*, 7 Mar. 56. 2. *NYT*, 7 Mar. 56. 3. *NYN*, 8 Mar. 56. 4. *DM*, May 56. 5. Goldner, *Nation*, 10 Jan. 72. 6. Mazo, *WWD*, 6 Dec. 71. 7. Merlin, *Le Monde*, 28 July 61.

174 THE STILL POINT

1. *DM*, May 56. 2. Martin, *NYT*, 18 Mar. 56. 3. Manchester, *DN*, Apr. 56. 4. Golea, *Informations et Documents*, 15 Mar. 57. 5. Koegler, *Die Welt*, Sept. 56.

176 DIVERTIMENTO NO. 15

1. *NYWTS*, 20 Dec. 56. 2. Kastendieck, *NYJA*, 20 Dec. 56. 3. Terry, *NYHT*, 20 Dec. 56 and 27 Nov. 58; *NYWJT*, 30 Nov. 66. 4. Martin, *NYT*, 20 Dec. 56 and 26 Nov. 58.

177 THE UNICORN,
THE GORGON, AND
THE MANTICORE

1. *NYHT*, 22 Oct. 56. 2. *DO*, Mar. 57. 3. *NYHT*, 27 Jan. 57. 4. *NYT*, 16 Jan. 57.

179 THE MASQUERS

1. *NYHT*, 30 Jan. 57. 2. Martin, *NYT*, 30 Jan. 57. 3. *Nation*, 30 Mar. 57; repr. Haggin, *Ballet Chronicle*, p. 41.

179 PASTORALE

1. *DN*, May 57. 2. Herridge, *NYP*, 15 Feb. 57. 3. Lloyd, *Monitor*, 2 Mar. 57. 4. Martin, *NYT*, 15 Feb. 57.

180 SQUARE DANCE

1. *NYT*, 3 Sept. 59 and 2 Feb. 58. 2. Biancolli, *NYWTS*, 3 Sept. 59. 3. *DN*, Jan. 58. 4. *NYT*, 3 Sept. 59. 5. *NYHT*, 22 Nov. 58. 6. *DM*, Jan. 58. 7. Manchester, *DN*, Jan. 58. 8. *DN*, Jan. 58. 9. *NYT*, 22 May 76.

182 AGON

1. Clement Crisp, *Financial Times*, 73. 2. Martin, *NYT*, 2 Feb. 58. 3. Interview, *Syracuse Post Standard*, 19 Sept. 54. 4. Interview, WNET-TV, 1964. 5. Interview, *Syracuse Post Standard*, 19 Sept. 54. 6. Merlin, *Stravinsky*. 7. Merlin, *Stravinsky*. 8. Interview, WNET-TV, 1964. 9. Coleman, "Apostle of the Pure Ballet," *NYT*, 1 Dec. 57. 10. Barnes, *NYT*, 30 May 70. 11. *NYT*, 2 Feb. 58. 12. *NYT*, 28 Nov. 57. 13. *NYHT*, 2 Dec. 57. 14. *DN*, Jan. 58. 15. Denby, *Dancers, Buildings and People*, pp. 96–100. 16. Kirstein, *Movement and Metaphor*, pp. 242–243. 17. *Times*, 31 Aug. 65. 18. Zakharov, *Pravda*, 14 Oct. 62.

186 GOUNOD SYMPHONY

1. *DN*, Feb. 58. 2. *NYHT*, 9 Jan. 58. 3. *NYT*, 9 Jan. 58, 26 Aug. 59, and 2 Apr. 60. 4. *NYHT*, 9 Jan. 58. 5. Merlin, *Le Monde*, 6 Mar. 59.

187 STARS AND STRIPES

1. Siegel, *DM*, Mar. 74. 2. *DN*, Oct. 58. 3. Manchester, *DN*, Feb. 58. 4. Terry, *NYHT*, 18 Jan. 58. 5. Hering, *DM*, Nov. 58. 6. Barnes, *NYT*, 27 Nov. 67. 7. *NYT*, 2 Feb. 58. 8. Kennedy, *Guardian*, 31 Aug. 65. 9. Porter, *Financial Times*, 31 Aug. and 2 Sept. 65. 10. Buckle, *Sunday Times*, 5 Sept. 65. 11. Baignères, *Le Figaro*, 29 and 30 June 65. 12. Osins, *Mainichi Daily News*, 10 Apr. 58. 13. Robinson, *Sydney Morning Herald*, 6 June 58.

190 WALTZ-SCHERZO

1. *NYT*, 2 Sept. 59. 2. *DN*, Oct. 58. 3. *NYT*, 10 Dec. 59. 4. *DM*, Nov. 58. 5. *DN*, Oct. 58. 6. *DN*, Feb. 64.

190 MEDEA

1. *NYT*, 14 May 59. 2. *DN*, Jan. 59. 3. *NYT*, 27 Nov. 58. 4. Todd, *D&D*, Feb. 59. 5. Manchester, *DN*, Jan. 59. 6. Hering, *DM*, Jan. 59. 7. *D&D*, Apr. 51. 8. Biancolli, *NYWTS*, 9 Nov. 60. 9. Terry, *NYHT*, 9 Nov. 60. 10. Martin, *NYT*, 14 May 59.

192 OCTET

1. *NYHT*, 6 and 3 Dec. 58. **2.** Herridge, *NYP*, 3 Dec. 58. **3.** Martin, *NYT*, 3 Dec. 58. **4.** unsigned, *NYWTS*, 3 Dec. 58. **5.** *NYT*, 3 Dec. 58.

192 THE SEVEN DEADLY SINS

1. *N.Y. Staats-Zeitung und Herold*, 26 Dec. 58. **2.** Martin, *NYT*, 5 Dec. 58. **3.** Terry, *NYHT*, 5 Dec. 58. **4.** Martin, *NYT*, 18 Jan. 59. **5.** *NYHT*, 5 Dec. 58. **6.** *NYT*, 5 Dec. 58. **7.** *DN*, Jan. 59. **8.** Hering, *DM*, Jan. 59. **9.** Terry, *NYHT*, 5 Dec. 58. **10.** Harrison, *NYHT*, 5 Dec. 58. **11.** Martin, *NYT*, 18 Jan. 59. **12.** Hering, *DM*, Jan. 59. **13.** Martin, *NYT*, 18 Jan. 59. **14.** *NYWTS*, 5 Dec. 58. **15.** *NYT*, 10 Dec. 59. **16.** *NYWTS*, 3 Sept. 59.

195 NATIVE DANCERS

1. *DN*, Feb. 59. **2.** *NYN*, 15 Jan. 59. **3.** Terry, *NYHT*, 15 Jan. 59. **4.** Kastendieck, *NYJA*, 15 Jan. 59. **5.** Martin, *NYT*, 15 Jan. 59. **6.** Terry, *NYHT*, 15 Jan. 59. **7.** Johnson, *NYP*, 15 Jan. 59.

195 EPISODES

1. Balanchine, *New Complete Stories*, p. 133. **2.** *NYHT*, 15 May 59. **3.** *NYT*, 7 June 59. **4.** *DM*, July 59. **5.** *NYT*, 15 May and 7 June 59. **6.** *NYT*, 7 June 59. **7.** *NYP*, 15 May 59. **8.** Denby, *Dancers, Buildings and People*, p. 121. **9.** *NYHT*, 9 Dec. 59. **10.** Hering, *DM*, July 59. **11.** Martin, *NYT*, 7 June 59. **12.** Manchester, *DN*, June 59. **13.** Martin, *NYT*, 7 June 59. **14.** Hering, *DM*, July 59. **15.** Martin, *NYT*, 7 June 59. **16.** Martin, *NYT*, 7 June 59. **17.** Hering, *DM*, July 59. **18.** Martin, *NYT*, 7 June 59. **19.** Hering, *DM*, July 59. **20.** Kennedy, *Guardian*, 6 Sept. 65. **21.** *Times*, 4 Sept. 65. **22.** Brunner, *Express*, 24 Aug. 65. **23.** Merlin (reporting from Frankfurt), *Le Figaro Littéraire*, 8 Sept. 62. **24.** Ruppel (reporting from Salzburg), *Süddeutsche Zeitung*, 24 Aug. 65.

199 NIGHT SHADOW

1. Denby, *Looking at the Dance*, p. 199. **2.** *NYHT*, 7 Jan. 60. **3.** *NYT*, 7 Jan. 60. **4.** Manchester, *DN*, Feb. 60. **5.** Kisselgoff, *NYT*, 29 Nov. 69. **6.** Hering, *DM*, Feb. 60. **7.** Lederman, *ModMus*, Spring 46. **8.** "Beyond Technique," *DP* 36 (Winter 68). **9.** *Playbill*, Jan.–Feb. 70.

201 PANAMERICA

1. *DM*, Mar. 60. **2.** Terry, *NYHT*, 21 Jan. and 6 Apr. 60. **3.** Terry, *NYHT*, 8 Apr. 60. **4.** Terry, *NYHT*, 21 Jan. 60. **5.** Terry, *NYHT*, 21 Jan. 60. **6.** Hering, *DM*, Mar. 60. **7.**

Manchester, *DN*, Feb. 60. **8.** *NYJA*, 21 Jan. 60.

202 THEME AND VARIATIONS

1. *NYT*, 14 Feb. 60. **2.** Manchester, *DN*, Mar. 60. **3.** *NYT*, 14 Feb 60. **4.** *DN*, Jan. 48. **5.** *NYHT*, 7 Dec. 47. **6.** *NYT*, 15 Dec. 47.

203 PAS DE DEUX

1. Manchester, *DN*, May 60. **2.** Terry, *NYHT*, 30 Mar. 60. **3.** Martin, *NYT*, 30 Mar. 60.

203 THE FIGURE IN THE CARPET

1. Manchester, *DN*, May 60. **2.** *NYT*, 14 Apr. 60. **3.** *NYT*, 14 Apr. 60. **4.** *NYHT*, 10 Nov. 60. **5.** Hering, *DM*, June 60. **6.** Hering, *DM*, June 60. **7.** Manchester, *DN*, May 60. **8.** Martin, *NYT*, 14 Apr. 60. **9.** Manchester, *DN*, May 60. **10.** Hering, *DM*, June 60. **11.** Hering, *DM*, June 60. **12.** Martin, *NYT*, 14 Apr. 60. **13.** Terry, *NYHT*, 14 Apr. 60. **14.** Manchester, *DN*, May 60. **15.** Hering, *DM*, June 60.

205 VARIATIONS FROM "DON SEBASTIAN"

1. Martin, *NYT*, 17 Nov. 60. **2.** *NYT*, 1 May 75. **3.** *NYHT*, 17 Nov. 60. **4.** *DM*, Jan. 61. **5.** *NYT*, 30 Apr. 71. **6.** Porter, *Financial Times*, 2 Sept. 65.

206 MONUMENTUM PRO GESUALDO

1. *NYWTS*, 17 Nov. 60. **2.** *NYT*, 30 Aug. 61. **3.** *NYT*, 25 Oct. 65. **4.** *NYP*, 17 Nov. 60. **5.** Porter, *Financial Times*, 7 Sept. 65. **6.** Geitel, *Die Welt*, Aug. 65.

207 LIEBESLIEDER WALZER

1. Martin, *NYT*, 23 Nov. 60. **2.** *Times*, 1 Sept. 65. **3.** *NYT*, 23 Nov. 60. **4.** *Guardian*, 1 Sept. 65. **5.** *NYHT*, 23 Nov. 60. **6.** *DN*, Jan. 61. **7.** *NYT*, 23 Nov. 60. **8.** Hering, *DM*, Jan. 61. **9.** Croce, *Playbill*, Jan.–Feb. 70. **10.** Hering, *DM*, Jan. 61. **11.** Kisselgoff, *NYT*, 14 Jan. 74. **12.** *DN*, Jan. 61. **13.** Porter, *Financial Times*, 2 Sept. 65. **14.** Geitel, (reporting from Hamburg), *Die Welt*, Sept. 62.

210 JAZZ CONCERT

1. *D&D*, Feb. 61. **2.** *NYT*, 8 Dec. 60.

210 CREATION OF THE WORLD

1. *NYHT*, 16 Mar. 61. **2.** *NYT*, 8 Dec. 60.

211 RAGTIME (I)

1. *DN*, Jan. 61. **2.** *NYT*, 29 Jan. 67.

211 LES BICHES

1. *DM*, Jan. 61.

211 EBONY CONCERTO

1. White, *Stravinsky*, p. 398. **2.** *DN*, Jan. 61. **3.** *DM*, Jan. 61. **4.** *NYT*, 22 June 72.

212 MODERN JAZZ: VARIANTS

1. *DN*, Feb. 61. **2.** *NYN*, 5 Jan. 61. **3.** *NYT*, 5 Jan. 61. **4.** *Hudson Review*, Spring 61; repr. Haggin, *Ballet Chronicle*, p. 54. **5.** *NYHT*, 5 Jan. 61. **6.** Denby, *Dancers, Buildings and People*, pp. 162, 167, 168.

213 ELECTRONICS

1. *NYN*, 23 Mar. 61. **2.** *NYWTS*, 23 Mar. 61. **3.** Haggin, *Hudson Review*, July 61; repr. Haggin, *Ballet Chronicle*, p. 56. **4.** Denby, *Dancers, Buildings and People*, p. 195. **5.** *NYT*, 23 Mar. 61. **6.** *NYHT*, 1 Sept. 61.

214 VALSE ET VARIATIONS

1. *NYT*, 5 Apr. 67. **2.** *NYT*, 8 Dec. 61. **3.** *DN*, Jan. 62. **4.** Crisp, *Financial Times*, 6 Sept. 65. **5.** Geitel, *Die Welt*, Sept. 62. **6.** Ilupina, *Moscow News*, 19 Oct. 62.

215 A MIDSUMMER NIGHT'S DREAM

1. *Playbill*, June 73. **2.** Terry, *NYHT*, 9 Mar. 66. **3.** Manchester, *DN*, Feb. 62. **4.** Terry, *NYHT*, 18 Jan. 62. **5.** Kisselgoff, *NYT*, 29 June 73. **6.** *NYT*, 28 Jan. 62. **7.** *DM*, Mar. 62. **8.** *NYT*, 9 Apr. 66. **9.** *DN*, Feb. 62. **10.** Manchester, *DN*, Feb. 62. **11.** Manchester, *DN*, Feb. 62. **12.** *NYT*, 28 Jan. 62. **13.** Martin, *NYT*, 18 Jan. 62. **14.** *NYT*, 28 Jan. 62.

218 BUGAKU

1. Bowers, *DM*, Mar. 50. **2.** *Chicago Tribune*, 16 Nov. 65. **3.** Lombardi, *Mainichi Daily News*, 9 July 63. **4.** *Time*, 29 Mar. 63. **5.** *NYWTS*, 30 Sept. 63. **6.** *NYT*, 30 Aug. 63. **7.** *DN*, Apr. 63. **8.** Porter, *Financial Times*, 1 Sept. 63. **9.** Kennedy, *Guardian*, 1 Sept. 63. **10.** Baignères, *Le Figaro*, 30 June 65. **11.** Geitel (reporting from Salzburg), *Die Welt*, Aug. 65.

220 ARCADE

1. White, *Stravinsky*, p. 278. **2.** *DN*, May 63. **3.** *NYT*, 5 Sept. 63. **4.** *NYHT*, 13 Dec. 63.

220 MOVEMENTS FOR PIANO AND ORCHESTRA

1. *Times*, 8 Sept. 65. **2.** *Ballet Review*, III, 4,

NOTES

70. **3.** Henahan, *Chicago Tribune*, 8 Aug. 63. **4.** Hughes, *NYT*, 10 Apr. 63. **5.** Terry, *NYHT*, 10 Apr. 63. **6.** Manchester, *DN*, May 63. **7.** Porter, *Financial Times*, 7 Sept. 65. **8.** Geitel (reporting from Salzburg), *Die Welt*, Aug. 65.

222 THE CHASE

1. *NYT*, 19 Sept. 63. **2.** *NYT*, 23 Sept. 63. **3.** Biancolli, *Mozart Handbook*, p. 444. **4.** *NYHT*, 19 Sept. 63. **5.** Hughes, *NYT*, 19 Sept. 63.

222 FANTASY

1. *NYHT*, 25 Sept. 63. **2.** *DN*, Nov. 63. **3.** *Monitor*, 28 Oct. 63.

223 MEDITATION

1. Freedley, *Morning Telegraph*, 11 Dec. 63. **2.** Kastendieck, *NYJA*, 11 Dec. 63. **3.** Terry, *NYHT*, 12 Dec. 63. **4.** Watt, *NYN*, 12 Dec. 63. **5.** Manchester, *DN*, Feb. 64. **6.** Hughes, *NYT*, 11 Dec. 64. **7.** Manchester, *Monitor*, 16 Dec. 63. **8.** Freedley, *Morning Telegraph*, 11 Dec. 63. **9.** Bland (reporting from Edinburgh) *Observer WR*, 3 Sept. 67.

223 TARANTELLA

1. Terry, *NYHT*, 8 Jan. 64. **2.** Kastendieck, *NYJA*, 8 Jan. 64. **3.** Hughes, *NYT*, 8 Jan. 64. **4.** Manchester, *DN*, Feb. 64, and *Monitor*, 22 Jan. 64. **5.** Porter, *Financial Times*, 31 Aug. 65.

224 QUATUOR

1. *DM*, Mar. 64. **2.** *Providence Sunday Journal*, 22 Jan. 64. **3.** *DN*, Feb. 64.

227 CLARINADE

1. *DN*, June 64. **2.** *NYT*, 30 Apr. 64. **3.** *NYT*, 24 May 64. **4.** Sargent, *New Yorker*, 9 May 64.

227 DIM LUSTRE

1. *NYT*, 16 Oct. 65. **2.** *NYHT*, 7 May 64. **3.** *DN*, June 64. **4.** *NYT*, 16 Oct. 65.

228 IRISH FANTASY

1. Bland, *Observer WR*, 12 Sept. 65. **2.** *DN*, Nov. 64. **3.** *NYT*, 5 May 71. **4.** Porter, *Financial Times*, 8 Sept. 65. **5.** *Times*, 8 Sept. 65.

228 PIÈGE DE LUMIÈRE

1. *NYT*, 2 Oct. 64. **2.** *DN*, Nov. 64. **3.** *NYHT*, 13 Oct. 65 and 2 Oct. 64.

230 PAS DE DEUX AND DIVERTISSEMENT

1. *DN*, Feb. 65. **2.** *NYHT*, 16 Oct. 65.

3. *NYT*, 14 Oct. 65 and 11 Jan. 67.

230 SHADOW'D GROUND

1. *DN*, Mar. 65. **2.** *NYHT*, 22 Jan. 65. **3.** *NYT*, 22 Jan. 65.

232 HARLEQUINADE

1. *NYT*, 31 Jan. 72. **2.** *NYT*, 7 Apr. 66. **3.** *NYT*, 11 Jan. 73. **4.** *DN*, Mar. 65. **5.** *NYJA*, 5 Feb. 65. **6.** *NYP*, 5 Feb. 65.

234 DON QUIXOTE

1. *NYT*, 6 Feb. 75. **2.** *NYHT*, 29 May 65. **3.** Campbell, *Chicago Daily News*, 28 May 65. **4.** Hughes, *NYT*, 29 May 65. **5.** Gottfried, *WWD*, 1 June 65. **6.** Denby, *Dancers, Buildings and People*, p. 123. **7.** Barnes, *NYT*, 29 Jan. 65. **8.** Cassidy, *Chicago Tribune*, 26 Feb. 68. **9.** Goldner, *DN*, Mar. 70. **10.** Barnes, *NYT*, 13 Feb. 70. **11.** Porter, *New Yorker*, 17 Feb. 73. **12.** *NYT*, 29 May 65. **13.** *Chicago Tribune*, 26 Feb. 68. **14.** Denby, *Dancers, Buildings and People*, p. 128. **15.** Interview with Eugene Palatsky, 1965. **16.** *NYHT*, 29 May 65. **17.** *WWD*, 1 June 65. **18.** *Chicago Tribune*, 26 Feb. 68. **19.** *NYT*, 6 June 65. **20.** *New Yorker*, 17 Feb. 73. **21.** *New Yorker*, 17 Feb. 73. **22.** *New Yorker*, 17 Feb. 73.

240 VARIATIONS

1. Kerner, *VV*, 7 Apr. 66. **2.** White, *Stravinsky*, p. 497. **3.** *NYT*, 2 Apr. 66. **4.** *NYHT*, 1 Apr. 66. **5.** *DN*, May–June 66. **6.** Leonard Harris, *NYWTS*, 1 Apr. 66.

241 SUMMERSPACE

1. *DN*, June 66. **2.** *DM*, June 66. **3.** *NYT*, 15 Apr. 66. **4.** *Newark News*, 15 Apr. 66. **5.** *Ballet Review*, III, 4, 70.

242 BRAHMS-SCHOENBERG QUARTET

1. *NYHT*, 22 Apr. 66. **2.** *NYT*, 30 Nov. 70 and 2 Dec. 74. **3.** *Boston Globe*, 6 Dec. 70. **4.** Manchester, *DN*, June 66.

244 JEUX

1. Kirstein, *Movement and Metaphor*, p. 202. **2.** Sokolova, *Dancing with Diaghilev*, pp. 41, 43. **3.** *NYT*, 2 May 66. **4.** *NYWJT*, 23 Nov. 66. **5.** *DN*, Jan. 67.

245 NARKISSOS

1. *DN*, Jan. 67. **2.** *NYT*, 25 Nov. 66 and 25 Nov. 67.

245 LA GUIRLANDE DE CAMPRA

1. *NYT*, 2 Dec. 66. **2.** *NYP*, 2 Dec. 66.

245 PROLOGUE

1. *NYT*, 13 and 17 Jan. 67. **2.** *NYWJT*, 13 Jan. 67. **3.** *NYP*, 13 Jan. 67. **4.** *DM*, Mar. 67.

246 RAGTIME (II)

1. *NYWJT*, 18 Jan. 67. **2.** *DM*, Mar. 67. **3.** *NYT*, 18 Jan. 67.

247 TROIS VALSES ROMANTIQUES

1. *NYT*, 7 Apr. 67. **2.** *Newark News*, 7 Apr. 67. **3.** *DM*, June 67.

247 JEWELS

1. *NYT*, 14 Apr. 67. **2.** *Time*, 21 Apr. 67. **3.** *DN*, May 67. **4.** *NYT*, 14 Apr. 67. **5.** *Partisan Review*, Fall 68. **6.** *New York City Ballet*, p. 202. **7.** Dodd, *DT*, Sept. 69. **8.** Merlin, *Le Monde*, 24 June 69. **9.** Schmidt-Garre, *Münchner Merkur*, 14–15 Aug. 72. **10.** Krieger, *Sovetskaya Kultura*, 19 Oct. 72.

250 GLINKIANA

1. *NYT*, 24 Dec. 67. **2.** *NYT*, 24 Nov. 67. **3.** *DM*, Jan 68.

251 METASTASEIS AND PITHOPRAKTA

1. *NYT*, 19 Jan. 68. **2.** *DN*, Mar. 68. **3.** *SR*, 3 Feb. 68. **4.** *DN*, Mar. 68. **5.** Stewart (reporting from New York), *Guardian Weekly*, 23 May 68. **6.** Barnes, *NYT*, 1 Feb. 69. **7.** Hering, *DM*, Mar. 68. **8.** Jowitt, *VV*.

253 HAYDN CONCERTO

1. Barnes, *D&D*, Apr. 68. **2.** *NYP*, 26 Jan. 68. **3.** *DM*, Mar. 68. **4.** *D&D*, Apr. 68.

253 SLAUGHTER ON TENTH AVENUE

1. *DM*, July 68. **2.** *VV*, May 68. **3.** *NYT*, 4 May 68. **4.** *NYT*, 18 July 68.

255 REQUIEM CANTICLES (I)

1. *NYP*, 3 May 68.

255 STRAVINSKY: SYMPHONY IN C

1. *NYT*, 24 Jan. 69. **2.** *DM*, Apr. 68 and Apr. 69. **3.** Barnes, *NYT*, 20 May 68. **4.** *Ballet Review*, II, 5, 69. **5.** *DM*, July 68.

256 LA SOURCE

1. *NYT*, 25 Nov. 68. **2.** *DN*, Jan. 69. **3.** *NYT*, 10 Feb. 69. **4.** *NYT*, 24 May 73.

257 TCHAIKOVSKY SUITE

1. *NYT*, 10 Jan. 69. **2.** *LI Press*, 10 Jan. 69. **3.** *DN*, Feb. 69.

258 FANTASIES

1. *DM*, Apr. 69. **2.** *NYT*, 24 Jan. 69. **3.** *NYT*, 29 May 72. **4.** *Ballet Review*, II, 5, 69.

259 PRELUDE, FUGUE, AND RIFFS

1. Baker, *Chicago Tribune*, 2 June 69. **2.** *DM*, Aug. 69. **3.** *New Yorker*, 31 May 69.

259 DANCES AT A GATHERING

1. *NYT*, 25 Apr. 69. **2.** *DM*, July 69. **3.** *LI Press*, 3 June 69. **4.** *Monitor*, 23 May 69. **5.** *NYT*, 24 May and 1 June 69. **6.** *Washington Post*, 24 May 69. **7.** *VV*, 29 May 69. **8.** *Nation*, 5 June 72. **9.** *Hudson Review*, Fall 69. **10.** Interview with McDonagh, *Ballet Review*, III, 5, 69. **11.** Dodd, *DT*, Sept. 69. **12.** Geitel, *Die Welt*, 17 Aug. 72. **13.** Koegler, *Süddeutsche Zeitung*, June 69. **14.** Baignères, *Le Figaro*, 24 June 69. **15.** *Izvestia*, 14 Oct. 72.

265 REVERIES

1. *NYT*, 7 Dec. 69. **2.** *DM*, Apr. 70. **3.** *DN*, Jan. 72. **4.** *NYT*, 23 Nov. 71.

266 IN THE NIGHT

1. Interview with Terry, *SR*, 21 Feb. 70. **2.** Interview with Croce, *Albany Times-Union*, 71. **3.** *Ballet Review*, III, 3, 70. **4.** *SR*, 21 Feb. 70. **5.** *NYT*, 30 Jan. 70. **6.** Gale, *Newark News*, 8 Feb. 70. **7.** *Harper's*, Apr. 71. **8.** *Albany Times-Union*, 71.

268 WHO CARES?

1. *Nation*, 2 Mar. 70. **2.** *Newsweek*, 16 Feb. 70. **3.** *DM*, Apr. 70. **4.** *NYT*, 6 and 15 Feb. 70. **5.** *Ballet Review*, III, 3, 70. **6.** *Monitor*, 13 Feb. 70.

270 SARABANDE AND DANSE (I)

1. *NYT*, 21 June 70. **2.** *NYT*, 23 May 70. **3.** *DM*, Aug 70.

271 SUITE NO. 3

1. *Nation*, 28 Dec. 70. **2.** *Newsweek*, 14 Dec. 70. **3.** *Newsday*, 4 Dec. 70. **4.** *Monitor*, 19 Dec. 70. **5.** *NYT*, 13 May 73. **6.** Ruppel, *Süddeutsche Zeitung*, 16 Aug. 72. **7.** Liepa, *Literaturnaia Gazeta*, 25 Oct. 72.

272 KODÁLY DANCES

1. *DN*, Mar. 71. **2.** *Boston Herald*, 16 Feb. 71.

273 CONCERTO FOR TWO SOLO PIANOS

1. *NYT*, 23 Jan. 71. **2.** *NYP*, 22 Jan. 71. **3.** *LI Press*, 22 Jan. 71.

273 FOUR LAST SONGS

1. *Nation*, 22 Feb. 71. **2.** *Boston Herald*, 5 Feb. 71. **3.** *NYP*, 22 Jan. 71.

274 CONCERTO FOR JAZZ BAND AND ORCHESTRA

1. *DN*, June 71. **2.** *NYT*, 8 May 71.

275 OCTANDRE

1. *NYT*, 15 May 71. **2.** *NYP*, 14 May 71. **3.** *Boston Herald*, 16 June 71.

275 THE GOLDBERG VARIATIONS

1. *New Yorker*, 19 June 71. **2.** Interview with Croce, *Albany Times-Union*, 71. **3.** Geiringer, *Bach Family*, pp. 277–278. **4.** Rich, *New York*, 5 July 71. **5.** *Nation*, 5 July 71. **6.** Webster, *Philadelphia Inquirer*, 6 June 71. **7.** *NYT*, 29 May 71. **8.** *DN*, Sept. 71. **9.** *VV*, 10 June 71. **10.** *Monitor*, 7 June 71. **11.** *Monitor*, 7 June 71. **12.** *VV*, 10 June 71. **13.** *Washington Star*, 27 Jan. 72. **14.** *NYT*, 29 May 71. **15.** *Ballet Review*, III, 6, 71. **16.** *Ballet Review*, IV, 2, 72. **17.** *Nation*, 5 July 71. **18.** *D&D*, Aug. 71. **19.** *Ballet Review*, II, 6, 71. **20.** Kisselgoff, *NYT*, 10 Jan. 74. **21.** *DN*, Sept. 71. **22.** *D&D*, Aug. 71. **23.** *DN*, Sept. 71. **24.** *Ballet Review*, III, 6, 71. **25.** *Ballet Review*, IV, 2, 72. **26.** Schmidt-Garre, *Münchner Merkur*, 14–15 Aug. 72. **27.** Liepa, *Literaturnaia Gazeta*, 25 Oct. 72.

280 PAMTGG

1. *NYT*, 27 June 71. **2.** *DM*, Aug. 71.

281 PRINTEMPS

1. *NYT*, 16 Jan. 72. **2.** *DN*, Mar. 72. **3.** *DM*, Apr. 72.

281 CHOPINIANA

1. *NYT*, 22 Jan. 72. **2.** *NYP*, 3 May 72. **3.** *DN*, Mar. 72. **4.** *Ballet Review*, IV, 2, 72.

282 WATERMILL

1. *Nation*, 6 Mar. 72. **2.** *NYT*, 13 Feb. 72. **3.** *NYP*, 19 Feb. 72. **4.** *Nation*, 6 Mar. 72. **5.** *NYT*, 13 and 4 Feb. 72. **6.** Henahan, *NYT*, 10 Feb. 72. **7.** *NYT*, 20 Feb. 72. **8.** *Washington Star*, 18 Feb. 72. **9.** *NYT*, 20 Feb. 72. **10.** *Ballet Review*, IV, 2, 71.

286 STRAVINSKY FESTIVAL

1. Goldner, *Stravinsky Festival*, p.

246. **2.** *Ballet Review*, IV, 3, 72.

287 LOST SONATA

1. *Washington Post*, 20 June 72.

287 SCHERZO FANTASTIQUE

1. *NYT*, 28 Nov. 72. **2.** *Ballet Review*, IV, 3, 72. **3.** *Washington Post*, 20 June 72.

287 SYMPHONY IN THREE MOVEMENTS

1. *Nation*, 26 Feb. 73. **2.** *NYT*, 14 Nov. 74. **3.** *NYT*, 10 May 74. **4.** *Nation*, 26 Feb. 73. **5.** *Ballet Review*, IV, 3, 72. **6.** *Nation*, 26 Feb. 73. **7.** *Ballet Review*, IV, 3, 72.

289 VIOLIN CONCERTO

1. *NYT*, 16 Nov. 72. **2.** *Nation*, 4 Dec. and 10 July 72. **3.** *NYN*, 16 Nov. 72. **4.** *WWD*, 16 Nov. 72. **5.** Vecheslova, *Leningradskaia Pravda*, 30 Sept. 72.

291 SYMPHONY IN E-FLAT

1. Herridge, *NYP*, 21 June 72. **2.** *NYT*, 21 June 72. **3.** *Ballet Review*, IV, 3, 72.

292 CONCERTO FOR PIANO AND WINDS

1. *NYT*, 21 June 72. **2.** *NYT*, 19 Jan. 73.

292 DANSES CONCERTANTES

1. *NYHT*, 17 Sept. 44. **2.** *NYT*, 23 Feb. 45. **3.** *ModMus*, Nov.–Dec. 44. **4.** *NYT*, 21 June 72. **5.** *Ballet Review*, IV, 3, 72. **6.** *NYN*, 28 Nov. 72. **7.** *Ballet Review*, IV, 3, 72. **8.** *NYT*, 19 Feb. 73. .

293 OCTUOR

1. *Newsday*, 26 June 72. **2.** *NYT*, 22 June 72. **3.** *Ballet Review*, IV, 3, 72.

294 SERENADE IN A

1. *NYT*, 22 June 72 and 3 Feb. 73. **2.** *Newsday*, 26 June 72. **3.** *Ballet Review*, IV, 3, 72.

294 DIVERTIMENTO FROM "LE BAISER DE LA FÉE"

1. *NYT*, 15 June 74. **2.** *NYT*, 22 June 72. **3.** *Ballet Review*, IV, 3, 72. **4.** Kisselgoff, *NYT*, 4 Feb. 74. **5.** *NYT*, 17 Nov. 74. **6.** *New Yorker*, 2 Dec. 74.

296 SCHERZO À LA RUSSE

1. *NYT*, 22 June 72 and 9 June 74. **2.** *Ballet Review*, IV, 3, 72. **3.** Goldner, *Stravinsky Festival*, pp. 113–114.

296 CIRCUS POLKA

1. *Ballet Review*, IV, 3, 72.

297 SCÈNES DE BALLET

1. Repr. White, *Stravinsky*, p. 382. **2.** *NYT*, 29 Nov. 74. **3.** *NYT*, 20 Nov. and 6 Dec. 72.

298 DUO CONCERTANT

1. *Ballet Review*, IV, 3, 72. **2.** *New Yorker*, 9 Dec. 72. **3.** *DM*, May 74. **4.** *Ballet Review*, IV, 3, 72. **5.** *Nation*, 10 July 72, and Goldner, *Stravinsky Festival*, p. 134.

299 THE SONG OF THE NIGHTINGALE

1. Repr. White, *Stravinsky*, p. 192. **2.** *NYT*, 23 June 72. **3.** *NYT*, 3 Feb. 73. **4.** *Ballet Review*, IV, 3, 72.

301 PIANO-RAG-MUSIC

1. *NYT*, 4 Feb. 73. **2.** *NYN*, 5 Feb. 73.

301 ODE

1. *Ballet Review*, IV, 3, 72. **2.** *NYT*, 24 June 72.

301 DUMBARTON OAKS

1. *NYT*, 24 June 72. **2.** *VV*, 29 June 72. **3.** *Ballet Review*, IV, 3, 72.

302 PULCINELLA

1. Quoted in Goldner, *Stravinsky Festival*, pp. 241–242 **2.** Goldner, *Stravinsky Festival*, p. 150. **3.** Goldner, *Stravinsky Festival*, p. 152. **4.** *Ballet Review*, IV, 3, 72. **5.** *NYT*, 24 June and 22 Nov. 72. **6.** *VV*, 29 June 72. **7.** *Ballet Review*, IV, 3, 72. **8.** Goldner, *Stravinsky Festival*, p. 151. **9.** Goldner, *Stravinsky Festival*, p. 152.

304 CHORAL VARIATIONS ON BACH'S "VOM HIMMEL HOCH"

1. *NYT*, 26 June 72. **2.** Goldner, *Stravinsky Festival*, p. 182–183.

305 REQUIEM CANTICLES (II)

1. *NYT*, 26 June 72. **2.** *Washington Post*, 27 June 72. **3.** *Ballet Review*, IV, 3, 72. **4.** *NYT*, 12 Jan. 74. **5.** *Nation*, 10 July 72.

306 CORTÈGE HONGROIS

1. *Monitor*, 4 June 73. **2.** *Boston Globe*, 23 May 73. **3.** *VV*, 31 May 73. **4.** *NYT*, 9 Jan. 75.

307 AN EVENING'S WALTZES

1. *Monitor*, 4 June 73. **2.** *NYT*, 26 May 73. **3.** Micklin, *Newsday*, 25 May 73.

308 FOUR BAGATELLES

1. *NYT Sunday Magazine*, 8 Dec. 74. **2.** *New Yorker*, 11 Feb. 74. **3.** *Nation*, 2 Mar. 74. **4.** *NYT*, 12 Jan. 74. **5.** *SR/W*, 4 May 74. **6.** *HiFi/MusAm*, May 74. **7.** *NYT*, 12 Jan 74.

309 VARIATIONS POUR UNE PORTE ET UN SOUPIR

1. *Nation*, 16 Feb. 74. **2.** *NYT*, 19 Feb. 74. **3.** Siegel, *DM*, May 74. **4.** McDonagh, *NYT*, Nov. 74.

310 DYBBUK

1. (reporting from New York) *Observer*, May 74. **2.** Joseph C. Landis, trans., ed., and intro., *The Dybbuk and Other Great Yiddish Plays* (New York: Bantam, 1966), pp. 18–19. **3.** *NYT*, 17 May 74. **4.** Herridge, *NYP*, 17 May 74. **5.** *Monitor*, 24 May 74. **6.** *NYT*, 17 May 74. **7.** *Monitor*, 24 May 74. **8.** *VV*, 6 June 74. **9.** *NYT*, 15 Nov. 74. **10.** (reporting from New York) *Observer*, May 74. **11.** *Nation*, 24 May 74. **12.** *NYT*, 17 May 74. **13.** *NYP*, 17 May 74. **14.** *VV*, 6 June 74. **15.** *Washington Post*, 17 May 74.

313 BARTOK NO. 3

1. *NYT*, 25 May 74. **2.** *NYP*, 24 May 74. **3.** *Newsday*, 24 May 74.

313 SALTARELLI

1. *Newsday*, 3 June 74. **2.** *NYP*, 5 June 74. **3.** *NYP*, 5 June 74. **4.** *NYT*, 1 June 74.

314 COPPÉLIA

1. *DM*, Feb. 58. **2.** Kirstein, *Movement and Metaphor*, p. 170. **3.** *Nation*, 28 Dec. 74. **4.** *Nation*, 28 Dec. 74. **5.** *NYT*, 18 May 75. **6.** *NYT*, 23 Nov. 74 and 20 Jan. 75. **7.** *New Yorker*, 5 Aug. 74. **8.** *Soho Weekly News*, 28 Nov. 74. **9.** *NYT*, 23 Nov. 74. **10.** *Jersey Journal*, 22 Nov. 74. **11.** *New Yorker*, 5 Aug. 74.

319 SINFONIETTA

1. *NYT*, 11 Jan. 75. **2.** Kimball, *NYP*, 10 Jan. 75.

319 SONATINE

1. *DL*, Fall 75. **2.** *New Yorker*, 2 June 75. **3.** *Boston Sunday Globe*, 1 June 75. **4.** *NYT*, 16 June 75. **5.** *DM*, Aug. 75. **6.** *Nation*, 7 June 75.

320 CONCERTO IN G

1. *DL*, Fall 75. **2.** *NYT*, 16 May 75. **3.** *Boston Sunday Globe*, 1 June 75. **4.** *Nation*, 7 June 75.

321 INTRODUCTION AND ALLEGRO FOR HARP

1. *NYP*, 23 May 75. **2.** *NYT*, 24 May 75.

321 SHÉHÉRAZADE

1. *NYT*, 24 May 75.

321 ALBORADA DEL GRACIOSO

1. Stuckenschmidt, *Maurice Ravel*, p. 84. **2.** *New Yorker*, 9 June 75.

322 MA MÈRE L'OYE

1. *New Yorker*, 9 June 75. **2.** *NYP*, 23 May 75. **3.** *NYT*, 23 May 75. **4.** *DM*, Aug. 75. **5.** *Monitor*, 28 May 75.

323 DAPHNIS AND CHLOE

1. *DM*, Aug. 75. **2.** *DL*, Fall 75. **3.** *NYT*, 23 May 75.

324 LE TOMBEAU DE COUPERIN

1. *DM*, Aug. 75. **2.** *DL*, Fall 75. **3.** *NYT*, 22 Nov. 75. **4.** *Washington Star*, 8 Sept. 75. **5.** *Nation*, 21 June 75.

325 PAVANE

1. *New Yorker*, 16 June 75. **2.** *NYT*, 31 May 75. **3.** *DM*, Aug. 75. **4.** *DL*, Fall 75.

325 UNE BARQUE SUR L'OCÉAN

1. *DM*, Aug. 75. **2.** *New Yorker*, 16 June 75. **3.** *VV*, 16 June 75.

326 TZIGANE

1. Stuckenschmidt, *Maurice Ravel*, p. 216. **2.** *DM*, Dec. 75. **3.** *New Yorker*, 16 June 75. **4.** *DM*, Aug. 75. **5.** *DL*, Fall 75. **6.** *VV*, 16 June 75.

327 GASPARD DE LA NUIT

1. Stuckenschmidt, *Maurice Ravel*, p. 111. **2.** *NYT*, 31 May 75. **3.** *New Yorker*, 16 June 75. **4.** *VV*, 16 June 75. **5.** *New Yorker*, 16 June 75. **6.** *DN*, Oct. 75. **7.** *DM*, Aug. 75.

327 SARABANDE AND DANSE (II)

1. *VV*, 16 June 75. **2.** *DN*, Oct. 75.

328 CHANSONS MADÉCASSES

1. *New Yorker*, 16 June 75. 2. *DN*, Oct. 75. 3. *DL*, Fall 75. 4. *NYT*, 31 May 75. 5. *VV*, 16 June 75. 6. *Nation*, 21 June 75.

329 RAPSODIE ESPAGNOLE

1. *New Yorker*, 16 June 75. 2. *DN*, Oct. 75. 3. *Washington Star*, 5 Sept. 75. 4. *New Yorker*, 16 June 75. 5. *NYT*, 31 May 75. 6. *DM*, Aug. 75.

329 THE STEADFAST TIN SOLDIER

1. *NYT*, 1 Aug. 75. 2. *NYT*, 1 Aug. 75. 3. *DM*, Oct. 75. 4. *New Yorker*, 9 Feb. 76.

330 CHACONNE

1. Barnes, *NYT*, 24 Jan. 76. 2. *Washington Post*, 28 Feb. 76. 3. *DN*, Mar. 76. 4. *New Yorker*, 2 Feb. 76. 5. *DN*, Mar. 76. 6. *NYT*, 8 Feb. 76. 7. *DN*, Mar. 76. 8. Andersen, *DM*, Apr. 76. 9. Goldner, *Nation*, 28 Feb. 76. 10. Goldner, *DN*, Mar. 76. 11. *New Yorker*, 2 Feb. 76. 12. *DN*, Mar. 76. 13. *Washington Post*, 28 Feb. 76.

332 UNION JACK

1. Bender, *Time*, 24 May 76. 2. Siegel, *Soho Weekly News*, 20 May 76. 3. *NYT*, 13 May 76. 4. *NYT*, 13 May 76. 5. "The Feet of Fighters: A Measure of Metrical Verse" and "Union Jack," essays in booklet prepared for preview performance, 13 May 76. 6. *New Yorker*, 31 May 76. 7. *NYT*, 13 May 76. 8. Kisselgoff, *NYT*, 13 May 76. 9. *NYT*, 13 May 76. 10. *NYT*, 13 May 76. 11. *Nation*, 5 June 76. 12. *Nation*, 5 June 76. 13. *Newsweek*, 24 May 76. 14. *New Yorker*, 31 May 76. 15. *NYP*, 14 May 76. 16. *New Yorker*, 31 May 76. 17. *WWD*, 14 May 76. 18. *NYP*, 14 May 76. 19. *Newsday*, 14 May 76. 20. *NYT*, 23 and 14 May 76. 21. *Nation*, 5 June 76. 22. *Nation*, 5 June 76. 23. *Nation*, 5 June 76.

INDEX

Note: Photographs of performers in index entries are indicated by *italic* numerals.

A

Aaronson, Boris, 135
Aasen, Muriel, 234, 259, 313, 314, 322, 324
Adams, Diana, 46, 47, *49*, 66, *67*, 72, *82*, *84*, 87, 101, 103, *104*, 110, 117, 119, *120*, 132, 134, 136, 137, 138, *139*, 140, 144, *145*, 149, 151, 161, *162*, 164, 167, 170, 176, *182*, *183*, 186, 187, 195, *198*, 201, 203, 206, *207*, *209*, *211*, *212*, *213*
Afternoon of a Faun, 147–149
Age of Anxiety, 108–110
Agon, 182–186
Air and Variations, 59–60
À la Françaix, 126–127
Alborada del Gracioso, 321–322
Allegro Brillante, 170–172
Alma Mater, 39
Alonso, Alicia, 60
Alsop, Lamar, *298*, 326
Alvarez, Rafael, 169
Amboise, Jacques d', *47*, 48, 58, *59*, 64, 69, 72, *84*, 96, *99*, 101, 115, 116, 138, *139*, 140, 144, 146, 147, 149, 151, 153, 161, 164, 167, 168, 174, *175*, 179, 186, 187, *189*, 190, 191, 195, *198*, 201, 203, *204*, 205, 213, 214, *216*, 220, *221*, 222, 223, 224, 228, 230, 234, 242, 245, 247, 249, 257, 268, *306*, 313, 319, 321, 322, 327, 332, *333*
Amboise, Paul d', 69
American Ballet Caravan, 63–70
American Ballet Ensemble, 34, 45
American Concert Ballet, 34
American in Paris, An, 34
Anchutina, Leda, 36, 41, 42, 45, 50, 51, 55, 59
Andersen, Hans Christian, 51, 299–300, 330
Anderson, Jack, 254, 256, 270
Andriessen, Juriaan, 114
Ansermet, Ernst, 135
Ansky, S., 310
Antheil, George, 36, 42
Apollo (Stravinsky), See *Apollon Musagète*.
Apollon Musagète, 7, 16, 46–51, 73
Applebaum, Stan, 280
Arcade, 220, 292
Ariadne (Rieti), 83
Armistead, Horace, 81, 102, 140, 153, 186, 214
Arnell, Richard, 81
Aroldingen, Karin von, 47, 66, 84, 96, *100*, 103, 110, 140, 151, 161, 182, 187, 195, 199, 207, 215, 220, 227, 234, 242, *243*, 244, 245, 247, 255, 268, *269*, 271, 275, 277, *280*, 281, *290*, *296*, 304, *306*, 309, *310*, 323, 327, *329*, 332, *333*
Arshansky, Michael, 103, 153, *154*, 232, *233*, 302, 314
Ashley, Merrill, 64, 72, 84, 172, *176*, 187, 228, 234, 242, 247, 250, 257, 259, 268, 271, 287, 305, 313, 314, *317*, 323

Asquith, Ruby, 53, 54, 56, 57, 62
Ashton, Frederick, 110, 111, 138
Auden, W. H., 108, 192
Auric, Georges, 245
Austin, Debra, *313*, 319, *328*
Avedon, Michael, 329
Avila, Juan de, 41, 69

B

Bacarro, Mario, 117
Bach, Johann Sebastian, 59, 66, 275, 304
Baignères, Claude, 190, 219, 264–265
Bailey, Sally, 151
Baiser de la Fée, Le, 51–53, 97, 294
Baker, Alan, 139
Baker, Robb, 259
Balanchine, George, 1–22, 25–28, 31–36, 39, 91–92, *286*, *304*, 337–338; performing, 103, 116, *154*, *217*, 234, *237*, *238*, *302*, *306*; rehearsing, *xiii*, *182*, *254*; works choreographed, *passim*
Ballade, 135–136
Ballet Caravan, 15, 34, 53–62
Ballet Imperial, 64–66
Ballet Russe de Monte Carlo, 15, 33, 36, 43, 68, 199, 292
Ballet Society, 33–34, 71–89
Ballets 1933, Les, 2–3, 13, 43
Ballets Russes de Diaghilev, 12, 46, 102–103
Ballets Russes de Monte Carlo, 2–3, 13
Banfield, Raffaello de, 107
Baranova, Irina, 3
Barber, Samuel, 84, 168
Barnes, Clive, 68, 72, 74, 86, 100, 112, 163, 183, 189, 207, 211, 214, 216, 226, 227, 228, 230, 232, 235, 240–257 passim, 262, 265, 266, 267, 269, 270, 272, 273, 274, 275, 276, 278, 280, 281, 283, 284, 285, 292, 293, 294, 295, 296, 297, 300, 301, 302, 304, 305, 308, 310, 311, 312, 313, 317, 320, 321, 323, 324, 327, 331, 335, 336
Barnes, Patricia, 278, 279
Barnes, Virginia, 79
Barnett, Robert, 58, 84, 110, 115, 136, 139, 144, 153, *154*, 161, 168, 170, 172, *173*, 179, 187
Barque sur l'Océan, Une, 325–326
Bartók, Béla, 125, 190, 313
Bartók No. 3, 313
Barzin, Jane, 71
Barzin, Leon, 34, 160
Bat, The, 44–45
Bate, Stanley, 79
Battey, Jean, 262. *See also* Lewis, Jean Battey
Baum, Morton, 14, 35
Bax, Sir Arnold, 139
Bayou, 136–137

Beard, Dick, 84, 93, 108
Beaton, Cecil, 110, 119, 129, 139
Beattie, Herbert, 207
Beatty, Talley, 81
Beaudet, Marc, 79, 81
Beaumont, Cyril, 55, 89, 113, 122, 132, 137
Becker, Lee, 177
Beethoven, Ludwig van, 138, 308
Behn, Mrs. Aphra, 149
Bellini, Vincenzo, 199
Belt, Byron, 100, 258, 273, 318
Bender, William, 332
Bennett, Grena, 45
Bennett, Tracy, 64, 71, 206, 234, 273, 282, 292, *293*, 310, 322
Benois, Nicolas, 271
Bérard, Christian, 43, 137
Berger, Arthur V., 72
Berman, Eugene, 10, 66, 166, 292, 294, 302
Bernstein, Aline, 71
Bernstein, Leonard, 108, 259, 310
Bertrand, Aloysius, 327
Bewley, Lois, 168, *210*
Bianco, Erico, 71
Biancolli, Louis, 55, 56, 176, 181, 192, 194, 207, 214
Biches, Les, 211
Bigelow, Edward, 58, 63, 78, 79, 81, 96, 103, 108, *109*, 115, 129, 149, 153, 230
Billy the Kid, 60–61, 71
Bivona, Elena, 278–279
Bizet, Georges, 84, 166, 170, 329
Blackface, 81
Blaisdell, Frances, 136
Bland, Alexander, 223, 228
Blaustein, Sylvia, 153
Bliss, Herbert, 34, 72, 76, *81*, *83*, 84, 87, 93, 95, 96, 100, 103, 108, 114, 116, 117, *120*, 134, 136, 139, 140, *143*, 144, 151, *152*, 153, 161, *162*, 164, 168, 176
Blitzstein, Marc, 93, 94
Blum, Anthony, 72, 84, 170, 172, 176, 182, 195, 199, 207, 211, 215, 218, 220, 222, 227, 228, 234, *241*, 242, 247, 255, *256*, 257, *258*, 259, *261*, *263*, 265, 266, 271, 273, 277, 304, 313
Bocher, Barbara, 95, 120
Bodrero, James, 151
Boelzner, Gordon, 220, 242, 247, 259, 266, 268, 273, 275, 281, 292, *298*, 321
Bogan, James, 259, 265, 273
Bohm, Jerome D., 60, 61
Bolender, Todd, 34, 40, 45, 50, 58, 60, 62, 69, 72, *75*, *76*, 77, 79, *80*, 82, 84, 93, 95, 101, 108, *109*, 125, 126, 127, 134, 141, *142*, *143*, 144, 146, 149, 161, 164, *165*, 168, 172, *173*, 174, 179, 182, 210, 294, 301
Bolger, Ray, 253
Bolt, James de, 207

Bonazzi, Elaine, 302, 305
Bonnefous, Jean-Pierre, 84, 87, *88*, 96, 117, 140, 182, *185*, 203, 207, 214, 216, 218, 220, 232, 234, 247, 259, 266, 268, 269, 271, 280, 287, *290*, 294, *297*, 302, *306*, *307*, *308*, 314, *320*, 332, *333*
Boris, Ruthanna, 39, 41, 44, 46, 54, 55, 56, 57, 120, 143, 146
Borne, Bonita, 273
Borree, Susan, 170, 176, 203
Boureé Fantasque, 100–102, 247
Bowers, Faubion, 218
Bowles, Paul, 56, 69
Boyt, Jean, 161
Braden, John, 230, 241, 245, 255, 257, 273, 313, 319, 322, 327
Bradley, L. J. H., 95, 96, 110
Brahms, Johannes, 207, 242
Brahms-Schoenberg Quartet, 242–244
Brant, Henry, 41, 62
Braunstein, Jack, 82, 161
Brecht, Bertolt, 192
Breckenridge, Doris, 50, 66, 136, 138
Breyman, Annia, 43
Britten, Benjamin, 70, 95, 110, 149
Brogan, James, 293
Brown, Lewis, 190, 192
Brown, Vida, 116, 117, 119
Browse, Lillian, 107
Brozak, Edith, 58, 151
Bruhn, Erik, 168, *176*, *199*, 201
Brunner, Gerhard, 50, 198
Bry, Theodore de, 55
Buckle, Richard, 38, 50, 86, 98, 100, 108, 113, 114, 115, 116, 190, 311, 312
Bugaku, 218–220
Buonincontro, Maurizio, 86
Burkhalter, Jane, 46
Burton, Scott, 230
Busch, Herman, 161
Butler, John, 177
Buttignol, Val, 95
Byrd, William, 245

C

Cabin in the Sky, 7
Caccialanza, Gisella, 34, 35, 36, 39, 41, 42, 43, *44*, 45, 51, 52, 53, 54, 55, 58, 59, 62, 63, 64, 66, 69, 70, 72, 73, 77, 79, *80*, 81
Cadmus, Paul, 58
Cage, The, 122–125
Cage, John, 80
Cagli, Corrado, 83
Cakewalk, 120–122
Campbell, Mary, 234
Campra, André, 245
Capriccio Brillante, 120
Capricorn Concerto, 84
Caracole, 137–138
Caras, Stephen, 172, 287
Card Party, The, 50–51
Carlson, Stanley, 192
Carlyss, Earl, 153
Carter, Bill, 117, 161, 207, *209*, *211*, 215, *217*
Carter, Elliott, 55, 57, 78

Cassidy, Claudia, 218, 235, 236
Castelli, Victor, 64, 103, 164, 176, 182, 199, 234, 259, 280, 282, 287, 292, 309, *310*, 324, 326, 327, 332, *333*
Caton, Edward, 42
Chabrier, Emmanuel, 56, 100, 247
Chaconne, 330–332
Chagall, Marc, 96
Chanel, Coco, 3
Chaney, Stewart, 46
Chansons Madécasses, 328–329
Chapman, John, 55
Charade, 61–62, 71
Chase, The, 222
Chausson, Ernest, 132
Chavez, Carlos, 201
Chloe (Ravel), 323
Chopin, Frédéric, 44, 172, 259, 266, 281
Chopiniana, 281–282
Choral Variations on Bach's "Vom Himmel Hoch," 304–305
Chotzinoff, Samuel, 45
Christensen, Harold, 54, 55, 57, *58*, 60, 62
Christensen, Lew, 14, 34, 35, 40, 44, 45, 46, *48*, 49, 53, 54, 55, 57, 58, 59, 60, 61, 62, 63, 69, 70, 72, 76, 77, *80*, 81, 84, 95, 103, 150, 153
Christensen, Willam, 192, 294
Chujoy, Anatole, 46, 47, 51, 62, 69, 73, 77, 79, 81, 84, 86, 87, 88, 93, 95, 97, 101, 103, 107, 111, 114, 117, 118, 120, 122, 127, 136, 139, 144, 156, 195, 202
Circus Polka, 296–297
City Portrait, 62–63
Clarinade, 227
Clifford, John, 72, 85, 164, 182, *184*, 187, 211, 215, 218, 223, 228, 232, 234, 242, 247, 250, 255, 256, 257, 258, 259, *263*, 265, 270, 271, 272, 273, 275, 280, 287, *288*, 291, 292, *293*, 301, 302, 306, 307, 309, 313
Cohen, Selma Jeanne, 224
Colette, 71
Colman, John, 149
Colt, Alvin, 61, 69, 125, 143
Columbine (Debussy), 136; (Drigo), 143; (Scarlatti), 54
Con Amore, 150–151
Concert, The, 172–173
Concertino, 144–145
Concerto, 44
Concerto Barocco, 6, 66–69
Concerto for Jazz Band and Orchestra, 274–275
Concerto for Piano and Winds, 292
Concerto for Two Solo Pianos, 273
Concerto in G, 320–321
Concurrence, La, 33
Condé, Hermes, 282, 310, 324, *328*
Connolly, Joseph, 71
Consoer, Diane, 170
Contreras, Gloria, 201
Cook, Bart, 122, 149, 172, 180, 182, 195, 215, 234, 242, 257, 259, 271, 273, 274, 275, 282, 287, 290, 306, 307, 310, 319, 321, 323, 327, 332, *333*
Copland, Aaron, 60, 63, 134, 230
Coppélia, 314–319

Corelli, Arcangelo, 180
Corsa, Preston, 69
Cortège Hongrois, 306–307
Cotillon, 7, 33, 62, 118, 247
Coton, A. V., 68, 166
Coudy, Douglas, 55, 56, 57, 58
Craft, Robert, 301
Cranko, John, 115
Creation of the World, 210–211
Crisp, Clement, 182, 215
Croce, Arlene, 74, 76, 105, 118, 200–201, 275–276, 279, 285, 295, 308, 317–318, 320, 322, 323, 326–335 passim
Crowell, Ann, 170
Cullberg, Birgit, 190
Cunningham, Merce, 80, 241
Curley, Wilma, 168, 172

D

Damase, Jean-Michel, 228
Dance Drama Company, 174, 179
Dance Index, 13
Dances at a Gathering, 173, 259–265
Danieli, Fred, 55, 57, 58, 59, 60, 61, 62, 64, 69, *70*, 71, 73, 75, 76, 77, 81
Danilova, Alexandra, 24, 27, 29, 30, 47, 281, 306, 313
Danses Concertantes, 292–293
Daphnis and Chloe, 323
Daydé, Bernard, 327
Debussy, Claude, 135, 147, 174, 244, 270, 281, 327
Delibes, Léo, 116, 230, 256, 313
De Mille, Agnes, 14, 106
Denby, Edwin, 15, 34, 43, 44, 48, 51, 52, 61, 65, 68, 73, 82, 87, 105, 119, 137, 144, 157, 164, 165, 167, 184, 185, 197, 199, 213, 214, 235, 236, 239, 256, 258, 259, 260, 261, 292
Derain, André, 42, 93
Diaghilev, Sergei Pavlovich, 1–4, 12, 281, 323
Diamond, David, 63
Dickson, Charles, 63, 69
Dim Lustre, 227–228
Divertimento (Haieff), 77–78
Divertimento (Rossini), 70
Divertimento from "Le Baiser de la Fée," 294–296
Divertimento No. 15, 176–177
Djorup, Joan, 72, 79
Doboujinsky, Mstislav, 64
Dodd, Craig, 250, 264
Doering, Jane, 57, *58*
Dohnányi, Ernö, 146
Dollar, William, 34, 36, 39, *40*, 41, *42*, 44, 45, 50, *51*, *52*, 54, 58, 59, *60*, 64, 66, 67, 70, 71, 72, 79, 101, 107, 114, 146, 153
Don Quixote, 234–239
Donizetti, Gaetano, 205
Donizetti Variations. See *Variations from "Don Sebastian"*
Dorris, George, 105
Doubrovska, Felia, 27, 29, 30, 105, 106, 306
Downes, Edward, 45
Doyle, James, 69
Dreams, 42

Drew, Robert, 81, 120, 211
Drigo, Riccardo, 143, 232
Dryden, Richard, 258, 324
Dudin, Helene, 27–28
Dudleston, Penny, 161, 195, 282, 299
Duel, The, 107–108
Duell, Daniel, 176, 187, 250, 275, 287, 292, 293, 322, 323, 326
Dufy, Raoul, 126
Dulcinea (Nabokov), 234
Dumas, Alexandre, 119
Dumbarton Oaks, 301–302
Duncan, Isadora, 7
Dunkel, Eugene, 39
Dunleavy, Rosemary, 222
Dunphy, Jack, 63
Duntiere, Victor, 81
Duo Concertant, 11, 298–299
Dushok, Dorothy, 95, 116
Dybbuk, 310–313
Dybbuk Variations, The, 310–313
Dying Swan (Fokine), 4

E

Ebony Concerto, 211–212
Eglevsky, André, 45, 46, *49*, 91, *116*, *117*, 120, 126, *127*, 129, *131*, 137, 140, *143*, 144, *145*, 161, 166, *167*, 168, 190
Eguchi, 37
Electronics, 213–214
Élégie, 87
Eliot, T. S., 174
Elizabeth, Queen of England, 195
Ellyn, Lois, 82, 84
Encounter, 53
Enfant et les Sortilèges, L'. See *Spellbound Child, The*
Engel, Lehman, 41
Episodes, 195–199
Erkkila, Dan, 282
Errante, 40–41
Escobar, Luis, 201
Estópinal, Renee, 72, 182, 195, 232, 247, 255, 265, 275, *293*, 330
Eula, Joe, 259, 265, 266, 270, 273, 275, 323, 326
Eurydice (Gluck), 45
Eurydice (Stravinsky), 87, *88*, *89*
Evening's Waltzes, An, 307–308

F

Fairy's Kiss, The. See *Baiser de la Fée*
Falla, Manuel de, 55
Fallis, Barbara, 120, 145, 168, 170
Fanfare, 149–150
Fantasia Brasileira, 71
Fantasies, 258–259
Fantasy, 222–223
Farrell, Suzanne, 47, *50*, 64, 66, 72, 84, 103, 117, *118*, 140, 161, 164, 170, 176, 182, 195, 199, 203, 206, 207, 214, 215, *217*, 218, 220, *221*, 223, 224, 227, *228*, 230, 234, 235, *237*, *240*, 242, 246, *247*, *249*, 250, 251, 252, 253,

254, *255*, 266, 268, *320*, 321, 322, 323, *326*, 330, *331*, 332, *333*
Farnaby, Giles, 245
Faull, Eileen, 83
Fauré, Gabriel, 247
Fedorova, Nina, 110, 232, 242, 323
Feldman, Morton, 241
Fernandez, José, 69
Ffolkes, David, 79, 140
Figure in the Carpet, The, 203–205
Filling Station, 58–59
Filly, The, 149
Fiorato, Hugo, 82, 102, 132, 160, 161
Firebird, 96–100
Five Gifts, The, 146
Flagg, Elise, 161, 164, 215, 232, 234, 242, 265, 275, 293, 299, 330
Fletcher, Robert, 138, 149, 177
Flomine, Deborah, 176, 228, 253, 255, 257, 268, 293
Fokine, Michel, 3, 5, 6, 7, 14, 38, 39, 96, 98, 172, 281
Folk Dance, 56–57
Fontaine, Edwina, 117
Foster, Stephen, 61, 81
Four Bagatelles, 308–309
Four Last Songs, 273–274
Four Temperaments, The, 72–76
Françaix, Jean, 126, 144
Francés, Esteban, 76, 79, 84, 127, 146, 151, 168, 170, 199, 201, 203, 205, 234, 245, 250
Frangini, Gualtiero, 119, 148, 149, 150
Frankel, Emily, 174, 179
Frankenstein, Alfred, 58, 60
Frankfurt, Wilhelmina, 195, 313, 324, 330
Free, Karl, 55
Freedley, George, 223
French, Jared, 60
Frohlich, Jean-Pierre, 71, 110, 153, 215, 282, 293, 324, 330
Fugate, Judith, 250, 322, 323, 324

G

Gale, Joseph, 242, 247, 266, 291, 293, 310
Galindo, Blas, 69
Garfield, Constance, 120, 168
Garis, Robert, 248, 249, *320*, 321, 323, 324, 325, 326, 328
Gaspard de la Nuit, 327
Gassmann, Remi, 213
Gates, Penelope, 153, 215
Geiringer, Karl, 276
Geitel, Klaus, 207, 209, 210, 215, 219, 220, 221, 264
Gellen, Paul, 286, 287, 288, 289, 292–305 passim
Gelles, George, 278, 285, 324, 325, 329
Genauer, Emily, 129, 283
Genêt (Janet Flanner), 192
George, Carolyn, 101, 120, 144, 146, 149, 161, 168, 187
Georgov, Walter, 58, 63, 170
Gephart, William, 76
Gershwin, George, 11, 268
Gesualdo of Venosa, 206
Geva, Tamara, 33, 40, 41, 254

Gianoli, Luigi, 125, 132
Gibert, Ruth, 63, 66
Gifford, Walter, 59
Ginastera, Alberto, 201
Giordano, Matthew, 322
Glazounov, Alexander, 168, 214, 223, 306
Glinka, Mikhail, 116, 145, 167, 250
Glinkiana, 250–251
Gloire, La, 138
Gluck, Christoph Willibald von, 45, 46, 330
Godard, Benjamin, 41
Godkin, Paul, 81
Goldberg Variations, The, 275–280
Goldner, Nancy, 173–174, 235, 261–262, 265, 269–270, 271–272, 273, 274, 276, 278, 279, 281, 282, 283, 284, 286, 288–289, 290–291, 296, 299, 303–312 passim, 316, 317, 320, 321, 323, 325, 327, 328, 329, 331, 334, 336; essay by, 21–32
Goldwyn Follies, 7, 34
Golea, Antoine, 176
Goodman, Benny, 134, 144
Gordon, Meg, 273
Gottesman, Ellen, 149
Gottfried, Martin, 235, 236
Gottschalk, Louis Moreau, 61, 120, 223
Gould, Morton, 39, 144, 227
Gounod, Charles, 186
Gounod Symphony, 186
Govrin, Gloria, 47, 72, 84, 87, 96, 103, 122, 151, 153, 161, 164, 182, 187, 195, 203, 207, 214, 215, 227, 232, *233*, 234, 242, 247, 255, 265, 301
Graeler, Louis, 180, 190
Graham, June, 63
Graham, Martha, 11, 18, 34, 80, 195, *196*
Graham-Lujan, James, 151
Grant, Alberta, 127, 153, *154*
Greco, José Luis, 153
Green, Judith, 167, 176, 186, 192, 195, 203
Gregg Smith Singers, 304
Greskovic, Robert, 318
Groman, Janice, 122, 168
Guest, Ivor, 314
Guests, The, 93–95
Guirlande de Campra, La, 245

H

Haakon, Paul, 33, 39, 41, 42
Haas, George, 253
Haddow, Ardith, 313
Haggin, B. H., 51, 53, 72, 81, 82, 97, 98, 119, 152, 158, 165, 166, 212, 213, 214, 262, 263
Haieff, Alexei, 77
Haigney, Kathleen, 275
Halicka, Alice, 51
Hall, Claudia, 83
Hamlet (Beethoven), 138
Handel, George Frederick, 203, 332
Harlequin (Debussy), 136; (Drigo), 143, 232; (Rieti), 199; (Scarlatti), 54
Harlequin for President, 54
Harlequinade, 232–234
Harlequinade Pas de Deux, 143
Harmon, Carter, 81
Harris, Dale, 282

Harris, Leonard, 241
Harrison, Jay S., 178, 193, 194, 195
Hartley, Russell, 95
Harvey, Peter, 215, 234, 242, 245, 247
Hasburgh, Rabana, 45, 51, 54, 55, 56, 57
Hastings, Baird, 79
Hawkins, Erick, 54, 55, 56, 57, 58
Hawkins, Frances, 34, 35
Hayden, Melissa, 47, 64, 66, 72, 75, 78, 82, 84,
    87, 88, 94, 95, 96, 101, 102, 107, 108, 110,
    111, 114, 115, 116, 117, 122, 125, 126, 134,
    136, 137, 139, 140, 143, 145, 146, 147, 151,
    161, 162, 164, 167, 168, 170, 174, 175, 176,
    177, 179, 182, 183, 185, 186, 187, 189, 191,
    195, 203, 204, 206, 207, 212, 214, 215, 217,
    228, 230, 242, 243, 244, 245, 247, 250, 257,
    259, 266, 304, 306
Haydn, Franz Joseph, 253
Haydn Concerto, 253
Hays, David, 176, 179, 187, 195, 201, 206,
    207, 210, 211, 213, 215, 218, 220, 222, 228
Heath, Percy, 212
Held, John, Jr., 39
Henahan, Donal J., 221, 284, 285, 311
Hendl, Susan, 75, 176, 182, 206, 207, 215,
    247, 253, 259, 265, 268, 274, 275, 277, 281,
    287, 294, 305, 307, 314, 324, 330
Henry, Pierre, 309
Hériat, Philippe, 228
Hering, Doris, 37, 48, 51, 52, 64, 68, 73, 78,
    81, 82, 94, 95, 96, 97, 98, 101, 102, 109, 114,
    116, 118, 121, 126, 133, 136, 137, 138, 140,
    142, 144, 146, 147, 150, 168, 169, 170, 175,
    181, 189, 190, 191, 193, 196, 197, 198, 200,
    201, 205, 208, 209, 211, 212, 216, 246, 247,
    250, 252, 253, 256, 258, 265, 268, 281, 298
Herridge, Frances, 72, 82, 161, 180, 197, 207,
    233, 245, 246, 253, 255, 273, 274, 275, 281,
    282, 292, 311, 312, 313, 314, 321, 323, 335
Hess, William, 76, 110
Hicks, Gloriann, 110, 172
Hiden, Georgia, 63, 71, 72, 95
Highland Fling, 79, 80
Hindemith, Paul, 72, 141, 319
Hinkson, Mary, 203
Hinton, James, Jr., 117
Hlinka, Nicol, 232
Hobi, Frank, 66, 67, 94, 95, 101, 103, 114,
    116, 117, 120, 121, 125, 126, 127, 129, 141,
    143, 146, 149, 153
Hoffmann, E. T. A., 153, 314
Hollman, Gene, 192
Honnegger, Arthur, 245
Horosko, Marian, 151, 168
Hoskinson, Richard, 84, 117, 207, 322, 324
Hound and Horn, 33
Howard, Holly, 36, 41, 42, 43, 44, 45, 46, 48
Hughes, Allen, 219, 220, 221, 223, 224, 227,
    229, 231, 234, 236, 238
Humphrey, Doris, 68 n., 122
Hunkins, Sterling, 224

I

Illuminations, 110–114
Ilupina, Anna, 163, 215

Imperial Gagaku, 159
Interplay, 144
In the Night, 266–268
Introduction and Allegro for Harp, 321
Irish Fantasy, 228
Irving, Robert, 160, 207, 245
Iseult (Bax), 139
Ito, Genji, 282
Ito, Teiji, 282
Ivanov, Lev Ivanovich, 129, 132, 157
Ives, Charles, 11, 164
Ivesiana, 164–166

J

Jackson, Brooks, 119, 127, 132, 136, 139, 149
Jackson, Milt, 212
Jantzen, 114
Jazz Concert, 210–212
Jeux, 244–245
Jeux d'Enfants, 170, 330
Jewels, 247–250
Jillana, 38, 47, 49, 50, 103, 110, 117, 120, 126,
    134, 143, 146, 151, 152, 161, 168, 174, 176,
    187, 191, 195, 199, 201, 203, 207, 210, 215,
    230, 234
Jinx, 95–96
Johannsen, Christian, 17
Johnson, David, 310
Johnson, Harriet, 195
Johnson, Louis, 136
Johnson, Nancy, 151
Jolley, Jay, 161, 164, 322, 326, 330
Jones, John, 212
Jones Beach, 114–115
Jowitt, Deborah, 158, 252–253, 254, 262, 276,
    278, 302, 304, 307, 308, 311, 312, 326, 328,
    329
Juke Box, 70–71
Junyer, Joan, 78

K

Kabalevsky, Dmitri, 143
Kahrklyn, Hortense, 37, 43, 50
Kai, Una, 93, 122, 138, 139, 170
Kaleidoscope, 143–144
Kallman, Chester, 192
Kantarjian, Gerard, 224
Karinska, 36, 46, 64, 84, 100, 116, 117, 120,
    132, 140, 141, 143, 144, 145, 153, 161, 167,
    176, 186, 187, 190, 195, 201, 203, 205, 207,
    211, 214, 215, 218, 222, 223, 228, 230, 242,
    247, 256, 268, 296, 297, 330
Karlin, Rita, 72
Kaskas, Anna, 45
Kastendieck, Miles, 170, 176, 202, 224, 233
Kauflin, Jack, 63
Kaufman, Susan, 153
Kavan, Albia, 54, 56, 57
Kawase, Kensuke, 282
Kay, Hershy, 120, 161, 187, 223, 253, 268, 332
Kaye, Nora, 91, 93–94, 101, 108, 110, 117,
    122–123, 124, 132, 133, 136, 138
Keeler, Elisha C., 180–181

Kellaway, Roger, 280
Kendall, Elizabeth, 331
Kennedy, James, 107, 189, 198, 208, 219
Kent, Allegra, 47, 49, 66, 67, 72, 84, 87, 101,
    116, 117, 122, 131, 140, 141, 144, 145, 147,
    153, 161, 164, 165, 167, 168, 170, 172, 176,
    177, 179, 180, 182, 185, 186, 187, 190, 192,
    193, 194, 195, 197, 199, 200, 201, 203, 215,
    216, 218, 219, 220, 222, 228, 230, 242, 243,
    244, 247, 250, 257, 258, 259, 263, 266, 275,
    301
Kerner, Leighton, 240
Khachaturian, Aram, 38, 163
Kidd, Michael, 60, 62
Killebrew, Gwendolyn, 328
Kimball, Robert, 319
King and I, The, 124
King, Martin Luther, 255
Kirkland, Gelsey, 66, 84, 96, 99, 100, 122, 161,
    187, 203, 206, 215, 223, 228, 232, 234, 242,
    247, 250, 256–257, 259, 261, 265, 266, 270,
    271, 272, 273, 277, 280, 287, 291, 294, 299,
    300, 307, 308, 310
Kirkland, Johnna, 258, 265, 270, 273, 275
Kirstein, Lincoln, 13–15, 20, 21, 33, 34, 35,
    41, 42, 43, 45, 50, 54, 55, 56, 57, 60, 61, 62,
    64, 70, 71, 77, 78, 103, 111, 121, 129, 138,
    182, 185, 192, 225, 244, 249, 250, 268, 285,
    286, 316, 332; essay by, 1–12
Kisselgoff, Anna, 36, 66, 132, 182, 200, 209,
    216, 232, 234, 249, 255, 257, 258, 270, 275,
    279, 280, 281, 288, 290, 292, 293, 295, 305,
    307, 309, 311–312, 314, 317, 319, 333
Klotz, Florence, 308
Kochno, Boris, 103
Kodály, Zoltán, 272
Kodály Dances, 272–273
Koechlin, Charles, 40
Koegler, Horst, 176, 264
Kolodin, Irving, 40, 62
Koolish, Deborah, 274, 310, 322
Kopeikine, Nicholas, 44, 72, 108, 115, 120,
    144, 170, 172
Kova, Margit de, 60
Kova, Marija, 215
Kovnat, Susan, 127
Kramer, Helen, 45, 51
Krevitsky, Nik, 72, 127, 147–148
Krieger, Victoriana, 250
Kriegsman, Alan M., 331, 332
Kriza, John, 63, 69, 70
Krokover, Rosalyn, 83–84, 109
Kursch, Judy, 81

L

Labisse, Felix, 228
Lady of the Camelias, 119–120
Laing, Hugh, 91, 103, 108, 110, 119, 120, 125,
    127, 132, 136, 138
Lamont, Deni, 85, 87, 151, 153, 164, 170, 187,
    199, 201, 215, 228, 232, 233, 234, 241, 245,
    257, 268, 282, 302
Lang, Ariel, 50
Lang, Harold, 95, 101, 116
Larkin, Peter, 149, 195, 245

Larsson, Irene, 120, 122, 139, 146, 147, 149, 153, 168, *169*

Laskey, Charles, 36, *37*, *39*, 40, 41, 42, 43, 44, 45, 54, 55, 56, 81, 83

Lawrence, Robert, 133

Lazowski, Yurek, 116

Leavitt, Gerard, 79

LeClerq, Tanaquil, 35, *38*, *49*, 51, *63*, 66, *67*, 71, *72*, 77, 78, 79, 80, *82*, *83*, 84, *85*, 87, 88, 89, 94, 100, *101*, 102, 108, *109*, 110, *113*, 114, 117, *118*, 119, 120, 122, 132, 134, 136, *137*, 141, *142*, 144, *145*, 147, *148*, 151, 153, 159, 161, *162*, 164, 166, *167*, *170*, 172, *173*, 176

Lederman, Minna, 52, 65, 66, 200, 292

Lee, Tom, 70

Leitch, Helen, 36, 45

Leland, Sara, 47, 66, 84, 110, 117, 140, 144, 164, 172, *174*, 176, 182, *184*, 195, 207, 210, 211, 215, 223, 227, 234, 241, 242, 244, 247, 250, 253, *258*, 259, *263*, 266, 268, 271, 273, 275, 280, 287, 288, 292, 304, 307, 313, 321, 327, 332, *333*

Lengyel, Melchior, 125

Lenya, Lotte, 192

Lesur, Daniel, 245

Levasseur, André, 199, 228

Levinoff, Joseph, 41, 43

Levins, Daniel, 161

Lewis, George, 203

Lewis, Jean Battey, 132, 287, 305, 312

Lewis, John, 212

Li, George, 153

Lieberman, Rolf, 274

Liebeslieder Walzer, 207–210

Liepa, Maris, 272, 280

Lilac Garden, 132–134

Lindgren, Robert, 96, 161, 180, 192

Lishner, Leon, 76, 83

Liszt, Franz, 42, 43

Littlefield, Catherine, 14, 33

Lland, Michael, 117, 180

Lloyd, Margaret, 53, 56, 162–163, 180

Lombardi, Michael, 218

London, Lorna, 36, 59, 62, 63, 70

Longchamp, Gaston, 36, 42, 138

Lopez, Luis, 69, 81

Loring, Eugene, 14, 34, 39, 41, 42, 54, *56*, 57, 58, 60, *61*, 62

Losch, Tilly, 192

Lost Sonata, 287

Love, Kermit, 71

Loyola, Andrew, 253

Lubell, Roberta, 192

Lüders, Adam, 84, 242

Ludlow, Conrad, 47, *49*, 64, 66, *67*, 84, 96, 101, 144, 151, 176, 195, 201, 203, 206, 207, 210, 213, 214, 215, *217*, 228, 230, 234, 242, *243*, 245, *248*, 255, 258, 265, 266, *271*

Lurçat, Jean, 36

Lyon, Annabelle, 36, 41, 42, *43*, 45, 50, *51*, 53, 54, 56

M

Magallanes, Nicholas, 34, *38*, 40, 51, 52, 53, 64, 66, 70, 71, 72, *83*, 84, 87, *89*, *94*, 100, 110, *111*, 114, 116, 117, *118*, 122, *124*, *131*, 134, *137*, 141, *145*, 149, 151, 153, 161, *162*, 170, *171*, 176, 177, *178*, 180, *181*, 195, *197*, 199, *200*, 201, 203, 207, 215, *217*, 234

Maiorano, Robert, 84, 110, 122, 161, 195, 215, 224, 230, 258, 259, *261*, *263*, 265, 268, 273, *274*, 275, 282, 292, 294, 301, 305

Malaieff, M., 50

Malraux, Madeleine, 287, 294, 301, 320

Ma Mère l'Oye, 322–323

Manchester, P. W., 83, 87, 105, 129, 130, 132, 133, 140, 142, 146, 148, 150, 151, 161, 163, 167, 168, 170, 171, 175, 180, 181, 184, 188, 190, 191, 193, 197–198, 200, 202, 203, 204, 205, 208, 209, 211, 212, 215, 216–218, 219–224 passim, 227–231 passim, 232–233, 241, 244, 245, 247–248, 249, 251, 252, 257, 258

Mandia, John, 58, 122, 136, 139, 166, 168, *169*, 172, 174, 177, *178*

Marie-Jeanne, 34, 36, 43, 45, 46, 48, 53, 55, 56, *57*, 58–59, *60*, 61, *62*, 63, *64*, 66, *67*, 70, 72, *83*, 85, 93, 110, 146

Marks, Marcia, 251, 259, 280

Martin, John, 15, 34, 37, 39, 40, 41, 42, 43–44, 47, 51, 52, 55, 56, 57, 59, 60, 61, 62, 63, 64, 72, 76–77, 78, 79, 80, 82, 84, 86, 87, 88, 92, 93, 94–95, 96–97, 101, 102, 103, 104, 107, 108–109, 112, 114, 118, 120, 122, 126, 128, 130, 133, 134, 136–142 passim, 144, 145, 146, 148, 149, 151, 152, 156, 161, 162, 163, 165, 168, 169, 170, 171, 172–173, 175, 177, 179, 180, 181, 183, 187, 189–195 passim, 197, 198, 200, 202, 203, 204, 205, 207, 208, 211, 212, 214, 217, 292

Martin, Keith, 45, 54, 57, 120

Martinez, José, 69, 72, 79

Martins, Peter, 24, 26, 47, *50*, *64*, 66, 84, 96, *100*, 147, 170, *176*, 182, 203, 207, 214, 216, 234, 242, 247, 256, 259, *261*, *266*, 268, 271, 275, *277*, 281, *282*, 290, *291*, *298*, 299, 304, 306, 307, 314, *320*, 321, 323, *326*, 330, *331*, 332, *333*

Marty, Jean-Pierre, 223

Mary, Queen of Scots (Webern), 195

Maryinsky Theater (St. Petersburg), 2, 27, 41

Maskey, Jacqueline, 309

Mason, Jane, 151, 168

Masquers, The, 179

Massine, Léonide, 2, 7, 62, 101, 150

Massine, Lorca, 96, 273, 281, 301

Mathis, Joyce, 273

Matthews, Laurence, 195, 324, 326

Maule, Michael, 58, 59, 93, 96, 115, 117, 122, *141*, 144, 149

Mayuzumi, Toshiro, 11, 218

Mazo, Joseph H., 174, 291, 335

Mazurka from "A Life for the Tsar," 116

Mazzo, Kay, 47, 84, 87, 117, 140, 144, 147, 180, 182, 195, 199, 205, 206, 207, 214, 215, 218, 220, 227, 230, 234, *237*, 241, 242, 245, 247, 250, 253, 255, 256, 257, *258*, 259, *263*, 266, 268, *271*, 280, 281, *282*, 290, *291*, *296*, *298*, 299, 306, 321, 332, *333*

McBride, Pat, 79, 83, 87, 96, 108

McBride, Patricia, 47, *49*, *50*, *64*, 65, 66, 84, 99, 101, 117, 122, *131*, 140, 144, 147, 153,

161, 164, 170, *171*, 176, 182, *185*, 187, 195, 199, *203*, 205, *206*, 207, 210, 211, 214, 215, 218, 222, 223, 227, 228, 232, 233, 234, 242, 245, 247, *249*, 250, *253*, 259, *261*, *263*, *266*, 267, 268, 271, 275, 294, *295*, *297*, 306, *307*, 310, 312, 314, *315*, *317*, 321, 325, 328, 329, *330*, 332, *333*

McBride, Robert, 57

McConnell, Teena, 241

McDonagh, Don, 251, 287, 295, 297, 310

McHugh, John, 179

Medea, 190–192

Meditation, 223

Meier, Roberta, 168

Mejia, Paul, *85*, 182, 215, 228, 242, 245, 247, 250, *251*

Mendelssohn, Felix, 120, 140, 215

Menotti, Gian Carlo, 177

Merlin, Olivier, 76, 125, 141, 148, 163, 166, 174, 187, 198–199, 250

Merrill, Linda, 110, 253, 257, 259, 268

Metamorphoses, 141–143

Metastaseis & Pithoprakta 251–253

Metcalf, William, 302, 305

Micklin, Bob, 272, 293, 294, 308, 313, 314, 335

Midas (Rieti), 83

Midsummer Night's Dream, A, 215–218

Mielziner, Jo, 253, 268, 280

Mignone, Francisco, 71

Mikeshina, Adriana, 54

Milberg, Barbara, 47, 95, 110, 166, 170, 177, *178*, 182

Milhaud, Darius, 210

Miller, Margo, 243

Minkus, Leon, 117

Minotaur, The, 78–79

Miraculous Mandarin, The, 125–126

Mironowa, Eudokia, 59

Mishkin, Leo, 123

Mitchell, Arthur, 72, 75, 87, 101, 144, *145*, 147, 161, 164, 168, 176, *177*, *178*, 182, *185*, 187, 191, 195, 201, 203, 206, *210*, 211, 212, 215, *217*, 218, 220, 227, 228, 234, 245, *246*, *247*, 251, *252*, 253, *254*, 255, 274

Mitchell, David, 71, 327, 329

Modern Jazz: Variants, 212–213

Monahan, James, 38, 89, 93, 95, 96, 98, 101, 124, 125, 132, 135

Moncion, Francisco, 35, 63, 66, 72, 76, *77*, 78, 83, 84, 85, 87, 88, 93, 94, 95, 96, *99*, 102, 103, *104*, 107, *108*, *109*, 115, 117, *118*, 122, 136, 138, 139, 143, *147*, *148*, 151, 153, 164, 170, 172, *174*, 179, *180*, 195, 199, 201, 203, 211, 215, 234, *237*, 246, 247, 257, *266*, *267*, 275, 299, *300*, 302

Monteverdi, Claudio, 87

Montresor, Beni, 227

Monumentum pro Gesualdo, 206–207

Moore, Bonnie, 273

Moore, Hanna, 54

Moore, Lillian, 98, 104, 107

Moore, Marjorie, 40, 46, *58*, 59, 69, 70

Morcom, James Stewart, 63, 82, 176

Mordkin, Mikhail, 14

Morell, Karen, 153, 164, 215

Morris, Marnee, 47, 64, 66, 71, 72, 75, 84, 103, *154*, 167, 176, 187, 195, 199, 215, 223,

Morris, Marnee (*continued*)
228, 234, 242, *245*, 247, 255, *256*, *257*, 259,
268, 271, 287, 313
Mosarra, Francesca, 103
Mother Goose Suite, 93
Mounsey, Yvonne, 102, 103, 108, 114, 117,
120, 122, 129, 132, *139*, 146, 151, 153, 161,
168, 172, 179
Movements for Piano and Orchestra, 220, 221
Moylan, Mary Ellen, 34, 66, 72, *75*, 77
Mozart, Wolfgang Amadeus, 53, 82, 137, 176,
222
Mozartiana, 43–44, 137
Mullowny, Kathryn, 36, *37*, 39, 41, 42, 51
Munson, Marjorie, 57

N

Nabokov, Nicolas, 59, 234
Nagy, Ivan, 84
Narkissos, 245
Native Dancers, 195
Naumann, Peter, 195, 292, 299
Neary, Colleen, 26, 64, 66, 71, 72, 84, 96, 149,
161, 176, 182, 187, 215, 242, 271, 273, 282,
301, 314, *319*, 332, 327
Neary, Patricia, 47, 64, 66, 72, 75, 84, 96, 103,
122, 140, 161, 164, 176, 182, 195, 214, 215,
228, 234, *241*, 245, 247
Nichols, Betty, 79, 81
Nichols, Kyra, 228, 327
Nickel, Paul, 153
Night Shadow, 199–200
Nijinsky, Waslaw, 6, 7, 12, 147, 244
Nillo, David, 40
Noguchi, Isamu, 80, 87, 88
Norton, Elliott, 53, 57, 58
Nuitter, Charles, 314
Nutcracker, The, 153–158

O

Oboukhoff, Anatole, 27
O'Brien, Shaun, 58, 103, 108, 110, 153, 168,
172, 191, 199, *222*, 228, 232, *233*, 302, 314,
315
O'Connor, John J., 285
Octandre, 275
Octet, 192, 294
Octuor, 293–294
Ode, 301
Odette, Queen of the Swans, 129, 130, 131,
132
Offenkranz, Paul, 71
Officer, Harvey, 76
O'Hearn, Robert, 258
Ohman, Frank, 64, 72, 161, 170, 176, 182,
195, 207, 215, *227*, 228, 234, 245, 247, 253,
255, 268, 271, 275, *280*, 292
Ondine, 102
Opus 34, 151–152
Orbon, Julian, 201
Orpheus (Stravinsky), 87-90
Orpheus and Eurydice (Gluck), 45–46
Osins, Witaly, 190
Ostendorf, John, 255, 310
Otis, Cynthia, 321

P

Paganini, Nicolò, 42
Page, Ruth, 14, 15–16
Palais de Cristal, Le, 79
PAMTGG, 280
Panamerica, 201–202
Parente, Alfredo, 132, 141
Parney, Evariste, 328
Pas de Deux (Tchaikovsky), 203
Pas de Deux and Divertissement, 230
Pas de Deux Romantique, 114
Pas de Dix, 168
Pas de Trois (Glinka), 167
Pas de Trois (Minkus), 117
Pastorale, 179–180
Pastorela, 69
Patterson, Yvonne, 70
Paul, Mimi, 47, 66, *75*, 84, 96, 101, 110, 147,
161, 176, 186, 195, 206, 207, 215, 218, 224,
227, 230, 234, 245, *246*, 247, 250, *251*
Pavane, 325
Pavlova, Anna, 4–5, 12, 27
Pene Du Bois, Raoul, 244, 253
Pengelly, Jeanne, 45
Perkins, Francis D., 45
Perrault, Charles, 322
Peters, Delia, 172, 191, 259, 275, *293*, 322,
324
Petipa, Marius, 17, 43, 66, 72, 85, 129, 132,
168, 204, 215, 232, *233*, 235, 306, 313
Phaedra (Beethoven), 138
Piano-Rag-Music, 301
Picnic at Tintagel, 138–140
Pied Piper, The, 134–135
Piège de Lumière, 228–230
Pierrot (Debussy), 136; (Drigo) 232
Pietrucha, Roger, 228
Pilarre, Susan, 140, 176, 182, 187, 256, 259,
265, 268, 273, 281, 324
Pillersdorf, Susan, 191
Pitts, Bryan, 273, *274*, 275, 287, 323
Pocahontas, 55
Pope, Arthur Upham, 203
Poretta, Frank, 192, 207
Port, Terri Lee, *315*
Porter, Andrew, 47, 85, 150, 163, 190, 207,
209, 219, 221, 224, 228, 236, 238–239, 298
Portinari, Candido, 36
Potteiger, Jack, 43
Poulenc, Francis, 179, 211, 245
Prelude, Fugue and Riffs, 259
Prince, Robert, 245
Printemps, 281
Prinz, John, 110, 161, 223, 234, 242, 245, 247,
250, 253, 255, 256, *257*, 259, *263*
Prodigal Son, 7, 102–107
Producing Company of the School of American
Ballet, 33
Prokofiev, Sergei, 102, 161, 307
Prokovsky, André, 84, 140, 186, 187, 203, 214,
222, 228, *230*, 242
Prologue, 245–246
Promenade, 54–55
Pulcinella, 302–304
Punch and the Child, 81–82
Purchet, Maurice, 85–86

Purl, Mara, 282
Pushkin, Alexander, 103

Q

Quartet, 161
Quatuor, 224

R

Ragtime (I), 211
Ragtime (II), 246
Raibouchinska, Tatiana, 3
Rain, Charles, 55, 56
Rambert, Marie, 132
Rapp, Richard, 24, 26, 27, 29, 72, 75, 117, 122,
153, 161, 164, 168, 170, 176, *177*, 182, *185*,
192, 215, 227, 230, 234, *235*, *238*, 246, 253,
268
Rapsodie Espagnole, 329
Rasmussen, Angeline, 207
Rauschenberg, Robert, 241
Rauschning, Hans, 38, 87
Ravel, Maurice, 54, 71, 93, 115, 117, 270;
Festival (1975), 319–329
Ray, Charlotte, 110, 179
Raymonda Variations. See *Valses et
Variations*.
Redpath, Christine, 71, 85, 161, 172, 187, 234,
242, 247, 257, 265, 271, 273, 275, 281, 287,
292, *293*, 294, 296, 301, 302, 307, 313, 314,
319
Reed, Janet, 50, 58, 59, 66, 67, 84, 93, 95, 100,
114, 116, 120, 126, 134, 136, 143, 144, 151,
153, 161, 164, *177*, *210*
Reeves, Jean, 79
Reiman, Elise, 27, 28, 29, 36, 41, *42*, 43, 46,
48, 71, 72, 77, 78, 79, *80*, 84
Reminiscence, 41–42
Renard, 76–77
Reppa, David, 282
Requiem Canticles (I), 255
Requiem Canticles (II), 305
Reveries, 265–266
Revil, Rudi, 79
Revueltas, Silvestre, 201
Ribere, Lisa de, 273, 293
Rice, Newcomb, 62, 63
Rich, Alan, 276
Richardson, David, 26, 153, 195, 265, 273,
296, 324
Rieti, Vittorio, 83, 195, 199
Rimbaud, Arthur, 110
Rittmann, Trude, 59, 61
Rivas, Elena de, 36, *37*, 41, 43
Robberts, William D., 245
Robbins, Jerome, 16, 20, 63, 85, 93, *94*, 96,
100, 103, 104–105, *106*, 108, *109*, 114, 122,
127, *128*, 134, 135, 137, 144, 147, 149, 151,
161, 172, 226, 259, 266, 275, *277*, 282, 296,
297, 301, 302, 305, 307, 308, 310, 320, 321,
322, 325, 328
Roberge, Giselle, 85, 176, 273
Robinson, Roland, 132, 163, 170, 190
Rockefeller, Nelson, 69

Rodgers, Richard, 253
Rodham, Robert, 153, 182, *185*, 215, 227, 234
Roland-Manuel, Alexis, 245
Roma, 166–167
Roman, Janice, 79
Rorem, Ned, 71
Rosenfield, John, 58
Rosenthal, Jean, 95
Ross, Bertram, 195, *196*
Rossini, Gioacchino, 70, 151
Rouault, Georges, 102, 103
Ruppel, K. H., 119, 199, 272
Russell, Francia, 47, 176, 182, *189*, 203
Ryder, Mark, 174, 179

S

Saal, Hubert, 272, 334
Sabin, Robert, 47–48, 53, 63, 64, 80–81, 82, 88, 104, 109, 133, 145, 149, 152, 163, 167, 178
Sackett, Francis, 161, 176, 207, 275, 313, 319, 324, 327
Sackett, Paul, 96
Sadoff, Simon, 64, 71, 144
St. Denis, Ruth, 325
Saint-Saëns, Camille, 228
Sala, Oskar, 213
Saland, Stephanie, 259, 314
Salas, Juan Orrego, 201
Sale, Mary, 42
Saltarelli, 313–314
Sancho Panza (Nabokov), 234
Sandberg, Herbert, 190
Sanders, Job, 79
Sandré, Irma, 79
Santa Rosa, Tomás, 46
Sarabande and Danse (I), 270
Sarabande and Danse (II), 327–328
Saratoga Performing Arts Center, 225, 314
Sargent, Kaye, 153
Sargent, Winthrop, 227, 259
Satie, Erik, 11
Sauguet, Henri, 245
Savoia, Patricia, 172
Sayers, Dido, 110, 192
Scaasi, Arnold, 321
Scancarella, John, 79
Scarlatti, Domenico, 54
Scènes de Ballet, 297
Schadow, J. G. von, 53
Schaufuss, Peter, 85, 140, 199, 214, 242, *271*, 306, 307, 321, 323, 329, *330*
Scherzo à la Russe, 296
Scherzo Fantastique, 287
Schmidt-Garre, Helmut, 250, 280
Schoenberg, Arnold, 11, 151, 242
Schonberg, Harold C., 164
School of American Ballet, 3, 18, 19, 21–33, 80, 159–160
Schor, Joseph, 224
Schorer, Suki, 24, 26, 27, 28, 47, 49, 64, 66, 68, 84, 85, 101, 153, 161, 164, 176, *177*, 187, 199, 203, 214, 215, *217*, 222, 223, *224*, 227, *230*, 232, *233*, 234, 242, 247, 250, 256
Schubert, Franz, 222

Scotch Symphony, 140–141
Scott, Dorothy, 144, 145, 161
Schubert, Franz, 40, 222
Schuller, Gunther, 212
Sealy, Robert, 100, 211, 266–267, 269
Seasons, The, 80–81
Segarra, Ramon, 227
Seligmann, Kurt, 72
Serenade, 6, 15, 21, 33, 36–39
Serenade in A, 294
Sergeev, Konstantin, 87
Seven Deadly Sins, The, 192–194
Severinsen, "Doc," 274
Shadow'd Ground, 230–232
Shakespeare, William, 215
Sharaff, Irene, 108, 144, 147, 149, 172, 253, 280, 281
Shea, Mary Jane, 63, 66
Shéhérazade, 321
Shelton, Polly, 258, 274
Sherman, Louise, 207
Shire, Ellen, 210
Show Piece, 57–58
Shostakovich, Dimitri, 224
Siegel, Marcia B., 188, 273, 274, 275, 307, 310
Siegl, Henry, 161
Sieveling, Earle, 64, 84, 153, 176, 182, 197, 206, 234, 242, *243*, 247, *253*, 259, 266, 268, 270, *271*, 274, 280, 301
Sills, Bettijane, 161, 172, 176, 268, 294
Silverstein, Joseph, 290
Simmons, Stanley, 272, 273, 291, 294, 301, 322
Simon, Victoria, 117, 153, 176, 180, 214
Sinfonietta, 319
Sirvin, René, 107
Slaughter on Tenth Avenue, 253–255
Slonimsky, Yuri, 38–39, 270
Smith, Cecil, 37, 94, 128–129
Smith, Oliver, 108
Sobotka, Ruth, 63, 79, 95, 122, 127, *145*, 179, 211, 220
Sokolova, Lydia, 244
Soldier and the Gypsy, The, 55–56
Sonatine, 319–320
Song of the Nightingale, The, 299–300
Sonnambula, La. See *Night Shadow*.
Sorell, Walter, 224; essay by, 13–20
Soudeikine, Sergei, 41
Source, La, 256–257
Sousa, John Philip, 11, 187
Souvenirs, 168–170
Spellbound Child, The, 71–72
Spohn, Marjorie, 176, 324
Square Dance, 180–182
Stars and Stripes, 187–190
Steadfast Tin Soldier, The, 329–330
Steele, Michael, 87, 153, 161, 245, 246, 253, 275
Steinberg, Michael, 320, 321
Steinberg, Saul, 172
Stellman, Maxine, 45
Stetson, Lynne, 246, 255, 258, 273
Stevenson, Robert, 107, 114
Stewart, Helen, 53, 56, 57
Stewart, Malcolm, 252
Still Point, The, 174–176

Stone, Bentley, 14
Stowell, Kent, 85, 144, 151, 161, 176, *177*, 186, 187, 207, 210, 215, 234, 242, 247
Strauss, Johann, 45
Strauss, Richard, 127, 227, 273
Stravinsky, Igor, *xiii*, 10, 11, 15, 16–17, 34, 46, 50–51, *52*, 76, 87, 96, 122, 182, 192, 206, 211, 220, 225, 226, 240, 246, 247, 255, 273; Festival (1972), 286–305
Stravinsky: Symphony in C, 255–256
Stuart, Muriel, 27
Stuart, Virginia, 164, 281
Stuckenschmidt, H. H., 100, 107, 326
Suarez, Olga, *44*, 45, 46, 70, 71
Sugar Plum Fairy (Tchaikovsky), 158
Suite No. 3. See *Tchaikovsky Suite No. 3*.
Summerspace, 241–242
Sumner, Carol, 26, 28, 47, 66, 75, 110, 117, 161, 168, 176, 182, *184*, 187, 203, 214, 230, 232, 234, 241, 256, 294, 302, *303*, 324
Swan (Fokine). See Dying Swan.
Swanilda (Delibes), 314
Swan Lake, 129–132
Swift, Kay, 39
Sylphide, La, 79–80
Sylphides, Les, 6, 173, 281
Sylvester, Robert, 152
Sylvia: Pas de Deux, 116–117, 230
Symphonie Concertante, 82–83
Symphony in C, 84–87
Symphony in E-Flat, 291–292
Symphony in Three Movements, 287–289

T

Tailleferre, Germaine, 245
Tallchief, Maria, 34, 46, *49*, 51, *52*, 53, 66, 72, 76, 77, 78, 82, *89*, 91, *94*, 96, 97, 98, 100, 103, 110, 114, *116*, *117*, 120, 126, 129, *131*, 137, 140, *143*, 149, 153, *168*, 170, *171*, 186, 200, 201, 228, *229*
Tanner, Eugene, 101, 168, 170, 177, *178*
Tanner, Richard, 273, 275, 293
Tanning, Dorothea, 115, 136, 146
Taper, Bernard, 17
Tarantella, 223–224
Taras, John, 70, 76, 77, 78, 199, 201, 211, 220, 222, 228, 230, 244, 245, 253, 292, 297, 299, 323
Taylor, Paul, 195
Tchaikovsky, Peter Ilyitch, 36, 43, 51, 64, 129, 153, 170, 190, 202, 223, 247, 257, 265, 271
Tchaikovsky Suite, 257–258
Tchaikovsky Suite No. 1. See *Reveries*.
Tchaikovsky Suite No. 3, 271–272
Tchelitchew, Pavel, 40, 45, 72, 73
Ter-Arutunian, Rouben, 64, 129, 153, 168, 192, 232, 255, 292, 299, 304, 306, 307, 309, 310, 314, 321, 332
Terpsichore (Stravinsky), 46
Terry, Walter, 34, 36, 37, 54, 56, 57, 59, 60, 61, 62, 64, 65, 69, 73, 77–83 passim, 86, 88–89, 93, 95, 96–97, 98, 101, 102, 103, 104, 107, 108, 109, 110, 112, 114, 116–117, 120, 121, 122, 126, 127, 129–130, 133, 134, 136, 138, 139–140, 143, 144, 145, 146, 148,

Terry, Walter (*continued*)
  149, 150, 151, 158, 161, 165, 171, 172,
  176–177, 178–179, 181, 183–184, 187, 188,
  189, 192, 193, 195, 197, 199, 201, 202, 203,
  204–205, 208, 211, 213, 214, 216, 220, 221,
  222, 224, 227–228, 229, 230, 231, 234, 236,
  241, 243, 245, 246, 252, 266, 267, 309
Thayr, Forrest, Jr., 62
Theme and Variations, 202
Theseus (Carter), 78
Thom, Brigette, 330
Thomas, Richard, 153, 168, 170, 172, 177, *178*
Thomson, Virgil, 58, 59, 136, 146
Time Table, 63–64
Tobias, Roy, *63*, 93, 108, *109*, 120, 122, 125,
  126, 134, 144, 149, 153, 161, 166, 168, *170*,
  174, 176, 177, 179, 182, 201
Tobias, Tobi, 330
Todd, Arthur, 191, 193
Tomasson, Helgi, 85, 103, 147, 187, 203, 205,
  206, 214, 215, 223, 256, 257, 259, *263*, 271,
  275, *277*, 287, 294, *295*, 307, 308, 310, *311*,
  312, 314, *315*, *317*, 321, 328, 332, *333*
Tombeau de Couperin, Le, 324–325
Tompkins, Beatrice, 45, 51, 62, 63, 69, 72, 77,
  79, 80, 81, 84, 87, 93, 95, 96, 108, 114, 120,
  127, *128*, 138
Tosar, Hector, 201
Toumanova, Tamara, 3, 42
Tristram (Bax), 139
Triumph of Bacchus and Ariadne, The, 83–84
Trois Valses Romantiques, 247
T'Sani, Nolan, 66, 84, 242, 271, 273, 275, 326,
  327, 329
Tudor, Antony, 63, 119, 132, *133*, 138, 227
Tumkovsky, Antonina, 24, 27, 28
Turner, Charles, 179
Twain, Mark, 146
Tyler, Veronica, 215
Tyven, Sonja, *145*, 151, 161, 187
Tzigane, 326

U

Ulenspiegel, Tyl, 127–129
Unicorn, the Gorgon and the Manticore, The,
  177–179
Union Jack, 332–336
Upshaw, William, 76

V

Valse, La, 117–119
Valse Fantaisie, 145–146
Valses et Variations, 214–215

Vane, Daphne, 40, 45, *46*, *48*
Vardi, Emanuel, 87
Varèse, Edgar, 275
Variations, 240–241
Variations from "Don Sebastian," 205–206
Variations pour une Porte et un Soupir,
  309–310
Vauges, Gloria, 153
Vaughan, David, 166, 320, 323–327, 329
Vaughan Williams, Ralph, 258
Vazquez, Roland, 139, 153, 161, 168, 170, 199,
  201, 215, *217*, 222, 224, 230
Vecheslova, Tatiana, 291
Verdi, Giuseppe, 119
Verdy, Violette, *64*, 84, 87, 96, *99*, *131*, 140,
  151, 161, 167, 170, 176, 182, *186*, 187, 190,
  191, 195, 199, 201, 202, 203, 205, 207, 213,
  214, 215, 228, 242, 245, 247, *248*, *251*, 253,
  256, 259, *263*, *266*, 270, 281, *302*, 304, *308*,
  320
Vernet, Horace, 54
Villa-Lobos, Heitor, 201
Villella, Edward, 47, *50*, 85, 87, *103–104*, 105,
  131, 140, *141*, 147, *151*, 161, 167, 182,
  186–187, 190, 192, 195, 199, 201–202, *203*,
  205, 213–215, *217*, 218, *219*, 222–223, *224*,
  227, 230, *232–233*, 242, *244*, 245, 247, *249*,
  250, *256*, 259, *263*, 271, *272*, 282, *284–285*,
  287, *302–303*, 321
Vilzak, Anatole, 41–42
Violin Concerto, 289–291
Vivaldi, Antonio, 102, 180, 313
Vladimiroff, Pierre, 27
Vlady, 153
Voight, Caroline, 224
Vollmar, Jocelyn, 82
Vosseler, Heidi, 36, 39

W

Walczak, Barbara, 95, 101, 107, 116, 140, 145,
  146, 161, 166, 168, 170, 176, 182, 187, 192
Wall, Edmund, 134
Waltz-Scherzo, 190
Warburg, Edward M. M., 33, 39, 45, 50
Ware, Sheryl, 140
Watermill, 282–285
Watkins, Franklin, 42
Watt, Douglas, 112, 173, 213, 223
Watts, Heather, 84, 195, 275, 287
Watts, Jonathan, 58, 72, 84, 101, *154*, 168,
  170, 176, *177*, 179, *182*, 186, 195, 201, 202,
  203, 205, *206*, 207, 214
Weber, Carl Maria von, 114, 141
Webern, Anton, 11, 195
Webster, Daniel, 276

Weill, Kurt, 192
Weiss, Robert, 85, 110, 172, 187, 205, 215,
  223, 242, 247, 250, 259, 271, 275, *277*, 287,
  294, 302, 327, 329
Welles, Parmelee, 320
Wells, Bruce, 182, 257, 259, *263*, 265, 275,
  292, 294, 305, 307
Wells, Mary Ann, 227
Wescott, Glenway, 46, 49
Weslow, William, 110, 170, 187, *188*, 192, 199
Western Symphony, 161–164
White, Eric Walter, 87, 88, 96, 212, 220
White, Robert, 302
White, Terry, 282
Who Cares?, 268–270
Wilbur, Kathleen, 222
Wilde, Patricia, 47, *49*, 50, 66, 72, 84, 96, 101,
  107, 116, 117, 120, *121*, 129, 137, 140, *141*,
  143, *145*, 146, 151, *154*, 161, 164, 167, 168,
  170, 180, *181*, 186, 190, 195, 201, 205, *214*,
  215
Wilder, Alec, 70
Williams, Grant, 192
Williams, Stanley, 24, 27, 29, 30, 31
Willis, Thomas, 66, 68
Will O' the Wisp, 146
Wilson, Margaret, 255
Wilson, Mitzi, 207
Wilson, Sallie, 110, 122, 161, 187, 195, 199
Witch, The, 115–116
Woloshin, Sid, 280
Wood, Margaret, 153, 215
Wortham, Tomi, 127
Wright, Marilyn, 223

X

Xenakis, Iannis, 11, 251

Y

Yankee Clipper, 56
Yourth, Lynda, 85, 176, 195, 242, 281, 287,
  292

Z

Zakharov, Rostislav, 186
Ziegfeld Follies, 7
Zimmerman, Jerry, 172, 273, 308, 327
Zipprodt, Patricia, 282, 301, 310
Zivier, Georg, 68, 69, 76, 132, 135
Zodiac, 79
Zoete, Beryl de, 113
Zompakos, Stanley, 58, 120, 139

Printed by Holyoke Lithograph Co., Inc.

Photograph on page xiii by Michael Avedon

Photographs on pages 1, 21 by Martha Swope

Photograph on page 13 by Paul Hansen